Comparative Government and Politics

COMPARATIVE GOVERNMENT AND POLITICS

Published

Rudy Andeweg and Galen A. Irwin
Governance and Politics of the Netherlands (3rd edition)

Tim Bale
European Politics: A Comparative Introduction (2nd edition)

Nigel Bowles
Government and Politics of the United States (2nd edition)

Paul Brooker
Non-Democratic Regimes (2nd edition)

Robert Elgie
Political Leadership in Liberal Democracies

Rod Hague and Martin Harrop
* Comparative Government and Politics: An Introduction (8th edition)

Paul Heywood
The Government and Politics of Spain

Xiaoming Huang
Politics in Pacific Asia: An Introduction

B. Guy Peters
Comparative Politics: Theories and Methods
[*Rights: World excluding North America*]

Tony Saich
Governance and Politics of China (2nd edition)

Anne Stevens
The Government and Politics of France (3rd edition)

Ramesh Thakur
The Government and Politics of India

Forthcoming

Tim Haughton and Darina Malová
Government and Politics in Central and Eastern Europe

Robert Leonardi
Government and Politics in Italy

* Published in North America as **Political Science: A Comparative Introduction (5th edition)**

**Comparative Government and Politics
Series Standing Order
ISBN 0–333–71693–0 hardback
ISBN 0–333–69335–3 paperback**
(*outside North America only*)

You can receive future titles in this series as they are published by placing a standing order. Please contact your bookseller or, in the case of difficulty, write to us at the address below with your name and address, the title of the series and one of the ISBNs quoted above.

Customer Services Department, Macmillan Distribution Ltd
Houndmills, Basingstoke, Hampshire RG21 6XS, England

8th Edition

Comparative Government and Politics

AN INTRODUCTION

ROD HAGUE
and
MARTIN HARROP

First edition 1982
Second edition 1987
Third edition 1992
Fourth edition 1998
Fifth edition 2001
Sixth edition 2004
Seventh edition 2007
Eighth edition 2010

Published by
PALGRAVE MACMILLAN

Palgrave Macmillan in the UK is an imprint of Macmillan Publishers Limited,
registered in England, company number 785998, of Houndmills, Basingstoke,
Hampshire RG21 6XS.

Palgrave Macmillan in the US is a division of St Martin's Press LLC,
175 Fifth Avenue, New York, NY 10010.

Palgrave Macmillan is the global academic imprint of the above companies
and has companies and representatives throughout the world.

Palgrave® and Macmillan® are registered trademarks in the United States,
the United Kingdom, Europe and other countries

ISBN 978-0-230-23101-6   hardback
ISBN 978-0-230-23102-3   paperback

This book is printed on paper suitable for recycling and made from fully
managed and sustained forest sources. Logging, pulping and manufacturing
processes are expected to conform to the environmental regulations of the
country of origin.

A catalogue record for this book is available from the British Library.

A catalog record for this book is available from the Library of Congress.

10   9   8   7   6   5   4   3   2   1
19   18   17   16   15   14   13   12   11   10

Printed and bound in China

Summary of Contents

Contents

List of illustrative material

Tables

Preface

This edition retains the purpose of its predecessors: to provide a wide-ranging, contemporary and clearly written introductory text for courses in comparative politics and other introductory courses in politics and political science.

We have made some significant changes to this edition. First, we have sought to broaden the introduction to the study of politics in Part I by extending the discussion of some of the concepts in Chapter 1 and by providing separate chapters on theoretical approaches (Chapter 2) and research strategies (Chapter 3). Part I is relevant to the broad church of comparative politics but is written with a general politics audience in mind, including more advanced students undertaking dissertations and projects. This Part may also prove a useful introduction for students coming to politics for the first time at a later stage in their studies. These chapters are logically positioned at the start but pedagogical considerations may of course point in a different direction, particularly for beginning undergraduates.

Second, we have added a number of new sections to reflect recent developments and rectify old omissions. The new material includes ideology, security and surveillance, studying political culture, media structures, legal pluralism, regulation and the financial crisis. Although the book remains centred on the state, we have also tried to take more note throughout of the European Union.

Third, we have revised and edited the entire text in an attempt to keep the book clear, accessible and contemporary. We have restructured the parts, in particular moving political economy to follow the chapter on public policy so that these two more applied chapters are located together. To forestall an appreciable increase in the book's length, we have removed some older content and, to increase focus on the main text, we have marginally reduced the amount of illustrative material. In particular, we have absorbed the debates into the main text. However, the debate sections from the previous edition have been added to our website for those users who use this material in their teaching.

This edition is the work of many hands. At Palgrave Macmillan, we would like to thank Stephen Wenham for his helpful assistance and Steven Kennedy for his continuing guidance. We thank Keith Povey and Nick Fox for their vigilant copy-editing; Ian Wileman for his skilful typesetting; and Russell Foster for his impeccable editorial and research assistance. We owe a special debt to the publishers' anonymous reviewers for their careful and constructive comments.

We are grateful, too, for the many suggestions of the teachers and students from around the world who use the book, whether in its English or translated form. Mistakes of fact and interpretation inevitably creep into each new edition and we continue to welcome corrections. Please feel free to contact Martin Harrop at:

School of Geography, Politics and Sociology
University of Newcastle
Newcastle upon Tyne
England
NE1 7RU
e-mail: martin.harrop@newcastle.ac.uk

ROD HAGUE
MARTIN HARROP

Guide to learning features

This book contains a range of features designed to aid your learning. These are outlined below.

Profiles

Profiles offer an outline of specific countries and regions to complement our thematic approach. For each country or region covered, our profile provides:

- A standard set of demographic, economic and political indicators;
- A capsule description of the country's main political institutions;
- A short account of its overall political configuration.

Spotlights

Spotlights follow on from profiles, providing a detailed case study of how the chapter theme operates in the country profiled.

Learning resources

The learning resources at the end of each chapter offer guidance on exploring the topic in more depth. These sections should come in useful over the entirety of a politics degree. They cover:

- Next step: the one source which, in our opinion, represents your natural next move.

- Further reading: around a dozen major publications on the chapter topic. Even a selection of these should provide highly detailed coverage.
- Internet sources: selected websites on the topic, often with a focus on factual or practical information which is useful for further research. For clickable links to these sources, visit our website.

Further reading on more detailed topics is also included in the profiles and spotlights.

Note: All the references in this book from this and the previous edition are listed by chapter on our website, offering a comprehensive guide to the topic of each chapter.

Definitions

The first time a technical term is used, it appears in red and is separately defined on the same page. In the index, these terms are also listed in orange so that they can be located easily. All these definitions, and more, are also available in our on-line dictionary.

Boxes and tables

Boxes are used mainly to define, contrast and illustrate particular political processes. Tables display statistics, again usually with a comparative theme.

Hague and Harrop on the Web

Access to our website is free and unrestricted. Resources include:

- An extended dictionary of comparative politics;
- Links to websites, by chapter;
- Interactive quizzes by chapter;
- Guide to comparative politics on the Internet;

- Chapter summaries;
- Essay questions by chapter;
- Debate topics by chapter;
- The book's references listed by chapter.

http://www.palgrave.com/politics/hague

Guide to profiles

In addition to a profile on the European Union, we have included 15 country profiles which contain a number of figures, rankings and scales to indicate the social and political conditions of the country. These indicators and their sources are as follows.

Population (annual growth rate)

The median country's population is 4.5m. A high positive or negative growth rate can be destabilizing. Based on 2009 data.

Source: CIA (2009), itself based on US Bureau of the Census estimates

Income group

The World Bank's four-fold classification, based on 2008 data, is more precise than the traditional distinction between developed and developing countries:

▶ 66 high income countries (gross national income per head at least $11,906). Examples: France, USA.
▶ 46 upper middle income countries ($3,856–$11,905). Examples: Jamaica, Poland.
▶ 55 lower middle income countries ($976–$3,855). Examples: Egypt, India.
▶ 43 low income countries ($975 or less). Examples: Ghana, Vietnam.

Source: World Bank (2009a)

Human development index (HDI)

HDI is based on averaging three dimensions: life expectancy, education (enrolment, adult literacy) and gross domestic product per head. Of 177 countries ranked in the 2008 report, based on 2007 data, Iceland scored highest (rank = 1) and Sierra Leone lowest.

Source: United Nations Development Programme (2009)

Regime type, political rights, civil liberties

Hague and Harrop classify governments as liberal democracies, illiberal democracies or authoritarian (as at 2009). Freedom House judges political rights and civil liberties, as at 2008, on a scale from 1 (most rights or liberties) to 7.

Source: Freedom House (2009a)

Freedom of the press

Freedom House assesses the freedom of print, broadcast and internet-based media in each country, based on the legal, political and economic environment for these media. Of 195 countries ranked in the 2008 report, based on 2008 data, Finland scored highest (rank = 1) and North Korea lowest.

Source: Freedom House (2009b)

Perceived transparency

Transparency International ranks countries by their perceived level of corruption, as determined by expert assessments and opinion surveys. Of 180 countries ranked in the 2008 report, based on 2007–08 data, Denmark, New Zealand and Sweden scored equal highest (least corrupt) and Somalia lowest.

Source: Transparency International (2009)

Part I
STUDYING POLITICS

The foundations of political analysis lie in the concepts, approaches and methods through which we understand the subject. In this part, we introduce core ideas that are central to the study of politics of any kind, comparative or otherwise. In Chapter 1, we examine the key vocabulary of the discipline, including terms such as politics, government, power and authority. We also address the classification of governments used in this book: liberal democracy, illiberal democracy and authoritarian rule. Chapter 2 considers major approaches to political analysis, covering the study of institutions, political behaviour, structures, rational choices and ideas. Chapter 3 outlines specific research strategies and methods, including case studies, comparisons, statistical methods and historical analysis.

This part will enable you to:

- ▶ Define key terms used in political analysis;
- ▶ Appreciate contrasting approaches to the study of politics;
- ▶ Consider some methods to use in research projects in politics.

Chapter 1
Political concepts

This book examines the organization of politics in countries around the world. We focus on how nations solve the core problem of reaching collective decisions, paying particular attention to the institutions of government which serve this purpose. But we cannot jump straight into our subject. For just as what astronomers see in the sky depends on the type of telescope through which they peer, so too does any interpretation of politics depend on the concepts through which we approach the topic. Indeed, in politics it often seems as though everyone has his or her own telescope – and claims that their instrument is the best!

In this chapter, therefore, we introduce some core **concepts** used in political analysis. A concept is simply an idea, term or category; for instance: democracy, power or authority. Concepts are best approached with definitions restricted to their inherent characteristics. What, for example, are the features which a government must necessarily possess to qualify as a democracy? We can agree, surely, that some measure of popular control over the government forms part of this concept; if there were no way of holding the rulers to account, there would be no democracy. A good definition of a concept, in this narrow but important sense, will be clear, concise and pointed.

Conceptions, by contrast, are broader in character. They are understandings, perspectives or interpretations of a concept. We might, for instance, conceive of democracy as self-government or as representative government; as majority rule; or as the protection of minority rights. Conceptions build on definitions by moving on to a fuller discussion and consideration of alternative positions. This chapter addresses both concepts and conceptions but, as befits an introduction, our emphasis is on the former.

What is politics?

To start at the beginning: what is politics? We can easily list, and agree on, some examples of political activity. When an American president starts his annual tussle with Congress over the federal budget, he is clearly engaged in politics. When people join a protest against a war, they are patently participating in politics. The heartland of politics, as represented by such examples, is clear. However, the boundaries are less precise. When one country invades another, is it engaged in politics or merely in war? When a court issues a ruling about abortion, should its judgement be construed as political or judicial? Is politics restricted to governments or can it also be found in families, universities and even seminar groups?

A **concept** is a term, idea, or category. A **conception** is a broader understanding or interpretation of a concept (Gallie, 1956).

> **Politics** is the activity or process by which groups reach and enforce binding decisions affecting the collectivity as a whole.

A crisp definition of politics – one which fits just those things we instinctively call 'political' – is difficult. The term possesses varied uses and nuances. But three aspects of politics are clear:

◆ Politics is a collective activity, occurring within and between groups. A castaway on a deserted island could not engage in politics.
◆ Politics involves making decisions on matters affecting the group. These decisions can be reached by a variety of means, from informed deliberation to violent imposition.
◆ Political decisions become authoritative policy for the group as a whole, binding and committing its members. These decisions are enforced.

The necessity of politics arises from our social nature. We live in groups that must reach collective decisions about using resources, about relating to others and about planning for the future. A country deliberating on whether to go to war, a family discussing where to take its vacation, a university deciding whether its priority lies with teaching or research – all are examples of bodies seeking decisions impinging on all their members. Politics is a fundamental activity because a group which failed to reach any such decisions would soon cease to exist.

Once reached, decisions must of course be put into effect. Means must be found to ensure the acquiescence and preferably the consent of the members. Once agreed, taxes must be raised; once declared, wars must be fought. Public authority – ultimately, force – is used to implement collective policy. If you fail to contribute to the common task, the authorities may imprison you; at any rate, they are the only people empowered to do so. So politics possesses a hard edge, reflected in the word 'authoritative' in Easton's famous definition (1965b, p. 21):

A political system can be designated as the interactions through which values are authoritatively allocated for a society; that is what distinguishes a political system from other systems lying in its environment.

As a concept, then, politics can be defined as the process of making and executing collective decisions. But, as with many political terms, contrasting conceptions can be constructed on this simple definition. At this broader level, the key contrast is between those who see politics as the pursuit of the interests of the whole community and those who view the activity as a collision between groups pursuing their own narrow goals. This difference is summarized in the dictionary's two definitions of the adjective 'political': either 'sagacious and judicious' or 'crafty and scheming'. It is worth comparing these two conceptions since they provide different starting points for understanding politics.

The interpretation of politics as a community-serving activity can be traced to the ancient Greeks. For instance, the Greek philosopher Aristotle (384–322 BC) argued that 'man is by nature a political animal' (1962 edn, p. 28). By this he meant not just that politics is unavoidable but also that it is the highest human activity, the feature which most sharply separates us from other species. For Aristotle, people can only express their nature as reasoning, virtuous beings by participating in a political community which seeks to identify the common interest through discussion and to pursue it through action to which all contribute. In Aristotle's model constitution, 'the ideal citizens rule in the interests of all, not because they are forced to by checks and balances, but because they see it as right to do so' (Nicholson, 1990, p. 42). Politics is the pursuit of common goals and citizens should contribute to their achievement.

From this somewhat idealized perspective, violence and domination are sometimes wholly removed from the political domain. For Crick (2000, p. 30), politics is 'that solution to the problem of order which chooses conciliation rather than violence and coercion'. A similar view is advanced by Goodin and Klingemann (1996, p. 8): 'pure force, literally speaking, is more the province of physics than of politics. Thus, an absolute dictator in quest of complete power could rightly be said to be engaged in an (inevitably futile) attempt to transcend politics'.

The difficulty with this benign conception is that it provides an ideal of what politics should be rather than a description of what it actually is. At its best, no doubt, politics is a process of deliberation and conciliation; but politics as it exists is surely more conflictful. A party in pursuit of power engages in politics, whether its strategy is peaceful, violent or both. To say that wars and dictatorships are not forms of politics is to narrow the subject in a way that runs counter to common sense, to much of human history (including the twentieth century), and to politics as it operates in much of the contemporary world. Such a lens can too easily become a blindfold – and the conception can obscure the underlying concept.

So we must also give weight to the competing conception – that politics is, in truth, the use of the public arena to advance private interests. On this account, narrow interests take precedence over collective benefits and those in authority place their own goals above those of the community. Within this framework lie those who see power as an intrinsic value and politics as a competition for its acquisition and retention. This more pragmatic reading also extends to those who see politics as a battle for other resources, including wealth. Thus, Lasswell (1936) famously defined politics as 'who gets what, when, how' and Marx and Engels (1848) depicted the executive of the modern state as 'a committee for managing the whole affairs of the common bourgeoisie'. Discussion occurs in the context of fundamental differences in power, and conciliation serves to reinforce existing inequalities.

This realist conception surely possesses descriptive merit. Particularly in large, complex societies, politics is a competition between groups – ideological as well as material – either for power itself or for influence over those who wield it. Note, however, that because political decisions touch the community as a whole, policies favouring particular groups must (in most systems) be presented as best for the group as a whole. In this way, the interests of the whole often do re-enter the political calculus, and public dialogue (where permitted at all) moderates the pursuit of private concerns.

What emerges, we suggest, is the multifaceted nature of politics. The subject involves both shared and competing interests, both cooperation and conflict, both reason and force. Each of our conceptions is necessary but both together are sufficient. The essence of politics lies in the interaction between conceptions and we should not narrow our vision by reducing politics to either one. Laver (1983, p. 1)

makes the point: 'pure conflict is war. Pure cooperation is true love. Politics is a mixture of both'.

Government or governance?

Small groups can reach collective decisions without any special procedures. The members of a family or sports team can reach an understanding by informal discussion. And these agreements can be self-executing: those who make the decision implement it themselves. However, such simple mechanisms are impractical for larger units such as the countries which provide the focus of this book. Countries must develop standard procedures for making and enforcing collective decisions. By definition, decision-making organizations formed for this purpose comprise the **government**: the arena for resolving political issues.

A **government** consists of institutions responsible for making collective decisions for society. More narrowly, government refers to the top political level within such institutions.

In popular use, 'the government' refers just to the highest level of political appointments: to presidents, prime ministers and others at the apex of power. But in a wider conception, government consists of all organizations charged with reaching and implementing decisions for the community. By this definition the police, the armed forces, public servants and judges all form part of the government, even though such people are not usually appointed by political methods such as election. In this broader sense, government is the entire terrain of institutions endowed with public authority.

The classic case for government was made in the seventeenth century by Thomas Hobbes (Box 1.1). His view was that government provides us with protection from the harm that we would otherwise inflict on each other in our quest for gain and glory. By granting a monopoly of the sword to a government, we transform anarchy into order, securing not only peace but also the opportunity for cooperation.

In modern terms, a government offers security and predictability to those subject to it. In a well-governed society, citizens and firms can plan for the

BOX 1.1

Hobbes's case for government

The case for government was well-made by the English philosopher, Thomas Hobbes (1588–1679). His starting point was the fundamental equality in our ability to inflict harm on others:

For as to the strength of body, the weakest has strength enough to kill the strongest, either by secret machination, or by confederacy with others.

So arises a clash of ambition and fear of attack:

From this equality of ability, arises equality of hope in the attaining of our ends. And therefore if any two men desire the same thing, which nevertheless they cannot both enjoy, they become enemies; and in the way to their end, which is principally their own conservation, and sometimes their own delectation, endeavour to destroy or subdue one another.

Without a ruler to keep us in check, the situation becomes grim indeed:

Hereby it is manifest, that during the time men live without a common power to keep them all in awe, they are in that condition which is called war; and such a war, as is of every man, against every man.

People therefore agree (by means unclear) to set up an absolute government to escape from a life that would otherwise be 'solitary, poor, nasty, brutish and short':

The only way to erect such a common power, as may be able to defend them from the invasion of foreigners, and the injuries of one another ... is, to confer all their power and strength upon one man, or one assembly of men, that may reduce all their wills, by plurality of voices, unto one will ... This done, the multitude so united is called a COMMONWEALTH.

Source: Hobbes (1651).

Governance denotes the activity of making collective decisions, a task in which government institutions may not play a leading, or even any, role. In world politics, many issues are resolved by negotiation: governance without government.

---

long-term, knowing that laws will be stable and applied consistently.

An additional argument for government, much favoured by economists, is the efficiency to be gained by establishing a standard way of reaching and enforcing decisions (Coase, 1960). If every decision had to be preceded by a separate agreement on how to reach and apply it, politics would become tiresome indeed. These efficiency gains give people who disagree on what should be done an incentive to agree on a general mechanism for resolving disagreements.

Of course, establishing a government creates new dangers. The risk of Hobbes's commonwealth is that it will abuse its own authority, creating more problems than it solves. As one of Hobbes's critics pointed out, there is no profit in avoiding the dangers of foxes if the outcome is simply to be devoured by lions (Locke, 1690).

A key aim in studying politics must therefore be to discover how to secure the undoubted benefits of government while also controlling its inherent dangers. We must keep in mind Plato's question of long ago: 'who is to guard the guards themselves?'. And here the notion of governance becomes relevant.

Governance is an old notion undergoing a revival in popularity. The term is nonetheless difficult to pin down, perhaps because it is in essence a conception rather than a concept. As Jordan, Wurzel and Zito (2005, p. 478) observe, 'there is no universally accepted definition of governance'. In general terms, though, the concept fits between politics and government; it is less than the former but, in a way, more than the latter. To be more specific, governance refers to regular procedures for resolving political issues, and thus focuses only on an aspect of politics, but it also draws attention to the wide range of non-governmental actors involved in such procedures, thus broadening our perspective beyond government. Let us expand on this summary statement.

Governance directs our attention away from government's command-and-control function towards the broader task of public regulation, a role which ruling politicians in liberal democracies share with other actors. Depending on the particular sector, these actors can include employers, trade unions, the judiciary, professional employees, journalists, scientists and even academics. In areas such as health care, law and sport, expert practitioners – doctors, lawyers, sports administrators – engage in substantial self-regulation. Because such professions do not take kindly to instructions from government, institutions such as the executive and the legislature are at most particular actors in governance networks and by no means always the commanding players. Most of the time, for example, a particular sport will be run by its governing body, with the government itself intervening only in extreme situations. Hence the need for the wider term – not to replace government but rather to broaden and supplement it.

Understood as the task of managing complex societies, governance involves the coordination of both public and private sector bodies; it is the ability to get things done without the capacity to command that they are done (Rhodes, 1996). Governance positions government as one actor in a network, rather than as a body with direct control over the levers of power. The term suggests a merging of public and private authority, a blurring that helps to explain the difficulty in giving a precise definition of the term. 'In the early days,' said a British entrepreneur who founded his business in 1992, 'people took decisions and had authority. Today it is just one mindless, circuitous working group' (Guthrie, 2008).

The concept of governance grew in popularity in the final two decades of the twentieth century as Western democracies lost some confidence in the ability of their governments to manage economic production and welfare provision directly. As a result, more emphasis was placed on government as a regulator (e.g. of privately owned telecommunications networks) rather than as a provider (e.g. through a state-owned telephone company). Similarly, in the financial crisis of 2008/09, the call was for improved governance – regulation – of the financial sector rather than permanent nationalization of failed investment banks.

Significantly, the concept of governance rose to prominence in discussion of the European Union, which relies almost exclusively on regulation and negotiation to influence its member states. The European Union is surely the prime example of a governance framework built on the foundation of national governments (Hooghe and Marks, 2001).

Because governance refers to the activity of ruling, it has become the preferred term when examining the quality and effectiveness of rule. In this context, governance refers to what governments do and to how well they do it. For example, many international agencies suggest that 'effective governance' is crucial to economic development in new democracies (World Bank, 1997). Driving home this theme, President Obama told Ghana's parliament in 2009 that 'development depends upon good governance' (BBC News, 2009). In this sense of governance, the focus is on government policies and activities rather than the institutions of rule themselves.

However, it is world politics which offers the most striking examples of governance. The reason is clear: no world government exists to make enforceable decisions yet many aspects of global relations are regulated by agreement. One example is the Internet, a massive network of linked computers beyond the control of any one government. Yet standards for connecting computers and data to the Internet are agreed, mainly by private actors. Thus we can speak only of the governance, but not the government, of cyberspace – and similarly of telecommunications, epidemics, copyright protection and the numerous other areas where human interaction activity spills across national boundaries (Goldsmith and Wu, 2006).

Classifying governments

With 'government' defined, we can turn to the question of how governments should be classified in comparative politics generally and in this book specifically. We should not be too ambitious here. As Huntington (1991, p. 8) advises, 'political regimes will never fit neatly into intellectually defined boxes, and any system of classification has to accept the existence of ambiguous, borderline and mixed cases'. Even so, classification is an important tool, especially in comparative politics: it enables us to group similar cases together and to examine the origins and consequences of each type.

We must begin with the most influential classification ever devised: Aristotle's analysis of the 158 city-states of Ancient Greece. These communities were small settlements showing considerable variety in their forms of rule during the period between approximately 500–338 BC. Such diversity provided an ideal laboratory for Aristotle to consider which type of political system provided what he sought in a government: namely, an optimal combination of

---

BOX 1.2

Aristotle's classification of governments

		Rule by		
		One	*Few*	*Many*
	Genuine	Kingship	Aristocracy	Polity
Form				
	Perverted	Tyranny	Oligarchy	Democracy

Source: Aristotle (1962 edn) book 3, ch. 5.

---

stability and effectiveness. His analysis offers one of the earliest examples of comparative politics at work.

Aristotle based his scheme on two dimensions (Box 1.2). The first was the number of people involved in the task of governing: one, few or many. This dimension captured the breadth of participation in a political system. His second dimension, more difficult to apply but certainly no less important, was whether rulers governed in the common interest ('the genuine form') or in their own interest ('the perverted form'). This dimension links to the differing conceptions of politics we have already discussed. For Aristotle, the significance of this second aspect was that a political system would be more stable and effective when its rulers governed in the long-term interests of the community, rather than in the narrow interests of their own social group.

Cross-classifying the number of rulers (one, few or many) with the nature of rule (genuine or perverted) yields the six types shown in Box 1.2. It is worth outlining each cell in this highly influential table. In the case of rule by a single person, Aristotle took kingship as the genuine form and regarded tyranny as its degraded equivalent. For government by the few, Aristotle distinguished between aristocracy (which he defined as rule by the virtuous) and its base form of oligarchy (rule by the rich). And within the category of rule by the many, he separated the ideal form of 'polity' – broadly equivalent to rule by the moderate middle class, exercised through law – from the debased form of 'democracy', which he interpreted unsympathetically as government by the poor in their own self-interest.

Modern classifications continue to be informed by Aristotle's work. Not surprisingly, however, Aristotle's categories now need supplementing to yield a classification more sensitive to the modern world. In this book, we distinguish between three types of government – liberal democracy, illiberal democracy and authoritarian – and we use this scheme to organize our discussion in Chapters 7–19. For now we will introduce these types as simple concepts, with fuller conceptions developed in Chapters 5 and 6.

Although unknown to Aristotle, **liberal democracy** is the most familiar category today. In this format, rulers are chosen through free, fair and regular elections. Nearly all citizens are entitled to vote and, to permit effective choice, electors can join and form political parties. Further, independent media allow electors to obtain an 'enlightened understanding' of the issues before as well as during election campaigns (Dahl, 1998, p. 39).

But – and here we reach the 'liberal' part – the government of a liberal democracy is subject to constitutional limits. Individual rights, including freedom of assembly, property, religion and speech, are effectively defended in independent courts. A clear boundary between public and private spheres keeps the elected government in its place. In office, rulers are subject to explicit, constitutional limits.

So the adjective 'liberal' in the phrase 'liberal democracy' is not used in the American sense to denote a supporter of progressive policies associated with the Democrats. Rather, the term refers to the philosophy of liberalism, a doctrine which regards individual autonomy as the cardinal value. In this

BOX 1.3

A classification of governments

	Characteristics	Examples
Liberal democracy	Representative and limited government operating through law provides an accepted framework for political competition. Regular elections based on near universal suffrage are free and fair. Individual rights, including freedom of expression and association, are respected.	Affluent Western countries such as Australia, Canada, France and Germany. India is an example of a predominantly liberal democracy in what is still mainly a poor country.
Illiberal democracy	Leaders are elected with no or minimal falsification of the count. However, the rulers exploit their position to prevent a level playing field. To keep potential opponents off-balance, rulers interfere with the rule of law, the media and the market. Individual rights are poorly entrenched and the judiciary is weak.	Many post-military states in Africa and Latin America (e.g. Venezuela). Several Asian states (e.g. Malaysia). Some post-communist states (e.g. Russia). Note that Venezuela under Chávez and Russia under Putin returned to a more authoritarian version of democracy.
Authoritarian regime	Rulers stand above the law and are free from effective popular accountability. The media are controlled or cowed. Political participation is usually limited and discouraged. However, the rulers' power is often constrained by the need for tacit alliances with other power-holders such as landowners, the military and religious leaders.	Military governments, ruling monarchies and personal dictators. Authoritarian rule is the most common form of rule in history.
	In the **totalitarian states** of the twentieth century, participation was compulsory but controlled as the government sought total control of society, justified by an ideology seeking to transform both society and human nature. These regimes placed heavy reliance on party members, the secret police and other informers as agents of social control.	Communist and fascist regimes subscribed to totalitarian thinking but the model was rarely fully implemented, except for a time in the Soviet Union. More recently, Iran after the Islamic revolution of 1979 showed some totalitarian characteristics.

way, the constitution of a liberal democracy provides not only an accepted framework of political competition but also an effective shield for defending individual rights against government excess.

We now turn to the opposite end of the spectrum. **Authoritarian regimes** are neither liberal nor democratic. The population lacks any effective and regular means of controlling its rulers. Elections may not take place at all, as in military regimes, or else the choice may be artificially restricted: vote for us or go to jail. Whole swathes of the population may be excluded from voting, as with the continued denial of the ballot to women in several Middle

Eastern kingdoms. Political parties may be banned altogether; or only one may be permitted; or 'independent' parties may only be permitted if they accept their subservience. In any event, the rulers exploit the advantages of office (including influence over the media) to prevent a level playing field at elections. Communication between rulers and ruled is low in quantity and quality. Furthermore, the leaders of authoritarian regimes – unlike those of any type of democracy – are prepared to falsify the election result if necessary.

Although orthodox communist states have slipped into history and military rule is currently rare, authoritarian rule remains an important form of government. China, after all, is the world's most populous nation while the Middle East contains a clutch of significant authoritarian regimes (as well as most of the world's oil reserves).

We must also note, in parentheses, the distinction often drawn between authoritarian and **totalitarian** regimes (Linz, 1975). The latter term is frequently used to denote communist and fascist regimes. The leaders of these systems sought tight control and total transformation of society. Most authoritarian rulers, however, seek to insulate themselves from the wider society and are rarely dictators in the sense of possessing unlimited control. Thus it is certainly possible to regard authoritarian and totalitarian regimes as distinct systems. However, because most totalitarian regimes now belong to the past, we have chosen in this book to use the term 'authoritarian rule' to refer to all forms of non-democracy. We include totalitarian regimes as a subgroup within this broader heading.

Finally, to the grey zone. Here lie the many hybrid regimes which combine democratic and authoritarian elements. Many phrases are used to capture this form of regime: semi-democracy, electoral democracy, delegative democracy and even semi- or electoral authoritarianism (O'Donnell, 1994). Simplifying decisively, the most important type of hybrid regime in today's world is what we call **illiberal democracy** (Zakaria, 2003). Many low-income post-communist, post-military and post-colonial countries take this form.

In an illiberal democracy, rulers run non-fraudulent but still controlled elections; they 'make' the result, even though they do not 'steal' it (Mackenzie, 1958). In Russia, for instance, President Putin's re-election victory in 2004 reflected authentic popular support for a strong leader; in that sense, Russia was at least an electoral democracy. Even so, no observer would have described Russia under Putin as a liberal democracy. As a graduate of the KGB, Putin showed a fine appreciation of the mechanics of power, dominating the broadcasting media, rewarding his friends and ruthlessly punishing his enemies. Because elections in an illiberal democracy only rarely deliver a change in government, turnover arises more from resignation or – as in Russia and much of Latin America – from constitutional limits on re-election.

Illiberal democracy is a common form of government in the world's political landscape, even if its intermediate status means it receives insufficient attention. We should also beware of assuming that the type is new. Finer (1970), for instance, discussed the comparable notion of quasi-democracy, using Mexico as his main illustration. However, examples are less stable than the type; political systems can move in and out of the category en route to fully democratic (or fully authoritarian) status. At the national level, for instance, Finer's favourite example of Mexico now qualifies as a liberal democracy.

Power

Power is the currency of politics. Just as money permits the efficient flow of goods and services through an economy, so power enables collective decisions to be made and enforced. Without power, a government would be as useless as a car without an engine. Power is the key political resource that enables rulers both to serve and to exploit their subjects.

Many authors go so far as to define politics in terms of power. Hay (2002, p. 3), for instance, suggests that politics is 'concerned with the distribution, exercise and consequences of power'. On such

Power is the capacity to bring about intended effects. The term is often used as a synonym for influence, to denote the impact (however exercised) of one actor on another. But the word is also used more narrowly to refer to the more forceful modes of influence: for example, getting one's way by threats.

accounts, politics is found not just in governments but also in the workplace, the family, the university and indeed in any other arena in which power is exerted. Such a view is probably too broad; in reality, those who study politics are primarily interested in the flow of power in and around government. But the difference here is minor; all are agreed that power is central to politics. How then should this term be understood?

The word itself comes from the Latin *potere*, meaning 'to be able'. One conception, then, sees power as simply the capacity to bring about intended effects (Russell, 1938). The greater our ability to determine our own fate, the more power we possess. In this sense, describing the United States as a powerful country means that it has the ability to achieve its objectives, whatever those may be. Similarly, to lack power is to be prey to circumstances. Notice that the emphasis here is on power *to* rather than power *over* – on the ability to achieve goals, rather than the more specific exercise of control over other people or countries.

This 'power to' approach is associated with the American sociologist, Talcott Parsons (1902–79). Parsons developed a conception of power as the capacity of a government to draw on the obligations of its citizens in order to achieve collective purposes such as order and environmental protection. Other things being equal, the more powerful the government, the more effective it will be at achieving community goals. For Parsons (1967), political power is a desirable collective resource which enables rulers to implement the common interest.

In defining power as 'not just the ability to act but the ability to act in concert', the German-born political theorist Hannah Arendt (1906–75) adopted a similar perspective (1970, p. 44). A group whose members are willing to act together possesses more horsepower – an enhanced capacity to achieve its goals – than does a group dominated by suspicion and conflict. For Arendt, as for Parsons, to be in power is to be empowered by a group's members to pursue joint objectives. Thus Arendt viewed power and violence as enemies rather than siblings: 'power and violence are opposites; where the one rules, the other is absent. Violence can destroy power; it is utterly incapable of creating it' (1966, p. 56). This view of power reflects a conception of politics as the expression of the community's shared interests.

The benign conception of power developed by Parsons and Arendt had some impact, but it surely remains incomplete. As we saw in discussing wider conceptions of politics, power is not just a technical task of implementing a vision shared by a whole society. It is also a struggle over what goals to pursue. The question of whose vision triumphs is surely relevant to any assessment of power. In large part, power consists in the ability to get one's way and to impose one's opinions, whether by force or persuasion. That is, one actor exercises power over others. In Dahl's famous definition (1957), power is a matter of getting people to do what they would not otherwise have done. In this interpretation, power is synonymous with influence over others.

Power as influence can be exerted through a variety of means, including threats, bribes, negotiations and commitments. Rather confusingly, the term 'power' is often confined to influence achieved by the threat of sanctions: 'your money or your life'. In this narrower sense, power would not normally be applied to influence achieved by negotiating a deal (which might benefit both parties) or by persuading the other party that acting in a certain way is simply the right thing to do (altering preferences). In these cases, the relationship involved is more naturally understood as one of influence than power.

It is clear, then, that the concept of power gives rise to a number – perhaps an excessive number – of conceptions (Lukes, 1974). At its simplest, power is just the production of intended effects. As we move beyond this core definition, our view of power will reflect our assumptions about politics. If we view politics as the pursuit of shared goals, we will see it as a resource of the political community as a whole. But if we interpret politics as an arena in which competing groups pursue their own particular objectives, we are more likely to measure power by the group's ability to overcome opposition.

Authority and legitimacy

Authority is a broader concept than power. Where power is the capacity to act, authority is the acknowledged right to do so. It exists when subordinates accept the capacity of superiors to give legitimate orders. Thus, a general may exercise power

Authority is the right to rule. Authority creates its own power so long as people accept that the person in authority has the right to make decisions.

over enemy soldiers but his authority is restricted to his own forces.

When writers such as Parsons and Arendt argue that power is a collective resource, they mean that power is most effective when converted into authority. The German sociologist Max Weber (1864–1920) suggested that in a relationship of authority the ruled implement the command as if they had adopted it spontaneously, for its own sake (1922, p. 29). Yet authority remains more than voluntary compliance. To acknowledge the authority of rulers does not always mean you agree with their decisions; it means only that you accept their right to make decisions and your own duty to obey. Relationships of authority are still hierarchical.

Just as there are various sources of power, so too can authority be built on a range of foundations. Weber developed a particularly influential conception of authority in distinguishing three ways of validating political power: by tradition, by charisma and by appeal to legal–rational norms (Box 1.4). This classification remains a useful starting point for comparing the nature of political authority in contemporary states.

Weber's first type, **traditional authority**, is based on 'piety for what actually, allegedly or presumably has always existed' (1923, p. 296). Traditional rulers do not need to justify their position; rather, obedience is required as part of the natural order. For example, monarchs rule because they always have done so; to demand any further justification would itself challenge tradition.

Traditional authority is usually an extension of patriarchy – the authority of the father or the eldest male. Weber (1923, p. 296) offers numerous examples of such relationships:

Patriarchy means the authority of the father, the husband, the senior of the house, the elder sibling over the members of the household; the rule of the master and patron over the bondsmen, serfs, and freed men; of the lord over the domestic servants and household officials, of the prince over house- and court-officials.

BOX 1.4

Weber's classification of authority

	Basis	Illustration
Traditional	Custom and the established way of doing things	Monarchy
Charismatic	Intense commitment to the leader and his message	Many revolutionary leaders
Legal–rational	Rules and procedures. The office, not the person	Bureaucracy

Source: Weber (1922).

Traditional authority remains the model for many political relationships, especially in authoritarian regimes. In Arabic, for example, the term 'sheikh' refers to the head of both a kingdom and an extended family; the word carries positive overtones such as maturity, experience and wisdom. In this way, the traditional authority of the father is projected onto the political system as a whole, providing a foundation for rule which subjects are expected to accept unconditionally – just like children.

Charismatic authority is Weber's second form. This type contrasts sharply with authority based on tradition. Where traditional allegiance is founded in the past, charismatic authority spurns history. The charismatic prophet looks forward, convincing followers that the promised land is within reach. Such leaders are obeyed because they inspire their followers, who credit their saviour with exceptional and even supernatural qualities.

Contrary to popular use, charisma is not for Weber an intrinsic quality of a leader. Rather, the term refers to how followers perceive their redeemer: as inspirational, heroic and unique. So there is little point in searching for the distinctive personal qualities of charismatic leaders; in any case, research suggests that their personalities are quite ordinary (Oakes, 1997). The key is demand rather than supply: which political conditions bring forth a requirement for authority to be expressed in such messianic terms?

Typically, charismatic leaders emerge in times of crisis and upheaval. Jesus Christ, Mahatma Gandhi, Martin Luther King and Adolf Hitler are illustrations. Yet the base of charismatic authority in a specific individual is also its weakness. Unlike the traditional form, charismatic authority is short-lived: it fades either with the particular leader or with its transfer to a more permanent structure. This latter process is called the **routinization of charisma**. The religious leader founds a church; the politician establishes a party. 'It is the fate of charisma', wrote Weber (1922, p. 129), 'to recede with the development of permanent institutional structures'.

The **routinization of charisma** is the process through which the individual authority of an inspirational leader is transferred to a permanent office or institution.

Consider the case of revolutionary Iran. Ayatollah Khomeini was a charismatic Muslim cleric and exiled hero who returned in triumph to his Iranian homeland to take over the government following the overthrow of the Shah in 1979. Khomeini did succeed in establishing a theocratic regime in Iran, dominated by the Islamic clergy, which outlasted his own death in 1989. But as memories of the regime's founder receded, so younger generations increasingly questioned the political authority of corrupt religious leaders, leading to public protests following a disputed election in 2009. It remains to be seen whether the regime created by the charismatic prophet can survive in the long term.

Legal–rational authority is the third and final element of Weber's scheme. Here obedience is owed to rules rather than rulers, resulting in government based on regulations rather than tradition or charisma. Legal–rational authority inheres in a role or a position, not a specific person. Because it derives from the office rather than the person, we can speak of officials 'going beyond their authority'. Setting out the extent of an officeholder's authority reveals its limits and so provides an opportunity for redress. In this way, legal–rational authority offers a foundation for individual rights and provides an essential component of liberal democracy.

Weber judged that legal–rational authority was becoming predominant in the modern world, both in the political realm and beyond. A public servant proceeding in accordance with written rules, a politician acting within the constitution, a judge methodically applying the law – all are examples of individuals implementing an explicit rationality. While all liberal democracies have a base in legal–rational authority, Weber's German homeland is one of the fullest examples. Its written constitution and extensive administrative codes provide a political and social framework, justifying Germany's designation as a *Rechtsstaat*: a state based on law.

Returning to the broader notion of authority, we must now introduce its close cousin, **legitimacy**. The terms are similar in meaning, but legitimacy is the wider concept. Where authority inheres in a specific role, such as that of a judge, legitimacy is an attribute of the wider system of government within which these offices exist. When a regime is widely accepted by those subject to it, we describe it as legitimate. Thus we speak of the authority of an official but the legitimacy of a regime.

Although the word legitimacy comes from the Latin *legitimare*, meaning to declare lawful, legitimacy is much more than mere legality. Legality is a technical matter. It denotes whether a rule was made correctly – that is, following regular procedures. By contrast, legitimacy is a broader and more political concept. It refers to whether people accept the validity either of a specific law or of the political system as a whole.

A **legitimate** system of government is one based on authority: that is, those subject to its rule recognize its right to make decisions.

Regulations can be legal without being legitimate. For instance, the majority black population in white-run South Africa considered the country's apartheid laws to be illegitimate, even though these regulations were made according to the existing constitution. The same could be said of many laws passed by communist states: properly passed and even obeyed but not accepted as legitimate by the people.

While legality is a topic for lawyers, political scientists are more interested in legitimacy: in how a regime gains, retains and sometime loses public faith in its right to rule. Weber's classification of authority is useful here too. Among other factors, a regime's legitimacy may rest on tradition, on a charismatic leader, or on conformity to the constitution. In any event, public opinion, not a law court, is the arena in which the battle for legitimacy is fought.

The state and sovereignty

The **state** is now the dominant principle of political organization on the world's landmass. There are, of course, a few intriguing exceptions (Wilde, 2007). These include territories still under colonial control (e.g. Britain's Gibraltar) or administered by the United Nations (e.g. Bosnia) or voluntarily subject to partial external authority (e.g. Puerto Rico is affiliated to the United States) or granted substantial autonomy within a larger state (e.g. Hong Kong within China).

> The **state** is a political community formed by a territorial population subject to one government.

Leaving such anomalies to one side, the world is parcelled up into separate states which, through mutual recognition and interaction, form the international system (Figure 1.1). These units are the main focus of this book and for this reason we will devote Chapter 4 to conceptions of the state's evolution and significance. Here we focus on the concept itself.

Figure 1.1 Member states of the United Nations, 1949–2009

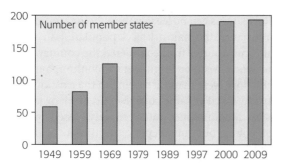

The state is a unique institution, standing above all other organizations in society. It alone claims not just the capacity but also the right to employ force. As Weber noted, the exclusive feature of the state is precisely this integration of force with authority: 'a state is a human community that (successfully) claims the monopoly of the legitimate use of physical force within a given territory' (quoted in Gerth and Mills, 1948, p. 78). When the state's monopoly of legitimate force is threatened, as in a civil war, its very existence is at stake. As long as the conflict continues, there is no legitimate authority. Hence, in cynically describing states as nothing more than 'bodies of armed men', the Russian revolutionary Vladimir Lenin (1870–1924) was only partly correct. Contrary to Lenin, a body of armed men does not constitute a state: for the law of the gun is no law at all.

How does a state differ from a government? In essence, the state defines the political community of which government is the managing agent. By successfully claiming a monopoly of authorized force, the state creates a mandate for rule which the government then puts into effect. This distinction between state and government is reflected in the characteristic separation of the roles of head of state and of head of government. European monarchs, for example, symbolize the state but their prime ministers are in charge of the government.

Since much of the theoretical justification for the state is provided by the European idea of **sovereignty**, we must unpack this related notion. As developed by the French philosopher Jean Bodin (1529–96), sovereignty refers to the untrammelled and undivided power to make laws. In a similar vein, the English jurist William Blackstone (1723–80) argued that 'there is and must be in every state a supreme, irresistible, absolute and uncontrolled authority, in which the right of sovereignty resides'.

The word 'sovereign' originally meant one seated above. So the sovereign body is the one institution unlimited by higher authority: the highest of the high. By definition, that body is the state. As Bodin wrote, the sovereign can 'give laws unto all and every one of the subjects and receive none from them'.

> **Sovereignty** refers to the ultimate source of authority in society. The sovereign is the highest and final decision-maker within a community.

Sovereignty originally developed in Europe to justify the attempt by monarchs to consolidate control over kingdoms in which authority had previously been shared with the feudal aristocracy and the Catholic church. Indeed, the British monarch is still known as the 'sovereign'. By consecrating central authority in this way, the legal concept of sovereignty contributed powerfully to the development of the European state.

But as democracy gained ground, so too did the belief that elected parliaments acting on behalf of the people are the true holders of sovereignty. The means of acquiring sovereignty evolved although the theoretical importance of Blackstone's 'supreme authority' remained unquestioned, especially in centralized European countries such as Britain and France. To this day, the notion of 'parliamentary sovereignty' remains an important theme in British political debate.

Beyond Europe, the notion of sovereignty remained weaker. In the federal United States, for instance, political authority is shared between the central and state governments, all operating under a constitution supposedly made by 'we, the people' and nourished by the Supreme Court. In these circumstances, the idea of sovereignty is diluted and so too, significantly, is the concept of the state itself. Americans more often use the word 'state' to denote the 50 states of the union rather than the federal government in Washington. Hemmed about with checks and balances, America's central government lacks the 'absolute and uncontrolled authority' which Blackstone judged so essential to the state.

Contemporary discussion distinguishes between **internal** and **external sovereignty**. External sovereignty is important because it allows a state to claim the right not just to regulate affairs within its boundaries but also to participate as an accepted member of the international order. In this way, the development of the international system strengthens the authority of states in the domestic sphere. Internal and external sovereignty normally reinforce each other. Thus Kosovo, which declared independence from Serbia in 2008 but has struggled to

Internal sovereignty refers to law-making power within a territory. **External sovereignty** refers to international recognition of the sovereign's territorial jurisdiction.

achieve full external recognition, finds itself in an uncertain position.

First and foremost, sovereignty is a theoretical construct. The formal right to make laws does not imply that the sovereign is omnipotent. All sovereigns are influenced by events beyond and within their borders. For this reason, claims that sovereignty has become a myth in an interdependent world should be treated with scepticism. Sovereignty always was a myth; that is its nature and significance. Mexico, for instance, depends more on the United States than vice versa but the two countries remain formally equal as sovereign nations. France (population 64.1 million) is more autonomous than Belgium (population 10.4 million) but both are sovereign entities. A state's control over its destiny is a matter of degree but its sovereignty is by its nature unlimited. The essence of sovereignty lies exactly in an unqualified legal title:

Constitutional independence, like marriage, is an absolute condition. People are either married or not married; they cannot be 70 per cent married. The same with sovereignty: a country either has the legal title of sovereignty or it does not; there is no in-between condition (Sørensen, 2004, p. 104).

Nations and nationalism

A **nation** is a more elusive concept than a state. Nations are imagined communities and a nation is often viewed as any group that upholds a claim to be regarded as such (Anderson, 1983). In two ways, though, we can be a little more precise. First, nations are peoples with homelands. As Eley and Suny (1996, p. 10) put it, a nation – like a state – implies 'a claim on a particular piece of real estate'. Here the origin of the word 'nation', deriving from a Latin term meaning place of birth, is relevant. The link between nation and place is one factor distinguishing a nation from a tribe or ethnic group. A tribe can easily move home but a nation remains tethered to its motherland, changing shape mainly through expansion and contraction.

Second, when a group claims to be a nation, it professes a right to **self-determination** within its homeland. It seeks sovereignty over its land, using or inventing a shared culture to justify its claim. This

Self-determination is the choice of acts without external compulsion. The right of national self-determination is the right of a people to possess its own government, democratic or otherwise. The principle was expressed in the influential Atlantic Charter (1941), a joint statement by Franklin Roosevelt and Winston Churchill, which underpinned decolonization.

assertion of self-rule (not to be confused with democratic rule) gives the idea of the nation its political character. A group becomes a nation by achieving or seeking control over its own destiny, whether through independence or devolution. Nations have either achieved statehood or are states in waiting.

Some examples will illustrate how demands for nationhood integrate territory, culture and politics. To describe French-speaking Canadians as a separate nation, as opposed to a linguistic community, indicates a claim for autonomy if not independence for this culturally distinct and geographically concentrated group. Similarly, the campaign for a Palestinian state since 1948 has strengthened what was previously a more amorphous Palestinian national identity.

Because the concept of nation is political, nations need not be united by a common language. A common tongue certainly eases the task of cultural unification yet Switzerland, for instance, is indisputably a nation even though French, German and Italian are used there. Similarly, speaking English does not suffice to qualify for membership of the English nation; if it did, the English nation would still sit astride the world.

In developing conceptions of the nation, discussion has centred on whether nations should be seen as modern or ancient. On the one hand, nations are often viewed as attempts by peoples to assert their essentially modern right to self-determination. On

A portion of mankind may be said to constitute a **nationality** if they are united among themselves by common sympathies . . . which make them cooperate with each other more willingly than with other people, desire to be under the same government, and desire that it should be government by themselves or a portion of themselves exclusively (Mill, 1861, p. 391).

the other hand, nations are also seen as creatures of antiquity, emerging from the primeval soup of past times. What are the arguments advanced on each side of this controversy?

To view nations as modern is to suggest that they are made rather than found. Nations assert statehood and, since states themselves are products of modernity, so too are nations. Specifically, a national identity serves several modern functions. It unites people who do not know each other but who nonetheless find themselves yoked together under common rulers and markets. A shared nationality, it is suggested, provides an emotional bond for an increasingly rational world. It allows the losers from the transition to a market economy to take comfort in the progress of their country as a whole. In a similar way, national identity provides a rationalization for participation in war, encouraging people 'to die for the sake of strangers' (Langman, 2006).

Certainly, many nations have been constructed in the course of recent struggles. In the nineteenth and especially the twentieth centuries, colonial peoples marched to independence under a nationalist banner. These assertions of national identity were often as artificial as the boundaries originally imposed by colonial rulers. It was 'the presence and power of the colonial regime that stimulated the development of a national identity as the basis of resistance' (Calhoun, 1997, p. 108). In a process aptly termed nationalism from above, the leaders of independence movements established national movements which did indeed prove to be the gravediggers of empire.

The opposed conception, that nations are ancient rather than modern, is propounded by Anthony Smith (2009). He points out that several large ethnic groups ('nations'?) are indeed of distant origin; examples include the Greeks, Serbs and Chinese. For Smith, nations draw on a tradition – real or mythical – of a shared descent, history and culture. This position is the primordial view of nations, meaning existing from the beginning.

Several other authors suggest that a sense of nationality is a natural part of the human condition, not a response to modern conditions. Geertz (1963), for example, believes that human beings inherently develop an emotional or spiritual affinity to a larger grouping than their immediate neighbours (whether this wider entity need be a nation is another matter). In similar vein, Van den Berghe (1981, p. 27) links nationalism to the primordial notion of kinship. He judges that we are cultural beings bound together by the shared recognition of common descent. But this recognition cannot just be invented but 'has to be rooted in historical reality'. So nations are extended kinship groups answering our cultural need to know who we are. They are universal, not specifically modern, in character.

As with many debates in politics, there are probably elements of truth in both positions. Overall, while some large nations may possess a long history as ethnic groups, rather more seem to have been created in the twentieth-century rush to statehood. Dating the precise origin of nations is impossible but their starring role is surely in modern times.

Even more than nations themselves, **nationalism** is a doctrine of modernity. Like many 'isms', nationalism emerged in the nineteenth century to flourish in the twentieth. But unlike these other 'isms', the principle of nationalism is reassuringly straightforward. It is simply the doctrine that nations do have a right to determine their own destiny – to govern themselves. In this way, nationalism is a universal idea even though each individual nation is unique, rooted in a particular place.

The United Nations Covenant on Civil and Political Rights (UNHCR, 1966) offers a succinct statement of the principle of national self-government:

All peoples have the right to self-determination. By virtue of that right they freely determine their political status and pursue their economic, social and cultural rights.

This principle proved to be highly influential throughout the twentieth century. Early on, with the final collapse of the Austro-Hungarian and Ottoman Empires, nationalism provided a justification for redrawing the map of Europe and the Middle East. Then, in the decades after 1945, national liberation allowed colonies in Africa and Asia to achieve political independence from their colonial masters. And towards the century's end, the collapse of communism initiated a resurgence of national expression throughout the Soviet Union and its satellite states. A strong case can be made for viewing nationalism as the twentieth century's driving force.

Nationalism, the key ideology of the twentieth century, is the doctrine that nations are entitled to self-determination. Gellner (1983, p. 1) writes that nationalism 'is primarily a political principle, which holds that the political and national units should be congruent'. National identity is politically vital because it answers a question beyond the reach of democracy: who are 'the people' who are to govern themselves?

Yet even today nations and states continue to cut across each other in untidy fashion. Whatever our instincts may tell us, we err if we imagine that each state contains only one nation, or that each nation is restricted to one state. Box 1.5 sets out four ways in which nations and states combine in practice. The first two rows in this box describe types of state (nation-state, multinational state) while the latter two rows denote additional possibilities for national groups (stateless nation, diaspora). To understand these categories is to appreciate some political complexities of the contemporary world.

The first and most straightforward category in Box 1.5 is the traditional **nation-state**. Here each country contains only the people belonging to its nation. The French Revolution of 1789 established the idea that the state should articulate the interests and rights of citizens bound together by a single national identity. The British philosopher John Stuart Mill (1806–73) was an early and influential advocate of the conjoined nation-state. He argued that 'where the sentiment of nationality exists in any force there is a *prima facie* case for uniting all the members of the nationality under the same government, and a government to themselves apart' (1861, p. 392). In today's world, Iceland is an example of a pure nation-state. Its population shares such a well-documented descent from within a compact island that the state's birth records provide a perfect laboratory for genetic research.

Even though few countries today are as homogeneous as Iceland, the nation-state is probably still an appropriate term when discussing the many countries in which one nationality remains politically and numerically dominant. In France, Germany and Israel, for instance, the state remains rooted in the soil of a strong national identity despite the presence of significant minorities: Algerians and Moroccans in France, Turks in Germany and Palestinians in

---

BOX 1.5

Nations and states

	Type of	Definition	Example
Nation-state	State	A state with its own nation	Iceland
Multinational state	State	A state with more than one nation	The United Kingdom contains the Scottish and Welsh nations, as well as England and Northern Ireland
Stateless nation	Nation	A nation which lacks its own state and whose homeland is spread across several countries	Kurds
Diaspora	Nation	A nation dispersed beyond its homeland	Jews, Armenians

---

Israel (Smooha, 2002). France, in particular, remains an archetypal nation-state: the government is expected to articulate the interests of the nation as a whole and all French nationals are deemed to share equally in the rights and duties of citizenship.

The second category in Box 1.5 is the **multinational state**. Here, more than one nation is fundamental to a country's politics and assimilation to a dominant nationality is not a realistic option. International migration is moving many, perhaps most, states in this direction. Even so, we should not regard the phenomenon of multinationalism as new. Britain, for instance, has long been divided between English, Welsh, Scottish and Irish nationals; Canada between English- and French-speakers; and Belgium between Dutch- and French-speakers. These examples demonstrate that multinational states can achieve internal peace and political stability.

However, there are many other cases where national divisions within a country have led to conflict. For instance, Balkan states such as Bosnia and Croatia experienced vicious conflicts between Croat, Muslim and Serbian national groups in the 1990s.

This book centres on states, whether nation-states or multinational in character. But there is a danger in such a state-centred approach: namely, that we ignore how national groups cut across state boundaries. The two lower rows in Box 1.5 address this possibility.

Our third category, the **stateless nation**, refers to a situation where a home state is lacking. The Kurds, for example, have inhabited a mountainous region of Asia for over 4,000 years and their national identity is well-established. Yet their homeland of Kurdistan is divided between Iran, Iraq, Syria and Turkey, with little prospect of an independent Kurdish state (Map 1.1). The 20 million Kurds seem likely to continue as the world's largest stateless nation.

Our final category is the **diaspora**, defined by Esman (1996, p. 316) as 'a minority ethnic group of migrant origin which maintains sentimental or material links with its land of origin'. The term was originally associated with the dispersal of the Jews from their Palestinian homeland following their defeat by the Romans in 70 AD. The Jews are the archetypal case, with only a minority of the world's Jews now living in the ancient homeland.

But there are many other examples. The Armenian genocide of 1915/16 scattered the survivors to the four winds – and in particular to Russia, France, USA, Argentina and Iran. Of a worldwide Armenian population of perhaps 10 million, only around 3 million live in Armenia itself.

Diasporas can exert a substantial influence on the homeland, not just through a flow of remittances but also through their impact on policy. India's 20 million non-resident Indians (NRIs) have become a powerful lobby for economic reform in the home country. Such transnational networks are growing in importance, encouraging the emergence of virtual nations and demonstrating the practicality of 'nationalism from a distance' (Anderson, 1998).

Map 1.1 A stateless nation: the Kurds

Ideology

The concepts reviewed so far have mainly been *about* politics, but ideas also of course play a role *in* politics. Political action is motivated by the ideas people hold about it. One traditional way to approach the role of ideas is via the notion of ideology. Our purpose here is to introduce this term without attempting an account of each specific ideology.

Unlike most political concepts, the terms 'ideology', 'left' and 'right' have a specific origin. We can therefore best proceed historically. Ideology was a word coined by the French philosopher Antoine Destutt de Tracy (1754–1836) during the 1790s, in the aftermath of the French Revolution. De Tracy employed the term to denote the science of ideas: idea-ology. His notion was to found a rigorous new discipline which would create a blueprint for political and social organization. This subject would start with our sensations, and our ideas about them, as

> Hamilton (1987) defines **ideology** as a system of collectively held beliefs and attitudes advocating a particular pattern of social arrangements, which its proponents seek to promote and maintain.

they emerge from our relationship with our physical environment. From this foundation, *idéologues* would construct a plan for a just and rational society.

The point is not so much de Tracy's detailed project but rather his conception that once ideas were liberated from their moorings in religion and tradition they could acquire their proper independence and importance. Like the French Revolution itself, the science of ideas was to be modern, secular and rational, constructed without reference to the old regime. The notion of ideology as a systematic design for a new political order remains an important theme in the concept's use.

Unsurprisingly, de Tracy's radical scheme soon came under attack. Napoleon Bonaparte (ruler of France 1804–14, 1815) sought to sustain his dictatorship with a more traditional religious appeal. He dismissed de Tracy's *idéologues* as windbags seeking to overturn the hallowed authority of throne and altar. Napoleon suggested that laws should be derived not from arrogant ideologists but from 'knowledge of the human heart and of the lessons of history' (Eagleton, 1991, p. 67). Napoleon wanted no truck with the 'cloudy metaphysics' of ideology. This perspective, in which a humanistic outlook based on respect for experience is contrasted with the naïve folly of forward-looking ideological systems, is also commonly encountered in political argument.

However, it was in the work of the communist philosopher Karl Marx (1818–83) that the concept of ideology received most criticism. Marx dismissed ideology as the illusions peddled by the ruling class to legitimize its own position: 'the ideas of the ruling class are in every epoch the ruling ideas' (Marx and Engels, 1845/6). Ideology, for Marx, served to paper over the cracks in the capitalist system. Although we now regard Marxism as itself an ideology, Marx himself saw ideology and science as opposed concepts. The function of ideology, he alleged, was simply to rationalize the class structure of existing society. In condemning ideology as illusion, Marx's treatment contrasts sharply with de Tracy's original notion.

In appreciating the contemporary use of 'ideology', the key point is that the term has ceased to denote the analysis of ideas. Instead, it has come to denote packages of ideas themselves. The core modern use of ideology is to describe any system of ideas offering an explicit account of:

▶ Human nature;
▶ The proper organisation of, and relationship between, state and society;
▶ The individual's position within this prescribed order.

Liberalism, for instance, regards individuals as the best judges of their own interests, advocates a tolerant society which maximizes personal freedom and favours a government which is limited but freely elected.

Which specific political outlooks should be regarded as ideologies is a matter of judgement. Marxism is surely one example and fascism is usually taken as another, even though fascist leaders themselves saw their doctrine as giving priority to action rather than reflection. It is doubtful, however, if every 'ism' should be judged an ideology. For instance, the central tradition within conservatism is sceptical of political blueprints, creating the potential paradox of an ideology against ideology. Even liberalism, the dominant outlook in the contemporary Western world, prefers to allow individuals to choose their own way of life rather than to impose a single ideological formula.

In any case, the era of explicit ideology beginning with the French Revolution surely ended in the twentieth century with the defeat of fascism in 1945 and the collapse of communism at the end of the 1980s. Bell first pronounced *The End of Ideology* in 1960:

The problem for the [recent post-college] generation is less the 'fear of experience' than an inability to define an 'enemy'. One can have causes and passions only when one knows against whom to fight. The writers of the twenties . . . scorned bourgeois mores. The radicals of the thirties fought 'capitalism', and later, fascism, and for some, Stalinism. Today, intellectually, emotionally, who is the enemy that one can fight? (1960, p. 286)

Fukuyama followed with *The End of History and the Last Man* in 1992:

What we may be witnessing is not just the end of the Cold War, or the passing of a particular period of post-war history, but the end of history as such: that is, the end point of mankind's ideological evolution and the universalization of Western liberal democracy as the final form of human government. (1992, p. 4)

We must always beware of claims that things are not as they were. Intellectual currents such as environmental concerns, feminism, Islamic fundamentalism and Islamic critiques of Western materialism continue to swirl in the twenty-first century. To their adherents, these causes define friends and enemies; they surely suffice to ward off the end of history.

Still, it must be doubted whether these ideas, values and priorities of the current century constitute ideologies in the classical sense. In particular, there seems little point in describing Islam as an ideology when it can accurately be called a religion. And why call environmental concern an ideology when we could just term it a policy? To describe any perspective, position or priority as an ideology is to extend the term in a manner that bears little relation to its original interpretation as a coherent, modern, secular system of ideas.

Left and right

Although the age of ideology may have passed, the terms **left** and **right** continue to be useful in understanding contemporary, and especially comparative, politics. Rather like ideology, the terms left and right require elaboration so that we can use them with as much clarity as they can bear.

Left and **right** (or left wing and right wing) imply opposite positions on an ideological dimension. However, the content of this dimension varies across countries and time. Broadly, the left is associated with equality, human rights and reform while the right favours tradition, established authority and the pursuit of the national interest. In the past, the left supported public ownership of industry; today it remains sympathetic to regulation of business.

BOX 1.6

Themes in the election programmes of left- and right-wing parties, 1945–98

Left	Right
Peace	Armed forces
Internationalism	National way of life
Democracy	Authority, morality and the constitution
Planning and public ownership	Free market
Trade protection	Free trade
Social security	Social harmony
Education	Law and order
Trade unions	Freedom and rights

Note: Based on party programmes in 50 democracies.
Source: Adapted from Budge (2006), p. 429.

Again like ideology, the origins of the concepts lie in revolutionary France. In the legislative assemblies of the era, noble royalists sat to the right of the presiding officer, in the traditional position of honour; radicals and commoners were positioned on the left. To be on the right implied support for aristocratic, royal and clerical interests; the left, by contrast, favoured a secular republic and civil liberties. To this day, seating arrangements in both chambers of France's parliament continue to reflect a party's ideological outlook.

The words left and right are still commonly encountered in classifying political parties, especially in Western Europe. The concepts continue to resonate with party activists and they will recur in this book. There remains some truth in Sartori's comment (1976, p. 78) that 'what compels us to utilize the left–right distinction is that this appears to be the most detectable and constant way in which not only mass publics but also elites perceive politics'.

Surveys suggest that most electors in Western democracies can situate themselves as being on the left or right, even if many simply equate these labels with a particular party or class – socialists to the left, conservatives to the right (Mair, 2009, p. 210). Certainly, the terms have survived the decline of the ideologies they long served to summarize. They travel well throughout the democratic world,

enabling us to compare many parties and programmes across countries and time.

The specific issues over which these tendencies compete have of course varied. Left and right are best seen as labels for containers of ideas rather than as well-defined ideas in themselves. The vessel on the left is marked 'reformers and modernizers'; the one on the right, 'traditionalists and conservatives'.

In Western Europe, especially, the terms were also long associated with the issue of public ownership; the left (as socialists and communists) favouring nationalization and the right (with exceptions on the extreme) a free market. It is here, with the now widespread acceptance of the market economy, that the concepts of left and right have lost some bite. Even so, other more diffuse contrasts continue. Generally, the left supports the principle of equality and policies to reduce inequality; the right is more accepting, and welcoming, of natural inequalities. We might also judge that the left is more ideological; the right, less so. It would, though, be a mistake to fix the terms with an artificial precision that denies the natural evolution of the political agenda.

Examining the period 1945–98, Budge (2006) usefully summarizes themes in the programmes adopted by parties of the left and right in 50 democracies (Box 1.6). His analysis puts flesh on the bones of the distinction between left and right. Budge notes not just the familiar contrast between public ownership and the free market (though some rightists, such as fascists, never favoured a free market). He also identifies broader political and philosophical divisions: for example, between the left's support for internationalism and the right's emphasis on protecting a national way of life. Where the left embraces democracy, the right highlights respect for authority and traditional morality.

To be sure, in another 50 years, the content of Box 1.6 might be quite different. However, the underlying contrasts in disposition – between progress and order, reform and stability, science and tradition – may well remain.

Learning Resources for Chapter 1

Next step

Crick (2000) is a lively examination of the nature of politics.

Further reading

Stoker (2006) and Hay (2007) are readable alternatives to Crick. Governance is covered by Kjær (2004). On the classification of governments, see Dahl *et al.* (2003) for democracy; Brooker (2009) and Linz (1975) for non-democracy; and Zakaria (2003) for points in-between. For the state, van Creveld (1999) traces the state's rise while Hay *et al.* (2005) focus on recent issues. Jackson (2007) examines the evolution of sovereignty. Calhoun (1997) provides an accessible overview of nationalism. On power, see Lukes (1974) for a radical interpretation; Smith (2009) discusses power and the state. Watt (1982) addresses authority, Lipset (1960) examines legitimacy, Heywood (2007) introduces ideology and Mair (2007) reviews left and right.

Internet sources

Global Gateway, Library of Congress
Links to resources on the world's countries
http://www.loc.gov/rr/international/portals.html

IPSAportal
Top 300 sites in political science
http://ipsaportal.unina.it/final.html

Political Resources on the Net
Links to politics sites
http://www.politicalresources.net

Richard Kimber's Political Science Resources, Keele University
Links to politics sites
http://www.psr.keele.ac.uk/

World Factbook, CIA
Country profiles and more, regularly updated
https://www.cia.gov/library/publications/the-world-factbook/

Zárate's Political Collections
World leaders since 1945
http://terra.es/personal2/monolith/home.htm

Chapter 2
Theoretical approaches

In this chapter, we introduce major theoretical approaches to the study of politics. The contemporary study of politics is marked by a variety of perspectives that developed at distinct stages in the discipline's history and which continue to be influential alongside each other to this day. By studying these approaches, we can gain a sense of the different ways in which politics can be studied.

How should 'approaches' be defined? They are ways of understanding: 'sets of attitudes, understandings and practices that define a certain way of doing political science' (Marsh and Stoker, 2010, p. 18). Approaches are schools of thought that influence how we go about political research, structuring the questions we ask and constraining the answers we can obtain.

The value of addressing approaches is that it enables us to be their master rather than their victim. Keynes's famous comment (1936, p. 381) about economics impinges also on our endeavours: 'practical men, who consider themselves to be exempt from any intellectual influences, are usually the slaves of some defunct economist'. Approaches deserve explicit consideration because they highlight topics worth studying and enable us to position our research within established frameworks.

This chapter examines five such approaches: institutional, behavioural, structural, rational choice and interpretive. For simplicity, we avoid all subdivisions and crossovers within each perspective (Lichbach and Zuckerman, 2009; Marsh and Stoker, 2010). Our order of discussion reflects the historical evolution of politics as an academic discipline rather than a specific logical progression.

We will suggest that the institutional approach offers a natural route into the study of comparative government in liberal democracies while the structural approach provides a historical framework for analysing comparative politics more broadly. The behavioural approach also contributes useful findings, an increasing number of which are comparative, and many of these are introduced in Part II. The rational choice and interpretive approaches, while still fundamental to political analysis, are less directly focused on comparative politics.

The institutional approach

The study of governing **institutions** is a central purpose of political science in general and of comparative politics in particular. It provided the original foundation of the discipline and so created a baseline from which other approaches have developed and against which they can be compared. An appreciation of institutions remains part of the tool-kit of most political scientists – including those who would not wish to be labelled as institutionalists.

An **institution** is a formal organization, often with public status, whose members interact on the basis of the specific roles they perform within the organization. In politics, an institution typically refers to an organ of government mandated by the constitution.

In addition, an institutional approach is core to the discipline (and to this book), taking us to the area that distinguishes politics as a distinct field of study. As Eulau (1963, p. 10) wrote:

If there is any subject matter at all that political scientists can claim exclusively for their own, a subject matter that does not require acquisition of the analytical tools of sister fields and that sustains their claim to autonomous existence, it is, of course, formal political structures.

Institutions are particularly important in liberal democracies since the 'decisive step towards democracy is the devolution of power from a group of people to a set of rules' (Przeworski, 1991, p. 14). Any study of government and politics in liberal democracies must in part be a study of institutions.

Their importance notwithstanding, there is no single theory of institutions. The institutional approach points to an area of study rather than offering a programme with its own methods. Still, its proponents have considered the nature of institutions and examined their role in political systems, and it is these observations that we review here.

Usually, the term 'institution' refers to the major organizations of national government, particularly those specified in the constitution. Such entities often possess legal personality, acquiring privileges and duties under law; in this sense, they are treated as literal actors. Implicitly, a specific emphasis on institutions in political analysis affirms the origins of political studies in the examination of constitutions and the state.

However, the concept of an institution also radiates outwards in three directions. The first extension is to other governing organizations which may have a less secure constitutional basis, such as the bureaucracy and local government.

The second extension is to other important political organizations which do not form part of the government, notably political parties. Note that as we move away from the heartland of constitutional structures in these directions, so the term 'organization' tends to supplant the word 'institution', enabling the study of political structures to draw on wider traditions of organizational analysis (Scott, 2007).

The third extension of the concept is both more important and debatable. We define institutions concretely, as bodies with addresses, telephone numbers and websites. But the term is sometimes used more broadly, to denote any established and well-recognized political practice. For instance, scholars refer to the institutionalization of corruption in Russia, a usage implying that the abuse of public office for private gain has become an accepted routine of political life – an institution – in its own right. This book is primarily concerned with formal institutions of government and we use words such as 'regimes' or 'practice' to denote informal arrangements such as corruption. When 'institution' is equated with any political or social practice, the term is stretched too far (Rothstein, 1996).

Institutional analysis assumes that positions within organizations matter more than the people who occupy them. This axiom enables us to discuss roles rather than people: presidencies rather than presidents, legislatures rather than legislators, and the judiciary rather than judges. So the capacity of institutions to affect the behaviour of their members means that politics, like other social sciences, is more than a branch of psychology.

Institutions possess rules their members are expected to follow. These rules provide the skeleton to which members attach informal practices of their own. A supplementary focus on individuals is therefore needed to understand the unwritten conventions which are needed for the organization to function but, within the institutional tradition, these codes are taken to build on the formal organization itself.

The institutional approach offers two main reasons for supposing that organizations do indeed shape behaviour. First, because institutions provide benefits and opportunities they shape the interests of their staff. Employees acquire interests such as defending their organization against outsiders and ensuring their own personal progress within the structure. As soon as an organization pays salaries, it possesses its own defence force. As March and Olsen (1984, p. 738) wrote:

The bureaucratic agency, the legislative committee and the appellate court are arenas for contending social forces but they are also collections of standard operating procedures and structures that define and defend interests. They are political actors in their own right.

Second, sustained interaction among employees encourages the emergence of an institutional culture, or house view, which welds this force into an effective fighting unit. Institutions generate norms which in turn shape behaviour. One strength of the institutional approach is exactly this capacity to account for the origins of interests and cultures, rather than just taking them for granted.

In operation, institutions bring forth activity which takes place simply because it is expected, not because it has any deeper political motive. When a legislative committee holds hearings on a topic, it may be more concerned to be seen to be doing its job than to resolve the issue itself. The institutional approach, more than any other, suggests that much political action is best understood by reference to this **logic of appropriateness** rather than the **logic of consequences**.

For instance, when a president visits an area devastated by floods, he is not necessarily seeking to direct relief operations or to achieve any purpose other than to be seen performing his duty of showing concern. In itself, the tour achieves the goal of meeting expectations arising from the actor's institutional position. 'Don't just do something, stand there,' said Ronald Reagan, a president with a fine grasp of the logic of appropriateness. When an institution faces a requirement to act, its members are as likely to be heard asking 'what did we do the last time this happened?' as 'what is the right thing to do in this situation?'.

This emphasis within the institutional framework on the symbolic or ritual aspect of political behaviour contrasts with the view of politicians and

> The **logic of appropriateness** refers to actions which members of an institution take to conform to its own norms. For example, a head of state will perform ceremonial duties because it is an official obligation. By contrast, the **logic of consequences** denotes behaviour directed at achieving an individual goal such as promotion or re-election.

bureaucrats as rational, instrumental actors who define their own goals independently of the organization they represent. At the least, institutions provide the rules of the game within which individuals pursue their objectives (Shepsle, 2006).

Institutional analysis can be static, based on examining the functioning of, and relationships between, institutions at a given moment. But writers within this approach show increasing interest in institutional evolution and its effects. Institutions possess a history, culture and memory, frequently embodying traditions and founding values. In a process of **institutionalization**, they often grow 'like coral reefs through slow accretion' (Sait, 1938, p. 18). Many institutions thicken naturally over time, developing their internal procedures and also becoming accepted by external actors as part of the governing apparatus; in other words, the institution becomes a node in a network and, in so doing, entrenches its position.

> **Institutionalization** is defined by Huntington (1968) as 'the process by which organizations acquire value and stability' over time. An organization such as a legislature is institutionalized if it is clearly distinguished from its environment, possesses internal complexity and follows clear rules of procedure.

As particular institutions come to provide an established and accepted way of working, so they acquire resilience and persistence (Pierson, 2004). Many doubts will be expressed at a constitutional convention about the wisdom of adopting parliamentary government but a generation later few will be found favouring a switch to a presidential system (or vice versa). So, like constitutions, institutions are devices through which the past constrains the present. Institutional inertia can eventually damage performance but, even so, considerable coordination among a range of actors is needed before a restructuring of the institutional landscape becomes feasible. 'Better the devil you know' is a norm that keeps many leaky vessels afloat. Thus, the study of institutions is the study of political stability rather than change. As Orren and Skowronek (1995, p. 298) put it:

Institutions are seen as the pillars of order in politics, as the structures that lend the polity its integrity, facilitate its routine operation and produce continuity in the face of potentially destabilizing forces. Institutional politics is politics as usual, normal politics, or a politics in equilibrium.

What is the value of institutions to a political system? Answering this question will help us to understand both their ubiquity in liberal democracies and to identify some limitations of illiberal democracies and authoritarian regimes, which are less institutionalized. The contribution of institutions lies in their capacity to make long-term commitments which are more credible than those of any single employee, thus building up trust. For example, governments can borrow money at lower rates than are available to individual civil servants. Similarly, a government can make credible promises to repay its debt over a period of generations, a commitment that is necessarily beyond the reach of any individual debtor.

Institutions also offer predictability. When we visit a government office, we do so with expectations about how the member of staff will behave even though we know nothing about the individual concerned. A shared institutional context eases the task of conducting business between strangers. So in and beyond politics, institutions help to glue society together, extending the bounds of what would be possible for individuals acting alone (Johnson, 2001).

An institutional approach, like all others, can become inward-looking. Two particular limits need highlighting. First, some institutions are explicitly created to resolve particular problems. We should perhaps focus more on these key historical moments which permit institutional creativity. Such periods, even though uncommon, enable us to view institutions as a product of, rather than just an influence on, political action by individuals.

Second, governing institutions rarely act independently of social forces, especially in poorer, simpler and non-democratic countries. Sometimes, the president *is* the presidency and the entire superstructure of government is a facade behind which personal networks and exchanges continue to drive politics forward – or backward. In the extreme case of communist party states, for instance, the formal institutions of government were controlled by the ruling party and the party was itself carefully monitored by

the secret police. Government was the servant, not the master, and its institutions carried little independent weight.

Even in liberal democracies, it is always worth asking whose interests benefit from a particular institutional set-up. Just as an institution can be created for specific purposes, so too can it survive by serving the wealthy and the powerful. For instance, the policy inertia inherent in Washington's separation of powers surely works to the advantage of those who benefit most from the existing structure of American society. Institutions can strengthen their foundations by providing a collective benefit but we should not forget that the support of powerful interests in the wider society provides additional stability. A narrow focus on institutions and their evolution risks ignoring this broader underpinning.

Overall, institutions must be seen as central to liberal democratic politics. The institutions of government are the device through which political issues are shaped, processed and sometimes resolved. They provide a major source of continuity and predictability. They shape the environment within which political actors operate and, to an extent, structure their interests, values and preferences. The institutional approach offers no developed theory but it does provide observations about institutional development and functioning which can anchor studies of specific cases.

The behavioural approach

In the 1960s, the favoured unit of analysis, particularly in American political science, moved away from institutions and towards individual behaviour. The focus changed from electoral systems to voters, from legislatures to legislators, from presidencies to presidents. The central tenet of **behaviouralists** was

---

Behaviouralism was a school of thought in political science which emphasized the study of individuals rather than institutions. The focus was on voters rather than elections, legislators rather than legislatures, and judges rather than the judiciary. The aim of the movement was to use scientific methods to discover generalizations about political attitudes and behaviour.

that 'the root is man' rather than institutions (Eulau, 1963). This new programme invited us to study what people actually do, rather than the constitutional documents and organization charts which institutionalists examine and sometimes celebrate.

Labels notwithstanding, political behaviouralists certainly did not ignore attitudes and opinions. On the contrary, the study of public opinion became an important dimension of their research, just as the field of electoral behaviour extends to studies of voters' attitudes – to include what people think, not just how they act in the polling booth. Rather than implying an exclusive concern with actions, the word 'behaviour' expressed a focus on political reality rather than official discourse, on individuals rather than institutions, and on scientific explanation rather than the loose descriptions of the institutionalists. It provided a rallying cry for a new project (Farr, 1995).

Why did the leading approach to political research shift in this way? One influence was decolonization. In newly independent countries, the institutions of government proved to be of little moment. Presidents, and then ruling generals, quickly dispensed with the elaborate constitutions written in haste by Western experts before the final departure of the colonial power. A fresher and wider approach, rooted in social, economic and political realities rather than constitutional fictions, was needed to understand politics in the developing world.

In the United States, furthermore, the post-war generation of political scientists was keen to apply innovative social science techniques developed in the Second World War, notably interview-based sample surveys of ordinary individuals. In this way, the study of politics could be presented as a social science and be eligible for research funds made possible by that designation.

Within the behavioural tradition, institutions were not ignored altogether. Rather, the study of assemblies, for instance, moved away from formal aspects (e.g. the procedures by which a bill becomes law) towards legislative behaviour (e.g. how members defined their role). Thus, researchers investigated the social backgrounds of representatives, their individual voting records, their career progression and their willingness to rebel against the party line. In the study of the judiciary, too, scholars began to take judges rather than courts as their level

of analysis, using statistical techniques to assess how the social background and political attitudes of justices shaped their decisions and – at the highest level – how they interpreted the constitution (Segal and Spaeth, 2002). What mattered was the full complexity of how people behaved within their institutional setting.

In practice, it was in the study of ordinary people that the behavioural approach really earned its spurs. Initially in the USA, and then in many other Western democracies, survey analysis yielded useful generalizations about voting behaviour, political participation and public opinion. In contrast to the focus of institutional analysis on government, these studies looked at the relationship between politics and society, showing for example how race and class impinged on whether, how and to what extent people took part in politics. In this way, behavioural research placed politics in its social setting.

As these studies extended across countries and over time, so behaviouralists began to rediscover the importance of differences across nations, gaining more insight into which regularities were truly regular and which were specific to the locale where they were conducted. In this way, political behaviour began to reconnect with the institutional approach, broadly defined. For instance, because voting behaviour depends on features of an electoral system such as the incentives it provides for tactical voting, there can be no simple, universal model of voting behaviour. Rather, the comparative requirement is to understand how electoral rules influence the voters' response.

In a similar way, voters are more likely to punish a governing party for a poor economy if the party is the sole occupant of office, rather than part of a coalition (Duch and Stevenson, 2008). Thus, we cannot expect to discover universal laws about the impact of the economy on electoral behaviour; we must recognize that national institutions intervene between economic performance and the voters' response (Anderson, 2009).

The behavioural approach generated the research foundation for several chapters in this book. In its own terms, behaviouralism delivered: 'there are few areas in political science where scholarly knowledge has made greater progress in the past two generations' (Dalton and Klingemann, 2007, p. vii). Yet as a model for the entire discipline, the behavioural revo-

BOX 2.1

The person, not the post: political behaviour in the White House

In the study of political elites, Barber's *The Presidential Character: Predicting Performance in the White House* (1972) provided an influential example of the focus on individuals rather than institutions. Barber assumes that 'who the president is at a given time can make a profound difference in the whole thrust and direction of national politics'. Even superficial speculation, he suggests, 'confirms the commonsense view that the man himself weighs heavily among other historical factors' (1972, p. 3).

We can add that each president leaves his mark on the White House, so our assumptions about the office reflect the achievements (or lack of them) of its previous occupants. The office shapes the man but, over time, the men also shape the office.

Barber did not adopt the quantitative approach of most behavioural research: he examined his subjects in the round, rather than as collections of variables. Nonetheless, his qualitative analysis was informed by a desire to understand, explain and even predict, rather than merely to describe. He examined personality but with the goal of understanding behaviour.

Specifically, Barber argued that the key differences in presidential behaviour can be predicted in advance of new incumbents taking office. Two dimensions, he suggested, are key. The first is how much energy a president invests in his work, leading to a distinction between active and passive types. The second is whether a president experiences political life as enjoyable or discouraging, affirming or draining, leading to a distinction between positive and negative presidents. Cross-classifying these factors leads to a four-fold classification: active-positive, active-negative, passive-positive and passive-negative presidents.

Barber's classification of American presidents

	Active	Passive
Positive	e.g. John Kennedy	e.g. Ronald Reagan
Negative	e.g. Richard Nixon	e.g. Dwight Eisenhower

Source: Barber (1972).

Barber then applied his scheme to individual presidents. John Kennedy exemplified the confident active-positive: 'This is a damned good job,' said Kennedy of his office. Richard Nixon – one of Barber's most successful predictions – was the dangerous active-negative: 'he very nearly got away with establishing a presidential tyranny', claims Barber. Ronald Reagan is the genial passive-positive; as he famously said, 'I hear hard work never killed anyone but I figure why take the chance?' And Dwight Eisenhower is the reluctant passive-negative; Barber's judgement is 'a sucker for duty'.

The Presidential Character exemplifies the application of an individual-level approach to the study of elites. It examines systematically variations in how presidents behave in office, demonstrating in the process that the analysis of the individual in politics is more than either a psychological study of personality formation or a historical account of great leaders.

lution eventually ran its course. Its focus on mass political behaviour took the study of politics away from its natural concern with the institutions of government. Its methods became more and more technical and its findings more and more specialized.

Behaviouralism produced a political science with too much science and too little politics. Amid the protests of the late 1960s, behaviouralists were criticized for fiddling while Rome burned. Rather like the institutional approach before it, behaviouralism seemed unable to address the political changes then occurring. The research programme had become orthodox rather than progressive; it was time to add something new.

The structural approach

In political analysis, the **structural approach** has served, in part, as a corrective to the limitations of individual-level analysis. In downplaying the individual, structuralists resemble institutionalists. However, the notion of structure is much broader, and possibly deeper, than that of an institution; we can send a text message to an institution but not to a structure. The starting point, then, is to grasp what is meant by the term 'structure'.

> In politics, a **structural approach** emphasizes the objective relationships between social groups, including social classes and the state. The varying interests and positions of these leading groups shape the overall configuration of power and provide the dynamic of political change.

The dictionary defines a structure as 'the construction of a whole; its supporting framework'. Political structuralists follow this definition by focusing on the relationships between powerful groups in society, such as the bureaucracy, political parties, social classes, churches and the military. This constellation of interests provides the structure underlying the institutional politics of parties and government; it is the framework which underpins, and ultimately determines, actual politics. The approach is sociological, always giving due weight to class interests but, unlike much Marxism, not confining its attention to them.

Each group seeks to protect its own interests and sustain its own political influence in the context of a society which is always evolving in response to economic change, ideological developments, international politics and the effects of group conflict itself. Because the configuration of interests is always evolving, structuralists can also embrace change more easily than institutionalists.

Like a system, a structure is defined by the relationships between its components. The elements themselves, their internal organization and especially the individuals within them, are of a lesser interest. Structuralists look exclusively at the big picture; their instrument is the macroscope rather than the microscope. Here we see the contrast with the behavioural approach. As Skocpol (1979, p. 291) put it, structuralists 'emphasize objective relationships and conflicts among variously situated groups and nations, rather than the interests, outlooks, or ideologies of particular actors'.

Individuals are seen as a product of, rather than prior to, their social location; they are secondary to the grand political drama unfolding around them. The assumption is that over a period of time, groups will defend their real interests within the structure, irrespective of the beliefs and acts of their leaders and members at any particular moment. The emphasis is on social rather than individual actors.

But 'real interests' and 'social actors' are, of course, terms imposed by the researcher. Who is to say where a group's true interests lie and how can we refer to the 'actions' of a group rather than a person? In execution, the structural approach is broad-brush, making large if plausible assumptions about the nature of conflict in a particular society, and drawing conclusions about causes without considering counterfactual questions about what would have happened had the supposed causes not been present. The interpretive narratives that result are plausible but rarely supported by evidence that would overcome either a social scientist's caution about drawing causal inferences or a historian's commitment to primary sources.

We can draw a sharp contrast between structural and cultural analysis (Chapter 7). The structural perspective regards culture as a factor of little independent significance. For instance, a structural explanation of poverty might emphasize the contrasting interests and power positions of property-owners, the working-class and the underclass. By contrast, a cultural explanation might place more weight on the values of poor people themselves, showing how limited aspirations trap the poor in a cycle of poverty that can persist across generations. For the structuralist, the important factor is the framework of inequality itself, not the values that confine particular families to the bottom of the hierarchy. This point, and the overall thrust of structuralism, is well-summarized by Mahoney (2003, p. 51):

BOX 2.2

The structural approach: Skocpol on revolutions

Skocpol's account of the French, Russian and Chinese revolutions (1979) offered an influential example of a structural approach focused on relationships between classes and states rather than on individuals. Before her study, much research on revolutions had employed a behavioural perspective, using concepts such as relative deprivation to understand the conditions under which people come to see themselves as deprived (Gurr, 1980). Skocpol, however, was keen to distinguish her structural approach from one focused on the perceptions of the masses and the motives of political leaders:

The fact is that historically no successful revolution has ever been 'made' by a mass-mobilizing, avowedly revolutionary movement . . . As far as the causes of historical social revolutions are concerned, Wendell Phillips was quite correct when he once declared: 'Revolutions are not made; they come'. (1979, p. 17)

She quoted with approval (1979, p. 18) the structuralist observation of Hobsbawm: 'The evident importance of the actors in the drama . . . does not mean that they are also dramatist, producer and stage-designer'. Skocpol regarded structural conditions – the relationships between groups within a state and, equally important, between states – as fundamental to the arrival of the classic revolutions. Specifically, she judged that regimes which were internationally weak and domestically ineffective became vulnerable to insurrection when well-organized agitators succeeded in exploiting peasant frustration with an old order to which the landed aristocracy offered only limited support.

Like other structuralists, but in contrast to traditional Marxists, Skocpol viewed the state – in its strength or its weakness – as a major player in the overall array of forces:

We can make sense of social-revolutionary transformations only if we take the state seriously as a macro-structure. The state properly conceived is no mere arena in which socioeconomic struggles are fought out. It is, rather, a set of administrative, policing, and military organizations headed, and more or less supported by, an executive authority. (1979, p. 29)

Skocpol's statement of her approach to revolutions provided an important declaration of the structuralist approach to politics generally:

One must be able to identify the objectively conditioned and complex intermeshing of the various actions of the diversely situated groups – an intermeshing that shapes the revolutionary process and gives rise to the new regime . . . To take such an impersonal and nonsubjective viewpoint – one that emphasizes patterns of relationships among groups and societies – is to work from what may in some generic sense be called a structural perspective on sociohistorical reality. (1979, p. 18)

Nearly 25 years later, Skocpol could look back approvingly at the achievements of the structural approach and its method of comparative history:

Comparative historical analysis has certainly come of age over the past quarter century. By now, comparative historical analysis has claimed its proud place as one of the most fruitful research approaches in modern social science, side by side with behavioralism, rational choice and interpretive genres. (2003, p. 424)

At the core of structuralism is the concern with objective relationships between groups and societies. Structuralism holds that configurations of social relations shape, constrain and empower actors in predictable ways. Structuralism generally downplays or rejects cultural and value-based explanations of social phenomena. Likewise, structuralism opposes approaches that explain social outcomes solely or primarily in terms of psychological states, individual decision-making processes, or other individual-level characteristics.

In principle, structures can be examined without reference to history. The essence of any structure, physical or political, lies in the way its parts form a stable equilibrium. How the structure emerged in the first place is, for a strict advocate of this approach, a secondary or even irrelevant issue. To appreciate why a bridge is stable, we need to understand how its components maintain themselves in equilibrium; the history of the structure's construction is of no moment (at least until it collapses and blame is to be apportioned).

As if to keep us on our toes, however, the best-known structural work in politics has adopted an explicitly historical approach, seeking to understand how competition between powerful groups leads to specific outcomes such as a democratic or authoritarian regime and a two-party or a multiparty system. The authors of such studies recognize that, in reality, politics is struggle rather than equilibrium. The approach is structural in spirit but the method, in practice, is comparative history, giving us another contrast with the non-historical generalizations favoured by behaviouralists and the sometimes static descriptions of the institutionalists.

Barrington Moore, Jr's *Social Origins of Dictatorship and Democracy: Lord and Peasant in the Making of the Modern World* (1966) is the work which did most to shape this format. Moore sought to understand why liberal democracy developed earlier and more easily in France, England and the United States than in Germany and Japan. He suggested that the strategy of the rising commercial class was the key variable. Where the bourgeoisie avoided entanglement with the landowners in their battles with the peasants, as in the United Kingdom, the democratic transition was relatively peaceful. But where landlords engaged the commercial classes in a joint campaign against the peasantry, as in Germany, the result was an authoritarian regime which delayed the onset of democracy.

Although later research qualified many of Moore's judgements, his study demonstrated the value of studying structural relationships between groups and classes as they evolve over long periods (Mahoney, 2003). He asked important comparative questions and answered them with an account of how and when class relationships develop and evolve. Not only does Moore exemplify the structural approach, he helped to define it.

The structural approach has led to, and emerged strengthened from, wide-ranging historical studies such as Barrington Moore's and Skocpol's. It is an approach which has built on its Marxist foundations without confining itself to class analysis. It asks big questions and, by selecting answers from the past, it interrogates history without limiting itself to chronology. Many authors working in this tradition do make large claims about the positions adopted by particular classes and groups; interests are often treated as actors, leading to ambitious generalizations which need verification through historical research. Even so, the structural approach, in the form of comparative historical studies, has proved to be a constructive approach to political research.

The rational choice approach

Rational choice analysis returns us to individuals, but of the abstract, calculating kind found in economics. It is not that this approach regards all others as irrational; rather, the distinctive feature of this framework is that politics is conceived as consisting of strategic interaction between individuals, with all players seeking to maximize the achievement of their own particular goals. Where behaviouralists seek to explain political behaviour through statistical generalization, the rational choice approach focuses solely on the interests of the actors as the explanatory factors. The assumption is that people can appraise the alternatives available to them in any specific situation and can consistently choose the option that ranks highest in their preference order.

The potential value of rational choice analysis lies in its ability to model the essentials of political action, and hence make predictions, without all-encompassing knowledge of the actors. We just need to identify the actors' goals and how these objectives can best be advanced in a given situation. All else, including the accounts actors give of their own behaviour, is detail. The aim is to model the essentials of human interaction, not to provide a rich account of human motives.

Nor are rational choice analysts concerned to provide an accurate account of the mental process leading to actual decisions; the test is just whether behaviour is correctly predicted. The underlying philosophy – that explanation is best achieved by predictive models that are both simple and fundamental – is a distinctive feature of the approach, reflecting its origins in economics.

What goals can people pursue within the rational choice framework? Most analysts adopt the axiom of self-interest. As stated by John Calhoun in his *Disquisition on Government* (1851), the assumption is that each person 'has a greater regard for his own safety of happiness, than for the safety or happiness of others: and, where they come into opposition, is ready to sacrifice the interests of others to his own'.

At the cost of increased complexity, we could broaden the range of permitted goals. We could imagine that people take satisfaction in seeing others achieve their ends or even permit our subjects to pursue altruistic projects. Yet just as markets are best analysed by assuming self-interest among the participants, so too do most rational choice advocates believe that the same assumption gives us the essence of politics. It is rationality and self-interest in combination which facilitate prediction: 'if people are rational and self-interested it becomes possible to explain and even predict their actions in ways that would allow rational choice theorists to claim a mantle of scientific credibility' (Hindmoor, forthcoming).

Rational choices are not necessarily all-knowing. Operating in an uncertain world, people need to discount the value of going for a goal by the risk they will fail to achieve it. In situations of uncertainty, we may prefer to eliminate the risk of a bad outcome than to go for broke by staking all on a single bet. Thus a rational choice needs to be distinguished from a knowledgeable one.

Also, we may find the effort of researching our options exceeds the benefit from the knowledge gained, leading to short cuts such as just considering a few possibilities (known as bounded rationality) or relying on expert opinion – for instance, to help us evaluate party policies before deciding how to vote. It is not always rational to be fully informed, a fact that brings the approach closer to the real world. However, the full rational model – the version which allows us to predict most easily – takes actors to be knowledgeable as well as rational and self-interested.

The subject of rational choice analysis is typically the individual. Indeed, the starting point is sometimes **methodological individualism**: the principle that explanations in politics must be found in the

> As stated by Elster (1989, p. 13), **methodological individualism** is the principle that 'the elementary unit of social life is individual human action. To explain social institutions and social change is to show how they arise as the result of the actions and interaction of individuals'. The term was first used by the Austrian-born economist, Joseph Schumpeter (1883–1950).

preferences and behaviour of individuals. The existence and functioning of larger units – institutions, governments, classes and states – must, it is argued, finally be understood as the collective outcome of individuals pursuing their own interests. Even if individuals did not create an organization, it would be subject to change if it served no one's interests (and everyone could agree on a replacement). 'Society, not being human, cannot have preferences', write Riker and Ordeshook (1973, p. 78). Riker (1990, p. 171) adds that consistent generalizations in the social sciences are only possible when 'the central propositions are about individuals'. This determination to seek explanations of political outcomes in individual interests provides the starkest contrast with institutional and structural approaches.

But in the study of politics, the rational choice framework is often extended to the larger units that are our stock in trade. In his analysis of political parties, for example, Downs (1957, p. 28) imagines that all members 'act solely in order to attain the income, prestige, and power which come from being in office'. For ease of analysis, he treats parties as if they were single actors, in the same way that students of international politics often regard a government as a single entity making foreign policy decisions on the basis of the national interest. In both cases, the aim is accurate prediction, not a detailed reconstruction of the actual decision process. These 'as if' accounts of parties and states depart from the principle of methodological individualism but they do so in search of the simplicity and predictions which are valued within the rational choice approach.

A major contribution of the approach lies in highlighting **collective action problems**. These refer to the difficulties which arise in coordinating the actions of individuals so as to achieve the best outcome for each person. For instance, many people

BOX 2.3

Comparing approaches: studying the Cuban missile crisis

Allison's study of the Cuban missile crisis (1971) is the best-known comparison of different approaches to understanding a particular topic. His work shows that we do not need to adopt one fixed framework but can add value through looking at the same subject through different lenses.

Allison's Model I, the rational choice approach, treats states as single actors pursuing clear goals by making strategic choices. This is the dominant mode of analysis in international politics and Allison finds that it does provide a 'productive shorthand' in comprehending American and Soviet actions during the missile crisis. However, he suggests that 'it is not itself a full analysis and cannot stand alone' (1971, p. 246).

Model	Label	Description
I	Rational actor	Explain international events by identifying the goals and strategies of the states involved
II	Organizational process (institutional approach)	Explain government 'acts' as the outputs (rather than decisions) of loosely allied departments which rely heavily on their standard internal procedures
III	Governmental politics (court or palace politics approach)	Executive decisions emerge from a circle of senior individuals who meet, discuss and compromise in a flexible and political fashion

Rather, Model II – the organizational process or institutional approach – comes into play. This lens helps to account for aspects of the Soviet installation of missiles in Cuba. The physical layout of the weapons, and the obsessive secrecy of their installation, reflected standard procedures of the agencies involved, separate from any overall Soviet objectives. They were the products of institutions, not strategy.

Similarly, Model III – which in the case of the USA examines the politics of the top decision-making group around the president – adds additional purchase. For example, some of this group's discussions with military commanders were not genuine consultations so much as a political attempt to prepare a defensible record.

Although Allison himself argues for a 'shift of gears' away from the rational choice approach, the impression left by his study is that Model I provides the core understanding, with II and III adding only supplementary appreciation of detail. The results from a comparable analysis of decision-making in domestic politics might well differ but it is surely difficult to begin any political analysis without addressing the goals of the main actors involved. In that sense, the assumption of rational choice is fundamental.

Further reading: Allison (1971), Allison and Zelikow (1999).

persist with a polluting lifestyle, aware that their own behaviour will make no decisive difference to overall environmental quality. Yet the collective outcome from everyone behaving in this way is climate change damaging to all. Individual rationality leads to a poor result for everyone.

Similarly, in the financial crisis of 2008–09, many investment bankers took on highly risky investments to increase their bonuses; their employers, too, were

happy enough as long as their firms' profits carried on increasing. When these investments eventually turned bad, the effect was not only a problem for the original investors but also, and more importantly, a threat to an important **public good** – the stability of the Western financial system. Some form of coordination, such as stricter regulation of banks by governments in this example, is needed if private actions are to be rendered compatible with a desir-

Collective action problems arise when rational behaviour by each person produces an outcome which is suboptimal overall. The issue typically arises when people seek to free ride on the efforts of others in providing **public goods** – those which cannot be restricted to contributors alone. Public statues, national defence and clean air are examples of public goods.

able collective outcome. The lesson for political analysis is that individual preferences and collective outcomes are two different things; politics lies between and a government is usually needed to bridge the gap.

One of the most influential studies within the rational choice tradition is Anthony Downs's *An Economic Theory of Democracy* (1957). By outlining part of Downs's analysis, we well see both the strengths and the limits of the framework within which he worked. Downs defines a party as 'a team of people seeking to control the governing apparatus by gaining votes in a duly constituted election'. We are asked to imagine that parties act as if they were motivated by power alone. Voters, too, are assumed to want only a government which reflects their own policy preferences. Downs's question is: under these conditions, what policies should parties adopt to maximize their vote?

To answer this question, Downs assumes that voters' policy preferences can be represented on a simple left–right scale. For him, the left end represents full government control on the economy; the right end, a completely free market. How vote-maximizing parties will position themselves depends on the distribution of public opinion along the left–right scale. In his best-known scenario, Downs imagines that public opinion forms a symmetrical, bell-shaped distribution around the midpoint (Figure 2.1). Again, this assumption is simple but plausible: except in polarized societies, more people are probably found at the centre than anywhere else. In these circumstances, vote-maximizing parties in a two-party system will converge at the midpoint. A party may start at one extreme but it will move towards the centre because there are more votes to be won there than there are to be lost to abstention at the extreme. Once parties have converged at the position of the **median voter**, they reach a position of **equilibrium** and have no incentive to change their position.

Figure 2.1 A bell-shaped distribution: parties converge at the centre

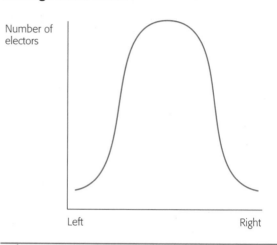

The **median voter** has an equal number of voters on either side when voters are positioned on a dimension such as left and right. When this dimension is the sole cleavage, and the distribution of preferences along it is bell-shaped (i.e. possesses a single peak), rational parties will converge on the position represented by the median voter.

When more than two parties are allowed into the model, the possibility arises of blackmail parties forming to force a major party back towards an extreme. Thus, many protest parties aim to remind them, the big parties, not to forget us, the ordinary folk. Downs uses an American example to illustrate this point: the States' Rights Democratic Party. This Southern right-wing splinter group ('Segregation Forever!') gained just 2.4 per cent of the vote in the 1948 presidential election. However, the Dixiecrats' purpose was not to win the election but rather to provide a **shock** to the system – to threaten the Democrats because of their liberal policy on civil rights.

Equilibrium is a position of balance. A political equilibrium exists when no significant actors feel they would gain appreciably from changing the current position. For example, an electoral system is in equilibrium if no significant party prefers any alternative. **Shocks** (unanticipated events, often external to the system) temporarily disturb or permanently alter the equilibrium point.

Whether parties (or other actors) behave rationally is of course an open question. The crucial question is how accurate are the predictions from Downs's model? In reality, do parties in two-party systems converge on the centre? Often they do. Bill Clinton and Tony Blair are just two examples of leaders who won elections by steering their parties to the middle ground. In such cases, Downs's analysis provides a sufficient explanation.

But sometimes parties go astray. Leaders occasionally take their parties away from, rather than towards, the centre. Barry Goldwater, right-wing Republican candidate for the American presidency in 1962, claimed that 'extremism in the defence of liberty is no vice'. Another example, from the left rather than the right, is Michael Foot's radical leadership of Britain's Labour Party. His lurch to the left was reflected in a party manifesto for the 1983 election which was described as the longest suicide note in history (Kelly, 2003).

As Downs would have anticipated, these politicians paid an electoral price for moving away from the median voter. Goldwater was crushed and the Labour Party remained out of office for another 14 years. However Downs's model does not easily explain these journeys to the extremes. Further, other right-wing leaders – notably Ronald Reagan and Margaret Thatcher – have achieved electoral success despite an ideological position to the right of the median voter.

In such cases, we need to introduce considerations that take us beyond Downs's model. These factors include the ideologies of party leaders, the attitudes of party members and the willingness of voters to support strong candidates perceived as capable of addressing national problems even if they are seen as extreme. As with Downs, so with the rational choice approach generally: the predictions are far from flawless but they do enable us to identify exceptional cases in need of further investigation.

In that way, the approach is useful even when it is inaccurate: 'you can sit in your armchair and try to predict how people will behave by asking how you would behave if you had your wits around you. You get, free of charge, a lot of vicarious, empirical behavior' (Schelling, quoted in Allison, 1971, p. 35).

Thus, when we explain how a politician seeks to gain from a particular action, our mind comes to rest. We have our explanation, an account rooted in

a simple but plausible assumption about why we do what we do. In that sense, the rational choice approach is an indispensable tool in our kitbag.

Yet the approach, like any other, also takes too much for granted. It fails to explain the origins of the goals that individuals hold; it is surely here, in understanding the shaping of preferences, that society re-enters the equation. Our aspirations, our status and even our goals emerge from our interactions with others ('I'll have what she's having') rather than being formed beforehand. Certainly, we cannot take people's goals and values as given.

Also, since the rational choice approach is based on a universal model of human behaviour, it possesses limited relevance in understanding variation across countries. Just as individual goals are taken for granted, so too are the varying national settings within which individuals pursue their strategies.

Finally, it is worth noting three areas where deviations from rationality may be systematic:

▶ As individuals, we must all temper our rationality with the need to maintain a positive self-image. Examining ourselves objectively leads only to madness.

▶ Not all action is instrumental: we sometimes value behaviour for itself but by definition spontaneity can never be set as a goal.

▶ Groups sometimes seem to make decisions which are more polarized, and less rational, than those which would have been taken by their individual members (Box 2.4).

Yet we naturally assume that such cases are exceptional for the belief that the world is fundamentally rational is one to which we are psychologically committed – perhaps beyond all reason.

The interpretive approach

An important and challenging question to ask about politics is the extent to which it is driven by ideas. To what degree should our research focus on the ideas and interpretations – the assumptions, constructions, identities, meanings and values – within which politics operates?

On the one hand, we could regard ideas as an outgrowth of, rather than an independent influence on,

---

BOX 2.4

The limits of rationality: groupthink

The German philosopher Friedrich Nietzsche (1844–1900) claimed that madness is the exception among individuals but the rule in groups. Janis's work (1982) on groupthink offers support to the latter part of this proposition, thereby encouraging us to recognize the limits of applying individual-level rational choice models to groups.

For Janis, groupthink emerges when a team's concern with maintaining internal harmony overrides its motivation to appraise realistically alternative courses of action, leading to decisions inferior to those the group's members would have made if acting alone. This syndrome is most likely to emerge when:

- The group is under stress;
- The group is isolated from the rest of the organization;
- The group's members share a similar background and ideology.

In such conditions, the group stereotypes the opposition, becomes convinced of its own invulnerability and loses its capacity to assess risk. Later research added the point that even in normal conditions group discussion tends to strengthen the predominant opinion among the members, leading to a shift to riskier decisions (Rothwell, 1986).

Groupthink is not just an academic label; it can lead to policy fiascos. Janis cites failures from five American administrations:

- Franklin Roosevelt: Pearl Harbor;
- Harry Truman: the invasion of North Korea;
- John Kennedy: the Bay of Pigs invasion;
- Lyndon Johnson: the escalation of the Vietnam War;
- Richard Nixon: the Watergate cover-up.

But these cases are well-known, partly because they are exceptional, and in any case groupthink is far from inevitable even when conditions are ripe. During the Cuban missile crisis, for instance, many of the same policy-makers involved in the Bay of Pigs failure engaged in more honest and successful deliberation. In this case, several improvements were made to the decision-making process:

- Group members were charged with looking at the problem as a whole, leading to sharp discussion of all proposals;
- New members were brought in as appropriate, allowing different viewpoints to emerge;
- To encourage give and take, the president sometimes absented himself from meetings.

Rationality in groups can be achieved, it seems, but it has to be worked at in order to overcome the negative aspects of group dynamics.

---

political practice, as with Karl Marx's materialist reading of history: 'the ideas of the ruling class are in every epoch the ruling ideas' (Marx and Engels, 1845, p. 12). On the other hand we could, with the German philosopher Georg Hegel (1770–1831), adopt an idealist account, in which ideas take on an autonomous existence and history is seen as the movement of spirit through the world.

The relationship between ideas and politics can itself be approached in several ways. Political ideology is one traditional lens (see p. 19); political culture offers another perspective (Chapter 7). Here, we will examine the general notion of an **interpretive approach**. In its strongest version, this position holds that politics itself consists of the ideas participants hold about it. There is no political reality separate from our mental constructions which can be examined for the impact of ideas. Rather, politics is formed by ideas themselves. The true political constitution is the complex of shared ideas.

The **interpretive approach** assumes '(1) that the structures of human association are determined primarily by shared ideas rather than material forces, and (2) that the identities and interests of purposive actors are constructed by these shared ideas rather than given by nature' (Wendt, 1999, p. 1, defining the related notion of the constructivist approach).

In a more restrained version, the argument is not that ideas comprise our political world but that they are an independent influence upon it, shaping how we define our interests, our goals, our allies and our enemies. We act as we do because of how we view the world; if our perspective differed, so would our actions. Where rational choice focuses on how people go about achieving their individual objectives, the interpretivist examines the framing of objectives themselves and regards such interpretations as a property of the group rather than the individual.

Furthermore, many interpretivists imagine that we can restructure our view of the world. For instance, there is no intrinsic reason why individuals and states must act (as rational choice theorists imagine) in pursuit of their own narrow self-interests. To make such an assumption is to project concepts onto a world that we falsely imagine to be independent of our thoughts. 'Interests are not just "out there" waiting to be discovered; they are constructed through social interaction' (Finnemore, 1996, p. 2). Specifically, ideas come before material factors because the value placed on material things is itself an idea.

For example, states are often presented as entities existing independently of our thoughts. But the state is not a physical entity like a lake or a mountain; it is an idea built over a long period by political thinkers as well as by practical politicians. Borders between blocs of land were placed there not by nature but by people. In remote areas, there may be nothing on the ground to indicate the presence of a boundary; in a sense, the map is the reality.

States did not come into existence as if produced by a volcanic eruption, to be followed later by political philosophers who invented the notion of sovereignty in justification. Rather, the idea and the reality emerged together as part of a single conception. True, the consequences of states – such as taxes and wars – are real enough, but these are the effects of the world we have made – and can remake.

Similarly, the class relationships emphasized by the structuralists, and the generalizations uncovered by the behaviouralists, are based not on physical realities but on interpretations that can, in principle, be changed. For instance, a finding about women's under-representation in legislatures can generate a campaign that leads to increased female participation, thus altering the relationship between gender and involvement. For this reason, interpretivists often focus on historical narratives, examining how understandings of one event influence later events.

Parsons (forthcoming) provides a useful definition of the related notion of constructivism:

A constructivist argument claims that people do one thing and not another due to the presence of certain 'social constructs': ideas, beliefs, norms, identities or some other interpretive filter through which people perceive the world. We inhabit 'a world of our making' (Onuf, 1989) and action is structured by the meanings that particular groups of people develop to interpret and organise their identities, relationships and environment.

All versions of the interpretive approach draw a sharp distinction between social studies and natural science. The former alone studies human action – and action is meaningful behaviour that both describes and explains what is taking place. When we enquire 'what is a person up to?' we seek an account of the motives which constitute the action itself. Weber gives the example of a wood-cutter at work: the same act may mean that the woodsman is earning a living, building up a personal supply of timber, or working off a temper (Parkin, 2002, p. 20). Geertz (1973, p. 5) concludes from such examples that since we are suspended in webs of meaning that we ourselves have spun, the social analyst is not engaged in a behavioural science seeking laws but an interpretive one seeking meaning: 'what we call our data are really our own constructions of other people's constructions of what they and their compatriots are up to'.

In politics, as in other disciplines concerned with groups, many interpretivists consider not so much the meanings attached to behaviour by individuals but rather how such meanings form, reflect and sustain the traditions, cultures, codes, narratives and

Ideas and politics: Valentino on mass killing and genocide

In his prize-winning study of mass killing and genocide in the twentieth century, Valentino (2004, p. 3) suggests that mass murder of civilians is a product of the ideas of the instigators. 'Mass killing is an instrumental policy designed to accomplish leaders' most important ideological and political objectives' (p. 67). Valentino is a student of elite ideas, which he takes to encompass both their goals and their assessments of how to achieve them; he is less concerned with structural relationships or government institutions existing in the wider society:

> To identify societies at high risk for mass killing, we must first understand the specific goals, ideas and beliefs of powerful groups and leaders, not necessarily the broad social structures or systems of government over which these leaders preside. (p. 66)

Specifically, Valentino contends that 'mass killing occurs when powerful groups come to believe it is the best available means to accomplish certain radical goals, counter specific types of threat or solve difficult military problems' (p. 66).

Unlike rational choice thinkers, Valentino does not assume that politicians are accurate in their perceptions of their environment. He suggests that it is their interpretations themselves that matter:

> An understanding of mass killing does not imply that perpetrators always evaluate objectively the problems they face in their environment, nor that they accurately assess the ability of mass killings to resolve these problems. Human beings act on the basis of their subjective perceptions and beliefs, not objective results. (p. 67)

But it is not just ideas and perceptions that are Valentino's concern. Rather, he examines how leaders are driven by actual and perceived changes in the political environment to regard mass killing as the final solution for achieving their ends. Thus, his approach is not purely interpretive but instead consists of a fruitful examination of the interaction over time between elite ideas and perceptions, on the one hand, and political realities, on the other.

Valentino carries through his interest in ideas to a consideration of how we can best prevent future occurrences of mass killing. He rejects the relevance of behavioural or structural generalizations suggesting that mass killings only occur in dictatorships or war. Rather, he suggests that leaders in any type of structure, institution or political system may come to see mass killing as the best, most effective or sole method of achieving their goals. Effective prevention therefore requires us to return again to leaders' ideas: 'if we hope to anticipate mass killing, we must begin to think of it in the same way its perpetrators do' (p. 141).

discourses of a social group or an entire society. The concern is social constructs rather than the ideas of leaders and elite groups as studied by Valentino (Box 2.5). For example, by acting in a world of states – by, say, applying for passports and supporting national sports teams – we routinely reinforce the concept of the state itself. By practising statehood in these ways, as much as by direct influences through education and the media, the idea itself is socially reinforced or, as is often said, socially constructed. Further, these understandings can also be socially contested – 'why should I need a visa each time I visit this country?' – leading to gradual changes in the ideas themselves.

There is an obvious but useful lesson for students of politics, and of comparative politics especially, in the interpretive approach. When we confront a political system for the first time, our initial task is to engage in political anthropology: to make sense of the activities that comprise the system. What are the moves? What do they mean? What is the context that provides this meaning? And what identities and values underpin political action? Behaviour which has one meaning in our home country may posses a different significance, and constitute a different action, elsewhere. For example, offering a bribe may be accepted as normal in one place but be regarded as a serious offence in another. Casting a vote may be an act of partisan choice in an established democracy, an act of courage in a democracy under threat and an act of obedience in a dictatorship. Criticizing the president may be routine in one country but treason in another. Because the consequences of these acts vary, so does their very nature.

So far, so good. Yet in studying politics we want to identify patterns that abstract from detail; we seek general statements about presidential, electoral or party systems which go beyond the facts of a particular case. We want, further, to examine relationships between such categories so as to discover overall associations. We want to know, for instance, whether a plurality electoral system always leads to a two-party system. Through such investigations we can acquire knowledge which goes beyond the understandings of the participants in a particular case.

We must recognize, also, that events have unintended consequences: the Holocaust was a product of Hitler's ideas but its effects ran far beyond the Führer's own intentions. An interpretive approach gives us a grounding in meaning but risks missing the commonplace observation that much social and political analysis studies the unintended consequences of human activity.

In short, unpacking the meaning of political action is best regarded as the starting point but not the end point of political analysis. It provides a practical piece of advice: to ensure we have grasped the meaning of political behaviour, thus enabling us to compare like with like. Yet it would surely be unsatisfactory to regard a project as complete at this preliminary point.

Compared to the other approaches reviewed in this chapter, the interpretive approach remains more of an aspiration than an achievement. Some studies conducted within the programme focus on interesting but far-away cases when meanings really were different: when states did not rule the world, when money-lending was considered a sin, or when the political game consisted of acquiring dependent followers rather than independent wealth (de Goede,

2005). Yet such studies do little to confirm the easy assumption that the world we have made can be easily dissolved. As the institutionalists with whom we began this chapter are quick to remind us, most social constructs are social constraints, for institutions are powerfully persistent.

Conclusion

How can we judge the value of the approaches reviewed in this chapter? The measure is not the conventional lens of truth or falsity; while theories can be tested against evidence, approaches must be assessed in a broader way. But neither should approaches be judged against some abstract, fixed standard of philosophical adequacy; in the final analysis, what matters is what works best in delivering new and important research findings.

In our view, the key question is whether an approach is fruitful. The cash value of a school of thought lies precisely in its ability to generate a progressive research programme – innovative studies which shape new problems and cast fresh light on old ones (Lakatos, 1978). A fertile approach will identify a manner of looking at politics which is fresh, revealing and productive. It will generate truths, and sometimes provide a pragmatic account of what it will accept as evidence, even though it is neither true nor false in itself (Lichbach, 2009).

As research programmes, theoretical approaches are not for all time. Rather like people, they are born, develop, tire and decay. But each approach, like each person, leaves a legacy. Our discussion of theoretical approaches in politics has therefore introduced some themes in the history of politics as an academic discipline and outlined some major tides of opinion that have flowed through it. In politics, though, established approaches tend to remain on the menu rather than being replaced altogether, thus offering a continuing set of choices for researchers as they go about their studies.

Learning Resources for Chapter 2

Next step

Lichbach and Zuckerman (2009) cover rationality, culture and structure in their detailed study of approaches in comparative politics.

Further reading

Marsh and Stoker (2010) contains useful essays on many of the approaches reviewed in this chapter. Like Lichbach and Zuckerman, this book also covers overlaps and subtypes we have ignored. For the institutional approach, see Peters (1999) and, for enthusiasts, Rhodes *et al.* (2006). Anderson (2009) usefully assesses the contemporary contribution of the behavioural approach; see also Dalton and Klingemann (2007). Mahoney and Rueschemeyer (2003) is an excellent review of structural analysis from a comparative history perspective. Tsebelis (2002) uses a rational choice framework to examine how political institutions work, while Green and Shapiro (1994) offer a critique of rational choice applications in political science. Green (2002b) and Parsons (forthcoming) examine the interpretive approach.

Internet sources

Committee on Concepts and Methods
A research committee of the International Political Science Association
http://www.concepts-methods.org/

Comparative Politics
Sites of working papers in political science
http://sitemason.vanderbilt.edu/files/f3oFgI/2007%20LAPOP%20among%20the%20links%20of%20Comparative%20Politics%20Political%20Science%20Sites%20of%20Working%20Papers.pdf

New Political Science
An organized section of the American Political Science Association
http://www.apsanet.org/~new/

Rational Choice Theory
An essay by John Scott
http://privatewww.essex.ac.uk/~scottj/socscot7.htm

www.palgrave.com
Companion Website
Visit the Companion Website to 'click and go'
www.palgrave.com/politics/hague

Chapter 3
Research strategies

How do we find out about political systems, processes and behaviour? Books such as this one are replete with accounts of research findings but the methods used to create these results usually receive less attention. By outlining the main research strategies used in politics, and in comparative politics in particular, this chapter provides a background in the varied methods adopted by the academic studies reported in this book. Our goal is not to cover specific techniques such as interviewing. Rather, our aim is to examine the territory lying between narrow research techniques, on the one hand, and broad theoretical approaches, on the other. This is a space where many student dissertations are located and we hope, too, that some of the strategies we discuss here will be relevant to the design of such projects.

Political research is not an area where one size fits all and we will cover a range of strategies. These methods vary principally in the number of cases included in the analysis (Box 3.1). We begin with the flexible and straightforward device of the case study, where the object is to provide a detailed account of a single example of a wider phenomenon. We then introduce comparison proper before discussing the qualitative comparison of a small number of instances. We next discuss quantitative analysis, where the number of cases is large and the object is to demonstrate relationships between variables rather than to provide intense scrutiny of one or a few cases. Here we will rest content with outlining the nature, rather than the techniques, of statistical research. We conclude with a discussion of historical analysis within political research – a distinct topic, to be sure, but one which has attracted recent attention and which does raise the often puzzling question of how research strategies used in politics differ from those employed in history.

Case studies

Case studies are one of the most widely used strategies in political research, providing the lion's share of articles published in journals of comparative politics (Hull, 1999). Such studies combine a qualitative investigation of a topic, using all appropriate techniques, with a link to wider themes in the study of politics.

One key to a successful case study is to be clear what the study is a case of. A case is an instance of a more general category. By its nature, to conduct such a study is to undertake an investigation with significance beyond its own boundaries. Lawyers study cases which are taken to illustrate a wider legal principle. Physicians study a case of a particular ailment because they want to learn how to treat similar instances in the future. For example, an account of the Japanese election of 2009 which does not venture beyond the

BOX 3.1

Some research designs in politics

	Number of cases	Case-, variable- or process-centred?	Strategy
Case study	One	Case	Intensive study of a single instance with wider significance
Qualitative comparison (small-N)	A few	Case	Qualitative comparison of a few instances
Quantitative analysis (large-N)	Many	Variable	Search for causes by making statistical assessments of the relationships between variables
Historical analysis (small-N)	One	Process	Often, tracing the process leading to a known outcome

Note: N is the statistician's term for the number of cases.

topic itself is a study, not a case study. But an analysis which takes this election as an example of the fall of a previously dominant party is a case study.

So a case study adds value by offering a detailed illustration of a theme of wider interest, turning history and journalism into political science. For instance, we could take the United States as an example of presidential government, Canada as an illustration of federalism and Ireland as an example of a country employing the single transferable vote.

By their nature, case studies are multimethod, using the range of techniques in the political scientist's toolbag. The kit includes:

- Reading the academic literature;
- Examining secondary documents;
- Scrutinizing primary sources;
- Conducting interviews with participants and other observers in the country, organization or other unit under scrutiny;
- Experiencing, or at least visiting, the unit under study.

In other words, scholars of cases engage in 'soaking and poking, marinating themselves in minutiae' (King *et al.*, 1994, p. 38). They aim to

provide a description which is both rounded and detailed, a goal which Geertz (1973) called 'thick description'. This approach contrasts with specific methods seeking to understand the matter in hand through a single lens, such as a statistical analysis or an experiment. Unlike statistical analysis, which seeks to identify relationships between variables measured across a series of observations, case analysis aims to identify how a range of factors interact to produce specific outcomes in the case under scrutiny.

Case studies possess broader significance by definition but this added value can be acquired in various ways. Box 3.2 outlines five types of case study. A case can be useful because it is representative, prototypical, deviant, exemplary or critical (or a combination of these).

Of these designs, the **representative case** is by far the most common. It is the workhorse of case studies, as useful as it is undramatic. Often researchers will use their own country as a representative example. For instance, researchers may be interested in coalition formation in general but choose to study the phenomenon in their own country in detail. The home country is the research site but the hope is that the results will contribute to a broader understanding. A collection of representa-

BOX 3.2

Some types of case study

	Definition	Example
Representative	Typical of the category	Coalition government in Finland
Prototypical	Expected to become typical	The United States as a pioneering democracy
Deviant	The exception to the rule	India as a case of democracy in a poor country
Exemplary	Creates the category	The French Revolution
Critical	If it works here, it will work anywhere	Promoting democracy in post-invasion Iraq

Further reading: Yin (2003, 2004).

tive case studies can provide the raw material for later distillation by other scholars.

By contrast, a **prototypical case** is chosen not because it is representative but because it is expected to become so. As Rose (1991a, p. 459) puts it, 'their present is our future'. Studying a pioneer can help us to understand a phenomenon which is growing in significance elsewhere. In the nineteenth century, the French scholar Alexis de Tocqueville (1835, ch. 1) studied America because of his interest in the new politics of democracy. He wrote, 'my wish has been to find there [in the USA] instruction by which we [in Europe] may ourselves profit'. De Tocqueville regarded the United States as a harbinger of democracy and therefore a guide to Europe's own future. Another example of a prototypical case would be studying HIV/Aids policy in one of the first countries where the infection became prevalent.

The purpose of a **deviant case** study is very different. Here we deliberately seek out the exceptional and the untypical, rather than the norm: the countries which remain communist, or which are still governed by the military, or which seem to be immune from democratizing trends. Deviant cases are often used to tidy up our understanding of exceptions and anomalies: why does India contradict the thesis that democracy presupposes prosperity? Why did tiny Switzerland adopt a federal architecture when most federations are found in large countries? Why does turnout stay high in Denmark as it falls elsewhere (Elkit *et al.*, 2005)?

Deviant cases always attract interest and, by providing a contrast with the norm, enhance our understanding of typical examples. But since the exceptional tends to the exotic, the danger is overstudy. Comparative politics should be more than a collection of curios.

Exemplary cases are archetypes that generate the category of which they are taken, in a somewhat circular way, as representative. For instance, the French Revolution altered the whole concept of revolution, reconstructing the idea as a progressive, modernizing force. In this way, the French Revolution made possible all the modern revolutions which followed. In similar fashion, the American presidency does far more than illustrate the presidential system of government: it is the model which influenced later creations of similar systems, notably in Latin America. While an exemplar is often defined as an example to be emulated, in research design the term refers more neutrally to an influential example which illustrates the essential features of a phenomenon.

Finally, a **critical case** (also called a crucial case) enables a proposition to be tested in the circumstances least favourable to its validity. The logic is simple: if true here, then true everywhere. For instance, attempting to introduce democracy to Iraq following the American invasion was a difficult assignment. If democracy could be imposed successfully in that case, it could surely also be built in more favourable situations, for example in countries with prior experience of democracy and fewer internal divisions. Thus Iraq provides a critical case for the proposition that democracy can be imposed.

Similarly, if we find that political participation is low even among a sample of politics students, we can be fairly sure that it will be more limited still among the wider population. Thus a small survey of politics students might yield results applicable to a wider population without the expense of sampling the larger group. In this way, critical case studies can be highly efficient, providing exceptional returns on the research investment. However, there is a risk: a critical case design builds a potential for generalization into a single investigation but involves a bet that the relevant proposition will, in fact, be confirmed in unfavourable conditions.

In the absence of overarching theory, case studies are the building blocks from which we construct our understanding of the political world (Yin, 2003). Rather like judges in common law systems, political scientists (and politicians more so) usually proceed by comparing cases rather than by making deductions from first principles. In consequence, much comparative political analysis takes the form not of relating cases to abstract theory, but simply of drawing analogies between the cases themselves. For instance: how did the process of state-building differ between post-colonial states of the twentieth century and the states of early modern Europe? What are the similarities and differences between the Russian and Chinese revolutions? Why does the plurality electoral system produce a two-party system in the USA but a multiparty system in India? In such examples, we see how a series of cases can provide a base for comparative understanding.

Comparative studies

A comparative design is well-established in politics, more so than in most disciplines. In this section, we will first raise the obvious question: what is the value of comparing politics in different countries? We will then go on to consider some of the difficulties in implementing comparative designs.

Why compare? The answer is that it broadens our understanding of the political world, leading to improved classifications and giving potential for explanation and even prediction (Box 3.3). We discuss each purpose in turn.

BOX 3.3

The value of comparing

▶ Learning about other governments broadens our understanding, casting fresh light on our home nation;
▶ Comparison permits us to classify political structures and processes;
▶ Comparison enables us to test hypotheses about politics;
▶ Comparison gives us some potential for prediction and control.

Broadening understanding

The first strength of a comparative approach is straightforward: it enables us to find out more about the places we know least about. This point was well-stated by Munro (1925, p. 4). He described the purpose of his book on European governments as aiding 'the comprehension of daily news from abroad'. This ability to interpret overseas events grows in importance as the world becomes more interdependent. In an era of international terrorism, no one can afford the insular attitude of Mr Podsnap in Dickens's *Our Mutual Friend*: 'Foreigners do as they do sir, and that is the end of it'. In any case, Munro was perhaps a shade modest; even when the focus is just on one overseas country, an implicit comparison with the homeland helps to broaden our horizons.

Understanding politics in other systems not only helps to interpret new developments there, it also assists with practical political relationships. For instance, British ministers have a patchy track record in negotiations with their European partners partly because they assume that the aggressive tone they adopt in the Commons chamber will work as well in EU meeting rooms. Their assumption is incorrect, showing ignorance of the consensual political style found in many Continental democracies. What works at home often fails when playing away.

Similarly, American students sometimes puzzle at how the British parliamentary system can deliver stable government when the prime minister, unlike their own president, is constantly at the mercy of a vote of confidence in the Commons. Because American parties are so decentralized, the tendency is to underestimate the ability of a British governing party to control its own Members of Parliament. Conversely, British students are so accustomed to the importance of party that they experience difficulty in understanding why Congress and the White House continue to quarrel even when the same party nominally controls both institutions.

The general point is made by Dogan and Pelassy (1990): through comparison we discover our own ethnocentrism and the means of overcoming it. In this respect, comparative politics is a virtual trip abroad – and the object of foreign travel, said the British critic G. K. Chesterton (1874–1936), is not so much to set foot overseas as to see one's own country as a foreign land.

Enabling classification

A second advantage of comparison is that it enables us to classify government structures and political processes. We can distinguish between liberal and illiberal democracies and contrast both with authoritarian regimes. We can group constitutions into written and unwritten, and electoral formulae into proportional and non-proportional. We can then search for the factors which incline countries to one form rather than the other.

Similarly, once we classify executives into presidential and parliamentary systems, we can look at which type is more stable and effective.

Classification is inherently comparative, turning what is often a constant within a single country into a variable between them. In this way, classification provides the raw material from which explanatory ventures can be launched.

Testing hypotheses

Comparative researchers seek to understand a variety of political systems not just for their own sake but also to formulate and test **hypotheses**. Comparative analysis enables us to develop and scrutinize such questions as: do first-past-the-post electoral systems always produce a two-party system? Are two-chambered assemblies only found

A **hypothesis** is a relationship posited between two or more factors or variables: for example, between electoral and party systems, or between war and revolution.

under federalism? Are revolutions more likely to occur after defeat in war?

Confirmed hypotheses are valuable not just for their own sake but because they are essential for explaining the particular. Consider, for example, one specific question: why did a major socialist party never emerge in the United States? An obvious answer is because the USA was built on, and retains, a strongly individualistic culture. This explanation may seem to be particular but in fact it is quite general. It implies that other countries with similar values would also lack a strong socialist party. It also suggests that countries with a more collective outlook will be more likely to sustain a party of the left. These hypotheses would need to be confirmed comparatively by looking at a range of countries before we could claim a full understanding of our original question about the USA. So explaining the particular calls forth the general; only theories explain cases.

Potential for prediction

Generalizations, once validated, have potential for prediction. Here we come to our fourth reason for studying politics comparatively. If we find, say, that introducing proportional representation (PR) in New Zealand did indeed lead to coalition government, we can reasonably predict at least one effect of introducing PR to countries such as Canada which still use the plurality method. Equally, if we know that subcontracting the provision of public services to private agencies raises the quality of delivery in one country, we can advise governments elsewhere that here is an idea at least worth considering.

The ability to predict provides a base for drawing lessons across countries (Rose, 2004). Rather than resorting to ideology or guesses, we can use comparison to address 'what would happen if…?' questions. This function of comparative research perhaps underpinned Bryce's comment on his own study of modern democracies (1921, p. iv):

Many years ago, when schemes of political reform were being copiously discussed in England, it occurred to me that something might be done to provide a solid basis for judgment by examining a certain number of popular governments in their actual working, comparing them with one another, and setting forth the various merits and demerits of each.

Of course, any approach brings its own difficulties and the breadth inherent in comparative designs brings its own risks (Box 3.4). Again, we proceed by examining these potential pitfalls one by one.

Understanding meaning

Building on our discussion of the interpretive approach in Chapter 2, we should remember that the meaning of an action depends on the conventions of the country concerned. For instance, styles of political representation are highly variable. Where Nigerian politicians seek to impress by acts of flamboyant extravagance (such as seducing their competitors' female companions), Swedish politicians set out to affirm their very ordinariness. The same goal of impressing constituents is achieved by culturally specific means. What works in Lagos would be disastrous in Stockholm and what succeeds in Stockholm would be met with apathy in Lagos. Similarly, when members of the legislature vote against their party's line, the consequences can vary by country from complete indifference to expulsion from the party. What appears to be the same act carries varying significance. Meaning depends on context.

This problem of the meaning and significance of action is particularly important in politics because the activity is partly conducted through coded language. Were the people who attacked the World Trade Center and the Pentagon murderers, martyrs or both? Were American civil rights activists also black militants? Were active members of the Irish Republican Army terrorists or freedom fighters? How such actors are described reflects existing political opinions, raising doubts about whether we can find a wholly neutral language for interpreting our subject matter.

Globalization

Globalization poses a considerable challenge to comparative political research, understood as the comparison of separate states. Although 191 'independent' countries belonged to the United Nations by 2009, in reality these states are interdependent, or even dependent, rather than independent. Countries learn from, copy, compete with, influence and even

---

BOX 3.4

The difficulties of comparison

⯈ The 'same' phenomenon can mean different things in different countries, creating difficulties in comparing like with like;

⯈ Globalization means that countries cannot be regarded as independent of each other, thus reducing the effective number of cases available for testing theories;

⯈ Any pair of countries will differ in many ways, meaning we can never achieve the experimenter's dream of holding all factors constant apart from the one whose impact we wish to test;

⯈ The countries selected for study may be an unrepresentative sample, limiting the significance of the findings.

---

invade each other in a constant process of interaction. States did not develop independently; rather, the idea of statehood diffused outwards from its proving ground in Europe. As Dogan and Pelassy (1990, p. 1) say, 'there is no nation without other nations'.

The major transitions of world history – industrialization, colonialism, decolonization, democratization – unfolded on a world stage. In that sense we have one global system rather than a world of independent states. Green (2002a, p. 5) puts the point well when he says the world is arranged 'as if national politics are in fact cells of a larger entity with a life all its own'. The implication is that we should study this larger organism rather than comparing its component parts as if they were independent.

Specific institutional forms also reflect diffusion. The communist model was often imposed by force of Soviet arms; the presidential system in Latin America was imported from the United States; the ombudsman was a device copied from Sweden. The development of international organizations, from the United Nations to the European Union, also creates a newer layer of governance to which all member states must react.

Why do connections between states constitute a pitfall for students of comparative politics? The answer is provided by Tilly (1997): comparative politics traditionally presumes distinct and separate units of comparison, most often states, which can be treated as if they were independent. That assumption was always a simplification but in an interdependent world such a presumption has become positively misleading. Technically, treating countries as independent entities artificially inflates the effective sample size in statistical analysis, resulting in exaggerated confidence in the significance of the results obtained.

Too many variables, too few countries

This is a major problem for those who conceive of comparative politics as a version of the experimenter's laboratory, in which researchers patiently seek to isolate the impact of a single variable. Even with 191 sovereign states, it is impossible to find a country which is identical to another in all respects except for that factor (say, its electoral system) whose effects we wish to detect. For this reason, political comparisons can never be as precise as laboratory experiments. We just do not have the countries to go round.

To make the same point from another angle, we will never be able to test all the possible explanations of a political difference. For example, why was New Zealand particularly sympathetic to introducing the private sector into the running of public services during the 1990s? Perhaps the strength of the reforms there reflected the pro-market thinking of the country's political and business elite (Boston *et al.*, 1995). Or perhaps the public sector in New Zealand was vulnerable to reform because, unlike many democracies in continental Europe, its structure was not protected by the constitution and civil law codes (Hood, 1996).

Here we have two potential explanations for New Zealand's distinctiveness, one based on ideology and the other on law. Both interpretations are broadly consistent with the facts. But we have no way of isolating which factor is decisive. Ideally, we would want to discover whether the public sector had been reformed in a country just like New Zealand except that only one of these two factors applied. But there is no such country; we have run out of cases.

In such circumstances, we can of course resort to asking hypothetical 'what if' questions. What would the outcome have been in New Zealand had its reforming elite confronted an unsympathetic legal framework? Would public sector reform still have

proceeded? We should not shy away from such **counterfactuals** for they must form part of any attempt to estimate the impact of unique events. To help us in this task, Tetlock and Belkin (1996) have developed useful guidelines for judging the plausibility of any particular counterfactual. However, by definition the outcome of such thought experiments can never be tested against reality.

A **counterfactual** is a thought experiment speculating on possible outcomes if a particular factor had been absent from a process or an absent one had been present. What would our world be like if Hitler had died in a car crash in 1932 or if his invasion of Russia had succeeded? (Rosenfeld, 2005). Who would rule China today if its leaders had not embraced economic reform?

Selection bias

We turn finally to a more technical difficulty in comparative research which nonetheless has implications for all those who practise the art. **Selection bias** is at issue whenever the units of study (such as countries, democracies or electoral systems) are chosen other than randomly. In these circumstances the danger is that the units studied are unrepresentative of a wider population and results cannot be generalized to the wider category from which the cases were drawn. Given the rarity of random sampling in qualitative comparisons, the point is not so much to eliminate such bias as to be aware of its presence.

The danger often emerges as an unintended result of haphazard selection. For example, we choose to study those countries which speak our language, or which have good exchange schemes, or in which we feel safe. As a result, large, powerful countries are studied more intensively than small, powerless ones, even though the politics of large and small states may differ. Similarly, more studies are conducted in

Selection bias arises when the choice of what to study produces results that are unrepresentative of the wider class from which the cases and variables are drawn. Studies of English-speaking democracies are unrepresentative of all democracies; studies of communist parties that remain in power today are untypical of ruling communist parties in the twentieth century.

Western than Eastern Europe, which should give us pause before we generalize to Europe as a whole.

A virtue of statistical designs covering a large number of countries is that they reduce the risk of selection bias. Indeed, if the study covers all current countries, selection bias disappears – at least so long as generalization is restricted to the contemporary world. But, alas, the problem may just resurface in another form, through an unrepresentative selection of variables rather than countries. To appreciate this version of selection bias, consider an illustration. Much statistical research in comparative politics, including the scores used in the country profiles in this book, relies on existing data collected by governments and international bodies with different interests from our own. The priorities of these organizations are often economic rather than political. So the availability of data means that financial and economic variables receive more attention than they justify, and politics runs the risk of being treated as a branch of economics.

A particularly important form of selection bias comes from examining only positive cases, thus eliminating all variation in the phenomenon we seek to explain. Because this is a common, noteworthy and avoidable mistake, it deserves careful consideration. King *et al.* (1994, p. 129) explain the problem:

The literature is full of work that makes the mistake of failing to let the dependent variable vary; for example, research that tries to explain the outbreak of wars with studies only of wars, the onset of revolutions with studies only of revolutions, or patterns of voter turnout with interviews only of non-voters.

The problem here is that when only positive cases of a phenomenon are studied, conclusions about the causes and consequences of the phenomenon are ruled out. Contrast is needed to give variation, so that we can then consider what distinguishes times of war from times of peace, periods of revolution from periods of stability, and abstainers from voters.

Even without variation in the dependent variable, we can still identify common characteristics of the cases. For example, we may find that revolutions are always preceded by war, or that all non-voters are cynical about politics. However, we have no contrast to explore and explain. We do not know whether the conditions leading to revolution often exist without

triggering a revolution, or whether the political cynicism we find among abstainers is equally prevalent (or conceivably even more so) among those who do turn out on election day (Geddes, 2003). The fact that Y is always preceded by X does not show that X is always followed by Y.

Survivorship bias is a particular form of this problem. It arises when non-survivors of a temporal process are excluded, leading to biased results. Studying contemporary communist states or military governments as representative of the entire class of such regimes (past as well as present) is an error because those that have survived are likely to differ from those that disappeared. We should not treat those who complete a journey as typical of those who started out, for to do so would be to ignore the casualties along the way. In designing our research, we should look through both ends of the telescope – at starters as well as finishers, at casualties as well as survivors.

Qualitative comparisons

Implementing a comparative design involves making qualitative or quantitative comparisons. In this section, we examine qualitative comparisons, leaving quantitative analysis to the next section.

Qualitative comparisons fall between case studies and statistical analysis. They are the standard form of comparison, consisting of small-*N* studies concentrating on the intensive comparison of an aspect of politics in a few countries. Most often, the number of countries is either two, a paired or binary comparison, or three, a triangular comparison. The concern with predefined aspects of the cases explains why George (1969) calls this method 'structured, focused comparison'. Countries are normally selected to introduce variation into the dependent variable, thus overcoming an inherent limit of the single case study.

To illustrate the technique, consider two examples using paired comparison. First, Kudrle and Marmor (1981) compared the growth of social security programmes in the United States and Canada. They sought to understand Canada's higher levels of spending and programme development, concluding that the elements of left-wing ideology and conservative paternalism found there were the key contrasts with the USA.

Second, Heclo (1974) compared the origins of unemployment insurance, old age pensions and earnings-related supplementary pensions in Britain and Sweden. In both countries, Heclo concluded, the bureaucracy was the main agent of policy formulation. In contrast to Kudrle and Marmor, and indeed to many qualitative comparisons, Heclo's project sought to explain a similarity rather than a difference between the countries examined.

Qualitative comparisons such as these have proved to be a success story of comparative politics. Like case studies, they remain sensitive to the details of particular countries and policies but in addition they demand the intellectual discipline inherent in the comparative enterprise. The dimensions of comparison must be addressed; similarities and differences identified; and an effort made to account for the contrasts observed. For these reasons, qualitative comparisons allow research findings to cumulate whereas the conclusions of case studies often languish in their covers.

Unlike many statistical studies, qualitative comparisons remain sensitive to history. As we saw in discussing the structural approach in Chapter 2, the format works particularly well when, as with Heclo, a few countries are compared over time, examining how they vary in responding to common problems or arriving at distinct outcomes.

How should countries be selected for a qualitative comparison? A common strategy is to select countries which, although differing on the factor under study, are otherwise similar. This is a **most similar** design. With this approach, we seek to compare countries which are as similar as possible in, say, their history, culture and political institutions, so that we can clearly rule out such common factors as explanations for the particular difference of interest to us. For instance, we might seek to explain why Britain managed a more peaceful transition to

democracy than Germany, examining a contrast between two large countries which nonetheless share a common European heritage.

However, even with a most similar design many factors will remain as possible explanations for an observed difference and usually there will be no decisive way of testing between them. The problem of too many variables and too few countries cannot be sidestepped; in practice, the value of a qualitative comparison lies in the journey rather than the destination.

A **most different** design seeks to test a relationship by discovering whether it can be observed in a range of different countries. If so, our confidence that the relationship is real, and not due to both factors depending on an unmeasured third variable, will increase (Peters, 1998). For example, Rothstein (2002) examines the evolution of social and political trust in two contrasting democracies, Sweden and the United States, assuming that any trends shared between these two different countries should also be observable in other democracies. In a similar way, if we were to find that the plurality method of election were associated with a two-party system in the diverse group of countries employing that method, our confidence in the robustness of this relationship would increase. The most different design is the basis of much statistical research, to which we now turn.

Quantitative analysis

In political research, quantitative comparison or statistical analysis is now less common than at the height of the behavioural era but it remains a significant and worthwhile strand. Statistical research is inherently comparative but possesses strong conventions. In this section, we outline some of these principles without attempting a full guide (for which see Pennings *et al.*, 2006).

In contrast to the techniques reviewed so far, the quantitative approach is based on variables rather than cases. Specifically, the object is to explore the extent to which variables or factors covary, such that knowing a country's score on one variable (for instance, its literacy rate) allows us to predict its score on another (for instance, its electoral turnout). In such analyses, one variable is **dependent** while

A **most similar** design takes similar countries for comparison on the assumption, as Lipset (1990, p. xiii) put it, that 'the more similar the units being compared, the more possible it should be to isolate the factors responsible for differences between them'. By contrast, the **most different** design seeks to show the robustness of a relationship between two factors by demonstrating its validity across diverse settings (Przeworski and Teune, 1970).

In a statistical analysis, the **dependent variable** is the factor we wish to account for: for example, party voted for. The **independent variable** is the factor believed to influence the dependent variable: for example, level of education.

the others are **independent** or explanatory. Examples of such work in comparative politics include tests of the following hypotheses:

- The more educated a population, the higher its proportion of post-materialists;
- The higher a person's social status, the greater his or her participation in politics;
- The more affluent a country, the more likely it is to be a liberal democracy;
- Presidential government is less stable than parliamentary government.

To illustrate the statistical approach, consider an example. Figure 3.1 is a scatterplot showing the relationship between the number of members in a national assembly (the dependent variable) and a country's population, within the 10–60 million range (the independent variable). The graph reveals a **positive correlation**: the larger the population, the larger the assembly.

The **correlation** coefficient measures the accuracy with which we can predict from one statistical variable to another. A **positive** correlation means that scores on the variables go up (or down) in tandem. A **negative** correlation means that when one variable goes up, the other goes down.

However, the content of the graph can be summarized more precisely. This is achieved by calculating a **regression line**: the line giving the best fit to the data. This line, also shown in Figure 3.1, is defined by a formula linking the variables. In this case, the formula reveals that, on average, the size of an assembly increases by about seven members for each increment of 1 million in a country's population. Given such an equation, which also gives a base estimate for assembly size given a notional population of zero, we can use the population of any particular country to predict its assembly size.

One important virtue of a regression equation is that it allows us to identify **outliers** or off-the-line

Figure 3.1 Population and assembly size, 2009, showing the line of best fit and highlighting two outliers

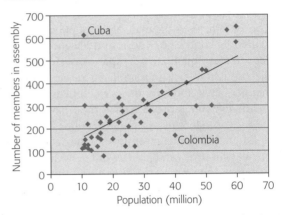

Note: For bicameral assemblies, the size of the lower chamber is used.
Source: CIA (2009).

cases. The larger the difference between the predicted and the actual assembly size, the greater the need for additional explanation, thus providing a link to deviant case analysis. In our example, Cuba's National Assembly of People's Power is far larger than would be expected for a country with a population of just 11 million.

How can we account for this outlier? The answer is probably that communist states adopted large assemblies as a way of reducing any threat they might pose to the party's power. Such an interpretation offers a plausible starting point for further investigation, giving us a case selection strategy in which the case is nested within a statistical framework (Lieberman, 2005). It may be, for example, that the weakening of Fidel Castro's grip on power in Cuba will stimulate political liberalization and eventually a smaller and on-the-line assembly.

The value of quantitative comparisons is that they can provide precise summaries of large amounts of data using standard techniques whose application can be checked by other researchers. But interpretation requires attention to two main dangers. First, a strong correlation between two variables may arise simply because both depend on a third, unmeasured

The **regression line** is the line of best fit in a scatterplot. **Outliers** are the observations furthest away from the value predicted by the regression line.

factor. For example, a correlation between proportional representation (PR) and multiparty systems might arise because both factors emerge in divided societies, not because PR itself increases the number of parties. Or a correlation between ethnic minority status and abstention at elections might arise because both factors are concentrated among the poor, not because ethnic status itself reduces turnout.

In principle, the solution to **spurious correlation** is simple: include all relevant variables in the analysis, for advanced statistical techniques can effectively control for such problems. In practice, however, not all relevant variables will be known and spurious correlation is a continuing danger. Note, though, that even a spurious correlation may be a practical if risky basis for prediction.

A **spurious correlation** is one which arises because both factors depend on a third variable. For instance, the relationship between the proportion of immigrants in an area and its crime rate may be spurious because poverty is the real cause of crime and both variables score highly in poor areas.

The second issue in interpreting statistical results is that even if a relationship is genuine, the direction of causation remains to be established. Take an example. Suppose we find that liberal democracies secure higher rates of economic growth than authoritarian regimes. We still face a problem of interpretation. Does the correlation arise because democracies facilitate economic growth or because a high rate of growth fosters a stable democracy? A case can be made either way, or both, and by itself a statistical correlation will not provide the answer. In itself, a correlation does not prove a relationship of cause and effect (though in a non-experimental discipline, neither does anything else).

Worthwhile quantitative comparisons can be made even when the variables take the form of categories (e.g. yes/no) rather than numerical scores. For example, are federations less likely than unitary states to develop welfare states? Is proportional representation linked to coalition government? Are non-Muslim countries more likely than Islamic ones to be democratic? Here we are dealing with categories rather than numerical scales: a country is either a federation or not, a government is either a

coalition or not. In these circumstances, a straightforward cross-tabulation is the qualitative equivalent of the scatterplot in Figure 3.1 and can be equally useful. Correlation-like statistics can be calculated for such tables (Pennings *et al.*, 2006).

Not all statistical work is concerned with estimating the impact of one factor on another. Simple counts provide a useful beginning. As Miller (1995) says, asking the plain question 'how many of them are there?' is worthwhile. For instance: how many federations are there? How many states are democratic? What is the probability that an authoritarian regime in 1980 has become democratic today? Such questions must be answered if we are to achieve a comparative understanding of the political world. Just as straightforward case studies often contribute more to comparative politics than elaborate attempts at theory testing, so simple counts can provide more useful results than sophisticated statistical analyses.

Historical analysis

Most studies in politics, and in comparative politics especially, focus on the contemporary world; in the main, we leave history to the historians. But this division of labour is of course arbitrary; today's present is tomorrow's past. Political science can and perhaps should make more use of the past as a treasure trove of additional cases, whether of rare events such as genocide and revolution or of particular episodes that exemplify, challenge or refine existing theories. History can enlarge our database, enabling us to employ the most different design to examine the robustness of findings across different time periods.

Quarrying the past by political scientists in this way is rather different from the approach adopted by traditional historians. According to the German historian Leopold von Ranke (1795–1886) history 'merely wants to show how essentially things happened'. For von Ranke (1824, p. iv), 'a strict representation of facts, be it ever so narrow, and unpoetical, is, beyond doubt, the first law'. From this perspective, the obligation is to present the past in its own terms – as a narrative pieced together from primary sources. Many political scientists, however, would be concerned with the past as a source of generalization: in other words, with case studies rather than studies.

The further and more interesting question, though, is how students of politics should understand temporal sequences as such. That is, how can we make the transition from taking snapshots of the present – the traditional focus of most political research – to developing moving pictures of change over time? This section addresses this question, beginning with the specific notion of an analytic narrative and then introducing some broader notions which help us to locate politics in the context of time.

The **analytic narrative** (Bates *et al.*, 1998) is an attempt to combine the historian's concern with the story with the political scientist's interest in explaining outcomes using explicit approaches. The task of an analytic narrative, typically based on rational choice, is to show how actors' interests and understanding create strategies which, interacting over time, generate the outcome of interest. In contrast to a case study, an analytic narrative is necessarily concerned with sequences; however, it does not aim to provide a comprehensive rounded description of the process but rather to identify the key factors driving towards the outcome. Such narratives are an equivalent within a rational choice framework to the comparative histories favoured by the structuralists discussed in Chapter 2.

> An **analytic narrative** attempts to integrate historical and political science methods. It examines how a particular sequence of moves, made by calculating actors aware of the options available to them, generates a particular result (Bates *et al.*, 1998).

Two examples will help to clarify the design. First, Weingast (1998) shows how slavery was maintained in the USA until the Civil War by a balance between Northern and Southern interests – both within parties and in the Senate. According to Bates, this balance provided an equilibrium in which even Northerners lacked strong incentives to advance anti-slavery initiatives. So here we have two actors – Northerners and Southerners – interacting over time to yield a stable situation in which Northerners opposed to slavery were nonetheless prepared to accept it.

Second, Bates (1998) narrates the birth, life and death of the International Coffee Organization

(ICO, 1962–89). He seeks to explain why the government of a coffee-consuming nation – the USA – supported a body which was essentially a cartel of coffee producers. The answer involves a range of actors, including producers, roasters and bureaucrats. Their interactions over the Cold War period produced and maintained an equilibrium – the ICO – until the balance was destroyed by shifts in market taste and by the emergence of new producers who did not join the organization.

Although analytic narratives provide a way of examining politics over time, especially using the rational choice approach, broader approaches are still needed. Pierson (2004) brings together some terms for thinking about politics in the context of time; this vocabulary renders explicit our often submerged thoughts about political change. We will now introduce each notion in Box 3.5 in turn.

A political process is **path dependent** when its outcome depends on earlier decisions; that is, the destination depends on the route. Path dependence implies an emphasis on history generally and branching points specifically. By contrast, path independence means that 'all roads lead to Rome', that the same destination will be reached, irrespective of the route. Path independence implies an emphasis on underlying structures and resources rather than historical sequences. For instance, the result of a football game is path dependent if the first score is vital; it is path independent if the better team is sure to win in the end, no matter who scores first. To take a more political illustration, the outcome of a war is path dependent if a battle proves decisive; it is path independent if the stronger side is sure to win eventually, whatever the results of an initial confrontation.

It is important to recognize that much political research imagines path independence. If all rich countries are liberal democracies, **tracing the process** by which a particular wealthy nation

> **Process tracing** involves identifying and describing the historical sequences linking a cause to an effect. For example, what were the steps leading from Hitler's anti-semitism to the Holocaust? Through what mechanisms does defeat in war lead to a change of regime? Process tracing reconnects political science with history, providing a mode of explanation based on causal chains rather than general laws or statistical relationships.

BOX 3.5

History matters: politics in time

Concept	Definition	Example
Path dependence	The outcome of a process is not inevitable but depends on initial decisions which lead down a particular path	Britain's decision after the war to adopt a tax-funded health system, free at the point of service, was a choice that set the country on a one-way road of socialized medicine
Critical juncture	A turning point which establishes interests, structures or institutions that persist through time	The constitutional convention which established the USA
Sequencing	The order of events, not just their occurrence, affects the outcome	Communist regimes which introduced economic reform before political liberalization (e.g. China) were more likely to survive than those beginning the reform process with political change (e.g. the USSR)
Slow-moving cause	An influence which changes slowly but, over a long period, dramatically	The gradual expansion of higher education eventually culminates in a student revolt

Source: Adapted from Pierson (2004).

---

became democratic would not cast light on the general relationship. If all wealthy states end up as democracies, whatever their starting point, we should concentrate on why affluent countries select democracy in and select dictatorship out. When all roads lead to Rome, in short, we should look for underlying causes; in these circumstances, historical narratives can describe the route but not account for the destination.

Often, however, the outcome is far from predetermined. It is here that the concepts of critical junctures, sequences and slow-moving causes provide tools for thinking about how the political past influences the political present.

Critical junctures, for example, can initiate a path dependent process. These key moments clear a new path that continues to be followed long after the juncture itself has passed. During the critical phase (often a moment of crisis), all options really are on the table and history is indeed written. Revolutions are one example; constitutional conventions another.

Once the new order has consolidated, politics settles down and the choices realistically available to decision-makers shrink in importance. The revolutionary generation gives way to the pragmatic operators of the new regime. As ideas are displaced by institutions, so the constitution as choice is supplanted by the constitution as constraint.

By dividing history into critical and normal eras, we arrive at a plausible perspective on the old debate about whether people make their own history. The answer is perhaps that they do but only occasionally. That is, critical junctures are choice points in which human agency really can be decisive.

Ideas, in particular, rise to prominence during critical junctures. In normal times, much political discussion is what Schmidt (2002, p. 252) calls cheap talk, expressing negotiating positions which defend established interests. But sometimes the existing stock of ideas becomes incapable of responding to a shift in circumstances, creating pressures for established procedures to be revised or completely rethought. A country may experience economic decline, a party a fall in votes, a trade union a collapse in membership. Suddenly, ideas that had previously received scant consideration are propelled to centre stage.

Not all the outcomes from a critical juncture are shaped by political choice; for example, revolutions exert unintended consequences far removed from the rebels' intentions. Similarly, institutions created in a critical juncture continue to consolidate and thicken over time, often transforming their character in the process. America's constitutional convention established the presidency, to be sure, but the Founding Fathers would be dismayed by the office's contemporary scale. The executive office has been transformed over the centuries; a series of small steps has led to a massive change in the White House. So we should not draw too sharp a line between critical and normal times (Mahoney and Rueschmeyer, 2003).

Sequencing, the order in which events unfold, can help to account for path dependence. For example, in European countries where trade unions developed before socialism became a full-blooded ideology (notably Britain), the labour movement took on a moderate reformist character. But where Marxist thought was already established, as in France, communist unions developed with a more radical political agenda. So whether trade unions emerged before or after the onset of Marxism helps to explain whether particular European countries developed a reformist or radical labour movement. The outcome was not predetermined but depended on the order of events.

In a similar way, the sequence in which government departments are created influences their contemporary status. Those created earliest, such as the finance and justice ministries, typically constitute the core of government, with later ministries such as the environment or transport occupying a more peripheral position. Thus, the functioning of the central government is likely to be incompletely understood if this historical sequence is ignored and all departments are treated as equal.

One form of 'sequence' is a conjuncture in which separate events occur at the same time, enlarging their political impact. The collision of the First World War with the emergence of working-class socialism, or of the Vietnam War with the student movement, generated political effects which were greater than would have been the case had these events unfolded separately. These confluences are typically made by history; they are another contributor to path dependence.

Slow-moving causes, finally, are processes that unfold over a long period. Examples include modernization, technological advance, the spread of education and the growth of the mass media. Such processes often need to reach a **threshold** before exerting a visible, dramatic effect. The emergence of students as a force in national politics, for instance, can be explosive, but this rapid onset may reflect decades of gradual expansion in higher education. A critical mass is needed before the student voice becomes strong enough to be heard.

A **threshold** is a level or tipping point above which a variable begins to exert a critical effect. The point at which sliding snow turns into an avalanche is an illustration. In politics, the number of women representatives in an assembly may need to reach a critical mass before the change in gender composition exerts significant impact.

Similarly, the election of the first member of an ethnic minority to the legislature will usually indicate that long-run changes in attitudes to and among minorities have passed a threshold at which their representation becomes a practical possibility. When thresholds are involved, long-term but otherwise slow-moving causes need to be understood historically. Contemporary explosions have long fuses and political scientists need to search into the past to uncover them.

Learning Resources for Chapter 3

Next step
King *et al.* (1994) offer a stimulating account of qualitative research design from a social scientific perspective.

Further reading
Yin (2003) is the standard source on case studies; see also his selection of examples (2004). For case selection in political research, see George and Bennett (2004) and especially Geddes (2003). Peters (1998) and Mair (1996) provide thorough and judicious discussions of comparative methods. Qualitative comparisons are considered in Ragin (1987, 1994) and Ragin *et al.* (1996). Pennings *et al.* (2006) look at statistical methods in the context of comparative politics. Mahoney and Rueschmeyer (2003) and Pierson (2004) address the incorporation of history into political analysis.

Internet sources
Committee on Concepts and Methods
A research committee of the International Political Science Association
http://www.concepts-methods.org/

Comparative Methods in Political and Social Research
David Levi-Faur's course materials
http://poli.haifa.ac.il/~levi/method.html

Society for Political Methodology
The political methodology section of the American Political Science Association
http://polmeth.wustl.edu/

www.palgrave.com
Companion Website
Visit the Companion Website to 'click and go'
www.palgrave.com/politics/hague

Part II
STATES AND REGIMES

The state remains the fundamental political unit in the world and Chapter 4 introduces this central concept, examining the state's emergence, restructuring and contemporary challenges.

The other chapters in this Part discuss the two main ways of governing states: by democratic or authoritarian means. Chapter 5 reviews the development of democracy in the modern world and unfolds the distinction between liberal and illiberal democracies. For comparison with contemporary democracy, we also consider direct and deliberative democracy. Chapter 6 examines the nature of non-democratic rule and introduces the main power bases of authoritarian rulers: in a personal despotism, a monarchy, a political party, a presidency, the armed forces or religion.

This part will enable you to:

▶ Understand the nature of the state and its historical evolution;
▶ Appreciate the origins of democracy and its transformation into forms suitable for large states;
▶ Recognize both the nature of authoritarian rule and the diverse forms of its expression.

Chapter 4
The state

Although we now take for granted the division of the world into states, we should not assume that the state always was the dominant principle of political organization, nor that it always will be. There was a world before states and, as advocates of globalization tirelessly point out, there may be a world after them too.

Before the state, government consisted, in the main, of kingdoms, empires and cities. Most such units were governed in a highly decentralized fashion but some were substantial in area and population. For example, the ancient Chinese empire 'proved capable of ruling a population that eventually grew into the hundreds of millions over a period of millennia – albeit control was not always complete and tended to be punctuated by recurring periods of rebellion' (van Creveld, 1999, p. 36). Ancient history quickly dispels the idea that all modern states are larger and more stable than every traditional political system.

Yet the modern state remains a unique political form, distinct from all preceding political formations. Today's states possess sovereign authority to rule the population of a specific territory, a notion which contrasts with the more personal and non-centralized rule by traditional kings and emperors. It is this difference which enables Melleuish (2002, p. 335) to suggest that 'the development of the modern state can be compared to the invention of the alphabet. It only happened once but once it had occurred it changed the nature of human existence for ever'.

This modern idea of the state developed in Europe between the sixteenth and eighteenth centuries, with the use of the word 'state' as a political term coming into common use towards the end of this period (Dyson, 1980, p. 26). In this chapter, we portray some of the historical and contemporary forces shaping this central unit of the contemporary world. Our aim is to present not just an abstract idea but also a force that has moulded, and is in turn shaped by, its environment.

Emergence, expansion and restructuring

The state emerged from the embers of medieval Europe (c.1000–1500). In the Middle Ages, European governance had been dominated by the Roman Church and feudal lords. The Church formed a powerful transnational authority placed above mere monarchs, with kings acting only as secular agents of the Church's higher authority. Even within their nominal territories, 'rulers' were further limited by feudal noblemen who exerted extensive authority over men of lower rank within their domain. Sandwiched between these forces – the one supranational and the other subnational – monarchs occupied a far weaker position than do today's rulers. The initial problem before us, then, is to explain how modern states escaped from the dual constraints of church and feudalism to create the core political entity of our world.

Emergence

If any single force was responsible for the transition to the modern state, that factor was war. As Tilly (1975, p. 42) writes, 'war made the state, and the state made war'. The introduction of gunpowder in the fourteenth century transformed military scale and tactics, as organized infantry and artillery replaced the knight on horseback. The result was an aggressive, competitive and expensive arms race. Between the fifteenth and eighteenth centuries, for instance, military manpower in France and England grew almost tenfold (Opello and Rosow, 2004, p. 50).

New technology forced fresh thinking from rulers. In continental Europe, kings needed administrators to recruit, train, equip and pay for standing armies, thus laying the foundation of a modern bureaucracy. Reflecting the new benefits to be secured from a large army, units of rule increased in size. Between 1500 and 1800, the number of independent political units in Europe fell from around 500 to just 25 as the medieval architecture of principalities, duchies and bishoprics gave way to a more recognizable framework of larger countries. (Note, however, that two major European states, Germany and Italy, did not unify until the second half of the nineteenth century.)

With the growth of bureaucracy, local patterns of administration and justice became more uniform. As feudal ties decayed, standard rules applying across a territory eased the growth of commerce, especially in post-feudal cities. In addition, rulers began to establish formal diplomatic relations with their counterparts abroad, a central feature of the modern state system. The outcome of these changes was the more centralized monarchies which developed in England, France and Spain in the sixteenth century to flourish in the seventeenth. In France, for instance, Louis XIV of France (reign 1643–1715) became known as the Sun King: the monarch around whom the realm revolved.

Just as war-making weakened the feudal pillar of the medieval framework, so the Reformation destroyed its religious foundations. From around 1520, Protestant reformers led by Martin Luther condemned what they saw as the corruption and privileges of the organized Church. This reform movement exerted profound political consequences, shattering the Christian commonwealth as antagonism developed between Protestant and Catholic rulers, notably in the Thirty Years' War (1618–48) in German-speaking Europe.

This conflict was finally ended by the **Peace of Westphalia** (1648), an important if occasionally overstated chapter in the book of the state (Osiander, 2001). Westphalia is considered pivotal because it gave territorial rulers more control over the public exercise of religion within their kingdoms, thus rendering national secular authority superior to religious edict from Rome. The threat posed by Westphalia to papal supremacy doubtless explains the vigour of Pope Innocent X's reaction to it. He condemned the treaty as 'null, void, iniquitous, unjust, damnable, reprobate, inane, empty of meaning and effect for all time' (van Creveld, 1999, p. 82). But even this spirited tirade could not hold back the decline in papal authority.

> The **Peace of Westphalia** (1648) is judged to be a significant moment in the emergence of the state. In bringing an end to the Thirty Years' War, the peace treaties gave territorial rulers more control over the exercise of religion within their boundaries, thus confirming the diminished transnational authority of the Church.

As central authority developed in Europe, so did the need for its theoretical justification. The crucial idea here was sovereignty (see p. 14), as later tamed by the notions of contract and consent. The French philosopher Jean Bodin made the key contribution to this new centralizing ideology. Bodin argued that within society a single authority should be responsible for legislation, war and peace, public appointments, judicial appeals and the currency. Such a concentration of political authority is clearly far removed from the decentralized medieval framework of Christendom and feudalism.

Sharing Bodin's belief in the need for a powerful sovereign, the English philosopher Thomas Hobbes drove the argument forward. Without a central authority to enforce the peace, claimed Hobbes, society would regress to civil war. But where Bodin's sovereign still derived his authority from God, Hobbes's analysis was distinctively secular. He located the sovereign's authority in a contract between rational individuals seeking protection from each other's mischief. If the sovereign failed to deliver order, people would no longer be under any obligation to obey. In this way, the sovereign came to serve the people, no longer the other way round, and religion became a matter of inner conviction.

The vision of a government made by and for the governed was further developed by John Locke (1632–1704), an English philosopher whose thinking shaped the liberal vision of the Western state that underpinned the American Revolution of the 1770s. Locke argued that citizens possess **natural rights** to life, liberty and property and that these rights must be protected by rulers governing through law. Citizens consent to obey the laws of the land even if only by tacit means such as accepting the protection which law provides. But should rulers violate these natural rights, the people 'are thereupon absolved from any further Obedience, and are left to the common Refuge, which God hath provided for all Men against force and violence' – the right to resist (Locke, 1690, p. 412). So in Locke's work we observe a modern account of the liberal state, with sovereignty limited by contract and consent. Society is now placed above rather than beneath government.

These ideas of sovereignty, contract and consent were reflected, in contrasting ways, in the American and French revolutions – the two momentous affirmations of modernity. In America, the colonists established their independence from Britain and went on to fashion a new republic, giving substance to Locke's liberal interpretation of the state. In Lockean fashion, the Declaration of Independence (1776) boldly declared that governments derive 'their just authority from the consent of the gov-

erned' while the American constitution (drafted 1787) famously begins, 'We, the people of the United States'. But the powers delegated to the federal government are expressly limited and strictly enumerated, reflecting a liberal desire to limit the centre's scope.

It was the French Revolution of 1789 that made the most daring attempt to reinterpret sovereignty in democratic rather than just liberal terms. Described by Finer (1997, p. 1516) as 'the most important single event in the entire history of government', the French experience mapped out the contours of modern democracy. Where the American federal government remained strictly limited in its authority, the French revolutionaries regarded a centralized, unitary state as the sovereign expression of a national community consisting of citizens with equal rights. Where the American revolution was built on distrust of power, the French revolutionaries favoured universal suffrage and a government empowered to pursue the **general will**. The principles of France's modernizing revolution were articulated in the Declaration of the Rights of Man and the Citizen, a document described by Finer as 'the blueprint of virtually all modern states' (Box 4.1). The Declaration served as a preamble to the French constitution of 1791 and forms part of the country's current constitution.

The **general will** is followed when citizens make decisions for the good of society as a whole rather than for the interests of particular groups and individuals within it. The term was central to the thought of the French philosopher Jean-Jacques Rousseau (1712–78) and its affirmation of a collective interest still finds echoes in some distrust within France of special interests.

True, these democratic pretensions were soon swept aside in France as violence, terror and war stimulated the return of authoritarian rule under Napoleon. However, the revolution in ideas was irreversible. As national identity joined forces with the state, so sovereignty – once the device used by monarchs to establish their supremacy over popes and noblemen – was decisively reinterpreted for a new democratic age.

Natural rights (e.g. to life, liberty and property) are supposedly given by God or by nature; in either case, their existence is taken to be independent of government. In seventeenth-century political thought, natural rights functioned to limit the authority of government, thus establishing the basis for the liberal component of liberal democracy.

BOX 4.1

Declaration of the Rights of Man and the Citizen, France, 1789

ARTICLES 1–6

1 Men are born and remain free and equal in rights. Social distinctions may be based only on considerations of the common good.

2 The aim of every political institution is the preservation of the natural and imprescriptible rights of man. These rights are liberty, property, security and resistance to oppression.

3 The source of all sovereignty lies essentially in the Nation. No corporation or individual may exercise any authority that does not expressly emanate from it.

4 Liberty is the capacity to do anything that does not harm others. Hence the only limitations on the individual's exercise of his natural rights are those which ensure the enjoyment of these same rights to other members of society. These limits can be established only by legislation.

5 The law is entitled to forbid only those actions which are harmful to society. Nothing not forbidden by legislation may be prohibited and no one may be compelled to do what the law does not ordain.

6 Law is the expression of the general will. All citizens have a right to participate in shaping it either in person, or through their representatives. It must be the same for all, whether it punishes or protects.

Note: Article 6 is an extract. For the Declaration's full text, see Finer (1997, p. 1538).

Expansion

With the thinking of the French Revolution, the theoretical foundations of the Western democratic state were, in essence, complete. The detailed construction work was completed in the nineteenth and the first three quarters of the twentieth centuries, supported by growing nationalist sentiment. Only in the final decades of the twentieth century did the state begin to transform its shape, reducing its direct participation in the economy while still quietly expanding its regulatory role.

During the nineteenth century, the cage of the state became more precise, especially in Europe. Borders slowly turned into barriers as precise maps marked out defined frontiers. Lawyers established that a country's territory should extend into the sea by the reach of a cannonball and, later, above its land to the flying height of a hot-air balloon. Reflecting this new concern with national boundaries, passports were introduced in Europe during the First World War. To travel across frontiers became – as it had not previously been – a rite of passage, involving official permission as expressed in a passport stamp. Such documents remained necessary for overseas travel at least until some member countries of the European Union abolished mutual border controls through the Schengen Agreement (1985).

Economically, too, the second half of the nineteenth century saw the end of an era of relatively liberal trade. Stimulated by economic depressions, many European governments introduced protectionist trade policies in the second half of the nineteenth century. By the century's end, the United Kingdom was the only developed country practising free trade (Winham, 2005, p. 90). As national markets gained ground against local as well as international exchange, so the economy became more susceptible to regulation by central government. Internally, the domestic functions performed by the state began to expand. Many tasks we now take for granted as public responsibilities emerged in the nineteenth century, including education, factory regulation, policing and gathering statistics (literally, 'state facts').

For most of the twentieth century, Western states bore deeper into their societies (Box 4.2). As with the original emergence of European states, this expansion was again fuelled by the demands of war. The 1914–18 and 1939–45 conflicts were **total wars**,

Total war, a significant notion in the twentieth century, required the mobilization of the population to support a conflict fought with advanced weaponry on a large geographical scale. Such wars were fought between countries, not just between armed forces, with citizens mobilized in the name of nationalism. Total war required state leadership, intervention and funding.

BOX 4.2

The Western state: expansion and restructuring

Aspect	Expansion (1789–1974)	Restructuring (1975–2000)
Centralization The penetration of central power over a specified territory.	Emergence of national police forces. Introduction of border controls.	Migrants and asylum-seekers loosen border controls. Agreed elimination of border controls within some EU states.
Standardization Greater uniformity within society.	Common language. Standard weights and measures. Consistent time zones.	Strengthening of regional autonomy and identities. Increased support for a multicultural society.
Force Strengthened monopoly of legitimate force.	Emergence of national police forces, backed by the military.	
Mobilization Increased capacity to extract resources from society.	Military conscription. Introduction of income tax. Increased public spending.	Reduced rates of income tax. Tax-payers' revolts in a few countries.
Differentiation State institutions and employees become increasingly distinct from society.	The idea of public service as the even-handed application of rules.	The idea of governance as collaboration between state and society. Public employees encouraged to mimic private sector styles.
Functions Growth in the state's tasks and its intervention in society.	War-making. Welfare provision.	Privatization reduces state's direct economic role. Welfare provision reduced modestly; some public tasks contracted out.
Size Expansion of the state's budget and personnel.	Growth of public sector.	Public sector stabilizes. Fiscal deficits increase. Military spending falls.

Source: Adapted from Clark (1995), Table 1, p. 12.

fought between entire nations rather than just between specialized armed forces. To equip massive forces with the industrial weapons of tanks, planes and bombs required unparalleled mobilization of citizens, economies and societies. Because such conflicts were extraordinarily expensive, tax revenues as a proportion of national product almost doubled in Western states between 1930 and 1945 (Steinmo, 2003, p. 213). The twentieth century was an era of the state because it too was an age of war.

Initially, the onset of peace in 1945 did not lead to a corresponding reduction in the state's role. Rather,

Western governments sought to apply their enhanced administrative skills to domestic needs. In economic policy, many governments drew on the counter-cyclical policies recommended by British economist John Maynard Keynes (1883–1946) to secure full employment (see Chapter 19). Throughout Europe, the warfare state gave way to the welfare state, with rulers accepting direct responsibility for protecting their citizens from the scourges of illness, unemployment and old age. In this way, the European state led a post-war settlement – the Keynesian welfare state – which integrated full employment and public welfare with an economy in which the private sector continued to play a substantial part.

> The **Keynesian welfare state** (KWS) combined counter-cyclical government policies to limit fluctuations in unemployment with state guarantees of health care, housing and income maintenance. The KWS peaked in Western Europe in the 1970s.

Restructuring

Eventually, the post-war expansion of the Western state proved to be unaffordable. Warfare states are temporary but welfare states involve long-term commitments extending across generations. By 1980, the average share of gross domestic product spent or transferred by the governments of 13 developed democracies reached 46 per cent, a substantial increase on the proportion just ten years earlier (Table 4.1). With social democratic governments redistributing income in the name of greater equality, the average top rate of income tax in Western countries reached an inhibiting 63 per cent by the mid-1970s (Steinmo, 2003, p. 221). As public employment continued to expand, so financial pressures mounted. Following the oil crises of the 1970s, speculation even began to emerge about whether governments might go bankrupt. Rather like the empires of old, no sooner had Western states reached their full extent than they began to look overstretched.

In consequence, the 1980s and to a lesser degree the 1990s witnessed significant restructuring. This refocusing was particularly pronounced in English-speaking countries, stimulated by the right-wing agenda of Ronald Reagan (American president,

Table 4.1 Total government expenditure in selected democracies as a proportion of gross domestic product, 1970–2007 (%)

	1970	1980	1990	2004	2007
Denmark	40.2	56.2	56.0	56.3	53.2
Sweden	43.3	61.6	60.5	57.3	52.5
France	38.5	46.1	49.6	53.4	52.3
Belgium	36.5	50.7	50.8	49.3	48.3
Finland	30.5	36.6	44.5	50.7	47.3
Netherlands	43.9	57.5	49.4	48.6	45.3
United Kingdom	38.8	44.8	41.9	43.9	44.3
Germany	38.6	48.3	43.8	46.8	43.8
Norway	41.0	48.3	52.3	46.4	40.9
United States	31.6	33.7	33.6	36.5	37.3
Canada	34.8	40.5	46.0	41.1	37.0*
Japan	19.4	32.6	31.3	38.2	36.3
Ireland	39.6	50.8	39.5	34.2	35.4
Average	36.7	46.7	46.1	46.4	44.1

* Data for 2006.

Note: Gross domestic product is the total value of goods and services produced within a country over a year. Averages are unweighted by size of economy.

Sources: Adapted from Vartiainen (2004), Table 7.1; for 2004 onwards, from OECD (2009).

1981–89) and Margaret Thatcher (British prime minister, 1979–90). Nationalized industries were sold, welfare provision was trimmed, the highest rates of income tax were reduced and the state increasingly sought to supply public services indirectly, using private contractors. Fiscal policies to contain unemployment lost ground to monetary policies aimed at limiting price increases. Across the Western world as a whole, the state's share of total expenditure peaked in 1980 (Table 4.1). In financial terms, a century of state expansion was coming to its end.

Two additional factors encouraged the restructuring of the state in the final decades of the twentieth century. First, military demands were for once consistent with a diminished state: spending on the armed forces declined after the Cold War. Second, in an increasingly global economy, trade grew more rapidly than overall production, leading many commentators to speculate about the fundamental irrelevance of the state in a new order dominated by

BOX 4.3

Some major attacks by Islamic terrorists on civilian Western targets, 2001–08

Date	Targets attacked	Approximate number killed	Perpetrators
11 September 2001	World Trade Center, New York; Pentagon, Washington, DC	2,974	19 hijackers, mainly from Saudi Arabia, in an attack coordinated by al-Qaeda
12 October 2002	Nightclubs, Bali, Indonesia	202*	Three Indonesian Muslims, out of 30 people convicted, were executed in 2008
11 March 2004	Commuter trains, Madrid	191	21 people, mainly from North Africa, were convicted in 2007
7 July 2005	Underground trains and a bus, London	52	Four Muslims born or raised in the UK

* Mainly Western tourists.

multinational corporations. For instance, Guehenno (1995, p. 7) suggested that 'territory is of dwindling importance' in a weightless world economy where the value of a product bears no relation to its bulk. Bets, deals, films, ideas, money, music, news, pornography, software – all could be transacted electronically with no regard to customs posts. Ohmae (1995) even claimed that states had become 'dinosaurs waiting to die', overwhelmed by unconstrained movements of talent, capital and corporate headquarters across national boundaries.

We should avoid conflating restructuring with retreat. At the same time as the state's direct engagement in the economy declined, its role as a regulator continued and even expanded. Regulation, of course, is a relatively cheap activity for governments. It is this shift in the state's focus, often summarized as a transition from government to governance (see p. 5), which is captured in the notion of restructuring.

Security and surveillance

At the end of the new century's first decade, how should we portray the standing of the Western state?

Clearly, predictions of the state's irrelevance in a peaceful twenty-first century world of global trade have failed. On the contrary, the state has returned to centre stage as it leads the response to the multiple risks of the new century. In particular, the state's traditional role as protector of national security has reasserted itself at the core of the political agenda.

Predictions of the 'state's backbone turning to jelly' in a new century of peace were shattered on 11 September 2001 (Mann, 1997, p. 492). The attacks on New York and Washington were the first foreign assault on the continental United States in the modern era; they demonstrated the vulnerability of even the world's most powerful country to organized terrorism. Other attacks on Westerners proved that 9/11 could not be dismissed as a one-off (Box 4.3). Once more, international threats led to a stronger, better-organized and more assertive state.

Consider, for example, the American response. There, the consequences of 9/11 included not just George W. Bush's 'war on terror' but also the passage of the Patriot Act (2001, amended 2006). The Patriot Act gave federal law enforcement agencies considerable powers to investigate anyone thought to be directly engaged in terrorism or just associated with terrorist suspects. The bill is so-called because its full title is The Uniting and Strengthening America by Providing Appropriate Tools Required to Intercept and Obstruct Terrorism Act. The bill was signed into law by the president in the month following the 9/11 attacks and within 72 hours of its introduction in Congress.

The 9/11 strike also led to the creation of the Department of Homeland Security (DHS) in 2002 with a mission to 'lead the unified national effort to secure America'. By absorbing several existing agencies, the DHS became one of the largest and most expensive federal departments, with an authorized budget of $53 billion by 2008. McKay (2009, p. 285) describes the DHS's founding as the 'biggest single reorganization of the federal government since the creation of the Department of Defense after the Second World War'. It represented an attempt to improve the effectiveness and especially the coordination of federal responses to terrorist threats.

Other Western states also showed a heightened response to terrorist dangers. In the United Kingdom, where British suicide bombers killed 52 people in attacks on public transport in London in 2005, a series of laws was introduced that built on initiatives already implemented in response to the long-standing conflict in Northern Ireland. For example, the Terrorism Act (2006) introduced new criminal acts such as encouraging terrorism and participating in training for it.

Influenced by the London bombings, Australia responded similarly. Its government passed the Anti-Terrorism Act (No. 2) in 2005. This law provided for short-term preventative detention in the context of terrorist incidents, introduced court-approved control orders which restricted the movement of people when such limits would help to prevent a terrorist act, and outlined a crime of **sedition** for those who urge the government's violent overthrow.

> To engage in **sedition** is to advocate insurrection or rebellion against a state. By contrast, treason is the act of violating an allegiance to a state, including aiding its enemies.

The emergence of what is sometimes called the security state naturally produced a reaction. Interest groups expressed particular concerns about:

- ▶ The development of a surveillance society;
- ▶ Threats to civil liberties;
- ▶ The limited accountability of intelligence services (O'Harrow, 2005).

Monitoring by closed-circuit television, and of telephones and Internet use, offers new tools for the state to track its population, including ordinary citizens, terrorists and 'terrorist suspects'. In the USA, National Security Letters (which required organizations such as Internet providers to supply the government with access to their records about individual users) came under particular attack from civil liberty organizations. Exchanges of information between the intelligence services of different countries raised further concerns.

In Britain, anxiety centred on the length of time suspected terrorists could be detained without charge. During vigorous debates, Prime Minister Blair declared in 2005: 'we are not living in a police state but we are living in a country that faces a real and serious threat of terrorism' (Saward, 2006, p. 212). An Australian judge claimed that her country's anti-terrorist laws were 'striking at the most fundamental freedoms in our democracy' (Pelly *et al.*, 2005).

Clearly, the state was back. In addition to administrative, legislative and budgetary changes, the voice of multiculturalism rapidly weakened as notions of a common citizenship regained lost ground in response to the threat of terrorism. Furthermore, the idea of security itself broadened, coming to embrace more than terrorism. In the first decade of the century, several Western states sought to reassert their functional significance by offering a wider conception of threats to their country.

The UK is again an illustration. As its National Security Strategy (2008) report stated, 'our view of national security has broadened to include threats to individual citizens and to our way of life, as well as the integrity and interests of the state'. The strategy document identified a series of challenges which went well beyond military threats from foreign powers (Box 4.4).

Of course, a list of risks is not in itself a strategy for dealing with them. Nonetheless, such statements show states positioning themselves as the overall risk manager for society, not least in protecting citizens from threats combining international and domestic elements.

BOX 4.4

The broadening security landscape: Britain's national security strategy, 2008

Security challenge	Government statement in report
Terrorism	The UK faces a serious and sustained threat from violent extremists, claiming to act in the name of Islam
Weapons of mass destruction	Nuclear weapons remain potentially the most destructive threat to national security
Transnational crime	The threat to the UK from serious and organized crime is high
Global conflict, fragile states	Most of the major risks and threats emanate from failed or fragile states
Civil emergencies	The highest risk is an influenza-type epidemic like the outbreak in 1918 which killed 228,000 people
State-led threats	For the foreseeable future, no state or alliance will have both the intent and capability to threaten the UK militarily

Source: Cabinet Office (2008).

The post-colonial state

The state was born in Europe and then exported to the rest of the world by colonial powers, notably Britain, France and Spain. Consequently, most states in today's world are post-colonial. As Armitage (2005, p. 3) points out, 'the great political fact of global history in the last 500 years is the emergence of a world of states from a world of empires. That fact fundamentally defines the political universe we all inhabit'. Countries without a history as a colony, leaving aside the ex-colonial powers themselves, are few and far between; they include China, Ethiopia, Iran, Japan and Saudi Arabia.

Although the term 'post-colonial' is usually confined to the many states achieving independence in the aftermath of the Second World War, settler societies such as Australia, Canada, New Zealand and the United States provide early examples of states formed from colonies. In settler societies, the new arrivals sought to supplant indigenous communities, a goal ruthlessly achieved. The founders brought with them segments of a European tradi-tion which they recreated and adapted for a frontier environment. Even though the standing of the state in settler countries is less elevated than in Europe, their political organization remains recognizably Western. Settler societies are from, though not in, Europe (Hartz, 1955; Huntington, 2004). In the far larger number of non-settler colonies, by contrast, the imperial rulers sought to exploit local labour and resources without establishing new nations in the territory.

How then did non-settler colonies emerge into statehood? The major part of this process took place in four waves spread over two centuries (Box 4.5, p. 71). The retreat from empire by European powers after 1945 was certainly the largest of these waves, stimulating a massive increase in the world's stock of states. However, each wave deposited particular kinds of state on the post-colonial shore.

The *first* wave of decolonization occurred early in the nineteenth century, in the Spanish and Portuguese territories of Latin America, where colonial settlers had dominated without eliminating indigenous peoples. These early wars of independence occurred soon after the American and French revolutions but lacked the liberal, egalitarian basis of their more famous predecessors. Rather, the Latin American wars took the form of republican movements against monarchical rule from Europe. New constitutions were produced but they were neither democratic nor even fully implemented.

The outcome of this first wave of decolonization in Latin America was not a Lockean constitutional state authorized by the citizens and subject to their consent. Economic exploitation of native populations, the poor and descendants of slaves continued in the post-colonial era. In the capital, power lay with autocrats; in the interior, where natural resources were gathered for export, strongmen known as **caudillos** held sway (McCreery, 2002). The resulting inequalities created endemic conflicts within Latin American societies which remain important to this day.

> A **caudillo** is a political boss who rules the roost in a particular territory, providing order and expecting allegiance. These local strongmen remain important figures in rural Latin America, where they reflect and reinforce the limited penetration of central state institutions.

The *second* wave of post-colonial states emerged in Europe and the Middle East with the final collapse of the multinational and religiously diverse Austro-Hungarian, Russian and Ottoman empires around the end of the First World War. The principle of national self-determination, espoused by American President Woodrow Wilson and reflected in nationalist sentiment within the imperial territories themselves, played a key role in this major redrawing of the European map. The Austro-Hungarian Empire, for instance, dissolved into five separate states: Austria, Hungary, Poland, Czechoslovakia and Yugoslavia.

However, with the exception of the Turkish state which eventually emerged from the ruins of the Ottoman empire, strong and stable states failed to develop. Rather, international politics continued to intrude, preventing those countries on the European periphery from experiencing the continuous state development found in the continent's core. Most of the new states formed from the Austro-Hungarian Empire were incorporated into Hitler's Germany and, after the war, into the Soviet sphere of influence. Only with the collapse of communism in the 1990s and the entry of many of these post-colonial countries into the European Union in 2004 was independent statehood finally consolidated, creating new opportunities to construct effective states on the base provided by historic nations.

The *third* and largest wave of state creation occurred after 1945, with the retreat from empire by European states diminished by war (Spruyt, 2005). Asian countries such as the Philippines (1946) and India (1947) were the first to achieve independence; many other colonies, in Africa, the Caribbean and the Middle East, followed suit. This wave of decolonization grew into a veritable tsunami. Between 1944 and 1984, over 90 new independent states – almost half the world's current stock – were created. This transition was truly a rush to statehood. Eighteen emerged in 1960 alone, a year in which the United Nations declared that lack of preparation for independence was no reason for delaying it (Mayall, 1996, p. 44).

But here it is crucial to distinguish between form and substance. The state form has been successfully exported from Europe to ex-colonies but effective functioning has rarely followed. Most post-1945 countries lacked any previous experience as a coherent entity; rather, statehood was superimposed on ethnic, regional and religious groups that had themselves been strengthened by the rigid classifications of the colonialists.

Often, the post-colonial state has become a prize for which the traditional leaders of such groups compete, resulting in the government's lack of autonomy from social interests. The prizewinners distribute the rewards to their own supporters, reinforcing circuits of personal rule which are incompatible with government by law. The state is both coercive and weak, lacking the drive of its European forebears. For such reasons, Davidson (1992, p. 188) suggests that the post-colonial state in Africa has proved to be the 'black man's burden' rather than 'Europe's last gift' to the continent.

The *fourth* and final wave of state formation occurred in the final decade of the twentieth century, triggered by the collapse of communism. The dissolution of the communist bloc previously dominated by the Soviet Union led to independence for the Baltic states and for a dozen Soviet satellites

BOX 4.5

States from empires: waves of decolonization

Wave of decolonization	Main imperial powers	Main locations of colonies	Approximate number of new states created by decolonization	Examples of newly independent states
1810–38	Spain, Portugal	Latin America	15	Argentina, Brazil
After the 1914–18 war	Ottoman, Russian and Austro-Hungarian empires	Europe (beyond its Western core), Middle East	12	Austria, Finland, Poland, Turkey
1944–84	UK, France, Belgium, Portugal	Mainly Africa, Asia and the Caribbean	94	Algeria, Congo, India, Philippines
1991	Russia	Soviet Union republics in the Baltics, East Europe and central Asia	15	Kazakhstan, Latvia, Ukraine

Sources: Adapted from Derbyshire and Derbyshire (1999) and Opello and Rosow (2004).

in Eastern Europe such as Hungary, Poland and Romania. In addition, the Soviet Union itself – in effect, a Russian empire – dissolved into 15 successor states, including the Ukraine, Uzbekistan and of course Russia.

The experience of these new post-communist states has again been mixed. The Baltic states gained economic and political stability from their proximity to, and now their membership of, the European Union. However, central Asian republics such as Uzbekistan reveal a more typical post-colonial syndrome: small size, ethnic divisions, a preindustrial economy and autocratic rule. In the successor states to the Soviet Union, these problems are again reinforced by the absence of precolonial experience as an independent state.

Overall, then, the contrasts between West European parent states and their post-colonial progeny are deep-rooted. Post-colonial states rarely possess the strength and autonomy which their European predecessors acquired during their own development. This contrast can be seen in the treatment of borders. While European rulers were keen to mark off their own frontiers, they invented borders for their colonies which bore little relation to natural or social features. In the Middle East,

many of the new states exhibited a somewhat artificial appearance, with their new names, their new capitals, their lack of ethnic homogeneity and their dead-straight boundaries that were so obviously the result of a British or French colonial official using a ruler. (Owen, 2004, p. 11)

Africa reveals a similar pattern. The boundaries of half its states contain at least one straight section and, reflecting the low value of land, many national borders are treated with indifference by governments and people alike. Some are completely unguarded, hardly the sign of a state concerned to demonstrate its mastery of territory. Sovereignty remains important as a title, securing international recognition and access to aid. But the label's significance is largely symbolic, with little to prevent the movement of people, soldiers, goods and terrorists across boundaries.

The rulers of many post-colonial states – again, in Africa particularly – are constrained by limited penetration through their territory. Control may not extend far beyond the capital, with government outposts falling under the influence of local strongmen. Regional groups and powerful caudillos jostle to control central government offices located in their zone of authority (Migdal, 2001). The authority of political rulers is sometimes subject to further competition from ethnic groups, organized criminal gangs, powerful companies and vigilante groups, all of which may operate across frontiers. As far as the post-colonial state is concerned, Latouche's (1996) 'Westernization of the world' may be limited to form rather than substance.

Collapsed states and state building

As a counterpoint to our discussion of strong European states, it is useful to consider **collapsed states** and efforts to (re)build them. Western governments demonstrate a growing concern with what are variously termed collapsed, criminal, disrupted, failed, failing, fragile, fragmented, vulnerable, quasi-, weak or **failed states**. The USA's National Security Strategy, for instance, suggested that 'America is now threatened less by conquering states than we are by failing ones' (President of the United States, 2002, p. iv). Writing from a human rights perspective, Ignatieff (2002, p. 114) claims that 'the human rights dilemmas of the twenty-first century derive more from anarchy than tyranny'. In addition, examining collapsed states broadens our understanding of the state, avoiding the danger of focusing only on successes.

A **collapsed state** is often defined institutionally, to denote the crumbling of state organization and its effective replacement by private and subnational bodies. The concept of a **failed state** is closely related but is usually defined functionally as the state's inability to perform its key role of monopolizing the legitimate use of force within its territory.

Where a revolution involves a temporary failure of state authority, based on a competition for the contract to rebuild, a collapsed state is a decayed regime that no longer fulfils its core task of securing order and welfare. In Zaire, for example, Reno (2003, p. 86) reports in a chilling sentence that 'expenditures

Table 4.2 Countries scoring highest on the Fund for Peace Failed States Index, 2009

Rank	Country
1	Somalia
2	Zimbabwe
3	Sudan
4	Chad
5	Democratic Republic of Congo
6	Iraq
7	Afghanistan
8	Central African Republic
9	Guinea
10	Pakistan

Note: The failed states index is based on social and economic indicators (e.g. number of refugees, sharp economic decline) as well as political factors (e.g. distrust of state institutions). A rank of one indicates the most complete failure.

Source: Fund for Peace (2009).

on education and health care reached zero in 1992'. Collapse may not involve civil war and does not usually result in a new regime. Rather, order is typically retained in private hands. Wealthy people arrange their own protection and the black, informal or parallel economy takes over. Even some international trade is sustained as armed groups, sometimes led by the nominal political rulers themselves, control the export of natural resources such as timber, gems and drugs. Thus, against Hobbes, the disintegration of state institutions does not imply the triumph of disorder. Nor indeed does the economy become completely detached from global markets. A collapsed state need not entail a failed society.

Most examples of state collapse come from post-colonial Africa and especially from smaller countries with no precolonial experience as an independent entity. Seven of the ten countries which top the Fund for Peace (2009) list of failed states are in Africa (Table 4.2). As Zartman (1995a, p. 2) comments, such geographical concentration provides an opportunity 'not just to learn about Africa but to learn from Africa – a project of much wider importance'. Outside Africa, many instances of state 'collapse' are cases of state weakness rather than complete failure. In Afghanistan and Colombia, for

BOX 4.6

Some cases of state collapse in Africa

Country	Year of independence	Start of collapse	Initiation of collapse
Uganda	1962	1979	The overthrow of the tyrant Idi Amin left a power vacuum
Chad	1960	1980	Collapse was brought about by factional conflict within a guerrilla movement that had itself overthrown the previous regime
Liberia	1847*	1990	A rebellion against the concentration of power under Samuel Doe who had himself led a military coup in 1980
Somalia	1960	1990	Opposition clans rose up against the governing clan led by the military ruler Siyad Barre

* Liberia was founded in 1821 as a settlement for blacks from the United States. These 'Americo-Liberian settlers' declared an independent republic in 1847.

Source: Adapted from Zartman (1995a) which includes a chapter on each example listed above.

instance, leaders may share authority with drug dealers and warlords but the state continues, at least as a lame leviathan.

(Re)building states after a period of collapse is a difficult exercise, showing in particular the danger of imposing a Western form in non-Western conditions. State building cannot easily be imposed from outside; indeed, aid agencies providing services in a failed state may for that reason inhibit the growth of government (Fukuyama, 2004). It is one thing for external might to overthrow rulers such as the Taliban in Afghanistan and Saddam Hussein in Iraq. It is quite another to secure effective indigenous leadership and to build legitimate national institutions, such as an army, a police force, a judiciary, a central bank, government departments, local administration, and a tax collection agency, and functioning education, transport, energy and health care systems. 'You, the people' is less compelling than 'we, the people'. A state is not a prefabricated building, to be constructed on site from imported parts.

The difficulties of state building, particularly from outside, raise a fundamental question: does the effort make sense? Perhaps alternative forms of

organization should be permitted to evolve in the developing world, finally ending the West's obsession with the state as a universal institution.

Certainly, many contemporary 'states' seem to lack the capacity to achieve real independence. As many as 45 developing countries possess populations below 1.5 million, surely below the size needed to function with significant autonomy (Commonwealth Secretariat, 1997). Many are quasi-states, pretending to sovereignty and sometimes reduced to cashing in on its value by providing flags of convenience for the disreputable. In particular, many vulnerable island states possess no resilience to external shocks, no economic diversification, no military force, and limited capacity to participate in international organizations.

Some specialists on African politics query the value of statehood altogether. Clapham (2003, p. 29) suggests that territorial states are an expensive burden in an African setting where most national populations are widely scattered over infertile land. In these conditions, the traditional tribal model of an interdependent group united by a shared ethnic identity may be more appropriate than the imposed Western model of a territorial state governing a

COUNTRY PROFILE

UGANDA

Form of government ■ a unitary republic with 69 districts, many with substantial practical autonomy.

Legislature ■ the 332 current members of the unicameral Parliament include 215 constituency members and 79 district representatives reserved for women. Additional seats are reserved for groups such as the armed forces and workers. The president can appoint additional members. Members are elected for a renewable five-year term.

Executive ■ the president is both chief of state and head of government; he is assisted by the prime minister in supervising the cabinet. Semi-presidential elements notwithstanding, the system is effectively presidential. The president is directly elected for a five-year renewable term.

Constitution and judiciary ■ the current constitution dates from 1995. The judiciary is headed by the Court of Appeal whose members are appointed by the president and approved by the legislature. The legal system is based on English common law and customary law.

Electoral system ■ single-member plurality.

Party system ■ the 1995 constitution was revised in 2005 to permit a multiparty system. President Yoweri Museveni's vehicle, the National Resistance Movement (NRM), won 207 seats in the 2006 parliamentary elections. The main opposition came from the Forum for Democratic Change (FDC), led by Dr Kizza Besigye, which won 37 seats. The FDC consists of figures who have fallen out with Museveni; they accuse him of 'corruption and nepotism, because of weak and dictatorial leadership' (FDC, 2007).

Population (annual growth rate): 31.4m (+3.6%)	
World Bank income group: low income	
Political Rights score: ⑤	
Civil Liberties score: ④	
Human development index (rank/out of): 154/177	
Freedom of the press index (rank/out of): 112/195	
Perceived corruption index (rank/out of): 126/180	

Note: For meaning and sources of scales and indexes, see p. 00. In all cases a score and rank of 1 is 'best'.

Located on a plateau in east Africa, **UGANDA** is a landlocked but fertile country with large freshwater lakes and rivers; Churchill called it 'the pearl of Africa'.

By population, it is one of the largest countries in sub-Saharan Africa. Despite an effective anti-Aids campaign, about 500,000 people are still living with HIV/Aids. Reflecting this Aids factor, the population is exceptionally young, with a median age of just 15 (USA: 37).

The economy remains mainly agricultural, with coffee the main export but there are also substantial deposits of

copper, cobalt and oil. In 2008, the economy grew by 7 per cent. Nonetheless, the level of human development remains comparatively low, with one in five men, and two in five women, still illiterate.

The country is a typical colonial construct, bringing together a wide variety of ethnic and language groups under a British protectorate consolidated during the 1890s from a series of traditional kingdoms.

The largest of these groups, but comprising no more than a fifth of the current population, is Buganda. Located

in the centre and south of the country, the kingdom of Buganda dates back to at least the fourteenth century ('Uganda' is a Swahili term for Buganda). The original colonial settlement was with the Kabaka, the Bugandan king, and Buganda's leaders also opened the door to independence.

Aspirations for an independent Bagandan state have gone unfulfilled, however, and the position of Buganda within post-independence Uganda has been a major source of conflict, contributing to the country's recent history of instability and violence.

Further reading: Ocitti (2006), Tripp (2000).

State collapse and reconstruction in Uganda

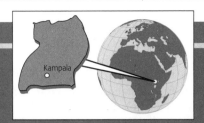

Kampala

Uganda provides an interesting example of the difficulties and dangers of imposing the Western concept of the state on a region historically ruled in a more traditional and decentralized fashion. If European countries such as France provide us with examples of strong states, Uganda (like many other sub-Saharan countries) tells us about the state's limits.

Independence in 1962 bequeathed to the new leaders 'a state groping with rudimentary tasks of broadening its authority over an uncertain territory, against a background of scarce resources and unrefined administration' (Khadiagala, 1995, p. 33). The first post-independence government was an alliance between the Kabaka, serving as ceremonial president, and Milton Obote, a member of the Lango tribe, who was executive prime minister. Obote soon became the dominant figure, with assistance from General Idi Amin, an ethnic Kakwa, only for Amin himself to seize power in 1971.

Amin was a crude military despot who ignored weak state institutions in creating a personal dictatorship that led to the deaths of about 300,000 people. With the economy in decay, Amin was himself removed from power in 1979 by a combined force of Ugandan exiles and an invading army from neighbouring Tanzania. The subsequent state collapse led to violent conflict between competing guerrilla groups, pro-

ducing another 100,000 deaths and numerous internal refugees.

Because state collapse lacks the self-limiting character of revolution, it poses the puzzle of whether, how and by whom public authority should be reconstructed. In the absence of established institutions, the key to state rebirth seems to be good domestic leadership.

Uganda illustrates the point. The country began to recover after Yoweri Museveni's National Liberation Army secured control in 1979. Under Museveni's skilled but increasingly

authoritarian leadership, and with substantial international support, Uganda's economy recovered considerably. The country has received praise from the World Bank as an example of successful development in fragile states (Manor, 2006).

Today, Uganda is best classified as an illiberal democracy – no small achievement given the country's history and continuing low standard of living. Freedom of speech and assembly are at least partially respected.

In 2005, however, parliament abolished a constitutional limit on presidential terms, paving the way for

Museveni to win a third term in 2006 with 59 per cent of the vote. Such self-serving constitutional modifications are a sign of a president who stands above, rather than sits beneath, the constitution. Despite the reintroduction of political parties, the president's National Resistance Movement remains pre-eminent, with some harassment of opposition figures and groups. The president increasingly governs through patronage rather than persuasion; critics allege that he has become a barrier rather than a contributor to further national progress.

Self-designation of 'Dada' Amin:

His Excellency President for Life Field Marshal Al Hadj Doctor Idi Amin Dada, VC, DSO, MC, Lord of All the Beasts of the Earth and Fishes of the Sea and Conqueror of the British Empire in Africa in General and Uganda in Particular

---

Above all, though, Uganda has still finally to resolve the problem of the Lord's Resistance Army (LRA), a violent northern cult whose members prey on the Acholi people, causing many to flee their homes and demonstrating thereby the continuing difficulty experienced by the central government in ensuring its control over all its territory.

Further reading: Keitetsi (2004), Manor (2006).

united citizenry. Clapham concludes that the project of attempting to restore universal statehood may be a pipe dream.

Similarly, Herbst (2004) invites the West to adopt a more flexible stance in responding to issues of boundaries and secession. In his view, the long-run solution is for the West to overcome its obsession with statehood and to encourage experiments in Africa with new (or old) models of political organization. His view is that when states collapse, we should 'let them fail'.

However, such radical views are not universally shared. Zartman (1995c, p. 268), for instance, argues that 'both the cause and remedy of state collapse relate to socio-political structures within a given sovereign territory and people, not to the shape of the state itself. It is better to reaffirm the validity of the existing unit and make it work'. Perhaps so, but we should remember both that statehood developed in response to the conditions of early modern Europe and that the states that exist there today are themselves survivors of a competitive struggle. There is no necessary reason why the form should fit the different circumstances elsewhere.

Beyond the state

We live, it is often said, in an era of globalization, during which the constraints of geography on economic, cultural and political arrangements have receded (Waters, 2000). In truth, there never was a time when states were self-contained, independent silos, but that is perhaps all the more reason to place states in an international context.

In this section, we divide our discussion of this **international** and **supranational** setting into three parts. We look first at **intergovernmental organizations** (IGOs), then at the European Union (EU) and finally at non-governmental organizations (NGOs). Our main focus will be the impact of these bodies on states, though we will also examine the EU as a unique entity – more than an IGO but less than a

Intergovernmental organizations (IGOs) are bodies whose members include states. IGOs are established by treaty and usually operate by consent, with a permanent secretariat.

BOX 4.7

Beyond the state

Term	Definition
International ('inter' = 'between')	Between states (e.g. international politics) but also used more generally, to refer to anything extending beyond one country
Multinational ('multi' = 'many')	Operating in or composed of several countries (e.g. multinational corporations)
Transnational ('trans' = 'beyond')	Beyond countries (e.g. transnational terrorist networks)
Supranational ('supra' = 'above')	Above the state, especially the transfer of formal authority to a supranational body

---

conventional state – which is important in its own right.

Intergovernmental organizations

The majority of established states belong to most of the 250 or so intergovernmental organizations (IGOs) which now populate the international environment. IGOs include single purpose entities (e.g. the International Telecommunications Union), regional organizations (e.g. the Union of South American Nations) and universal bodies (e.g. the United Nations).

Such bodies are an appropriate response to global problems by states operating in a world which lacks a world government. IGOs perform useful functions for states, sharing information, coordinating policies and developing international infrastructure. For instance, everyone gains from a sustainable environment, from a world telephone network and from the ability to use bank cards overseas. Operating in an informal and flexible manner, with high levels of trust among participants, the distance of IGOs from democratic pressures within their member states may contribute to their efficacy. In a sense, IGOs are as much an outgrowth of state power into the international realm as a constraint on individual govern-

Map 4.1 The European Union

Founding members (1952 ECSC; 1958 EEC and Euratom): Belgium, France, (West) Germany, Italy, Luxembourg, Netherlands. The territory of the German Democratic Republic (East Germany) was incorporated into a united Germany in 1990.

First enlargement (1973): Denmark, Ireland, United Kingdom.

Mediterranean enlargement: Greece (1981); Portugal, Spain (1986).

EFTA enlargement (1995): Austria, Finland, Sweden.

2004 enlargement: Cyprus, Czech Republic, Estonia, Hungary, Latvia, Lithuania, Malta, Poland, Slovakia, Slovenia.

2007 enlargement: Bulgaria, Romania.

Key
1 Croatia
2 Bosnia and Herzegovina
3 Serbia-Montenegro
4 Former Yugoslav Republic of Macedonia
5 Albania
6 Switzerland
7 Moldova
8 Slovenia

Source: Adapted from Nugent (2006), p. xxiv.

ments; they represent a pooling of public authority as much as a threat to it.

Our main concern here is the impact of IGOs on states themselves. At the very least, belonging to so many IGOs complicates the task of governance. States must arrange to pay their subscriptions, attend meetings, identify their national interest, consult with domestic interest groups, initiate some proposals, respond to others and implement agreements. IGOs bore into the daily activities of national governments, posing a particular challenge for many small states. Even for large countries, IGOs dilute the distinction between domestic and foreign policy, giving an international dimension to many, perhaps most, government activities. We should recognize that any attempt to analyse national policy-making without considering the impact of IGOs will be a considerable oversimplification.

In addition, IGOs have affected the balance of forces within national political systems. Specifically, they tend to fragment domestic policy-making. Slaughter, in particular, has emphasized the segmenting effect of public officials communicating with colleagues from other countries. Noting how judges, administrators, regulators, central bankers, legislators, police forces and heads of state 'are all networking with their foreign counterparts', she suggests that:

the state is not disappearing; it is disaggregating into its component institutions. The primary state actors in the international realm are no longer foreign ministries and heads of state but the same government institutions that dominate domestic politics. The disaggregated state, as opposed to the mythical unitary state, is thus hydra-headed, represented and governed by multiple institutions in complex interaction with one another abroad and at home. (Slaughter, 2003, p. 190)

These horizontal linkages between departments deepen as a club-like spirit develops among ministers in 'their' IGO. For instance, finance ministers – never popular at home – are among friends at meetings of bodies such as the International Monetary Fund (Figure 4.1). Domestically, ministers of agriculture must defend the farmers' interest against other departments but at IGO meetings, they meet only other ministers of agriculture, all of whom

Figure 4.1 The segmented state: horizontal links between ministries

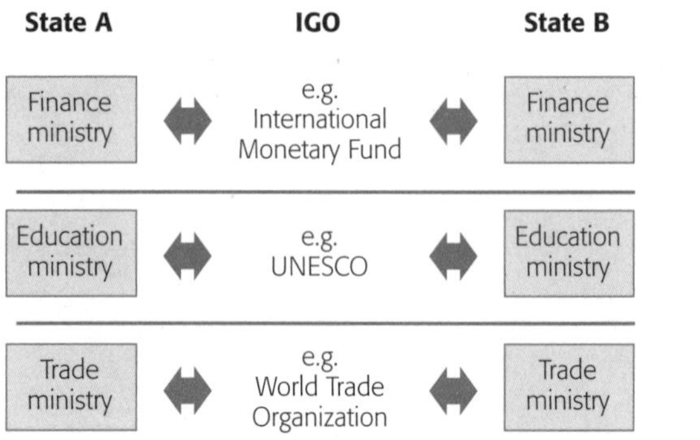

agree on farming's importance (Andeweg and Galen, 2002, p. 169)

Given such fragmentation within national political systems, we must ask which governing institutions gain, and which lose, from such interdependence. Among the winners are the executive and the bureaucracy (Box 4.8). These bodies provide the representatives who attend IGO meetings and conduct negotiations; they therefore occupy pole position. The judiciary is also growing in significance as a result of IGO activity, partly because some influential IGOs such as the World Trade Organization adopt a highly judicial style, issuing judgements on the basis of reviewing cases. In addition, national judges are increasingly willing to use international agreements to strike down the policies of their home government.

As for losers, the most significant is surely the legislature, which may only learn of an international agreement after the government has signed up to it.

BOX 4.8

The impact of IGOs on national politics: winners and losers

Winners	Losers
Executive	Legislature
Bureaucracy	Parties
Judiciary	

▶ TIMELINE

THE EUROPEAN UNION

1951	Treaty of Paris signed by France, West Germany, Italy, Belgium, the Netherlands and Luxembourg. This Treaty set up the European Coal and Steel Community (ECSC) which included a supranational High Authority.
1957	The ECSC members sign the Treaty of Rome, establishing the European Economic Community (EEC) and Euratom.
1965	The Merger Treaty combines the ECSC, EEC and Euratom.
1973	Britain, Denmark and Ireland join the EEC.
1979	The European Monetary System (EMS) is agreed, linking currencies to the European Currency Unit (ECU). First direct Europe-wide elections to the European Parliament.
1981	Greece joins the EEC.
1986	Spain and Portugal join the EEC. Signing of the Single European Act, to streamline decision-making and set up a single market by 1992.
1992	Treaty of Maastricht launches provisions for Economic and Monetary Union (EMU) and replaces the EEC with the European Union (EU) from 1993.
1995	Austria, Finland and Sweden join the EU.
1997	Treaty of Amsterdam extends the Union's role in justice and home affairs and enhances the authority of the European Parliament.
1999	Launch of European Monetary Union (EMU), initially linking 11 national currencies to the euro. Launch of the euro as a virtual currency.
2000	Treaty of Nice agrees on institutional reforms to prepare for enlargement, including a reallocation of member states' voting power and a reduction in the issues requiring unanimity.
2002	The eurozone withdraws national currencies.
2003	Publication of a draft constitutional treaty for Europe.
2004	Cyprus, the Czech Republic, Estonia, Hungary, Latvia, Lithuania, Malta, Poland, Slovakia and Slovenia join the EU.
2005	Referendums in France and the Netherlands reject the constitutional treaty.
2007	Bulgaria and Romania join the EU.
2008	Referendum in Ireland rejects the constitutional treaty.
2009	Treaty of Lisbon, successor to the ill-fated constitutional treaty, comes into effect.

Note: nomenclature of the 'European Union' has varied over time, reflecting institutional and constitutional developments.

In some countries, Australia for one, international treaties are an executive preserve, enabling government to bypass the assembly by signing treaties on proposals opposed by parliament. Similarly, 'Europeanization has strengthened the central executive at the expense of parliaments, despite the increased involvement of the latter in EU policy-making' (Börzel and Sedelmeier, 2006, p. 56). In international matters, parliaments are more reactive than proactive. Political parties, too, seem to have lost ground under pressure from IGOs. Like assemblies, their natural habitat is the state, not the international conference.

The European Union

In a world of states supplemented by international organizations, the European Union (EU) stands alone. It is a unique hybrid blending **supranational** and intergovernmental elements. The EU is the world's most developed example of regional integration. It represents a deliberate attempt by European politicians to bring peace to a continent with a long history of war. From modest beginnings in the 1950s, the Union has developed its institutions, acquired considerable policy-making authority, reduced national barriers to trade, established a new currency and broadened its membership.

Statistically, the EU now stands comparison with the USA (Table 4.3). Less than half the area of the United States, its population and economy are somewhat larger, though American productivity remains well ahead. But of course the key contrast is political: the EU is a union of states, not a state in itself. Certainly, the EU has acquired state-like attributes including a flag, an anthem, a mention in its citizens' passports, and its own entry in the CIA's World Factbook. It also sought, though without success, to convert its founding treaties into a single Constitutional Treaty. Further, it possesses developed institutions, including an elected parliament, an influential court and a commission to initiate and supervise policy.

It is important to note, however, that the depth of integration varies between members. Britain and Ireland, for instance, have not joined the **Schengen Agreement** (1985) scheme to eliminate border controls, and by 2009 11 countries had not adopted the euro as their currency. The equivalent to this **differentiated integration** in the USA would be if a

Table 4.3 The European Union and the USA, 2007

	European Union	USA
Area (million sq. km)	4.3	9.9
Population (million)	491	304
Member states	27	50
Median population of member states (million)	10.2	4.2
Gross domestic product (trillion $)	14.4	13.8
Gross domestic product per head ($)	32,700	45,800

Note: As a result of the range of sources used, GDP per head multiplied by population in the above data does not equal the figure shown for GDP.

Sources: BEA (2008), CIA (2009), Eurostat (2008)

> The **Schengen Agreement** is a scheme to remove controls on persons – including third-country nationals – at internal borders. Originally signed by five EU members in 1985, it now encompasses a majority of EU states, plus Norway and Iceland.

few states still required entry visas and used their own currency.

Above all, the EU neither levies personal taxes nor possesses its own armed forces. The traditional dynamic of the European state – to raise taxes so as to wage war – is therefore absent. Rather, the Union was founded as a mechanism for ensuring peace through economic integration. Thus, the original declaration proposing the European Coal and Steel Community explicitly sought to render war between France and Germany 'not merely unthinkable but materially impossible' (Schuman Declaration, 1950). Coal and steel production were placed under a new high authority in the hope that member countries would no longer have an incentive to invade each other so as to control the material for weapons production. The underlying mission of the Union has remained broadly constant: economic integration,

> **Differentiated integration** occurs when only some members of a community join together in a scheme to strengthen the union as a whole.

especially through a single market, in the service of broader political objectives.

This mission has given the EU a strong regulatory character, distinguishing it from the broader functions performed by traditional states. Its primary mode of governance is to issue regulations, especially in areas such as trade and competition policy that facilitate its key objective of a single market. Lacking any requirement to equip and pay military personnel, the EU's budget of €134 billion in 2009 remains relatively small, amounting to just 2.5 per cent of total public expenditure in the member states (Nugent, 2006, p. 430). Its funds are raised mainly by a levy on member states, not by direct taxes of persons, and are largely spent subsidizing farmers and poorer regions within its member states.

Lack of hard military power notwithstanding, the EU has still become a significant player on the world stage. This position derives from economic rather than military muscle. It is the world's largest trading bloc and negotiates trade agreements with other countries as the external dimension of its pursuit of a coherent internal market.

In comparing the EU with other political systems, we should resist the temptation of assimilating it to more familiar units. As it continues to develop, the EU may or may not move closer to a United States of Europe. It may or may not become a more traditional intergovernmental body. The EU cannot be characterized by placing bets on its future but only by examining its current status. As such, the EU makes a unique contribution to the ecology of comparative politics.

Non-governmental organizations

As private and unofficial bodies lacking the status offered by a membership of governments, **international non-governmental organizations** (NGOs) exert less influence than IGOs on domestic politics, at least for the more powerful states. However, the number and significance of NGOs has also expanded significantly, particularly since 1945 when the United Nations granted consultative status to international organizations that are not established by international treaty. On a reasonably consistent basis, the number of NGOs increased from 176 in 1909 to 1255 in 1960 and to 4830 in 1993. On looser definition, about 40,000 NGOs were said to be operating internationally by the turn of the century (Kegley

> **International non-governmental organizations** (usually called NGOs) are private institutions with members or groups drawn from more than one country. Examples include the International Red Cross, Greenpeace and the Catholic Church.

and Blanton, 2009). The impact of NGOs on postcolonial countries can be considerable. Leading NGOs such as the Red Cross and Médecins Sans Frontières can apply substantial pressure to national governments where the international community is already engaged in supplying services as a result of civil war or humanitarian crisis (Adams, 2003).

In such conditions, NGOs have become important actors as executors of IGO, especially United Nations, policy. As early as the mid-1990s, over 10 per cent of all public development aid was distributed through NGOs, compared to less than 1 per cent in 1970 (Weiss and Gordenker, 1996). About ten super-NGOs, including CARE, Save the Children and Oxfam, dominate the distribution of aid in complex emergencies.

In acting as UN subcontractors, NGOs can partially substitute for government. For instance, NGOs coordinated primary education in northern Sri Lanka after civil war started there in 1987. As a channel for distributing aid and implementing associated policy, NGOs possess clear attractions to outside donors: they are more efficient and less corrupt than many domestic governments and they are also more sensitive than armies to local political conditions.

These points mean NGOs, and the Western governments on which many are financially dependent, possess considerable clout in the least developed countries on which aid is concentrated. Fernando and Heston (1997, p. 8) go so far as to suggest that 'NGO activity presents the most serious challenge to the imperatives of statehood in the realms of territorial integrity, security, autonomy and revenue'. The danger is not only that NGOs inhibit the strengthening of the domestic government but that they become an economic force themselves, offering relatively well-paid jobs to a privileged minority within the local population and supplying an injection of demand into the economy. If state building rather than state substituting really is the objective, then NGOs – just like an invading army – also need an exit strategy.

Learning Resources for Chapter 4

Next step

Opello and Rusow (2004) is a wide-ranging but accessible historical introduction to the state.

Further reading

Van Creveld (1999) and Pierson (2004) examine the rise of the state, while Finer (1997) offers a monumental history of government. Both Sørensen (2004) and Paul (2004) examine the state's alleged transformation in the contemporary era. For Africa, see Hyden (2006, ch. 3) and Jackson (1990) on quasi-states. Collapsed states and state building are covered in Chesterman *et al.* (2005), Rotberg (2004) and Zartman (1995a). See Slaughter (2004) for emerging styles of world governance. Among many introductions to the EU are Cini (2006), McCormick (2008) and Nugent (2006).

Internet sources

Europa
European Union Gateway to the European Union
http://europa.eu

Global Policy Forum
Useful material on nations and states
http://www.globalpolicy.org/

Human Development Report
Publishes the Human Development Index
http://hdr.undp.org/

Third World Network
Development and the Third World
http://www.twnside.org.sg

Transparency International
Publishes the Corruption Perceptions Index
http://www.transparency.org/

World Bank
Ranks countries by income and ease of doing business
http://www.worldbank.org

World Trade Organization
Administers the rules of international trade
http://www.wto.org

Chapter 5
Democracy

We live in an era of democracy; for the first time in history, most people in the world live under tolerably democratic rule. This fact reflects the dramatic transformation of the world's political landscape in the final quarter of the twentieth century. Over this short period, the number of democracies more than doubled – from less than 40 to more than 80. Democracy expanded beyond its core of Western Europe and former settler colonies to embrace Southern Europe (e.g. Spain), Eastern Europe (e.g. Hungary), Latin America (e.g. Brazil), more of Asia (e.g. Taiwan) and parts of Africa (e.g. South Africa). This expansion began before, but was accelerated by, the collapse of communism (Figure 5.1). Mandelbaum (2007, p. xi) goes so far as to claim that 'this global democratic surge in the last quarter of the twentieth century has a strong claim to being the single most important development in a century hardly lacking in momentous events and trends'.

Once the Cold War had passed, and the principle of unconditional state sovereignty came into question, so the promotion of democracy became a more explicit ideological objective of the West. The United States, in particular, periodically talked the talk: 'it is the policy of the United States to seek and support democratic movements and institutions in every nation and culture, with the ultimate goal of ending tyranny in our world' (White House, 2006). International law, which previously had little to say on political organization within states, also began to address the topic of democracy. The West began to speak the language of democracy with a louder voice than during the Cold War.

As democracy continues to spread, so it becomes more varied. Understanding the forms taken by democracy in today's world is therefore a

Figure 5.1 The number of democratic countries in the world, 1946–2008

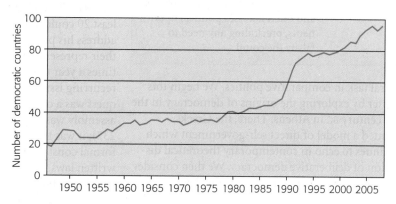

Source: Adapted from Polity IV Project (2009).

large states. Finally, we examine the two main forms of representative democracy in today's world – liberal and illiberal – and the waves of democratization from which they emerged (Box 5.1).

BOX 5.1

Forms of democracy

Form	Definition
Direct democracy	The citizens themselves assemble to debate and reach decisions on matters of common interest.
Deliberative democracy	A perspective on democracy which emphasizes the value of public discussion among free, equal and rational citizens in giving legitimacy to decisions and in enhancing their quality.
Representative (indirect) democracy	Citizens elect a parliament and, in presidential systems, a chief executive. These representatives are usually held to account at the next election.
Liberal democracy	A version of representative democracy in which the scope of democracy is limited by constitutional protection of individual rights, including freedom of assembly, property, religion and speech. Free, fair and regular elections are based on near universal suffrage.
Illiberal democracy	A version of representative democracy in which rulers, once elected, govern with few limits and little respect for individual rights. To assist re-election, the president ensures favourable media coverage and often harasses political opponents, precluding any need to falsify the count.

central task in comparative politics. We begin this chapter by exploring the origins of democracy in the fifth century BC in Athens. There, the Greeks invented a model of direct self-government which continues to echo in contemporary theoretical discussion of deliberative democracy. We then consider the emergence of representation as the device enabling a measure of democracy to be achieved in

Direct democracy

The core principle of democracy is self-rule; the word itself comes from the Greek *demokratia*, meaning rule (*kratos*) by the people (*demos*). From this perspective, democracy refers not to the election of rulers by the ruled but to the denial of any separation between the two. The model democracy is a form of self-government in which all adult citizens participate in shaping collective decisions in an environment of equality and open deliberation. In a direct democracy, state and society become one.

Direct democracy was born in ancient Athens. Between 461 and 322 BC, Athens was the leading *polis* (city-community) in ancient Greece. *Poleis* were small independent political systems, typically containing an urban core and a rural hinterland. Even though Athens only comprised about 40,000 citizens, it was one of the larger examples. Especially in its earlier and more radical phase, the Athenian *polis* operated on the democratic principles summarized by Aristotle (Box 5.2). This ethos applied to all institutions of government within the community. All citizens could attend meetings of the assembly, serve on the governing council and sit on citizens' juries. Because ancient Athens continues to provide the archetypal case of direct democracy, we will discuss its operation in more detail (Figure 5.2).

History has judged there to be no more potent symbol of direct democracy than the Athenian *Ekklesia* (People's Assembly). Any citizen aged at least 20 could attend assembly sessions and there address his peers; meetings were of citizens, not their representatives. The assembly met around 40 times a year to settle issues put before it, including recurring issues of war and peace (imperial conquest was a core objective). In Aristotle's phrase, the assembly was 'supreme over all causes' (1962, p. 237); it was the sovereign body, unconstrained by a formal constitution or even, in the early decades, by written laws. As far as we can tell, meetings were lengthy, factional and vigorous, with the talking – and hence probably the subsequent show of hands –

BOX 5.2

Aristotle's characterization of democracy

- All to rule over each and each in his turn over all;
- Appointment to all offices, except those requiring experience and skill, by lot;
- No property qualification for office-holding, or only a very low one;
- Tenure of office should be brief and no man should hold the same office twice (except military positions);
- Juries selected from all citizens should judge all major causes;
- The assembly should be supreme over all causes;
- Those attending the assembly and serving as jurors and magistrates should be paid for their services.

Source: Aristotle (1962), book VI.

dominated by influential orators known as demagogues (Dahl, 1989, p. 21).

The assembly did not exhaust the avenues of participation in Athens. Administrative functions were the responsibility of an executive council consisting of 500 citizens aged over 30, chosen by lot for a one-year period. Through the rotation of members drawn from the citizen body, the council was

regarded as exemplifying a principle of community democracy: 'all to rule over each and each in his turn over all'. Hansen (1991, p. 249) suggests that about one in three citizens could expect to serve on the council at some stage, an astonishing feat of self-government entirely without counterpart in modern representative democracies.

A highly political legal system provided the final leg of Athenian democracy. Juries of several hundred people, again selected randomly from a panel of volunteers, decided the lawsuits which citizens frequently brought against those considered to have acted against the true interests of the *polis*. The courts functioned as an arena of accountability through which top figures (including generals) were brought to book.

Thus the scope of the Athenian democracy was extraordinarily wide, providing an enveloping framework within which citizens were expected to develop their true qualities. For the Athenians, politics was intrinsically an amateur activity, to be undertaken by all citizens in the interest of the community at large and to enhance their own development. To engage in democracy was to become informed about the *polis* – and an educated citizenry meant a stronger whole.

Nevertheless, Athens's little democracy did possess serious flaws:

- Citizenship was restricted to men whose parents were themselves citizens. So most adults –

Figure 5.2 The direct democracy of Ancient Athens

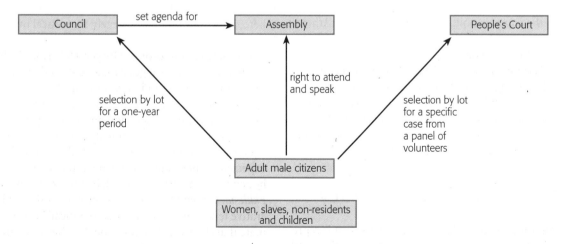

Note: citizenship was a birthright which could not normally be acquired by other means.

including women, slaves and foreign residents – were excluded. Women played no significant public role and critics allege that slavery provided the platform from which the citizen elite could make time for public affairs (Finley, 1985).

- ► Participation was not in practice as extensive as the Athenians liked to claim. Most citizens were absent from most assembly meetings even after the introduction of an attendance payment.
- ► Athenian democracy was hardly an exercise in lean government. A management consultant would surely conclude that the system was time-consuming, expensive and overcomplex, especially for such a small society. Its applicability to a modern world in which people are committed to paid work, and the affluence resulting therefrom, is questionable.
- ► The principle of self-government did not always lead to decisive and coherent policy. Indeed, the lack of a permanent bureaucracy eventually contributed to a period of ineffective governance, leading to the fall of the Athenian republic after defeat in war.

Perhaps Athenian democracy was a dead end in that it could only function on an intimate scale which limited its potential for expansion and, worse, increased its vulnerability to larger predators. Finer (1997, p. 368) adopts just this position: 'the *polis* was doomed politically if it expanded and doomed to conquest if it did not. It had to succumb and it did'. Yet the Athenian democratic experiment prospered for over 100 years. It provided a settled formula for rule and enabled Athens to build a leading position in the complex politics of the Greek world. Athens proves that direct democracy is, in some conditions, an achievable goal.

Certainly Finer (1997, p. 371) was correct in acknowledging the Athenian contribution to Western politics: 'the Greeks invented two of the most potent political features of our present age: they invented the very idea of citizen – as opposed to subject – and they invented democracy'.

Deliberative democracy

Although modern democratic government is representative rather than direct, the Greek tradition still

---

BOX 5.3

Deliberative democracy: Leib's proposal for a third, popular branch of government in the United States

- ► The new popular chamber to consist of 525 citizens selected at random for compulsory service. A fresh sample to be drawn for each topic.
- ► The chamber to divide into 35 panels of 15 people.
- ► Each panel to discuss the same topic face-to-face over several days.
- ► Topics to emerge from an initiative signed by 10 per cent of the population or by a majority vote in the House of Representatives and Senate.
- ► Panels to conclude their deliberations with a secret vote.
- ► Transcripts to be published but anonymity to be respected.
- ► If a two-thirds majority is achieved when the votes of all panels are combined, the proposal is to become law unless vetoed either by the House and Senate or by the courts.
- ► An administrative agency to support the panels by, for example, summarizing materials. Some members of this agency are to be elected; others to be chosen by political parties.

Source: Adapted from Leib (2004).

---

finds echoes in the current concern with deliberative democracy. Because of this link, we will explore the contemporary notion of deliberative democracy here. This notion remains largely theoretical but has not lacked academic influence for that.

The German philosopher Jürgen Habermas is the key figure here. He suggests that we should view democracy as a method of communication. Specifically, democratic legitimacy arises from free, public and rational discussion among competent citizens deliberating in a context of openness and equality (Habermas, 1975). This ideal situation is expected to inculcate civic virtue in the manner hoped for, and partly achieved, by the Athenian *Ekklesia*. Cohen (1997, p. 79) summarizes the deliberative tenet: 'outcomes are democratically legitimate if and only if they could be the object of a free and reasoned argument among equals'.

The underlying idea is straightforward. In an open debate, arguments based on private interests are soon recognized and discredited; public reason involves appeal to the public good. Free and sincere discussion delivers reasons on which all can agree, allowing the stronger argument rather than the stronger speaker to prevail. Authentic debate also enables public opinion to be formed and not merely expressed, thus providing a crucible for developing the collective will. In such conditions, a consensus should emerge about what is truly in the public interest, with reason triumphing over interests. Even if deliberation does not yield consensus, voting should follow the debate rather than serving as a substitute for it. In common with the ancient Greeks, deliberative democrats encourage the weighing of judgements among debaters rather than the crafting of compromises between interests.

Unfortunately, few advocates of deliberative democracy offer specific guidance on institutional arrangements to secure their objective. The problem here is that creating the conditions in which a debate can be truly free and open is by no means straightforward (Meehan, 1995). Indeed, some critics allege that, just as women, slaves and non-citizens were excluded from the *Ekklesia*, so the voices of similar groups today will remain unheard in public discourse as long as society continues to be based on inequalities such as race, class, gender and education. A free debate to which sections of society feel unable to contribute is not a free debate at all.

Clearly, however, deliberative thinking points in the direction of discussion in small groups, perhaps building on formats such as university seminars and town meetings. In a world of large states, such aspirations may seem utopian. However, Leib (2004) has suggested a method of integrating deliberation among citizens within the existing framework of representative democracy. His proposed scheme – based on the United States but, he claims, with wider applicability – repays examination (Box 5.3).

Leib proposes to add a new third branch to the American system. This popular chamber would consist of citizens selected at random so its deliberations would truly articulate the voices of the people, albeit with a rather large sampling error. The new body would not however control its own agenda;

> ### BOX 5.4
>
> ## Degrees of democracy: from unanimity to plurality
>
> **Unanimity**   All to agree, assent or at least acquiesce
>
> **Concurrent majority**   More than one majority required: for example, a double majority of voters and states in a federation
>
> **Qualified majority**   More than a simple majority: typically, two-thirds
>
> **Weighted majority**   A majority after adjusting votes for differences in voting power: for example, shareholders may have one vote per share
>
> **Absolute majority**   More than half of those entitled to vote
>
> **Majority (simple majority)**   More than half of those voting
>
> **Plurality**   The largest number of votes but not necessarily a majority

rather, topics would be set for it, either by a popular initiative or by a reference from the existing chambers. Any proposal supported by a **qualified majority** of two-thirds in this new popular house would become law unless vetoed by the legislature or the courts (Box 5.4).

Why will Leib's scheme fail to progress? Leaving aside the difficulty of amending an entrenched constitution, the answer seems to be that deliberation is only one value among several we want to incorporate into our democratic designs. America's constitution has proved fit for purpose in providing a framework for encouraging compromises between interests and in contributing to stability. This success creates an understandable bias against radical reform: 'if it ain't broke, don't fix it'. In addition, a new chamber would further complicate policy-making in a system already loaded with checks and balances. Also, in contrast to the *Ekklesia*, only a trivial proportion of a population of about 300 million would be a member of the popular chamber, even over the course of a lifetime. In that respect, the new body would be a mechanism of representative rather than direct democracy.

Representative democracy

At national level, all contemporary democracies are **representative** rather than direct. The democratic principle has transmuted from self-government to elected government, with barely a nod to ancient tradition. To the Greeks, the very idea of a representative democracy would have seemed preposterous: how can the people be said to govern themselves if they are ruled by a separate government? As late as the eighteenth century, the French philosopher Jean-Jacques Rousseau propounded the same point: 'the moment a people gives itself representatives, it is no longer free. It ceases to exist' (1762, p. 145).

> A **representative** stands for another person, group or entity. A flag represents a nation, a lawyer represents a client and elected politicians represent their electors, districts and parties.

Yet as large modern states emerged, so too did the requirement for a new form of democracy. In contrast to the little democracy of Athens, any modern version had to be compatible with the much larger states found in today's world. In addition, citizenship ceased to be an elite status as it extended to the vast majority of the adult population, including women.

One of the first authors to graft representation onto democracy was Tom Paine (1737–1809), a British-born political activist who experienced both the French and the American revolutions. In his *Rights of Man* (1791/2, p. 180), Paine wrote:

The original simple democracy ... is incapable of extension, not from its principle, but from the inconvenience of its form. Simple democracy was society governing itself without the aid of secondary means. By ingrafting representation upon democracy, we arrive at a system of government capable of embracing and confederating all the various interests and every extent of territory and population.

Scalability has certainly proved to be the key strength of representative institutions. The conventional wisdom in ancient Athens was that the upper limit for a republic was the number of people who could gather together to hear a speaker. However,

modern representative government allows massive populations (such as a billion Indians and 300 million Americans) to exercise some popular control over their rulers. And there is no upper limit. In theory, the entire world could become one giant representative democracy. To adapt Tom Paine's phrase, representative government has indeed proved to be a highly convenient form.

As ever, intellectuals were on hand to validate this thinning of the democratic ideal. Prominent among them was Joseph Schumpeter (1883–1950), an Austrian-born economist who became an academic in the United States. In *Capitalism, Socialism and Democracy* (1943), Schumpeter conceived of democracy as nothing more than party competition: 'democracy means only that the people have the opportunity of refusing or accepting the men who are to rule them'. He wanted to limit the contribution of ordinary voters because he was sceptical of their political capacity:

The typical citizen drops down to a lower level of mental performance as soon as he enters the political field. He argues and analyzes in a way that he would recognize as infantile within the sphere of his real interests. He becomes a primitive again. (1943, p. 269)

Reflecting this jaundiced view, Schumpeter argued that elections should not even be construed as a device through which voters elect a representative to carry out their will; rather, the role of elections is simply to produce a government. From this perspective, the elector becomes a political accessory, restricted to selecting from broad packages of policies and leaders prepared by the parties. Representative democracy is merely a way of deciding who shall decide, a system far removed from the intense, educative discussions in Athens's assembly, Habermas's debating forum and Leib's popular branch:

The deciding of issues by the electorate [is made] secondary to the election of the men who are to do the deciding. To put it differently, we now take the view that the role of the people is to produce a government ... And we define the democratic method as that institutional arrangement for arriving at political decisions in which individuals acquire the power to decide by means of a competitive struggle for the people's vote. (Schumpeter, 1943, p. 270)

Liberal and illiberal democracy

Although all modern democracies are representative, the diffusion of democracy around the world has created a requirement for an additional distinction between liberal and illiberal democracies.

Like representative democracy itself, **liberal democracy** is a compromise. Specifically, it seeks to integrate the authority of democratic governments with simultaneous limits on their scope. By definition, liberal democracy is limited government. The goal is to secure individual liberty, including freedom from unwarranted demands by the state. In this way, the population can be defended against its rulers and minorities can be protected from democracy's inherent danger: tyranny by the majority.

In place of the all-encompassing scope of the Athenian *polis*, liberal democracies are governments of laws rather than men. Elected rulers are subject to constitutions that usually include a statement of individual rights. Should the government become overbearing, citizens can in theory use domestic and international courts to uphold their rights. In these respects, a liberal democracy is democracy disarmed. At the same time, rights to free speech and association permit political opinion to form and to receive expression through political parties, for 'without liberty, there can be no democracy' (Beetham, 2004, p. 65).

Liberal democracy is a settlement between individual liberty and collective politics which reflects the key issues involved in its emergence in Western political systems. These issues included the desire to entrench religious freedom and to secure property rights against encroachment by the poor. These elements were especially important to the design of the American system of government, the most liberal (and perhaps the least democratic) of all liberal democracies.

With the collapse of communist and military rule in the final decades of the last century, **illiberal democracy** (also called electoral or semi-democracy) became a more common and recognized form.

In this type of regime, the elected ruler or rulers pay little attention to individual rights, at least when dealing with political opponents. Ballot stuffing is avoided but democracy does not extend far beyond the election itself. Even the election outcome is conditioned by the ruler's influence over the media and by the use of state resources to favour his own organization, factors which exert influence long before the formal campaign gets underway.

The result is what Huntington (1991, p. 306) describes as 'democracy without turnover and competition without alternation'. Hence illiberal democracy is less democratic – as well as less liberal – than its liberal cousin. Given that liberal democracy 'is a system in which parties lose elections' (Przeworski, 1991, p. 10), illiberal democracy is a system in which they don't. Rather, change at the top usually results from a constitutional limit on tenure or the occasional resignation.

The illiberal character of these regimes emerges most clearly once an election is won. The government, typically dominated by a strong president, shows only a limited sense of constitutional restraint; such concepts as fair play and a loyal opposition barely register. O'Donnell (1994, p. 59) describes the format: 'whoever wins election to the presidency is thereby entitled to govern as he or she sees fit, constrained only by the hard facts of existing power relations and by a constitutionally limited term of office'. Illiberal democracy authorizes power without limiting it.

Illiberal democracy is based on a powerful leader rather than strong institutions. In this respect, the system resembles authoritarian rule more than liberal democracy. Rather than serving as a representative agent, the president – or, less often, prime minister – plays the part of personal ruler, taking care of the people's needs and claiming their respect, deference and support in exchange. Having elected a saviour, the voters are expected to cheer from the stands, only entering the political field at their own risk. In view of this 'poisoned partnership' between ruler and ruled, some commentators prefer to speak of electoral or competitive authoritarianism rather than illiberal democracy (Korosteleva, 2004; Schedler, 2006). Yet we must beware of double standards here. If we set the standard needed to qualify as a democracy too high, we may end up with no passes at all (Box 5.5).

BOX 5.5

Is this country a liberal or an illiberal democracy? Which country is it?

- Over 20 million adults living in this country are not entitled to vote;
- At most elections in this country, most of those entitled to vote abstain;
- Members of the legislature manipulate electoral boundaries to secure their own re-election;
- Incumbents use public and private resources to ensure their re-election and are rarely defeated;
- The law protects the existing major parties against newcomers;
- The presidential candidate coming second in votes is sometimes deemed to have won the election;
- The president has no personal electoral account-ability for up to half his tenure;
- The constitution of this country has never been ratified by vote of the people;
- A president of this country once said, 'in the working out of a great national program which seeks the primary good of the greater number, it is true that the toes of some people are being stepped on and are going to be stepped on. But these toes belong to the comparative few who seek to retain or to gain position or riches or both by some short cut which is harmful to the greater good'

The country is, of course, the United States. Nonetheless, the USA is a clear example of a liberal democracy. The moral is that we do not expect a country to be perfectly democratic in order to qualify as a liberal democracy. By the same token, neither should we set an unrealistic standard in judging whether a country such as Russia qualifies as an illiberal democracy.

Note: In 2008, the voting-age population included 3.4 million ineligible felons and an estimated 19.9 million non-citizens (United States Elections Project, 2008). Second-term presidents cannot stand for re-election. The passage above from President Franklin Roosevelt was quoted by Vladimir Putin in his address to Russia's Federal Assembly in 2006. Putin added, 'these are fine words and it is a pity that it was not I who thought them up'.

Because the judiciary in an illiberal democracy is under-resourced, it is unable to enforce the individual rights documented in the constitution. The law is used selectively, as a tool of power. Political opponents are subject to detailed legal scrutiny but supporters find the law rarely intrudes on their activities: 'for my friends, everything; for my enemies, the law,' said Getúlio Vargas, President of Brazil, 1930–45 and 1951–54. The state intervenes in the workings of the market, with political connections influencing economic rewards; politics occupies more space in an illiberal democracy than in a liberal one. And, in contrast to most authoritarian regimes, the leader often does provide effective governance, thus earning as well as manipulating popular support.

Illiberal democracy is commonly found in recent democracies. Zakaria (2003, p. 61) notes how 'since the fall of communism, countries round the world are being governed by regimes like Russia's that mix elections and authoritarianism – illiberal democracy'. The form is particularly common in democracies with continuing poverty, with ethnic, religious or economic divisions, with government revenue derived from natural resource (e.g. oil) revenues, and with real or constructed external threats.

For instance, many Latin American countries are characterized by extreme inequality, with the urban poor seeking salvation through a strong, populist leader. Asian illiberal democracies such as Malaysia and Singapore combine an overriding commitment to further economic development with ethnic divisions between Chinese and Malays (Bourchier, 2006). Governments in Venezuela and Russia claim to be engaged in oil-funded projects to restore national prestige in a hostile international environment. In these circumstances, a national father figure or dominant party can be presented as a protector against external threats, a bulwark against domestic disintegration and an engine of development. The head, it is claimed, must be allowed to rule the body politic.

How widespread is illiberal democracy? According to Freedom House (2009), 63 out of 193 countries could only be classified as 'partly free' in 2008. These states, containing 20 per cent of the world's population, included Nigeria, Singapore, Turkey, Uganda and Venezuela. Many other exam-

BOX 5.6

Huntington's three waves of democratization

	Period	Examples
First	1828–1926	Britain, France, USA
Second	1943–62	India, Israel, Japan, West Germany
Third	1974–91	Southern and Eastern Europe, Latin America, parts of Africa

Note: The first wave partly reversed between 1922 and 1942 (e.g. in Germany and Italy) and the second wave similarly between 1958 and 1975 (e.g. in much of Latin America and post-colonial Africa). Many such reversals have now themselves reversed.

Source: Huntington (1991). For some criticisms of the wave approach, see Grugel (2002, pp. 32–7).

ples come from new democracies in Africa, Latin America and Asia.

To the extent that illiberal democracies are personal in character, they might be expected to be unstable in the long run. Huntington (1991, p. 137), for example, claims 'this half-way house cannot stand'. Yet we cannot wish illiberal democracies out of existence by just deeming them to be transitional. So far illiberal democracy seems to have provided a stable method of governing poor and unequal societies, particularly since the end of communism rendered blatant dictatorship less defensible. Once set, illiberal democracy can be a strong amalgam, not least in an Islamic setting where liberal democracy is equated with Western permissiveness. Crouch (1996, p. vii) shows how Malaysia's 'repressive-responsive' regime 'provides the foundation for a remarkably stable political order'. Similarly, Borón (1998, p. 43) argues that in the 'faulty democracies' of Latin America, democracy 'endures but does not consolidate'. When one strong leader departs, his regime may be replaced not by a liberal democracy but just by another dominant leader.

Writing on sub-Saharan Africa, Herbst (2001, p. 359) judges that 'it is wrong to conclude that African states are travelling between democracy and authoritarianism simply because a majority of them belong to neither category. Rather, the current condition of African states could well prevail for decades'.

The heart of the matter is perhaps that illiberal democracy is a tacit, but stable, compromise between domestic elites and international organizations. Illiberal democracy is usually sufficient for the ruling elite to meet the conditions of aid set by the World Bank, the IMF and donor governments. While these international bodies may welcome democracy, in practice they give higher priority to economic reform. Non-fraudulent elections, even if neither completely free nor fair, are regarded as sufficient tests of democracy. Such reasoning led Case (1996, p. 464) to conclude that illiberal democracy is not 'a mere way station on the road to further democracy'. His prediction has proved to be sound; the number (if not the exact composition) of partly free countries in Freedom House ratings (2009) has remained stable since 1993.

Waves of democratization

When and how did modern democracies emerge? Here we review the historic transition to democracy, looking not just at the emergence of liberal democracy in such countries as the USA and the UK but also at more recent transitions. As with the phases of decolonization discussed in the preceding chapter, so too did democracies emerge in a series of distinct waves (Box 5.6).

First wave

The earliest representative democracies emerged in the 'first long wave of democratization' between 1828 and 1926. During this first wave nearly 30

A **wave** of democratization is a group of transitions from non-democratic to democratic regimes that occurs within a specified period of time and that significantly outnumbers transitions in the opposite direction during that period (Huntington, 1991, p. 15).

Figure 5.3 Liberal democracy: checks and balances in American government

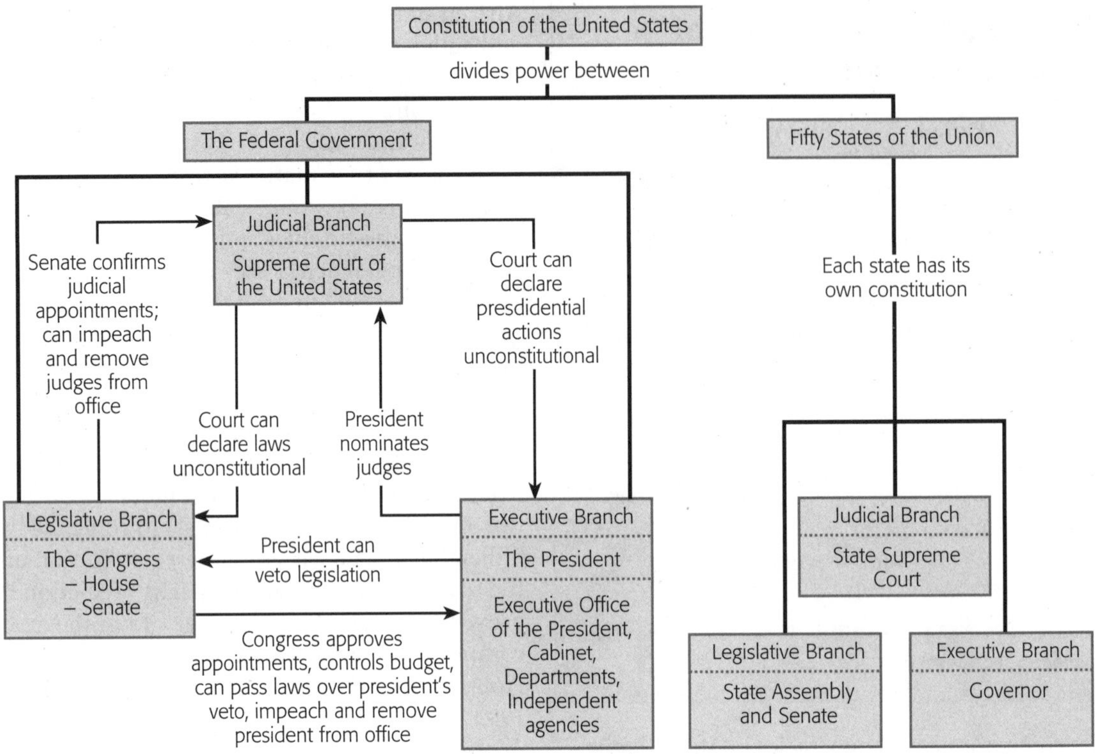

```
                    ┌─────────────────────────────────────┐
                    │   Constitution of the United States  │
                    └─────────────────────────────────────┘
                              divides power between

        ┌──────────────────────────┐              ┌──────────────────────────┐
        │   The Federal Government  │              │   Fifty States of the Union │
        └──────────────────────────┘              └──────────────────────────┘
```

Judicial Branch
Supreme Court of the United States

Senate confirms judicial appointments; can impeach and remove judges from office

Court can declare presdidential actions unconstitutional

Each state has its own constitution

Court can declare laws unconstitutional

President nominates judges

Legislative Branch
The Congress
– House
– Senate

President can veto legislation

Executive Branch
The President

Executive Office of the President, Cabinet, Departments, Independent agencies

Congress approves appointments, controls budget, can pass laws over president's veto, impeach and remove president from office

Judicial Branch
State Supreme Court

Legislative Branch
State Assembly and Senate

Executive Branch
Governor

countries established at least minimally democratic national institutions, including Argentina, Australia, Britain, Canada, France, Germany, the Netherlands, New Zealand, the Scandinavian countries and the United States. However, some **backsliding** occurred as fledgling democracies were overthrown by fascist, communist or military dictatorships during Huntington's 'first reverse wave' from 1922 to 1942.

> **Backsliding** occurs when a democratic transition is reversed, in whole or especially in part.

However, democracy did consolidate in the earliest nineteenth-century cases, including the United States and the United Kingdom. We will examine these two transitions in more detail, not least because they resulted in some subtle but significant differences in how liberal democracies operate.

The emergence of democracy in the United States was rapid but it was a transition nonetheless. The republic's founders had thought of political leadership in non-democratic terms, as the duty of a disinterested, leisured gentry. They favoured an elite-led republic, not an Athenian-style democracy. But the idea that citizens could only be represented fairly by those of their own sort quickly gained ground in the states, strengthened by the egalitarian spirit of a frontier society. The suffrage soon extended to nearly all white men. Of course, some groups had to wait until the twentieth century for the full franchise. Women were not offered the vote on the same terms as men until 1919 and the black franchise was not fully realized until the Voting Rights Act of 1965. In that sense America's democratic transition was completed in the last 50 years.

Today, the USA gives us the clearest picture of a liberal democracy in which the liberal dimension is entrenched by design. The Founding Fathers wanted, above all, to prevent a dictatorship of any kind, including tyranny by the majority. To prevent any government – and especially elected ones – from acquiring excessive power, the constitution set up an intricate system of checks and balances between institutions (Figure 5.3). Even the administration itself experiences difficulty in passing reforms which are widely recognized to be necessary but are opposed by an organized minority. The constitution placed government under law above government by the people. In this way, the liberal dimension of America's democracy emerged victorious over its representative aspect. Only during periods of external threat, such as after 9/11, do individual liberties come under threat (Lyon, 2003).

In Britain, by contrast, the outcome of the transition was originally a less liberal implementation of democracy. By the eighteenth century, the power of the monarch had been checked by the growing authority of parliament. However, the rights of the individual citizen were never stated as clearly as in the USA. The widening of the suffrage also occurred more gradually in the United Kingdom, with each step easing the fears of the propertied classes about the dangers of further reform (Table 5.1). As the House of Commons acquired democratic legitimacy, so both the monarchy and the non-elected House of Lords retreated into the background, unable to provide American-style checks and balances.

Where American democracy diffuses power across institutions, British democracy emphasizes the sovereignty of Parliament. The electoral rules normally ensure a secure majority of seats for the leading party, which then forms the government. This ruling party retains firm control over its own members in the House of Commons, enabling it to ensure the passage of its bills into law. In this way, the hallowed sovereignty of Britain's parliament is leased to the party in office. Except for the government's sense of self-restraint, the institutions that limit executive power in the United States – including a codified constitution, the separation of powers and federalism – are absent.

Far more than the United States, Britain exemplifies Schumpeter's model of democracy as an electoral competition between organized parties. 'We are the masters now,' trumpeted a Labour MP after his party's triumph in 1945; similar thoughts must have occurred to many Labour MPs after their party's

Table 5.1 The expansion of the British electorate, 1831–1931

Year	Electorate (as a percentage of population aged 20+)
1831	4.4
1832	First Reform Act
1832	7.1
1864	9.0
1867	Second Reform Act
1868	16.4
1883	18.0
1884	Third Reform Act
1886	28.5
1914	30.0
1918	Vote extended to women over 30
1921	74.0
1928	Equal Franchise Act
1931	97.0

Note: In 1969, the voting age was reduced from 21 to 18.

Source: Adapted from Dahl (1998), Figure 2.

equally emphatic victory in 1997. Certainly, the country's judiciary has now become more active and independent, stimulated in part by the European Court of Justice, while the 1980s privatizations reduced the state's direct control over the economy. Reflecting international trends, even Britain's party-dominated democracy has moved in a liberal direction. But from a comparative perspective, a winning party in Britain is still rewarded with an exceptionally free hand. The contrast with the United States remains clear.

Second wave

Huntington's second wave of democratization began in the Second World War and continued until the 1960s. Like the first wave, some of the new democracies created at this time did not consolidate. For example, elected rulers in several Latin American states were quickly overthrown by military coups.

But established democracies did emerge after 1945 from the ashes of defeated dictatorships, not just in West Germany but also in Austria, Japan and Italy. These post-war democracies were introduced by the victorious allies, led by the USA, acting with the

COUNTRY PROFILE

MEXICO

LIBERAL DEMOCRACY

Form of government ■ a federal and presidential republic.

Legislature ■ the 500 members of the Chamber of Deputies are elected for a single three-year period and the 128 members of the Senate for a single six-year tenure.

Executive ■ the president, directly elected for a non-renewable six-year term, heads both the state and the government, choosing the members of the Cabinet.

Constitution and judiciary ■ headed by the Supreme Court of Justice, the judicial system mixes American constitutional principles with the civil law tradition. In practice, both judicial independence and police enforcement of law have been weak.

Electoral system ■ 300 members of the Chamber represent single-member districts; the other 200 are elected by a list system of proportional representation. The Senate also operates a mixed electoral system.

Party system ■ dominated by the Institutional Revolutionary Party (PRI) until the 1990s. The conservative National Action Party (PAN), which formed part of Vicente Fox Quesada's successful Alliance for Change in the 2000 elections, retained the presidency in 2006 with a narrow and disputed victory over the left-wing Revolutionary Democratic Party (PRD).

Population (annual growth rate): 110.1m (+1.1%)
World Bank income group: upper middle
Political Rights score: ②
Civil Liberties score: ③
Human development index (rank/out of): 52/177
Freedom of the press index (rank/out of): 108/194
Perceived corruption index (rank/out of): 72/180

Note: For meaning and sources of scales and indexes, see p. xvi. In all cases a score and rank of 1 is 'best'.

Although **MEXICO** achieved independence from Spain as early as 1821, the decisive moment in its history was the civil conflict that erupted in 1910 against a ruling oligarchy established by President Díaz. His powerful elite was supported by foreign capital and the military but provided few opportunities for an emerging middle class. The revolution was led by younger elements of this class though peasants and workers were eventually drawn in. The initial outcome was the constitution of 1917, a left-wing document which limited the authority of the Catholic Church. However, the revolution's radical spirit was best expressed under the presidency of Lázaro Cárdenas in the 1930s. His administration undertook radical land reform, breaking up many large estates and granting land to over a million peasants.

Cárdenas also established the system of rule built round the Institutional Revolutionary Party (PRI). Founded in 1929 in an attempt to rein in regional political machines, the PRI was transformed into a structured patronage organization capable of mobilizing and channelling mass support. The party was organized into three sectors, representing workers, peasants and 'popular' (mainly public sector) groups. Leaders of these sectors distributed favours to their members, creating incentives to continue supporting the party. As a ruling party, the PRI also used the considerable perks of office to further reward its clients. PRI rule could also be ruthless: it repressed opposition and manipulated election results, becoming 'one of the world's leading manufacturers of electoral fraud' (Schedler, 2005, p. 9).

Gradually, the PRI's left-wing principles weakened as it established a 'perfect dictatorship' based on its entrenched patronage networks. Especially in the 1950s and 1960s, the PRI seemed to have found the recipe for stable rule by a dominant party. However, three problems recurred, eventually leading to the democratization discussed on the next page:

■ Continuing poverty for those excluded from the party's network, reflected in periodic revolts;

■ Increasing opposition from the expanding urban middle class created by economic growth;

■ Economic crises which sometimes occurred when the PRI placed its political objectives before sound economic policy.

Further reading: Edmonds-Poli and Shirk (2008), O'Neill (2009).

Democracy in Mexico

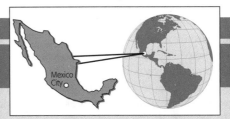

'Yes, it can be done,' shouted the crowds in Mexico City as they celebrated the downfall of the PRI after the presidential election of 2000. After 70 years in power, the PRI not only lost a presidential election for the first time but also ceased to control either house of the national legislature. The world's oldest ruling party had suffered an historic reverse, subsequently confirmed by its poor performance in 2006. This peaceful transfer of power decisively confirmed Mexico's status as a new democracy. For students of comparative politics, Mexico offers a remarkably successful example of democratization. How did this transition unfold?

With the political effectiveness of the PRI machine decaying, Carlos Salinas (president, 1988–94) initiated economic reforms, including privatizing major firms and opening the economy to international competition, not least through NAFTA. In contrast to the Soviet Union, where Gorbachev introduced political reform before economic change, in Mexico economic liberalization preceded political change. In this respect, the comparison is with China rather than the USSR.

As the PRI lost direct control of economic resources, so its powers of patronage declined and voters became free to support opposition parties, especially in the cities. Independent trade unions began to form outside the enveloping embrace of the PRI.

Eventually, the PRI itself introduced political changes that served to

enliven a moribund opposition. By the 1990s, the party no longer felt able to manipulate election results. In 1997, it lost its majority in the Chamber of Deputies after relatively fair elections.

The next and decisive election, in 2000, was overseen by a powerful independent election commission, characterized by Lawson (2004, p. 146) as 'worthy of emulation by many established democracies'. The growing authority of the Federal

Election to the Chamber of Deputies, 2006		
	Votes (%)	*Seats*
National Action Party (PAN)	34.6	206
Party of the Democratic Revolution (PDR)	29.8	160
Institutional Revolutionary Party (PRI)	28.4	121
Others	7.2	13

Source: Adapted from Psephos (2006).

Electoral Institute, shown in a professional election count, sent a clear message that the era of PRI vote-rigging in federal elections had ended.

So the PRI's fall was partly self-induced: its leaders recognized that the tools needed to guarantee their party's continued grip on power were hindering the country's further development.

Mexico's gradual move to democracy seems to have avoided what Baer (1993, p. 64) described as 'the dilemma of all reforms from above, particularly in ageing regimes: how to avoid unleashing a revolution from below'. But it remains to be seen how

far, and at what speed, democracy will deepen in Mexico. Recent presidents sustained economic stability but put through few reforms of what remains a highly regulated economy.

Mexico's continuing problems – weak governance, low growth, urban squalor, drugs, crime, corrupt judges, incompetent police and inadequate education – mean that it is premature to regard the country as a consolidated liberal democracy. Indeed, the democratic transition has accelerated

some difficulties; drug cartels previously kept under control by the PRI killed over 6,000 people in 2008.

Also, a close and controversial presidential election in 2006, when the defeated candidate of the left refused to accept the result, showed that the electoral process is not yet fully authoritative. As in South Africa, however, progress should be judged not against an ideal standard but rather against what came before.

Further reading: Shirk (2005), Camp (2006).

support of partners in the countries concerned. Such second-wave democracies did establish firm roots, helped by an economic recovery which was itself nourished by American aid. During this second wave, democracy also consolidated in the new state of Israel and the former British dominion of India.

How did these second-wave democracies differ from those of the earlier wave? Their liberal traditions were somewhat weaker as representation through parties proved to be the stronger suit. Parties had gone unmentioned in the American constitution but by the time of the second wave they had emerged as the leading instrument of democracy in a mass electorate. Like many recent constitutions, Germany's Basic Law (1949) went so far as to codify their role: 'the political parties shall take part in forming the democratic will of the people'. In that respect, second-wave constitutions were built in the Schumpeter mould. However, in several cases effective competition was reduced by the emergence of a single party which dominated national politics for a generation: Congress in India, the Christian Democrats in Italy, the LDP in Japan and Labour in Israel.

Third wave

The third wave of democratization was a product of the final quarter of the twentieth century – within the memory of most people alive today. Its main and highly diverse elements were:

- The ending of right-wing dictatorships in Southern Europe (Greece, Portugal and Spain) in the 1970s;
- The retreat of the generals in much of Latin America in the 1980s;
- The collapse of communism in the Soviet Union and Eastern Europe at the end of the 1980s.

This third wave transformed the global political landscape. The predominance of democracy resulting from this wave provides an inhospitable environment for those non-democratic regimes that survive. Even in sub-Saharan Africa, presidents subjected themselves to re-election (though rarely to defeat). With the end of the Cold War and the collapse of any realistic alternative to democ-

racy, the European Union and the United States became more encouraging of democratic transitions (while keeping a close eye on their own shorter-term interests). Thus, although the third wave peaked in the early 1990s, some countries have continued to experience democratic or at least popular uprisings in the twenty-first century: for instance, Georgia's Rose Revolution in 2003 and Ukraine's Orange Revolution the following year (Wilson, 2006).

Within the third wave, the Southern European group provides the most secure cases of **consolidation**, aided by a desire to join the European Union and by economic development. These same factors also encouraged democratic deepening in those Eastern Europe countries which have entered the EU. Elsewhere, including much of Latin America and Africa, many democratic latecomers have not yet fully consolidated, if indeed they are to do so at all. The category of illiberal democracy is becoming a more plausible perspective on many third-wave regimes. As the euphoria of transition fades, so the assumption that consolidation of liberal democracy is just a matter of time begins to wear thin (Carothers, 2002).

A democracy has **consolidated** when it provides an accepted framework for political competition. Huntington (1991, p. 266) suggested a two turnover test: that is, consolidation occurs when each of the two main sides has given up power to the other through an election. But Przeworski's broader definition (1991, p. 26) has proved to be more useful: 'democracy is consolidated when ... a particular system of institutions becomes the only game in town and when no-one can imagine acting outside the democratic institutions'.

One reason for the sketchy consolidation of third-wave democracies is the inheritance from the old regime. After all, ruling communist parties and military councils had brooked no interference from the judiciary and paid no heed to constitutions, including statements of human rights. Even before the emergence of communist and military dictatorships, many such countries had no tradition of individual rights or formal restraints on rulers. In such conditions, an illiberal rather than a liberal democracy is an understandable outcome.

Lower levels of affluence, often combined with highly visible inequalities, are particularly important in hindering democratic consolidation in third-wave countries. As Vanhanen (1997) notes, such conditions favour neither the diffusion of power resources nor the development of mutual toleration and compromise which foster the consolidation of liberal democracy. Many authors hold that economic well-being is in fact the key to a stable liberal democracy.

In *Political Man* (1960, pp. 48–9), for instance, Lipset famously concluded that 'the more well-to-do a nation, the greater the chances that it will sustain democracy'. Although poor but democratic India is an exception, further economic development (especially when its fruits are widely diffused) may prove to be necessary for democratic deepening in third-wave states.

Learning Resources for Chapter 5

Next step

Dahl *et al.* (2003) is a wide-ranging collection on the nature, conditions, procedures and impact of democracy.

Further reading

Dahl (1989, 1998) offers lucid accounts of democracy. His 1989 book is more advanced but the 1998 volume is a useful introduction. Other overall assessments include Arblaster (2002) and Held (2006). For Athens, see Finley (1985) and Hansen (1991). Deliberative democracy is a more difficult and theoretical literature; see, for instance, Habermas (1978). In addition to Leib (2004), applied works include Mutz (2006), O'Flynn (2006) and Parkinson (2006). On illiberal democracy, O'Donnell (1994) sets the scene; for more recent assessments, see Carothers (2002), Ottaway (2003), Schedler (2006) and Zakaria (2003). Democratization has spawned an outstanding literature: Huntington (1991) and O'Donnell *et al.* (1986) were influential.

Internet sources

Freedom House
Widely used country ratings of democracy, civil liberties and the press
http://www.freedomhouse.org/

Democracy Coalition Project
Seeks open democratic societies around the world
http://www.demcoalition.org/2005_html/home.html

Direct Democracy, University of Geneva
An interdisciplinary approach to the study of direct democracy
http://c2d.unige.ch/

Journal of Democracy
Accessible scholarly articles on the current position of democracy around the world
http://www.journalofdemocracy.org/

National Endowment for Democracy
Supporting freedom around the world
http://www.ned.org/

Rights and Democracy
Seeks to develop democratic practices, institutions and culture at national and regional levels
http://www.ichrdd.ca/site/

www.palgrave.com
Companion Website
Visit the Companion Website to 'click and go'
www.palgrave.com/politics/hague

Chapter 6
Authoritarian rule

'The study of politics in **authoritarian** countries should be more valued by comparative scholars', comments Posusney (2005, p. 2). And the reason is straightforward: 'non-democratic government, whether by elders, chiefs, monarchs, aristocrats, empires, military regimes or one-party states, has been the norm for most of human history' (Brooker, 2009, p. 1). Certainly the brutal twentieth century will be remembered more for the dictatorships it spawned – including Hitler's Germany, Stalin's Russia, Mao's China and Pol Pot's Cambodia – than for the democratic transitions at its close.

However, studying non-democracies remains far more than a historical exercise. Nine of the 45 largest countries by population are still governed by authoritarian means (Table 6.1). Unlike some democracies, many authoritarian states possess young and expanding populations. Several such states are of international significance. China is one of the world's largest economies; Saudi Arabia provided most of the 9/11 terrorists; Iran's investment in nuclear technology has projected the country to the centre of world politics. Despite generally low living standards, non-democratic countries control most of the world's remaining oil, with high levels of military spending and corruption, a factor predisposing to political instability. Geographically, most authoritarian states are located in an arc running through North Africa, the Middle East and much of Asia. This location overlaps, albeit imperfectly, with the Islamic crescent (Map 6.1).

The nature of authoritarian rule

In approaching authoritarian rule, we should not assume that all such states place total, unlimited power in a despot who seeks to control the whole population through fear and surveillance. Even in the twentieth century, totalitarian regimes demanding explicit popular support of the supreme leader were the exception rather than the rule. Elements of the totalitarian method can still be found, particularly in the widespread use of the secret police for monitoring potential opposition. But with a few exceptions such as North Korea, totalitarian regimes are rarely observed today.

Most non-democracies are in fact authoritarian rather than totalitarian. That is, the rulers seek to maintain their own control (and increase their

Authoritarian rule is a broad category, used here to cover any form of non-democratic rule. Some authors use the term in a more restricted sense, to distinguish authoritarian regimes from totalitarian states which sought total penetration of society in an attempt, notional or real, at transformation (Linz, 1975).

Table 6.1 **The largest authoritarian states by population**

	Population (rank)	Form of rule	Gross domestic product, per head (rank)	Oil reserves (rank)	Perceived corruption (rank)
China	1	Communist party	133	14	72
Vietnam	14	Communist party	169	30	121
Egypt	16	Presidential	135	27	115
Iran	20	Contested theocracy	87	3	141
Burma	27	Military junta	206	78	178
Sudan	30	Presidential dictatorship (military links)	184	21	173
Algeria	34	Presidential (strong military influence)	126	15	92
Saudi Arabia	43	Royal family	59	1	80
Uzbekistan	45	Presidential dictatorship	170	46	166
(United States, for comparison)	(4)	(Liberal democracy)	(10)	(13)	(18)

Note: The table shows the largest countries by population of those classified by Freedom House as 'not free' in each year, 2001–05 and 2009. Ranks for population, gross domestic product and proven oil reserves are from CIA (2009) which ranks 229 entities, mainly countries (1 = largest). Perceived corruption is from Transparency International (2009) which ranks 180 countries (1 = least corrupt). Data are from 2006–09, depending on country and variable.

wealth) by limiting mass participation rather than by mobilizing the population. Ordinary people are unlikely to experience the knock on the door as long as they keep away from politics. Rulers operate within unspoken limits, recognizing the need to strike deals with other power-holders in business, the church and the regions. Typically, government takes the form not of a single dominant leader but rather of an elite group, such as a military council, with considerable internal jockeying. Ideology and policy are often absent. In such a situation, as perhaps in some totalitarian cases, rulership is an uneasy combination of formally unlimited authority and considerable political vulnerability.

Since non-democratic leaders stand above the law, the constitutional architecture (if any) is an uncertain guide to political realities. Laws are vague and contradictory, creating a pretext for bringing any chosen troublemaker to court. Special courts, often in the form of military tribunals, are often used for sensitive cases. Parliaments and the judiciary are under-resourced, unprofessional and ineffective. Civil rights are poorly respected and the state often requires private organizations to be licensed. The absence of constitutional constraint leads to callous treatment of the powerless, including minority groups, non-nationals, prisoners and women. The absence of a clear legal framework to protect private property rights is one reason why authoritarian rule is often associated with economic stagnation. The price of the rulers securing a large slice of the pie is that the pie itself fails to grow.

Inherited monarchies apart, the absence of a clear succession procedure is the central weakness of authoritarian regimes, providing much of their political dynamic. Because competitive elections do not provide a mechanism for refreshing the leadership, authoritarian leaders may continue in post until well past their sell-by dates. For this reason, a decline into personal despotism is an inherent danger of authoritarian regimes – though, as Brooker (2009, p. 130) observes, 'degeneration into personal rule is common among dictatorships, particularly among party regimes, but is far from being inevitable'. A more important consequence of uncertain succession is that authoritarian rulers can be removed by upstarts at any time, meaning that they must devote constant attention to shoring up their position.

Map 6.1 The largest authoritarian states by population

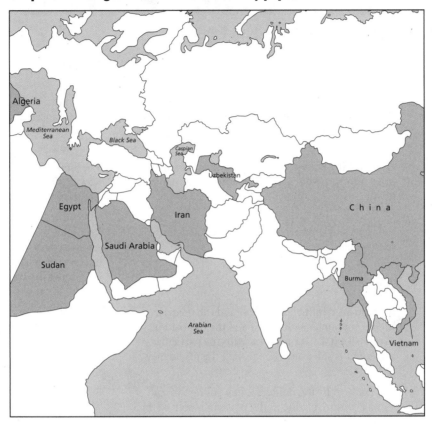

Identifying how authoritarian leaders respond to these inherent political uncertainties brings us to the essence of non-democratic rule. Leaders rely on control of three key resources: the military, patronage and the media. First, authoritarian rulers maintain a strong military and security presence. To sustain their position, they need to be perceived as willing to use this resource. For instance, the massacre of pro-democracy demonstrators in Tiananmen Square in Beijing in 1989 goes unmentioned in the Chinese media but, even today, its message is still understood. Similarly, Bellin (2005, p. 26) suggests that 'in the Middle East and North Africa, it is the stalwart will and capacity of the state's coercive apparatus to suppress any glimmers of democratic initiative that have extinguished the possibility of transition'.

High spending on the armed forces – often made possible by natural resource revenues – is typical of authoritarian states. Such investment buys off potential opposition, permits foreign adventures and provides the means for suppressing domestic dissent. Even when the military does not itself rule, it still provides a key support base for the political executive. Lavish treatment of the armed forces is therefore inevitable. Authoritarian regimes lack the separation of military and political spheres which characterizes liberal democracy.

Second, authoritarian rulers maintain their position through an unofficial patronage network in which other power holders are incorporated by providing them with resources (such as control over jobs and access to money-making opportunities) which they can distribute, in turn, to their own supporters. In this way, allegiance to one's immediate patron, and indirectly to the regime, becomes the key to a successful career. These patron-client pyramids extend throughout society, providing a web of

BOX 6.1

Forms of authoritarian rule

	Definition	Examples
Despots	A single individual, owing allegiance to no institution, rules though fear and rewards, relying on a personal security force to maintain power.	Dominican Republic (Trujillo), Haiti (François Duvalier)
Monarchs	A ruling king emerges from the royal family, with other family members in key political and military posts.	The Gulf States: Bahrain, Kuwait, Oman, Qatar, Saudi Arabia, United Arab Emirates
Political parties	Rule by a single party, often combined with a strong president.	Communist states. Many African states in the post-independence era. Pre-invasion Iraq under the Ba'ath Party.
Presidents	A president dominates politics (and the media), keeping opponents off-guard and the opposition marginalized. Power may rest with the particular leader but is still exercised through the presidency.	Uzbekistan
Armed forces	Government by the military, often ruling through a junta comprising the leader of each branch of the forces.	Burma
Religious leaders	A rare form of rule in which religious leaders rule directly. Also known as theocracy.	Iran

allegiances which overcomes the public–private divide. As long as the clients are politically sound, their patrons will ignore shady behaviour, a fact which helps to explain why most authoritarian regimes are corrupt. Institutions are weak but pragmatic alliances are strong, providing the regime's glue.

The allocation of resources such as jobs, contracts and investment through private patronage leads to substantial misallocation of capital, a weak banking sector, reduced foreign investment and a sharp distinction between insiders and outsiders (King, 2007). But as long as rulers continue to control key economic commodities (such as oil), they can carry on purchasing political loyalty.

Third, the media are subject to close scrutiny. Communist and fascist states claimed they would use the mass media to build a new and improved human being, fully committed to the regime's objectives. Contemporary authoritarian rulers have more modest goals. They rest content with ensuring favourable media coverage for their own achievements; their opponents are criticized or ignored. Censorship is implemented by catch-all offences such as threatening the dignity and effectiveness of the state. It is notable that even as the Chinese Communist Party introduced market mechanisms to many parts of its economy, it did not privatize the mass media (Esarey, 2006).

So authoritarian politics is typically driven by fear and vulnerability. The result is a repertoire of control mechanisms in which politics comes before economics and obedience before initiative. Communication is opaque, trust is lacking, government spending is misused, corruption is endemic, laws are ignored and foreign investors are scared away. In many cases, the outcome is a static society, an underperforming economy and a cynical population. In the long run, such a configuration may be a poor recipe for regime stability. Still, as the English economist John Maynard Keynes said in 1923, 'this long run is a misleading guide to current affairs. In the long run, we are all dead'.

Brooker (2009, p. 273) notes that 'historically, dictatorships have shown much greater political variety and creativity than democracies'. Our discussion must therefore focus on this diversity Box 6.1 lists pure types; many contemporary authoritarian regimes are a mixture. For instance, an army general may take the post of president or the president may rule through a one-party system.

Personal despots

In its original meaning, a despot is any barbaric and arbitrary ruler who treats his subjects as little more than slaves. Here we are concerned with a distinctive if rare type of rule: personal despotism. The adjective 'personal' implies that the source of power is the leader himself, together with his family, loyalists and bodyguards. In a personal despotism, links to a wider ideology, social forces and an organized party are at most intermittent. The leader retains discretion in his decisions, a resource which he uses to keep his opponents off-guard. He also takes care to fill not only his own boots but also those of his entourage. The despot's rule is exercised through the leader himself, rather than through institutions. Thus personal despotism displays, in stark and extreme fashion, features found in many authoritarian regimes.

Although personal despots have been most common in Central America and Africa, the syndrome was originally labelled 'sultanism' by the nineteenth-century German sociologist Max Weber (1921/2, p. 231). This term was also preferred by Chehabi and Linz (1998) in their wide-ranging study of the phenomenon.

Personal despotism typically arose in small, post-colonial countries with agricultural economies, particularly during the few-questions-asked era of the Cold War. The dictatorships of Rafael Trujillo in the Dominican Republic (1930–61) and of François Duvalier in Haiti (1957–71) are archetypal cases, illustrating many standard characteristics.

In Dominica, Trujillo (known as The Goat) acquired power through a military coup in 1930. He established a brutal dictatorship, rationalized by an unsophisticated concoction of Catholic, anti-Haitian and nationalist myths. Coming from a poor background, Trujillo accumulated enormous wealth, treating the sugar plantations as his own property. Torture was common. Like many despots, Trujillo was concerned with status as much as wealth. His statue was everywhere; schoolchildren prayed daily for 'God, country and Trujillo'. As the despot's abilities declined with age, so the repression became more arbitrary, the economy more impoverished and the wealthy more resentful. His circle of supporters narrowed, eventually leading to his assassination with American encouragement in 1961 (Hartlyn, 1998).

The story of François 'Papa Doc' Duvalier in Haiti is fundamentally similar. Although Duvalier came to power through an election in 1957, his rule proved to be extraordinarily despotic and gruesome. He maintained a personal presidential guard and created the notorious Tontons Macoutes – the bogeymen – as an instrument of terror. Unpaid but exempt from prosecution, the members of this militia were in effect invited to prey upon the population. They did so. Again like Trujillo, Duvalier enriched himself and his family through corruption. If the government was short of money, Papa Doc would simply imprison a chosen businessman in the presidential palace until the victim signed a cheque. Duvalier achieved his ambition of retaining power until his death, in 1971, when he was succeeded by his son, Baby Doc (Girard, 2006).

Other cases of personal despotism include Fulgencio Batista (Cuba, 1933–58), Anastasio Somoza (Nicaragua, 1936–56), Ferdinand Marcos (Philippines, 1965–86) and Mobutu Sese Seko (Zaire, now the Democratic Republic of Congo,

1965–97). Some of these dictators sought, and for a period succeeded, in ensuring a family successor to their own rule. But the personal nature of such regimes, as well as the damage they inflict on the economy, works against the establishment of a dynasty. Indeed, the virtual dismantling of any government institutions can result eventually in a collapsed state. While the Cold War provided a hospitable environment for personal despots, the current international environment is less well-disposed to this crude form of authoritarian rule.

Monarchs

Ruling monarchies are a more common and stable form of rule than personal despotism. Where a succession procedure is accepted, monarchy can provide a stable framework for the exercise of traditional authority, in which the ruler shows paternalistic concern for his or her allegiant subjects. In liberal democracies, of course, monarchs survive only as figureheads but ruling royal families remain the governing force in the oil-rich Arab states of the Persian Gulf (Map 6.2). We will consider the Gulf state monarchies (Bahrain, Kuwait, Oman, Qatar, Saudi Arabia and the United Arab Emirates (UAE) in more detail. These Muslim countries are of course politically important, providing a source of oil, gas and terrorists.

Typically, a leading tribe established a privileged relationship with the colonial power and exploited this connection to secure control of the Western-style state created at independence. The tribe itself may be ancient but its position at the head of the state is relatively recent.

The Gulf states make few concessions to democracy. The constitution of Oman, issued by the Sultan in 1996, makes clear that the person of the Sultan 'is inviolable and must be respected and his orders must be obeyed'. Several kingdoms, notably Kuwait, have now established *majlis* (consultative assemblies) but this reform is unlikely to presage a transition to a constitutional monarchy (Herb, 2005). Beyond the Gulf, however, parliaments have made more ground in two other Arab monarchies: Jordan and Morocco.

In three ways, use of the term 'monarchy' to describe the traditional political systems found in the Gulf is imprecise. First, the titles taken by Arab

Map 6.2 The Gulf states

'monarchs' themselves reflect tribal or Islamic tradition: 'emir' (leader or commander), 'sheikh' (revered leader of the tribe) or 'sultan' (a leader who possesses authority). The United Arab Emirates, a federation of seven emirates, is called just that – not the United Arab Kingdom.

Second, the leading members of the ruling dynasty, rather than a single monarch, often exercise authority. Governance is by princes, rather than just the king; these countries are run by family businesses rather than sole traders.

Third, while the king typically designates a crown prince as his preferred successor, custom requires that a clan council meets after the monarch's death to confirm or indeed change this appointment. Herb (1999, p. 491) judges that this element of selection is the 'glue that holds the dynastic monarchies together', enabling them to continue across the generations in a manner which is difficult to achieve when (as with most European monarchies) succession is based on **primogeniture**.

Weber's notion of traditional rule captures the nature of authority in these male-dominated Arab dynasties. Authority is owed to the ruler himself rather than to a more abstract entity such as a state or party. The people are subjects as much as citizens,

> **Primogeniture** means inheritance by the first born, particularly by the eldest male. A monarchy based on this succession rule is exposed to the risk that the designated individual will not be up to the job.

and the ruler is constrained neither by law nor by competitive election. This authority flows from the historic authority of nomadic tribal leaders. For example, the Al Bu Said dynasty has ruled Oman for longer than the United States has existed as an independent country. An Omani feels to his rulers as an American would, had the USA been governed since its inception by the clan of Kennedy.

Because the ruler is expected to take responsibility for his people, the right of ordinary people to petition on individual matters is well-established. But the petitioner requests benevolent treatment, not the implementation of constitutional rights. The abstract idea of a state linking rulers and citizens is weak, as are such modern notions as constitutions, rights, interest groups, the separation of powers and the rule of law. Politics is based on intrigue at the palace, with little distinction between public and private sectors.

We can use Saudi Arabia – the heartland of the Arab and Islamic worlds and the state with the world's largest oil reserves – to illustrate monarchical governance. The country's political style reflects the influence of King Abdul Aziz Ibn Saud. He led the Saudi state from its inception in 1902 until his death in 1953. In true patrimonial style, Ibn Saud ran his kingdom as a gigantic personal household, using marriage as a vital political tactic. He took several hundred wives drawn from all the powerful families in the state, a stratagem which solidified his control.

Saudi Arabia's ruling royal family, led by an influential group of around 200 princes, still constitutes the core of government. The Basic Law promulgated in 1992 declared that Saudi Arabia is a monarchy ruled by the sons and grandsons of Ibn Saud. The crown prince, designated by the king, serves as the monarch's temporary successor when the king dies. Reflecting Bedouin tradition, a permanent replacement is then chosen through negotiation within the group. Family members occupy key positions on the Council of Ministers, serving in particular as a bridge between the government, the military and the active security forces. This large ruling family, itself

divided into factions, populates and controls the leading institutions of state, providing a form of collective leadership and a barrier against radical change.

Although Saudi's rulers have reacted firmly to the terrorist threat in their midst, the regime is more authoritarian than totalitarian. The ruling family does not monopolize wealth but leaves space for lower-tier families. There is some separation of political and religious authority: 'the Al Saud have provided the sword and the purse while the Al Sheikh, the descendants of the founder of Wahhabism, have traditionally handled the religious establishment' (Seznec, 2003, p. 77). A tradition of consultation allows the royal family to incorporate other families, as well as technical experts, within its framework of rule.

Political parties are still banned but some mechanisms of representation have emerged, adding an institutional veneer to what is still a traditional regime. The Basic Law of 1992, an innovation in itself, introduced a Consultative Council, with a non-princely and technocratic membership, to 'advise the King on issues of importance'. The Council is a strengthened form of a body which dates back to 1927 yet it remains at most a proto-parliament. The royal family, and the traditional rule it represents, remains pre-eminent; reform is slow and halting.

In Saudi Arabia, as elsewhere in the Middle East, ruling monarchies have proved to be resilient. Hadenius and Teorell (2007, p. 153) report that in this region there were 'no transitions from governing monarchies to democracy, 1972–2003'. Nor are there many reasons to expect such changes: traditions of personal, paternalistic and princely rule remain entrenched; reserves of oil continue to offer a cushion of wealth; and Islam is not easily reconciled with liberal democracy.

Political parties

Like most authoritarian rulers, personal despots and ruling monarchs are unconcerned with national transformation and often even with economic development. The twentieth century, however, witnessed the birth, ossification and disintegration of party-based dictatorships which monopolized public authority in the name of economic modernization, social transformation and national revival.

Communist parties were of course the main example but fascist and nationalist parties also used ideological commitments to justify their exclusive hold on power. For instance, at least 20 one-party regimes were established in post-independence African countries in the 1960s (Brooker, 2009, p. 106). Even today, the legacy of one-party rule, and especially communist party rule, remains significant. In this section, we will look at ruling communist parties, past and then present, before turning to the few contemporary non-communist cases of single party rule.

Communist parties

The onset of communist party rule came, of course, with the 1917 October Revolution in Russia. This chaotic coup signalled the international advent of a regime, an ideology and a revolutionary movement which sought to overthrow the capitalist democracies of the West. Initially, communist power expanded dramatically in Eastern Europe and Asia. The Union of Soviet Socialist Republics (USSR) – effectively a new Russian empire – was formed in 1924. After 1945, Eastern European countries such as Poland and Romania became satellite territories of this new empire. Communism spread beyond the USSR to encompass other countries, such as China, North Vietnam and Cuba (see Timeline). Until the decisive collapse of the communist order in the late 1980s and early 1990s, 23 regimes claiming Marxist inspiration ruled more than 1.5 billion people: about one in three of the world's population (Holmes, 1997, p. 4).

In his theoretical writings, Karl Marx (1818–83) had acknowledged that a temporary period of 'dictatorship of the proletariat' would be required after the revolution:

Between capitalist and communist society there lies the period of the revolutionary transformation of the one into the other. Corresponding to this is also a political transition period in which the state can be nothing but the revolutionary dictatorship of the proletariat. (Marx, 1875)

Practical revolutionaries quickly seized on this rather vague observation. In particular, the Russian revolutionary Vladimir Lenin (1870–1924) developed the notion of a **vanguard party**. Lenin's proposition was that communist parties possessed a deeper understanding of the true interests of the working class than did the workers themselves. Accordingly, the party must place itself in the vanguard of the communist movement, leading the phase of dictatorship while the workers' revolutionary consciousness matured under the party's tutelage. In this way, an ideology aimed at ending inequality was held to justify the creation of a new, if supposedly temporary, ruling party elite.

In power, of course, ruling communist parties dominated all sections of society, wholly contra-

> As propounded by Lenin, a **vanguard party** consists of full-time revolutionaries whose understanding of Marxist thinking enables them to escape ideological indoctrination from the old order and to raise the consciousness of the masses both before and after revolution. Without this lead, workers will only develop trade union consciousness.

dicting Marx's aspiration that society would come to prevail over the state. Lenin's view that the workers must be forced to be free simply resulted in no freedom whatever. Communist regimes were strongly authoritarian, brooking no opposition, stage-managing elections, acting above the law, rewriting constitutions, determining all major appointments to the government, controlling the media and spying on their populations. Article 6 of the 1977 Soviet constitution articulates the party's leading role:

The leading and guiding force of the Soviet society and the nucleus of its political system, of all state organizations and public organizations, is the Communist Party of the Soviet Union. The CPSU exists for the people and serves the people. The Communist Party, armed with Marxism-Leninism, determines the general perspectives of the development of society and the course of the home and foreign policy of the USSR, directs the great constructive work of the Soviet people, and imparts a planned, systematic and theoretically substantiated character to their struggle for the victory of communism.

COMMUNISM'S KEY DATES

1848	Publication of the *Communist Manifesto*.
1917	October Revolution in Russia.
1928	Soviet Union introduces its first five-year plan.
1933	Stalin acquires supreme power in the Soviet Union.
1946–9	Communist rule established in Eastern Europe.
1949	Communist rule established in China.
1953	Stalin dies.
1954	Communist rule recognized in North Vietnam.
1956	Khrushchev denounces Stalin and tells the West, 'History is on our side. We will bury you'.* Soviet Union suppresses Hungarian uprising.
1959	Communist rule established in Cuba.
1966	Mao Zedong launches Cultural Revolution in China.
1968	Soviet Union suppresses uprising ('Prague Spring') in Czechoslovakia.
1976	Communist rule established in a reunited Vietnam. Mao Zedong dies.
1978	Deng Xiaoping begins economic reform in China.
1985	Gorbachev becomes General Secretary of the Soviet Communist Party.
1988	Gorbachev abandons Brezhnev doctrine of maintaining communist rule by force.
1989	China violently suppresses pro-democracy protests in Tiananmen Square, Beijing.
1989–91	Communist rule ends in Eastern Europe.
1991	Soviet Union disbands. Soviet Communist Party outlawed.
2001	China joins World Trade Organization.
2008	China hosts the Olympics.

* This is the standard translation but Pearl (2003) suggests 'We will outlast you' is more accurate.

Under state socialism, the party controlled and the government implemented – hence the compound term 'party state'. This form of dictatorship was more extensive in its organization, and more effective in its penetration of society, than any other form of non-democratic rule. Originally attractive to at least some idealists, the party increasingly drew its membership from ambitious careerists and from those who thought it safer to be in the party than out.

Although communist party states grew less totalitarian as they matured, the result was simply stagnation. Communism reached its dead-end as the system rotted from within. As the party lost its mission, its language became wooden and predictable; in the end it ruled only because it ruled. When Mikhail Gorbachev became General Secretary of the Soviet Communist Party in 1985, his intention was modernization, but the outcome was dissolution. In Eastern Europe, communist rule fell apart in 1989 once the new Russian leader made clear that the USSR would no longer intervene militarily to protect the puppet rulers of its satellites. The following year, the Soviet Union itself dissolved into 15 constituent republics. In Russia, by far the most important of these republics, the Communist Party was quickly outlawed, a humiliating fate for what had been the most powerful party on earth (Brown, 2004).

But what of those authoritarian regimes which continue to sail under the command of the communist party? With the exception of the decaying regime in Cuba, the surviving communist governments are clustered in Asia, far from the democratic hub (Box 6.2). China, Vietnam and Laos were traditionally poor and agricultural societies in which communist rulers have, over the last three decades, loosened their control over the economy while retaining a firm grip on political power.

This reform strategy has delivered substantial if uneven growth, particularly in China and Vietnam. By unleashing entrepreneurial initiative, ruling parties have averted the inertia which led to the fall of communism in the Soviet Union and Eastern Europe. As a result, Asian communist parties can still expound the nationalist agenda of catch-up with the West and, partly for this reason, their position remains intact and indeed largely unchallenged. As its Marxist legacy fades, China continues to offer a model to the rest of the world of development without democratization.

Historically, China is the most importance case of Asian communism. However, communism in the People's Republic has always possessed distinct national characteristics. Power has certainly been exerted through the Chinese Communist Party (CCP) but the party itself has been controlled by elite factions which have demonstrated considerable flexibility, especially in embracing the language of nationalism rather than class. Park (1976, p. 148) goes so far as to judge that 'the success of Chinese communism lies primarily in its emphasis on nationalism'. The revolution itself was led by the People's Liberation Army as much as by the CCP, leading to Mao's famous observation that 'political power grows out of the barrel of a gun'.

Yet corruption, cronyism and cynicism remain endemic in the party. As a result of reform, China possesses not so much a market economy as a political economy in which party members, alongside local bureaucrats and army officers, are on the make alongside more conventional entrepreneurs. Commercial rationality in China is less focused on identifying market opportunities than on creating strong ties to local officials that will in turn guarantee those opportunities.

This reform ensemble has delivered partial industrialization which may prove to be more successful than the Soviet Union was in meeting the demands of an advanced economy and a well-educated population. Even so, the party leaders in Beijing face a long list of domestic challenges, including some arising from economic development itself. These difficulties include environmental degradation; increasing inequality between provinces and between individuals; massive population movements from the countryside; an unruly peasantry; urban unemployment; an ageing population; inadequate availability of medical care; inefficient allocation of capital; pervasive corruption; popular cynicism about the party; and, in 2009, slower economic growth.

The management of such problems is more likely to involve choices for party leaders from a menu which includes reform and repression but not democracy. Indeed, China's very success in entering the world economy has established the world's dependence on its goods, reducing international pressures for democratization.

BOX 6.2

Communist party states, 2009

	Official title	Communist rule established	Comment
China	People's Republic of China	1949	The Communist Party has retained tight political control while leading substantial and successful economic reform.
Cuba	Republic of Cuba	1961	A communist regime long run as a personal despotism by Fidel Castro. In 2008, Raúl Castro succeeded his elder brother as president, creating the possibility of political reform.
Laos	Lao People's Democratic Republic	1975	An impoverished country with a partly liberalized economy and an ageing party leadership.
North Korea	Democratic People's Republic of Korea	1948	A despotic regime, based on the 'Dear Leader' Kim Jong-il, son of the 'Great Leader' Kim Il-sung, and the military. Political reform may follow Kim Jong-il's exit.
Vietnam	Socialist Republic of Vietnam	1976*	As in China, the Communist Party has initiated economic reform while retaining a political monopoly.

* North Vietnam: 1954.

Other ruling parties

Occasionally, single ruling parties other than communist ones provide the basis for authoritarian rule. As Huntington (1970, p. 9) pointed out, 'unless it can guarantee a low level of political mobilization, an authoritarian regime may have little choice but to organize and develop a political party as an essential structural support'.

An organized party is especially important in authoritarian regimes permitting a measure of electoral competition; after all, even a controlled election needs a party to control it. In Mexico, the Partido Revolucionario Institucional performed this election-winning role until the country's democratic transition in 2000. In the Asian island state of Singapore, the People's Action Party continues to dominate elections. In authoritarian regimes as well as democracies, parties are an essential feature of rule in nearly all large, complex societies.

But we must distinguish here between the supports of power and power itself. Often, the party is the vehicle rather than the driver, with real authority resting with a dominant president, military ruler or political elite. Today we find only a limited number of authoritarian regimes in which a single non-communist party sustains its position as an effective wielder of power. More often, the supposed ruling party is an arena within which more coherent actors compete.

The post-independence experience of many sub-Saharan countries shows the weakness of many 'ruling' parties. After independence, African presidents soon suggested that a single party – their party – would be the best means of expressing and

COUNTRY PROFILE

COUNTRY PROFILE

CHINA

Form of government ■ communist party state.

Legislature ■ the large National People's Congress (almost 3,000 members chosen by provincial congresses and the armed forces) meets for only brief periods though its committees now make some contribution to national governance.

Executive ■ the State Council, headed by the premier, is the top executive body, supervising the work of the ministries. A president serves as ceremonial head of state.

Judiciary ■ China has been moving in the direction of rule by law but the judicial system remains a branch of the administration and is underdeveloped in comparison with any democracy. Extensive corruption.

Elections ■ Elections have been introduced to many of China's 930,000 villages since 1987 and, more recently and tentatively, to some townships. However, elected officials still operate under the party's supervision. Indirect election is usual at higher levels.

Parties ■ The Chinese Communist Party (CCP) remains the dominant political force.

Population (annual growth rate): 1,330m (+0.6%)
World Bank income group: lower middle
Political Rights score: ⑦
Civil Liberties score: ⑥
Human development index (rank/out of): 81/177
Freedom of the press index (rank/out of): 181/195
Perceived corruption index (rank/out of): 72/180

Note: For meaning and sources of scales and indexes, see p. xvi. In all cases a score and rank of 1 is 'best'.

THE PEOPLE'S REPUBLIC OF CHINA (PRC) has attracted considerable Western interest since its emergence at the start of the twenty-first century as a powerful force in the global economy. China's population is already the world's largest. Its increasingly open economy has grown tenfold since 1978 and on some measures is already the world's second largest; it may surpass that of the United States in the first half of the current century.

The country already employs around a quarter of the world's workers, with particular strengths in manufacturing and assembly. Its international competitiveness has created an enormous trade surplus with the USA, allowing China to overtake Japan as the world's largest holder of US government bonds. Although the primary role of China's industry has been to serve as a low-cost subcontractor to the West, increasing technological sophistication enables many of its producers to offer goods (if not services) of increased complexity and value.

The country's entry into the World Trade Organization in 2001 demonstrated its more outward-facing character, a trend confirmed by the successful and tightly organized Olympics held in Beijing in 2008. China's burgeoning industrialization required massive imports of raw materials, contributing to a global boom in commodity prices. Its policy-makers show little compunction in importing resources such as oil from other authoritarian regimes. Rapid expansion combined with sheer scale mean that China is a major contributor to climate change without possessing the capacity to lead a global response. In all these ways, the world is learning the wisdom of Napoleon's observation from 1803: 'China is a sickly, sleeping giant. But when she awakes the world will tremble' (Safire, 1993).

In understanding China, it is crucial to recognize its internal diversity. A massive, increasing and destabilizing gulf exists between city and countryside; coastal zones and the interior; party and people; rich and poor; the corrupt and the honest; and between winners and losers. These inequalities have led to enormous population flows from rural areas to the cities, creating tensions within both importing and exporting regions. Environmental problems apparent within the country itself include air pollution, especially in the cities; water shortages in the north; water pollution from untreated waste; deforestation; soil erosion and desertification. Thus far, China's cautious authoritarian rulers have ridden the country's transformation, and its effects, with both skill and difficulty. However, at the end of the first decade of the twenty-first century, the political implications of these internal difficulties still remain to be established.

Further reading: Dittmer and Liu (2006), Hutton (2006), Saich (2004).

SPOTLIGHT

Authoritarian rule in China

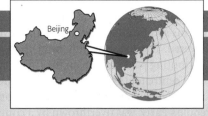

China's history differs fundamentally from that of the United States, where limits on central power were built into the republic, and from that of many Western European countries, where restraints on monarchical power were gradually imposed. China's political history is wholly non-democratic. Yet unlike the Soviet Union, the Chinese Communist Party (CCP) succeeded in jettisoning orthodox communist policies without destroying its own hold on power. As Dickson (2007, p. 828) notes, 'China has become a prime example of how authoritarian governments can employ strategic action to survive indefinitely despite rapid economic development'. So how has this trick been achieved?

The party devotes considerable energy to maintaining its monopoly position. Even with nearly 70 million members, the party remains an elite force, supervising the government, the justice system and the mass media. Belonging to the party involves a continuing commitment but, in exchange, membership provides access to the contacts, information and patronage needed to acquire power and wealth. Even in the absence of ideology, ambition still glues the party together.

As governance has stabilized, so the party has become somewhat less intrusive and more supervisory. This revised role has allowed some expansion in the role of other institutions. For example, the National People's Congress remains weak but its leaders have acquired a role in supporting reform. Similarly, the notion of a distinct legal sphere has begun to emerge. The immature judicial system still approves public executions but a measure of 'socialist legality' now prevails.

However, the media are still tightly controlled, with about 30,000 officials censoring Internet access for the country's 100 million or so users. Party members still occupy the key positions in all major political institutions, providing an additional mechanism of control.

In the wider political system, the crucial reform has been the reduction of central control from Beijing. In local communities, informal net-

'The continuing invocation of socialist values in an increasingly capitalist society has only deepened cynicism, allowing neither socialist nor capitalist values to gain a firm foothold' (Wang, 2002, p. 3).

works of power holders determine 'who gets rich first'. These collusive alliances are composed not just of well-placed men in the party but also of officials in the bureaucracy, local government and the army. Local officials can and do provide favoured businesses with contracts, land, favourable regulations, information, supplies, transport and other subsidies (Breslin, 2004).

So political and economic reform does not necessarily imply a shift towards a market economy operating within the rule of law. Currently, at least, reform empowers local elites to create a state-sponsored business class, whose members include public officials and party members. In this way, the new rich remain dependent on the political system and do not seek its transformation.

The loosening of central political control has led to an explosion of corruption. In the new environment, public employees are quick to recognize opportunities to earn extra money from their official position.

In one port city, a smuggling racket responsible for about 10 per cent of China's total gasoline imports included the deputy mayor, the head of customs and over 100 other officials, six of whom were sentenced to death after the scheme was uncovered (Gong, 2002).

Here, perhaps, is one of the party's major dilemmas: it can only attract members by offering opportunities to acquire resources but the dubious manner in which these are obtained increases the distance between party and society.

So, like China itself, the party faces considerable challenges in the years ahead. Its prospects must depend on its ability to maintain strong economic growth and an enhanced position for the country in the world order.

Further reading: Breslin (2004), Brodsgaard and Yongnian (2006).

encouraging national unity. But these one-party systems soon withered, if indeed they ever really flowered. They became little more than a vehicle for distributing patronage from the ruling ethnic group at the centre to its supporters in the regions. When Kwame Nkrumah, leader of Ghana's Convention People's Party, was overthrown by a coup in 1966, his party effectively disappeared with him. These one-party systems were far weaker than those in communist states.

Even when the single party does begin as an independent force, it can still be captured by a strong leader. In the Middle East, where parties in authoritarian regimes have generally retained more significance than in Africa, Iraq's Ba'ath party provides an example of this trajectory of decay. The Ba'ath began as a radical, secular, modernizing pan-Arab party with a strong, cellular organization. It provided the framework within which Saddam Hussein rose to power. But eventually Saddam stamped his authority on the party, building what became in part a personal despotism. His command was demonstrated at a party convention in 1979 when he read out the names of potential opponents and, as he did so, ordered each one to be taken out individually and shot. At the end of the meeting, in a speech given fulsome applause, the leader congratulated those remaining for their past and future loyalty.

Egypt is perhaps a more typical example of the rather passive role which a dominant party plays in non-communist authoritarian regimes. The National Democratic Party (NDP) forms part of an established, indeed ossified, structure of power based on a strong presidency and an extended bureaucracy. Within this framework, however, the NDP is the junior partner: 'the NDP has failed to serve as an effective means to recruit candidates into the elite. Rather, persons who are already successful tend to join the party in order to consolidate their positions' (Lesch, 2004, p. 600). With its close links to the state, the NDP is an arena for furthering political and business careers but not a major policy-making force. The Egyptian case thus confirms the value of distinguishing between actors and arenas. A 'dominant' party in an authoritarian state may simply be an arena within which particular elite groups express and perpetuate their control.

Presidents

We have already met several strong presidents in this chapter but their power has derived from a source external to the executive office: in a monarchy, the communist party or even the ruler's own family. But of course the office of president (or, less often, prime minister) can itself be the power base. Even if authority begins elsewhere, a president in an authoritarian system occupies a unique position, possessing a visibility which can be invested in an attempt to transfer the authority to his own post, typically by establishing a direct relationship through the media with the people he rules. When the presidential office has itself become the power base, we can speak of the presidential form of authoritarian rule.

True, a ruling presidency usually contains a strong element of personal rule. However, in contrast to a personal despotism, authority here remains based in a specific office which is likely to outlast the incumbent. The format is more institutional and thus better suited to larger and more complex societies.

The rapid concentration of powers in the president is a familiar process in Latin America, where it is known as an *autogolpe*. Typically, the president declares a state of emergency, removes the prohibition on re-election and extends his powers to govern by decree. In the Peruvian coup of 1992, President Alberto Fujimori suspended the constitution, the judiciary and Congress before introducing a new constitution (subsequently ratified by referendum) permitting his re-election. Fujimori did not lack popular support; indeed, he was re-elected in 1995 and 2000 but resigned later in 2000 following allegations of corruption (Carriûn, 2006). The fascist-influenced dictatorship established by President Getulio Vargas in Brazil in 1937 is another example of an *autogolpe*.

Although the concept of an *autogolpe* is Latin American in origin, examples can be found elsewhere, particularly if the notion is extended to include creeping centralization of power. Uzbekistan is a clear and significant case. The largest of the

An *autogolpe* (self-coup) is a 'coup launched by the chief executive himself in order to extend his control over the political system in some extra-constitutional way' (Farcau, 1994, p. 2).

central Asian republics, Uzbekistan formed part of the Soviet Union until the collapse of communism, becoming an independent state in 1991. The country's politics are dominated by Islam Karimov, a former First Secretary of the Uzbek Communist Party. In effect, the establishment of Karimov's dictatorship in Uzbekistan was a coup against the party he once led. In 1994, Karimov resigned from the communist successor party, claiming that only a non-partisan head of state could guarantee constitutional stability. By this route, he instituted a gradual change in the nature of authoritarian rule in his country: from a party-based to a presidency-based regime.

To forestall the emergence of opposition, Karimov regularly dismisses ministers and replaces regional leaders. He keeps tight control of the media, uses a traditional institution of local governance (the *mahalla*) as an instrument of social control, and also relies on the National Security Service for surveillance. Like other leaders of secular regimes in Islamic societies, Karimov has sought to prevent the mosque from becoming an explicit site of opposition. He has banned parties based on religion or ethnicity. The regime's nervousness about Islamic opposition was demonstrated by its indiscriminate massacre of hundreds of Muslim demonstrators at Andijan in 2005. Karimov also maintains an infamous gulag at Jaslyk, known as the prison-of-no-return, where a Muslim inmate was boiled to death (Khatchadourian, 2004).

Although there are elements of personal despotism in Karimov's rule, his power is primarily based on the presidency. Melvin (2000, p. 34) provides a summary:

As a result of the political change since independence, a system of one-man rule has been established in Uzbekistan. The President enjoys extensive powers including appointments and he resides at the pinnacle of a system of executive power that runs throughout the country and effectively subordinates all aspects of political life to its elements. The President takes all major, and many minor, decisions.

Armed forces

In the second half of the twentieth century, military government became an important form of authoritarian rule in Africa, Latin America and parts of Asia. In most cases the generals have now retreated to their barracks, and **military coups**, such as those in the West African states of Guinea and Mauritania in 2008, have once more become merely intermittent. Today, coups – when they occur – are more likely to be backed than to be fronted by the armed forces. However, a number of direct military governments do remain, including a particularly repressive regime in Burma.

A **military *coup d'état*** (or putsch) is a seizure of political power by the armed forces or sections thereof. Although the term conjures up images of a violent and unwelcome capture of power against civilian rulers, many coups replaced one military regime with another, involved little if any loss of life and were more or less invited by the previous rulers.

Although military governments shared the twentieth century with communist and fascist dictatorships, the contrasts between military and totalitarian rule are sharp. Most military coups came later in the century, between the 1960s and 1980s; more significantly they occurred in post-colonial countries where the state had not achieved the penetration found in Europe. Sub-Saharan Africa was the major arena, with 68 coups – including many counter-coups against existing military governments – between 1963 and 1987 (Magyar, 1992). While fascist and communist parties sought to exploit the power of the modern state, many military coups (especially in smaller African countries) were made possible precisely because the state remained simple and underdeveloped. An ambitious general just needed a few tanks, driven by a handful of discontented officers, to seize the presidential palace and the radio station.

Why did military coups cluster in these post-war decades? The Cold War was the key. During this period, the United States and the Soviet Union were more concerned with the global chessboard than with how client countries governed themselves. So ruling generals could survive through the political, economic and military backing of a superpower even though they might lack support in their own country.

The standard institutional form of a military regime is the junta (council), a small group made up of the leader of each branch of the armed forces. Within this structure, a strongman often emerges as a dominant figure. In Chile, for instance, following the coup of 1973, General Augusto Pinochet himself acted as chief executive within a classic four-man junta representing the army, navy, air force and national police. He soon reinforced his dominance, becoming the country's president in 1974 and remaining in post until 1990.

Many military rulers take civilian posts in this way, merging military and political authority. For example, Colonel Gadaffi seized power in a coup in Libya in 1969 but is now accepted as national leader – despite, in his case, occupying no official position whatever. Such transitions to a more civilian status may be real or just for presentation; in either case, the armed forces are likely to remain a significant political actor.

Just as military governments prospered during the Cold War, so too did they shrivel after its close. By the 1990s, ruling generals could no longer rely on their sponsoring superpower; instead, conditionality ruled the roost. Aid and technical assistance flowed to civilian regimes adopting democratic forms and offering at least some commitment to civil rights. In addition, many military regimes discovered that governance was a complex task for which an army background provided poor preparation; many ruling generals began to yearn for the simplicity of life in the barracks. The last Latin American generals were back in their quarters by 1993; coups since then have generally been short-lived affairs confined to smaller countries in the region (Figure 6.1).

What is the legacy of military rule for today's civilian leaders? The inheritance is far from uniform; the stronger the position of the military government when it leaves office, the better the deal it could negotiate for the post-authoritarian order. Nonetheless, Agüero (2004, p. 252) notes that 'in none of the countries considered [in post-military Latin America] were the patterns of previous periods of democratic rule simply reproduced in the new democracies'. Rather, many of the new regimes were characterized by ugly birth defects which continued to fester even as the new order matured.

The main problem was that long periods of army rule led to an interweaving of civilian and military power. In many Latin American countries, senior officers had become accustomed to such privileges

as guaranteed seats in the cabinet, a high level of military expenditure, sole control of the security agencies, personal profit from defence contracts, exemption from civilian justice and a formal role as guarantor of internal security. The ending of military government did not mean an end to these distortions. Indeed, some of these privileges were entrenched before military rulers could be persuaded to relinquish their occupancy of the state.

Chile illustrates the difficulties of full disengagement. Before returning power to civilians, General Pinochet ensured that a new constitution approved in 1980 secured military autonomy. The armed forces were granted exemption from prosecution in civilian courts, given guaranteed seats in the Senate and retained their status as guarantors of 'institutional order' and 'national security'. Similarly, Ecuador's armed forces were guaranteed 15 per cent of the country's oil revenues until 2010. Such conditional transitions, characteristic of Latin America, helped the shift to, but weakened the depth of, the post-military democracy. As the era of military rule retreats into history, some of these conditions are being unwound but they undoubtedly left a difficult bequest for new democracies.

In the contemporary world, Burma provides one of the few remaining examples of military government. This impoverished South East Asian country has experienced virtually continuous military rule since 1962 when General Ne Win established a presidential dictatorship pursuing a state-dominated policy of national self-reliance. When elections in 1990 were won by Aung San Suu Kyi's National League for Democracy, the military simply disregarded them. Since 1989, the regime has confined Aung San Suu Kyi to her house for long periods.

Elsewhere, military influence is exerted over what are at least nominally civilian regimes. In Pakistan, for instance, the army sees itself as the guardian of the national interest, defending the country against corrupt politicians. Four military regimes have ruled Pakistan since independence in 1947, though the current regime is civilian following the removal of General Pervez Musharraf from the presidential office in 2008.

Algeria provides a further example of strong military influence on civilian government: 'every state has an army but in Algeria the army has a state' (Harbi, quoted in Bellin, 2005, p. 26). The army, the

Figure 6.1 The ending of military rule in Latin America

state and the leading party comprise a powerful elite ('*les décideurs*', '*le pouvoir*') forged in the fierce nationalist struggle against the French. When the Islamic opposition to this elite won a landslide victory in elections in 1991, the army cancelled the results, installing a new five-member High State Council the following year. With the Islamic opposition subdued by force, the state may now be securing more autonomy as a new generation of military officers emerges with no memories of the liberation struggle.

Alternatively, the military can replace one civilian leader with another, rather than directly taking office itself. The crisis in Honduras in 2009 is a recent example. In the context of a dispute about revisions to the constitution, soldiers arrested President Manuel Zelaya (in his pyjamas) and removed him from the country. Roberto Micheletti, next in the presidential line of succession, was sworn in as president on the same day. Military intervention was less surgical than this description might imply; in addition to the leadership change, civil liberties were suspended and troops patrolled the streets. Nonetheless, these events fell short of a full-blown coup and this fact, in itself, reflects changed attitudes to direct military rule in and beyond Latin America.

Religious leaders

Government by religious leaders is our final, and the rarest, form of authoritarian rule. A religious society is one thing; a clerical government is quite another. Even Muslim countries typically separate religious and civil leadership within the context of an overall commitment to Islam. Indeed, in much of the Middle East, the mosque has become a source of opposition to authoritarian rulers; a divide which would not be possible if religious and civil leadership belonged in the same hands.

At least since the fall of the Taliban in Afghanistan, the Persian but non-Arab Islamic Republic of Iran stands alone as an example of a constitutional **theocracy**. Even here, rule by religious leaders (ayatollahs and mullahs) possesses limited legitimacy, especially among the young and educated. Public protests disputing the result of the 2009 presidential election confirmed not only popular disaffection but also divisions between reformers and hardliners within the ruling elite itself.

> **Theocracy** is government by religious leaders. In ancient Israel, for example, God's laws were expounded and applied by holy men. Although most Islamic countries separate religious and political roles, the regime established in Iran after the overthrow of the Shah in 1979 is a recent example of a theocracy.

Iran's theocracy was a child of the 1979 revolution, the last great insurrection of the twentieth century. In this revolution, Ayatollah Khomeini, a 76-year-old cleric committed to Islamic fundamentalism, overthrew the pro-Western Shah of Iran. The revolutionaries advocated a traditional Islamic republic free from foreign domination; 'neither East nor West' was the slogan (Martin, 2003). In power, the ayatollahs created a unique Islamic state in which they governed directly rather than under the oversight of secular rulers.

Iran's post-revolutionary constitution did incorporate a directly elected presidency and assembly. Yet real power still lies with the clerics, expressed in part through a 12-member Council of Guardians which certifies that all bills and candidates conform with Islamic law. In strictly enforcing traditional, male-dominated Islamic codes, the ayatollahs permeate society in a manner reminiscent of totalitarian regimes. The Interior Ministry still makes extensive use of informants while the state employs arbitrary arrests and even assassination as a form of control through terror.

As with many authoritarian regimes, Iran's rulers offer no clear direction on such practical maters as economic development, monetary policy and overseas trade (Chehabi, 2001). Unsurprisingly, therefore, rule by ayatollahs has failed to deliver economic growth, even in a country awash with oil revenues. Instead, the clerics have grown wealthy by establishing *bonyads* – tax-exempt 'charitable' trusts – for their own benefit. These foundations monopolize many sections of an inefficient, state-dominated economy. Since Khomeini's death in 1989, Iran's theocratic establishment has consisted of competing factions of middle-aged to elderly men exploiting the revolutionary heritage in a successful effort to acquire and retain power and wealth. Neither a strong party nor a royal family exists to impose direction on these elements (Keshavarzian, 2005).

Unsurprisingly in a country where the median age is just 26 years (compared to 37 in the USA), rule by this theocratic elite has intensified the generational divide. Well-educated young people, including many female graduates, chafe at the restrictions imposed by a hypocritical religious establishment. 'I write a weblog so that I can shout, cry and laugh, and do the things that they have taken away from me in Iran today', wrote Lolivashe in her blog in 2004 (Alavi, 2005). The young rely on the Internet, satellite television and mobile phones to circumvent official censorship, at some risk. To distance themselves from the regime, they follow Western icons such as Mariah Carey who have long lost credibility in the West itself. This affirmation of freedom is not necessarily rooted in a secular outlook; rather, it reflects opposition to the cultural repression imposed by a religious leadership which, in common with most authoritarian rulers, lacks a positive vision for the country's future.

Learning Resources for Chapter 6

Next step

Brooker (2009) is a wide-ranging source on authoritarian regimes.

Further reading

Linz (1975) is an influential and insightful guide to authoritarian rule, while Palmer (2003) adopts a more practical approach, as shown by his title, *Breaking the Real Axis of Evil: How to Oust the World's Last Dictators by 2025*. For twentieth-century authoritarianism specifically, see Perlmutter (1981, 1997). Chebabi and Linz (1998) examine personal despotisms. For military disengagement, consider Howe (2001) for Africa, Cottey *et al.* (2003) for Eastern Europe and Silva (2001) for Latin America. Posusney and Angrist (2005) provide an excellent collection on authoritarian persistence in the Middle East. On China, Saich (2004) is a thorough guide. For authoritarian legacies, see Hite and Cesarini (2004) on Latin America and Elster *et al.* (1998) on post-communist states.

Internet sources

The Central People's Government of the People's Republic of China
The Chinese government's website
http://english.gov.cn

Dictator of the Month
A rogue's gallery
http://www.dictatorofthemonth.com/English/English_welcome.htm

Marxists Internet Archive
Background on Marxist thinking
http://www.marxists.org/

Transparency International
Focuses on corruption, which inevitably overlaps with authoritarian rule
http://www.transparency.org/

Part III
POLITICAL MOBILIZATION

In this part we examine the mechanisms through which society influences government and people are drawn into the political process. We begin in Chapter 7 with political culture, where we examine the values that people bring to their engagement with politics. Chapter 8 discusses the role of communication in politics, while Chapter 9 examines how, and to what extent, citizens participate in non-electoral politics. The remaining chapters in this part examine specific devices through which society, or elements within it, influence the political process: elections and voters (Chapter 10), political parties (Chapter 11) and interest groups (Chapter 12).

This part will enable you to:

- Understand the roles of political culture and communication in politics;
- Appreciate how people participate (if at all) in politics;
- Become aware of the significance of elections, parties and interest groups as links between society and government.

Chapter 7
Political culture

Culture is defined by UNESCO (2002) as 'the set of distinctive spiritual . . . intellectual and emotional features of society or a social group. It encompasses, in addition to art and literature, lifestyles, ways of living together, value systems, traditions and beliefs'. In other words, culture is the essential human characteristic, expressing our nature as aware social beings. Unlike nature (with which it is often contrasted), culture involves values, symbols, meanings and expectations. It tells us who we are, what is important to us and how we should behave.

While we can usually identify major themes in a nation's political culture, we must also recognize that any large country will contain a number of culturally distinctive social groups within it. The result may be either a national culture with one or more subcultures or even a multicultural society. At any rate, cultures do not always map accurately on to countries.

A definition of **political culture** flows easily from this account of 'culture'. The term refers to the overall pattern of beliefs, attitudes and values in a society towards the political system. The concept can be usefully compared with political ideology. Political culture is a broader, more diffuse but also more widely applicable notion. Where an ideology refers to an explicit system of ideas, political culture comes closer to Linz's notion of mentalities: 'ways of thinking and feeling, more emotional than rational, that provide non-codified ways of reacting to different situations' (Linz, 1975, p. 162). With the decay of ideology, political culture offers a potentially major highway into understanding the role of beliefs and attitudes in politics.

It is possible to view political culture not as an aspect of politics but as an entire approach to political science (Ross, 2009). In this respect, political culture links to the interpretive approach discussed in Chapter 2, though much of the research reviewed in this chapter is in fact conducted within a behavioural framework. At any rate, we can clearly contrast cultural analysis with the structural approach examined in Chapter 2. Where an emphasis on structure entails a concern with underlying, objective interests as a political force, a cultural approach emphasizes the importance of values and the symbolic meaning of political behaviour.

> **Political culture** denotes 'the sum of the fundamental values, sentiments and knowledge that give form and substance to political processes' (Pye, 1995, p. 965). It can be understood as either the sum of individuals' attitudes or as an attribute – the culture – of a group which gives shared meaning to political action.

Studying political culture

Political culture has a natural appeal for comparativists. Studying and especially visiting another country for the first time, we are naturally drawn to the differences between its own culture and our own. Furthermore, Gabriel Almond, the father of modern studies of political culture, claimed that the sentiments and mentalities we observe can be an independent force in political life: 'political values, feelings and beliefs are not simple reflections of social and political structure … the political content of the minds of citizens and political elites is more complex, more persistent and more autonomous than Marxism and liberalism would suggest' (1993, p. 14).

Yet it is dangerously, even seductively, easy to use cultural contrasts as an explanation for political differences. For one thing, culture can influence how the political game is played – the rituals, the moves, the language – without necessarily affecting the content of politics. Group and class conflict may underpin politics in two countries even though the manner of their expression in each local culture differs.

In addition, the dominant culture – as expressed in the national media to which the visitor is exposed – may reflect only the values of the political elite. The powerful naturally seek to validate inequalities of power; the wealthy always seek to legitimize the economic system from which they benefit. Underlying this dominant discourse, but less visible to the superficial observer, we often find layers of cynicism and opposition to the pre-eminent culture.

Thus, commenting on the class structure of nineteenth-century England, Marx's collaborator Friedrich Engels (1820–95) felt that the workers had become a 'race wholly apart' from the business owners who employed them:

The workers speak other dialects, have other thoughts and ideas, other customs and moral principles, a different religion and other politics from those of the bourgeoisie. Thus there are two radically dissimilar nations, as unlike as differences of race could make them. (Engels, 1844, p. 124)

We can illustrate these points by considering Almond and Verba's classic study, *The Civic Culture* (1963). In this book, the authors sought to identify the political culture within which a liberal democracy is most likely to develop and consolidate. Their landmark investigation became a political science equivalent of Weber's attempt (1905) to discover the cultural source of modern capitalism. Where Weber located the spirit of capitalism in protestant values, Almond and Verba found the source of stable democracy in what they called a **civic culture**.

> In a **civic culture**, many citizens are active in politics but a passive minority serves to stabilize the system, preventing it from overheating. Further, participants are not so involved as to refuse to accept decisions with which they disagree. Thus the civic culture resolves the tension within democracy between popular control and effective governance: it allows for citizen influence while retaining flexibility for the government.

In thinking about liberal democracy, it is easy to assume that people with participant attitudes form the model citizen army of a stable system. Nearly everyone imagines that a healthy political system is one whose citizens believe they can contribute to, and are affected by, government decisions. But the interest of Almond and Verba's study rested precisely in its rejection of such a proposition. The authors proposed that democracy will prove most stable in societies blending different cultures in a particular mix they term the 'civic culture'. The ideal conditions for democracy, they suggested, emerge when attitudes leading to low levels of participation provide ballast for an essentially participant culture.

Armed with this theory, Almond and Verba set out to discover which countries in their study came closest to their conception of a civic culture. In 1959 and 1960 they conducted sample surveys in the USA, Britain, Italy, Mexico and West Germany. Their research method presumed a view of political culture as the sum of individual attitudes within each nation. Of the countries surveyed, Britain and to a lesser extent the United States came closest to the civic ideal. In both these states citizens felt they could influence the government but often chose not to do so, thus conferring on the government its required agility. By contrast, the political cultures of

Italy, Mexico and West Germany all deviated in various ways from the authors' prescription.

Like most original work, Almond and Verba's study attracted considerable scrutiny (Barry, 1988). Two criticisms, in particular, highlighted the limitations of the concept of political culture itself. First, critics alleged that the whole notion of a national political culture was inherently vague and that the authors should have focused more on subcultures of race and class. Had they done so, suggests Macpherson (1977, p. 88), they would have discovered that the participants are the educated middle class while the poorly educated working class is less engaged with formal politics. These critics claimed that the civic culture was simply a sanitized reformulation of class rule.

Second, critics pointed out that Almond and Verba failed to offer a detailed account of the origins and evolution of political culture. Rather, political culture was taken as a given, raising the suspicion that the concept is little more than a sophisticated restatement of simplistic assumptions about national character. In addition, the authors initially had little to say about the evolution of political culture over time, a theme which – as we shall see – characterized much later discussion in this area, not least in Germany. Underlying these criticisms, then, is the notion that a country's political culture should not be seen as fixed and stable but rather should be regarded as a dynamic entity which is at least partly shaped by the operation of politics itself. As we will see in the next section, this position has been confirmed by later research.

Political trust and social capital

Times move on. In the half century following Almond and Verba's study, many established democracies hit turbulent waters: Vietnam and student activism in the 1960s, the oil crisis of the 1970s, the anti-nuclear and ecology movements of the 1980s, privatization and cutbacks to the welfare state in the 1990s and terrorism in the 2000s.

As Almond and Verba (1980) noted in an update to their original study, such events left their mark on Western political cultures. More recent research in the area has therefore focused on whether liberal democracies have suffered a decline in political and social trust. And the answer, in general, is that they have, although the fall focuses on the public's confidence in the performance of democratic institutions rather than in the principle of democracy itself.

In a comparative study, Norris (1999a, p. 20) concluded that overall public confidence in such institutions as parliament, the civil service and the armed forces declined between 1981 and 1991 in each of the 17 countries she examined. Just as worrying, other surveys show that European publics place less trust in agencies of representation such as parties than in the forces of law and order, such as the military and police (Inoguchi, 2002). Yet although electors have grown somewhat cynical about the operation of democracy, support for the underlying principle remains widespread even among today's disillusioned democrats. Democratic values command widespread acceptance within liberal democracies as an ideal, but at the same time citizens have become more critical of the workings of the core institutions of representative democracy.

The United States dramatically illustrates the decline of trust in government. In 1964, three-quarters of Americans said that they trusted the federal government 'to do the right thing'; by 1994, at the bottom of the cycle, only a quarter did so (Figure 7.1). Much of this decline was brought about by specific events such as the Vietnam War and Watergate, with partial recoveries during periods of peace and prosperity. Thus, trust recovered somewhat as the economy and stock market boomed in the late 1990s. Despite the intelligence failings exposed by 9/11, Americans rallied round the flag following the attacks; faith in government received a boost (Brewer et al., 2003). But this effect was short term. By 2007, trust in national government had fallen back, remaining far below the levels recorded in the late 1950s when Almond and Verba issued their broadly positive appraisal of America's civic culture. This responsiveness to events shows the danger of generalizing about a country's political culture on the basis of a single survey.

The long-term trend on political trust slopes downwards in other democracies too. In the UK, the proportion of people saying they would 'trust a British government of any party to place the needs of this country above the interests of their own

Figure 7.1 Americans' trust in the government in Washington, 1964–2007

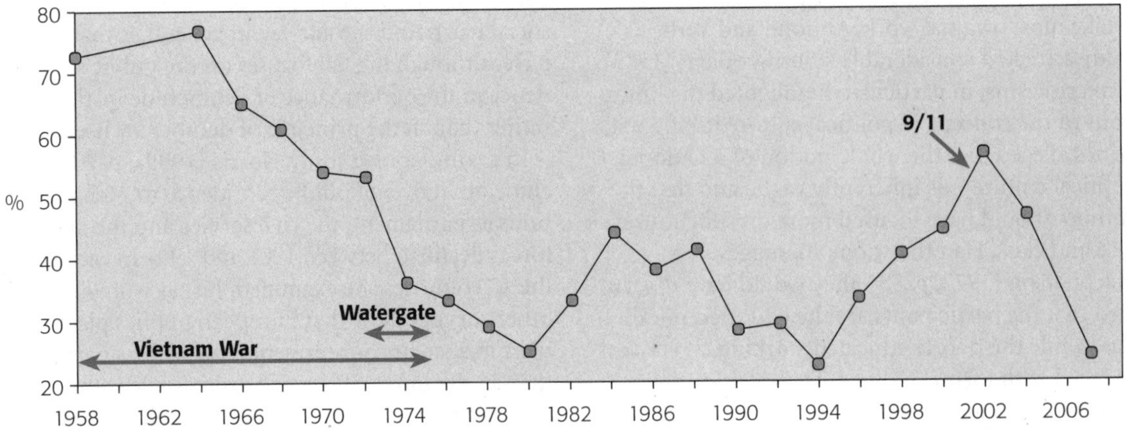

Note: Per cent trusting 'the government in Washington to do what is right' just about always or most of the time.

Sources: American National Election Studies (2009); Mackenzie and Labiner (2002); McKay (2009), Figure 12.1, citing a CBS/New York Times poll, 2007 (which may not be directly comparable with earlier results).

political party' halved from 38 per cent in 1986 to a low point of 16 per cent in 2000 before recovering somewhat to 29 per cent in 2007 (BSA, 2009). So since Almond and Verba's study both the American and the British 'civic' cultures have witnessed a shift towards more sceptical and instrumental attitudes but without threatening the survival of liberal democracy itself.

Are there other, more subtle consequences of falling confidence in political institutions? Putnam (2002) answers in the affirmative. He suggests that declining faith in government represents a deflation of the political culture, reducing the capacity of the political system to achieve shared goals. The argument here is that trust encourages solidarity among strangers. For example, as trust in government falls, so we might expect people to become less willing to: believe what their leaders say; vote at elections; fight in wars; and support any public projects in which they do not see a sure return for themselves (Hetherington, 2004).

By contrast, a culture of trust oils the wheels of collective action, enabling projects to be initiated which are impractical in a society where mutual suspicion prevails. It is ironic, suggest Putnam and Gross (2002, p. 1), that 'just at the moment of liberal democracy's greatest triumph, some fundamental social and cultural conditions for effective democracy may have

eroded in recent decades, the result of a gradual but widespread process of civic disengagement'.

In an influential study using Italy as his laboratory, Putnam (1993) attempted to test these ideas by showing how a supportive political culture directly enhances the performance of a political system. In their original work, Almond and Verba had portrayed Italy as a country whose people felt uninvolved in, and alienated from, politics. The culture was distinctly uncivic, lacking positive and supportive attitudes among the majority.

Putnam revisits Italy's political culture, paying more attention to diversity within the country. He demonstrates how cultural variations within Italy influenced the effectiveness of the 20 new regional governments created in the 1970s. Similar in structure and formal powers, these governments nonetheless varied greatly in performance. Some (such as Emilia-Romagna in the North) proved stable and effective, capable of making and implementing innovative policies. Others (such as Calabria in the South) achieved little. What, asks Putnam, explains these contrasts?

He finds his answer in political culture. He argues that the most successful regions have a positive political culture: a tradition of trust and cooperation which results in high levels of **social capital.** By contrast, the least effective governments are found in

> **Social capital** refers to a culture of trust and cooperation which makes collective action possible and effective. As Putnam (2002) writes, it is the ability of a community to 'develop the "I" into the "we"'. A political culture with a fund of social capital enables a community to build political institutions capable of solving collective problems.

regions lacking any tradition of collaboration and equality. In such circumstances, supplies of social capital run low and governments can achieve little. National studies, such as Almond and Verba's, are insufficiently sensitive to these regional contrasts.

But where does social capital itself come from? How does a region establish a foundation of mutual trust? Putnam's answer is historical: he attributes the uneven distribution of social capital in modern Italy to events deep within each area's history (Morlino, 1995). The more effective governments in the north draw on a tradition of communal self-government dating from the twelfth century. The least successful administrations in the south are burdened with a long history of feudal, foreign, bureaucratic and authoritarian rule. Thus, Putnam's analysis illustrates how political culture can be a device through which the past influences the present. Although his interest in rebuilding trust might prompt him to disagree, the implication seems to be that social capital is an inherited trait. It cannot be made to order.

Generational analysis and postmaterialism

The concept of political culture has been criticized for its static quality. Sometimes, indeed, a nation's culture is presented as a never-changing constraint on the operation of its government. Sensitive to this comment, some advocates of the cultural approach have sought to address changes in political culture through the analysis of **political generations**.

The idea here is that each generation has the potential to develop a perspective on politics which distinguishes it from both the one before and the

> A **political generation** is an age cohort sharing distinctive experiences and values which shape its outlook throughout its life course.

one afterwards. Typically, this distinctive outlook reflects the formative experience of the generation as it matures. For example, growing up in an environment of war or depression colours political attitudes in a manner that persists throughout life.

In other cases, values may shift across generations in a more gradual fashion, producing the slow-moving causes discussed in Chapter 3. Thus, each new cohort may show greater sympathy for causes such as gay rights or environmental protection. Through generational turnover, a political culture can be slowly transformed without any single person changing their opinion – a point often ignored in analysis of cultural change.

In studying political generations, life-cycle or ageing effects must be incorporated. As a generation ages, its values will inevitably adjust (becoming more conservative, for instance), so any differences between generations can only be identified by comparing two or more generations at the same life stage (Figure 7.2, p. 128). So the fact that the young are more left wing than the old at a particular time does not demonstrate a generational divide. This difference may reflect a life-cycle effect; it is entirely possible that a cohort of elderly conservatives might in its youth have been more left wing than the new radicals coming up behind. The lesson is that capturing a generational divide requires long-term data enabling like to be compared with like.

One factor which has been measured over a long period, and which illustrates how political scientists have sought to incorporate change into their understanding of political culture, is **postmaterialism**. As well as providing an example of political generations, this concept also addresses the nature of political values in affluent democracies – both now and in the future.

From the late 1940s to the early 1970s, the Western world witnessed a period of unprecedented economic growth. 'You've never had it so good' became a cliché

> **Postmaterialism** is a commitment to radical quality of life issues (such as the environment) which can emerge, especially among the educated young, from a foundation of personal security and material affluence. Postmaterialists participate extensively in politics but are inclined to join elite-challenging promotional groups rather than traditional political parties.

COUNTRY PROFILE

GERMANY

Form of government ■ a constitutional and parliamentary federal republic.

Legislature ■ the 622-member Bundestag is the lower house. The smaller upper house, the Bundesrat, represents the 16 federal *Länder* (states).

Executive ■ the chancellor leads a cabinet of between 16 and 22 ministers. A president serves as ceremonial head of state.

Constitution and judiciary ■ Germany is a state based on law (a *Rechtsstaat*). The Federal Constitutional Court has proved to be highly influential as an arbiter of the constitution and as an international model of a constitutional (rather than an American-style supreme) court.

Electoral system ■ the Bundestag is elected through the influential mixed member proportional system which has now been adopted in over 20 countries. Members of the Bundesrat are nominated by the *Länder*; hence, the Bundesrat is never dissolved.

Party system ■ the leading parties are the SPD (Social Democratic Party) and the CDU (Christian Democratic Union). Other significant parties are the Greens, the liberal FDP (Free Democratic Party) and The Left party. A CDU/FDP coalition has been in power since 2009.

Population (annual growth rate): 82.3m (-0.1%)	
World Bank income group: high income	
Political Rights score: ❶	
Civil Liberties score: ❶	
Human development index (rank/out of): 22/177	
Freedom of the press index (rank/out of): 17/195	
Perceived corruption index (rank/out of): 14/180	

Note: For meaning and sources of scales and indexes, see p. xvi. In all cases a score and rank of 1 is 'best'.

Among all the European liberal democracies, **GERMANY** has experienced the most fragmented history. Although a German-speaking people has existed since time immemorial, Germany did not become a single entity until the formation of the German 'Empire' in 1871. Since then, the country's boundaries have been subject to frequent change, with losses of territory at the end of both world wars and a division of the remaining core into separate communist and democratic states in 1949. Germany was not reunited until 1990 when the communist east was successfully absorbed into the Federal Republic.

Aware of its difficult history, Germany has been a motor for a united Europe in the post-war period. Its European commitment is entrenched in its consti-

tution. For most of its existence (if less so now) the Federal Republic has been willing to support the EU with hard cash, to the detriment of its own budget. Because Germany naturally views European developments through the lens of its own system of government, the country's political institutions are of continental significance.

Seeking to avoid the political instability of the Weimar Republic, which had contributed to the Nazi seizure of power, the framers of the post-war constitution made the chancellor the key figure in the new republic. The chancellor determines government policy, appoints cabinet ministers, heads a staff of 500 and can be removed from office only when the Bundestag simultaneously demonstrates a majority for a named

successor. Within a parliamentary framework, Germany offers a distinctive form of 'chancellor democracy'.

Germany boasts the largest economy in Europe and the fifth largest in the world. Its skilled employees, working in capital-intensive factories, produce manufactured goods for export at premium prices. Germany is the world's largest exporter, ahead of the United States, China and Japan. By the late 1990s, however, the post-war German miracle had begun to fade. As the costs of reunification mounted, unemployment grew in the west while becoming entrenched in much of the east. Modest reforms increased the flexibility of the labour market without exempting the economy from the global recession which emerged in 2008.

Further reading: Conradt (2008), Helms (2000).

Political culture in Germany

As well as studying the impact of political culture on government, it may be just as fruitful to examine how regimes affect values. Here the post-war division of Germany provides a rare natural experiment, allowing us to gauge how the contrasting structures of government in the capitalist west and communist east affected popular thinking. Did political cultures diverge under these regimes and converge after reunification?

Three main processes can be observed. The first is the positive impact of post-war economic recovery on political culture within the west. Between 1959 and 1988 the proportion of Germans in West Germany expressing pride in their political institutions increased from 7 to 51 per cent. Over a similar period, support for a multiparty system grew from 53 to 92 per cent. The emergence of a supportive public over this period certainly offers hope to other transitional countries seeking to build a democratic culture on an authoritarian history. Post-war West Germany shows how economic growth can deliver political legitimacy.

The second process is the impact of the communist German Democratic Republic (GDR) on political culture. Just after reunification, people in the east were significantly less trusting of parliament, the legal system and indeed each other than were people in western Germany. In 1991, for

example, Germans who had lived in the east were 11 percentage points less trusting in these respects. The experience of living under a communist regime, and particularly one which engaged in such extraordinarily close surveillance of the population, had left its mark (Rainer and Siedler, 2006).

The third process is the impact of reunification on political culture in the former GDR. Here, there is strong evidence of declining contrasts between east and west. Trust in parliament and the legal system increased dramatically in the east following the transition to a democracy. Among those in the east who have not experienced unemployment,

uniform but varies with their success in coping with a market economy.

Broader cultural contrasts (and stereotypes) between east and west remain significant. Even in the decades after reunification, easterners and westerners remain, like Britons and Americans, divided by a common language. 'Ossis' tend to perceive 'Wessis' as bourgeois, patronizing, materialistic and individualistic. Conversely, many westerners seem to look down on east Germans – and certainly are perceived to do so by easterners themselves.

Overall, however, the natural experiment provided by post-war Germany shows that a country's political

Ostalgie, nostalgia for the German Democratic Republic, was a German cultural phenomenon of the early 2000s. It mocked Western seriousness by presenting a rose-tinted but also self-deprecating image of life in the communist East, focusing on such GDR icons as:

- *Ampelmännchen*: the little man on the traffic light;
- *Trabant cars*: highly polluting, highly unreliable;
- *Vita Cola*: communism's answer to Coca-Cola.

trust in other people is also converging towards western levels. However, among the substantial number of easterners who have experienced unemployment since reunification, social trust seems to have declined rather than increased. Thus, the cultural reaction of east Germans to living in a liberal democracy is not

culture is not a constant but rather is continually influenced by political and economic developments.

Further reading: Berg-Schlosser and Rytlewski (1993), Kolinsky (2002), Rainer and Siedler (2006).

Figure 7.2 Political generations

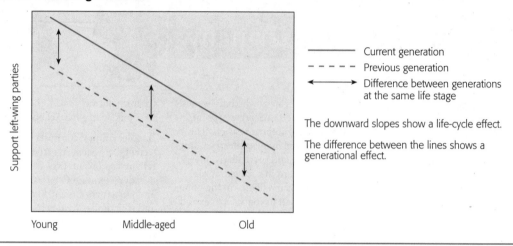

The downward slopes show a life-cycle effect.

The difference between the lines shows a generational effect.

that summarized the experience of the post-war generation. This era was also a period of relative international peace, enabling cohorts to grow up with no experience of world war. In addition, the newly instituted welfare state (and increasing property prices in some countries) offered increased security to many Western populations against the demands of illness, unemployment and old age.

According to Inglehart (1971), this unique combination of affluence, peace and security led to a silent revolution in Western political cultures. He suggests that the priority accorded to economic achievement made way for increased emphasis on the quality of life: 'in a major part of the world, the disciplined, self-denying and achievement-oriented norms of industrial society are giving way to the choices over lifestyle which characterize post-industrial economies' (Inglehart, 1997, p, 28).

From the 1960s, a new generation of postmaterialists emerged: young, well-educated people focused on lifestyle issues such as ecology, nuclear disarmament and feminism. Where pre-war generations had valued order, security and fixed rules in such areas as religion and sexual morality, postmaterialists gave priority to self-expression and flexible rules, for themselves if not always for their own children. Postmaterialists were elite-challenging advocates of the new politics rather than elite-sustaining foot soldiers in the old party battles. They were more attracted to single-issue groups than to the broader packages offered by political parties.

Based on extensive survey evidence, Inglehart showed that the more affluent a democracy, the higher the proportion of postmaterialists within its borders. The United States was in the vanguard. In the early 1970s, American postmaterialists were concentrated among 'yuppies' – young, upwardly mobile, urban professionals, especially those in the wealthiest state of all, California. Three decades later, this affluent generation retains a relatively progressive outlook, suggesting a genuine generational effect.

In Europe postmaterialism came first to, and made deepest inroads in, the wealthiest democracies such as Denmark, the Netherlands and West Germany. Norway apart, the affluent Scandinavian countries also proved receptive to these values (Knutsen, 1996). Postmaterialism was less common in poorer European democracies with lower levels of education, such as Greece.

Assuming a generational effect, postmaterial values will become more prominent. When Inglehart began his studies in 1970–71, materialists out-numbered postmaterialists by about four to one in many Western countries. By 2000 the two groups were much more even in size, a major transformation in political culture. Even allowing for some decay of radicalism with age, generational replacement will continue to work its effect. As Inglehart (1999, p. 247) notes, 'as the younger birth cohorts replace the older more materialist cohorts, we should observe a shift towards the postmaterial orientation'.

The unerring expansion of education gives postmaterialism a further boost. Experience of higher

▶ **TIMELINE**

GERMANY

1871	Germany is united under the leadership of the Prussian Chancellor, Otto von Bismarck.
1919	Treaty of Versailles imposes harsh conditions on Germany following its defeat in the First World War.
	The Weimar Republic, Germany's first experience with a fully democratic regime, is established.
1923	Hyperinflation begins. At its peak, prices double every 48 hours.
1931	Unemployment reaches six million. About one in two families are directly affected.
1933	Adolf Hitler is appointed Chancellor and institutes the Third Reich.
1941	Initiation of the holocaust in which at least five million Jews are killed.
1945	Allies occupy Germany as the Third Reich collapses.
1949	The Federal Republic of Germany (FDR, West Germany) is established in the Western-occupied zone.
	The German Democratic Republic (GDR, East Germany) is established in the Soviet-occupied zone.
1990	Germany is reunited following the collapse of the GDR.
1999	The German capital moves from Bonn, in the west, to Berlin.
2005	The CDU and SPD form a grand coalition under Angela Merkel (CDU).
2009	The CDU and the liberal Free Democrats form a coalition.

education is the best single predictor of a postmaterial outlook. Indeed postmaterialism can probably be best understood as the liberal outlook induced by degree-level education, especially in the arts and social sciences. These liberal values are then sustained through careers in expanding professions where knowledge rather than capital or management authority is the key to success (Farnen and Meloen, 2000). The never-ending march of higher education may be the key sociological underpinning of postmaterialism, leading to a gradual change in the population's values as poorly educated older people are replaced by younger generations of graduates.

Although postmaterialism is normally interpreted as a generational value shift among the general public, its most important political effects may be through elite values. Inglehart's shock troops have moved into (and in some cases already out of) positions of power, securing a platform from which their values can directly affect government decisions. For instance, the 1960s generation retained touches of radicalism even as it secured the seductive trappings of office. Thus, Bill Clinton (born 1946, the first president to be born after the war) offered a more liberal agenda to the American people than did his predecessor in the White House, George Bush (born 1924). These two men represented different generations as much as different parties. A similar claim can be made about Britain by comparing Tony Blair (born 1953) with his predecessor John Major (born 1943).

However, the later political successes of conservative leaders such as George W. Bush (born, like

Clinton, in 1946) and Angela Merkel (born even more recently, in 1954) reminds us that postmaterialism will not carry all before it. Even if the diffusion of postmaterialism continues, this advance certainly does not rule out periods of conservative ascendancy. After all, the distinctive challenges of the twenty-first century include security issues such as terrorism, energy supply, global warming and pensions. These issues threaten individual security and also possess a clear collective dimension. In short, issues force themselves on to the political agenda with a force that overwhelms gradual cultural change across generations.

Political culture in authoritarian states

In the mature democracies of the West, a supportive political culture still offers broad encouragement to those charged with the task of ruling. By contrast, authoritarian rulers face characteristic problems arising from their unwillingness to confront the challenge of the ballot box. Lacking the legitimacy flowing from free election, such rulers must find other ways of responding to the political culture of the societies they govern. Broadly speaking, their options are threefold: to ignore, exploit or seek to reconstruct the existing political culture.

The first option, ignoring political culture, is exemplified by many military regimes. Most generals rode to power on a tank and showed little concern for the niceties of political culture. Their task was to protect their own back against challengers seeking to supplant them. Far from seeking to draw support from the wider culture, military rulers typically sought to isolate the mass population from engagement with government, thus shrinking the political arena. 'We rule because we rule' remains the implicit message of many a military regime.

The second option, exploiting political culture, is much more common. As with democratic rulers, authoritarian leaders seek to emphasize those aspects of the culture that support their hold on power. In many Islamic countries, political leaders can present democracy as an alien Western concept which in practice leads to licence rather than freedom; to an emphasis on material rather than spiritual values; and to the pursuit of individual self-interest rather than social harmony. For example, Mahathir bin Mohamad, Prime Minister of Malaysia, 1981–2003, condemned Western democracies in which 'political leaders are afraid to do what is right, where the people and their leaders live in fear of the free media which they so loudly proclaim as inviolable'. In this way, authoritarian rule can be presented as an indigenous cultural tradition opposed to Western liberalism. Religion, then, continues to be a strong cultural force which can be used in defence of authoritarian rule.

The third option, seeking to reconstruct political culture, is both the least common and the most interesting response of authoritarian rulers. By definition, totalitarian rulers sought to transform the political values of their subjects. Communist regimes made a particularly systematic and long-lasting effort at transforming political culture. Communist revolutions were, after all, originally intended as cultural revolutions. Almond (1983) describes the communist experience as a 'natural experiment in attitude change' in which the party set out to disprove the proposition that mass political culture resists transformation by the elite. If communist propagandists really could build a new communist personality, then political culture would clearly not possess the entrenched character attributed to it by authors such as Almond and Verba in *The Civic Culture*.

What then did the communist experiment reveal? Take the Soviet Union as an example. Propaganda there was endlessly repeated not just in speeches but also in public arenas such as factories and schools. Most other ruling communist parties adopted a similar approach, though attempts at indoctrination were less extensive in Eastern Europe where communist rule resulted from invasion rather than revolution.

Yet nowhere did the anticipated transformation of political culture come about. Some radical idealism may have existed at first in the Soviet Union, at least among urban youth, but eventually mass participation took on a purely ritual form, based on passive obedience to power rather than active commitment to communism. Fear created conformity without cultural transformation. Before long, the endless repetition of lies became a way of demonstrating the party's ability to control public discourse rather than a genuine attempt to transform political culture. Everyone knew the experiment had failed but no one could say so.

Whatever legitimacy communist states possessed seemed to owe more to traditional factors such as inherent patriotism and the party's success at delivering industrialization, welfare services, public order and, in the case of the Soviet Union, superpower status. The new communist men and women never left the drawing board. Almond's conclusion (1983, p. 137) regarding the twentieth century's largest experiment with political culture seems to be fully justified:

What the scholarship of comparative communism is telling us is that political cultures are not easily manipulated. A sophisticated movement ready to manipulate, penetrate, organise, indoctrinate and coerce, and given an opportunity to do so for more than a generation, ends up as much or more transformed than transforming.

Political culture in illiberal democracies

In illiberal democracies, presidents find themselves in an awkward position in relation to political culture. As elected leaders, they can hardly embrace the anti-democratic strategies associated with Marxist and many Islamic regimes. Yet neither can they embrace the full Western package of liberal democracy, with its emphasis on limited government, powerful institutions and individual rights.

In practice, such rulers exploit the political culture by selectively emphasizing its authoritarian elements; their skill in doing so is often part of the reason for their political success. As O'Donnell (1994, p. 61) writes, such tendencies are widespread beyond the West: 'whether it is called culture, tradition, or historically structured learning, the plebiscitary and *caudillista* tendencies toward delegative democracy are detectable in most Latin American (and, for that matter, many Central/East European, post-Soviet, African and Asian) countries'.

Traditions of deference, and of personal allegiance to powerful individuals, are a cultural resource which many leaders in Africa, Asia and Latin America exploit to the full. Loyalty to the national

leader is presented as an outgrowth of the natural allegiance of the tribe to its leader; of the submission of the landless peasant to the powerful landowner; or of the unforced obedience of the child to its parent. In Africa, for example, Chabal and Daloz (2006, p. 30) boldly claim that 'most people in Africa conceive of "democracy" in terms of personalised politics and not in terms of institutionalisation'. Where institutional development facilitates liberal democracy, a culture of personal politics fosters at best illiberal democracy.

Once elected (and then re-elected), the ruler of an illiberal democracy functions as father and chief patron to the nation, providing security and stability but not day-to-day democratic accountability. Some authors view this cultural desire for a strong leader as the outgrowth of experience with authority within the family. In Asia, suggests Pye (1985), strong family traditions encourage a group-centred style of adult politics in which deference to authority places a leading role. The child respects and accepts parental authority, leading – it is claimed – to similar deference to benevolent rulers later in life. The difficulty with the cultural expectation that the president will provide for his people is that he often lacks the means of doing so, producing an unstable cycle of high expectations, mass disappointment and the search for a new and equally personal saviour.

Post-communist Russia provides an example of a political culture which currently seems more consistent with an illiberal than a liberal form of democracy. Gitelman (2005, p. 248) writes that

the authoritarian traditions of Russia mean that people are not used to democratic behaviours and values, such as welcoming pluralism in thinking and behaving, tolerating dissent and supporting seemingly less efficient methods of democratic decision-making. They do not easily see the advantages of debate, discussion and non-conformity, and not deferring to a class of 'superiors'.

Inglehart (2000) also judges that Russian culture is exceptionally stony ground on which to nurture a liberal democracy. Drawing on a survey conducted in 1999/2000, he finds that Russians are less trusting, tolerant and happy than people in most other countries – cultural features which were reinforced but not created by communist realities. Since he also argues that 'cultural factors are ultimately more decisive than economic ones', his conclusion is that the prospects for a transition from an illiberal to a liberal democracy in Russia are limited.

Yet the Russian case also illustrates the dangers of relying on a broad-brush notion such as political culture in explaining specific trends. When communism collapsed, some scholars doubted whether Russia's political culture was consistent with democracy of any kind (Eckstein, 1998b); now, with a post-communist constitution created and elections occurring on a regular basis, few would doubt that a regime with at least some formal democratic elements has been established. If internal order and economic growth continue, and in particular become taken for granted, it is surely possible that the culture itself will gradually become more sympathetic to a more liberal democracy. Here, then, is the wisdom of Almond's observation (1993, p. 16) that political culture is an effect as well as a cause: 'the advocates of political culture recognise that causality works both ways: attitudes influence structure and behaviour, and structure and performance in turn influence political attitudes'.

Elite political culture

Although the impact of mass political culture on political stability has been widely debated, the significance of elite political culture has been addressed less often. Yet even where mass attitudes to politics are well-developed, as in liberal democracies, it is still the views of the elite which exert the most direct effect on political decisions. In this section, we examine elite political culture, focusing on its consequences for political stability.

It is of course the case that in a liberal democracy parties offer competing values and policies. Underlying these contrasts, however, we often find

Elite political culture consists of the beliefs, attitudes and ideas about politics held by those who are closest to the centres of political power. The values of elites are more explicit, systematic and consequential than are those of the population at large (Verba, 1987, p. 7).

tacit agreements and shared understandings. In defining his related idea of an operational code, Leites (1960, p. 18) also articulates the notion of elite political culture: 'a set of general beliefs about fundamental issues of history and central questions of politics as these bear, in turn, on the problem of action'.

Elite culture is far more than a representative fragment of the values of the wider society. The ideas of elites are distinct from, though they overlap with, the national political culture. For example, the leaders of liberal democracies generally take a more liberal line on social and moral issues. Stouffer's (1966) famous survey of American attitudes to freedom of speech, conducted in 1954, demonstrated this point. Stouffer showed that most community leaders maintained their belief in free speech for atheists, socialists and communists at a time when the public's attitudes were much less tolerant. It was crucial to the cause of free speech in the United States during the 1950s that a majority of the political elite resisted the strong pressure from Senator Joe McCarthy's populist anti-communist witch-hunt.

One reason for the liberal and sophisticated outlook of political leaders is their education: in most democracies, politics has become virtually a graduate profession. The experience of higher education nurtures an optimistic view of human nature, strengthens humanitarian values and encourages a belief in the ability of politicians to solve social problems (Farnen and Meloen, 2000). Indeed the contrast between the values of the educated elite and those of the least educated is itself a source of tension in many political cultures.

Elite political culture has a substantial bearing on political stability in two main ways. First, a political order is more likely to survive if the ruling group genuinely believes in its own right to govern. Second, a willingness to compromise among the leaders representing different groups in divided societies can contain intergroup hostility, securing stability against the risk of disintegration. We examine each element in turn.

The first theme of elite self-confidence (or rather its absence) can be illustrated with an example from authoritarian regimes. The revolutions of 1989 in Eastern Europe dramatically illustrated how a collapse of confidence among the rulers themselves helped to precipitate major political change. As Schöpflin (1990) points out,

an authoritarian elite sustains itself in power not just through force and the threat of force but, more importantly, because it has some vision of the future by which it can justify itself to itself. No regime can survive long without some concept of purpose.

In the initial phase of industrialization, communist rulers in the Soviet Union and Eastern Europe had good reason to believe their new planned economies were producing results. By the late 1980s, however, progress had given way to decline; industrial planning had reached a dead end. As any remaining support from intellectuals faded, so party officials began to doubt their own legitimacy. Communist rulers were aware that they had become a barrier to, rather than a source of, progress. Elite values had ceased to underpin the system of government. By contrast, economic growth continues apace in contemporary China, sustaining the elite's confidence in its own authority. It is elite political culture, as much as mass opinion, which explains why most communist regimes collapsed but some survived.

The second way in which elite culture contributes to stability draws on the analysis of divided societies, especially in Continental Europe. The classic analysis here is by Lijphart (1968, 1977, 2002). His concern remains of vital importance today in such areas as the Balkans, Iraq and Sri Lanka.

Lijphart suggested that even a society separated into potentially hostile **pillars** can achieve political stability as long as party and group leaders are willing to compromise at elite level. A culture of compromise is expressed in agreements over the distribution of state resources, with each group retaining autonomy over how it uses the resources it receives. This solution allows each community to continue to regulate itself on those matters not directly affecting other groups (Figure 7.3).

Just such an accommodating attitude, Lijphart suggests, prevailed among group leaders in European **consociational democracies** such as Austria (1945–66), Belgium (from 1919) and the Netherlands (1917–67). These societies were divided by religion and ideology. In the Netherlands, for

Figure 7.3 How elite compromise can deliver political stability to divided societies

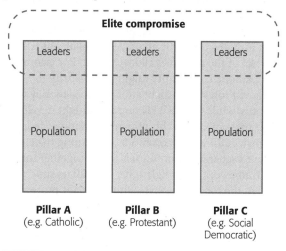

instance, Catholics and Protestants constituted separate religious pillars while the Social Democrats and Liberals formed less densely organized secular groups. Andeweg and Irwin (2009, p. 21) describe how the religious pillars structured lives in the 1950s: a typical Catholic would have been born of Catholic parents in a Catholic hospital, received a Catholic education, joined the Catholic Boy Scouts, played soccer for a Catholic team, married another Catholic, joined a Catholic trade union, read a Catholic newspaper, died in a Catholic home for the elderly and been buried in a Catholic graveyard by a Catholic undertaker.

The leaders of all the pillars negotiated among themselves on how to slice the national pie. This elite accommodation operated on the basis of two informal rules: first, that distributions should reflect the relative population size of each group, and, second, that each group should retain a minority veto over matters it judged vital to its own interests. Such discussions resembled international diplomacy,

A **consociational democracy** is an arrangement in which agreements between the national leaders of separate pillars in a divided society help to secure political stability. **Pillars** are organized communities, typically based on religion (e.g. Catholic) or ideology (e.g. socialist).

with the leaders of each pillar acting almost as if they represented a separate country. Discussions took place in secret and were treated for what they were: serious political business.

As with the international norm of non-intervention in states' domestic affairs, each pillar was left in control of the resources allocated to it. For example, the Catholic community might give priority to welfare; Protestants might allocate more money to schools; while the Social Democrats might develop their mass media. In this informal version of federalism, a culture of accommodation among the elite allowed separate communities to live together under the framework of a single state. The pillars supported the roof of the state while the roof protected the pillars.

Today, the pillars have crumbled as religious divisions have weakened. Nonetheless, elite compromise remains a key theme in many European democracies, not just the Netherlands. On Belgium, for instance, Deschouwer (2009, p. 7) reports that despite a 'depillarization of the minds' in a country previously divided into Catholic, socialist and liberal segments, 'the pillar organizations are still very visible and do play a role in political decision-making'. So Lijphart's formulation remains a practical demonstration of how elite political culture can be detached from the wider group in a way that contributes to overall stability.

Three qualifications are in order. First, the key role of elite culture means that consociational democracy is more than a matter of institutional arrangements; it cannot be expected to flourish in all conditions. What worked for the Netherlands in the 1950s will not necessarily succeed elsewhere. Second, elite accommodation can also be seen as an elite cartel, limiting popular influence in national politics. Third, there is a danger that empowering the pillars will just reinforce them, slowing the long-term process of integration (McGarry and O'Leary, 2006).

A clash of civilizations?

To conclude this chapter, we examine the value of political culture in understanding the relationship between Islam and the West. Such a comparison acquired added significance after 9/11 but also pos-

sesses two further advantages. First, it takes us beyond the state towards a more global perspective, and, second, the comparison raises the topic of religion, a dimension of culture that we have not yet addressed in detail. To what extent, then, should the current division between the Muslim and the Western worlds be viewed as a conflict of political cultures?

Huntington (1996) is the main proponent of the proposition that the division between Islam and the West is cultural or, to use his term, 'civilizational'. Huntington's view derived from a broader analysis, published before September 11, 2001, in which he suggested that cultures based on civilizations rather than countries would become the leading source of conflict in the twenty-first century.

According to Huntington, the end of the Cold War did not mean the end of cultural divisions. Rather the focus shifted from a battle of ideologies to a clash of civilizations, including Islam and the West (Box 7.1). Since such groupings are supranational, Huntington (1996, p. 20) implies that political culture has escaped its national moorings to embrace wider but still competing identities:

A civilization-based world order is emerging: societies sharing cultural affinities cooperate with each other; efforts to shift societies from one civilization to another are unsuccessful; and countries group themselves around the lead or core states of their civilization.

Between the contradictory worldviews of these civilizations, suggests Huntington, there is little common ground or room for compromise. He anticipates that as globalization proceeds, friction and conflict will intensify, reversing the 'McWorld' thesis – the proposition that the world will converge on American norms (Barber, 1995). Huntington notes, for example, how cultural kinship influenced the choice of sides in the wars of the 1990s: 'in the Yugoslav conflicts, Russia provided diplomatic support to the Serbs ... not for reasons of ideology or power politics or economic interest but because of cultural kinship' (1996, p. 28). In 2006, similarly, the Russian defence minister warned the West to steer clear of Belarus, citing cultural affinities: 'Belarusans and Russians are one people' (Shepherd, 2006, p. 19). Huntington is also sceptical of prag-

BOX 7.1

A clash of civilizations?

Huntington defines civilizations as the broadest cultural entities in the world; they are 'cultures writ large'. He divides the world into seven or eight major civilizations:

1 Western;
2 Japanese;
3 Islamic;
4 Hindu;
5 Slavic-Orthodox;
6 Latin American;
7 Chinese;
8 (possibly) African.

Source: Huntington (1996).

BOX 7.2

Relationships between states and civilizations

Type of state	Relationship to civilization	Example (civilization)
Core state	The most powerful and culturally central state in a civilization	India (Hindu)
Member state	A state fully identified with a particular civilization	UK (Western)
Lone state	A state lacking cultural commonality with other societies	Japan (Japanese)

Source: Huntington (1996), pp. 135–54.

matic efforts to switch civilizations, suggesting that the reason Australia failed to reinvent itself as an Asian country was just that, culturally speaking, it's not.

Huntington draws on these civilizational themes in discussing the specific relationship between Islam and the West. The transnational character of civilizations is indeed exemplified by these religions, each of which predates the emergence of states. Thus, in medieval Europe, Christendom stood above kingdoms in the political hierarchy. Similarly, Muslim countries form an Islamic domain in which a shared religious commitment transcends national divisions. Although the origins of the conflict between Islam and the West may lie in religion, Huntington argues that the contemporary division is cultural or civilizational rather than religious. With the Islamic world falling ever further behind the West in science and technology, it is no longer the West's Christian foundations which have become the target of Islamic criticism. Rather the Muslim critique rests on the West's secular culture as exemplified by American materialism.

How do states relate to these civilizations? Huntington provides an intriguing classification, though countries can fall into more than one category (Box 7.2). A **core state** leads a civilization, a **member state** is identified with a single civilization, while a **lone state** either forms its own civilization or stands, like Haiti, in a class of its own. Perhaps the

most interesting category is the mixed or torn state whose leaders may attempt the difficult assignment of moving their country from one civilization to another. Turkey, an Islamic society whose leaders traditionally pursued a secular Western course, is the classic case. Russia, positioned between Western and Slavic-Orthodox civilizations, provides another example of perpetual ambivalence.

As would be expected for a civilizational divide, differences in education and upbringing underpin and perpetuate these cultural differences. Western education is avowedly secular, allowing schooling to concentrate on scientific knowledge and technical training. But in many Muslim countries, literal instruction in the Koran (Islam's holy text) remains a major theme, ill-preparing young people – male as well as female – for the modern world.

The upshot is that Huntington (1996, p. 217) portrays Islam and the West as civilizations locked in permanent cultural conflict:

The underlying problem of the West is Islam, a different civilization whose people are convinced of the superiority of their culture and are obsessed with the inferiority of their power. The problem for

Islam is the West, a different civilization whose people are convinced of the universality of their culture and who believe that their superior, if declining, power imposes on them the obligation to extend that culture throughout the world.

Many of Huntington's critics reject his essentialist reading of Islam which is focused on that religion's inherent characteristics and which assumes all believers speak with one voice. Stepan (2001, p. 234) is surely closer to the mark when he interprets Islam as multivocal, capable of varying its voice across place and time. In similar fashion, Gregorian (2004) describes Islam as 'a mosaic, not a monolith', while Fuller (2002, p. 52) suggests that

Islam is not a butterfly in a collection box or a set of texts prescribing a single path. The real issue is not what Islam is but what do Muslims want. People of all sorts of faiths can rapidly develop interpretations of their religion that justify practically any quest.

Thus, both Turkey and Saudi Arabia are Muslim countries. However, Turkey's state is secular and substantially democratic, whereas Saudi Arabia's authoritarian regime leads a society constrained by a severe form of Islam. The reaction to 9/11 confirms Islam's multivocal character: the hijackers undoubtedly drew on one anti-Western dialect within Islam but most Muslims, like most Christians, regarded the attacks as morally unjustified (Saikal, 2003, p. 17). Furthermore, any assumption of a monolithic Islam was invalidated by violent conflict between Sunni and Shia Muslims in post-invasion Iraq.

The political character of Islam, and its relationship with the West, has varied over time. The possibility of conflict with the West may be inherent but this potential often remains latent. Saikal (2003, p. 24) writes that 'since the advent of Islam in the early seventh century, relations between its domain and the largely Christian West have been marked by long periods of peaceful coexistence but also by many instances of tension, hostility and mutual recrimination'. As long as civilizations are conceived as static, it is difficult to account for variability in the relationship between them. Huntington's expansive claim (1996, p. 210) that the West's problem is 'not Islamic fundamentalism but Islam' surely involves a breathtaking dismissal of peaceful centuries.

Rather than regarding the current wave of Muslim fundamentalism as an inherent feature of Islam, we should seek to locate its emergence in the events of the twentieth century, an approach which takes us away from political culture towards more specific themes in political history. Brzezinski's list (2002, p. 18), for instance, would be accepted by many:

Arab political emotions have been shaped by the region's encounter with French and British colonialism, by the defeat of the Arab effort to prevent the existence of Israel and by the subsequent American support for Israel and its treatment of the Palestinians, as well as by the direct injection of American power into the region.

So political culture (or equivalent terms such as civilization) can only take us so far. Culture identifies the general climate but fails to offer specific forecasts. As Roy (1994, p. viii) observes, 'culture is never directly explanatory and in fact conceals all that is rupture and history: the importation of new types of states, the birth of new social classes and the advent of contemporary ideologies'. Over time, political debate itself shapes the political culture as leaders selectively exploit its themes in pursuit of their own goals. By itself, terms such as 'political culture' and 'civilization' are blanket explanations, offering wide initial coverage but also obscuring the crucial detail beneath.

Learning Resources for Chapter 7

Next step

Pharr and Putnam (2000) is an important comparative study of political culture in established democracies, focusing on increased dissatisfaction with the performance of government.

Further reading

Norris (1999b) is a useful supplement to Pharr and Putnam. On political culture generally, Crothers and Lockhart (2002) is a wide-ranging reader, Chabal and Daloz (2006) offer a more interpretive perspective and Ross (2009) discusses the contribution of culture to comparative political analysis. For social capital, see Putnam (1993); Putnam (2002) is an interesting comparative attempt to apply the concept beyond the United States. The key source on postmaterialism is Inglehart (1971, 1990, 1997). Norris and Inglehart (2004) study the relationship between religious and political values. Huntington (1993, 1996) is the main source on the clash of civilizations, but see also more grounded works such as Saikal (2003).

Internet sources

Bowling Alone.com
More Americans are bowling but not in leagues
http://www.bowlingalone.com/

Civic Practices Network
A learning collaborative for civic renewal
http://www.cpn.org/

Daniel Elazar Papers Index, Jerusalem Center for Public Affairs
Papers on American political culture
http://www.jcpa.org/dje/index-apc.htm

Saguaro Seminar, Harvard University
Building civic engagement in America
http://www.hks.harvard.edu/saguaro

Chapter 8
Political communication

Society, and with it politics, is created, sustained and modified through communication. Without a continuous exchange of information, attitudes and values society would be impossible. As Williams (1962, p. 11) wrote, 'what we call society is not only a network of political and economic arrangements, but also a process of learning and communication'. Communication is therefore a core political activity, providing opportunities to educate, inform, manipulate and persuade. Through communication, meaning is constructed and culture transmitted.

Awareness of the importance of communication led Aristotle (1962) to provide the earliest systematic treatment of the topic through his analysis of the rhetorical techniques used by orators in their speeches to the assembly and juries of ancient Athens. Where Aristotle asked how speakers influenced the reactions of their audience, contemporary scholars investigate who controls, and the influence of, the **mass media**. But in studies ancient and modern, the underlying assumption is the same: that communication is where politics does (and should) take place.

Assessments of the quality of political communication enter into the fundamental issue of classifying governments. A free flow of information is one test in discriminating between liberal democracies, illiberal democracies and authoritarian regimes. For example, Dahl (1998, p. 37) judges that a liberal democracy must provide opportunities for what he calls enlightened understanding: 'within reasonable limits as to time, each member [of a political association] must have equal and effective opportunities for learning about relevant alternative policies and their likely consequences'. In an illiberal democracy, by contrast, dominance of major broadcasting channels is a tool through which leaders maintain their ascendancy over potential challengers. An authoritarian regime may permit no explicit dissent at all.

In examining political communication, it is useful to break the activity into its component parts. This task leads to what is known as the transmission model (Figure 8.1), an account that interprets communication as consisting of who says what to whom, through which media and with what effects. So the model distinguishes five components:

- A sender: who?
- A message: what?
- A channel: how?
- A receiver: to whom?
- A presumed impact: with what effect?

The '**mass media**' refers to methods of communication that can reach a large and potentially unlimited number of people simultaneously. These channels include television, newspapers, radio, books, magazines, cinema, blogs, websites and posters.

Figure 8.1 The transmission model of political communication

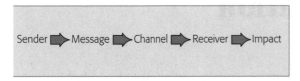

For example, a local party (the sender) might distribute a leaflet (the channel) advocating voting at a forthcoming election (the message) to its own supporters (the receivers), with the result that turnout goes up (impact).

Even though much recent research in political communication focuses on one component only – namely the message and the meanings embedded within it – the transmission model still provides a helpful reminder of the existence of receivers and, sometimes, an impact. The danger of focusing solely on content is that we learn nothing about the receivers and even less about whether the communication has the slightest effect on them.

In this chapter, we focus on the key channel of political communication in modern societies: the mass media. We begin with an account of the development of the media before turning to contemporary variations in how the media are structured in liberal democracies. We next explore the issue of media impact, followed by a discussion of a notion which is, to some extent, a media construct: public opinion. The final sections examine the role of the media in authoritarian states and illiberal democracies.

Media development

The intimate connections between communication and politics are revealed by examining the early development of the media. The expansion of communication facilitated the emergence of a common national identity and the growth of the state, especially in the nineteenth and twentieth centuries. The mass media, in particular, delivered a shared experience for dispersed populations, providing a glue to connect the citizens of large political units. We cannot understand the development of either the media or the state without appreciating the interaction between them.

The Timeline outlines the major developments in the history of the media. Here we discuss one of the key innovations: the extension of literacy to the wider population that marked off the modern era of both communication and states. Mass literacy in a common language was central to the successful development of contemporary states, facilitating the administration of large areas, encouraging a common national identity and enabling ordinary people to participate in cultural life. By the end of the eighteenth century, 'signing literacy' had reached about 80 per cent in innovative Sweden. Other European countries, and New England, achieved mass literacy in the nineteenth century, following the introduction of compulsory primary education. Mass literacy was a function, an achievement and an affirmation of the modern state, just as it has become an important success in many contemporary low income countries. By 2007, the world's literacy rate had reached at least 80 per cent, a considerable increase on the figure of around 63 per cent in 1970 (CIA, 2009).

Newspapers

Widespread literacy in a shared language permitted the emergence of popular newspapers in Western states, the key development in political communication during the nineteenth and early twentieth centuries (Dooley and Baron, 2001). Advances in printing (e.g. the steam press) and distribution (e.g. the railway) opened up the prospect of transforming party journals with a small circulation into populist and profitable papers funded by advertising. By growing away from their party roots, papers became not just more popular but also, paradoxically, more important to politics.

In compact countries with national distribution, such as Britain and Japan, newspapers built enormous circulations. Newspaper owners became powerful political figures. In interwar Britain, for example, four newspaper barons – Lords Beaverbrook, Rothermere, Camrose and Kemsley – owned newspapers with a total circulation of over 13 million, amounting to one in every two daily papers sold. Stanley Baldwin, a prime minister of the time, famously described such proprietors as

▶ **TIMELINE**

THE DEVELOPMENT OF COMMUNICATION MEDIA

Fifth millennium BC	Writing systems develop in the earliest urban civilizations of the Near East, notably Phoenicia.
About 750 BC	The first modern alphabet, based on sounds rather than symbols, emerges in Greece.
AD 1450	In Mainz, Johannes Gutenberg invents printing with movable metal type. Book production is aided by new techniques for the mass manufacture of paper.
19th century	Compulsory primary education introduced, and mass literacy achieved, in Western states.
	The telegraph - a way of sending information across wires using electric signals - permits international dissemination of news, decisions and instructions.
Later 19th and early 20th century	Popular newspapers emerge, often with mass circulation. New railway networks allow national distribution.
1930s	Radio's golden age. For the first time, politicians broadcast directly into electors' homes.
1950s–1960s	Television becomes the most popular, and usually the most trusted, medium in Western countries. By regulation or state ownership, politicians secure access to the medium. Entertainment programmes from the USA are widely exported, diffusing American values.
1970s–1980s	The television audience begins to fragment, with an increase in the number and commercialization of channels; distribution by cable and satellite; widespread use of video.
1990s	Internet access reaches more affluent and educated groups in Western societies, representing a further expansion of international communication. Mobile telephony emerges.
2000s	Mobile telephony becomes standard and provides the only form of telephony in many low-income countries. The Internet reaches the mass population in Western societies, extending horizontal communication among citizens (e.g. through social networking sites). Sharp decline in physical newspaper readership.

'aiming at power without responsibility – the prerogative of the harlot throughout the ages' (Curran and Seaton, 2003, p. 64).

Broadcasting

Although newspapers remain significant channels of political communication, in the twentieth century their role was of course supplanted by broadcasting. Cinema newsreels, radio and then television enabled communication with the mass public to take place in a new form: spoken rather than written, personal rather than abstract, and, on occasion, live rather than reported. Oral communication reasserted itself, though now in a form which could escape the confines of an assembled group, as found for instance in ancient Athens. Broadcasting

---

Contemporary trends in mass communication

Commercialization The decline of public broadcasting and the rise of for-profit media treating users as consumers rather than citizens

Fragmentation More channels and an enhanced ability to download and consume programmes on demand

Globalization Improved access to overseas events and media in the global village

Interaction Increased use of interactive channels (e.g. email, games), reducing passive exposure to politics through top-down communication

---

was the central communications revolution of the last century.

Broadcasting's impact in Western liberal democracies was relatively benign. A small number of national television channels initially dominated the airwaves in most countries, providing a shared experience of everything from national events to popular entertainment. By offering some common ground to societies which were, in these early post-war decades, still strongly divided by class and religion, the new media initially served as agents of national integration.

However, the impact of broadcasting on politicians themselves was immediate. Leaders had to acquire new communication techniques. A public speech to a live audience encouraged expansive words and dramatic gestures but a quieter tone was needed for transmission from the broadcasting studio direct to the living room. The task was to converse with the unseen listener and viewer rather than to deliver a speech to a visible audience gathered together in one place.

The art was to talk to the millions as though they were individuals. President Franklin Roosevelt's fireside chats, broadcast live by radio to the American population in the 1930s, exemplified this new approach. The impact of Roosevelt's somewhat folksy idiom was undeniable. He talked not so much to the citizens but as a citizen and was rewarded with his country's trust. In this way, broadcasting –

and the forgotten medium of radio specifically – transformed not just the reach but also the style of political communication (Barber, 1992).

Broadcasting is also making a substantial contribution to political communication in most low-income countries but for different reasons. In the developing world, broadcasting (whether radio or television) possesses two major advantages over print media. First, it does not require physical distribution to each user; second, it is accessible to the one in five of the world's population who cannot read. In low income countries, these factors initially encouraged the spread of radio. Villagers could gather round the shared set to hear the latest news, not least on the price of local crops. Today, around half the population in developing countries also has access to television: there are more TV sets in China than in the USA.

Just as some developing countries are moving directly to mobile telephony, eliminating the need for an expensive fixed-wire infrastructure, so also have many poorer countries developed large broadcasting networks without passing through the stage of mass-circulation newspapers. The capacity of ruling politicians to reach out to poor, rural populations through these radio and television networks is an important component of governance in illiberal democracies, particularly in Latin America.

In the first decade of the twenty-first century, the four major trends in communications in the developed world are commercialization, fragmentation, globalization and interaction (Box 8.1). These factors are discussed below but their joint effect is to reduce national political distinctiveness in media structures. In addition, governments lose control over broadcasting as consumers either choose their own political programming or increasingly escape from politics altogether. If the mass media performed a nation-building function in the twentieth century, their emerging impact in the new century is to splinter the traditional national audience, fragmenting a shared experience and perhaps contributing thereby to the decline of participation in formal national politics.

Commercialization

Communication is increasingly treated as the important business it has become. It allows new media moguls, such as Rupert Murdoch, to build transnational broadcasting networks, achieving on a global scale the prominence which the newspaper barons of the nineteenth century acquired at national level. Even in northern and southern Europe, where the state traditionally exerted substantial influence over the media, the 1970s and 1980s saw the introduction of new commercial channels; in addition, advertising was added to many public stations.

Such developments threatened previously cosy links between national parties and national broadcasters. They represented a shift to seeing the viewer in less political terms, as a consumer rather than a citizen. Parties no longer called the shots and politics had to justify its share of screen time. In this increasingly commercial environment, Tracey (1998) claimed that public service broadcasting had become nothing more than 'a corpse on leave from its grave'.

In a similar way, McChesney argued in *Rich Media, Poor Democracies* (1999) that commercialization shrinks the public space in which political issues are discussed. Channels in search of profit will devote little time to serious politics; instead, they concentrate on soft news – news you can use. Certainly, profit-seeking media have no incentive to supply public goods such as an informed citizenry and a high electoral turnout, which were the traditional concerns of public media. For those who view democracy as a form of collective debate, media commercialization is a challenge indeed. Against this, commercial broadcasters reply that it is preferable to reach a mass audience with limited but stimulating political coverage than it is to offer extensive but dull political programming which, in reality, only ever reached a minority with a prior interest in public affairs (Norris, 2000).

Fragmentation

Consumers are increasingly able to watch, hear and read what they want, when they want. Long gone are the days when American viewers were restricted to three large networks (ABC, CBS and NBC) and British viewers could choose only between the public BBC and the commercial ITV. Distribution by cable, satellite and telephone wire allows viewers to receive a greater range of content, local and overseas as well as national. Content can also be stored for playback on demand, reducing reliance on what

Table 8.1 World internet usage, 2006-08

	Percentage of population in region using internet		Percentage of world's internet users, by region	
	2006	2008	2006	2008
North America	70	73	21	16
Australia and Oceania	54	60	2	1
Europe	39	49	29	25
Latin America and Caribbean	15	30	8	11
Asia	10	17	35	41
Middle East	10	23	2	3
Africa	4	6	3	3
World	17	24	100	100

Source: Internet World Stats (2009).

the broadcasters make available at a specific moment. Not least among younger age groups in the developed world, an increasing share of screen time is spent on the internet, further fragmenting the audience across a range of specialized virtual communities. In the USA, the ratio of time spent watching television compared to the internet halved from 8:1 in 2000 to 4:1 in 2005; this ratio has continued to fall subsequently (Murrie, 2006). Significantly, internet use continues to expand in all regions of the world (Table 8.1).

The combined result of these developments is a more splintered audience, with advertising revenue divided between more channels. During the 1990s, for instance, the audience share of the big three American television networks dropped by a third. Newspaper circulations are also declining in the developed world: by 8 per cent for dailies in the USA and by 6 per cent in the European Union, between 2003 and 2007 (WAN, 2008). Local and evening newspapers are closing, with some shift to less political free papers.

The political implications of this shift from broadcasting to narrowcasting are substantial. Governments, parties and commercial advertisers encounter more difficulty in reaching a mass audience when viewers can defend themselves by simply choosing another channel via their remote control.

Where earlier generations would passively watch whatever appeared on their television screen, the Internet is inherently user-driven; people choose which sites to visit. News junkies tune in but most people tune out.

Overall, exposure to politics falls as the electorate (especially young electors) becomes harder to reach. Political parties are forced to adopt a greater range and sophistication of marketing strategies, including the use of personalized but expensive contact techniques such as direct mail, email, social networking sites and telephone. These techniques were brilliantly exploited by Barack Obama in his successful campaigns for the Democratic nomination and the White House in 2008 (Johnson, 2009).

In this more fragmented environment, politicians have to communicate in a manner, and at a time, of the voters' choosing. They must continue their migration from television news to higher-rated talk shows, blurring the distinction between politician and celebrity (Jones, 2005). Politicians find themselves in a competition for eyeballs with entertainers ranging from sports personalities to movie stars. The sound bite, never unimportant, becomes even more vital as politicians learn to articulate their agenda in a brief interview or an even briefer commercial.

In short, just as the balance within the media industry has shifted from public service to private profit, so the emphasis within political communication has moved from parties to voters. Politicians rode the emergence of broadcasting with considerable success in the twentieth century but they are experiencing tougher going in the new millennium of fragmented media.

Globalization

'The empires of the future will be empires of the mind,' said Winston Churchill in 1943. Certainly, in the global village, the world has been compressed into a television screen. In 1776 the English reaction to the American Declaration of Independence took 50 days to filter back to the United States. In 1950 the British response to the outbreak of the Korean War was broadcast in America after 24 hours. In 2003 British and American viewers watched live broadcasts of the Iraq War at the same time. We now take for granted the almost immediate transmission of newsworthy events around the world.

It is now harder than ever for governments to isolate their populations from international developments. Even before the internet, communist states found it difficult to jam foreign radio broadcasts aimed at their people. Discussing the collapse of communist states, Eberle (1990, pp. 194–5) claimed that 'the changes in Eastern Europe and the Soviet Union were as much the triumph of communication as the failure of communism'.

Recent technological developments also facilitate underground opposition to authoritarian regimes. A small group with internet access now has the potential to draw the world's attention to political abuses, providing source material for alert journalists. Burma's military rulers, China's communist government, Iran's clerics and Saudi Arabia's ruling families have all suffered from overseas groups in this way. Significantly, however, and testifying to the limited impact of information as such, all four regimes remain in place (Atton, 2004).

Interaction

A particular aspect of fragmentation is the growing exposure to interactive channels of communication. Radio phone-ins allow ordinary people to listen to their peers discussing current issues, without mediation by a politician; blogs perform the same function in electronic space. Messaging systems and social networking sites are inherently interactive. Such media allow peer-to-peer interchanges which tend to crowd out top-down, one-way politician-to-voter communication. Even when voters do watch a politician, it may be through an embarrassing extract posted on YouTube rather than the original broadcast from which the clip is taken. In short, screen time is up but passive exposure is down.

In response to the threat from these new media, traditional broadcasters have added an interactive element to some of their output, for example in the internationally successful *Idol* series. These shows give many young people their first experience of voting, yet, far from stimulating turnout in national elections, their freshness seems to give traditional participation through the ballot box a somewhat old-fashioned air.

The expansion of interactive channels sits uneasily alongside the rather passive role expected of most voters in a representative democracy. Implicitly, a young generation schooled on interactive media is raising an important question to which politicians have yet to find an adequate answer: why should we listen to you when we have the option to interact electronically with people of our own age and interests?

Media structures

Technological innovations such as broadcasting are potentially universal, applying to all countries. Nonetheless, the way in which the mass media have developed, and been integrated into national politics, varies significantly across liberal democracies, yielding distinctive **media structures**. By exploring these systems, we will demonstrate the value of moving beyond a uniform characterization of the media in liberal democracies as consisting of a 'free press' pursuing 'independent journalism'.

> The **structure of the media** refers to overall patterns of media use and, in particular, the relationships between media, the state and the economy. For example, the extent of newspaper circulation, the scope of public broadcasting and the partisanship of the press are structural components of the media.

In an important comparative classification, Hallin and Mancini (2004) distinguish between Anglo-American, northern European and southern European media structures within the liberal democratic world (Box 8.2). In the Anglo-American model, market mechanisms predominate and the mainly private media respond to commercial considerations. Reflecting the early achievement of mass literacy, newspaper circulation remains relatively high. The notion of journalism as a news-gathering profession is entrenched, while the media and political worlds inhabit distinct spheres, with the former acting – or liking to think it acts – as a watchdog over the latter. This liberal model underpins many instinctive conceptions of the proper relationship between media and politics in a free democracy, not least the USA.

But the Anglo-American model is not the only one on offer. In the Northern European structure, the media are interpreted as responsible social actors with their own contribution to make to society in general and to political stability in particular.

BOX 8.2

Media structures in liberal democracies

	Anglo-American structure	Northern European structure	Southern European structure
Newspaper circulation	High	High	Low
Journalistic professionalism	High	High	Low
Links between media and politics	Low	High	High
State intervention	Low	High	High
Examples	Britain, Canada, Ireland, USA	Denmark, Finland, Norway, Sweden	Greece, Portugal, Spain

Source: Adapted from Hallin and Mancini (2004) who also refer to these structures as, from left to right across the columns, 'liberal', 'democratic corporatist' and 'polarized pluralist'.

Newspapers and even television networks represent particular groups (e.g. religions, trade unions, political parties) but do so in an environment shaped by an interventionist state. For example, public broadcasting is significant and the government subsidizes private media in support of both their information and representation functions. Regulations governing media coverage, such as the right to privacy and to reply, are also more extensive than in the Anglo-American structure.

This northern European format, which to a degree extends beyond Scandinavia to Belgium, Germany and the Netherlands, is an element of a wider settlement in which the political system emphasizes the search for accommodation between strong social groups. In this sense, the role of the media is similar to that of such mechanisms as proportional representation and coalition government: to facilitate the expression of, and agreement between, different groups. Journalistic professionalism is fully supported but is tempered by an awareness of the media's role as an actor in, and not just an observer of, politics and society.

The southern European structure is in many ways the opposite of the northern European model. In such Mediterranean countries as Greece, Portugal and Spain, an authoritarian tradition acted as a brake on the development of universal literacy, mass circulation newspapers and a vibrant civil society. Even after the democratic transitions of the 1970s, governing parties still strongly influence public broadcasting, while newspapers and other television stations are subject to party political influence. Television becomes a potent vehicle of popular entertainment but newspaper circulation remains low, with journalists seeing themselves as providing ideologically loaded commentary rather than hard news. In these party-dominated southern European structures, the political position of the media remains even more subdued than in the northern European format.

Hallin and Mancini demonstrate the danger of discussing the media in liberal democracies without reference to national, or in this case regional, traditions. As with many categories in comparative politics, the 'same' role is understood differently in different areas. Consider conceptions of the journalist's task. In the Anglo-American world, the journalist is a reporter: a news-gathering professional, speaking truth to power and engaged in a combative relationship with the government. In northern Europe, journalists are expected to add greater sensitivity to the national interest, political stability and to the outlook of their newspaper and the social group it serves. In southern Europe, journalism focuses less on information and more on commentary from an ideological perspective.

Of course, Hallin and Mancini's classification obscures variation within each category. For example, in the Anglo-American format public broadcasting and partisan national daily newspapers remain far more significant in the UK than in the USA, where commerce dominates the media and newspapers are primarily local. Equally important, like many classifications in comparative politics, the value of Hallin and Mancini's scheme is being

eroded by the contemporary media trends discussed in the previous section. The tendency is to a more Anglo-American approach, not least in understanding the journalist's task.

Media impact

What is the media's impact on those exposed to it? One way of thinking about this question is counterfactually. Clearly, politics would change substantially if all mass media were suddenly outlawed; for example, we would surely observe the denationalization of politics, with a revival of local campaigning in particular. But such mental experiments are as hypothetical as imagining a house without walls: there is perhaps more credibility in describing the media as the house within which many people (especially young people) live their political lives. Jones (2005, p. 17) expresses this viewpoint:

Media are our primary point of access to politics – the space in which politics now chiefly happens for most people, and the place for political encounters that precede, shape and at times determine further bodily participation (if it is to happen at all) ... Such encounters do much more than provide 'information' about politics. They constitute our mental maps of the political world outside our direct experience. They provide a reservoir of images and voices, heroes and villains, sayings and slogans, facts and ideas that we draw on in making sense of politics.

For example, the clutch of American movies about Vietnam, 9/11 and Iraq provided a stimulus for political discussion which was, in its way, as much a form of political participation as volunteering to take part in an election campaign or paying a subscription to an interest group. The underlying notion here – that following politics in the media is a form of political behaviour rather than just an influence on political behaviour – captures the importance of the media in today's world.

Mechanisms of impact

It is worthwhile examining how scholarly thinking about specific media effects has evolved. Box 8.3 outlines four main mechanisms: reinforcement,

---

BOX 8.3

Media effects

	Definition	Comment
Reinforcement	The media strengthen existing opinions	People read newspapers which support their existing outlook (selective exposure). In addition, people interpret information to render it consistent with their prior opinions (selective interpretation) and forget information that runs counter to existing beliefs (selective recall).
Agenda-setting	The media influence what we think and talk about	The compressed nature of news, especially on television, means coverage is highly selective. Reported events are widely discussed by the public but non-reported events lose visibility.
Framing	How an event is narrated as a coherent story highlights its particular features	A frame focuses on particular aspects of a problem, its origins, remedies and evaluation. It encourages viewers and readers to interpret the topic in a similar way.
Priming	Media coverage influences how we interpret events beyond those in the particular story	Priming extends media impact beyond the particular topic. For example, coverage of a crime story in the national media may encourage electors to judge candidates by their law and order policies.

---

agenda-setting, framing and priming. At various times since 1945, each of these has contributed to academic thinking about the impact of broadcast and print media in particular.

In the 1950s, before television became pre-eminent, the **reinforcement** thesis – also known as the minimal effects model – held sway (Klapper, 1960). The argument here was that party loyalties initially transmitted through the family acted as a political sunscreen protecting people from media effects. People saw what they wanted to see and remembered what they wanted to recall. In Britain, for instance, where national newspapers were strongly partisan, many Labour supporters read left-wing papers while most Conservatives bought right-wing papers. Given such self-selection, the most the press could do was to reinforce readers' existing dispositions while also, perhaps, crystallizing the partisanship of some uncommitted readers.

The reinforcement theory proved its value half a century ago when voting was more stable than today. Even now, many studies of media impact on voting find only limited effects during the short period of an election campaign (Gavin and Sanders, 2003). The reinforcement thesis still offers effective medicine for the vast range of people and organizations blaming the 'biased' media for the public unpopularity of their particular cause. Even so, the reinforcement account has surely become too limited as a contemporary perspective on media effects. Party loyalties have long been weaker, and television more pervasive, than in the 1950s. For this reason, the agenda-setting view of media impact gained ground in the 1970s and 1980s.

The **agenda-setting** perspective contends that the media (and television in particular) influence what we think about, though not necessarily what we think. The media write certain items onto the agenda and by implication keep other issues away from the public's gaze. As Lazarsfeld and Merton (1948) pointed out in an earlier era, 'to the extent that the mass media have influenced their audiences, it has stemmed not only from what is said but more significantly from what is not said'.

SPAIN

Form of government ■ a parliamentary liberal democracy, with strong regions and a hereditary monarch playing a largely ceremonial role.

Executive ■ the prime minister appoints the cabinet (typically 16–20 strong). Cabinet members need not be drawn from parliament. The monarch – Juan Carlos I since 1975 – is head of state.

Legislature ■ the bicameral legislature (Cortes Generales) consists of the Congress of Deputies (350 members) and the Senate (264 members; 208 directly elected and 56 chosen by regional assemblies). Parliament is dominated by well-organized parties; the Senate is particularly weak.

Constitution and judiciary ■ The Constitutional Court consists of 12 members appointed by parliament, the government and the judiciary itself. The legal system is based on civil law.

Electoral system ■ deputies are elected by PR with closed party lists. A small district magnitude gives large parties an advantage. For the Senate, electors can vote for up to three candidates for their province. The four obtaining the highest number of votes are elected.

Party system ■ the 1978 constitution places parties at the centre of the new democracy. The party system has now stabilized, with the Spanish Socialist Workers' Party (PSOE)

Population (annual growth rate): 40.5m (+0.1%)	
World Bank income group: high income	
Political Rights score: ①	
Civil Liberties score: ①	
Human development index (rank/out of): 13/177	
Freedom of the press index (rank/out of): 47/195	
Perceived corruption index (rank/out of): 28/180	

Note: For meaning and sources of scales and indexes, see p. xvi. In all cases a score and rank of 1 is 'best'.

and the centre right People's Party (PP, Popular Party) together securing 84 per cent of the vote in the 2008 elections to the lower chamber. The PSOE was confirmed in office with just under half the seats.

SPAIN'S political transition following the death of General Franco in 1975 is one of democratization's great success stories. As Heywood (1995, p. 4) writes, 'Franco's death was followed not by bloody conflict, as many had feared, but by a remarkably rapid and skillfully engineered transition to democracy'.

Favourable conditions included the country's location in Western Europe; the considerable economic modernization that had already taken place under the old regime; and the significant contribution made by King Juan Carlos.

Spain's delayed democratization came all the easier for its late arrival. All the power centres such as the Catholic Church and the military wanted to avoid

reopening old conflicts, leading to the triumphant compromise of the 1978 constitution.

Spain now scores highly on the Human Development Index. It is securely integrated into Europe, joining the European Union in 1986 and using the euro currency since its inception. Reflecting a highly regulated labour market, average living standards do remain significantly below those of Europe's wealthiest economies; unemployment is stubbornly high.

Although Spain is one of Europe's oldest states, regional divergences remain central to its politics. Specifically, the country has granted extensive devolution to historic regions and identities while retaining what is, in

theory, a unitary rather than federal framework.

The constitution established a complex mechanism by which regions could aspire to varying levels of autonomy. The historic communities of the Basque Country and Catalonia quickly proceeded to the most autonomous level, with other regions offered the prospect of a later upgrade. In 2006, even greater devolution was agreed for Catalonia, including recognition of its status as a distinct nationality. In the same year, the Basque nationalist organization ETA (Basque Homeland and Freedom) declared a 'permanent' ceasefire, having killed about 900 people since the 1970s. However, the ceasefire ended the following year; bombings continue.

Further reading: Gunther *et al.* (2004), Magone (2008).

The media in Spain

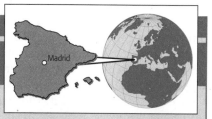

The development of the Spanish media over the era of democratization in some ways follows a typical pattern. The monotonous coverage offered under the dictatorship gives way to a flowering of free expression, followed by a media restructuring in which broadcasting increasingly dominates the press. Media structures follow the southern European pattern, with extensive links between media outlets and political parties, and a continuing emphasis on partisan advocacy in media coverage.

Under the authoritarian leadership of General Franco, the position of the media had been wholly subservient. Rigid censorship ensured that newspapers offered only the dullest of political coverage, largely confining themselves to reprinting official press releases. The fare provided by the broadcasters was little better. Monopoly channels under state control offered an inoffensive diet of operetta, sport and soap operas. The media formed an essential part of the dictatorship's 'culture of evasion' (Heywood, 1995, p. 76).

With liberalization, independent media burst into life, offering all shades of opinion through a diverse range of publications. As in many post-communist countries, television quickly established itself as the key medium. This pattern reflected not just the indifferent quality and poor reputation of the press but also the greater accessibility of television to an electorate with variable education; until the 1990s, illiteracy remained a significant issue.

The dominance of broadcasting over print in Spain is exceptional within Western Europe and more typical of the pattern found in the country's former colonies in Latin America. According to a 2005 survey, nine out of ten Spaniards watch television daily while only 41 per cent read newspapers – and many of these confine themselves to sports journals or free papers. In 1996, 66 per cent of respondents said that television was their main source of political information while only 17 per cent mentioned the press (Gunther *et al.*, 2004, p. 146).

Media use in Spain, 2007

	Average minutes per day
Television	220
Radio	108
Newspapers	17
Internet	36
Magazines	4

Source: Adapted from WARC (2009).

Reflecting an authoritarian and corporate tradition, membership of social organizations and political parties is low. When combined with reliance on television, the effect is an electorate which is mobilized cognitively rather than socially. That is, links between politicians and voters operate not so much through social networks such as trade unions and churches as through the mass media, especially television. The result is an

individualized style of politics which gives considerable weight to the personality of party leaders (Magone, 2008, p. 39).

This pattern is common among new democracies but in Spain it has not led to an illiberal democracy in which one key politician dominates the airwaves. Rather, political parties now compete for influence over a pluralistic media environment in which large commercial media organizations coexist alongside diminished state channels.

The leading parties have sought influence over broadcasting, relying in part on a constitutional statement that interprets broadcasting as an essential public service requiring government regulation. In addition, antiterror legislation and large libel awards against newspapers have placed pressures on editorial freedom. Such difficulties lower the country's position in international rankings of media freedom.

Supporting these quantitative judgements, Hallin and Mancini (2004, p. 120) comment that 'intervention by the state in media markets is almost always seen – and with much reason – as a cynical attempt at political control'. However, these characteristics surely do not seriously threaten Spain's status as an established and successful liberal democracy.

Further reading: Balfour (2005), Gunther and Montero (2009).

In an election campaign, for example, television directs our attention to major candidates and to the race for victory; by contrast, fringe candidates and the issues are often treated as secondary. Walter Lippman's (1922) view of the press articulates well the agenda-setting account: 'it is like a beam of a searchlight that moves restlessly about, bringing one episode and then another out of the darkness and into vision'.

Agenda-setting is forced by the limited length of news broadcasts. It is through their assumptions about newsworthiness that news editors resolve their daily dilemma of reducing a day's worth of world events to less than 30 minutes on the evening news. In deciding what to cover, in what order, and what to leave out, programme editors set the agenda and exert their impact.

Because news programmes focus on the exceptional, their content is invariably an unrepresentative sample of events. For example, policy fiascos receive more attention than policy successes. Similarly, corruption is a story but integrity is not. A fresh story gathers more coverage than a new development of a tired theme. Necessarily, agenda-setting creates a distorting mirror on the world. The shorter news bulletins become, the more selective the TV lens must be and the greater the distortion becomes.

But we should recognize two limitations to the agenda-setting perspective. First, editors do not select stories on a whim (Box 8.4). In deciding whether to pursue a story, editors take into account their assessment of the significance their audience will attach to it. Editors are also sensitive to the item's potential impact on audience size and appreciation.

Editors are paid to demonstrate their news sense; if they consistently fail to do so, they lose their jobs. It is therefore naïve to attribute broad agenda-setting power to editors simply because they make the specific judgements about what is to appear on screen or on the front page. The wider cultural context enters into their calculation of what to cover. Just as we do not blame the newsreader for the news, neither should we condemn the news selector for the agenda.

The view that the media circulate opinions more than they create them is implicit in Newton's wise comment (2006, p. 215) about the relationship between journalists and society:

BOX 8.4

Some tests used by journalists to determine newsworthiness

- ▶ Will the story have a strong impact on our audience?
- ▶ Does the story involve violence? ('If it bleeds, it leads.')
- ▶ Is the story current and novel?
- ▶ Does the story involve well-known people?

Source: Adapted from Graber (2005), pp. 106–8, based on studies in the USA.

Implicit in many statements about media effects on society is the idea that somehow the media are quite separate from society, firing their poison arrows from a distance. In fact, the media are part of society; journalists and editors do not arrive on Earth from Mars and Venus, they are part of society like the rest of us.

Second, the explosion of channels in the electronic era means that agenda control is no longer as strict as in the heyday of broadcast television. People can follow even the most specialized political interests through some media outlet. As the media becomes more pluralistic, so consumers acquire the capacity to follow their noses and shape their own agendas.

The **framing** of a story – the way in which reports construct a coherent narrative about an event – is a more recent attempt to understand media impact. The idea here is interpretive in character, reflecting Plato's observation that 'those who tell the stories also rule society'. The journalist's words, and the camera's images, help to frame the story, providing a narrative which encourages a particular reaction from the viewer. For example, are immigrants presented as a stimulus to the economy or as a threat to society? Does the American media portray a war critically (Vietnam in its later stages) or positively (Iraq in the invasion phase)? Is a criminal who has been sentenced to die getting his just deserts or a cruel and unusual punishment? As the concept of a 'story' suggests, the journalist must translate the event covered into an organized narrative which connects with the receiver. The shorter the report, the greater the reliance on the shared, if sometimes simplistic, presuppositions termed 'consensus frames' by Jamieson and Waldman (2003).

Finally, the media's agenda and frames may exert a **priming** effect, encouraging people to apply the criteria implicit in one story to new information and topics. In an American study, Iyengar *et al.* (1982) noted how 'problems prominently positioned in television broadcasts loom large in evaluations of presidential performance'. This indirect, cueing effect may have been understated in research focused on direct media effects. For example, the more the media focuses its coverage on foreign policy, the more likely it is that voters will be primed to judge parties according to their policies in this area and to vote accordingly.

To take another example, it is possible that coverage of racist attacks may prompt some individuals to engage in similar acts themselves, should the opportunity arise in their neighbourhood. Bear in mind, however, that priming is more often asserted than demonstrated – it is, again, often claimed by those who seek to blame the media for behaviour that in fact has its roots elsewhere. To attribute one racist incident to media coverage of another is surely to ignore underlying causes.

The effects we have outlined here – reinforcement, agenda-setting, framing and priming – are precise and, in principle, measurable. Their importance is that they offer insight into how the content and tone of media coverage can impinge on the audience. In this way, they take us beyond blanket assertions of media power to a more subtle interpretation of media effects.

Television and newspapers

One danger in discussing the mass media lies in treating its various channels as uniform – as if books, films, magazines, press, radio, television and websites were similar in their partisanship and effects. As an antidote to such treatments, in this section we contrast the impact of the two key channels of the mass media age: television and newspapers.

By the 1980s, television had become the preeminent mass medium in all liberal democracies. It remains a visual, credible and easily digested format which reaches almost every household. Consider election campaigns as an example. Here the television studio has become the main site of battle. The party gladiators participate through appearing on interviews, debates and talk shows; merely appearing on television confirms some status and recognition on candidates. Ordinary voters consume the election, if at all, through watching television.

Local party activists, once the assault troops of the campaign, have become mere skirmishers. The British Member of Parliament who found that he could no longer canvass effectively on the doorstep because his constituents were too engaged with the campaign on television tells a plausible tale about the impact of television on local campaigning (Mitchell, 1982). Television has ceased to cover the campaign, it has become the campaign.

To say that the television studio is the site of battle is one thing; to say that it determines the outcome is quite another. It is difficult to demonstrate a strong connection between television coverage of campaigns and the voters' response. For instance, one frequent observation about the electoral impact of television is that it has primed voters to base their decision more on personalities, especially those of the party leaders. To which an obvious riposte is: compared to when? Before television, after all, came the now forgotten media of radio and, in some countries, cinema. Even the claim that the broadcasting media as a whole have led voters to decide on personality neglects the importance of personalized press coverage of the parties in the era before broadcasting.

To be sure, some studies have shown a modest increase in recent decades in the focus of media coverage of election campaigns on party leaders. However, it is far from proven that votes are increasingly cast on the basis of leaders' personalities and even less clear that any such increase is attributable to television. Certainly, research does not support the proposition that television, even in the USA, has rendered the images of the leaders the key influence on electoral choice (Mughan, 2000; King, 2002; Langer, 2006).

Where television may initially have made a broader but larger contribution is in partisan dealignment: the weakening of party loyalties among electors. Because of the limited number of channels available in television's early decades, governments required balanced and neutral treatment of politics. The result was an inoffensive style that contrasted with the more partisan coverage previously offered in many national newspapers, especially outside the USA. As a result, television may originally have weakened party loyalties, particularly among generations growing up with the medium.

In the Netherlands, for instance, television helped to break down the separate pillars composing Dutch society in the 1950s, providing a new common ground for citizens exposed to the single national channel: 'Catholics discovered that Socialists were not the dangerous atheists they had been warned about, Liberals had to conclude that orthodox Protestants were not the bigots they were supposed to be' (Wigbold, 1979, p. 201).

More recently, however, the multiplication of channels and more relaxed regulation has led to a more partisan tone to some television coverage, especially in the USA. Fox News, for example, made its name with its explicitly patriotic coverage of the Iraq War, treatment which contrasted with the more traditional approach of, say, CNN. At the very least, the differing coverage of these channels reflected and reinforced renewed ideological conflict between liberals and conservatives (Mason, 2006).

Despite the primacy of television, it would be wrong to discount the political impact of the second mass medium, newspapers. Despite their falling circulation, quality newspapers possess an authority springing from their longevity. In nearly all democracies, newspapers are freer with comment than is television. In an age when broadcasters still lead the provision of instant news, the more relaxed daily schedule of the press allows print columnists to offer more interpretation and evaluation.

Television tells us what happened; at their best, newspapers place events in context. Broadcast news can only cover one story at a time whereas newspapers can be scanned for items of interest and can be read at the user's convenience. Newspapers offer a luxury which television can rarely afford: space for reflection. For such reasons, quality newspapers remain the trade press of politics, read avidly by politicians themselves. In countries with a lively press tradition, newspapers retain a political significance greatly in excess of their circulation.

Newspapers also influence television's agenda: a story appearing on TV's evening news often begins life in the morning paper. This agenda-influencing role, it is worth noting, does not depend on a newspaper's circulation. But when an elector does see a story covered both on television and in the press, the combined impact exceeds that of either medium considered alone.

In several liberal democracies – notably Britain, Germany, Japan, Korea, the Netherlands, Scandinavia and Switzerland – readership of national newspapers remains substantial (Norris, 2002, p. 130). In Japan, unusually, some studies indicate that the public still relies more on the national press than on television and that in consequence newspapers exert more influence over the electorate's agenda (Feldman, 1993, p. 24).

Public opinion

Especially in liberal democracies, the business of politics is in part a battle for influence over the important but imprecise terrain of **public opinion**. Governments, parties and interest groups seek to persuade the public to adopt their agenda, their frame of reference and their policy preferences. Yet although the notion of public opinion remains somewhat opaque, it is an important element in political communication, constructed and measured by the media. In this section, we discuss the definition, measurement and impact of public opinion.

Defining public opinion

Where political culture refers to the sum of political attitudes in a community, the notion of public opinion focuses more on the specific issues, policies and problems of the day. Reflecting this contrast, one definition is highly pragmatic: public opinion is simply what the adult population thinks about a given issue, nothing more and nothing less. From this viewpoint, public opinion can be measured by a straightforward opinion poll surveying the adult population.

Public opinion can refer to (1) 'the range of views on some controversial issue held by some significant portion of the population' or (2) the informed judgement of a community on an issue of common concern, where that judgement is formed in the context of shared political goals (Qualter, 1991).

While this definition is certainly clear, it does not fully capture what most politicians understand by public opinion. Their use of the term usually denotes structured and organized opinion – as expressed for example in the media – that impinges on their decisions. This more political account of public opinion can be used to link the idea of a 'public' to the views of an informed community sharing basic political principles. This more elaborate perspective was expressed by the British statesman W. E. Gladstone (1809–98): 'public opinion represents the sum or balance of the abstract moral principles of the persons forming the community' (quoted in Hare, 1873, p. xix). From this viewpoint, a community is only regarded as capable of a public opinion if its people are settled on the ends of government and the range of means for pursuing them. Here public opinion is interpreted as the considered will of a cohesive group.

Measuring public opinion

The idea of public opinion has gained further currency as opinion polls, citizens' juries and focus groups have developed to study it. Indeed, there are few areas where a concept is so closely linked to its measurement. In liberal democracies, public opinion is both assessed by, and partly composed of, investigations into its content (Box 8.5).

Consider **opinion polls** and **sample surveys**, the most accurate methods of identifying what people profess to believe. Although the public itself remains resolutely sceptical of samples, their accuracy is now well-attested, at least in predicting election outcomes. In the United States, the average error in predicting the major parties' share of the vote at post-war national elections is around 1.5 per cent. This accuracy is impressive even if not always sufficient for the television networks to pick the right winner on election night. The level of precision is similar in other democracies.

Counter-intuitive it may be, but 1,000 people carefully selected for an opinion poll can accurately represent the whole population. The key phrase here is 'carefully selected'. The procedure must be systematic, such as selecting every nth name from a list of electors. Self-selected samples such as viewers who respond to television polls, or constituents who contact their representative about their pet topic, are not a valid basis for estimating public opinion – at

---

> **BOX 8.5**
>
> ## Measuring public opinion
>
> ▶ An **opinion poll** is a series of questions asked in a standard way of a systematic sample of the population. The term usually refers to short surveys on topical issues for the media. Polls are usually conducted face to face, by telephone or by email (Bishop, 2004).
> ▶ A **sample survey** is conducted using the same methods as an opinion poll but involves a more detailed questionnaire. Such surveys are often commissioned by governments or academic researchers (Fink, 2005).
> ▶ A **focus group** is a moderated discussion among a small group of respondents on a particular topic. It is a qualitative open-ended device used to explore the thinking and emotions lying behind people's attitudes. The technique has found favour with party strategists (Krueger and Casey, 2000).
> ▶ In a **deliberative opinion poll**, or **citizens' jury**, people are briefed by, and can question, experts and politicians on a given topic before their own opinions are measured. This technique seeks to measure what public opinion would be if the public were fully informed on the issue (Fishkin and Laslett, 2003).

---

least when public opinion is taken to include the non-attentive public as well as the **issue public**.

Yet even when a sample is chosen systematically, it would be wrong to overstate the reliability of opinion polls in measuring the opinions of individual respondents. Like students taking a test, interviewees in a survey are answering questions set elsewhere. Polls are commissioned by journalists and party officials in the capital city, not by the ordinary people who answer the questions. They are a form of agenda-setting.

As a result, people may never have thought about a topic before they are invited to answer questions on it (Althaus, 2003). They may give an opinion when they have none or they may agree to a state-

> The **issue** or **attentive public** consists of the minority with a particular interest in or knowledge of a given topic.

ment because it is the easiest thing to do ('yea-saying'). Certainly, one danger of opinion polls is that they help to construct public opinion even as they measure it.

A **focus group** overcomes some of these difficulties. Here, a researcher gathers together a small group of people – typically eight to ten – for a general discussion of a topic in which the participants normally share a particular interest: for instance, lapsed Republicans, non-voters or protest participants. The idea is to explore in open-ended style the perspectives through which the participants view the issue. A focus group is a qualitative version of an opinion poll, smaller in scale and to a greater extent self-selected, but aiming at a fuller understanding than is possible with the pre-coded answers used in an opinion poll.

Because opinion polls do not give respondents a chance to discuss the issue before expressing their views, their results are criticized by those who favour more ambitious interpretations of the public's role. Building on a richer view of the public's capacity, scholars have developed the idea of a **deliberative opinion poll** or **citizens' jury** (Fishkin, 1991). This technique involves exposing a small sample of electors to a range of viewpoints on a selected topic, perhaps through presentations by experts and politicians. With the background to the problem established, the group proceeds to a discussion and a judgement. Opinion is only measured when the issues have been thoroughly aired in this way. As Fishkin (1991, p. 1) explains:

an ordinary opinion poll models what the public thinks, given how little it knows. A deliberative opinion poll models what the public would think, if it had a more adequate chance to think about the questions at issue.

Deliberative polling can therefore be used to anticipate how opinion might develop on new issues. It is also particularly useful on issues with a large technical content, for example global warming and genetic testing. In such areas, expert explanation can usefully precede an expression of opinion. Though not widely used, citizens' juries are an ingenious attempt to overcome the problem of ill-informed replies, which bedevils conventional opinion polls.

The impact of public opinion

Given that public opinion is an important element of democratic politics, how exactly does it exert its influence? In a sense public opinion pervades all policy-making. It forms the environment within which politicians work, sitting in on many government meetings even though it is never minuted as a member.

In such discussions public opinion usually performs one of two roles: acting either as a prompt or as a veto. 'Public opinion demands we do something about traffic congestion' is an example of the former; 'public opinion would never accept restrictions on car use' illustrates the latter. So, as Qualter (1991, p. 511) suggests, 'while public opinion does not govern, it may set limits on what governments do'.

Yet public opinion is never all-powerful, even in liberal democracies. It informs agendas rather than policy. Four factors limit its influence:

▶ Public opinion offers few detailed policy prescriptions. A few important objectives preoccupy the public but most policies are routine and uncontroversial. In detailed policy-making, expert and organized opinion matters more than public opinion.

▶ The public as a whole is often ill-informed, especially but not only on foreign policy. Asked before the Iraq invasion, 'To the best of your knowledge, how many of the September 11 hijackers were Iraqi citizens?', only 7 per cent of Americans gave the correct answer: none (Pryor, 2003).

▶ Public opinion can evade trade-offs but governments cannot, though they sometimes try. The public may want lower taxes, more government spending and a lower budget deficit but rulers must choose between incompatible objectives. Further, the risks associated with a policy are poorly assessed by the public but require close attention from decision-makers (Weissberg, 2002).

▶ Politicians typically respond to organized opinion rather than to public opinion. Their perceptions of the public's views are in any case often inaccurate, derived as they are from the distorting lenses of interest groups and the natural tendency to project one's own views onto the wider electorate (Herbst, 1998).

Public opinion is most influential when it is seen to change. Only foolhardy politicians disregard developments in the overall climate of opinion and many politicians are wisely sensitive to changes in the national mood (Stimson, 1991, 2004). Climate change can be an irrelevance one year and the topic everyone is talking about the next; a skilled politician can spot and respond to such agenda shifts.

The media in authoritarian states

Just as democracy thrives on the flow of information, so authoritarian rulers limit free expression, leading to media coverage which is subdued and usually subservient. Far from acting as the fourth estate, casting a searchlight into the darker corners of government, journalists in authoritarian states defer to political authority. Lack of resources within the media sector usually increases vulnerability to pressure. Official television stations and subsidized newspapers reproduce the regime's line while critical journalists are harassed and the entire media sector develops an instinct for self-preservation through self-censorship.

However, the consequence is that inadequate information flows to the top, increasing the gap between state and society and leading ultimately to incorrect decisions. A thoughtful dictator responds to this problem by encouraging the media to expose malfeasance at local level, thus providing a check on governance away from the centre. But there is no escaping the paradox of authoritarianism. By controlling information, rulers may secure their power in the short run but they also reduce the quality of governance, potentially threatening their own survival over the long term. The more developed the country, the more severe is the damage inflicted by an information deficit at the top.

How exactly do authoritarian rulers limit independent journalism? The constraints are varied and often more subtle than explicit censorship. An understanding of these limitations contributes to an appreciation of authoritarian rule. In her study of sub-Saharan Africa before the wave of liberalization in the 1990s, Bourgault (1995, p. 180) identified a typical roster of control mechanisms, including:

- Declaring states of emergency which formally limit media freedom;
- Licensing of publications and journalists;
- Heavy taxation of printing equipment;
- A requirement to deposit a bond with the government before new publications can launch;
- Restricted access to newsprint;
- The threat of losing government advertising;
- Broad libel laws.

As we saw in Chapter 6, authoritarian states are, of course, most often found in low-income countries. Lack of resources undoubtedly holds back the development of the media. Limited means stifle journalistic initiative and increase vulnerability. Sometimes impoverished journalists are reduced to publishing favourable stories (or threatening to write critical ones) in exchange for money.

Pressures from authoritarian leaders are by no means restricted to Africa. In much of post-communist central Asia, large parts of the media remain in state hands, giving the authorities direct leverage. The state also typically retains ownership of a leading television channel. The outcome is subservience:

From Kazakhstan to Kyrgyzstan and Tajikistan to Belarus and Ukraine, the story is a dismal one: tax laws are used for financial harassment; a body of laws forbids insults of those in high places; compulsory registration of the media is common. In Azerbaijan, as in Belarus, one-man rule leaves little room for press freedom. (Foley, 1999, p. 45)

The justification for restricting the freedom of the media is typically built on an overriding national requirement for social stability, nation-building or economic development. The subtext is that we cannot be like the West until we have caught up, and perhaps not even then. In Egypt, for instance, the government expects that 'the press should uphold the security of the country, promote economic development, and support approved social norms' (Lesch, 2004, p. 610). A free press, like a competitive party system, is presented as a recipe for squabbling and disharmony.

Even though many of these justifications for controlling the media are simply excuses for authoritarian government, we should not assume that the

Western idea of a free press garners universal appeal. Islamic states, in particular, stress the media's role in affirming religious values and social norms. A free press is seen as an excuse for licence: why, the question is posed, should we import Western, and particularly American, ideas of freedom if the practical result is the availability of pornography? When society is viewed as the expression of an overarching moral code, whether Islamic or otherwise, the Western tradition of free speech appears alien and even unethical.

As with other aspects of politics, totalitarian states developed a more sophisticated approach to the media. Mass communication was expected to play its part in the transformation of political culture. The media were therefore brought under tighter control than in other authoritarian systems. Unrelenting penetration of mass communication into everyday life was a core component of the totalitarian system. It is significant, however, that neither communist nor fascist regimes regarded the media, by themselves, as a sufficient means of ideological control. Communist states, in particular, supplemented mass **propaganda** with direct agitation in places where people gathered together.

On the one hand, propaganda explained the communist party's mission and instructed both the elite and the masses in the teachings of Marx, Engels and Lenin. To achieve their propaganda objectives, ruling communist parties developed an elaborate media network with radio, posters, cinema, television and 'socialist art' all reinforcing each other. Agitation, on the other hand, operated at local, person-to-person level. The party sought to place an agitator in each factory, farm and military unit, encouraging the workers to ever greater feats of production. Together, propaganda and agitation dominated the flow of information; the theory was that the combined effect would be all the greater

> **Propaganda** is communication by an organization which seeks to promote support for its cause by influencing the attitudes and especially the behaviour of large numbers of people. The word is religious in origin: in 1622 the Catholic Church established a College of Propaganda to propagate the faith.

because, in the nature of a total regime, no dissenting voices were permitted.

What was the impact of the communist attempt to use the media as a tool for influencing the public? Propaganda does seem to have helped with agenda-setting by disguising local problems such as accidents, poverty and pollution which could be hidden from people beyond the affected area. It may also have scored some success in highlighting achievements such as industrialization (Oates, 2005, p. 118). And, just as advertising by parties in democracies is often aimed at their own activists, so communist propaganda may have helped party members to keep the faith.

But at a more fundamental level the communist experience revealed the limits of media power. A cynical public was not easily fooled. Grandiose statements about national progress were too often contradicted by the grim realities of daily life. In any case, as communist states became inert, so propaganda became empty ritual. No one believed that a new order of socialist fraternity was under construction. So the major lesson of communist propaganda is that even rulers who monopolize the media cannot guarantee their own legitimacy.

It is noteworthy, however, that the remaining states with a nominal communist allegiance have kept close control over the means of mass communication. In China, access to information has traditionally been provided on a need-to-know basis. The country's rulers remain keen to limit dissenting voices even as the party's tolerance of non-political debate increases. Although the regime is keen to promote e-commerce, internet users who search for 'inappropriate' topics such as democracy or Tibetan independence will find their searches blocked and their access to search engines withdrawn. In 2004, Reporters without Borders described China as the 'world's largest prison for cyber-dissidents' (Zhao, 2006). The excuse offered is that the authorities are merely protecting state security: 'managing the internet will affect national culture, information security and the long-term stability of the state', said Hu Jintao, China's president, in 2007 (Dickie, 2007). Western companies themselves have gone along with such limitations in order to secure access to the large Chinese market (Box 8.6).

BOX 8.6

China and the internet

This extract is a summary of China's *Public Pledge of Self-Regulation and Professional Ethics for the Chinese Internet Industry* (Internet Society of China, 2002). Yahoo! and other Western providers signed this document despite the limitations it places on the free flow of information.

'We internet service providers pledge to abide by state regulations on internet information service management to fulfil the following disciplinary obligations:

▶ *To refrain from producing, posting or disseminating pernicious information that may jeopardize state security and disrupt social stability, contravene laws and regulations and spread superstition and obscenity;*
▶ *To monitor the information publicized on websites according to law and remove harmful information promptly;*
▶ *To refrain from establishing links to websites containing harmful information'.*

John Chambers, chairman of Cisco, said, 'one thing technology companies cannot do, in my opinion, is involve themselves in politics within a country'.

Further reading: Goldsmith and Wu (2006), Dickie (2007).

The media in illiberal democracies

In illiberal democracies, control over the media is far less extensive than in authoritarian states. Citizens who lived though a preceding era of communist or military rule become aware of the greater range and vigour of channels operating in a newly competitive sector. The press, in particular, is often left substantially alone, offering a forum for elite debate which is perhaps of value even to the rulers.

Yet the leading political force also dominates broadcast coverage, even where explicit or implicit censorship is absent. To some extent, such an emphasis reflects political reality: viewers are naturally most interested in those who exert most influence over their lives. Latin America provides a good example. In many countries on the continent, a tradition of personal and populist rule lends itself well to expression through broadcasting media which reach the many poor and illiterate people who seek salvation through 'their' leader.

Foweraker *et al.* (2003, p. 105) describe the origins of this tradition in the twentieth century when 'populist leaders in Latin America made popular appeals to the people through mass media in newspapers and especially radio'. These authors comment that contemporary populism continues in the same vein, albeit now operating through television more than radio. Leaders hold out promises of 'a consumer lifestyle that is intimately familiar to their publics through television advertising and television soap operas' (ibid., p. 107).

The political style of Hugo Chávez, president of Venezuela since 1998, is a good example. Many callers to his Sunday morning broadcast show, *¡Aló, Presidente!,* petition the president for help in securing a job or social security benefit, usually citing in the process the callousness of the preceding regime. The president created a special office to handle all such requests. Aware of Chávez's communication skills, the opposition sought to restrict the president's access to state-owned broadcasting, though the regime continues to intimidate journalists (Hellinger, 2003, p. 49). In Chávez's governing style, we see how the leader of an illiberal democracy can strengthen his authority through the media even against the opposition of many media professionals themselves.

Even in many post-communist illiberal democracies, pressures on the media – from powerful business people as well as politicians – remain intense. In Russia, for instance, this influence derives precisely from the centrality of television to political communication. As in Latin America, broadcasting is the main way of reaching a dispersed population for whom free television has more appeal than paid-for papers. In a 2004 survey, 82 per cent of Russians said they watched television routinely, compared to just 22 per cent who said the same about national newspapers (Oates, 2005, p. 124). The television audience in Russia for nightly news programmes is substantial, matching that in the United States for the Super Bowl. In the size and interest of its audience, television news is the equivalent of soap operas elsewhere. By comparison, the press and the internet are less explicitly controlled, at least on non-political matters, an important change to the all-embracing censorship of the communist era.

Vladimir Putin's success in the presidential election of 2000 owed much to his control of public television, whose news broadcasts in the final days of the campaign portrayed his opponents as sympathetic to gays and Jews. Subsequently, Putin took steps to tighten his control over the main television channels, in some ways re-establishing an authoritarian level of dominance. Some channels are state-owned; others are controlled by friendly business interests; and one channel that did offer more independent coverage now finds itself covering sport only. Particularly but not only during elections, television showcases the achievements of the administration and its favoured candidates; opposition figures receive less, and distinctly less flattering, attention. This strong pro-regime bias continued after Dimitry Medvedev succeeded to the presidency in 2008.

With over 100 laws governing media conduct, and the occasional journalist still found murdered by unknown assailants, self-censorship – the voice in the editor's head which asks 'am I taking a risk in publishing this story?' – remains rife. Because editors know which side their bread is buttered, there is no need for politicians to take the political risk involved in explicit instruction. The internal censor allows the president to maintain deniability. 'Censorship? What censorship?' he can ask with a smile.

The interesting point – and one that is characteristic of illiberal democracy – is that the Russian public seems to prefer control of the media by established authority to the liberal model of independent journalists searching out the truth (Oates, 2005, p. 127). Russians regard state television as one of the most unbiased and reliable sources of information, even though they are aware of political interference in its coverage. Perhaps influenced by the communist era, most Russians raised no objections to the highly controlled treatment of either the war in Chechnya or the country's many social problems. These attitudes to the media reflect an underlying preference for order and in particular for a strong president who delivers it.

Learning Resources for Chapter 8

Next step

Norris (2000) offers an interesting comparative account of the media's role in Western democracies.

Further reading

Gunther and Mughan (2000) and Esser and Pfetsch (2004) offer comparative collections; see also Bennett and Entman (2001), Hallin and Mancini (2004) and Street (forthcoming). On the USA, Graber (2005) is an authoritative text, while Jamieson and Waldman (2003) look at the 'press effect' specifically. Norris *et al.* (2003) compare the frames used in media coverage of 9/11 with earlier terrorist incidents. On public opinion, Glynn *et al.* (1998) is a wide-ranging collection while Bishop (2004) examines whether public opinion is fact or illusion. Away from Western democracies, Willnat and Aw (2009) examine the media in Asia; Bourgault (1995) discusses sub-Saharan Africa; and Oates (2006) portrays television, democracy and elections in Russia.

Internet sources

Communication, Cultural and Media Studies Infobase
A useful resource for students of communication
http://www.ccms-infobase.com/

Reporters without Borders
For press freedom
http://www.rsf.org/

Freedom House
Press freedom by country
http://www.freedomhouse.org

International Federation of Journalists
The world's largest organization of journalists
http://www.ifj.org/

Index on Censorship
For free expression
http://www.indexonline.org/

Pew Center for Civic Journalism
Advancing good journalism
http://www.pewcenter.org/

UNESCO Information and Communication
Communication from a cross-national and policy perspective
http://www.unesco.org

www.palgrave.com
Companion Website
Visit the Companion Website to 'click and go'
www.palgrave.com/politics/hague

Chapter 9
Political participation

Political participation refers to any of the many ways in which people can seek to influence the composition or policies of their government. Clearly, citizens contacting their representative and activists canvassing for their favoured candidate are participating in the formal political process. But participation can also take less conventional forms such as signing a petition, taking part in a demonstration or even engaging in terrorist acts against the state. One distinction in the study of participation, then, is between its more conventional and less conventional forms.

In a liberal democracy, people can choose whether to get involved in politics, to what extent and through what channels. But participation is also found in many non-democratic regimes. Totalitarian states required citizens to engage in regimented demonstrations of support for the government. Other non-democratic regimes also demand at least a facade of participation, though this too is often manipulated so that it supports rather than threatens the existing rulers.

Participation in liberal democracies

What expectations should be brought to the study of participation in a liberal democracy? One perspective, dating back to Aristotle (1962) and the ancient Greeks, is that involvement in collective decision-making is both an obligation owed to the community and an exercise in personal development, broadening individual horizons and acting as a vehicle for collective education. From this point of view, participation is beneficial both to the community and to the individual, and non-participants are seen as freewheeling on the efforts of others. This approach finds echoes in the contemporary emphasis on the duties and rights of the citizen (Bellamy, 2008).

An alternative approach, rooted in practical realities more than high ideals, sets a lower standard for participation. Contrary to Aristotle, the suggestion is that man (and woman) is not naturally a political animal; rather, we should interpret universal participation as a sign of unresolved tension within a political system. Demonstrations, protests and even a high turnout may indicate a system that is overheating rather than in rude health.

From this viewpoint, all that is required in a liberal democracy is that citizens monitor political events with the realistic ability to become involved

Political participation is activity by individuals formally intended to influence who governs or the decisions taken by those who do. **Conventional participation** takes place within formal politics; **unconventional participation** is, to a degree, outside or even against orthodox politics.

when they want to do so. Schudson (1998, p. 311) suggests that citizens may appear inactive but remain poised for action when required, like parents watching their children play in the pool. In normal times, limited participation may indicate the success of a political system in meeting popular demands, thus allowing citizens to pursue more fulfilling activities. What matters is that the channels are open, not that they are in constant use. We first encountered this perspective in discussing Almond and Verba's view of political culture (see p. 122); it is useful to remind ourselves here that the simple equations, participation equals good and non-participation equals bad, should not be taken for granted.

Although this debate about participation raises issues of judgement rather than fact, the findings reviewed in this chapter are nonetheless relevant. If we should discover, for instance, that non-participants are clustered in lower social strata, then we might well want to conclude that lack of engagement reflects political cynicism rather than satisfaction. What then are the findings about individual participation in liberal democracies?

The most striking result is the limited extent of any form of participation other than voting. In a renowned analysis, Milbrath and Goel (1977, p. 11) divided the American population into three groups, a classification which has since been applied to participation in other liberal democracies. These categories, based on involvement with conventional politics, were:

◆ A small proportion of gladiators (around 5–7 per cent of the population) who fight the political battle – for instance, the activist campaigners;
◆ A large group of spectators (about 60 per cent) who observe the contest but rarely participate beyond voting;
◆ A substantial number of apathetics (about one-third) who are unengaged in formal politics.

Milbrath and Goel's labels were based on an analogy with Roman contests at which a few gladiators performed for the mass of spectators but with some apathetics not even watching the show (Figure 9.1).

As Schudson points out, it is important not to write off the large population of spectators: those

Figure 9.1 Patterns of participation in liberal democracies

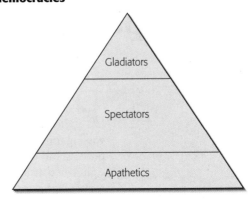

who keep an eye on politics without becoming involved other than through casting an occasional ballot. Especially among the young, political engagement may take the form of visiting websites, discussing an election with friends or watching a film about a current issue. To categorize such activity as 'spectating' is to take a rather narrow and perhaps old-fashioned view of participation. In Norway, for instance, despite a fall in turnout, 'the broader political activity of citizens has increased. The rise in political involvement is quite widespread, covering political interest and political discussion' (Listhaug and Grønftlaten, 2007).

The significance of this point is that any decline in narrow participatory behaviour such as contacting a representative does not necessarily indicate a fall in wider political interest and the spectating that forms part of it (Dalton, 2008). It is noteworthy here that 49 per cent of the British population said in a 2008 survey that it was essential or very important to being a good citizen to keep informed about current affairs, higher than the proportion saying the same about contacting politicians or joining a party (Ipsos-Mori, 2008). Participation as monitoring is a theme ignored in traditional studies focused on behaviour alone.

Whatever view we take on political spectators, the most striking fact about political participation in liberal democracies is the small proportion of gladiators. Voting in national elections is normally the only activity in which a majority of citizens engages. Table 9.1 shows some typical findings from a British study: apart from signing a petition, participation

Table 9.1 Political participation in Great Britain, 2008

Which, if any, of the things on this list have you done in the last two to three years?

	%
Voted in the last general election	61
Signed a petition	37
Boycotted certain products	18
Presented my views to a representative	17
Attended a political meeting	4
Taken part in a demonstration	3
Taken an active part in a political campaign	3
Donated money to a political party	3

Sources: Ipsos-Mori (2009); turnout from Kavanagh and Butler (2005), Table A1.2.

declines rapidly once we move beyond voting at national elections. Throughout the democratic world anything other than voting is the preserve of a minority of activists. Furthermore, the gladiators are outnumbered by the apathetics: people who neither vote nor even follow politics through the media.

It is easy to assume that different forms of participation form a scale, such that those who engage in the rarer forms of participation also perform the more popular acts. In fact, however, there is some tendency for people to specialize in particular forms of participation. In their classic study of the United States, Verba *et al.* (1978) identified four modes of conventional participation:

- Voting, e.g. participating in local as well as national elections;
- Campaigning, e.g. canvassing;
- Communal activity, e.g. participating in an organization concerned with a particular issue;
- Contacting, e.g. communicating with officials about an individual problem.

So participation is, to a degree, a matter of 'how?' and not just 'how much?'. This observed division of labour suggests the value of providing a menu of participation opportunities so that people can choose the channels of engagement with which they are most comfortable.

There is no denying that whichever mode of participation we examine, the gladiators are far from a cross-section of society. In most democracies, participation is greatest among well-educated, middle-class, middle-aged, white men. In addition, for all but protest behaviour, participation peaks among the middle-aged.

Furthermore, the highest layers of political involvement show the greatest skew. As Putnam (1976, p. 33) put it:

The 'law of increasing disproportion' seems to apply to nearly every political system; no matter how we measure political and social status, the higher the level of political authority, the greater the representation for high-status social groups.

This bias in participation towards upper social groups is significant because it suggests that apathy may not, after all, be a sign of satisfaction with the existing order. In that case, we would expect the well-heeled to be less involved in politics because they have relatively little to complain about. So why does participation increase as we move up the social scale? Two factors seem to be particularly influential: political resources and political interest (Verba *et al.*, 1995).

First, consider resources. People in high-status groups are equipped with such political assets as education, money, status and communication skills. Education gives access to information and, we trust, strengthens the ability to interpret it. Money buys the luxury of time for political activity. High status provides the opportunity to obtain a respectful hearing. And communication skills such as the ability to speak in public help in presenting one's views persuasively. Added together, these resources provide a useful toolkit for effective political intervention; their unequal distribution helps to account for under-participation by less privileged social groups.

Second, consider political interest. High-status individuals are more likely to be engaged with formal politics. They possess the motive as well as the means to become involved. No longer preoccupied with the daily struggle, they can take satisfaction from engagement in collective activity (Inglehart, 1997). The wealthy are also more likely to be brought up in a family, and to attend a school,

Table 9.2 Female representation in the national legislatures of liberal democracies, 2009

	Year of female suffrage	Current electoral system	Female representation	
			(%)	Rank (out of 146 countries)
Sweden	1919	List PR	47	2
Finland	1906	List PR	42	7
Netherlands	1919	List PR	41	8
Denmark	1915	List PR	38	9
Norway	1913	MMP	36	13
New Zealand	1893	MMP	34	17
Germany	1918	MMP	32	20
Australia	1902	AV	27	35
Canada	1917	Plurality	22	48
Italy	1945	PR	21	52
United Kingdom	1918	Plurality	20	59
France	1944	Majority	18	65
USA	1920	Plurality	17	71
Ireland	1918	STV	13	89

Note: Rwanda is ranked highest (56%). Based on single or lower house. AV: alternative vote; MMP: mixed member proportional; PR: proportional representation; STV: single transferable vote. For electoral systems, see Box 10.1.

Sources: McAllister and Studlar (2002), IPU (2009).

where an interest in current affairs is encouraged. They will probably see how politics can impact on their own wealth. So higher social groups have an interest in politics – in both senses of 'interest' – and can afford to put their concerns into practice. Conversely, those in the lower social strata are less likely to come from a background where an interest in formal politics is expected and they are more likely to be preoccupied with the struggles of ordinary life.

These factors of political resources and political interest help to explain the social bias in political participation, and potentially in political decisions, towards privileged groups. In addition, they assist in accounting for one continuing case of under-representation, helping to explain why women are still in a minority at higher political levels even though in most countries they form a majority of electors (and often, these days, of voters). In 2009, women made up just 19 per cent of the world's legislators, double the figure from 30 years earlier but still a large under-representation (Table 9.2).

There is no doubt that, as a group, women still possess fewer political resources than men. Across the world as a whole, they still have less formal education (even though this difference has reversed among the young in many liberal democracies). Further, interest in formal politics is sometimes limited by childbearing and homemaking responsibilities and, as we have suggested, political interest is a major influence on participation.

In addition, of course, there is a self-perpetuating mechanism at work: just because men predominate at the higher levels of politics, this state of affairs is seen as natural by many men and causes many women to seek opportunities elsewhere. By the same token, though, once change begins, it should become self-reinforcing (Stevens, 2007).

The emphasis of research on political participation is on explaining what distinguishes the gladiators from the spectators. But let us not ignore the apathetics, the people who do not participate at all. This group raises the problem of **political exclusion**. As Verba *et al.* (1995) write, the apathetics in effect exclude themselves – or perhaps are excluded – from the normal means by which citizens collectively shape their society.

A typical non-participant might be an unemployed young person with no qualifications, inhabiting a high-crime, inner-city neighbourhood, often from a minority culture and perhaps not even speaking the dominant language. Such a profile may encourage radical activity among a few but, in general, a preoccupation with everyday life limits or eliminates formal political participation.

Just as higher social groups possess both the resources and the interest to over-participate, so a shortage of resources and lack of interest in the remote goings-on of national politics explain the under-participation of those near the bottom of increasingly unequal Western democracies.

Overall, then, studies of political participation demonstrate the tension within liberal democracy between traditional participatory principles and prosaic reality. The aims of universal participation and political equality coexist alongside the facts of limited and unequal involvement. This gap provides room for concerned citizens to advocate measures to increase political involvement, a theme of some importance given the concentration of disengagement among the poor. For example, Macedo *et al.* (2005, p. 9) comment that 'persistent or even increasing inequalities in participation in the United States impoverish our public life and call into question the democratic credentials of our politics'.

However, such efforts will not close the gap between democratic aspirations and achievements. Because participation in a liberal democracy is an option rather than a requirement, it is unlikely ever to be equal; and, because inequalities in participation are deeply rooted in social differences in resources and interest, so the active minority is likely to remain unrepresentative of the passive majority. The gap may reflect inflated expectations of democracy more than its real, if limited, achievements.

Social movements

In 1996, 325,000 Belgians, 3 per cent of the country's population, marched through Brussels in a peaceful protest against an inadequate public investigation into a sexually motivated child murder. This 'White March' (white was worn as a symbol of purity) was an example of a social movement, a form of participation that has come to provide a significant challenge, or at least a useful supplement, to standard channels. In this section, we extend our discussion of political participation by examining the nature and interpretation of these movements.

Social movements (also called popular movements) consist of people from outside the mainstream who come together to seek a common objective through an unorthodox challenge to the existing political order. The White March was a typical example in that many participants considered themselves to be conventional citizens who would not ordinarily take an active part in politics. In criticizing an official investigation, their march was a political protest against politics.

Social movements espouse a political style which provides distance from established channels, thereby questioning the legitimacy as well as the decisions of the government. The members of social movements adopt a wide repertoire of protest acts, including demonstrations, sit-ins, boycotts and political strikes. Some such acts may cross the border into illegality but the actors' motives are political.

To appreciate the character of social movements, we can usefully compare them with parties (Box 9.1). Movements are more loosely organized, typically lacking the precise membership, subscriptions and leadership of both parties and interest groups. Like parties whose origins lie outside the legislature, movements emerge from society to challenge the political establishment. However, unlike parties, movements do not seek to craft distinct interests

---

BOX 9.1

Comparing social movements, political parties and protective interest groups

	Social movements	Political parties	Protective interest groups
Seek to influence the government?	Usually	Yes	Yes
Seek to become the government?	No	Yes	No
Focus on a single issue?	Yes	Rarely	Yes
Formally organized, led and funded?	Not usually	Yes	Yes
Tactics used	Unconventional	Conventional	Conventional
Main levels of operation	Global, national, local	National	National

Note: On protective interest groups, see Box 12.2.

---

into an overall package; rather, they claim the moral high ground in one specific area.

Movements can also be contrasted with interest groups. Like interest groups, social movements typically focus on a single issue: nuclear disarmament, feminism, the environment. Again like interest groups, social movements do not seek state power; rather they seek to influence the political agenda, usually by claiming that their voice has previously gone unheard. But the contrasts with interest groups are more important. Whereas protective interest groups seek precise regulatory objectives, movements are more diffuse, often seeking cultural as much as legislative change. For example, the gay movement might measure its success by how many gay people come out, not just by the passage of anti-discrimination legislation. Similarly, women's movements may emphasize consciousness-raising among women. By focusing on culture and identity, movements adopt a broader interpretation of politics – and of the purpose of political participation – than do protective interest groups.

Before the emergence of the modern state, much protest activity was local rather than national, aimed at landlords, tax collectors and other authority figures. However, the transition to modernity soon created a favourable environment for the emergence of broader and more sophisticated forms of protest. Urbanization brought people together, education expanded their concerns, the mass media enabled information to circulate, civil rights allowed people

to express their opinions openly, representative institutions gave people hope that their voice might be heard and, above all, the growth of central government made politics a more important theme in ordinary lives. All these factors encouraged the emergence of social movements engaged in collective protests aimed at national decision-makers.

Tilly (2004, p. 33) suggests that the British anti-slavery movement of the late-eighteenth and early nineteenth centuries should be regarded as the earliest example of a social movement as now understood. The techniques adopted in this campaign, including petitions and boycotts, established a palette of protest activities soon emulated by other reforming groups. It is clear, at any rate, that while social movements are a product of the modern era, they are not a recent phenomenon: **new politics** is a label that can mislead.

Even though movements themselves are far from new, perspectives on them have evolved. In the 1950s, mass movements, as they were then called, were perceived as a threat to the stability of liberal democracy. They were taken as a sign of a poorly integrated mass society 'containing large numbers of people who are not integrated into any broad social groupings, including classes' (Kornhauser, 1959, p. 14). Strong movements signalled weak institutions and the inability of the political system to process smoothly social demands into public policies. Movements were judged to be supported by marginal, disconnected groups: unemployed intellectuals, isolated workers, the peripheral middle class. 'Until the 1960s, most scholars who studied social movements were frightened of them' (Goodwin and Jasper, 2003a, p. 5).

Perspectives were transformed in the 1960s and 1970s. The American civil rights movement could hardly be dismissed as irrational, while Vietnam, and the draft specifically, propelled parts of the educated American middle class into anti-war movements. As intellectuals became more critical of the government, so their treatment of social movements became more positive. Especially in the United States, movements were judged to be engaged in 'rational, purposeful and organized action', mobilizing resources in pursuit of specific political goals (Tilly, 1978). Like public interest groups, they were now regarded as part of the normal political process. Reviewing this revised perspective, della Porta and Diani (1999, p. 10) conclude that 'it is no longer possible to define movements in a prejudicial sense as phenomena which are marginal and anti-institutional. A more fruitful interpretation towards the political interpretation of contemporary movements has been established'.

It is certainly worth noting that the movement activists of the era of protest in the West during the 1960s resembled the social profile of participants in orthodox politics. In the main, they were well-educated, articulate, young people from middle-class backgrounds. And more than a few leaders of social movements switched to orthodox politics as they aged: many a protest activist of the 1960s turned into a party leader by the century's end. Prominent examples included Joschka Fischer, Germany's foreign minister between 1998 and 2005, and Peter Hain, a minister in Tony Blair's government in Britain. For all the stylistic contrast between mainstream and movement politics, one function of the movements has been to provide a training ground for future national leaders. In this way, too, protest activism has entered the mainstream (Norris, 2002).

Developments in communications have lowered the barriers to entry for new movements. Take the protest in Britain in 2000 against the country's high tax on petrol (Joyce, 2002). A diverse network of British farmers and road hauliers blocked petrol refineries in a coordinated series of protests, quickly creating a national fuel crisis. This movement's rapid expansion, albeit building on foundations pre-

Table 9.3 Not in my name: the largest demonstrations against the Iraq War by city, 15–16 February 2003

City	Estimated number of protestors
Rome	Up to 3,000,000
Barcelona	1,300,000
London	1,000,000
Madrid	600,000
Berlin	500,000
Paris	200,000
Sydney	200,000
Damascus	Up to 200,000
Melbourne	160,000
New York	100,000

Source: Figures are estimates reported in the *Financial Times*, 17 February 2003.

viously established, owed much to mobile telephones. As Bennett (2005, p. 205) remarks, 'such applications of communication technology favour loosely linked distributed networks that are minimally dependent on central coordination, leaders or ideological commitment'.

Compared to parties and interest groups, movements can expand more easily from the national to the international level. Again, communications technology enhances this natural flexibility. A classic example is the protest in February 2003 against the American-led war in Iraq. Over a single weekend, an estimated six million people took part in demonstrations in 600 or so cities throughout the world (Table 9.3). Bennett (2005, p. 207) reckons that this event 'may well stand as the largest simultaneous multinational demonstration in recorded history'. The ability of social movements to mushroom in this way, even without any central organization or leader, confirms their capacity to articulate authentic public concern at a transnational level. Social movements are a form of participation well-suited to a more global world.

Liberal democracies hold no monopoly over social movements. In the 1970s and 1980s, they also became a significant feature in many authoritarian regimes in lower-income countries. In contrast to liberal democracies, however, these movements were the territory of the poor, as people facing acute problems of daily life collaborated to improve their living conditions in a hostile political environment. The urban poor organizing soup kitchens, the inhabitants of shanty towns lobbying for land reform, groups of mothers pressing for information on their sons who had 'disappeared' under military rule – all were examples of this blossoming of popular political activity.

However, many community-based movements in low income countries lacked the desire or the means to engage with national politics. A culture of anti-politics, also found in many post-communist countries, limited the movements' wider impact. Indeed the democratic transition has taken some wind from their sails. In Uruguay, for example, 'democracy brought, by a curious twist, the disappearance of many grass-roots movements that had been active during the years of dictatorship' (Canel, 1992, p. 290). In and beyond the developing world, there is nothing as dangerous to a protest movement as success.

Participation in political violence

The forms of participation we have examined so far operate within a broadly civil framework. Even when social movements engage in illegal acts, their protests take place within what has become an accepted framework of dissent. Yet when orthodox politics leaves conflicts unresolved, and sometimes even when it does not, the outcome can be **political violence** – by citizens seeking to change government policy, by one social group against another and by the state against its own people. To appreciate the full repertoire of activities falling under the heading of political participation, we must also consider the role of violence in politics.

The events of 11 September 2001 brought political violence and **political terror** into focus (Lutz and Lutz, 2004). The assaults on New York and Washington were unprecedented terrorist acts in the number of their victims but they built on a tradition of political violence that is as ancient as politics itself. Many terms used today in describing violence derive from these earliest instances. The Zealots (literally, those jealous on God's behalf) were Jewish

> **Political violence** consists of 'those physically injurious acts directed at persons or property which are intended to further or oppose governmental decisions and public policies' (LaPalombara, 1974, p. 379). **Political terror** occurs when such acts are aimed at striking fear into a wider population than the immediate victims.

activists who resisted Roman rule in Palestine. In the era of the Crusades, the Assassins (literally, hashish-eaters) were a Muslim sect who believed their religious duty was to hunt down Christians. The Thugs (literally, the deceivers) were religiously motivated bandits who operated in central and northern India between the seventeenth and nineteenth centuries. They specialized in befriending wealthy travellers during the day and strangling them at night, cutting up the corpses to aid disposal (van Woerkens, 2002).

The central point about political violence is that it must be viewed through the conventional lenses of political analysis, not through a distorting filter that 'explains' violence as the product of the irrational fanaticism of the participants. As Clausewitz said of war, violence is 'a continuation of politics by other means'. The threat and use of force is a way of raising the stakes; it extends but rarely replaces conventional politics. Most political violence is neither random nor uncontrolled but tactical. When farmers block a road, or when the secret police beat up a student activist, or even when terrorists blow up an aircraft, the act carries a deliberate political signal. The roots of violent participation are to be found not in the characteristics of individual perpetrators but rather in the wider conditions giving rise to the phenomenon. We illustrate this point with a brief discussion of participation in three forms of political violence: suicide missions, genocide and revolution.

Suicide missions

Suicide missions are an extreme form of violent participation that have acquired significance, notably in Iraq and Afghanistan, since their resurgence in the Lebanon conflict of 1973–86. In the nature of the case, research on individual attackers is

> A **suicide mission** is an assignment whose success is recognized to depend on the death of the perpetrator.

difficult, but as far as is known the participants in these missions are not psychologically disturbed and would not otherwise be expected to kill themselves.

A sociological profile is perhaps more promising: many are young, unmarried men with above average education and social status (Gambetta, 2005a). Even so, only a minute proportion of those fitting this profile take part in terrorist acts and the profile in any case varies, depending on whether participants are drawn from inside or outside an organization's established membership (Pedahzur, 2005). In the case of political violence, behavioural research on individual participants seems to provide only limited understanding.

A broader and more structural analysis, examining the context within which suicide missions are launched, is appropriate. After all, an established organization is needed to select and research the target and to recruit, train, motivate, arm and transport the attacker. The perpetrator is merely the final link in the chain.

Suicide missions typically arise when organized groups find themselves lacking other means of confronting a Western power. In that sense, such missions are weapons of the weak – cheap, simple and capable of generating publicity in the enemy's homeland. They provide an effective tactic which in many cases draws on Islamic traditions of martyrdom within the community as a whole.

Genocide

When we examine participation in genocide, we again see the requirement to place individual behaviour in a broader context. Confronting the **genocide** of the European Jews during 1941–45, or of the Tutsis in Rwanda in 1994, we naturally seek to understand why the people who carried out the killings did so. We initially seek to attribute evil behaviour to inherently evil individuals. But in all such cases, the perpetrators appear to be normal people in abnormal situations.

This point was graphically demonstrated by Stanley Milgram's famous experiments in Connecticut, USA, during 1961–63. In these studies

Genocide is the deliberate and systematic extermination of a large proportion of a people, nation, race or ethnic group.

most volunteers – none of them students, by the way – proved to be willing to deliver what they believed to be an extreme electric shock to other volunteers when instructed to do so by a white-coated administrator. Obedience to authority was the norm, even among this group of normal people (Milgram, 1974).

Milgram's study formed a critical case in that in the real world of genocidal organizations, such as the SS, members are under greater pressure to conform to orders than in a university experiment. In addition, they feel peer pressure to fulfil their killing quota and are motivated further by the opportunity of looting the victims' possessions. In short, to understand participation in genocide, we must focus on the conditions which lead to the emergence of the killing machine, not on the characteristics of the killers themselves.

The Rwandan genocide is particularly revealing. It was perpetrated by up to 200,000 Hutu peasants, many armed with nothing more than machetes. Closely organized by political militias, the peasants hunted down and 'chopped' at least 500,000 Tutsis in 100 days. In a heavily populated country, many of the victims were known personally to the killers. Yet few Hutus refused to take part in what they saw not as an orgy of violence but rather as hard, disciplined work (Hatzfeld, 2005). When almost one in five members of an ethnic group is willing to engage in killing, it is impossible to attribute such acts to abnormal, evil or deviant individuals.

Because conformity is the norm, an understanding of participation in cases of genocide requires a political rather than a psychological question: 'why were the orders given?', not 'why were the orders obeyed?'.

Revolution

Occasionally, participation in political violence extends to the governing framework itself as the entire political order becomes a matter for dispute. When the existing structure of power is overthrown, leading to a long-term reconstruction of the political, social and economic order, we can speak of a revolution. Such episodes are rare but pivotal, inducing broad and deep alterations in society. The major instances – France, America, Russia, China, Iran – have substantially influenced the modern world.

Skocpol (1979, p. 4) defines **revolutions** as 'rapid, basic transformations of a society's state and class structures; and they are accompanied and in part carried through by class-based revolts from below'. Goldstone (1991) suggests revolutions consist of three overlapping stages: state breakdown, the struggle for power and radical reconstruction of the state.

How far can we discover the roots of revolutions by studying individual participants? Certainly, the motivations that seek ordinary people to participate in revolutionary activity have received considerable attention. In his study of the French Revolution, for example, de Tocqueville (1856) noted that grievances patiently endured become intolerable once a brighter future seems possible. Gurr (1980) sought to develop de Tocqueville's insight, suggesting that political instability only results from deprivation when combined with a belief that conditions are worse than they could and should be. What matters is not absolute deprivation, a condition associated with a struggle for survival and therefore political passivity. As the Russian revolutionary Leon Trotsky wrote, 'the mere existence of privations is not enough to cause an insurrection; if it were, the masses would always be in revolt' (1932/3, p. 103). More important is **relative deprivation**. When relative deprivation is widespread, Gurr suggests, instability and revolution may result. Specifically, the most explosive situation arises when a period of improvement is followed by a decline in the ability of the regime to meet rising demands.

Relative deprivation arises when people believe they are receiving less than they feel they are entitled to. The sense of entitlement may be based on a comparison with past times, an abstract standard of justice or to the rewards accruing to other groups.

The contribution of this research lies in demonstrating that how people perceive their condition is more important than their actual situation. Relative deprivation is certainly a background factor motivating participation in many revolutions. Peasant frustrations, in particular, were involved in the French, Russian and Chinese examples. Note, however, that even relative deprivation may often be extensive without signalling uprisings of any kind.

Its status is more likely to be that of a necessary rather than a sufficient condition of revolution.

This social psychological account provides some insight into the conditions of political instability, and of participation in it, but it seems to be incapable of explaining revolutionary progress and outcomes. Whose discontent matters? How and why do uprisings turn into revolutions? How is discontent channelled into organized opposition movements? Why is such opposition usually suppressed but sometimes not? Because relative deprivation has no answer to these important questions, it is better regarded as a theory of political violence in general rather than of revolutions in particular. As with suicide missions and genocide, an understanding of participation in revolutions requires a broader, more structural approach to prevailing historical conditions and to the political relationships between major groups (see Box 2.2).

Participation in authoritarian states

This section examines political participation in authoritarian regimes. It can be concise since, in contrast to liberal democracies, authoritarian rulers seek either to limit genuine participation in politics or, in the case of totalitarian states, to direct it through tightly controlled channels. In either case, the object is to minimize any threat which unregimented participation might pose to the regime. Nonetheless, there is some interest in reviewing how participation is kept under control. Specifically, we examine the role of patron–client networks as a form of limited and dependent participation in authoritarian regimes before turning to the directed participation demanded by totalitarian regimes.

We should be careful to avoid stereotyping here. Even in non-democracies, the limits and nature of participation are often subject to an implicit dialogue as activists test the boundaries of the acceptable. Non-democratic rulers may allow free space in those areas such as local politics which do not directly threaten the central regime itself. Further, as societies governed by authoritarian rulers grow more complex, so rulers often come to realize that responding to popular pressure on non-sensitive issues can limit dissent and enhance political stability.

Patron–client networks

A major technique for controlling participation in authoritarian states is the patron–client network. **Clientelism**, as this practice is often called, is a form of political involvement which differs from both voluntary participation in liberal democracies and the regimented routines of totalitarian states. Although patron–client relationships are found in all political systems, authoritarian regimes offer the fullest expression of such relationships. Particularly in low income countries, personal networks of patrons and clients are the main instrument for bringing ordinary people into contact with formal politics; indeed, they are the central organizing structure of politics itself (Figure 9.2). Despite their informality, these networks underpin more formal channels of participation such as political parties.

So what exactly are patron–client relationships? They are traditional, informal hierarchies fuelled by exchanges between a high-status 'patron' and 'clients' of lower status. The colloquial phrase 'big man/small boy' conveys the nature of the interaction. Patrons are landlords, employers, party leaders, government ministers, ethnic leaders or anyone with control over resources. Lacking resources of their own, clients gather round their patron for protection and security. Political patrons control the votes of their clients and persuade them to attend meetings, join organizations or simply follow their patron around in a deferential manner. In Sri Lanka, for instance, patrons with access to the resources of the state largely decide how ordinary people vote. Personal insecurity gives a strong incentive to trade one's vote for a patron's protection (Jayanntha, 1991).

Patron–client relationships are often traditional and personal, as in the protection provided to tenants by landowners in low-income countries. But they can also be more instrumental, as with the

> **Clientelism** denotes politics substantially based on patron–client relationships. The patron provides protection to a number of lower-status clients who, in exchange, offer their unqualified allegiance and support.

Figure 9.2 A patronage network linking centre and periphery

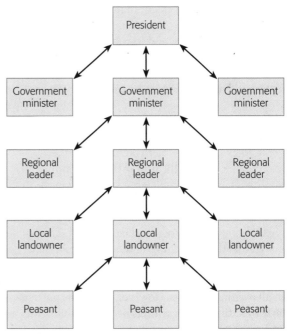

Note: Resources flow downwards, support flows upwards.

resources which the party machines in American cities once provided to new immigrants in exchange for their vote. In either case, the relationship affirms the inequality from which it springs.

In return for their clients' unqualified support, patrons offer access to jobs, contracts, subsidies, physical protection, medical care and even a guarantee of food in hard times. In other words, they provide an insurance policy for poor people who, lacking organized protection through collective insurance or the rule of law, would otherwise be vulnerable to life's dangers. Instead of paying premiums to an insurance company, clients offer political support to a patron. The boss then exploits his local power-base to strike deals with ministers in the national government, offering the votes of his clients in exchange for a share of the government's resources or simply a grant of a favourable licence. In this way, patronage networks grow and decline according to their patron's skill, just as more orthodox businesses rise and fall with the quality of their management. The president is typically the master patron, skilled in the art of supporting his clients but not to the extent that they become a threat.

The patron's power, and its inhibiting effect on democracy, is illustrated in this comment by Egypt's President Abdul Nasser, interviewed in 1957 when he was still a reforming leader (Owen, 1993):

We were supposed to have a democratic system between 1923 and 1953. But what good was this democracy to our people? You have seen the landowners driving the peasants to the polling booths. There they would vote according to the instructions of their masters. I want the peasants to be able to say 'yes' and 'no' without this in any way affecting their livelihood and daily bread. This in my view is the basis for freedom and democracy.

Participation through patronage is a device found in all political systems. However, it appeals particularly in authoritarian settings because it links elite and mass, centre and periphery, in a context of inequality. Although inequality provides the soil in which patronage networks flourish, these relationships still act as a political glue, binding the 'highest of the high' with the 'lowest of the low' through membership of a patron's network. The glue often works particularly well when the patron presents himself as a traditional patriarch.

By linking people across different levels within society, patron–client relationships limit the expression of solidarity among people at the same social level, such as peasants. For the elite, they are a useful tactic of divide and rule. The decay of such hierarchical networks of dependence can be an indication of a transition to a more sophisticated society in which ordinary people have acquired sufficient resources to be able to organize their political participation in a more autonomous, voluntary fashion. In other words, security means people no longer need to sell their votes. Poverty and authoritarian rule provide a setting in which patron–client relationships flourish; affluence and democracy generate a climate in which they decay.

Totalitarian governments

It is when we turn to totalitarian governments that we find the most ambitious attempts to develop mass participation in non-democratic systems. In communist and fascist states, participation was both more extensive and more regimented than in liberal democracies. **Regimented participation**, high in quantity but low in quality, was a central feature of totalitarian rule.

The most interesting examples come from communist states, particularly in their earliest and most vigorous decades. At first glance, participation in these regimes left liberal democracies in the shade. Under communism, citizen activity outscored the level found in today's liberal democracies. Ordinary people sat on comradely courts, administered elections, joined para-police organizations and served on people's committees covering local matters. This apparatus of participation derived from the Marxist idea that all power at every level of government should be vested in soviets (councils) of workers and peasants.

However, the calibre of participation in communist states did not match its extent. To ensure that mass engagement always strengthened the party's grip, communist party members guided all the avenues of political expression. At regular meetings of women's federations, trade unions and youth groups, party activists would explain policy to the people. But communication flowed only from top to bottom. So the members of these groups eventually behaved as they were treated: as passive rather than active. Because the party controlled participation so tightly, cynicism soon replaced idealism. Only careerist diehards were prepared to invest their full energy in the charade.

Regimented participation is elite-controlled involvement in politics designed to express popular support for the notional attempt by the rulers to build a new society. Its supposed purpose is to mobilize the masses behind the regime, not to influence the personnel or policies of the government.

Eventually, some ruling parties did allow more participation but only in areas that did not threaten their monopoly of power. Especially in Eastern Europe, industrial managers were given more say in policy-making. Political participation also became more authentic on local matters. But these modest reforms were not matched in national politics. Because no real channels existed for airing grievances, people were left with two choices: to shut up and continue with life or to air their complaints outside the system. For all the notional participation, communist governments chose to ignore popular indifference to their rule.

The trajectory of participation in communist China illustrates these themes but with the added complexity caused by Mao Zedong's distrust of party routines. In the 1950s and 1960s, participation through accepted channels was required as a way of demonstrating active support for the party's goals. The question was not whether citizens participated but to what extent. This format was comparable with that of other communist states.

In contrast to most other communist leaders, however, Mao remained dissatisfied with the caution of the party establishment. In 1966, he launched the Cultural Revolution, encouraging the masses to turn on corrupt power holders within the party, the workplace and the family. Even harmless intellectuals found themselves condemned as 'the stinking ninth category'. The outcome was an orgy of uncontrolled participation, including violent score-settling, which threatened the country's social fabric and caused permanent damage to the party's reputation. In 1969, Mao called on the army to restore order.

Following this remarkable episode, political participation in China developed along more predictable lines. After Mao's death in 1976, the leadership favoured economic reform over political purity, discouraging any form of participation which might threaten growth. Political passivity became acceptable. More recently, the party has opened some social space in which sponsored groups in areas such as education and the environment can operate with relative freedom. For example, more than 150,000 civic associations were registered by 2007, providing an opportunity for citizen-to-citizen communication under the watchful eye of the party-state (Guo, 2007). The level and pattern of participation has come to resemble that of an authoritarian rather than a totalitarian regime, with both the regimented routines and the political excesses of Mao's era consigned to the past.

However, channels for explicit opposition to the party remain closed. Memories remain of the Tiananmen Square massacre of 1989, when the army's tanks turned on pro-democracy demonstrators in Beijing. At local level, however, unconventional and sometimes violent protests against corruption, unemployment, pollution, illegal levies or non-payment of wages or pensions continue to an extent which is unusual in an entrenched non-democratic regime. These local protests are not aimed at the party's national dominance; in fact, they are often directed at local failures to implement national policies.

Participation in illiberal democracies

The participation challenge facing illiberal democracies is considerable. The transition from authoritarian rule requires the population to learn new styles of political participation: votes must be cast, parties organized and leaders recruited to political office. Cynicism must give way to a measure of engagement. Yet the very nature of illiberal democracy means that political authority is delegated to a president who is expected to resolve severe national problems by dominating the political sphere.

Once the voting is done, the people return to their daily grind, called on only infrequently to express their support for the national leader in his battle against the enemies of the country and its people. Participation therefore tends to be intermittent, unstructured and predicated on political inequality: the leader leads and the masses follow. Individual needs are often met through the personal intervention of a local political figure or other patron, or by bribing a local official.

Consider, for example, post-communist illiberal democracies. The old style of regimented participation quickly disintegrated as communism fell apart, partly in response to dramatic street protests in the capital cities. Once new and nominally democratic institutions had been created, the task was to consolidate the new order by developing structured forms of voluntary participation through parties, elections and interest groups. This task has proved to be demanding. The populations of many East European states had experienced regimented participation under communist rule and seen mass participation on television during its collapse. But this

RUSSIA

ILLIBERAL DEMOCRACY

Form of government ■ a federation of 89 units, comprising 21 republics, 6 territories, 49 regions, two federal cities, one autonomous region and ten autonomous republics.

Legislature and electoral system ■ the State Duma (lower house) contains 450 members elected by party list PR for a five-year term. The Federal Council (upper house) contains two members from each federal unit.

Executive ■ semi-presidential. The prime minister heads the Council of Ministers and succeeds the elected president if needed (no vice president). Vladimir Putin moved from president to prime minister in 2008 where he remains a leading figure.

Judicial branch ■ based on civil law and the constitution of 1993. Headed by a Constitutional Court and, for civil and administrative cases, a Supreme Court. Substantial lawlessness.

Party system ■ parties are weak and unstable, reflecting rather than shaping power. The leading party is Putin's United Russia.

Population (annual growth rate): 140.1m (−0.47%)	
World Bank income group: upper middle	
Political Rights score: ⑥	
Civil Liberties score: ⑤	
Human development index (rank/out of): 67/177	
Freedom of the press index (rank/out of): 171/195	
Perceived corruption index (rank/out of): 147/180	

Note: For meaning and sources of scales and indexes, see p. xvi. In all cases a score and rank of 1 is 'best'.

RUSSIA is a vast country with an imperial and authoritarian past. By area it is the largest country in the world, almost twice the size of the United States. Russia's rulers have in the past been autocratic empire-builders, basing their imperial expansion on control of a serf society and a large conscript army. Thus Russia's experience with communist dictatorship represented a culmination of a familiar authoritarian pattern.

Russia is still best conceived as an empire whose leaders are concerned to extend the country's international influence. The Soviet Union's collapse led to the emergence of 25 million Russians living outside the country's new boundaries in 'the near abroad'. In the Kremlin, certainly, one objective seems to be to restore Russia's status as a great power. This goal is assisted by the country's huge reserves of oil, gas, timber and minerals. These resources comprise about 80 per cent of Russia's exports. Vladimir Putin (president,

2000–08) sought to increase state leverage over these resources. As elsewhere, an economy based on commodity exports encourages corruption and rent-seeking, inhibiting both economic and democratic development.

The transition from communism in the 1990s was characteristically turbulent, involving a chaotic restructuring. Life expectancy and population plummeted as unemployment and alcoholism soared; even in 2006, male life expectancy remained 15 years below that in the USA. Many state-owned entities were in effect stolen, creating a few wealthy oligarchs but also perceived links between capitalism, crime and corruption. This botched transition offers a powerful lesson: market economies must be underpinned by sound public institutions, including effective courts.

Russia remains an illiberal democracy but its authoritarian tendencies intensified during Putin's presidency, leading many authors to prefer the term 'elec-

toral authoritarianism' to 'illiberal democracy'. Certainly, the democratic designation sits uneasily alongside the country's low ratings by Freedom House for political rights and civil liberties. Exploiting the considerable powers accorded to the presidential office under the 1993 constitution, Putin strengthened his control over television, the judiciary and the provinces while dealing ruthlessly with potential opponents. At the same time, his centralizing policies were at least partly directed towards producing a more law-governed society in which corruption would be less prominent and property rights more secure.

Certainly, the economy recovered well under Putin's rulership and the president himself remained exceptionally popular throughout his term. Subject to a constitutional limit of two consecutive terms as president, Putin has occupied the position of prime minister since 2008; he remains the government's leading force.

Further reading: Sakwa (2002), White *et al.* (2005).

Participation in Russia

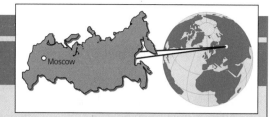

Russia presents a clear case of the limits of political participation in an illiberal democracy. On the one hand, Russia is an intensely political society with an educated people fully aware of national developments. On the other hand, political participation is extremely shallow, held back by pervasive cynicism about the capacity of ordinary people to make a difference. So how does political participation work in the setting of this large and important illiberal democracy?

Most Russians follow politics on television and in national and local newspapers. Two-thirds of Russians say they regularly or sometimes discuss the country's problems. They are well aware of the impact of politics on the country's development and, reflecting the communist era, are highly sophisticated in interpreting the nuances of news reports.

Yet in one survey, most Russians said that the country is not a democracy and that their vote would not change anything. In another study, 85 per cent said they had no power to influence overall government decisions (Rose, 1999). Authoritarianism, past and present, pervades current attitudes, creating a country with a silent majority.

Suspicion of organizations is endemic, with more people distrusting than trusting even the highest-rated institutions: the army and the church. Trust remains contained within personal networks of friends and family.

Political parties come near the bottom of the trust list, perhaps explaining why so many of them choose bland names such as 'Russia's Choice' and 'United Russia'. At just 1 per cent, membership of parties remains well below even declining Western levels. The parties themselves have proved to be unstable, with an insecure social base. They are, in the main, creatures of politicians or even of the Kremlin itself.

Low membership of parties reflects limited participation in social organizations. Civil society remains poorly developed. Most Russians belong to no voluntary public organizations; membership of trade unions is low; partly as a result of the communist war against God, regular church attendance is uncommon. Although some organizations that emerged during Gorbachev's era of *glasnost* (openness) have survived, few have acquired large memberships and others have been incorporated into the regime.

Particularly under President Putin, the government remained suspicious

of non-governmental bodies, especially those with foreign links. In a pattern characteristic of illiberal democracies, and also of some of the more liberal democracies in Eastern Europe, mass political participation in Russia is concentrated on national elections, with few organizations standing between citizen and state. Russia remains a distinctly uncivil society

Even in the post-communist era, participation is still constrained by the desire of the ruling elite, supported by the mass of the people, to construct a powerful and stable state with a strong international position. The Russian people remain subjects first, participants second.

Participation is cognitive, consisting in following and understanding the realities of power, but the effect of such perceptions is to diminish the likelihood of more active participatory behaviour.

Further reading: Fish (2005), Mickiewicz (2008), Remington (2004).

The paradox of participation in Russia

'When we examine the potential of conventional forms of political participation in Russia, it is quite high: 64 per cent of respondents are ready to participate in collective forms of political activities. At the same time, confidence in the effectiveness of various forms of public participation is rather low. Only a small share of respondents (between three and nine per cent) believe that any of the forms of public and political participation is efficient in the solution of problems.'

Source: Institute for Comparative Social Research (2003).

outburst of engagement did not last long. Few if any post-communist countries have established parties and interest groups with a large and stable membership.

The problem in illiberal democracies is the weakness of a **civil society** regulated by law but remaining separate from the state. Civil society provides opportunities for people to participate in collective activities that are neither pro-state nor anti-state but simply non-state. But developing such social capital is a conspicuous challenge in countries with a history of authoritarian rule. Under communist rule, for instance, civil society had been demobilized. It had been stood down so that the rulers could directly control the individual: 'everyone was supposed to be the same – working for the state, on a salary, on a leash' (Goban-Klas and Sasinka-Klas, 1992).

> **Civil society** consists of those groups which sit above the personal realm of the family but beneath the state. The term covers public organizations such as labour unions, interest groups and, on some definitions, recreational bodies. However, businesses are usually excluded because they are not voluntary bodies emerging from society.

The manipulated participation of the communist era left a bad taste, with 'the difficulties of starting afresh a major factor in accounting for the relatively low level of social and political participation' in the subsequent regimes (Rueschmeyer *et al.*, 1998, p. 270). There is a civic deficit rather than a civil society. An illiberal democracy, in which formal participation is largely confined to occasional voting at national elections, is an understandable response to this difficult legacy.

The weakness of civil society is also a factor limiting orthodox participation in some of Latin America's illiberal democracies, especially the smaller ones. Social problems such as poverty, inequality, drugs, crime and limited education do not encourage either a sustained interest in national affairs or the development of a means of political expression. Pervasive corruption breeds cynicism, further discouraging participation. Social organiza-

tion often takes the form of self-help or even vigilante groups which define themselves in opposition to formal politics. Some such movements emerge from indigenous populations which are isolated from the political mainstream.

Consider, for example, the case of crime in Guatemala. Seligson (2005, p. 226) points out that 'one has to go back to fourteenth-century London to find historical homicide rates as high as those found in contemporary Guatemala'. Lynchings are common. No wonder more citizens say in surveys that 'a strong-hand government' is more important than the 'participation of everyone' in solving national problems. In these conditions, it is impossible to consolidate the patterns of formal political participation found in liberal democracies. Indeed, it is remarkable that amid such disorder, Guatemala, El Salvador and Colombia have retained the status of even illiberal democracy (Hagopian and Mainwaring, 2005).

Despite the absence of a communist legacy, the story is similar in many of the African countries seeking to nurture new avenues of participation following the retreat of the generals in the 1980s. As in Latin America, the act of overthrowing military regimes did stimulate significant mass participation, at least in major cities, providing echoes of the original struggle for independence in the 1950s and 1960s. Yet the difficulties of entrenching voluntary participation in Africa's illiberal democracies remain substantial. As Chazan *et al.* (1999, p. 101) comment, 'in few countries has a strong civil society emerged'.

As in Latin America, the core problem of poverty narrows horizons while illiteracy provides a barrier to voluntary participation. Further, the national government in many African states has limited functions and weak penetration outside the capital. The political culture remains strongly parochial. Such participation as emerges, at least beyond voting, is directed towards informal politics in ethnic groups and is contained through patron–client networks. These factors all suggest that voluntary participation in African illiberal democracies is likely to remain limited.

Learning Resources for Chapter 9

Next step

Dalton (2008a) is a comparative account of citizen participation in liberal democracies.

Further reading

Verba *et al.* (1995) examine the United States in their major study of participation, while Putnam (2000) is an interesting assessment of the decline of social participation in the USA, with an eye to its political impact. For a British investigation of participation, see Pattie *et al.* (2004). On social movements, see Tarrow (1998) for a general account, Tilly (2004) for a history, Zirakzadeh (1997) for a comparative study, della Porta *et al.* (1999) for the global context, and Ibarra (2003) and Norris (2002) for the uncertain relationship between the movements and orthodox democracy. For an examination of participation in authoritarian states, see Lust-Oka and Zerhouni (2008).

Internet sources

American Sociological Association
Section on collective behavior and social movements
http://www2.asanet.org/sectioncbsm/

CIVNET, Civitas International
An online resource for civic education practitioners
http://www.civnet.org

International Institute for Democracy and Electoral Assistance (IDEA)
Includes valuable publications on political participation
http://www.idea.int/

www.palgrave.com
Companion Website
Visit the Companion Website to 'click and go'
www.palgrave.com/politics/hague

Chapter 10
Elections and voters

'Elections are the defining institution of modern democracy', writes Katz (1997, p. 3). For the brief moment of an election campaign, voters are the masters and are seen to be so. As liberal and indeed illiberal democracies grow in number, so elections become a more widespread instrument, with the total annual number of votes cast exceeding one billion by 2004 (Muñoz, 2006, p. 1).

Clearly, one function of elections is to provide a competition for office and a means of holding the government to account. But that is not their only role. An election campaign also permits a dialogue between voters and parties, and so between society and state: 'no part of the education of a politician is more indispensable than the fighting of elections', claimed Winston Churchill. Like coronations of old, competitive elections also endow the new office-holders with authority, contributing thereby to the effectiveness with which leaders can perform their duties (Ginsberg, 1982). In short, competitive elections facilitate choice, accountability, dialogue and legitimacy – a rich bounty for what is, after all, only an occasional event.

Competitive elections in a democratic setting provide the heart of this chapter. We begin with the neglected issues of the scope and franchise of elections. We then turn to electoral systems, referendums, turnout and voting behaviour. The final sections discuss elections in authoritarian states and illiberal democracies.

Scope and franchise

One neglected question about elections in liberal democracies is their scope. The number of offices subject to election varies considerably between, say, the United States and Europe. The USA possesses more than 500,000 elected offices, a figure reflecting a strong tradition of local self-government. By comparison, many democracies in Europe have traditionally confined voting to national assemblies and local governments, with regional and European elections added recently. To illustrate the contrast, Dalton and Gray (2003, p. 38) point out that 'between 1995 and 2000 a resident of Oxford, England, could have voted four times; a resident of Irvine, California, could have cast more than 50 votes in just the single year of 2000'. Similarly, Australia has many more elected posts than does New Zealand, even when Australia's larger population is taken into account.

Other things being equal, the greater the number of offices subject to competitive election, the more democratic a political system becomes. However, there are dangers in too many elections. One is voter fatigue, leading to a fall in interest, turnout and quality of choice. American estimates suggests that five additional trips to the polls over a five-year period are likely to depress turnout by around 4 per cent over that same period (Dalton and Gray, 2003, p. 39).

In particular, the least important contests tend to become **second-order elections**: typically, their outcomes reflect the popularity of national parties even though they do not install a national government. The difficulty with such second-order contests is that they weaken the link between the office-holder's performance and the voters' response: a competent local administration might find itself dismissed from office for no other reason than the unpopularity of its party at national level.

The franchise (who can vote) is another underemphasized aspect of contemporary elections. Following a reduction in the voting age in the 1960s and 1970s, the suffrage in most democracies now extends to nearly all citizens aged at least 18. This extensive franchise is fairly recent, particularly for women. Few countries can match Australia and New Zealand where women have been electors since the start of the twentieth century. In some countries, women did not gain the vote on the same terms as men until after 1945, reflecting male recognition of women's contribution to the war effort (see Table 9.2).

It can be argued, however, that even in liberal democracies there remains room to extend the suffrage. For instance, in a few countries many convicted criminals are still denied the vote. America is the prime exhibit. The number of disenfranchised felons and ex-felons in the USA exceeds 5 million; about one in seven black men cannot vote for this reason.

Although Weale (2007, p. 157) suggests that 'there are probably as many arguments against depriving prisoners of the right to vote as there are in favour', not everyone accepts that being locked up should also mean being locked out. Canada's highest court has ruled that prisoner disenfranchisement 'has no place in a democracy built upon the principles of inclusiveness, equality and citizen participation'. Israel's Supreme Court even restored the right to vote to the assassin of the country's prime minister, declaring that 'we must separate contempt for his act from respect for his right' (Manza and Uggen, 2008, p. 232).

There also remains a question about non-citizen residents such as temporary workers. Should such people be granted the vote in the country where they live, work and pay taxes alongside citizens? If so, should they also retain the vote in their home country? The slow trend here is to greater inclusiveness. More than a dozen countries approved varying forms of non-citizen voting rights between 1963 and 1992, often on a reciprocal basis (Immigrant Voting Project, 2009). Within the European Union, all EU citizens residing in a country of which they are not a national can nonetheless vote and stand as a candidate at local elections. This policy is a tangible step towards maintaining voting rights in an age of mobility.

Electing legislatures

Most discussion of **electoral systems** centres on the rules for converting votes into seats. Such rules are as important as they are technical. They form the inner workings of democracy, often little understood by voters but essential to the system's operation and never, ever ignored by politicians themselves (Box 10.1). In this section, we examine the rules for translating votes into seats in parliamentary elections, leaving presidential elections to the next section.

The key characteristic of an **electoral formula** is whether the parliamentary seats obtained by a party

---

Second-order elections are heavily influenced by the results of first-order contests, often occurring at the same time. Second-order contests are viewed as less important by voters because typically they do not determine the composition of the national legislature or government. For example, a party's votes at local contests may reflect its popularity at national level, thus degrading the link between local governance and local elections.

In a broad sense, an **electoral system** denotes all the rules governing an election. However, the term is usually restricted to three aspects: first, the **structure of the ballot** (e.g. how many candidates are listed per party); second, the **electoral formula** (how votes are converted to seats); third, **districting** (the division of the territory into separate constituencies).

BOX 10.1

Electoral systems: legislatures

PLURALITY AND MAJORITY SYSTEMS

1. Single-member plurality: first past the post

Procedure The candidate securing most votes (not necessarily a majority) is elected on the first and only ballot within each single-member district (SMD).

Where used Forty-seven countries, including Bangladesh, Canada, India, UK, USA.

2. Two-round system

Procedure If no candidate wins a majority on the first ballot, the leading candidates (usually the top two) face a second, run-off election.

Where used Twenty-two countries including Egypt, Iran, Mali, Vietnam.

3. Absolute majority: alternative vote (AV)

Procedure Voters rank candidates. If no candidate wins a majority of first preferences, the bottom candidate is eliminated and his or her votes are redistributed by second preferences.

Where used Australia, Fiji, Papua New Guinea.

PROPORTIONAL SYSTEMS

4. List system

Procedure Votes are cast for a party's list of candidates, though in some countries the elector can also express support for individual candidates on the list.

Where used Seventy countries including Brazil, Czech Republic, Israel, the Netherlands, Russia.

5. Single transferable vote (STV)

Procedure Voters rank candidates in order of preference. Any successful candidate needs a set number of votes – the quota. All candidates who exceed this quota on first preferences are elected. Their surplus votes are then distributed according to second preferences. When no candidate has reached the quota, the bottom candidate is eliminated and these votes are also transferred. This continues until all seats are filled.

Where used Ireland, Malta.

6. Mixed member proportional (MMP)

Procedure Electors normally have two votes. One is for the district election (which usually uses the plurality method) and the other for a PR contest (usually party list). The two tiers are linked so as to deliver a proportional outcome overall. The party vote determines the number of seats to be won by each party. Elected candidates are drawn first from the party's winners in the district contests, topped up as required by candidates from the party list.

Where used Nine countries, including Germany and New Zealand.

PARALLEL SYSTEM

7. Mixed member majoritarian (MMM)

Procedure As for MMP, except that the two tiers are separate, with no mechanism to achieve a proportional result overall.

Where used Twenty-one countries, including Japan, South Korea, Thailand.

Note: Based on elections to lower chambers. Count of countries using each system is based on the 199 countries and territories examined in Reynolds *et al.* (2005).

are directly proportional to the votes it receives. Proportional representation (PR) simply means that a mechanism to achieve this goal is built into the allocation of seats. In non-proportional systems, by contrast, parties are not rewarded in proportion to the share of the vote they obtain; instead, 'the winner takes all' within each district, whether a Canadian riding, an American district or a British constituency. These non-proportional systems take one of two forms: plurality or majority. We examine these older non-proportional formats before turning to the more common PR system.

We also discuss the recent trend to mixed systems, in which electors cast two ballots: one for a district representative and the other for a party. These systems, too, can take either a proportional or non-proportional form, depending on whether a mechanism is incorporated to achieve proportionality between the party vote and seats in the assembly.

Plurality system

In the single-member plurality (also called 'first past the post') format, the winning candidate is simply the one receiving most votes in a particular electoral district. A party's representation in the legislature then consists of those of its candidates who win these constituency contests.

Despite its antiquity and simplicity, the plurality system is becoming less common. It survives principally in Britain and British-influenced states such as Canada, various Caribbean islands, India and the United States. However, because India and the USA are so populous, the largest share of the world's people living under democratic rule still vote by this method.

The crucial point about the plurality system is the bonus in seats it offers to the party leading in votes. To see how this bias operates, consider an example in which just two parties, the Reds and the Blues, compete in every constituency. Suppose the Reds win by one vote in each district. There could hardly be a closer contest, yet the Reds sweep the board in seats.

The political significance of this amplifying effect lies in its ability to deliver government by a single majority party. In parliamentary systems with dominant national parties, the plurality method is a giant conjuring trick, pulling the rabbit of majority gov-

Table 10.1 The Canadian federal elections of 1993 and 2006

Party	1993		2006	
	Votes (%)	Number of seats	Votes (%)	Number of seats
Liberal	**42**	**177**	30	103
Conservative	**16**	**2**	36	124
New Democratic Party	7	9	**17**	**29**
Reform/Alliance	19	52		
Bloc Québécois	14	54	**10**	**51**
Other			6	1
Total	98	294	99	308

Note: **Bold** entries illustrate disproportional results between the major parties in 1993 and between the minor parties in 2006.

ernment out of a hat containing only minority parties. This amplifying characteristic is crucial for those who consider that the function of an electoral system is to deliver decisive majority government by a single party.

For example, all but one of the 17 general elections in Britain between 1945 and 2005 yielded a majority in the House of Commons for a single party, even though no party secured a majority of votes in any of these contests. A similar pattern holds for most federal elections in Canada. In 1993, for instance, the Liberals won 60 per cent of the seats on 42 per cent of the vote; their Conservative opponents gained a mere two seats despite winning 16 per cent of the vote (Table 10.1).

It is, however, important to note that this amplifier works best when two dominant parties compete throughout the country. The British contest between Labour and the Conservatives still fits this bill, enabling the swing of the pendulum to deliver a parliamentary majority first for one party, then for the other.

But where parties are more fragmented, majority government is less likely. The weak performance of Canada's two main parties in 2006, with neither the Liberals nor the Conservatives gaining much more than a third of the vote, meant that no majority government ensued (Table 10.1). Regional parties also limit the capacity of the plurality method to deliver majority government. Such parties win in their own strongholds but lack the national appeal needed for overall victory. In India's increasingly regional party system, plurality elections have not delivered majority government since 1989.

Because the plurality system is based on the representation of districts, it offers no guarantee that the party which leads in votes nationally will secure most seats in the legislature. Another party may achieve such an efficient distribution of votes that it wins a majority of seats with fewer votes.

Again, consider an example. Suppose the Blues pile up massive majorities in their own geographical stronghold while the Reds scrape home with narrow wins throughout the rest of the country. The Reds could well win more seats despite obtaining fewer votes, reflecting the greater efficiency of their vote distribution.

> **Gerrymandering** is the art of drawing seat boundaries to maximize the efficiency of a party's support. The term comes from a constituency designed by Governor Gerry of Massachusetts in 1812. It was so long, narrow and wiggly that it reminded one observer of a salamander – hence gerrymander.

The bizarre situation of coming first in seats but second in votes has arisen twice in post-war British general elections. In the more recent case, in February 1974, Labour won four more seats than the Conservatives and formed a minority administration, even though the Conservatives won 226,000 more votes (Kavanagh and Butler, 2005, p. 203).

For Lijphart (1999, p. 134), this possibility of 'seat victories for parties that are mere runners-up in vote totals is probably the plurality method's gravest democratic deficit'. In a democratic era, the expectation is that votes rather than seats should count. Thus, an election resulting in a government formed by the party coming second in votes is regarded as yielding the wrong winner. Certainly, if we were designing an electoral system from scratch, we would surely reject a method in which the party securing most votes can come second in seats.

Three other weaknesses of the plurality method deserve mention:

> **Tactical voting** occurs when electors vote instrumentally for a party or candidate other than their preferred choice. In plurality electoral systems, voters sometimes desert their favoured party when it has no chance of winning in their local district.

▶ It encourages **tactical voting** because electors may feel their favoured party stands no chance of victory in their particular district. Tactical voting at district level exaggerates the regional basis of party support, reducing the extent to which parties integrate different regions within a national party system.

▶ The plurality method treats minority parties inconsistently, according to the geographical concentration of their support. Small parties with even support are hit badly (the Liberal Democrats in the UK, the New Democrats in Canada). But parties with a concentrated vote can secure a nice bonus (the Bloc Québécois in Canada) (Table 10.1).

▶ The importance of constituency **districting** gives incentives for **gerrymandering**. In the United States, partisan districting has become a fine art in elections to the House of Representatives and state legislatures, enabling incumbents to choose their voters, rather than the other way round. The solution to this problem is to cede control of districting to an independent agency (Mann and Cain, 2005).

Majority systems

The plurality system is not the only form of non-proportional representation. There is also a less common but perhaps more democratic version: the majority method. As its name implies, this formula requires the winning candidate to obtain a majority of votes, an outcome normally achieved through a second round. If no candidate wins a majority on the first round, an additional ballot is held, usually a run-off between the top two candidates.

Many countries in Western Europe used majority voting before switching to PR early in the twentieth century. The system remains significant in France and its ex-colonies. The democratic argument for a majority system is quite strong: namely, that no candidate should be elected without being shown to be acceptable to a majority of voters.

Within the majority category, the alternative vote (AV) is an efficient way of achieving a majority outcome in a single round within single-member seats. This system was devised by W. J. Ware, an American academic, in 1873. Voters rank candidates in order of preference but lower preferences only come into play if no candidate gains a majority of first preferences on the first count. Compared to simple plurality voting, AV takes into account more information about voters' preferences but is not necessarily more proportional. AV is used for Australia's lower chamber, the House of Representatives.

AV encourages candidates to reach out beyond their natural supporters to secure the second preferences of voters in other social groups. For this reason, AV deserves particular consideration when tensions between races, religions and ethnicities run high. This virtue explains why ethnically diverse Papua New Guinea returned to AV in 2002, following a failed flirtation with the plurality method.

Proportional representation

We move now from non-proportional systems to proportional representation. PR is more recent than non-proportional systems: it emerged in Continental Europe towards the end of the nineteenth century, stimulated by the founding of associations dedicated to electoral reform. PR is now more common than plurality and majority systems; it has been the method of choice for most democratic countries since the early 1920s. PR is the norm in Europe, both West and East, and in Latin America.

The underlying principle of PR is to achieve representation for a range of parties rather than to elect representatives for a given territory. Given that parties rather than electoral districts form the centrepiece of modern politics, this principle is certainly plausible. In a perfectly proportional system, every party would receive the same share of seats as of votes; 40 per cent of the votes would mean 40 per cent of the seats. Although the mechanics of PR are designed with this principle in mind, most PR systems are not perfectly proportional. They usually offer at least some bonus to the largest party, though less than most non-proportional methods, and they also discriminate by design or practice against the smallest parties. It is wrong to assume that any system labelled 'proportional' is completely so.

A single party rarely wins a majority of seats under PR. Hence majority governments are unusual and coalitions become standard. Because PR usually leads to post-election negotiations in parliament about which parties will form the next government, it is best interpreted as a method of electing parliaments rather than governments.

How does PR achieve its goal? The most common method, first introduced in Belgium in 1899 and still used there, is the party list system. In a pure list system, an elector votes for a slate of the party's candidates rather than for a single person. The number of votes won by a party determines how many candidates are elected from that party's list while the order in which candidates appear on the list (decided by the party itself) governs which people are elected as the party's representatives. A simple example will clarify the procedure. Suppose a party wins 10 per cent of the vote in an election to a 150-seat assembly. Assuming perfect proportionality, that party will be entitled to 15 members and these will be the first 15 candidates on its list.

List systems vary in their **ballot structure** and specifically in how much choice they give voters between candidates on a party's list. Many, like Belgium, employ closed-party lists; as in our example above, voters have no choice over candidates but can only vote for a party. Portugal, South Africa and Spain are other examples. In this format, party officials exert enormous control over political recruitment, as well as the ability to include women and minorities near the top of the list. Closed party lists undoubtedly benefit female representation in parliament (see Table 9.2).

However, most list systems in Western Europe give voters at least some choice between candidates. This option, known locally as preference voting, allows or requires voters to select one or more candidates from the party list. The total of votes cast for a given list still determines the party's overall representation, but a candidate's preference votes influence (to varying degrees) the order of appointment. Switzerland and Luxembourg operate exceptionally free lists in which electors can vote either for a party's list or for as many candidates as there are seats to be filled in the district.

List systems require multimember constituencies. Normally, the country is divided into a set of multimember districts and seats are allocated separately within each district. Employing constituencies in this way preserves some territorial basis to representation but reduces the proportionality of the overall outcome. This bias arises because, when only a few seats are on offer, a small party may not receive any seats even with a significant vote. Many countries have therefore introduced a compensating mechanism by which some seats are held back from the district allocation to be reallocated at regional and/or national level. These seats go to parties with votes left over after the initial lower-level distribution. These additional tiers increase both the proportionality and the complexity of the system.

The number of members returned per district is known as its **district magnitude**. This figure – which varies between regions within a country as well as across countries – is a critical influence on how proportional PR systems are in practice. As Farrell (2001, p. 79) observes, 'the basic relationship for all proportional systems is: the larger the constituency size, and hence the larger the district magnitude, the more proportional the result'. For example, Spain is divided into 52 districts, returning an average of just seven members each. This small magnitude means that minor parties may be denied seats and that already large parties receive an artificial boost.

> **District magnitude** refers to the number of representatives chosen for each electoral district (not to its number of electors). The more representatives to be elected for a district, the more proportional the electoral system can be and the smaller the discrimination against minor parties.

However, in the Netherlands, Israel and Slovakia, the whole country serves as a single large con-

stituency, extending proportionality even to small parties. The Israeli election of 2009, for example, saw a total of 12 parties winning seats in the 120-member Knesset. Seven of these parties secured less than 5 per cent of the vote each.

Most PR systems add an explicit threshold of representation. If a party's vote share falls below the threshold, it receives no seats, whatever its entitlement under the list formula (Figure 10.1). Thresholds, operating at district or national level, help to protect the legislature from extremes. As Kostadinova (2002) observes, 'the threshold is a powerful mechanism for reducing fragmentation in the assembly. It can be and is manipulated by elites to cut off access to parliament for smaller parties'. Several Central and East European countries, including Poland, have now raised the threshold to reduce the large numbers of parties securing representation in early post-communist elections.

Mixed systems

Plurality and PR systems are usually considered alternatives, yet a hybrid form has emerged which combines the two. This mixed method combines geographical representation with party representation (Shugart and Wattenberg, 2000). The best-known blend, often known as mixed member proportional (MMP), retains a mechanism for achieving overall proportionality and is indeed a form of PR.

Germany has been the inspiration for MMP. Here, electors have two votes: one for a district candidate and the other for a regional party list. Half the seats in the Bundestag are filled by candidates elected by plurality voting within single member districts. However, the party list vote is more important because it determines the total number of seats to be

Figure 10.1 Explicit thresholds of representation in some PR systems (per cent of total votes cast)

Notes: Hungary and Germany use mixed electoral systems. German parties winning three district contests achieve representation in the Bundestag even if they fall below the 5 per cent threshold on the party vote.

Sources: Birch (2007), Colomer (2004b), Jasiewicz (2003).

Table 10.2 How the mixed member proportional system works: the German federal election, 2009

	A Party list vote (%)	B Number of district seats won	C Number of list seats awarded (to bring D closer to A)	D Seats won in the Bundestag (%)
Christian Democrats/ Christian Social Union	33.8	218	21	38.4
Social Democrats	23.0	64	82	23.5
Free Democrats	14.6	0	93	15.0
Left Party	11.9	16	60	12.2
Green Party	10.7	1	67	10.9
Others	6.0	0	0	0.0

Note: Total number of seats is 622.

Source: Álvarez-Rivera (2009).

awarded to each party. Candidates from the party's list are used to top up its directly elected candidates until proportionality is achieved. Should a party win more district seats in a region than is its entitlement under the party vote, it retains the extra seats for that region and the Bundestag expands in size.

Table 10.2 shows how the German electoral system operated in 2009. Column B shows that the Christian Democrats (CDU) dominated the district contests despite winning only a third of the party vote. Without compensation, they would have gained an overwhelming majority in the Bundestag. The distribution of list seats (column C) went a long way to restoring proportionality, in particular by favouring minor parties such as the Free Democrats which won few if any district seats. Even so, the electoral system still showed a small bias to the CDU as a result of the party's success in the districts.

Other countries have introduced the idea of parallel district and party list votes but without any top-up device to achieve a proportional outcome overall. This non-proportional mixed member majority (MMM) system can result in what amounts to two separate campaigns. In Russia, for instance, 'the two contests may be separately organized, with different headquarters and campaign headquarters and campaign staff even in the case of candidates from the same party' (White, 2005b, p. 324). Many independent candidates, often drawn

from local elites or reflecting local concerns, have been elected through the district contests. It was a desire to reduce the number of independents that led to the replacement of MMM by list PR in Russia in 2007.

Electoral systems and party systems

The relationship between electoral systems and party systems remains a matter of controversy. The question is whether a technical feature such as formulae for converting votes into seats can nonetheless exert a strong influence on the system of parties in a country. In a classic work, Duverger (1954, p. 217) answered in the affirmative. He argued that 'an almost complete correlation is observable' between the plurality method and a two-party system; indeed, he suggested that this relationship, based on **mechanical** and **psychological** effects, approached that of 'a true sociological law'.

Duverger (1954) distinguished two effects of electoral systems. The **mechanical** effect arises directly from the rules converting votes into seats. Example: the threshold for representation used in many proportional systems. The **psychological** effect is the impact of the rules on how electors cast their votes. Example: tactical voting in plurality systems when the first choice party has no prospect of winning in the elector's own district.

Table 10.3 Major changes to the electoral systems used in legislative elections, 1800–2002

From	To	Number of changes	Example (year)
Majority or plurality	Proportional representation	27	Belgium (1900)
Majority or plurality	Mixed	6	New Zealand (1996)
Proportional representation	Majority or plurality	7	France (1988)
Proportional representation	Mixed	6	Italy (1993)

Notes: Based on 94 countries with some democratic experience. Records are incomplete for the earlier years. Some countries have experienced multiple changes (e.g. in 2006, Italy returned to PR, albeit with a winner's bonus).

Source: Adapted from Colomer (2004a), Table 1.3, p. 55.

But a reaction set in against attributing weight to political institutions such as electoral systems. Writers such as Rokkan (1970) adopted a more sociological approach, pointing out that social cleavages had produced multiparty systems in Europe long before PR was adopted early in the twentieth century. Jasiewicz (2003, p. 182) makes exactly the same point about post-communist Europe: 'political fragmentation usually preceded the adoption of a PR-based voting system, not vice versa'. Miller (2005, p. 13) adopts a similar position in discussing New Zealand's move away from the plurality method in 1996: 'the fracturing of the two-party system occurred long before the advent of PR'.

And there, by and large, the matter rests. It appears that electoral systems result from a party system as much as they influence it. The lesson of this debate is that we should ask not only about the impact of an electoral system but also about the political calculations that led to its adoption in the first place.

Design and reform of electoral systems

Questions of electoral system design have come to the fore as new democratic institutions have been built in the transition from communist and military rule. As Bielasiak (2006, p. 408) comments, 'the previous preoccupation with the consequences of electoral rules has given way to ever-growing attention to the political origins of electoral laws'. So what advice can we give those charged with designing a new electoral system, particularly for countries with a legacy of instability and division?

It is worth bearing in mind that the history of electoral reform is, in the main, a story of the expansion of PR. Table 10.3 shows the direction of changes in 94 countries over the course of the nineteenth and twentieth centuries. By far the most common switch has been from a majority or plurality system to PR. This shift outnumbered moves in the reverse direction by almost four to one.

Because PR is not a winner takes all system, it is always a safe option for parties negotiating electoral reform. In the discussions preceding suffrage extension in Europe early in the twentieth century, conservative and liberal parties felt that a shift from a majority system to PR would at least guarantee their own survival into the new era of mass suffrage. Socialist parties, still uncertain of their electoral potential, also judged that PR would at least remove the bias of the majority system against them. So for all the major players, PR was the least bad option (Lewin, 2004).

PR has also predominated in the more recent wave of democratic transitions. With memories of communist and military dictatorships still fresh, democratic reformers were keen to see a wide range of interests represented in the assembly.

PR is also a safe choice for those designing an electoral system for a new regime. PR will usually provide at least some representation for parties based on minority groups and ideologies, typically leading to coalitions which offer further protection against domination by a single ruling party (Karp and Banducci, 2008). Explicit thresholds and small district magnitudes can limit fragmentation and discord by excluding small anti-system parties.

Because there are no wasted votes, PR also leads to higher turnouts than the plurality system (IDEA, 2006).

The list system of PR offers further advantages for designers. First, it is inherently party-based, encouraging the strong parties which are an important component of a stable democracy. It is this desire for a stable party system, more than for proportionality as such, that lies behind the adoption of list PR in post-communist Europe. Second, the list of candidates enables parties to construct an order of election balanced by gender and ethnicity without requiring the government to impose specific quotas (Tripp and Kang, 2008). Third, when the whole country serves as a single electoral district, PR also avoids the complexity of defining and revising constituency boundaries.

Yet an electoral system cannot be expected by itself to resolve underlying social conflicts. In general, a method of election is performing its function if it proves to be widely acceptable and therefore stable over time. Its purpose is to deliver an equilibrium such that no party with the power to change the rules feels it will obtain a long-run benefit from doing so. If the winners do not seek to modify the system to their own advantage, and the losers do not blame the election rules for their own defeat, then the electoral system has done its job. It has become, as it should be, taken for granted – part of the political furniture.

Electing presidents

Electoral systems for choosing presidents receive less attention than those for electing legislatures. Yet the presidential office is invariably elected in countries with presidential or semi-presidential government. The president is sometimes elected even when the post is mainly honorary; Ireland is an example. So this neglected subject certainly merits attention.

In one sense, the rules for electing presidents are straightforward. Unlike seats in parliament, a one-person presidency cannot be shared between parties; the office is indivisible. So PR is impossible and the main choice is between the plurality and the majority method. However, in another sense, presidential electoral systems are more complicated since many, including the USA, are still based on **indirect election** through a special college.

> **Indirect election** occurs when office-holders are elected by a body which has itself been chosen by a wider constituency. The device is employed in some presidential elections and for some upper houses of parliament.

We begin with directly elected presidents. As Figure 10.2 shows, 61 of the 91 directly elected presidents in the world are chosen by a majority system. This number is increasing as countries dispense not only with indirect election but also with the plurality method, matching the trend in parliamentary elections (Colomer, 2004b, p. 59). The reason for the pre-eminence of the majority system in presidential elections is that it is more important to confirm majority backing for a single president than for every single member of a legislature. Plurality contests, in which the candidate with most votes wins on the first and only round, can lead to victory with an unacceptably small share of the vote. For example, Fidel Ramos became president of the Philippines in 1992 with just 24 per cent of the vote.

Figure 10.2 Methods for selecting presidents

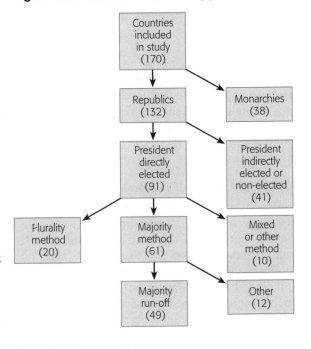

Source: Blais *et al.* (1997).

Most majority elections for presidents employ a run-off of the top two candidates, assuming neither wins a majority on the first round. France is a leading case. By their nature, run-offs create a possibility that the leading candidate in the first round fails to win election; this outcome occurred in 7 of 21 run-offs in Latin America between 1979 and 1992 (Peréz-Liñán, 2006). Such a result can occur when, for example, the right-wing vote is divided among several candidates in the first ballot but unites behind its single remaining candidate in the run-off, defeating the left-wing candidate who led in the preliminary round.

Given that most presidential elections are by national ballot, it is possible to require the winning candidate to obtain a certain level of support in the regions as well as nationally. Such **distribution requirements** are still uncommon but they do encourage candidates to broaden their support. This virtue is important in regionally divided societies. In Indonesia, for instance, a first-round victory requires at least 20 per cent of the vote in a majority of provinces. However, distribution rules introduce their own dangers, including the possibility of a **failed election**.

> **Distribution requirements** set out how a winning candidate's votes must be arranged across different sections of the electorate. The most common (but still unusual) requirement is for a minimum level of support in a certain number of provinces. Such requirements can lead to **failed elections** in which no candidate jumps through all the hoops.

As Figure 10.2 shows, almost a third of presidents manage to avoid the perils of direct election altogether. Many of these are chosen via indirect election in which a special body (which may itself be elected) supposedly acts as a buffer against the whims of the people. In the United States, for example, the Electoral College is still technically used to elect an incoming president. Today, the college survives only as a procedural and pre-democratic relic mandated by the constitution. Delegates to the College still assemble but, with the odd exception, they conscientiously follow the verdict of the state they represent.

Three other features of presidential elections are worthy of note: the length of term, the possibility of

---

BOX 10.2

Methods for electing presidents: some examples

	Method of election	Term (years)	Re-election permitted?
Argentina	Electoral college	6	After one term out
Brazil	Two round	5	After one term out
Finland	Plurality	6	Yes
France	Two round	5	Two-term limit*
Mexico	Plurality	6	No
Russia	Two round	5	One term out out required after two consecutive terms served
United States	Electoral college	4	Two-term limit

* Introduced in 2008 (previously no limit).

Sources: Adapted from Jones (1995b) and Nurmi and Nurmi (2002).

---

re-election and the link with other elections (Box 10.2). On the first point, the presidential term is sometimes longer, and is normally no shorter, than that served by members of the legislature. The longer the term, the easier it is for presidents to adopt a broad perspective free from the immediate burden of re-election. At just four years, the term of office of American presidents is unusually short. The danger is that year one is spent acquiring experience and year four campaigning, leaving only the middle years as a period of accomplishment.

Second, term limits are often imposed, restricting the incumbent to just one or two periods in office. The fear is that without such constraints presidents will be able to exploit their unique position in order to remain in office too long. Thus, the USA introduced a two-term limit after Franklin Roosevelt won four elections in a row between 1932 and 1944. Mexican presidents (like the deputies in the country's parliament) cannot stand for re-election.

As with many institutional fixes, term limits solve one problem at the cost of creating others. Clearly, a president who cannot be re-elected is no longer directly accountable to the voters. Also, **lame-duck** presidents lose clout as their term nears its end. And popular presidents, replete with confidence and experience, may be debarred from office at the peak of their careers.

> **Lame ducks** are elected officials reaching the end of their tenure. The term often refers specifically to those whose successors have been elected but are not yet in post. Authority tends to drain from lame ducks. Unlike incumbents facing re-election, their actions need not be governed by personal electoral considerations.

Third, the timing of presidential elections is also important. When these contests occur alongside elections to the assembly, the successful candidate is more likely to be drawn from the party that dominates the legislature. Without threatening the separation of powers, concurrent elections limit fragmentation, increasing the chance that congress will support the president's plans. This thinking lay behind the reduction of the French president's term to five years in 2000, the same tenure as the assembly's.

The referendum, initiative and recall

Elections are instruments of representative democracy; the role of the people is only to decide who will decide. But devices such as the **referendum**, the ini-

> A **referendum** involves a reference from another body, normally the legislature or the government, to the people. The device therefore provides a practical counter-example to the common argument that direct democracy is completely impossible in large states.

BOX 10.3

The referendum, initiative and recall

Referendum	a vote of the electorate on an issue of public policy such as a constitutional amendment. The vote may be binding or consultative.
Initiative	a procedure which allows a certain number of citizens (typically around 10 per cent in American states) either to initiate a popular vote on a given proposal or to place it on the legislature's agenda (an **agenda-setting initiative**).
Recall	a popular vote on whether an elected official should be removed from office during normal tenure.

---

tiative and the recall have now been introduced to many liberal democracies, supplementing but certainly not replacing representative elections (Box 10.3). These mechanisms are at the sharp end of democracy, allowing us to judge the practical effectiveness of direct democratic forms in a contemporary setting.

We first examine referendums, the most important of these devices. Referendums vary in their status (IDEA, 2008). They may be mandatory – meaning that they must be called on specified topics such as constitutional amendments – optional or even constitutionally forbidden on such subjects as taxation and public spending. Their outcomes may be binding, as with constitutional amendments requiring popular approval, or merely consultative, as with Sweden's vote in 1994 on membership of the European Union.

Referendums are growing in frequency. Most liberal democracies held at least one in the final quarter of the twentieth century, with the heaviest use in Europe, Australia and New Zealand (Morel, 2007) (see Table 10.4). Switzerland headed the list, holding 396 referendums between 1940 and 2006 on such issues as nuclear power, same-sex partnerships and immigration. However, few other countries have

Table 10.4 Western democracies holding most national referendums, 1940–2006

Country	Number of referendums
Switzerland	396
Italy	63
New Zealand	29
Ireland	28
Australia	27
Denmark	16
France	14
Sweden	5
Spain	4

Source: Morel (2007), Table 1.

made more than occasional use of referendums, while the American federal constitution makes no provision for national referendums at all.

What is the contribution of referendums to democracy and governance? How desirable is it to transform citizens into legislators? On the plus side, referendums do seem to increase voters' understanding of the issue, their confidence in their own political abilities and their faith in government responsiveness (Bowler and Donovan, 2002). Like elections themselves, referendums help with an important objective of any democracy: to educate the people.

Referendums can also inform the politicians. For instance, the rejection of the proposed European constitutional treaty by French and Dutch voters in 2005 informed the European Union elite that national electorates had grown weary of grand European projects.

A major benefit of optional referendums is to provide a safety valve. A referendum allows governments, particularly coalitions, to put an issue to the people when for some reason it is incapable of reaching a decision itself. Like a plumber's drain-rods, referendums resolve blockages. In this way, referendums supplement rather than supplant representative democracy (Qvortrup, 2005).

But there are also reasons for caution. As with elections, a surfeit of referendums can tire the voters, depressing turnout. In addition, a referendum treats an issue in an isolated way, ignoring the implications for other areas. The parlous state of

California's public finances, for example, owes something to the tendency of voters to support not just referendums involving extra spending but also those setting a cap on state taxes. There is no mechanism for ensuring consistency in referendum decisions, nor is it always clear for how long the results of a referendum should be considered decisive.

Also, voters' judgements are often informed by wider considerations than the specific proposition on the ballot. 'The answer was "Non" but what was the question?' asked one analyst after the French rejection of the European treaty in 2005 (Ivaldi, 2006). Further, voters are often reluctant to embrace change, turning referendums into instruments of conservatism as much as democracy (Kobach, 1997).

Despite their democratic credentials, the outcome of optional referendums can be influenced by government control of timing. In 2003, the European Union commenced a sequence of referendums on whether individual Eastern European states should join the EU. It began the series in Hungary, judging that a positive result there would influence the outcome in other Eastern European states where public opinion was more doubtful. The plan worked: all the accession countries holding referendums voted in favour.

More crudely, rulers can simply ignore the result of a referendum. In 1955, Swedes voted decisively to continue driving on the left; in 1963, the parliament passed a law introducing driving on the right. Alternatively, a referendum can be repeated until the desired outcome is obtained. Irish voters only ratified the Nice Treaty on the European Union in 2002, and the Lisbon Treaty in 2009, at the second time of asking.

In addition to these difficulties, referendums can easily be hijacked by:

▶ Wealthy companies waging expensive referendum campaigns on issues in which they have an economic interest;
▶ Government control over wording;
▶ Intense minorities seeking reforms to which the majority is indifferent.

What of the other mechanisms shown in Box 10.3: the initiative and the recall? Here the process is typically initiated from below rather than above,

COUNTRY PROFILE

UNITED STATES

Form of government ■ a presidential republic comprising a
federation of 50 states.

Legislature ■ the 435-member House of Representatives is the
lower house. The 100-member Senate contains two directly
elected senators from each state.

Executive ■ the president (who can serve a maximum of two
four-year terms) is supported by a massive apparatus,
including the Executive Office of the President and the
White House Office. However, the Cabinet is far less significant than in parliamentary systems. Despite administrative
support, presidents experience difficulty in achieving their
goals on domestic issues, with federal agencies and Congress
offering resistance.

Judiciary ■ the Supreme Court heads a dual system of federal
and state courts. This nine-member body can nullify laws
and actions running counter to the constitution. Many
political issues are resolved through the courts.

Electoral system ■ the USA is one of the few large countries
still employing the plurality method. The president is elected
indirectly through an electoral college. As in 2000, a candidate who wins the key states may be elected through this
college even though he comes second in the popular vote.
Re-election rates in Congress are exceptionally high.

Party system ■ the Democratic and Republican parties show
great resilience, despite periodic threats from third parties.

Population (annual growth rate): 307.2m (+1%)
World Bank income group: high income
Political Rights score: ❶
Civil Liberties score: ❶
Human development index (rank/out of): 12/177
Freedom of the press index (rank/out of): 24/195
Perceived corruption index (rank/out of): 18/180

Note: For meaning and sources of scales and indexes, see p. xvi. In all
cases a score and rank of 1 is 'best'.

The survival of the major parties reflects ideological flexibility, an entrenched position in law and the bias of plurality
elections against minor parties.

With the end of the Cold War, the
UNITED STATES became the world's
one remaining superpower. This
unique status is based partly on the
country's hard power: a large population, the ability to project military force
anywhere and a dynamic economy. Yet
America's soft power is also significant.
Its leading position in the media,
medical, technology and telecommunications sectors is underpinned by a
strong base in science and university
education, while its culture, brand
names and language have universal
appeal.

Yet hardly had commentators begun to
refer to the emergence of an American
'empire' than the global reputation of
the United States underwent a massive
decline during the presidency of George
W. Bush (2001–09):

■ The invasion of Iraq in 2003 was
widely condemned;

■ The country's failure to lead on environmental issues was judged a dere-
liction of its global duty;

■ Images of the initial reaction to
Hurricane Katrina in 2005 reminded
the world not just of poverty within
the USA but also of its concentration
among black people;

■ The emergence of China hinted at
the development of a bipolar international system.

However, the arrival in the White House
of Barack Obama on a promise of
change ensures the internal politics of
the United States will remain of vital
interest. Domestically, the world's No.1
operates a political system intended to
frustrate decisive policy-making. By

constitutional design, power is divided
between federal and state governments. The centre is itself fragmented
between the executive, legislature and
judiciary. American politics is extraordinarily pluralistic; reforms are more easily
blocked by interest groups than carried
through by the executive.

The president finds his plans obstructed
by a legislature which is the most powerful, and among the most decentralized, in the world. In normal times,
Washington politics is a ceaseless quest
for that small amount of common
ground on which all interests can agree.
In many respects, the president may still
lead the world but the separation of
powers mean that in domestic politics
even the country's chief executive is a
supplicant before Congress.

Further reading: Bardes *et al.* (2008), McKay (2009).

Elections in the United States

The United States is unique in its massive range of elected offices. At federal level, Americans can vote for the president and vice president, two senators per state and their member of the House of Representatives. But a much larger range of positions is subject to election at state and local level. These posts include auditors, judges, members of school boards, sheriffs, treasurers and, in North Dakota, the soil conservation supervisor. So why does the USA possess so many elected offices? And how successful has its national experiment with selection through election proved to be?

The exceptional array of elected posts in the USA reflects not just the practical requirements of governing a large, frontier society but also a culture that emphasizes equality, competence and a belief that administration is a practical matter. The task of those elected was, and is, to get the job done.

America played a pioneering role in extending the franchise for white men. As early as 1830, just 40 years after ratification of the constitution, property qualifications for voting had been withdrawn and nearly all states selected members of the Electoral College by direct popular ballot. In addition, traditions of direct democracy live on. Images of town meetings in New England form part of the political culture while most western states still employ some direct democratic devices such as the referendum, initiative and recall. Further, reforms to the distinctly American institution of primary elections have opened up the selection of a party's candidates to a remarkably wide proportion of the population.

Yet American experience with elections is far from an unconditional celebration of democracy. Southern blacks were effectively denied the vote until the Voting Rights Act of 1965. Felons and ex-felons are denied the vote in many states. The log cabin to White House ideal is widely accepted but money is increasingly necessary, though insufficient, for

Figure 10.3 Turnout at American presidential elections, 1948–2008

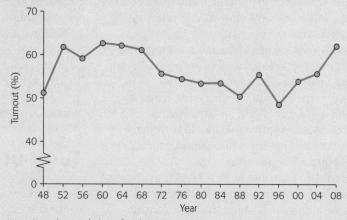

Note: Base is population of voting age.

Source: Adapted from McKay (2009), Table 6.2.

electoral success. The constitution does not allow national referendums. In many elections, advertising by interest groups overwhelms the candidates' voices.

The many confusions of the 2000 presidential election hardly contributed to the authority with which the eventual winner entered the White House. This election also drew attention once more to the fact that, under the cumbersome Electoral College procedure, American presidents are still not elected by a direct national ballot.

By contrast, the 2008 presidential election demonstrated the authority which can flow from a successful campaign. Barack Obama gained a convincing 68 per cent of the votes in the Electoral College, despite winning just 53 per cent of the popular vote. Obama's ethnicity, together with the expense and technological sophistication of his campaign, stimulated interest in and beyond the United States.

In a relatively close contest between two non-incumbents, turnout reached 62 per cent of eligible voters, high by recent American standards. The success of the 2008 election gave the new young president a powerful mandate to govern.

Sources and further reading: Bardes *et al.* (2008), Lewis-Beck *et al.* (2008).

allowing the public to influence, rather than just respond to, the agenda. These devices are therefore of some democratic interest, even though they are less common than the traditional referendum.

Where a referendum is typically initiated by the government itself, the initiative is a citizen-initiated ballot: a reference from some of the people to all the people. In Switzerland, again, 100,000 electors can propose a new law or an amendment to the constitution; the resulting ballot of the electorate succeeds if it is supported by a double majority of voters and cantons.

The initiative is a legal possibility in 37 countries, most of which are in Europe and Latin America. It is commonly included in post-authoritarian constitutions in an attempt to prevent a return to dictatorship. The initiative has also been adopted by many western states in the USA, notably California. Generally, however, in both the United States and beyond, initiatives have a low success rate (Qvortrup, 2008).

Sometimes the scope of the initiative is limited by linking it to legislation, actual or proposed. In Italy, five regional councils or 500,000 electors can initiate a popular vote but only on whether to repeal an existing law. Alternatively, initiatives can be held on whether legislative proposals should be rejected before they become law, a mechanism which inserts the popular will at an earlier stage.

The initiative can also be integrated into existing representative institutions by functioning as a petition to the authorities rather than as a decision-making device. The **agenda-setting initiative**, as this variant is known, allows electors to propose topics for discussion by the authorities. Specifically, a certain number of citizens can submit a proposal, within specified policy areas, which must then be considered but not necessarily approved by the legislature. No vote of the people is held to settle the issue; rather, the agenda-setting initiative builds on the familiar idea of a petition. One advantage of this technique is that it allows minorities to place their concerns on the table.

This mechanism was introduced to the constitutions of several European countries (e.g. Austria and Spain) after the First World War and has been extended to a number of other states (e.g. Poland and Thailand) since 1989 (IDEA, 2008). The agenda-setting initiative is well-established in Austria. In 2006, for example, over 250,000 signatories requested a national referendum in the event that Turkey be proposed for European Union membership by the EU, a demand accepted by the Prime Minister.

The recall, finally, is a ballot on whether an elected official should be removed from office during normal tenure. A vote is initiated by a petition signed by a minimum proportion (typically, around 25 per cent) of the votes cast for that office at the previous election. Unlike impeachment, the recall is a political rather than a legal device. Like referendums, it provides a method of resolving difficulties that have not been dealt with in the normal course of political events.

At national level, one of the few countries to employ the recall is Venezuela. There, a recall vote can be held on every elected official, including the president, on the initiative of 20 per cent of the relevant electorate. Some 18 American states also make provision for recall elections, where the mechanism was originally introduced as a weapon against corruption. However, the device has rarely been used – though Arnold Schwarzenegger did become governor of California following the successful unseating of the incumbent in 2003.

Turnout

Despite rising education, turnout has fallen in most of the democratic world. In 19 liberal democracies, turnout declined on average by 10 per cent between the 1950s and the 1990s (Wattenberg, 2000). Figure 10.4 shows the trend for one high-turnout country (Sweden), one traditionally middle-turnout country (the United Kingdom) and one low-turnout country (Switzerland). The pattern is clear, with the fall concentrated in the 1990s. In many countries, abstainers are now the majority at regional and local contests.

It is possible that the main fall in turnout has already taken place, at least for national contests. As the figure shows, participation increased modestly at recent elections in Switzerland and the United Kingdom. In the USA, too, turnout among the eligible population has recovered in the closer presidential elections of this century. But for now, prudence suggests that we should regard low turnout as a continuing issue.

Figure 10.4 Turnout at parliamentary elections, 1970-2007

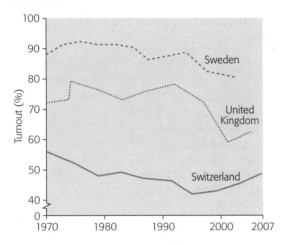

Source: Adapted from IPU (2009b).

Why the fall? The decline surely forms part of a wider trend in the democratic world: namely, a growing distance between voters on the one hand and parties and government on the other. It is surely no coincidence that turnout has reduced as **partisan dealignment** has gathered pace, as party membership has fallen and as the class and religious cleavages which sustained party loyalties in the early post-war decades have decayed.

In an influential analysis, Franklin (2004) links the decline of turnout to the diminishing significance of elections. He suggests that the success of many democracies in establishing welfare states and achieving full employment in the post-war era resolved long-standing conflicts between capital and labour. With class conflict disarmed, electors possessed fewer incentives to come out and vote on election day. As Franklin writes, 'elections in recent years may show lower turnout for the simple reason that these elections decide issues of lesser importance than elections did in the late 1950s' (2004, p. 174). When less is up for grabs, people are more likely to stay at home. This benign interpretation connects with the broader perspective that views participation as an option rather than an obligation (see p. 161).

Partisan dealignment refers to the weakening of bonds between (a) electors and parties and (b) social groups and parties.

But declining satisfaction with the performance of democratic governments has surely also played its part. Especially in the 1980s, popular trust in government and parties fell in many democracies, reflecting the growing complexity, internationalization and perhaps corruption of governance. Even though mass support for democratic principles remains strong, rising cynicism about government performance has probably encouraged more people to stay away from the polls (Putnam *et al.*, 2000).

Turnout varies not just over time but also between countries. How can we explain these cross-national differences? Here a cost–benefit analysis is useful (Downs, 1957). Turnout tends to be higher in those countries where the costs or effort of voting are low and the perceived benefits high. On the cost side, turnout is reduced when the citizen is required to take the initiative in registering as an elector, as in the USA. It is also lower when electors must vote in person and during a weekday (Box 10.4). So voting can be encouraged by allowing voting at the weekend, in advance, by proxy and by mail (Blais *et al.*, 2003).

On the benefit side, both election significance and vote significance contribute to higher turnout (Horiuchi, 2004). On the former, the more important the election, and the more cohesive the parties, the greater the turnout. On the latter, the greater the impact of a single vote, the more willing voters are to incur the costs of voting.

Thus, proportional representation enhances participation because each ballot affects the outcome. Several comparative studies find participation to be six to nine points higher among countries employing party list PR than in those states using the plurality method (Birch, 2007; Karp *et al.*, 2007).

At the level of the individual, variations in turnout reflect the pattern found with other forms of political participation. Specifically, high turnout reflects political resources and political interest. Thus, educated, affluent, married, middle-aged citizens with a job and a strong party loyalty, who belong to a church or a trade union, and are long-term residents of a neighbourhood, are highly likely to vote. These are the electors with both resources and an interest in formal politics. By contrast, abstention is most frequent among those with fewer resources and less reason to be committed to formal

---

BOX 10.4

Features of the political system and of individuals which increase turnout

Features of the political system	Features of individuals
Compulsory voting	Middle aged
Automatic registration	Home owner
Voting by post and by proxy permitted	Strong party loyalty
Advance voting permitted	Extensive education
Weekend polling	Attend church
Election decides who governs*	Belong to a trade union
Cohesive parties	Higher income
Proportional representation	Voted in previous elections
Close result anticipated	
Small electorate	
Expensive campaigns	
Elections for several posts held at the same time	

* Examples of elections which do *not* decide who governs are those to the American Congress and the European Parliament.

Sources: Blais *et al.* (2003), Endersby *et al.* (2006), Geys (2006), IDEA (2006).

---

party politics: young, poorly educated, single, unemployed men belonging to no organizations, lacking party ties and newly moved to their current address.

Attempts to boost turnout must remain sensitive to political realities. Conservative parties have reason to be cautious about such schemes, given their assumption (which is plausible if rarely directly substantiated) that abstainers would vote disproportionately for the left. Increased participation may benefit the system as a whole but impact unequally on the parties within it, thus delaying or preventing reform.

As turnout declines across most of the democratic world, so attention focuses on potential solutions. Technical fixes, such as locating polling stations in supermarkets and permitting voting by email, may have some role to play. Countries using plurality or majority voting could also boost turnout by introducing proportional representation, in which every vote counts. But has the time come to consider the most effective solution of all: compulsory voting?

There are arguments on both sides (Box 10.5). On the one hand, most citizens acknowledge obligations to the state such as paying taxes, serving on juries and even fighting in war. So why should we reject

what Hill (2002) calls the 'light obligation and undemanding duty' of voting at national elections? Currently, abstainers take a free ride on the efforts of the conscientious.

On the other hand, mandatory voting denies the liberty which is an essential part of liberal democracy. Requiring people to participate is a sign of an authoritarian regime, not a democracy. Paying taxes and fighting in battle are duties where every little helps and where numbers matter. However, elections in all democracies still attract more than enough votes on which to base a decision. There appears to be no evidence that high turnout increases the intrinsic quality of choices made.

Although compulsory voting does not guarantee a full turnout, it does make a difference: when the Netherlands made voting optional in 1970, turnout fell considerably. However, the reverse reform – introducing mandatory voting where it did not previously exist – has rarely been tried in recent times. The danger is that the reform would backfire, increasing political distrust between government and governed. When a Swedish minister floated the possibility in 1999, the reaction was firmly negative. There is surely a case for testing other turnout-enhancing reforms first.

BOX 10.5

Compulsory voting: for and against

FOR

▶ A full turnout means the electorate is representative;

▶ Disengaged groups are drawn into the political process;

▶ The authority of the government is enhanced by a full turnout;

▶ More voters will lead to a more informed electorate;

▶ People who object to voting on principle can be exempted;

▶ Blank ballots can be permitted for those who oppose all candidates;

▶ Voting is mandatory in over 20 countries already.

AGAINST

▶ The freedom to abstain should be part of a liberal democracy;

▶ Compulsory voting gives influence to less informed and engaged electors;

▶ Abstention may reflect contentment and is not necessarily a problem;

▶ In practice, turnout is not 100 per cent even when voting is mandatory;

▶ Voting (and deciding who to support) takes time;

▶ The best policy is to attract voters to the polls through their own volition.

Voting behaviour

Given that voters have a choice, how do they decide who to vote for? Although this is the most intensively studied question in all political science, there is no single answer. As a summary, however, we can suggest that since the 1960s electors in liberal democracies have moved away from group and party voting towards basing their decision on issues, the economy, leaders and party competence. Franklin (1992, p. 387) describes this process as 'the decline of cleavage politics and the rise of issue voting'.

For two decades after the Second World War, most studies of electoral behaviour disputed the intuitive proposition that voters do 'choose' which party to support. An influential theory of electoral choice, originally developed in the United States in the 1950s, argued that voting was an act of affirmation rather than choice (Campbell *et al.*, 1960). Voting was seen as an expression of loyalty to a party, a commitment which was both deep-seated and long-lasting.

In the USA, this **party identification** was confirmed by the traditional requirement to register as a party's supporter in order to be eligible to vote in its primaries. In this way, American electors learned to think of themselves as Democrats, Republicans or, in a minority of cases, as Independents. This view of American voters as habitual supporters of a partic-

> **Party identification** is a long-term attachment to a particular party which anchors voters' interpretations of the remote world of politics. It is measured by a standard survey question asking people whether they think of themselves as, for example, 'Democratic, Republican, Independent, or what?' (Bartle and Belluci, 2008).

ular party is called the socialization or party identification model.

The pattern in Western Europe was slightly different. Here voting expressed loyalty to a social group and only indirectly to the party representing it. The act of voting flowed from identification with a particular religion, class or ethnic group. Thus electors thought of themselves as Catholic or Protestant, middle class or working class; and they voted for parties which explicitly stood for, and doubtless reinforced, these interests. In short, party choice was anchored in social identity.

But whether the emphasis was placed on identification with a party (as in the USA) or with a social group (as in Europe), voting was viewed as a reflex, not a choice. The electoral 'decision' was an ingrained habit which, once acquired, was unlikely to change over a voter's lifetime. These psychological ties helped to account for the stability of parties in the early post-war decades.

However, models of party and group voting had become less useful by the 1970s. The 1960s and 1970s were decades of partisan dealignment. The ties which once bound voters, social groups and political parties together began to loosen. By the 1990s, the proportion of party identifiers had declined by over 10 per cent in such countries as Canada, Germany, Ireland, Sweden and the USA (Bentley *et al.*, 2000). Dalton (2008a, p. 189) judges that 'a general pattern of partisan decline is broadly affecting advanced industrial democracies' while Berglund *et al.* (2005, p. 110) conclude from a European study that 'partisanship is lower in all countries in the late 1990s than in the 1960s'.

Bear in mind that party loyalties have reduced in strength but they have not disappeared; electorates are dealigning rather than dealigned. Indeed, Stonecash (2005) argues that partisan and cultural conflict in the United States intensified at the start of the twenty-first century, stimulating a modest recovery of partisanship. Lewis-Beck *et al.* (2008) further suggest that the original party identification model remains a successful account of American voting behaviour.

What brought about this widespread weakening of party loyalties? Trends applying across many countries suggest common causes and Box 10.6 suggests some of the political and sociological factors at work.

Politically, reports of party-based scandal and corruption have probably played their part, as has some convergence in the policies of the major parties (Berglund *et al.*, 2005). A sense that major parties are all equally self-serving is unfavourable ground for young people, in particular, to develop a strong identification with one particular party.

Sociologically, the weakening of historic social divisions, the rise of television in place of the more partisan press and the expansion of education all contribute to a loosening of political identities. In this more relaxed environment, electors can form their own judgements about parties rather than relying on the cues provided by their social location and the loyalties flowing from it.

It is possible, of course, that the political factors will reverse but less likely that the sociological factors will do so. On balance, then, party loyalties in the electorate are unlikely to recover to the level of the 1960s.

The consequences of dealignment have proved to be substantial. Much of the democratic world has witnessed the emergence of new parties such as the Greens. Turnout, and active participation in campaigns, has fallen. Electoral volatility has expanded, split-ticket voting has increased and more electors

---

> ### BOX 10.6
>
> # Factors contributing to partisan dealignment
>
> | | Comment |
> | --- | --- |
> | Disillusionment with party politics | Events such as Watergate, and more recent publicity about corruption, reduce popular trust in parties |
> | Convergence of party policies | If policies diverge again, party loyalties may also recover |
> | Decay of social divisions | As cleavages of class and religion weaken, so too do loyalties to parties based on them |
> | Rising education | Educated voters can interpret events with less need for party cues |
> | Television becomes the dominant medium | Supplants the more partisan coverage in many newspapers |

are deciding how to vote closer to election day. Also, candidates and leaders seem to have grown in electoral importance relative to the parties they represent (Dalton *et al.*, 2000).

The decay of group and party voting has led political scientists to focus on the question of how voters do now decide. The contemporary emphasis is on four factors: political issues, the economy, party leaders and party image. Fiorina's account (1981) of **retrospective voting** captures many of these themes. From Fiorina's perspective, a vote is no longer an expression of a lifelong commitment. Rather it is a piece of business like any other. The elector asks of the government, 'what have you done for me (and the country) lately?'. Party identification is no longer a lens through which to view the polit-

> **Retrospective voting** means casting one's ballot in response to government performance. The phrase was introduced by Fiorina (1981); it tells us much about electoral choice in an age of dealignment.

ical world but just a running tally of how well different parties are judged to have performed in office. In Fiorina's framework, the electoral decision becomes an act of calculation rather than affirmation.

Retrospective voting helps to explain why economic conditions, particularly disposable income, unemployment and inflation, seem to have such a regular impact on the popularity of governments; as Duch and Stevenson (2008, p. 338) demonstrate, 'economic voting is persuasive in Western democracies'. Many voters proceed on the brutal assumption that governments should be punished for bad times and perhaps also rewarded for economic advance. Especially where a single party forms the government, many voters are happy to judge by results; they are fairweather supporters. The feel-good factor, however, is not just a matter of objective economic performance: voters' perceptions of the economy are the key battleground, and here politicians have some room for manoeuvre.

Electors assess the general competence of parties, asking not just what a party proposes to do but also how well it will do it. Given that parties are less rooted in ideology and social groups than in the past, their reputation for competence in meeting the unpredictable demands of office becomes a crucial marketing asset. So party image is vital, especially for opposition parties which do not have a recent record in government to brandish (Brewer, 2008). The skill is to generate trust in one's own side and to cast doubt on the opposition's capacity to govern. Given volatile and sceptical voters, gaining credibility – or at least more than one's opponents – is the cardinal objective.

Elections in authoritarian states

A few authoritarian regimes, including several ruling families in the Middle East, dispense with elections altogether, either because they do not possess an assembly or because members are appointed by the king. However, most non-democratic rulers recognize that elections can be a useful fiction. Elections satisfy international donors who are often happy enough if just the facade is democratic. We begin this section by looking at elections in totalitarian states before turning to their somewhat more subtle role in authoritarian regimes.

Elections in totalitarian regimes did not make much pretence of offering choice. There was no possibility that the ruling party could be defeated or even opposed through elections. In the Soviet Union, for instance, the official candidate was simply presented to the electorate for ritual endorsement. The voting act itself discouraged dissent. In Mao's China, voting took place in public. In some other communist states, voters who wanted to accept the party's choice could just place their ballot in the box whereas those who wanted to mark their ballot had to move, under the watchful eye of an official, to a special area. In such biased conditions, most votes really did go to the communist candidate even if the margin of victory was sometimes exaggerated when the results were announced.

Some communist states in Eastern Europe did eventually introduce a measure of choice to their elections by allowing a choice of candidates from within the ruling party. Central rulers found these candidate-choice elections useful in testing whether local party officials retained the confidence of their communities.

This local monitoring is one reason for the gradual introduction of such elections to many of China's 930,000 villages since 1987 and, more recently and tentatively, to some townships. Elected village committees help to build state capacity in a country where power has traditionally operated on a personal basis. However, even in contemporary China no explicit opposition to the party's policy platform is permitted. In many villages, real authority still resides with the local party official, who may in any case also serve as chair of the village committee. A revision to the election law in 1997 explicitly affirmed this supervisory role for the party. Neither in the countryside nor the towns are there signs of elections threatening the party's control. These tight limits on what elections can achieve may dash expectations raised by the original reform, thereby increasing popular frustration.

Elections in authoritarian rather than totalitarian regimes exhibit a different character. Here, competition is constrained rather than eliminated. Some opposition victories may be permitted but they are too few to affect the overall result. Independent candidates find themselves operating in a threatening environment. The secret police follow them around, breaking up some of their meetings. Using arbitrary registration rules, independent politicians may be banned from standing. Control over the media, the electoral system and the government is exploited to favour the ruling party. Through its conduct of campaigns, the regime projects both the illusion of choice and the realities of power, securing its victory without needing to falsify the count (though this option remains if all else fails).

Egypt provides an example of such biased processes. Since 1976, numerous parties have competed for seats in the People's Assembly, offering the appearance of a vigorous multiparty system. But the National Democratic Party (NPD), led by President Hosni Mubarak, has retained its dominant position throughout. Lesch (2004, p. 605) outlines the mechanisms employed:

- The Law of Political Parties (1977) requires new parties to be approved by the regime, which is dominated by the NPD itself;
- The Public Prosecutor must approve all candidates standing for election;
- Opposition poll watchers are often refused entry to polling places or arrested beforehand;
- The security forces sometimes bar electors lacking NDP-issued voting cards from entering the polling station;
- The assembly rejects challenges to the fairness of the election.

Elections in illiberal democracies

In an illiberal democracy, elections play a more important part in confirming the legitimacy of the ruler. The election outcome is more than just a routine acceptance by the people of the realities of power. Explicit vote-rigging is avoided, some candidates from non-governing parties gain election and the possibility of defeat cannot be entirely ruled out. Even so, elections do not operate on as free and fair a playing field as in a liberal democracy. In particular, the leading figure dominates media coverage,

using television to trumpet his often real achievements in office. The emphasis is as much on the carrot (providing reasons for voting for the dominant figure) as on the stick (threatening opposition supporters).

Incumbents seeking re-election can exploit unique resources. They are familiar to voters, draw on the state's coffers for their campaign, implement a favourable electoral system and call in political credits carefully acquired while in office. Anticipating the president's re-election, underlings carrying favour will seek to help the campaign along while credible opponents are deterred from embarking on a hopeless fight: why annoy the candidate who is sure to win?

In lower-income countries, patronage networks based on the leader's control of government provide a vote-gathering resource unavailable to the opposition. These networks are often supported by a culture which is sympathetic to rewarding the 'big man' who has supplied some crumbs from his table to an electoral district. For such reasons, Bratton (1998, p. 65) concludes that 'in a "big man" political culture, it is unclear whether the re-election of an incumbent constitutes the extension of a leader's legitimacy or the resignation of the electorate to his inevitable dominance'.

Africa still provides several examples where former dictators and military leaders have made the transition to an illiberal democracy, quickly mastering the arts of winning elections using patronage-based techniques similar to those employed in the pre-democratic era. Through such devices, a favourable result is manufactured well in advance, so that the growing army of independent election monitors may not find many if any irregularities on election day itself (Santa-Cruz, 2005).

President Vladimir Putin proved to be a skilled exponent of these techniques in ensuring both his own re-election in 2004 and the election of his successor, Dmitry Medvedev, in 2008. McFaul (2005) describes how Putin moved early to neutralize potential threats in three main areas: the media, the regions and business. In each sector, a few opponents were removed from office, yielding the desired servility among the remainder. McFaul's summary of the Russian president's strategy could be applied to election management in many other illiberal democracies:

The effect of these reforms occurred well before the votes were actually cast. The absence of independence within media, regional elite and oligarchic ranks reduced the freedom of manoeuvre for opposition political parties and candidates. At the same time, the state's larger role gave incumbents enormous advantages, be it national television coverage, massive administrative support from regional executives or enormous financial resources from companies like Gazprom. (McFaul, 2005, p. 77)

Such techniques presuppose weaknesses in the rule of law, the market economy and civil society in general. These deficits are not easy to measure: 'in an age of images and symbols, elections are easy to capture on film. But how do you televise the rule of law?' (Zakaria, 2003, p. 156). But it is precisely such constraints on opposition candidates that justify the distinction between elections in illiberal democracies such as Russia and those in liberal democracies such as the USA, even though American incumbents – like Russian presidents – also secure more media attention, political backing, financial support and electoral success than their challengers.

Learning Resources for Chapter 10

Next step

LeDuc *et al.* (2010) review a wide literature in their comparative study of elections and voting.

Further reading

On electoral systems, Farrell (2001) provides a clear introduction. Colomer (2004a) and Gallagher and Mitchell (2005) offer comparative collections. Lundell (2009) considers influences on the choice of electoral system, while Norris (2004a) examines the impact of electoral systems on party systems. Dalton and Wattenberg (2000) is a comparative study of voting trends; Franklin (2004) performs the same task for turnout; while IDEA (2006) adds practical suggestions. King (2002) examines the influence of leaders' personalities specifically. On referendums, see IDEA (2008) and Qvortrup (2005).

Internet sources

Inter-Parliamentary Union
The PARLINE database provides election results.
http://www.ipu.org

IFES
Supports the building of democratic societies.
http://www.ifes.org/

Center for Voting and Democracy
Promotes voter turnout, fair representation, inclusive policy and meaningful electoral choices in the USA.
http://www.fairvote.org/

Comparative Study of Election Systems
A collaborative program of survey research among election study teams from around the world.
http://www.umich.edu/~cses/

International Institute for Democracy and Electoral Assistance (IDEA)
Supports sustainable democracy worldwide. An informative site with a practical focus.
http://www.idea.int/

American National Election Studies
Data on voting, public opinion and political participation to serve research needs.
http://www.electionstudies.org/

Chapter 11
Political parties

'In this book I investigate the workings of democratic government. But it is not institutions which are the object of my research: it is not on political forms, it is on political forces I dwell.' So Moisei Ostrogorski (1854–1919) began his pioneering comparison of party organization in Britain and the United States. Ostrogorski was one of the first students of politics to recognize that **political parties** were becoming vital in the new era of democratic politics: 'wherever this life of parties is developed, it focuses the political feelings and the active wills of its citizens' (1902, p. 7).

Ostrogorski's supposition that parties were growing in importance proved to be fully justified. In Western Europe, mass parties battled for the votes of enlarged electorates. In communist and fascist states, ruling parties monopolized power in an attempt to reconstruct society. In the developing world, nationalist parties became the vehicle for driving colonial rulers back to their imperial homeland.

In the twentieth century, parties proved to be a key mobilizing device, drawing millions of people into the national political process for the first time. Parties jettisoned their original image as private factions engaged in capturing and even perverting the public interest. Instead, they became accepted as a necessary instrument in shaping the collective interest. In the second half of the twentieth century, parties began to receive explicit mention in newly written constitutions. Some countries banned independent candidates from standing for the legislature or prevented members from switching parties once elected (Reilly, 2007). By the century's end, most liberal democracies offered some public funding to support party work. Parties had become part of the system.

The question for the twenty-first century is whether we are witnessing a crisis of parties or merely a change in their role. No longer do parties seem to be energetic agents of society, seeking to bend the state towards their supporters' interests. Rather, they seem to be at risk of capture by the state itself. No longer do parties provide a home for the politically engaged; instead, social movements and promotional groups possess greater appeal for younger generations. Western publics still endorse the principle of democracy but they are increasingly unwilling to will its means: competing parties. Even in their Western European heartland, the European Union has reduced the scope of nationally based parties. Writing a hundred years after Ostrogorski, Mair (2008, p. 230) speculates that parties are now in danger of ceasing to be a political driving force.

Sartori (1976, p. 63) defines a **political party** as 'any political group identified by an official label that presents at elections, and is capable of placing through elections candidates for public office'. Unlike interest groups, serious parties aim to obtain the keys to government; in Weber's phrase, they live 'in a house of power'.

BOX 11.1

Typical elements of party organization in Western Europe

	Comment	Level
Party leadership	The leaders typically include government ministers when the party is in office	National
The party in parliament	Members of the parliamentary party, including backbenchers	National
The party's central organization	Officials at party headquarters	National
The party at regional and local levels	Party members elected to regional and local assemblies; local officials and ordinary party members	Subnational
The party in the European Union	Members of the European Parliament, where representatives of a national party join broader, transnational party groups	Supranational

Source: Adapted from Cotta (2000). See also Katz and Crotty (2006).

Even so, major parties continue to perform four important functions:

- Ruling parties offer direction to government, pursuing the vital task of steering the ship of state.
- By allowing voters to choose between parties with different teams of leaders and often with contrasting policies, a system of competing parties gives effect to liberal democracy.
- Parties function as agents of political recruitment, preparing and recruiting candidates for the legislature and the executive.
- Parties serve as devices of interest aggregation, filtering a multitude of specific demands into manageable packages of proposals. Parties select policies and combine them to form an overall programme.

Party organization and membership

Political parties are complex multilevel organizations, with their varied elements united by a common identity and, sometimes, shared objectives. 'A party is not a community but a collection of communities, a union of small groups dispersed throughout the country and linked by co-ordinating institutions' (Duverger, 1954, p. 17). It is a political system in miniature. Box 11.1 sets out the elements of a typical major party in Western Europe (Deschouwer, 2006). These elements typically come together at an annual conference which is often nominally supreme, at least in parties whose origins lie outside parliament.

At national level, the main distinction is between the party in parliament and the officials in party headquarters. But the top leaders often span and integrate these two arenas, spearheading the parliamentary party as well as heading the party organization. Below national level, many parties are also represented in both regional and local government. This superstructure is supported at the base by ordinary members, usually organized by area in branches. This array tends to become more complex as parties respond to decentralization within the state itself.

In Western Europe, parties typically possess a large if declining subscription-based membership, a coherent ideology and strong parliamentary discipline. Reflecting this importance, much of the most authoritative writing about parties in liberal democracies is based on this region. However, we should recognize that Western Europe is in some ways untypical. In federal North America, party organization is weaker and even more decentralized. Apart from the legislature (where party organization is strong), American and Canadian parties are largely devices for organizing elections; they often hibernate between campaigns. Volunteer helpers with campaigns, such as the multitude recruited by Barack Obama in 2008, often have no formal links with their party. Most new democracies, in Eastern Europe and beyond, also lack the Western European tradition of a large, dues-paying national membership.

As Panebianco (1988) reminds us, internal organization is a key issue in the study of parties. How is power distributed within the party? What is the relationship between leaders, members and parliamentarians? The answer to these questions, Panebianco claims, must be historical. He stresses the importance of the party's founding moment in dealing out the power cards between the elements of party organization. These 'continue in many ways to condition the life of the organization even decades afterwards'. In this section, we will examine a classification of parties based on their origins before turning to their internal distribution of power and an important current issue: declining membership.

Types of party organization

Adopting Panebianco's historical approach leads to a threefold distinction between cadre, mass and catch-all parties (Box 11.2). **Cadre** (or elite) parties are internally created. They are formed by groups of members within an assembly – the cadres – joining together to reflect common concerns and then fighting effective campaigns in an enlarged electorate. The earliest nineteenth-century parties were of this elite type: for example, the conservative parties of Britain, Canada and Scandinavia. The first American parties, the Federalists and the Jeffersonians, were also loose elite factions, based in Congress and state legislatures. Cadre parties are sometimes called caucus parties, the 'caucus' denoting a closed meeting of the party's members of parliament. Such parties remain heavily committed to their leader's authority, with ordinary members playing a supporting but not a sovereign role.

Mass parties are a later innovation. These originate outside the assembly, in groups seeking representation in the legislature as a way of achieving their goals. The working-class socialist parties that spread across Europe around the turn of the twentieth century epitomized these externally created parties. The German Social Democratic Party (SPD), founded in 1875, is a classic example. Such socialist parties exerted tremendous influence on European party systems in the twentieth century, stimulating many cadre parties to copy their extra-parliamentary organization. Mass parties acquired an enormous membership organized in local branches. Unlike cadre parties, they aimed to keep their representatives in parliament on a tight rein. They also sought influence over their members through affiliated organizations such as trade unions and sports clubs. Becoming a party member represented a distinct commitment, not least a formal statement of support for the party's ideological goals, but in exchange the organization would treat its members as part of the family, offering educational and leisure activities.

The **catch-all** party is more recent. Kirchheimer (1966) used this phrase to describe the outcome of an evolutionary path followed by many parties, both cadre and mass, in post-1945 conditions. The catch-all party responds to a mobilized political system in which governing has become more technical and in which electoral communication takes place through the mass media. Leaders communicate with the voters through television, bypassing the membership. Such parties seek to govern in the national interest rather than as representatives of a social group: 'a party large enough to get a majority has to be so catch-all that it cannot have a unique ideological program' (Kirchheimer, quoted in Krouwel, 2003, p. 29). Catch-all parties seek electoral support wherever they can find it; their purpose is to govern rather than to represent.

The broadening of Christian Democratic parties (such as the CDU in Germany) from religious defence organizations to broader parties of the centre-right is the classic case of the transition to catch-all status. The subsequent transformation of several radical socialist parties into leader-

---

BOX 11.2

Types of party organization

	Cadre party	Mass party	Catch-all party
Emergence	19th century	1880–1960	After 1945
Origins	Inside the assembly ('internally created')	Outside the assembly ('externally created')	Developed from existing cadre or mass parties
Claim to support	Traditional status of leaders	Represents a social group	Competence at governing
Membership	Small, elitist	Large card-carrying membership in local branches	Leaders become dominant
Source of income	Personal contacts	Membership dues	Many sources, including state subsidy
Examples	19th-century conservative and liberal parties, many post-communist parties	Socialist parties	Many modern Christian and Social Democratic parties in Western Europe

---

dominated social democratic parties, as in Spain and the United Kingdom, is another example.

Power within the party

Given the complex nature of modern parties, it is natural to ask where authority within them really resides. Of all the elements in Box 11.1, which one truly commands the party? The answer is far from clear, reflecting the blunt nature of the question. American parties, in particular, are sometimes seen as empty vessels waiting to be filled by fresh ideas and ambitious office-seekers. The American party is not controlled from any single point; no one pulls the levers, no one rules the party.

Yet much European research on parties does suggest that authority within the party flows from the top down, with the leaders who represent the party to the public playing a key role. In 1911, the German scholar Robert Michels (1875–1936) published *Political Parties*, certainly the most influential work on leadership within parties. Michels argued that even organizations with democratic pretensions become dominated by a ruling clique of leaders and supporting officials. Using Germany's Social

Democratic Party (SPD) as a critical case, Michels suggested that leaders develop organizational skills, expert knowledge and an interest in their own continuation in power. The ordinary members, aware of their inferior knowledge and amateur status, accept their own subordination as natural, even in an externally created party such as the SPD. Michels's pessimism about the possibility of democracy within organizations such as political parties was expressed in his famous **iron law of oligarchy**.

Certainly, party leaders in the legislature are normally the key actors within the parliamentary systems of Europe. When their party is in power, these leaders typically become government ministers. But even in opposition, a party's leaders are its public face, shaping perceptions of its strengths and weaknesses.

> Michels's **iron law of oligarchy** states that 'to say organization is to say a tendency to oligarchy' (often reproduced as, 'who says organization, says oligarchy'). Michels argued that even parties formally committed to democracy become dominated by a ruling elite (**oligarchy** is rule by and for the few).

We should note that the party organization outside the assembly does retain some useful cards. Most state financial aid normally goes to the party bureaucracy, not to the party in parliament. And only experts, working in or for the party, can cope with increasingly technical tasks such as raising funds through mail-shots, and arranging for advertising, briefings and press conferences during election campaigns. The contemporary importance of these tasks is captured in Panebianco's concept (1988) of an electoral-professional party centred on fighting elections through the mass media. Even this interpretation, however, privileges the party elite over ordinary members – just as Michels suggested.

Membership

The marked and often dramatic decline in party membership between the 1960s and the 1990s is shown in Table 11.1. In most countries, the proportion of the electorate belonging to a political party more than halved over the period. Denmark is a particularly extreme case, with membership falling from one in every five people in the 1960s to one in twenty by the 1990s.

This general subsidence seems to have continued into the 2000s, with membership of Sweden's Social Democrats falling from 177,000 in 1999 to just 125,000 in 2005 (Möller, 2007, p. 36). Even in Belgium, where parties remain central to the political process, membership had reached its lowest measured level by 2003 (Deschouwer, 2009, p. 100). Across the democratic world, millions of party foot soldiers have simply given up.

Furthermore, many new members do not engage with their party beyond paying an annual subscription; these credit-card supporters are especially likely to leave the party, resulting in increased turnover. Seyd and Whiteley's assessment (2002, p. 169) of trends in Britain's Labour Party is widely applicable:

Whatever activity one focuses on, participation has been declining over the past 10 years. The extent of the commitment of the average member is increasingly merely one of paying a yearly subscription and occasionally donating money to the party when asked to do so.

Lacking a steady flow of young members, the average age of members has increased. Nearly every-

Table 11.1 Falling party membership, 1960–99

	Total party membership as a percentage of the electorate		
	Beginning of 1960s	Beginning of 1980s	End of 1990s
Austria	26	22	18
Finland	19	13	10
Belgium	8	9	7
Norway	16	14	7
Denmark	21	8	5
Italy	13	10	4
Germany	3	4	3
Netherlands	9	3	3
New Zealand	23	9	3
UK	9	3	2

Note: Party membership in New Zealand is expressed as a proportion of votes cast, not the whole electorate.

Sources: Adapted from Mair (1994), Table 1.1; Mair and van Biezen (2001), Table 1; Sundberg (2002), Table 7.10; Miller (2005), Table 1.1.

where, those who belong to a party are older than those who vote for it. By the late 1990s, the average age of members of Canada's main parties was 59 (Cross and Young, 2004). Fewer than one in twenty members of Germany's Christian Democratic Union (CDU) are under 30. Membership may continue to fall as the oldest cohorts of members go unreplenished.

However, we must locate this recent decline in a longer perspective. If statistics were available for the entire twentieth century, they would probably show a rise in membership over much of the century followed by a fall in the final third. The recent decline is from a peak only reached, in many countries, in the 1970s. In other words, it is perhaps the bulge in membership after the Second World War, rather than the later decline, which requires explanation.

The reduction in membership has occurred in tandem with dealignment among electors and surely reflects similar causes. These include:

▶ The weakening of traditional social divisions such as class and religion;
▶ The loosening of the bond linking trade unions and socialist parties;

- The decay of local electioneering in an era of media-based campaigns;
- The appeal of social movements rather than parties to younger generations.

How should we appraise this fall in membership? As we suggested in discussing political participation generally (Chapter 9), we should not automatically assume that less is worse. Specifically, the fall may indicate an evolution in the nature of parties, rather than a weakening of their significance in government. Crotty (2006, p. 499), for one, notes how 'the demands of society change, and parties change to meet them'. Too often, perhaps, models of what parties ought to be like are drawn from the narrow experience of Western Europe in the twentieth century. Today, it is unrealistic to expect the rebirth of mass membership parties with their millions of members and their supporting pillars of trade unions and churches. Social change means that this organizational format has gone for good.

In its stead comes the modern format of parties found in the new democracies: lean and flexible, with communication from leaders through the broadcast media and the internet. Rather than relying on outdated notions of a permanent army of members, new-format parties mobilize volunteers for specific, short-term tasks, such as election campaigns. In addition, their funding increasingly comes from the state rather than the membership. Doubtless, the form of parties will continue to evolve but their purpose of giving direction to government continues unchallenged.

Selecting candidates and leaders

Elite recruitment is a vital and continuing function of parties. Even as parties decline in other ways, they continue to dominate elections to the national legislature from which, in most parliamentary systems, the nation's leaders are drawn. Given that candidates who are nominated for safe districts or who appear near the top of their party's list are virtually guaranteed a place in parliament, it is the **selectorate**, not the electorate, which makes 'the choice before the choice', opening the door to the house of power (Rahat, 2007).

> The **selectorate** consists of those who nominate a party's candidates for an election. This group often plays a more critical role than the electorate in determining who will represent the party in office.

Schattschneider (1942, p. 46) famously wrote that 'the nature of the nominating convention determines the nature of the party; he who can make the nominations is the owner of the party'. In similar vein, Duverger (1954, p. 353) commented that

the representative receives a double mandate: from the party and from his electors. The importance of each varies according to the country and the parties: on the whole the party mandate seems to carry more weight than that of the electors.

How, then, do parties select their candidates and leaders? In answering this question, we will observe an increasing role for ordinary members, a finding suggesting that Michels's iron law is showing signs of corrosion as parties seek to retain members by giving them a greater voice.

Candidates

A range of options is available for selecting candidates, ranging from the exclusive (selection by the leader) to inclusive (an open vote of the entire electorate) (Figure 11.1). Reflecting the complexity of party organization, the nomination process is generally decentralized. In Western Europe, certainly, a few parties do give control to the national leadership, though even here the leaders usually select from a list generated at lower levels. More often, though, local parties are the active force, either acting autonomously or with nominations ratified at national level. Small and extreme parties, and those in Scandinavia, are the most decentralized in their selection procedures (Lundell, 2004).

The nomination task is constrained by three wider features of the political system:

- The electoral system is a crucial influence. Choosing a series of candidates for individual constituencies in a plurality system is naturally a more decentralized task than preparing a single national list in a party list system.
- Incumbents (current members of parliament) possess an advantage almost everywhere,

usually achieving reselection without much ado. Often, candidates are only truly 'chosen' when the incumbent stands down.

◆ Nearly all countries impose conditions such as citizenship on members of the legislature while a few, including Belgium and several Latin American states, also impose gender quotas on party candidates.

Consider how the electoral system affects the nomination process (Box 11.3). Under the list form of proportional representation, parties must develop a ranked list of candidates to present to the electorate. This requirement forces central coordination, even if candidates are suggested locally. In the Netherlands, for example, each party needs to present a single list of candidates for the whole country. There, the major parties use a nominating committee to examine applications received either from local branches or directly from individuals. A senior party board then produces the final ordering.

In a few countries, candidate lists are prepared solely through a ballot of party members. This procedure is more democratic but, as Michels would have predicted, it causes difficulties of its own. Ballots advantage celebrity over competence, and wealth over party experience. Significantly, most of the Israeli parties that introduced ballots of members early in the 1990s soon withdrew the procedure.

In the few countries whose general elections use the plurality method, the nomination procedure is typically more decentralized. Candidates must win selection by a local party in a specific district. These bodies are invariably keen to guard their autonomy against encroachment from headquarters. In Canada, for instance, constituency parties show little concern for national needs; they seek candidates with an attractive local profile (Carty, 2002).

The manner of selection in local districts is also becoming broader. The nomination meeting was the exclusive preserve of the local party's management committee in Britain. However, here and elsewhere, the selection meeting is increasingly open to all members. Some parties in some countries now even choose their constituency candidates through a postal ballot of all members in the locality.

The USA has gone furthest in opening up the selection process. There, **primary elections** enable a party's supporters to choose their candidates for a particular office. In the absence of a tradition of direct party membership, a 'supporter' is generously defined in most states as anyone who declares, in advance, an affiliation to that party. An **open primary** extends the choice still further to any registered elector. Thus American primaries extend the power of nomination to a wider circle than the party members who now form the selectorate in some European democracies.

> A **primary election** is a contest in which a party's supporters select its candidate for a subsequent general election (a direct primary) or choose delegates to the presidential nominating convention (a presidential primary). A closed primary is limited to a party's registered supporters but any registered elector can participate in an **open primary**, though only for one party. To date, primaries are rarely encountered outside the United States.

Originally introduced to formalize selection procedures and to weaken the control of corrupt party bosses, primaries are now well-entrenched. Yet, as with membership ballots, primaries are at best a mixed blessing. By taking control over selection

Figure 11.1 Who selects candidates for legislative elections?

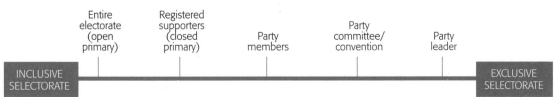

Source: Adated from Rahat (2008).

BOX 11.3

Selecting candidates for legislative elections

Electoral system used for national elections	How parties typically select candidates for these elections	Example
Proportional representation (party list)	Party officials or special party conventions draw up a ranked list of candidates	Netherlands
Plurality system	Local parties select the candidate, sometimes drawing from a list prepared by head office*	Canada, United Kingdom
Mixed system	The party draws up a list for the PR element while local parties select a candidate for the district contest	Germany

* In the USA, primary elections are held among a party's registered supporters in the district.

---

away from the party itself, they reduce its cohesion and give an advantage to better-known, well-financed candidates. In the process, parties become vehicles rather than drivers.

As we saw in Chapter 10, an increasing number of countries operate a mixed electoral system, in which electors vote for both a party list and a district candidate. These circumstances complicate the party's task of selecting candidates, requiring a national or regional list, plus local constituency nominees. In this situation, individual politicians also face a choice: should they seek election via the party list or through a constituency? Many senior figures ensure they appear on both ballots, using a high position on the party's list as insurance against restlessness in their home district.

Leaders

The method of selecting the party leader merits special attention, for in most cases the person selected becomes the party's nominee for prime minister or president, fronting its election campaign. There are a few exceptions: in Germany, the party's candidate for chancellor is appointed separately from the party leader and need not be the same person. In Belgium, party statutes normally preclude the party president from becoming a government minister. In the USA, too, the presidential candidate and chair of the party's national committee are separate posts; indeed, the former usually chooses the latter.

But whether these posts are combined or separate, parties collectively perform the important function of drawing up a shortlist of national leaders to put before the voters. One key test of these selection procedures should therefore be that they do deliver the best possible shortlist for the country. It is far from clear that most methods satisfy this test. The danger is that party selectorates will focus on the leader's ability to organize the party, heal internal divisions and campaign effectively. The capacity to lead the country may be a secondary consideration.

Just as many parties now afford their ordinary members a greater voice in candidate selection, so too has the procedure for selecting the party leader become broader. As Mair (1994) notes, 'more and more parties now seem willing to allow the ordinary members a voice in the selection of party leaders'. One factor here is the desire to compensate members for their declining role in media-driven election campaigns. Yet whether this wider selection process yields improved results is again debatable.

The most common way to choose the leader is still by a special party congress or convention (Box 11.4). American parties have long selected their presidential candidates through such conventions but these meetings are no longer the effective site of decision. The real choice is made by voters in the primaries, with the convention itself transformed since the 1970s into a media event for the party and its anointed nominee.

BOX 11.4

Selection of party leaders in liberal democracies

	Countries in which most major parties use this method	Total number of parties using this method
Party congress or convention	Finland, Norway, Sweden	37
Rank-and-file members	Belgium	19
Members of the parliamentary party	The Netherlands, New Zealand	17
Party committee	Italy	8

Note: Analysis based on 16 democracies.

Source: Adapted from Hazan (2002, p.124).

A ballot of party members is an alternative and increasingly popular method of selecting leaders. Such elections, often described as OMOV (one member, one vote) contests, provide an incentive for people to join the party and can also be used to limit the power of entrenched factions within it. In Belgium, for example, all the major parties have adopted this approach to choosing their party president. The new Conservative Party of Canada also adopted a membership election for its initial leadership contest in 2004, albeit with equal weight for each riding above a certain size rather than for each member.

Election by the parliamentary party is of course the traditional method, especially for cadre parties with their assembly origins. The device is still used in several countries, including Australia, Denmark and New Zealand. Britain's Conservative party adopts a two-stage process, giving ordinary members a choice but only between two candidates selected by the parliamentary party.

A vote of the party's members of parliament is of course a narrow constituency. And the ability of potential leaders to instil confidence in their parliamentary peers may say little about their capacity to win a general election fought on television. Even so, colleagues in the assembly will have a close knowledge of a candidate's abilities; they provide an expert constituency for judging the capacity to lead not only the party but also, more importantly, the country.

Party finance

Falling membership implies a smaller subscription income for parties in an era when party expenses (not least for election campaigns) continue to rise. The problem of funding political parties has therefore become highly significant (Box 11.5). Should members, donors or the state pay for the party's work? If funding is provided by the state, should taxpayers be given the right to opt out of supporting designated parties? Should private donations be encouraged (to increase funds and encourage participation) or restricted (to maintain fairness and reduce scandals)? Do limits on contributions and spending interfere with free speech? Underlying these questions is another deeper issue: are parties private or public entities?

In the main, the battle for public funding has been won. State support for national parties is now virtually universal in liberal democracies (Figure 11.2). As Fisher and Eisenstadt (2004, p. 621) comment, 'public subsidies have replaced private sponsorship as the norm in political finance'. State subsidies have also developed quickly in the new democracies of Eastern Europe, where party memberships are far

Figure 11.2 Introduction of public subsidies for parties' extra-parliamentary work, Western Europe, 1959–90

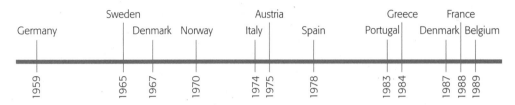

Source: Adapted from Scarrow, (2006), Table 1.

smaller than in the west. In both Eastern and Western Europe, public support reflects the role which most recent constitutions give to parties. In Germany, for example, parties are required under the constitution 'to participate in forming the democratic will'.

What forms does public funding take? Typically, support is provided for parliamentary groups, election campaigns or both. Campaign support, in turn, may be offered to parties, candidates or both. In an effort to limit state dependence, public funding may be restricted to matching the funds raised by the party from other means, including its members. In

any case, most funding regimes only reimburse a specified proportion of party spending.

Indirect subsidies are also on offer, usually in the form of free access to the mass media. Historically, this subsidy took the form of free political broadcasts on state-owned television and radio. Some countries also require commercial broadcasters to make free time available as a condition of their licence. This subsidy in kind is extremely valuable and almost certainly wasteful. A more efficient use of resources would surely ensue if parties were given the cash equivalent, thus freeing them to decide for themselves on the best use of the money.

BOX 11.5

Public funding of political parties: for and against

FOR	AGAINST
Parties perform a public function, supplying policies and leaders to the state.	Public funding is creeping nationalization, creating parties that serve the state, not society. Also, it requires a new regulatory body.
Parties should be funded to a professional level and not appear cheap. Marketing should match private-sector standards.	Public funding favours established and large parties, encouraging a cartel.
Public funding creates a level playing field between parties.	To maintain a level playing field, spending should be capped rather than subsidized.
Without public support, pro-business parties gain access to more funds.	Why should taxpayers fund parties against their wishes? A tax credit for voluntary donations is a preferable compromise.
Relying on private donations encourages corruption.	Corruption can be reduced by banning anonymous donations rather than adopting public funding.

Altering the way in which any organization obtains its funds is always consequential and state funding of parties is no exception. Three points are crucial here. First, public financing reduces a party's incentive to attract members. That is, party leaders know that their funding comes from the state and that they can appeal to the electorate directly through the mass media, limiting the political value of a membership army. Thus, the evolution of party funding contributes to a move away from mass parties and to a partial recovery of the old format of cadre parties.

Second, public funding tends to reinforce the status quo. Subsidies are normally restricted to parties gaining seats in the assembly; often, the more votes won in the previous election(s), the greater the payout. Thus large established parties have an advantage over new ones. Some authors have developed this point by suggesting that the transition to public funding has led to a convergence of the state and the top levels of major parties on a single system of rule, sometimes called a party state. Governing parties in effect authorize subsidies for themselves, a process captured by Katz and Mair's idea (1995) of **cartel parties**: 'colluding parties become agents of the state and employ its resources to ensure their own survival'. The danger of cartel parties is that they are viewed as part of the political establishment, further weakening their historic role as agents of particular social groups.

Third, public funding gives governments a device for influencing parties; those who pay the piper call the tune. The state may wish to use this lever in future in any number of ways: perhaps to promote democracy within parties, perhaps to encourage particular types of candidate, perhaps to discourage platforms judged unacceptable. To a degree, public funding is bound to turn parties into public utilities.

Issues of party finance extend beyond the provision of subsidies. What of donations: who can give how much and with what reporting requirements? This topic has become newsworthy, with increasing

> **Cartel parties** are leading parties that exploit their dominance of the political market to establish rules of the game, such as public funding, which reinforce their own strong position. In politics, as in business, the danger of cartels is that they damage the standing of the colluders over the longer term.

restrictions on **hard money** donations as a result of scandals in which cash-hungry parties have raised funds from private sources perceived by the public, rightly or wrongly, as in search of a payback. But as hard money is regulated more tightly, so **soft money** expands, with supporters running 'independent' campaigns. In the United States, the result can be less coherent campaigns, with potential confusion for the public (Cain and Goux, 2006).

> **Hard money** consists of campaign expenditure which is officially regulated. **Soft money** consists of campaign spending which is free of such regulation, often because it is made by organizations claiming to be independent of a party. The terms are American but the tendency for soft money to expand as hard money is regulated is universal.

Just as most democracies have introduced public funding, so too have most now banned anonymous contributions. A financial donation is treated as a public act, even though a vote is cast in secret (Nassmacher, 2006). Such transparency limits the freedom of citizens to use their money as they see fit and must surely scare off publicity-shy donors, reducing the funds raised. A few countries, including several new democracies, ban or limit contributions from public organizations, private companies, trade unions and overseas donors.

The issues involved in limiting donations emerge from considering the main outlier: the United States. American campaigns involve a relatively high proportion of private funding; indeed, Obama's extraordinarily expensive presidential campaign in 2008 was based entirely on private funds. The point here is not the high cost of the country's campaigns (expensive though they are) but the philosophical priority accorded to free speech. The judiciary has been especially concerned to enforce the first amendment: 'Congress shall make no law ... abridging the freedom of speech'. H. Alexander (2005, p. 7) summarizes the position:

The United States follows a more libertarian or free-speech approach, with more dependence upon private financing through more generous contribution limits from individual, political action committee and political party sources. Spending limits are provided only in presidential campaigns and according to a Supreme Court decision, *Buckley* v. *Valeo* (1976), are acceptable only when candidates voluntarily agree to them as a condition of their acceptance of public funding.

The waning social base

Most modern parties in Western Europe emerged from outside the assembly to express group interests, naturally developing a specific social base which continues to influence their policies and outlook. Although these foundations have weakened since the 1960s, most established Western European parties retain a bedrock of electoral support in the social structure. In the post-communist systems of Eastern Europe, by contrast, most contemporary parties lack secure anchors in society.

Western Europe

In a renowned analysis focused on Western Europe, Lipset and Rokkan (1967) showed how critical moments on the journey to a modern, developed state created **cleavages** which provided a long-term foundation for political parties.

> A **cleavage** is a social division creating a collective identity among those on each side of the divide. These interests are expressed in such organizations as trade unions, churches and parties. In Western Europe, class and religion have proved to be the widest and deepest cleavages (Mair, 2006).

Specifically, the decisive moment in the development of the state in Western Europe – the penetration of state authority throughout its territory – encouraged the formation of conservative parties representing the centralizing elite and, by reaction, regional parties representing the threatened periphery. Often, too, state-building led to the founding of Catholic parties seeking to defend the traditional autonomy of the Church against state encroachment, particularly in education.

At a later stage, beginning in the nineteenth century, the Industrial Revolution created further cleavages. The agricultural sector found itself threatened by the rise of industry, encouraging both farmers' parties and liberal parties representing the rising class of entrepreneurs. Then, class conflict intensified between industrial workers and employers, leading almost everywhere to socialist parties representing the new industrial working class.

Lipset and Rokkan claimed that in the 1960s West European parties still remained largely frozen in the framework established by the way these historic cleavages developed in particular countries. Even though the underlying cleavages had begun to fade, the parties based on them remained secure. However, considerable thawing has taken place since the 1960s. For instance:

- Many Catholic parties have repositioned themselves on the centre-right;
- Most agrarian parties have moved to the centre;
- Working-class socialist and communist parties have adopted a milder social democratic flavour.

These more open conditions have permitted the emergence and strengthening in many West European countries of **niche parties** appealing to a narrow segment of the electoral market. Prominent among these are extreme right parties such as France's National Front, Austria's Freedom Party and Switzerland's People's Party. By the mid-1990s, 15 far right parties had gained seats in national legislatures or the European parliament. A few had gained office at local level or even, as with Austria's Freedom Party, participated in national coalitions (Ignazi, 2006). More important, perhaps, the extreme right has often succeeded in influencing the agenda of mainstream conservative parties.

These parties of the extreme right are an exception to the thesis that parties emerge to represent well-defined social interests. So where exactly do these far right parties gain their votes? In the main, they draw heavily on the often transient support of

> **Niche parties** are those that appeal to a narrow section of the electorate. They are usually positioned away from the centre ground and highlight one particular issue. Unlike mainstream parties, they rarely prosper by moderating their position but instead achieve most, but still limited, success from exploiting their natural support group (Meguid, 2008). Far right, green and regional parties are examples.

uneducated and unemployed young men. Disillusioned with orthodox democracy and by the move of established right-wing parties to the centre, this constituency is attracted to parties that blame immigrants, asylum seekers and other minorities for its own insecurity in a changing world (Kitschelt, 2007). Far right voters take solace in a strong and exclusive nationalism.

However, many right-wing movements have proved to be short-lived flash parties whose prospects are held back by inexperienced leaders with a violent or even criminal background. Were the more extreme of these parties to expand to a point where they threatened the existing order, many protest voters would cease to vote for them, thus creating a natural ceiling to their support. In this sense, far right parties, like other niche organizations, lack the potential of those based on a more secure cleavage.

Although no one today would describe party systems as frozen, the plain fact is that in the political market (as in many others) the major players have retained their leading position. Decline does not imply disintegration. In New Zealand, for instance, 'despite the array of parties represented in parliament, the two major parties have continued to attract the lion's share of the vote' (Miller, 2005, p. 5). Sundberg (2002, p. 210) offers a similar appraisal of Northern Europe:

Parties in Scandinavia remain the primary actors in the political arena. To be old does not automatically imply that the party as a form of political organization is obsolete. The oldest car makers in the world are more or less the same age as the oldest parties in Scandinavia, yet nobody has questioned the capacity of these companies to renew their models. The same is true for political parties. They have developed their organizations and adapted their policies to a changing environment.

Eastern Europe

In post-communist Eastern Europe, parties have failed to develop the large memberships, strong extra-parliamentary organizations and tangible links with social groups that still characterize many of their equivalents in the west. Around the start of the twenty-first century, party membership was just 2.3 per cent of voters in Eastern Europe's new democracies, compared with about 5.5 per cent of electors in Western democracies (Webb and White, 2007, p. 352). Often, the successor to the old communist party remains the best-organized entity, with a loyal if ageing membership. Early predictions that parties in the east would develop along Western lines proved to be misplaced:

The weakness of new parties in Eastern Europe is important because it suggests that strong membership organizations are no longer necessary in contemporary conditions. The mass parties of Western Europe may be an increasingly unreliable guide to party developments elsewhere. (Lewis, 2007, p. 181)

As the national movements which initially seized power from the communists began to split, many new parties certainly appeared in the east, based on one of three main divisions: left against right, religious against secular, and European against nationalist. However, most of these east European parties are of the cadre type. Their base is in parliament or even the government itself. Steen's comment (1995, p. 13) about the Baltic countries – Estonia, Latvia and Lithuania – applies more generally to the post-communist world: 'the parties are more like campaigning institutions before elections, than permanent institutions propagating ideology'. In that respect, post-communist parties follow the American rather than the Western European model.

The failure of parties to penetrate post-communist societies reflected continuing suspicion of politics among the population. Even after communism fell, it remained difficult to enthuse electors who had been denied a political voice during, and often before, the communist era. In addition, parties lacked the incentives to build a mass organization that had stimulated socialist parties a century earlier. Since voting had already extended to virtually the whole population, there was no need for socialist parties to emerge to demand the suffrage for the working class. Also, parties in the Czech Republic, Poland, Hungary and Slovakia soon obtained state subsidies, eliminating the financial need to build a dues-paying membership. And the existence of television provided a ready-made channel of communication from the leader to the electorate, reducing the value of local activists.

BOX 11.6

Party systems in liberal democracies

	Definition	Examples
Dominant-party system	One party is constantly in office, governing alone or in coalition	South Africa (African National Congress)
Two-party system	Two major parties compete to form single-party governments	Great Britain (Conservative and Labour), United States* (Democratic and Republican)
Multiparty system	The assembly is composed of several minority parties, leading to government by coalition or a minority party	Belgium, Netherlands, Scandinavia

* However, divided government means one party can control the presidency while the other has a majority in either or both houses of Congress.

Kopecky (2006) points out that parties in post-communist Europe have found a home in the state rather than society. They are often led by people who were already in public office and who live from politics, rather than for it. The state provides parties with funding, access to the mass media, sympathetic regulation and a lucrative stream of jobs, subsidies and contracts. Whether ruling parties are colonizing the state, or the state is managing cartel parties, there is clear symbiosis between the two. What has emerged, in fact, is a new, post-communist version of the party-state. This system is viewed cynically by the population, placing even more distance between major parties and the wider society.

Party systems

To understand the political significance of parties, we must move beyond an examination of them individually. Just as the international system is more than the states that comprise it, so a **party system** refers to the overall pattern formed by the component parties, plus the interactions between them and the rules governing their conduct. Parties copy, learn from and compete with each other, with innovations in organization, fundraising and campaigning spreading across the party system. By focusing on

the relationships between parties, a party system denotes more than just the parties themselves. The United States, for instance, has a strong party system even though the parties themselves are weak by European standards (Bardi and Mair, 2008).

Like parties, structures of party competition persist over time, forming part of the operating procedures of democratic politics. We can distinguish three overlapping formats: **dominant, two-party** and **multiparty** systems (Box 11.6). Before we discuss each type, we should note that both dominant and two-party systems are now in decline. Multiparty systems, lacking a single dominant party, have become the most common configuration in liberal democracies.

Dominant party systems

In a dominant party system, one party outdistances

A **party system** denotes the overall configuration of parties in a particular country. Important features of a party system include the number of parties and their relative importance (just as we can examine a particular industry by identifying the number of companies and the market share of each). The interaction between parties (e.g. adversarial or consensual) and legal regulation are also features of the party system as a whole.

all the others and becomes the natural party of government, albeit sometimes in coalition with junior partners. In practice, such dominant parties use their control of the state to reward their supporters, thus building a more secure support base but also rendering themselves vulnerable in the long term to corruption and decline. For this reason, sustaining a predominant position is a difficult assignment for any party in a liberal democracy.

One of the few contemporary examples of a dominant party is South Africa's African National Congress (ANC). This party has multiple strengths, benefiting not just from memories of its opposition to apartheid and from its strong position among the black majority but also from its use of office to reward its own supporters. In the 2009 assembly elections, the party secured 66 per cent of both votes and seats, a remarkable achievement. The opposition parties, in contrast, are weak and divided, with a smaller social base.

Sweden provides an additional case of a party that continues to dominate, despite operating in what is clearly a competitive and well-regulated multiparty system. Even though the Social Democrats suffered a loss of power in 2006, they remained the largest party in both votes and seats. It would probably be premature to say their era of pre-eminence has come to an end. The oddity of the Swedish case is that, in contrast to South Africa, its dominant party does not usually possess a parliamentary majority but typically governs in a minority administration with parliamentary support from minor parties on the left.

Even so, the Social Democratic Workers' Party (Socialdemokraterna, SAP) has formed all but a handful of governments since the Second World War. It is the country's oldest party, gaining support from both the working class and the large public sector, and occupying a pivotal ideological position on the centre-left. More than most dominant parties, SAP has combined stable leadership with competent governance, enabling it to maintain its leading position in a genuinely competitive party system.

In the long run, however, most dominant parties fall victim to their own success. Figure 11.3 shows the decline in electoral support for India's Congress Party, Japan's Liberal Democrats (ejected from office in 2009) and even Sweden's Social Democrats. To avoid the error of concentrating only on survivors

(p. 50), we should also note that other dominant parties, notably Italy's Christian Democrats, have disappeared entirely. The very strength of a dominant party means that factions tend to develop within it, leading to an inward-looking perspective, a lack of concern with policy, excessive careerism, and increasing corruption.

India provides us with a diminished 'dominant' party. From independence in 1947, the country's politics was led by the Congress Party, an organization which under Mahatma Gandhi had provided the focus of resistance to British colonial rule. To maintain its leading position, the party relied on a patronage pyramid of class and caste alliances to sustain a national organization in a fragmented and religiously divided country. For two decades, Congress proved to be a successful and resilient catch-all party, drawing support from all social groups. Lacking access to the perks of office, no other party could mount a challenge to Congress's hegemony. But authoritarian rule during Indira Gandhi's State of Emergency (1975–77) cost Congress dearly. The party suffered its first defeat at a national election in 1977 and has received less than 30 per cent of the vote at every election since 1996.

Figure 11.3 The decay of some dominant parties, 1976–2009 (share of vote, %)

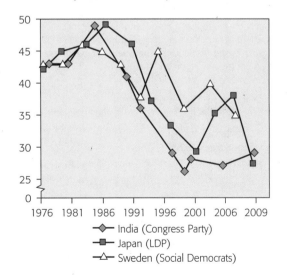

Note: Figures are for the lower or only house.

Source: IPU (2009b).

ITALY

Form of government ■ a parliamentary republic, with an indirectly elected president who can play a role in government formation.

Legislature ■ the Chamber of Deputies (630 members) and the Senate (315) are elected simultaneously by popular vote for a maximum of five years. A bill must receive the positive assent of both houses and (as in Australia) the Cabinet is equally responsible to both chambers.

Executive ■ the prime minister formally appoints, but cannot dismiss, the members of the large Cabinet. Coalition requirements limit the PM's choice of minister.

Judiciary ■ based on the civil law tradition, Italy has both ordinary and administrative judicial systems. A 15-member Constitutional Court has powers of judicial review.

Electoral system (Chamber of Deputies, 2006) ■ party list 'proportional' representation with the winning coalition guaranteed at least 340 seats.

Party system ■ the leading parties are Berlusconi's centre-right People of Liberty and the centre-left Democratic Party.

Population (annual growth rate): 58.1m (+0.05%)

World Bank income group: high income

Political Rights score: ❶

Civil Liberties score: ❶

Human development index (rank/out of): 20/177

Freedom of the press index (rank/out of): 65/195

Perceived transparency index (rank/out of): 55/180

Note: For meaning and sources of scales and indexes, see p. xv. In all cases a score and rank of 1 is 'best'.

ITALY was late to join the club of states, uniting only in 1861. As in many countries, unification preceded rather than followed the emergence of a common national identity. The powerful Catholic Church organized itself outside, and to an extent against, the new state. Acute regional contrasts, particularly between the more modern North and the underdeveloped South, remain important.

Since unification, Italy has experienced three systems of rule:

■ A constitutional monarchy which continued until 1922;
■ The fascist regime of Benito Mussolini, overthrown by an Allied invasion in 1943;
■ A parliamentary and republican democracy established in 1946.

The constitution taking effect in 1948 established a liberal democracy with a strong emphasis on checks and balances: two legislative chambers of equal status; a constitutional court; an independent judiciary; proportional representation; and provision for referendums and regional government. As a concession to the left, the constitution also emphasized social and economic rights and placed the state under an obligation to address inequality.

The most obvious feature of the new republic was its instability, with 62 governments by 2008 – an average of one per year. Coalitions emerged and collapsed, limiting the authority of the prime minister and the standing of government as a whole. Yet after a government fell, the same ministers would often return under a new administration (Giulio Andreotti was prime minister seven times) and public policy was rather more stable than government turnover might imply.

Government instability proved compatible with social modernization. Like other European countries, Italy underwent enormous development in the post-war decades. Although the economy became more industrial and open, contrasts persisted between a few large industrial companies (often politically well-connected) and a throng of smaller, family firms operating independently of the state.

The overall environment for business remains difficult by the standards of high income countries. Regulation is extensive, the non-wage costs of employment are high and the legal system remains extremely slow-moving.

The disparity between an increasingly sophisticated private sector and a spendthrift state with an inefficient bureaucracy provided part of the backdrop to the 1990s' transformation.

Further reading: Bull and Rhodes (2008), Ginsborg (2003).

Parties in Italy

The recent history of Italian politics is, first and foremost, a story about the fall of parties. In the 1990s, a dominant party system collapsed with astonishing speed, to be replaced after an interregnum by a more bipolar, but still not completely stable, system. Changes of this magnitude and speed are rarely encountered in liberal democracies.

Until 1992, Italy was a leading example of a dominant party system, with the Christian Democrats (DC) the leading player in all post-war governments. A patronage-based, Catholic, catch-all party that derived its political strength from serving as a bulwark against Italy's strong communist party, the DC slowly colonized the state, with particular ministries becoming the property of specific factions. The party used its control of the state to reward its supporters with jobs and contracts, creating a patronage network that spanned the country.

Between 1992 and 1994, this party system disintegrated. Still the largest party in 1992, the Christian Democrats had ceased to exist two years later. Its old sparring partner, the communists, had already given up the ghost, largely reforming as the Democratic Party of the Left (PDS) in 1991.

Why then did this party-based system collapse? Catalysts included the collapse of communism; referendums on electoral reform in the early 1990s

which revealed public hostility to the existing order; vivid attacks by President Francesco Cossiga on the patronage power of the leading parties; and the success of a newly assertive judiciary in exposing corruption. Like many other dominant parties, the DC's reliance on patronage also came under global and EU pressure for a genuinely open market.

Although the collapse of the old system was decisive, Italy's new order is only now beginning to deliver more stable government. The election of 1994, the first fought under a new electoral system designed to reduce fragmentation, fell apart after

tion won a majority in both legislative chambers, that stable government seemed to become a serious possibility. However, consolidation remained insecure partly as a result of Berlusconi's own volatile temperament. His miscalculations permitted a narrow victory in 2006 for Romano Prodi's coalition of the centre-left, though Berlusconi returned to power two years later, as head of the right-wing People of Liberty alliance.

Whatever the future may bring, Italy's old mass parties have disappeared, replaced by the looser, leader-dominated parties which are characteristic of the new democracies

Election to the Chamber of Deputies, 2008

Leader	Core party	Votes (%)	Seats
Silvio Berlusconi	People of Liberty	46.8	344
Walter Veltroni	Democratic Party	37.5	246

Turnout: 80.5% (−3.1)

Source: IPU (2009).

seven months. It was replaced by an astonishing crisis government of technocrats containing no parliamentary representatives at all. The next election, in 1996, did produce signs of consolidation. Two major alliances emerged: the centre-left Olive Tree Alliance and the more right-wing Liberty Pole.

But it was not until 2001, when Silvio Berlusconi's House of Freedom coali-

emerging in the 1990s. These weak parties do, however, operate in the context of competition between broad coalitions of the centre-left and centre-right.

Further reading: Bull and Newell (2005), Shin and Agnew (2008).

It remains the largest party, and the lead party in a minority coalition, but its glory days are gone.

Two-party systems

In a two-party system, two major parties of comparable size compete for electoral support, providing the framework for political competition. The remaining parties exert little if any influence on the formation and policies of governments. Neither major party dominates by itself but in combination they form the pillars of a strong party system. Rather like dominant parties, the two-party format is rare and becoming rarer.

Today, the United States is the surest example. Although American parties may lack the stable social foundations of their West European counterparts, a two-party system has been a constant feature of American history. The Republicans and Democrats have dominated electoral politics since 1860, assisted by the high hurdle that plurality elections set for minor parties. In particular, winning a presidential election is a political mountain which can only be climbed by major parties capable of assembling a broad national coalition. A presidential system is no friend of minor parties.

Legal regulation reinforces America's two-party system. From the 1880s, state legislatures and then the courts imposed a burden of regulation on America's parties, initially to root out corruption. These regulators have traditionally viewed parties as semi-official utilities performing the collective service of selecting candidates for public office. This perspective encourages sympathetic oversight of the major parties; minor parties, unable to present winning candidates, meet with such difficulties as including their party on the ballot (Lowenstein, 2006). So the position of the Republicans and Democrats is heavily entrenched. In the country of the free market, they form a powerful cartel strengthened by judicial policy.

Although Britain is often presented as emblematic of the two-party pattern, its contemporary politics barely passes the two-party test. Certainly, the Conservative and Labour parties regularly alternate in office, offering clear accountability to the electorate. However, third parties have gained ground; far more so, indeed, than in the United States. In 2005, the centre Liberal Democrats won 62 seats in a parliament of 646 members, the highest proportion for a third party in over 50 years. With 6 million votes, compared to 9.5 million for Labour and 8.8 million for the Conservatives, the Liberal Democrats can hardly be dismissed as also-rans. The Liberal Democrats have also progressed in local government and the new assemblies in Scotland and Wales. Today, Britain is best conceived as a two-and-a-half or even a multiparty system (Blondel, 1995, p. 165).

Like dominant party systems, the two-party format is in decline, kept alive only by the ventilator of the plurality electoral method and sometimes not even then. The long-term shift away from the plurality system has damaged the prospects for two-party systems. Even where a favourable electoral regime continues, as in Canada, the two-party system has buckled.

Multiparty systems

In multiparty systems, several parties – typically, at least five or six – achieve significant representation in parliament, becoming serious contenders for a place in a governing coalition. The underlying philosophy in many such systems is that political parties represent specific social groups (or, increasingly, opinion constituencies such as environmentalists) in historically divided societies. Parliament then serves as an arena of conciliation, with coalition governments forming and falling in response to often minor changes in the political balance. This emphasis on the representative and consensus-seeking function of parties contrasts sharply with the American notion of parties as post-fillers. The smaller European democracies, such as the Benelux countries and Scandinavia, exemplify the multiparty pattern.

In multiparty systems, the familiar competition between a social democratic party of the left and either a Christian Democratic or a conservative party of the right is supplemented by parties drawn from other families. These additional parties are rarely large but their combined representation in parliament, facilitated by proportional representation, suffices to yield a multiparty system.

The exact configuration of parties in a multiparty system varies by country. Typically, parties will be drawn from some but not all of the families identified in Box 11.7. In the left bloc are far left parties (usually with a communist origin), the greens and the social democrats. The centre and right bloc

---

BOX 11.7

Major party families in Western Europe

	Level of support	Trend in electoral support	Examples	Comment
LEFT				
Far Left	Low	↓	Communist Party (France). Left Party (Sweden).	Once a strong force in Finland, France and Italy, most communist parties have now reformed or decayed.
Green	Low	↑	Alliance '90/The Greens (Germany). Green League (Finland).	Ecology parties emerged from the late 1970s and have participated in coalition governments in such countries as Belgium, Finland and Germany.
Social Democrat	High	↑	Social Democratic Workers' Party (Sweden). Social Democrats (Finland).	Originally created to advance the working class, trade unions and socialist values, most such parties no longer challenge the free market.
CENTRE AND RIGHT				
Christian Democrat	High	↓	Christian Democratic Appeal (Netherlands). Christian Democratic Union (Germany).	Mainly Catholic in origin but with some Protestant cases. Christian Democratic parties now mainly represent the centre-right, with particular support from older people in the private sector.
Conservative	High	↔	Conservative Party (Britain, Norway).	These parties emphasize shared national loyalties and class unity, advocating a strong state as well as a market economy.
Centre	Medium	↔	Centre Party (Finland, Norway, Sweden).	Farmers' parties by origin, these parties have moved to the centre while often retaining traditional moral values.
Liberal	Medium	↔	Liberal Party (Netherlands). Venstre (Denmark).	Early advocates of universal suffrage, liberal parties favour individual rights and decentralization.
Far Right	Low	↑	Flemish Block (Belgium). National Front (France).	These racist and anti-immigration parties possess a strong nationalist and anti-establishment flavour.

Note: Level of support is assessed for countries in which a relevant party exists. Trend in support is from 1950 or from the year of foundation. Regional and New Left parties are also significant in some states.

Source: Adapted from Gallagher *et al.* (2006), Chapter 8.

Table 11.2 The Danish parliamentary election of 2007

	Votes (%)	Number of seats
Liberal Party (Venstre)	26.2	46
Social Democratic Party	25.5	45
Danish People's Party	13.9	25
Socialist People's Party	13.0	23
Conservative People's Party	10.4	18
Radical Liberal Party	5.1	9
New Alliance	2.8	5
Red–Green Alliance	2.2	4
Total	99.1	175

Note: Only parties winning seats are shown.

Source: IPU (2009c).

contains what are sometimes called bourgeois parties (Christian Democratic, conservative, centre and liberal) plus the far right.

Denmark provides a clear example. Here, no party has held a majority in the unicameral Folketing (People's Diet) since 1909. The country's complex party system has been managed through careful consensus-seeking but this practice has come under some pressure from the rise of new parties. Traditionally, the Danish party system comprised four main parties: the Social Democratic Party, the Social Liberal Party, the liberal Venstre Party and the Conservative People's Party. However, in an explosive election in 1973, three new parties achieved representation and since then a minimum of seven parties has been represented in parliament. The coalition that followed the 2007 election (Table 11.2) comprised the Liberal Party (Venstre) and the Conservative People's Party, with significant support in parliament from other parties, notably the far right Danish People's Party.

Clearly, multiparty governance, as in Denmark, is far removed from the concentration of power in Britain or even the focus of responsibility in the United States on the White House. To evaluate multiparty systems, we must therefore take a view on the nature of coalitions. How effective are they in delivering sound governance? Should we agree with

Herbert Asquith, British prime minister 1908–16, when he wrote, 'nothing is so belittling to the stature of public men, as the atmosphere of a coalition'?

Answers to this question have evolved over time, largely in response to economic performance. As the quotation from Asquith suggests, the English-speaking world has long treated coalitions with suspicion, regarding them as weak in operation and confused in their accountability. If things went wrong, which parties should be blamed? But opinions of coalitions became more positive as post-war economic recovery took hold in Continental Europe. In practice, coalitions seemed to produce policy continuity, while two-party systems such as Britain's now stood accused of an outdated adversarial approach.

However, the link between coalitions and weak government resurfaced in the 1990s. This reinterpretation reflected the tough 1990's agenda: welfare cuts, privatization and tax reductions. It was the traditional two-party systems, notably in Britain and New Zealand, that pursued the new policies with most energy. Continental Europe lagged behind, leading to doubts about whether multiparty systems were sufficiently flexible to produce the rapid policy changes needed to adapt to a more global economy. Blondel (1993, p. 12), for one, argued that 'the consensus mode of politics is not well-equipped to lead to long-term strategic action ... its value appears to lie primarily in its ability to handle deep social cleavages rather than policy development'.

A balanced conclusion is perhaps that multiparty systems, and the coalitions associated with them, produce continuity of policy which is helpful when the economy is growing naturally, but are slower, though not necessarily less successful in the long run, at reviving economies which have fallen on hard times.

Parties in authoritarian states

'Yes, we have lots of parties here,' says President Nazarbaev of post-communist Kazakhstan. 'I created them all' (quoted in Cummings, 2005, p. 104). This quotation indicates the secondary character of parties in most non-democratic settings. As Lawson (2001, p. 673) says of parties in dictatorships, 'the party is a shield and instrument of power. Its function is to carry out the work of government as directed by other agents with greater power (the military or the demagogue and his entourage)'. In this section, we examine the role of parties in non-totalitarian authoritarian regimes before turning to the much more powerful position of parties under communism.

A few authoritarian regimes, including ruling monarchies in the Middle East and some military governments, get by with no parties at all. However, most civilian authoritarian rulers have found a single party useful as a disguise for personal rule and as a technique for distributing patronage. In post-independence Africa, for example, the heroes of the nationalist struggle soon put a stop to party competition. With independence achieved, one-party systems were established, with the official party serving as the leader's personal vehicle. In defence of the one-party system, the tradition of the chief was skilfully exploited by dictators such as President Mobutu of the Congo:

In our African tradition, there are never two chiefs; there is sometimes a natural heir to the chief, but can anyone tell me that he has known a village that has two chiefs? That is why we Congolese, in the desire to conform to the traditions of our continent, have resolved to group all the energies of the citizens of our country under the banner of a single national party. (Quoted in Meredith, 2006, p. 295)

But it is important to recognize that most of these single parties proved to be weak, lacking autonomy from the national leader. Like government itself, they lacked presence in the countryside, were riven by ethnic and regional divisions and showed little concern with policy. True, the party was one of the few national organizations and proved useful in recruiting supporters to public office, but these functions could not disguise a lack of cohesion, direction and organization. Indeed, when the founder-leader eventually departed, his party would sometimes disappear with him. For instance, when a coup overthrew Kwame Nkrumah in Ghana in 1966, his Convention People's Party also collapsed.

Cases of authoritarian rule where the political party, rather than a dominant individual, is the true source of power are few and far between. One example is Singapore. There the People's Action Party (PAP) maintains a close grip despite permitting a modest degree of opposition. Thus Lee Kuan Yew, the island's Prime Minister from 1959 to 1990, acknowledged that his party post rather than his executive office was the real source of his authority: 'all I have to do is to stay Secretary-General of the PAP. I don't have to be president' (Tremewan, 1994, p. 184). Tremewan (p. 186) goes on to refer to the 'PAP-state' in which the party uses its control of public resources to ensure the quiescence of the citizens:

It is the party-state with its secretive, unaccountable party core under a dominating, often threatening personality which administers Singaporeans' housing, property values, pensions, breeding, health, media, schooling and also the electoral process itself.

Parties may be mainly an instrument of power in most authoritarian states but they are of course the leading institution in communist regimes. We discussed the theory of communist party rule in Chapter 6; here, we focus on the contemporary, and nominally communist, case of China.

Reforms notwithstanding, the Chinese Communist Party (CCP) still illustrates the elaborate internal hierarchy of ruling communist parties (Figure 11.4). At the party's base stand 3.3 million primary party organizations, found not just in local areas such as villages but also in factories and military units. At the top, at least in theory, is the sovereign National Party Congress, a body of around 2,000 people which meets infrequently and for short periods. In practice, the Congress delegates authority: to its 300-member Central Committee and, through that body, to the 22-strong Politburo ('political bureau') and its Standing Committee. This intricate pyramid allows the nine men on the Standing Committee to exert enormous influence over the political direction of the most populous country on earth – in itself, an astonishing political achievement.

The party is massive. In 2007, its membership reached 73 million, equivalent to the entire population of Turkey. And unlike most parties in the democratic world, the CCP's membership is still

Figure 11.4 Organization of the Chinese Communist Party

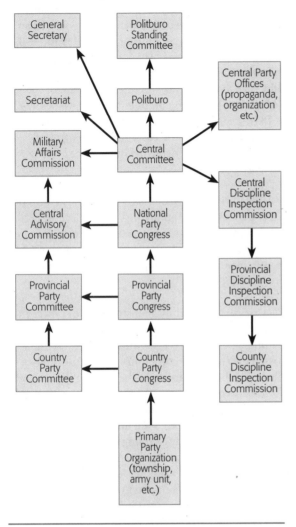

three million members work in the private sector, while 800,000 are self-employed; such statistics would be incomprehensible to Marx and Lenin.

Party members are united by ambition rather than ideology. The CCP remains an important academy for go-getters. A business route to worldly success has now emerged but even the most apolitical entrepreneur still finds value in close party links. Members are prepared to undergo a searching entry procedure, and the continuing obligation to participate in dull party tasks, in order to secure privileged access to education, travel, information, contacts and above all opportunities to acquire wealth. Those members who are particularly determined will seek out a patron to help them ascend the party hierarchy. Within the party's formal structure, it is these personal patron–client networks, not political ideologies or policy differences, that provide the integrating force.

Unlike many authoritarian parties, the CCP has sought since the 1990s to strengthen its control over its own members, the government and even public debate. Tighter political control is a response to economic liberalization. Although reform has created sustained growth, its side effects have included massive unemployment, rural depopulation and increased corruption. Party leaders fear that economic development will reduce the party's standing and eventually threaten its political monopoly. Experience elsewhere in the communist world suggests their anxiety is well founded.

Parties in illiberal democracies

The role of parties provides us with a fundamental contrast between liberal and illiberal democracies. In liberal democracies, a choice between coherent parties is the crucial instrument of representation, allowing voters to influence the direction of government. In an illiberal democracy, however, the choice becomes muddled. Either parties are not the true source of power or the selection on offer does not present alternative programmes to the electorate. To return to Ostrogorski's distinction, parties in an illiberal democracy are often as much a political form as a political force. They are shells for

growing, increasing by nine million between 2000 and 2007. Even in 2007, the membership was still only an elite 5 per cent of the total population; women, in particular, remain heavily under-represented (ChinaToday.com, 2009).

What accounts for the party's continuing control? The answer can hardly be ideology for the CCP's communist commitment is now nominal. Indeed, Saich (2004, p. 95) reports that on his travels he has met 'party members who are Maoists, Stalinists, Friedmanites, Shamans, underground Christians, anarchists, and social and liberal democrats'. Nearly ambitious politicians (and powerful presidents) rather than disciplined actors in their own right. The result is the appearance of democracy superimposed on the reality of at least soft authoritarianism.

Post-communist Russia provides an example of ineffectual parties in an illiberal democracy. The party system is unstructured and free-floating, with parties playing second or even third fiddle in the president's orchestra (Rose, 2000). At national level, power is focused on the political elite and at most confirmed by the Duma (lower chamber of the legislature). The party composition of the Duma is therefore only of secondary political interest. For example, Boris Yeltsin's dismissal of three governments in 1998–99 had no connection with the party balance in the Duma (White, 2005a).

In any case, the choice on offer in Duma elections is limited by the rapid turnover and limited coherence of parties. Where major Western parties have developed a recognized brand over the course of 100 or so years, Russian parties come and go with astonishing rapidity. Most parties competing in the 2003 parliamentary elections, a decade after the end of communist rule, were fighting their first campaign. What is more, these new parties succeeded in winning a majority of the list vote, showing the lack of entrenched party loyalties in the electorate. Only the dwindling communist successor party offered continuity and organization. Clearly, when parties cease to exist from one election to the next, it is impossible for them to be held to account. Not surprisingly, they are the least trusted public organizations in a distrustful country (White, 2007, p. 27).

Far more than in the United States, voters in Russia's presidential elections are choosing between candidates, not parties. The party is the vehicle but not the driver. When president, Vladimir Putin, did not even deign to belong to United Russia, an organization that had no clear vision other than to support him. Its guiding principle is 'common sense': the 'government should do what is best for the majority of citizens' (White, 2005a, p. 85). United Russia is what Russians term the 'party of power', meaning that the Kremlin uses threats and bribes to ensure it is supported by powerful ministers, regional governors and large companies. The equivalent in the USA would occur if the president were to start a new party just before his re-election

campaign, dragooning state governors and the CEOs of well-known corporations into supporting his new entity.

Given the weak position of Russia's parties, it is not surprising that they are poorly organized, with a small membership and minimal capacity to integrate a large and diverse country. In a manner typical of illiberal democracies, the rules concerning the registration of parties, the nomination of candidates and the receipt of state funding operate in favour of larger parties. Of course, the notion of cartel parties shows that similar processes are at work in liberal democracies too, but usually to the benefit of at least two major parties. In post-communist Russia (as in the communist era), there is only one party of power. Minor parties are trapped:

Having no significant power, parties cannot expect to establish stable links with constituencies, but without their support they cannot expect to play a significant role in the political system. (Kulik, 2007, p. 201)

Although the Russian story is distinctive in its details, the narrative is fundamentally similar in other illiberal democracies. In Latin American and Africa, too, the leading personality tends either to stand above the parties or to create a distinctly uneven playing field for the competition between them.

Venezuela under President Hugo Chávez is an example. From 1958, this oil-rich country was governed through the Pact of Punto Fijo – an agreement between the two major parties to marginalize other parties and to keep divisive issues off the agenda. This cartel gradually became corrupt and inefficient, allowing Chávez to promise in his 1998 presidential campaign that he would break the ossified puntofijismo system, thus empowering ordinary people. In reality, though, Venezuela has witnessed a transition from a system in which two parties were overpowerful to a populist regime in which parties are, by conventional democratic standards, insufficiently central to the political process. Chávez is first and foremost a populist leader of the country, using patronage and the media to maintain a relationship with his support base among the country's poor, rather than a leader of a party.

Learning Resources for Chapter 11

Next step   Katz and Crotty (2006) is a comprehensive handbook on party politics.

Further reading   Webb *et al.* (2002) examine the condition of parties in a range of liberal democracies; Gunther *et al.* (2002) is a more thematic collection. Scarrow (2002b) gathers historic writings on parties from Bolingbroke to Ostrogorski. Ignazi (2006) and Kitschelt (2007) consider extreme right parties in Western Europe. Kitschelt *et al.* (1999) cover post-communist parties, van Biezen (2003) and Webb and White (2007b) look at new democracies in Europe, and Brooker (2009) surveys one-party rule in non-democratic regimes. Nassmacher (2001, 2006) discusses party finance.

Internet sources

ECPR Standing Group on Political Parties
Facilitates communication among political scientists studying parties
http://www.keele.ac.uk/depts/spire/sgpp/index.html

Parties and Elections in Europe
Database on European elections, parties and leaders
http://www.parties-and-elections.de/

Political Organizations and Parties Section, American Political Science Association
Furthers scholarship on American and comparative political parties
http://www.apsanet.org/~pop/

Chapter 12

Interest groups

Interest groups, like political parties, are a major channel of communication between society and government, especially in liberal democracies. Both groups and parties represent their concerns upwards, but interest groups pursue more specialized concerns than the broad agendas followed by major parties. Interest groups are further distinguished from political parties by their narrower goal of seeking only to influence, without becoming, the government. They are not election-fighting organizations; instead, they typically adopt a pragmatic and low-key approach in dealing with whatever power structure confronts them.

Although many interest groups go about their work quietly, their activity is pervasive in liberal democracies. Their staff are to be found negotiating with bureaucrats over the details of proposed regulations, pressing their case in legislative committee hearings and seeking to influence media coverage. In authoritarian regimes, however, interests are articulated in a less public, more spasmodic and sometimes more corrupt fashion. Interests are still expressed to government but often through individual firms or powerful individuals rather than through pressure groups.

A major question about interest groups in liberal democracies is whether they supplement or supplant the democratic process. Certainly, interest groups have created a system of functional representation supplementing electoral representation. For their supporters, pressure groups provide expertise to government, give minorities a voice against the excesses of majority rule and are contained by the natural emergence of competition between different groups themselves. From this perspective, interest group representation now 'shares sovereignty' with elected institutions in a manner that is appropriate for a world based on expert knowledge (Klijn and Skelcher, 2007).

For critics such as Lowi (1969), on the other hand, groups are a 'corruption of democratic government'. When groups are too strong, politics becomes a matter of balancing particular interests rather than pursuing what Rousseau (1755) called 'the general will' – that is, the well-being of the body politic considered as a whole. The organized few triumph over the disorganized whole. Acting to defend the established order, interest groups serve as a barrier against the provision of solutions to long-term collective

Interest groups (also called pressure groups) are non-governmental organizations which seek as part of their purpose to influence public policy. Examples include employers' organizations, trade unions, consumer groups, professional bodies and broader campaigning associations. The term usually excludes bodies such as businesses and local authorities which, although they may lobby central government, are not created for that purpose.

BOX 12.1

Waves of interest group formation in the United States

	Wave	Examples
1830–60	Founding of first national organizations	YMCA and many anti-slavery groups
1880–1900	Creation of many business and labour associations, stimulated by industrialization	National Association of Manufacturers; American Federation of Labor
1900–20	Peak period of interest group formation	Chamber of Commerce; American Medical Association
1960–80	Founding of many environmental and public interest groups	National Organization for Women; Common Cause

Source: Adapted from Hrebenar (1997), pp. 13–15.

---

problems, such as the environment. Far from participating in a healthy competition among themselves, interest groups are arranged into a stable hierarchy of influence – in which the unorganized hold no sway at all. The result, it is alleged, is a dangerous supplanting of, rather than a helpful supplement to, democratic mechanisms.

Whichever view we adopt, we will suggest in this chapter that interest groups have become an indispensable component of governance in contemporary liberal democracies. The practical point at issue is surely not whether interest groups can be removed from the policy-shaping arena. Rather, the question is how to maximize the gains from interest group representation while minimizing the dangers – including those to democracy itself.

From a historical perspective, interest groups developed in a rather predictable way. In the West, they emerged in a series of waves formed by social change (e.g. industrialization) and the expansion of state activity (e.g. public welfare). Periods of social change raise new problems while an active government gives people more hope of gains from influencing public policy. Like many other aspects of modern politics, interest group activity is a response to the growth of public regulation. Those who support pruning the interest group undergrowth would be well-advised to begin by cutting back on government itself.

Box 12.1 summarizes the development of interest groups in the United States. Most Western nations have followed a similar if somewhat less vigorous course, resulting in the mosaic of independent group activity found in nearly all contemporary liberal democracies.

Classifying interest groups

When we think of interest groups, the bodies which first come to mind are **protective groups** articulating the material interests of their members: for instance, trade unions, employers' organizations and professional associations (Box 12.2). Sometimes called sectional or functional groups, these protective bodies give priority to influencing government and can invoke sanctions to help them achieve their goals. Workers can go on strike; medical practitioners can refuse to cooperate with a new prescription policy.

Protective groups seek selective benefits for their members and insider status with relevant government departments. Because they represent clear occupational interests, protective associations are often the most influential of all groups. They are well-established, well-connected and well-resourced.

But protective groups can also be based on local, rather than functional, interests. Geographic groups

---

BOX 12.2

Protective and promotional groups

	Protective groups	Promotional groups
Aims	A group *of*: defends an interest	A group *for*: promotes a cause
Membership	Closed: membership is restricted	Open: anybody can join
Status	Insider: frequently consulted by government and actively seeks this role	Outsider: consulted less often by government Targets public opinion and the media
Benefits	Selective: only group members benefit	Collective: benefits go to both members and non-members
Focus	Group aims to influence national government on specific issues affecting members	Group also seeks to influence national and global bodies on broad policy matters

---

emerge when the shared interests of people living in the same location are threatened by plans for, say, a new highway or a hostel for ex-convicts. Because of their negative stance – 'build it anywhere but here' – these geographical bodies are known as 'Nimby' groups (**n**ot **i**n **m**y **b**ack **y**ard) and are often accused of following a 'Banana' strategy: '**b**uild **a**bsolutely **n**othing **a**nywhere **n**ear **a**nyone'. Unlike functional organizations, Nimby groups come and go in response to specific threats.

Protective groups are not the only type of organized interest. Many associations founded since the 1960s are promotional rather than protective. **Promotional groups** advocate ideas, identities, policies and values. Also called advocacy, attitude, campaign and cause groups, promotional organizations focus on such issues as abortion, pornography and the environment. Their members are interested in the issue concerned without, in most cases, possessing a material stake.

In liberal democracies, promotional groups have undoubtedly grown in number, significance and recognition by government. Their increasing influence since the 1960s constitutes a major trend in interest politics. In the United States, for example, Common Cause (2006) describes itself as 'a non-profit, non-partisan citizen's lobbying organization promoting open, honest and accountable government'. Its 300,000 members, 35 state organizations

and $10 million annual budget are a tribute to the willingness of people to join a specific organization committed, ironically, to the public interest. However, even more than for members of political parties, many who join promotional groups are credit-card affiliates only. A financial contribution expresses the donor's commitment but also delegates pursuit of the cause to the group's leaders. For this reason, the effectiveness of promotional bodies as schools for democracy is often overstated (Maloney, 2009).

The boundary separating protective and promotional groups is poorly defined. For example, bodies such as the women's movement and the gay lobby seek to influence public opinion and are often classified as promotional. However, their prime purpose is to promote the interests of specific groups: they are, perhaps, best viewed as protective interests employing promotional means.

Interest groups do not always lobby government directly. Often, protective groups will join a **peak association**. Industrial associations and large firms

---

A **peak association** is an umbrella organization representing the broad interests of capital or labour to government. The members of peak associations are not individuals but other organizations such as firms, trade associations and labour unions.

Figure 12.1 A peak association: Britain's CBI

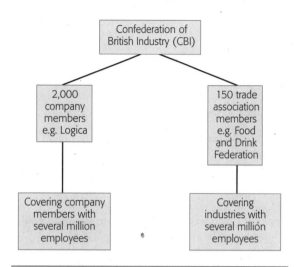

join a wider body representing the interests of capital to government. Examples include the National Association of Manufacturers in the USA, the Federal Organization of German Employers and the Confederation of British Industry in the UK (Figure 12.1).

Trade unions respond similarly. The Confederation of German Trade Unions (DGB) comprised eight unions with a total of 6.6 million individual members in 2006. In 2008, there were 55 unions affiliated to the Irish Congress of Trade Unions (ICTU) with a total membership of 833,486 from both sides of the border.

Peak organizations seek to influence public policy and often succeed. They are attuned to national government, possess a strong research capacity and talk the language of policy. In some states, the peaks play an integral role linking government with their own members and, through them, with society. The DGB (2009) defines its task thus:

The DGB brings together the individual unions, unites them in an effective whole and represents their joint interests. It is the voice of the unions in relation to political decision-makers, parties and associations on a federal, state and municipal level. It coordinates union activities but as an umbrella organization it does not conclude collective agreements.

When business and labour peak associations become centrally involved in negotiating broad policy packages (including such issues as price controls, wage increases and welfare benefits), the system is known as **corporatism** (Berger and Compston, 2002). Under corporatism, capital and labour become full social partners, working alongside government and playing a key role in implementing agreements reached. Here we see the clearest illustration of how functional interests, together with the government, can marginalize representation in parliament.

For the peaks to acquire such a strong position, however, they must achieve some autonomy from, as well as control over, their members. As the frequency with which peak associations label themselves 'federations' or 'confederations' suggests, such centralization is frequently lacking, especially in the English-speaking world.

With the decline of trade-union membership (see Table 12.1, p. 241), and the rise of pro-market thinking, international markets and smaller service companies, traditional corporate arrangements have decayed even in those European countries such as Austria where they were once entrenched (Tálos and Kittel, 2002). However, extensive consultation – if no longer joint decision-making – continues between the peaks and government, not least in Scandinavia. And some smaller countries, including Ireland and the Netherlands, have even developed or revived social partnerships as a route to improved economic efficiency.

Certainly, the political significance of peak associations continues to vary across the liberal democratic world, even though the general tendency is for them to become policy-influencing and service-providing bodies rather than organizations negotiating collectively with government on behalf of their members (Silvia and Schroeder, 2007).

In a democratic context, **corporatism** (often called social partnership in Europe) is a relationship between the state and interest groups in which major decisions on domestic matters emerge from discussion between the government and peak associations representing the major social partners: capital and labour.

Interest groups in liberal democracies

In this section we examine the role of interest groups in liberal democracies. Here, debate has centred on the concept of pluralism and we begin by outlining this significant idea. We then turn to more recent and detailed interpretations, discussing iron triangles and issue networks.

Pluralism

Pluralism provides an important perspective on the role played by interest groups in liberal democracy. This American-inspired view regards competition between freely organized interest groups as a form, rather than a denial, of democracy. In this way, pluralism offers not merely a claim about how interest groups operate but also, and significantly, an interpretation of liberal democracy itself.

What then is pluralism? It is a form of governance in which the state becomes an arena for competition between interest groups. The groups compete for influence over a government that is willing to listen to all the voices it can hear in the political debate. The government adds little of its own; it is an arbiter, not an initiator. For Arthur Bentley (1908), an American pioneer of this approach, 'when the groups are adequately stated, everything is stated. When I say everything, I mean everything'.

> Literally 'rule by the many', **pluralism** refers to a political system in which numerous competing interest groups exert strong influence over a responsive government. The state is more umpire than player. Each interest group concentrates on its own area (for example education or health care) so that no single elite dominates all sectors.

All kinds of interest have their say before the court of government. Groups compete on a level playing field, with the state showing little bias either towards interests of a particular type or towards specific groups within that type. As new interests and identities emerge, groups form to represent them, quickly finding a place in the house of power. In a pluralist system, politics forms an open, competitive market with few barriers to entry. Pluralist politics is transactional but not, in theory, corrupt.

Pluralism brings healthy fragmentation across the range of government activity since most interests are restricted to a single policy sector; in other words, power is non-cumulative. The influence of physicians is confined to health care; that of teachers, to education policy. Indeed the central tenet of pluralism is that no single elite dominates the entire sphere of government. Rather, different interest groups lead the way in each area of policy. Overall, pluralism depicts a wholesome process of dispersed decision-making in which government's openness allows its policies to reflect not just economic interests but also professional expertise.

The significance of pluralism lies in its implications for our understanding of contemporary democracy. Pluralists accept that majority rule is an insufficient account of how democracies work in practice. Rather, pluralists judge that democracy must, in reality, include a strong element of rule by minorities, each operating in a particular policy area but subject to the checks and balances of other groups operating in the same sector, with the government as broker.

Pluralists invite us to recognize that for all the froth of party competition, most policy decisions emerge from discussion between government departments and interest groups. At the level of detail practised in executive departments, governing parties experience mandate uncertainty; their manifesto and ideology provide little guidance. Interest groups fill this gap.

Pluralism weighs interests rather than votes, taking account of intensity of preferences by assuming, perhaps complacently, that organized opinion will in the main be strongly held opinion. In these ways, competing interest groups become a key instrument of democracy as rule by minorities, complementing the role played by parties in a traditional reading of democracy as majority rule.

The strengths of pluralistic governance are undoubtedly substantial. Dahl, for example, notes that

groups have served to educate citizens in political life, strengthened them in their relations with the state, helped to ensure that no single interest would regularly prevail on all important decisions, and, by providing information, discussion, negotiation and compromise, even helped to make public decisions more rational and more acceptable. (1993, p. 706)

In addition, interest groups help to scrutinize government activity, for example by monitoring whether governments do what they say. Gordon (2005, p. 5) notes that 'because their interests are focused on the policy effects of legislative outcomes and not just the political benefits of legislation, groups have significant incentives to make sure that the policies they support are duly instituted by the executive branch'. The media are a watchdog, too, but its attention is intermittent and selective. A specialist interest group will keep a beady eye on even the least newsworthy of policies within its zone of concern.

Both as an ideal and as a description of how politics works, pluralism draws on American experience. In the USA, interest group patterns come closer to the pluralist model than anywhere else. As de Tocqueville (1856) wrote, 'in no country in the world has the principle of association been more successfully used, or applied to a greater multitude of objects, than in America'. Petracca (1992, p. 3) makes the point succinctly: 'American politics is the politics of interests.'

Nowhere else are interest groups so numerous, visible, organized, competitive or successful. Tens of thousands of groups, ranging from Happiness of Motherhood Eternal to the United Autoworkers of America, seek to influence policy at federal, state and local levels. Nor are such groups confined to protective economic interests. Promotional groups are uniquely prominent in the USA, with over 500 focusing on environmental protection alone.

Washington politics reflects the competitive spirit that is pluralism's hallmark. Most of the time, American government is too fragmented to be anything more than an umpire of group demands. The separation of powers gives interest groups many points of leverage: congressional committees, executive agencies and the courts. Members of Congress realize they are under constant public scrutiny. In the House, a two-year election cycle means that politicians must be constantly aware of their ratings by interest groups. Representatives listen to group demands because it helps their re-election prospects.

Of course, all political systems generate myths, and America's is pluralism. In reality, pluralist

'competition' operates within an unquestioned acceptance of broad American values favouring the free market and the pursuit of individual self-interest. Policy debate works within a narrow ideological range, shaping and limiting the demands expressed. And although Washington politics is certainly competitive, the outcome is often – perhaps too often – a decision not to decide. The constitution deliberately fragments government authority, thus entrenching the interests of the wealthy and powerful. As Presidents Clinton and Obama discovered in their attempts to reform medical care, the voice of the status quo can sing as loud as that of reform.

But we would surely be wrong to dismiss the pluralist interpretation of interest groups in the USA as just a fairy tale. Overseas observers may interpret American politics as much ado about nothing but that view is rejected by the players themselves. To understand what happens in American politics, we must appreciate the vigorous competition between interest groups, no matter how narrow the terrain over which the battle is fought.

In general, pluralism remains an important perspective but many political scientists now accept that its portrayal of the relationship between groups and government is one-sided; some also claim that the pluralist portrait is superficial (Smith, 1995). Criticism focuses on four areas:

- Interest groups do not compete on an equal playing field. Some interests, such as business, are inherently powerful. Others, such as professional groups, are central to policy implementation. In reality, groups form a stable hierarchy of influence, with their ranking reflecting their usefulness to government.
- Pluralism neglects the bias of the political culture and political system in favour of some interests but against others. Groups advocating modest reforms within the established order are heard more sympathetically than those seeking radical change (Walker, 1991). Regulation is achievable; redistribution less so. Some groups, such as migrants, patients, the elderly and the low-paid, experience difficulty in organizing at all.
- The state is far more than a neutral umpire. In addition to deciding which groups to heed, it

may regulate their operation and even encourage their formation in favoured areas, thus shaping the interest-group landscape itself. In some democracies, notably France, the state is expected to embody and define the public interest, standing above more partial concerns.

➤ Pluralist conflict disguises interests shared by leaders of all the mainstream groups, such as their common membership of the same class and ethnic group. Thus, Wright Mills famously argued in *The Power Elite* (1956) that American leaders of industry, the military and government formed an interlocking power elite rather than separate power centres. This elite shared a commitment to the system which it commanded; disputes were restricted to detail.

From iron triangles to issue networks

While the debate about pluralism provides an overall perspective on the position of interest groups in liberal democracies, we must also examine how their role has evolved over time. In the United States, certainly, this pattern can be broadly characterized as a transition from **iron triangles** to **issue networks**. Significantly, elements of this trend can also be found in other liberal democracies.

American political scientists used the term iron triangle to describe the traditional relationship between groups and government in many (but not all) policy sectors in the USA. The three points on the triangle were government departments (or agencies within them), interest groups and congressional committees (Figure 12.2). Such triangles became an exercise in mutual exchange and support: the committee appropriated funds which were spent by the department for the benefit of interest group members. Thus, the Department of Agriculture, the

relevant committees in Congress and farmers' groups would collude on larger food subsidies. Each point on the triangle benefited considerably, even though the drain on the public purse as a whole was only small. This was a game without losers – except for the taxpayer who rarely knew what was going on.

Iron triangles were also called subgovernments, implying that each triangle formed a mini-government of its own, largely independent of policy-making in other sectors. Within each of these islands, a policy cartel presided. The effect was to reinforce the very fragmentation of the executive which made such triangles possible in the first place.

This system could deflect the political aims of the majority party in Congress or even of the president himself, providing a further example of the tension between interest groups and democracy. In contrast to the open and competitive debates assumed by pluralism, the idea of iron triangles suggests that a fragmented political system can sometimes just lead to closed, secretive policy-making.

Beyond the United States, the term policy community was sometimes used to describe a similar pattern of inward-looking policy-making (Marsh and Rhodes, 1992). Within a particular sector, it was alleged, interest group leaders and senior civil servants formed their own small communities. All the members in the policy village knew each other well, used given names and tried not to upset each other. The participants developed shared working habits and common assumptions about what could be achieved. They learned to trust each other and to respect each other's goals and confidences.

Shared interests predominated. For instance, the road builders and bureaucrats in the transport ministry would seek ever larger highway budgets, fully aware that similar coalitions in other sectors – defence, say, or education – would be seeking to maximize their own funding and autonomy. Village business was conducted behind closed doors to prevent political posturing and to allow a quiet life for all. Insiders were sharply distinguished from outsiders. The golden rule was never to upset the apple cart.

Fortunately, these cosy iron triangles and policy communities have decayed in many liberal democracies. Today, policies are subject to closer scrutiny by the media; new public interest groups protest loudly when they spot the public being taken for a ride; and some legislators are less willing to keep

Iron triangles, subgovernments and policy communities are terms used to refer to inward-looking coalitions of interests, based on senior bureaucrats, interest group leaders and sometimes relevant legislators, that dominate policy-making in particular sectors (e.g. agriculture). In many liberal democracies, these secretive and distinctly non-pluralistic cartels have given way to looser and more pluralistic **issue networks** which are more open to outside organizations and considered debate.

Figure 12.2 Iron triangles: how subgovernments operated in the USA

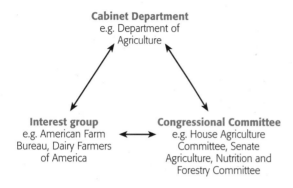

quiet when they see public money being wasted. As issues become more complex, so more groups are drawn into the policy process, making it harder to stitch together insider deals. In the United States, where this trend has gone furthest, the committee barons who used to dominate Congress have lost much of their power. The iron has gone out of the triangle; now influence over decisions depends on what you know as much as who you know.

Reflecting these trends, the talk now is of issue networks. These refer to the familiar set of organizations involved in policy-making: government departments, interest groups and legislative committees plus expert outsiders. However, the structure of an issue network is much looser than that of an iron triangle; the impact of a particular interest group varies from one topic within the field to the next, depending on its expertise. As Heclo (1978, p. 102) pointed out in an early statement:

The notions of iron triangles and subgovernments presume small circles of participants who have succeeded in becoming largely autonomous. Issue networks, on the other hand, comprise a large number of participants with quite variable degrees of mutual commitment . . . it is almost impossible to say where a network leaves off and its environment begins.

Clearly, the idea of issue networks enables us to portray policy-making in liberal democracies more positively. A wider range of interests participate in decisions, the bias towards protective groups is reduced, new groups enter the debate and a sound

argument carries greater weight. Because networks operate in a non-hierarchical way, we can portray their participants as engaged in a constructive exchange of resources such as knowledge (e.g. academic specialists), legitimacy (elected politicians), engagement in implementation (interest groups) and the capacity to draft bills and regulations (bureaucrats). An issue network remains more structured than the pluralist model of open competition implies but it is certainly more pluralist than an iron triangle.

Channels of influence

We turn now to the channels of communication between interest groups and the government. How do interest groups communicate with decision-makers? What are the channels through which this process takes place? Figure 12.3 sets out three mechanisms characteristic of liberal democracies: direct interaction with people in policy-making institutions; indirect influence through political parties; and indirect influence through public opinion. We will also look at specialist lobbying companies which help to pilot their interest group clients through these channels.

Direct discussion with policy-makers

A core activity of interest groups, especially protective ones, is influencing public policy. Those who

Figure 12.3 Channels of interest group influence

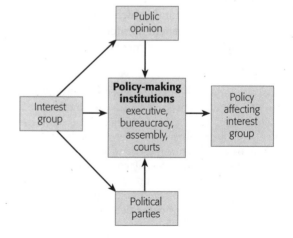

shape and apply policy are the ultimate target. So direct conversations with the ministers who form the political *executive* are ideal if access is available. Talking with ministers before specific policies have crystallized is particularly valuable because it enables a group to enter the policy process at a formative stage. But in many large political systems, such privileges are confined to a few well-connected individuals: the heads of the major peak associations, perhaps, or the chief executives of the country's largest corporations.

In practice, most interest group activity focuses on the bureaucracy, the legislature and the courts. Of these, the *bureaucracy* is undoubtedly the main pressure point. Interest groups follow power and it is in civil servants' offices that detailed decisions are formed. As Matthews (1989, p. 217) comments:

the bureaucracy's significance is reinforced by its policy-making and policy-implementing roles. Many routine, technical and 'less important' decisions, which are nonetheless of vital concern to interest groups, are actually made by public servants.

Shrewd protective groups focus on the small print because details are easier to modify. Access to ministers may be difficult but most democracies follow a convention of discussion over detail with organized opinion through consultative councils and committees. Often the law requires such deliberation. In any case, the real expertise frequently lies in the interest group rather than the bureaucracy and, from the government's viewpoint, a policy acceptable to all is politically safe.

While the bureaucracy is invariably a crucial arena for groups, the significance of the *assembly* depends on its political weight. A comparison between the United States and Canada makes the point. The American Congress (and especially its committees) forms a vital part of the policy process. A range of factors in the United States combine to create an ideal habitat for interest group operations: the separation of powers, the constitutional right 'to petition the government for a redress of grievances', weak party discipline and independent-minded committees within the legislature. Many interest groups have access to individual members of Congress and can arrange to contribute to

committee deliberations. The ability of interest groups to endorse particular candidates, and to indirectly support their re-election campaigns, renders legislators sensitive to group demands (Cigler and Loomis, 2006).

But the USA is a unique case. In most democracies, parliaments are more reactive than proactive; as a result, interest groups treat members of parliament as opinion-leaders rather than policy-makers. Where party voting is entrenched, lobbyists concentrate their strongest fire on the bureaucracy. As Landes (2002, p. 488) comments on Canada:

interest groups have an acute sense of smell when tracking the scent of power. Interaction with the bureaucracy and not with members of parliament is the goal of most groups and one reason why interest group activity is not highly visible to the untrained eye.

If interest groups feel slighted in the policy-making process, they may still be able to seek redress through the *courts*. In the European Union, an interest group that is unsuccessful at home can take its case to the European Court of Justice. In the United States, business corporations routinely subject government statutes and regulatory decisions to legal challenge. **Class action** suits are particularly common there.

A **class action** is a legal device initiated by complainants not just on their behalf but also for all others so situated. This mechanism enables legal costs and gains to be shared among a large group and so enables interest groups to pursue their goals through the courts.

But just as the USA is exceptional in the powers of its legislature, so too does it rely heavily on the courts to resolve disputes. Elsewhere, the courts are certainly growing in importance but they remain a remedy of last resort. In Australia, for instance, the requirement for litigants to prove their personal interest in the case hinders class actions. When the outcome of a legal case affects only the person initiating it, the policy and financial implications are more limited than in a class action. Inevitably, these specific cases are less important to interest groups.

EUROPEAN UNION

Form of government ■ a unique hybrid body in which policy is made partly by European Union institutions and partly through negotiations among the 27 member states.

Executive
- ■ The powerful *European Commission*, arranged into directorates, general departments and specialized service units, initiates many proposals and oversees their implementation; it is a cross between an executive and a bureaucracy, representing the common European interest.
- ■ The *Council of the European Union* ('Council of Ministers') is the meeting place for ministers from national governments; it must approve all Commission proposals before they become law.
- ■ The separate *European Council* is the EU forum for meetings of heads of government from the member states (the *Council of Europe* is a separate body again, unconnected with the EU).

Population of member states: 492m
Gross domestic product per head: $33,700 (+0.8%)

Assembly ■ the members of the large, unicameral multisite *European Parliament* are directly elected from each country for a five-year term. The number of MEPs from each country reflects its population, but with over-representation for small states. Though still lacking full legislative authority, the parliament has acquired greater rights of consultation and approval since the 1970s.

Judicial branch ■ the influential *European Court of Justice*, composed of one judge from each member country, has developed the EU's strong legal foundations, supporting the drive for European integration in the final decades of the twentieth century.

The **European Union**'s emergence owes much to the continent's history of conflict. After the 1939–45 war, many European leaders set out to create a unified continent within which war would no longer be feasible: a United States of Europe. However, economic factors were also fundamental. European economies needed to be rebuilt after 1945 and then, to achieve benefits of scale, integrated into a large, single market.

Later members, notably Britain, emphasized the economic basis of the Union while rejecting its federal vision. Margaret Thatcher said in 1988 that 'willing and active cooperation between independent sovereign states is the best way to build a successful European Community'. In developing this line, Britain has exploited the continental notion of subsidiarity to argue that decisions should be taken at the lower, national level whenever possible. While remaining sceptical about further efforts at deepening integration, Britain has

supported the admission of new members.

Even on the continent, some publics have grown sceptical of deepening integration. Proposals for a European constitutional treaty, expressing a commitment 'to forge a common destiny', were defeated by referendums in France (2005), the Netherlands (2005) and Ireland (2008). This rejection signalled the public's uncertainty about grand projects and deeper integration at a time of low growth and high unemployment. Following a 'period of reflection', the more modest Treaty of Lisbon was agreed in 2007 to 'enhance the efficiency and democratic legitimacy of the Union'. This Treaty came into effect in 2009. So the notion of an explicit constitution has been abandoned and the EU's basis still lies in treaties. In addition the euro currency is currently confined to 16 countries, reflecting a variable geometry in which integration proceeds at a different pace among particular groups of members.

Future developments in the EU remain uncertain. On the one hand, pressures to complete the single market, to provide an effective response to environmental and terrorist threats, and to counter American and Asian influence in the world, will surely continue, providing strong ammunition to those committed to further deepening.

On the other hand, more sceptical leaders and members (mindful of their often cynical electorates) will continue to suggest that such matters can be adequately addressed through intergovernmental means. Indeed, national governments rather than the EU took the lead in responding to the global financial crisis of 2008/09. What does seem likely is that the pace of expansion will slow, with the three candidate countries (Croatia, Macedonia and Turkey) facing an uncertain wait.

Further reading: Hix (2005), Nugent (2006).

Interest groups and the EU

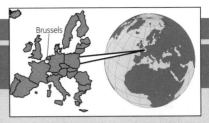

Brussels

One European Commission official said, 'My division is responsible for 44 directives and 89 regulations. And I have about nine staff to deal with all of this. The corresponding administration in the US has 600 people' (Greenwood, 2007, p. 6). It is no surprise therefore that the Commission has encouraged relevant interest groups to develop and has remained accessible to them. How then do interest groups operate in the unique hybrid that is the European Union?

Reflecting the European tradition of social partnership, the EU has encouraged interest groups. About 20,000 lobbyists work in Brussels, making the city the European equivalent to Washington, DC. The main peak associations are the Union of Industrial and Employers' Confederation of Europe (UNICE) and the European Trade Union Federation (ETUC). The European Round Table of Industrialists – a forum of 50 or so European industrial leaders – produces reports that are helpful to business, while influential sectoral groups include the European Chemical Industry Council and the Committee of Agricultural Organizations in the European Union.

Although the strengthened position of the European Parliament has extended the field for lobbyists, most work is still focused on the Commission, which has established an extensive system of consultative committees whose members are drawn from relevant interest groups. Even more than national governments, the Commission depends on interest groups not just for information, intelligence and advice but also

to back its proposals. As a regulatory body, it is difficult to envision how the Commission could function without specialist input from these groups.

Originally, the Commission preferred to deal with groups organized on a Europe-wide basis. However, many of these federations possess few resources and experience difficulty in taking prompt positions acceptable to members drawn from a range of countries. Increasingly, therefore, the Commission has turned not just to national peak associations but also to individual companies capable of offering greater insight into current market developments. In their turn,

the Commission retain a conditional quality.

■ Brussels remains at one remove from the glare of national politics. The focus is interest groups rather than social movements, and reasoned arguments rather than political grandstanding. Even more than at national level, effective lobbying depends on developing long-term relationships of trust combined with acute sensitivity to the Commission's agenda. The lobbying style is less aggressive than in the USA.

■ Because the European Union is a union of states, groups retain the option of seeking influence through their national govern-

How the ETUC views the European social model

'In the ETUC's view, social dialogue, collective bargaining and workers' protection are crucial factors in promoting innovation, productivity and competitiveness. This is what distinguishes Europe, where post-war social progress has matched economic growth, from the US model, where small numbers of individuals have benefited at the expense of the majority. Europe must continue to sustain this social model as an example for other countries around the world.'

Source: ETUC (2006).

many individual companies, including multinational corporations based outside the EU, have become more willing to lobby the Commission directly.

Compared to the lobbying of member governments, interest representation in the European Union differs in three main respects:

■ Policy is more frequently revised or dropped as it passes through the complex filters of the Union's institutions. For this reason, any initial agreements reached with

ments. Similarly, the Commission must depend on national governments for implementation – and on its interest group partners to monitor whether member states are, in fact, complying with EU policies and regulations.

Here, then, we see the complex reality of multilevel governance which allows skilled interest groups to influence the development of EU policy.

Further reading: Beyers *et al.* (2009), Greenwood (2007).

Indirect influence through political parties

In the past, many interest groups sought to use a favoured political party as a channel of influence, with group and party often bound together as members of the same family. For instance, Britain's labour movement historically regarded its industrial wing (the trade unions) and political wing (the Labour Party) as part of a single movement promoting broad working-class interests. In a similar way, the environmental movement has spawned both promotional interest groups and green political parties.

Today, however, such intimate relationships between interest groups and political parties are the exception. We have witnessed a growing specialization of function, as interest groups concentrate on their members and parties on their voters. As a result, most interest groups now seek to hedge their bets rather than to develop close links with a political party. Loose, pragmatic links between interests and parties are the norm. In the United States, this pattern is well-established. Business and organized labour gravitate towards the Republican and Democratic parties respectively but these have always been partnerships of convenience, not indissoluble marriages.

The traditional maxim of the American trade union movement has been to reward its friends and punish its enemies, wherever these are to be found. American business is equally pragmatic. Despite an ideological affinity with the Republican Party, business groups still contribute financially to the election campaigns of many Democratic members of Congress. Most interest groups give more to incumbents. They want access to legislators, whatever their ideological colours. They do not waste money on no-hopers.

The theme of pragmatic links with any party close to power is similar, if less explicit, in other countries. In Germany, for instance, the powerful Federation of German Industry certainly enjoys close links with the conservative Christian Democratic Union. However, it wisely remains on speaking terms with the more left-wing Social Democrats. The rule is that protective interests follow power, not parties.

Political parties, too, have weakened their links with the interests from which they originally emerged. The religious and class parties of Western Europe have broadened their appeal in the post-war era, seeking to be viewed as custodians of the nation as a whole. The distinction between parties bent on power and interest groups focused on influence has sharpened as marriages of the heart have given way to alliances of convenience.

Indirect influence through public opinion

Press, radio and television provide an additional resource for interest groups. By definition, messages through the media address a popular audience rather than specific decision-makers. Because promotional groups operate in society as much as government, the media are a central focus for such groups as they seek to steer public opinion and recruit a mass membership (Binderkrantz, 2005).

Many promotional groups lack both substantial resources and access to decision-makers, so free publicity becomes their stock-in-trade. For instance, environmental groups mount high-profile activities, such as seizing oil rigs, to generate footage shown on television across the world. In contrast to protective groups, many promotional groups view the media as sympathetic rather than a threat – and they may indeed be justified in their assumption (Dalton, 1994).

Traditionally, the media are less important to protective groups with their more specialized and secretive demands. What food manufacturer would go public with a campaign opposing nutritional labels on foods? The confidentiality of the government meeting room is a more appropriate arena for fighting rearguard actions of this kind; going public is a last resort. Keen to protect their reputation in government, protective groups steer away from disruptive tactics; they want to be seen as reliable partners by the civil servants on the other side of the table.

But even protective groups are now seeking to influence the climate of public opinion, especially in political systems where legislatures are important political actors. In the United States, most protective groups have learned that the surest route to the hearts of members of Congress is through their constituents. Therefore groups follow a dual strategy, going public and going Washington. In Denmark, too, 'decision makers seem to accept that groups seek attention from the media and the general public without excluding them from access to making their standpoint heard in decision-making'

(Binderkrantz, 2005, p. 703). Slowly and uncertainly, protective groups are emerging from the bureaucratic undergrowth into the glare of media publicity, thereby reducing the extent to which interest group and electoral representation run on separate tracks.

Lobbyists

Although interest groups are often their own best **lobbyists**, our focus in this section is on specialist companies whose aim is to open the doors of government to their interest group clients. These lobbying firms, sometimes known as contract lobbyists, are technicians of influence: hired guns in the business of interest-group communication. And they are growing in number, though not necessarily in influence.

> A **lobbyist** is defined by the United States Legislative Reorganization Act (1946) as any person or organization that receives money to be used principally to influence legislation before Congress. The term derives from the hall or lobby of Britain's House of Commons where people can and do approach Members of Parliament to plead their case.

Contract lobbyists are perceived by the public as operating at the unsavoury end of the persuasion industry (as some undoubtedly do) but a more balanced appreciation requires an understanding of the routine nature of much of their work. In politics, as in business, middlemen have their uses.

Why is lobbying an expanding profession? Three reasons suggest themselves:

- Government regulation continues to grow, often impinging directly on companies, interest groups and trade unions. A specialist lobbying firm working for a number of interest groups can often monitor parliamentary developments more efficiently than would be the case if each interest group undertook the task itself.
- Public relations campaigns are becoming increasingly sophisticated, often seeking to influence both the grass roots and the government in one integrated project. Professional advisers come into their own in planning and delivering multifaceted campaigns, which can be too complex for an interest-group client to manage directly.

- Many firms now approach government directly, rather than working through their trade association. Companies both large and small find that using a lobbying company to help them contact a government agency or a sympathetic legislator can yield quicker results than working through an industry body.

The central feature of the lobbying business is its intensely personal character. A legislator is most likely to return a call from a lobbyist if the caller is a former colleague. For this reason, lobbying firms are always on the look-out for former legislators or bureaucrats with a warm contact book. More than in most professions, lobbying is about who you know.

What then is the political impact of lobbying companies? Is it now possible for wealthy interest groups and corporations simply to pay a fee to a lobbying firm to ensure that a bill is defeated or a regulation deferred? On the whole, the answer is no. Lobbyists are inclined to exaggerate their own impact for commercial reasons but in reality most can achieve little more than access to relevant politicians and, perhaps, bureaucrats. Often, the lobbyist's role is merely to hold the client's hand, helping an inexperienced company find its way around the corridors of power when it comes to town.

Shaping the policy-maker's response to the message is a far greater challenge. Allegations of sleaze notwithstanding, influence can rarely be purchased through a lobbyist but must come, if at all, from the petitioning group itself. And impact depends first and foremost on the intrinsic strength of the case. To the experienced politician, a convincing case direct from the petitioner sings louder than yet another rehearsed presentation from a lobbying firm.

Rather than viewing professional lobbying in a negative light, we should recognize its contribution to effective political communication. It can focus the client's message on relevant decision-makers, ensuring that the client's voice is heard by those who need to hear it. In this way, lobbying enhances the efficiency of governance.

Of course, not everything in the lobby is rosy. Even if a company achieves no more for its lobbying fee than access to a decision-maker, perhaps that exchange in itself compromises the principle of equality which underpins democracy. Whatever the underlying realities, buying access and buying influence are rarely distinguished in the public's mind, damaging the legitimacy of the political process and generating a need, still largely unmet, for effective regulation (Box 12.3).

Conditions of influence

There is no doubt that some interest groups exert more influence over government than others. So what is it that gives particular groups the ability to persuade? Much of the answer is to be found in four attributes, ranging from the general to the specific: legitimacy, sanctions, membership and resources. The more general factors in this funnel (e.g. legitimacy) also influence the more specific ones (e.g. resources) (Figure 12.4)

First, the degree of *legitimacy* achieved by a particular group is clearly important. Interests enjoying high prestige are most likely to prevail on particular issues. Professional groups whose members stand for social respectability can be as militant on occasion, and as restrictive in their practices, as blue-collar trade unions once were. But lawyers and doctors escape the public hostility that unions continue to attract. Similarly, the voice of free enterprise usually obtains a sympathetic hearing in public

---

Figure 12.4 Conditions of interest group influence

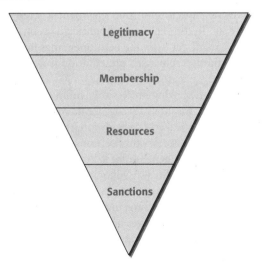

BOX 12.3

Regulating lobbyists

One way of securing the advantages of lobbying while reducing the risk of corruption is through public regulation. Currently, most countries have no such rules. Those that do (including Canada, the European Union, Germany and the United States) emphasize the following:

▶ Lobbyists must register as individuals on a public list;
▶ Expenditure on lobbying must be disclosed and be made public;
▶ A public agency audits the spending of lobbying firms;
▶ A cooling-off period is imposed on former legislators before they can become lobbyists.

Source: Chari *et al.* (2007).

debate, especially in the United States.

Second, a group's influence depends on its *membership*. This is a matter of **density** and commitment as well as sheer numbers. The highest penetrations are usually achieved when, as with many professional bodies such as physicians and lawyers, membership is a condition of practice. By contrast, the declining density of trade-union membership in the final quarter of the twentieth century, particularly marked in English-speaking countries, undoubtedly weakened labour's bargaining power (Table 12.1). At least in the private sector, union membership is now the exception in most Western democracies.

Influence is further reduced when membership is spread among several interest groups operating in the same sector. American farmers are divided between three major organizations with lower total coverage than Britain's National Farmers' Union. To be sure, the larger American food producers are politically well-connected but the interests of agriculture as a whole would be better

Density of membership refers to the proportion of all those who are eligible to join a group who actually do so. An encompassing membership enhances a group's authority and strengthens its bargaining position with government.

Table 12.1 Density of trade union membership in selected democracies, 1970–2003 (%)

	1980	1990	2000	2003
Sweden	78	81	79	78
Finland	69	72	75	74
Denmark	79	75	73	70
Norway	58	59	54	53
Ireland	57	51	37	35
Italy	50	39	35	34
United Kingdom	51	39	30	29
Canada	35	33	28	28
Australia	50	41	25	23
Germany	35	31	25	23
New Zealand	69	51	23	22
Netherlands	35	24	23	22
Japan	31	25	22	20
United States	20	16	13	12

Note: Density is union membership as a proportion of wage- and salary-earners in employment.

Source: Visser (2006).

served if all farmers belonged to a single national association.

The commitment of the membership is also important. For instance, the four million members of America's National Rifle Association (NRA) include many who are prepared to contact their congressional representatives in pursuit of the group's goal of 'preserving the right of all law-abiding individuals to purchase, possess and use firearms for legitimate purposes'. This well-schooled activism led George Stephanopoulos, former spokesman for President Clinton, to this assessment: 'let me make one small vote for the NRA. They're good citizens. They call their Congressmen. They write. They vote. They contribute. And they get what they want over time' (NRA, 2006).

Third, the financial *resources* available to an interest group affect influence. Here, money talks but not always loudly. Take the NRA once more. With an annual budget of $40 million, the NRA can afford to employ 275 full-time staff. Certainly, the coalition of gun control groups cannot match the NRA's fire power. Yet it would be naive to suppose that the cause of gun control in the USA is held back

solely by the NRA. To focus solely on its resources would be to ignore two factors in the wider environment: first, the difficulty of passing any legislation opposed by a significant minority within Congress; second, an ambiguous constitutional reference to the 'right of the people to keep and bear arms'. The NRA has used its resources to exploit both features but it has created neither.

Just as the impact of lobbying firms is often exaggerated, so too is the significance of the money available to an interest group. As a rule, finance is rarely decisive. Lack of resources may hold a group back but a surfeit does not guarantee political success.

Fourth, the ability of a group to invoke *sanctions* is clearly important. A labour union can go on strike, a multinational corporation can take its investments elsewhere, a peak association can withdraw its cooperation in forming policy. As a rule, promotional groups (such as environmental movements) have fewer sanctions available to use as a bargaining chip; and their influence suffers accordingly.

Interest groups in authoritarian states

The role played by interest groups in non-democratic states provides a sharp contrast to their position in liberal democracies. Authoritarian rulers see freely organized groups as a potential threat to their own power; hence, they seek either to repress such groups or to incorporate them within their power structure. In this section, we will examine the workings of these strategies in non-communist authoritarian regimes before turning to communist states, past and present.

In the latter half of the twentieth century, many authoritarian rulers had to confront the challenge posed by the new groups unleashed by economic development. These included labour unions, peasant leagues and educated radicals. How did rulers respond to these new conditions? On the one hand, one strategy was to suppress such groups completely. Where civil liberties were weak and many groups were new, this approach was feasible. For example, a strategy of repression was adopted by many military regimes. Military leaders often had their own fingers in the economic pie, sometimes in collaboration with overseas corporations; the rulers' goal was to maintain a workforce that was both compliant and poorly paid. Troublemakers seeking to establish labour unions were quickly removed.

This syndrome of forced exploitation continues in Burma. There, the military junta has outlawed independent trade unions, collective bargaining and strikes; imprisoned labour activists; and maintained strict control of the media. This repressive environment enables the regime to use forced labour, particularly from ethnic minorities, to extract goods such as timber which are exported through the black market for the financial benefit of army officers.

On the other hand, authoritarian rulers could seek to manage the expression of new interests. That is, they could allow interests to organize but seek to control them – a policy of incorporation rather than exclusion. By enlisting part of the population, particularly its more modern sectors, into officially sponsored associations, rulers hoped to accelerate the push towards modernization. This approach was common in Latin America, where the state licensed, funded and granted a monopoly of representation to favoured groups, reflecting a Catholic, corporate tradition inherited from colonial times (Wiarda, 2004).

Before the democratic and economic reforms of the 1980s and 1990s, Mexico offered a particular working of this format. Its governing system was founded on a strong ruling organization: the Institutional Revolutionary Party (PRI). This party was itself a coalition of labour, agrarian and 'popular' sectors (the latter consisting mainly of public employees). Favoured unions and peasant associations within these sectors gained access to the PRI. Party leaders provided state resources, such as subsidies and control over jobs, to these groups in exchange for their political support. In effect, Mexico became a giant patron–client network: a form of corporatism for a developing country. For the many people left out of the network, however, life was hard indeed.

Just as corporatism is decaying in liberal democracies, so Mexico's system – and many others like it – is also in decline. It was over-regulated, giving so much power to government and PRI-affiliated sectors as to deter business investment, especially from overseas. As the market sector expanded, so the patronage available to the PRI diminished. In 1997,

an independent National Workers Union emerged to claim that the old mechanisms of state control were exhausted, a point which was confirmed by the PRI's defeat in a presidential election three years later.

The position of interest groups in communist states was even more marginal than in other non-democratic regimes. This dependent position also provided a complete contrast to pluralism. For most of the communist era, independent interest groups did not exist. Their absence was a deliberate result of communist ideology. Communist states were led by the party, not by society. Groups served the party, not the other way round. Interest articulation by freely organized groups was inconceivable. Communist rulers sought to harness all organizations into transmission belts for party policy. Trade unions, the media, youth groups and professional associations were little more than branches of the party, serving the cause of communist construction.

The capacity to articulate interests did increase as communist economies matured. The use of coercion and terror declined and conflicts over policy became more visible. Institutional groups such as the military and heavy industry became more important as decisions became more technical. However, one sharp contrast with Western pluralism remained: ruling communist parties restricted interest articulation to safe technical matters. The party continued to crack down vigorously on dissent going beyond these confines. The objectives of the communist state remained beyond criticism. Thus 'socialist pluralism', to the extent that it existed, remained far more limited than its Western counterpart.

Even in reforming China, the Western notion of an 'interest group' still carries little meaning. China's Communist Party continues to provide the framework for most formal political activity. 'Mass organizations' such as the All-China Federation of Trade Unions and the Women's Federation are led by party officials and continue to transmit policy downwards rather than popular concerns upwards.

However, a new breed of non-governmental organizations did emerge in China in the 1980s, strengthening the links between state and society. Examples include the China Family Planning Association, Friends of Nature, the Private Enterprises Association and the Federation of Industry and Commerce (Box 12.4). Typically, only one body is officially recognized in each sector, indicating the

BOX 12.4

Examples of social organizations in contemporary China

	Type	Comment
All-China Federation of Trade Unions	Mass organization	A traditional transmission belt for the party
All-China Women's Federation	Mass organization	Traditionally a party-led body, this federation has created some space for autonomous action
China Family Planning Association	Non-governmental organization	Sponsored by the State Family Planning Commission, this association operates at international and local level
Friends of Nature	Non-governmental organization	Friends of Nature has mobilized student support in defence of habitats threatened by illegal logging

Source: Adapted from Saich (2004), pp. 186–92.

state's continuing control. From the party's viewpoint, this corporatist arrangement reduces the threat of wider links developing across sectors. The limited status of these new entities is shown by the use of the phrase, Government-Organized Non-Governmental Organization (GONGO).

Private business is intertwined with the state sector through personal and often corrupt links. This network of contacts operating through the back door leaves little space for policy-orientated interest groups. 'Rightful resistance' enables citizens to protest to higher authority about lower officials exceeding their proper powers, but again such appeals operate on an individual rather than a group basis and are often ignored anyway. As Manion (2009, p. 448) concludes, 'for the most part, the function of interest aggregation is monopolized by the communist party'.

Interest groups in illiberal democracies

By the nature of illiberal democracy, the borders between the public and private sectors are poorly policed, allowing the president and his allies to intervene in the economy so as to reward friends

and punish enemies. But this involvement is selective rather than comprehensive, operating to override normal business practices and not (in contrast to a communist state) to replace them.

At least in the more developed illiberal democracies, the result can be a dual system of representation, combining some role for interest groups on routine matters, with more personal relationships, nurtured by patronage, regarding matters that are key to the president and his ruling group. In these sensitive areas, employer is set against employer in a competition for political influence, leaving little room for the development of influential business associations. The general point is that even though illiberal democracies allow some interests to be expressed, interest groups as such are less significant than in a liberal democracy.

Russia, as always, is an interesting case. Certainly, the separation between public and private sectors, so central to the organization of interests in the West, has not fully emerged here. Particularly in the early post-communist years, ruthless business executives, corrupt public officials and jumped-up gangsters made deals in a virtually unregulated free-for-all. Individual financiers pulled the strings of their puppets in government but the politics were personal rather than institutional. In such an environment, interests were everywhere but interest groups were nowhere. 'Comrade Criminal' was disinclined to join trade associations.

As Russian politics stabilized and its economy has recovered, so some business associations of a Western kind have emerged, even if they have not yet secured extensive political influence. Peregudov (2001, p. 268) claims that 'in Russia a network of business organizations has been created and is up and running'. He suggests that this network is capable of adequately representing business interests to the state. However, it received limited attention from Vladimir Putin during his tenure as president. He continued to reward his business friends and, on occasion, to imprison his enemies.

We must be wary here of assuming that Russia will eventually develop a Western system of interest representation. Pluralism is not currently on the agenda. Evans (2005, p. 112) even suggests that President Putin 'sought to decrease the degree of pluralism in the Russian political system; it has become increasingly apparent that he wants civil society to be an adjunct to a strong state that will be dedicated to his version of the Russian national ideal'. In a manner similar to China's GONGOs, the state sought to collaborate with favoured groups while condemning any others to irrelevance.

The Russian government's strong nationalist tone led to particular criticism of those groups (such as women's associations) which depend on overseas support to survive in a hostile domestic environment. Few promotional groups in Russia have a significant mass membership and most groups operate solely at grassroots level, working on local projects such as education or the environment under the supervision of the public sector. Russia's combination of an assertive state and a weak society is not conducive to interest group development; authority is perceived as imposed from above rather than generated from below (Clément, 2008).

Yet the politics of illiberal democracies are rarely clear-cut. Dmitry Medvedev, Putin's successor as president, spoke more warmly about civil society. In a remarkable interview in 2009, he said:

And now there is the understanding that civil society is an integral non-governmental institution in any state. An institution that provides feedback. The organizations of people who do not hold office, but are nevertheless actively involved in the life of their country. Therefore meetings and contacts between the President and representatives of civil society are indispensable. (*Novaya Gazeta*, 2009)

Whether these liberal words are matched by action remains to be seen. They may be swallowed up by his country's strong state tradition.

Illiberal democracy frequently arises in polarized and relatively poor societies. This environment is again a difficult one in which to strengthen interest groups pursuing specialized and technical concerns. In many illiberal democracies in Latin America, deep-rooted issues of poverty, inequality, crime and drugs remain unresolved. These are political problems requiring political solutions. Certainly, social movements emerged to address such concerns but these groups were typically local groups founded on opposition to the state.

At national level, the leaders of illiberal democracies – such as Hugo Chávez in Venezuela – have often governed in a personal and populist way, seeking support through the media rather than through institutions such as interest groups (Crisp, 2000). Indeed, Chávez's political appeal rests partly on his rejection of the carefully crafted links between the oil industry, political parties and the government which characterized the preceding regime. Rather, Chávez has used oil revenues for a highly political form of redistribution to his predominantly poor supporters.

This personalist style of rule is long familiar to Latin America and has been further encouraged as privatization and market mechanisms have undercut the old corporatist channels. Also, the emergence of powerful indigenous movements in countries such as Bolivia raises political challenges which go beyond the technical, detailed concerns of protective interest groups. The relationship between state and society in much of Latin America remains one of mutual suspicion, providing difficult ground for nurturing interest groups.

In much of Africa, too, group politics in an era of post-military government continues to be based on ethnicity rather than interests generated through the workplace. Many poorer countries lack the complex economy needed to develop the interest group patterns found in affluent liberal democracies. In Botswana, for example, only two organizations – a business association and a conservation group – employ staff to lobby the government (Herbst, 2001).

When such economic resources as are available are parcelled out on ethnic lines, or in any other personal or unregulated way, incentives for orthodox interest groups to develop are limited. 'In this respect', suggests Rothchild (1997, p. 75), 'ethnic groups can be likened to the interest-defined groups that they compete with for state-controlled resources'. In addition, the space between state and society can be colonized by foreign non-governmental organizations, often providing needed services in collapsed states but also, by their presence and resources, inhibiting the development of domestic interest groups.

Learning Resources for Chapter 12

Next step

Many of the best studies of interest groups continue to be about the United States; Cigler and Loomis (2006) is an excellent collection.

Further reading

Wilson (1990) remains a clear and straightforward introduction to interest groups. Hrebenar (1997) is a good text on the USA; Beyers *et al.* (2009) examine interest group politics in Europe from a comparative perspective; M. Smith (1995) is a brief but helpful introduction to Britain. Two useful comparative studies are Wilson (2003) on the relationship between business and politics and Thomas (2001) on the links between parties and interest groups. Evans (2005) covers civil society in post-communist Russia.

Internet sources

Influence
Chronicles the relationship between lobbyists and their clients in the United States
http://www.influence.biz/

opensecrets.org
A guide to money in American elections
http://www.opensecrets.org/

National Rifle Association
Seeks to preserve the right of all law-abiding Americans to purchase, possess and use firearms
http://www.mynra.org/
http://www.nraila.org/About/

Brady Campaign
Leading the fight to prevent gun violence
http://www.bradycampaign.org/

www.palgrave.com
Companion Website
Visit the Companion Website to 'click and go'
www.palgrave.com/politics/hague

Part IV
GOVERNMENT AND GOVERNANCE

In this part we examine the major institutions of government and their constitutional basis. We begin with a chapter on constitutions and the legal framework (Chapter 13). We then analyse multilevel governance, reviewing the relationships between central, regional and local governments in federal and unitary systems (Chapter 14). Our focus next moves to the institutions of government, starting with the legislatures or parliaments which still serve as the key symbol of popular representation in national politics (Chapter 15). We then turn to what many people would naturally think of as 'the government': namely, the top political tier of leadership within the administration (Chapter 16). Chapter 17 examines the supporting tier of departments and agencies which gives effect to, and also helps to shape, political decisions. There we seek to map the complex terrain of contemporary public administration.

This part will enable you to:

▶ Understand the institutions of national government and the relationships between them;
▶ Become familiar with the various levels of authority within the state and, again, the relationships between them;
▶ Appreciate how political leaders in liberal democracies must seek influence through attempting to steer the complex governance networks which form the modern state.

Chapter 13
Constitutions and law

The academic study of politics began as a branch of law and belatedly these friends are now renewing an old acquaintance. Four factors are involved in this rebirth of interest in the legal dimension of politics:

◆ The late twentieth century witnessed an explosion of constitution-making among post-authoritarian states, with 85 constitutions introduced between 1989 and 1999 (Derbyshire and Derbyshire, 1999);
◆ Stimulated by the legal character of the European Union and by judicial activism in the USA, judges in many liberal democracies have become more willing to step into the political arena, not least in investigating corrupt politicians;
◆ Politicians have become more aware of the potential for a consistent legal framework to encourage political stability, investment and economic growth;
◆ The expanding body of international law increasingly impinges on domestic politics, with judges called on to arbitrate between the conflicting claims of supranational and national law.

In connecting law and government, the idea of the **rule of law** offers a useful entry point. In liberal democracies, the rule of law has succeeded in ensnaring absolute rulers in the threads of legal restraint. In the words of the nineteenth-century English jurist, A. V. Dicey (1885, p. 27), the purpose of the rule of law is to substitute 'a government of laws' for a 'government of men'. When law rules, governors cannot exercise arbitrary power, and the powerful are subject to the same laws as everyone else. More specifically, the rule of law implies that laws are general, public, prospective, clear, consistent, practical and stable (Fuller, 1969).

The gradual implementation of the rule of law and **due process** is an accomplishment of liberal politics, providing a basis for distinguishing liberal from illiberal democracies, and both from authoritarian regimes. That success, however, is never completely secure. The American constitution did not alter on 11 September 2001 but the rights of immigrants who found themselves imprisoned for several months without charge suddenly became less certain. As with all countries facing external threats, the rule of law takes second place to national security and needs to be rebuilt subsequently through the courts (Dempsey, 2002).

Within Western democracies, the two fundamental systems are **common law** and **civil law**. It is impossible to understand the differences in the

The **rule of law** is a Western and primarily Anglo-American term. Its varied dimensions include consistent application of the law; one law for all; and **due process** (respect for an individual's legal rights) (Kleinfeld, 2006).

The **common law**, found in England and many of its former colonies, consists of judicial rulings on matters not explicitly treated in legislation. Common law is based on precedents created by decisions in specific cases. In the more widespread **civil law** system, judges reach decisions by applying extensive written codes rather than by comparing cases. Civil law derives from the original **Roman law** codes (civil law is unconnected with a 'civil case', a term used to indicate a non-criminal action).

political role of judges in Anglo-American and Continental European democracies without some appreciation of this distinction. The common law is used mainly in the United Kingdom and its former colonies, including the USA. Originally based on custom and tradition, the common law consists of judges' decisions on specific cases. These decisions were first published as a way of standardizing legal decisions across a state's territory. Because judges abide by the *stare decisis* principle (stand on decided cases), their decisions create precedents and form a predictable legal framework, contributing thereby to nation-building.

Common law, then, is judge-made law. Of course, explicit statutes (laws) are also passed by the legislature in specific areas but these statutes usually build on case law and are themselves refined through judicial interpretation. The political significance of common law systems is that judges constitute an independent source of authority which is to some degree separate from the government itself.

Civil law, by contrast, is founded on written legal codes which seek to provide an overarching framework for the conduct of public affairs, including public administration and business contracts. The original codes were developed under Justinian, Roman Emperor between 527 and 565. **Roman law** has evolved into distinct civil codes, seen for example in the contrasting codes in France and Germany. These codes are then elaborated through laws passed by the national parliament. Civil law has shaped the legal character not just of Continental Europe but also of Latin America, the European Union – and, surprisingly, the US state of Louisiana.

In civil law, judges rather than juries identify the facts of the case (often indeed directing the investigation) before applying the relevant section of the code. The political importance is that judges are

viewed as impartial officers of state, engaged in an administrative task; they are merely *la bouche de la loi* (the mouth of the law). The courtroom is a government space rather than a sphere of independent authority; judge-made law would threaten legislative supremacy.

The underlying codes in civil law systems often emphasize social stability as well as individual rights. Indeed, the codes traditionally functioned as a kind of constitution, systematically setting out obligations as well as freedoms. However the more recent introduction of distinct constitutions (which have established a strong position in relation to the codes) has strengthened the liberal theme in many civil law countries. In addition, judges have found themselves filling gaps in the codes, providing decisions which function as case law even though they are not acknowledged as such. These developments have somewhat diluted the contrast between the two models (Stone Sweet, 2000).

Constitutions

We can look at **constitutions** in two ways. The first reflects their historic role as a regulator of the state's power over its citizens. For the Austrian philosopher Friedrich Hayek (1899–1992), a constitution was nothing but that – a device for limiting the power of government, whether unelected or elected. In a similar vein, Carl Friedrich (1901–84) defined a constitution as 'a system of effective, regularized restraints upon government action' (1937, p. 104). From this perspective, the key feature of a constitution is its statement of individual rights and its expression of the rule of law.

Certainly, a bill of rights now forms part of nearly all written constitutions (Box 13.1). Although America's Bill of Rights (1791) confines itself to such traditional liberties as freedom of religion, speech and assembly, recent constitutions are more ambitious, often imposing duties on rulers such as fulfilling citizens' social rights to employment and medical care. The Mexican constitution of 1917 was the first to introduce such provisions. Several post-communist constitutions have extended the list further, to include the right to childcare and a healthy environment. In consequence, the documents are expanding: the average (including amend-

BOX 13.1

The arrangement of constitutions

▶ A *preamble* seeks popular support for the document with a stirring declaration of principle and, sometimes, a definition of the state's purposes;
▶ An *organizational section* sets out the powers of government institutions;
▶ A *bill of rights* covers individual and perhaps group rights, including access to legal redress;
▶ *Procedures for amendment* define the rules for revising the constitution.

Further reading: Maddex (2007).

BOX 13.2

Entrenching the constitution: some examples

	Amendments require the approval of
Australia	Both houses of parliament, then a referendum achieving majority support (a) overall and (b) in a majority of states
Canada	Both houses of parliament and two-thirds of the states containing at least half the country's population
Germany	A two-thirds majority in both houses of parliament[1]
Spain	A two-thirds majority in both houses of parliament and, if demanded by a tenth of either house, a referendum achieving majority support[2]
Sweden	Majority vote by two successive sessions of parliament with an intervening election[3]
USA	A two-thirds majority in both houses of Congress and approval by three-quarters of the states[4]

Notes:
1. The federal, social and democratic character of the German state, and the rights of individuals within it, cannot be amended.
2. 'Fundamental' amendments to the Spanish constitution must be followed by an election, ratification by the new parliament and a referendum.
3. Sweden has four fundamental laws which comprise its 'constitution'. These include its Instrument of Government and Freedom of the Press Act.
4. An alternative method, based on a special convention called by the states and by Congress, has not been used.

ments) is now 29,000 words, compared to just 7,400 for the concise American constitution (Lutz, 2007).

The second but more fundamental role of constitutions is to specify a power map, defining the structure of government, articulating the pathways of power and specifying the procedures for lawmaking. As Sartori (1994, p. 198) observes, the key feature of a constitution lies in this provision of a frame of government. A constitution without a declaration of rights is still a constitution, whereas a document without a power map is no constitution at all. A constitution is therefore a form of political engineering, to be judged like any other construction by how well it survives the test of time. From this perspective, the American version, still standing after more than 200 years, is a triumph.

Much is made of the distinction between written and unwritten constitutions. Yet no constitution is wholly unwritten; even the 'unwritten' British and New Zealand constitutions contain much relevant statute and common law. A contrast between **codified** and **uncodified** systems is more helpful. Most

A **constitution** sets out the formal structure of the state, specifying the powers and institutions of central government, and its relationship with other levels. In addition, constitutions express the rights of citizens and in so doing create limits on government. A **codified** constitution is set out in a single document; an **uncodified** constitution is spread among a range of documents and is influenced by tradition and practice.

constitutions are codified: set out in detail within a single document, rather like a short civil law code. By contrast, the uncodified constitutions of Britain and New Zealand are spread out among several sources. Sweden falls in between: its constitution comprises four separate acts passed at different times.

Amendment

Procedures for amendment are an important building block of the constitutional structure. **Rigid**

constitutions offer the general benefit of a stable political framework. For current rulers, a rigid framework limits the damage should political opponents obtain power, for unless they can clear the amendment hurdle they too must abide by the values embedded in the settlement. Political enemies, coming together to agree a new constitution, thus find security in entrenchment. Put differently, a rigid constitution can deliver a political equilibrium.

Flexible constitutions, though rare, do offer the advantage of ready adaptability. In New Zealand, this flexibility permitted a recasting of the country's electoral system and government administration in the 1980s and 1990s. Similarly, the United Kingdom was able to devolve significant powers to Scotland and Wales in 1999 without much constitutional ado. In most other countries such radical changes would have required constitutional amendment.

> **Flexible constitutions** can be amended in the same way that ordinary legislation is passed; Britain is the major example. **Rigid constitutions** are entrenched, ring-fenced by a more demanding amendment procedure such as a qualified or concurrent majority.

Constitutions are entrenched by setting a higher level and wider spread of support for amendments than for ordinary bills. Typically, modification requires both a two-thirds majority in each house of parliament and additional endorsement from a broader constituency. In a federation, this extra ratification is from the component states; unitary countries usually employ a referendum (Box 13.2).

The amendment procedure offers clues as to the status of the constitution in relation to the legislature. When modifications cannot be approved by the legislature alone, the constitution stands supreme over parliament. In Australia, for example, amendments must be endorsed not just by the national parliament but also by a referendum achieving a concurrent majority: in most states and in the country as a whole.

In a few countries, however, special majorities within the legislature alone are authorized to make amendments. In such a situation, the status of the constitution is somewhat reduced and that of the assembly increased. Germany is a partial example: amendments there require only a two-thirds

majority in both houses. At the same time, however, the nucleus of Germany's Basic Law – the part setting out core rights – is accorded the ultimate entrenchment. It cannot be amended at all.

Although rigid constitutions may appear to be incapable of coping with change, in practice they adapt through judicial interpretation. As we will see, the American Supreme Court has shown particular skill at adjusting an old document to fit new times. It has reinterpreted a constitution designed in the eighteenth century for the fresh challenges of later eras. Thus one contrast between rigid and flexible constitutions is that in the former the judiciary manages evolution while in the latter politicians take the lead.

Origins

In the main, constitutions are a deliberate creation, designed and built by politicians. As the English political theorist John Stuart Mill wrote, constitutions 'are the work of men ... Men did not wake up on a summer morning and find them sprung up' (1861). How then do constitutions come into being? What conditions create the founding moment in which societies set about reconstructing their political order?

New constitutions typically form part of a fresh start after a period of disruption. Such circumstances include:

- ▶ Regime change: for example, the collapse of communist rule;
- ▶ Reconstruction after defeat in war: for example, Japan after 1945;
- ▶ The achievement of independence: for example, much of Africa in the 1950s and 1960s.

Most constitutions experience a difficult birth. Often, they are compromises between political actors who have merely substituted distrust for conflict. In Horowitz's terms (2002), constitutions are built from the bottom up rather than designed from the top down. For instance, South Africa's post-apartheid settlement of 1996 achieved an accommodation between leaders of the white and black communities against a backdrop of near slavery and continuing racial hostility. Acceptability was everything; elegance was nothing.

As vehicles of compromise, most constitutions are vague, contradictory and ambiguous. They are fudges and truces, wrapped in fine words (Weaver and Rockman, 1993). As a rule, drafters are more concerned with a short-term political fix than with establishing a resilient structure for the long run. In principle, everyone agrees with Alexander Hamilton (1788b, p. 439) that constitutions should 'seek merely to regulate the general political interests of the nation'; in practice, they are lengthy documents reflecting an incomplete settlement between suspicious partners.

The lauded American constitution of 1787, although shorter than most, is no exception to this general picture. Finer's description (1997, p. 1495) makes the point: 'the constitution was a thing of wrangles and compromises. In its completed state, it was a set of incongruous proposals cobbled together. And furthermore, that is what many of its framers thought'.

The main danger of a new constitution is that it fails to endow the new rulers with sufficient authority. Too often, political distrust means the new government is hemmed in with restrictions, limiting its effectiveness. Even the successful American constitution, for instance, divides power to the point where its critics allege that the administration, and specifically the president, can hardly govern at all.

The Italian constitution of 1948 is a further illustration of the tendency to underpower new settlements. Its hallmark is *garantismo*, meaning that all political forces are guaranteed a stake in the political system. Thus the document establishes a strong bicameral assembly and provides for regional autonomy. These checks on power were intended to prevent a recurrence of fascist dictatorship and to accommodate the radical aspirations of the political left. In practice *garantismo* led to ineffective governance, contributing to the transformation of the parties (but not the constitution) in the 1990s.

Judicial review and constitutional courts

Constitutions are no more self-implementing than they are self-made. Some institution must be found to enforce the constitution, striking down laws and practices that offend its principles. This review

power has fallen to the judiciary. With a capacity to override decisions and laws produced by democratic governments, unelected judges occupy a unique position both in and above politics. India's Supreme Court is even empowered to override constitutional amendments themselves. Through their power of review, constitutional courts express a liberal conception of politics, restricting the power of elected rulers. In this way, **judicial review** both stabilizes and limits democracy.

Judicial power, furthermore, is only partly limited by the constitution itself. Inevitably, judicial interpretation varies with the temper of the times, creating a living constitution. Justice Thurgood Marshall (1987, p. 181) gives the example of the American Supreme Court's evolving treatment of black Americans: they 'were enslaved by law, emancipated by law, disenfranchised by law; and, finally they have begun to win equality by law'. So, as another justice pointed out, 'we live under a constitution. But the constitution is what the judges say it is' (Hughes, 1916, pp. 185–6).

In three respects, though, judicial power is far from unqualified. First, constitutions do restrict what judges can plausibly say about them. Justices are only unfree masters of the document whose values they defend; like the hole in a doughnut, judicial discretion only exists as an area left open by a surrounding belt of restriction (Dworkin, 1977).

Second, judges are aware of the danger of converting their court into a continuous constitutional convention and will normally seek to decide a case on narrow grounds or assert that the issue should be resolved in the political arena. Like good generals, they like to keep their powder dry for the decisive battle.

Third, the impact of a court's judgements depends on its status among those who implement them. As the American President Andrew Jackson said of his Chief Justice, 'John Marshall has made his decision,

Judicial review empowers ordinary or special courts to nullify both legislation and executive acts that contravene the constitution. **Abstract review**, practised by constitutional courts only, is an advisory but binding opinion on a proposed law. **Concrete review**, practised by both constitutional and supreme courts, arises in the context of a specific case.

now let him enforce it'. Because decisions that are ignored damage a court's credibility, courts must follow a delicate course, heeding the climate of opinion without pandering to it. Ruth Ginsburg, an American Supreme Court justice, expressed her approach thus: 'an effective judge strives to persuade, not to pontificate' (1992, p. 194).

The function of judicial review can be allocated in two ways (Box 13.3). The first and more traditional method is for the highest or supreme court in the ordinary judicial system to take on the task of constitutional protection. A supreme court rules on constitutional matters just as it has the final say on other questions of common and statute law. Australia, Canada, India, the USA and much of Latin America provide examples of this approach. Because a supreme court heads the judicial system, its currency is legal cases which bubble up from lower courts.

A second and more recent method is to create a special constitutional court, standing apart from the ordinary judicial system. This approach originated with the Austrian constitution of 1920 and is now widely used. By 2005, almost half the world's constitutions made provision for such a court (Horowitz, 2006). Constitutional courts are much favoured in both Western and Eastern Europe. These special tribunals mean that many countries possess both constitutional and supreme courts. Spain, typically, has a Constitutional Tribunal to arbitrate on constitutional matters and a separate Supreme Court to oversee national criminal law. In civil law systems, the relationship between constitutional and ordinary courts is not always easy, but most constitutional courts have established the priority of the constitution over civil law codes. We will examine supreme and constitutional courts separately.

Supreme courts

The United States is the prototypical case of the supreme court approach. America's constitution vests judicial power 'in one Supreme Court, and in such inferior Courts as the Congress may from time to time ordain'. Although the Court possesses **original jurisdiction** over cases to which an American state or a representative of another country is a party, its main role is **appellate**. That is, constitutional issues can be raised at any point in the ordinary judicial system and the Supreme Court selects

---

> **BOX 13.3**
>
> ## Judicial review: supreme courts vs constitutional courts
>
> | | Supreme court | Constitutional court |
> |---|---|---|
> | Form of review | Concrete | More abstract |
> | Relationship to other courts | Highest court of appeal | A separate body dealing with constitutional issues only |
> | Recruitment | Legal expertise plus political approval | Political criteria more important |
> | Normal tenure | Until retirement | Typically one non-renewable term (six to nine years) |
> | Examples | Australia, United States | Austria, Germany, Russia |

for **concrete review** just those cases with broad significance. Thus, most petitions for the Court to review a case are turned down.

Contrary to popular belief, the American constitution does not itself specify the Court's role in adjudicating constitutional disputes. Rather, this function was gradually acquired by the justices themselves, with *Marbury* v. *Madison* (1803) proving decisive. In this case, Chief Justice John Marshall struck down part of the Judiciary Act (1789) as unconstitutional, thereby establishing the principle of judicial review. 'To what purpose are powers limited,' asked Marshall, 'and to what purpose is that limitation committed to writing, if these limits may, at any time, be passed by those intended to be restrained?' President Jefferson

> **Original jurisdiction** entitles a court to try a case at its first instance. **Appellate jurisdiction** authorizes a court to review decisions reached by lower courts.

expressed his displeasure, claiming that the judgement ran the danger of 'placing us under the despotism of an oligarchy'. But, whatever the constitutional basis of Marshall's decision, the principle of judicial review became established.

Stare decisis notwithstanding, the Supreme Court does occasionally strike out in new directions. This 'inconsistency' has proved to be a source of strength, enabling the Court to adapt the constitution to changes in national mood. For example, after its rearguard struggle against the New Deal in the 1930s, the Court conceded the right of the national government to regulate the economy.

At other times the Court has sought to lead rather than follow. The most important of these initiatives, under the leadership of Chief Justice Earl Warren in the 1950s and 1960s, concerned black civil rights. In its famous, unanimous decision in *Brown* v. *Topeka* (1954), the Court outlawed racial segregation in schools, dramatically reversing its previous policy that 'separate but equal' facilities for blacks fell within the constitution. Implementation proved to be tortuous but the decision itself was path-breaking (Riches, 2004).

Constitutional courts

Continental Europe, both west and east, favours constitutional rather than supreme courts. In Western Europe, such courts were adopted after 1945 in, for instance, West Germany and France (Figure 13.1). They represented a general attempt to prevent a revival of dictatorship, whether of the left or the right. In post-fascist states constitutional courts were also created to bypass ordinary judges who had remained in place in the existing courts. More recently, new regimes have created constitutional courts to overcome the inefficiency, corruption and opposition of judges from the old order.

Where a supreme court is a judicial body making the final ruling on all appeals (not all of which involve the constitution), a constitutional court is more akin to an additional parliamentary chamber. Hans Kelsen (1881–1973), the Austrian inventor of constitutional courts, argued that these courts should function as a negative legislator, striking down unconstitutional bills but leaving positive legislation to parliament. Certainly, the approach is more political, flexible and less legal than that of supreme courts. Constitutional courts practice **abstract review**, judging the validity of a law or issuing advisory judgements on a bill at the request of the government or assembly, often without the stimulus of a specific case. Judgements are often short and are usually unsigned, lacking the legal argument used by supreme courts.

Just as the USA illustrates the supreme court tradition, so Germany has become an exemplar of the newer constitutional court approach. Its Federal Constitutional Court provided an influential model for all post-communist countries in Eastern Europe (Kühn, 2006). Germany's court consists of 16 members appointed by the legislature for a non-renewable term of 12 years. The Court is divided into two specialized chambers of which one focuses on the core liberties enshrined in the Basic Law. The Court's public reputation has been enhanced by the provision of constitutional complaint, an innovative device permitting citizens to petition the Court directly once other judicial remedies are exhausted.

Because political power was still under a cloud after the Second World War, the Court was charged not just with constitutional review but also with maintaining the new order against groups seeking its overthrow. It has done just that, for instance by banning both communist and neo-Nazi parties in the 1950s. For this reason, among others, Kommers

Figure 13.1 Establishing constitutional courts in Europe

* These countries also possessed similar, but somewhat ineffective, courts in the interwar period.

Source: Adapted from Stone Sweet (2000, p. 31).

SOUTH AFRICA

Form of government ■ a liberal democracy with an executive president and entrenched provinces.

Legislature ■ the National Assembly, the lower house, consists of 400 members elected for a five-year term. The president cannot dissolve the assembly. The weaker upper house, the National Council of Provinces, contains ten delegates from each of the nine provinces.

Executive ■ a president heads both the state and the government, ruling with a cabinet. The National Assembly elects the president after each election.

Judiciary ■ the legal system mixes common and civil law. The Constitutional Court decides constitutional matters and can strike down legislation.

Electoral system ■ the National Assembly is elected by proportional representation using closed party lists. Provincial legislatures appoint the members of the National Council of Provinces.

Party system ■ the African National Congress (ANC; 264 seats and 66 per cent of the vote in 2009) has dominated the post-apartheid republic. The more liberal Democratic Alliance (67 seats), now the leading party in the Western Cape, forms the official opposition.

Population (annual growth rate): 49.1m (+0.3%)
World Bank income group: upper middle
Political Rights score: ②
Civil Liberties score: ②
Human development index (rank/out of): 121/177
Freedom of the press index (rank/out of): 64/195
Perceived transparency index (rank/out of): 54/180

Note: For meaning and sources of scales and indexes, see p. xv. In all cases a score and rank of 1 is 'best'.

South Africa was shaped by two groups of settlers: the Boers (farmers), descended from Dutch-speaking colonists of the seventeenth century, and a smaller group of British colonists. The discovery of diamonds and gold in the late nineteenth century consolidated a reliance on migrant labour, providing the economic foundation for the system of apartheid (apartness) institutionalized after 1945.

Apartheid defined three races – white, coloured and black – and outlawed inter-racial marriage. Apartheid's survival into the 1990s showed that governments based on brute power can last a long time. Yet change was eventually induced by three main factors:

■ The collapse of communism which destroyed the regime's bogeyman;
■ The imposition of sanctions by the EU and the United States;
■ Black opposition which began to encompass armed resistance.

As so often, initial reforms merely stimulated demands for more and faster change. In 1990, ANC leader Nelson Mandela was released from prison after 26 years, symbolizing recognition by the white rulers that the time had come to negotiate their own downfall. Four years later, the ANC won the first multiracial elections with 63 per cent of the vote. Mandela became president of a government of national unity, including the white-led National Party. South Africa returned to the family of nations, a transition later exemplified by the decision to hold the soccer World Cup there in 2010.

The ANC subsequently confirmed its position as a dominant party. It remains the natural party of the black majority and has proved adept at incorporating a range of other organizations, including trade unions, into its fold. Unlike many other liberation movements, the cohesiveness of the party survived the transition from opposition to government and the retirement of its hero-leader. Despite leadership conflicts and doubts about the quality of its governance, the party is still able to use its control of state resources to reinforce its support base.

Like many dominant parties, the ANC provides a measure of order in a country beset with social problems. These difficulties include not only the sensitive legacy of apartheid but also crime, inequality, poverty, unemployment, corruption, emigration, HIV/Aids, inadequate infrastructure and limited education. Average life expectancy is a mere 49 years and, unusually, is lower among women than among men.

Further reading: Buhlungu *et al.* (2007), Johnson (2009).

The constitution and the legal framework in South Africa

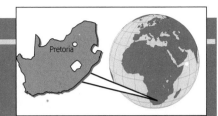

South Africa's transformation from a militarized state based on apartheid to a more constitutional order based on democracy was one of the most remarkable political transitions of the late twentieth century. What then was the nature of the political order established by the new constitution?

In 1996, after two years of hard bargaining between the ANC and the white National Party (NP), agreement was reached on a new 109-page constitution to take full effect in 1999. The NP expressed general support despite reservations that led to its withdrawal from government.

In a phrase reminiscent of the American constitution, South Africa's constitution declares that 'the Executive power of the Republic vests in the President'. As in the USA, the president is also head of state. Unlike the United States, though, the president is elected by the National Assembly after each general election. He can be removed through a vote of no confidence in the assembly (though this event would trigger a general election) or by impeachment. The system is therefore fundamentally parliamentary in character. The president governs in conjunction with a large cabinet.

Each of the country's nine provinces elects its own legislature and forms its own executive headed by a premier. But far more than in the USA, authority and funds flow from the top down. In any case, the ANC provides a glue linking not just executive and parliament but also national, provincial and municipal levels of government. So far, at least, the ruling party has dominated the governing institutions whereas in the USA the institutions have dominated the parties.

It remains to be seen how South Africa's rainbow nation will be able to reconcile constitutional liberal democracy with the political dominance of the ANC. Here, the modest reduction in the size of the ANC's parliamentary majority in the 2009 elections may exert some effect, reducing the ANC's desire and capacity to amend the constitution in its favour. In any case, the country's politics, more than most, should be judged by what preceded it. By that test the achievements of the new South Africa are remarkable indeed.

Further reading: Butler (2004), Sparks (2009).

Preamble to the South African constitution, 1999

We, the people of South Africa,
Recognise the injustices of our past;
Honour those who suffered for justice and freedom in our land;
Respect those who have worked to build and develop our country; and
Believe that South Africa belongs to all who live in it, united in our diversity.
We therefore, through our freely elected representatives, adopt this Constitution as the supreme law of the Republic so as to

- Heal the divisions of the past and establish a society based on democratic values, social justice and fundamental human rights;
- Lay the foundations for a democratic and open society in which government is based on the will of the people and every citizen is equally protected by law;
- Improve the quality of life of all citizens and free the potential of each person; and
- Build a united and democratic South Africa able to take its rightful place as a sovereign state in the family of nations.

May God protect our people.

Source: SouthAfrica.info (2009)

(2006) describes the Court as the 'guardian of German democracy'. One indicator of its success is its impact on the thinking of judges in ordinary courts, despite the formal separation of the constitutional court from the judicial hierarchy.

The Court has proved to be active. Its decisions have impinged on topics such as abortion, election procedures, immigration, party funding, religion in schools and university reform. Between 1951 and 1990, the Court ruled that 198 federal laws (nearly 5 per cent of the total) contravened the constitution.

Conradt (2008, pp. 253–4) offers an overall assessment of the Court's achievements:

More than any other postwar institution, the Constitutional Court has enunciated the view that the Federal Republic is a militant democracy whose democratic political parties are the chief instrument for the translation of public opinion into public policy. The court has become a legitimate component of the political system, and its decisions have been accepted and complied with by both winners and losers.

European Court of Justice

It would be remiss to conclude this discussion of constitutional courts without considering the Court of Justice of the European Communities (ECJ). Just as Germany's Federal Constitutional Court helped to shape the development of the postwar republic, so too has the Court of Justice contributed to building the European Union. From the 1960s to the 1980s, it was the decisive actor in expanding the EU's legal order. That regime, furthermore, is fundamental to the Union's functioning. The cumulative impact of the ECJ's decisions amounted to what Weiler (1994) terms a 'quiet revolution' in developing the founding treaties into something closer to a European constitution.

The Court's formal purpose is to ensure that those aspects of the Union's treaties subject to its jurisdiction, and the provisions concerning EU institutions, are correctly interpreted and applied. Cases can be brought by member states or by other institutions of the Union. As the final arbiter of European Union law, the ECJ also responds to requests from national courts for preliminary rulings on European law. Based in Luxembourg, it is unconnected with the European Court of Human Rights in Strasbourg.

The Court of Justice consists of one judge appointed from each member state for a renewable six-year term, with broad experience more important than specialized judicial expertise. Many cases are dealt with by small chambers of three to five judges; support is provided by eight advocates-general whose function is to make an initial recommendation on most cases before the Court. Even though a Court of First Instance was established in 1988 to share the workload, judgements are still slow to emerge: the time between lodging a case and final decision still averages almost two years (Nugent, 2006, p. 296).

In its early decades, the Court's decisions consistently and creatively strengthened the authority of central institutions (see Timeline). It achieved this goal in three ways, insisting that European law:

- Applies directly within member states (direct applicability);
- Must be enforced by national courts (direct effect);
- Takes precedence over national law (primacy).

In the 1990s, however, some member states began to question both the ECJ's procedures and further expansion of its authority. Some slippage occurred in implementing the Court's decisions and a few national courts grew restive. In particular, Germany's Federal Constitutional Court showed itself keen to retain jurisdiction over whether European treaties violated Germany's own constitution, an issue that may continue to be troublesome.

Even so, the ECJ remains the pre-eminent example of a judicial contribution to the emergence of a new political order, justifying Shapiro's comment (1987, p. 1007) that 'no other court has ever played so prominent a role in the creation of the basic governmental and political process of which it is a part'. Other courts, including America's, have strengthened the central authority; the European Court helped to create one.

Judicial activism

Perhaps with the exception of Scandinavia, judicial intervention in public policy has grown throughout the liberal democratic world since 1945, marking a

▶ **TIMELINE**

THE COURT OF JUSTICE OF THE EUROPEAN COMMUNITIES (ECJ)

1952	*Court of Justice of the European Communities* established as part of the European Coal and Steel Community.
1957	*Treaty of Rome*: the Court's jurisdiction extends to the new European Economic Community and Euratom treaties.
1963	*Van Gend en Loos*: European laws apply directly to individuals, creating rights and obligations that national courts must implement.
1964	*Costa* v. *Enel*: European law takes priority over national law.
1979	*Cassis de Dijon*: a product sold lawfully in one member state must be accepted for sale in other member states ('mutual recognition').
1987	*Foto-Frost*: national courts cannot invalidate EU measures but must refer their doubts to the ECJ for resolution.
1988	*Court of First Instance* established to reduce the ECJ's workload and to improve its scrutiny of factual matters.
1992	*Francovich and Bonifaci* v. *Italy*: when member states breach EU law, they must compensate those affected. *Maastricht Treaty* clarifies the ECJ's jurisdiction, e.g. to include treaty provisions for closer cooperation between member states but to exclude the Common Foreign and Security Policy.
2003	*Constitutional Treaty* for Europe published in draft.
2005	*Commission* v. *Council*: the Community can require member states to adopt criminal legislation. *Constitutional Treaty* rejected in referendums in France and the Netherlands.
2008	*Constitutional Treaty* rejected in a referendum in Ireland.
2009	The *Treaty of Lisbon*, a weaker replacement of the failed Constitutional Treaty, comes into effect.

Further reading: Alter (2009), de Burea and Weiler (2002).

transition from **judicial restraint** to **judicial activism**. Judges have become more willing to enter political arenas that would have once been left to elected politicians and national parliaments. For instance:

▶ The Australian High Court under Sir Anthony Mason (Chief Justice, 1987–95) boldly uncov-

ered implied rights in the constitution which had remained undetected by its predecessors (Mason, 1993);

▶ Even though the Dutch constitution explicitly excludes judicial review, its Supreme Court has produced important case law on issues where parliament was unable to legislate, notably in authorizing euthanasia (van Geffen, 2001);

◆ The Israeli Supreme Court has addressed conflicts between secular and orthodox Jews left unresolved by mainstream politics (Hirschl, 2002).

Judicial activism refers to the willingness of judges to venture beyond narrow legal reasoning so as to influence public policy. **Judicial restraint**, a more conservative philosophy, maintains that judges should simply apply the letter of the law, leaving politics to elected bodies.

What explanation can we offer for this significant judicialization of politics? Four reasons suggest themselves. First, the increasing reliance on regulation as a mode of governance encouraged court intervention. A government decision to deny gay partners the same rights as married couples is open to judicial challenge in a way that a decision to go to war or raise taxes is not.

Second, the decay of left-wing ideology enlarged the judiciary's scope. Socialists were suspicious of judges, believing them to be unelected defenders of the status quo and of property specifically. Now, the left has discovered that the courtroom can be a venue for harassing governments of the right.

Third, international conventions gave judges an extra lever they can use to break free from their traditional shackles. Documents such as the United Nations Universal Declaration of Human Rights (1948) and the European Convention on Human Rights (1950) provided a base on which judges could construct what would once have been viewed as excessively political statements.

Fourth, the continuing prestige of the judiciary encouraged some transfer of authority to its domain. The judicial process in most liberal democracies retained at least some reputation for integrity and impartiality, whereas the standing of many other institutions, notably parties, declined. Judicial status was reinforced when, as in Italy in the 1990s, civil law judges were seen to be investigating corrupt politicians (Inoguchi, 2002).

Whatever the factors lying behind the expansion of judicial authority, the process is self-reinforcing. Stone Sweet (2000, p. 55) makes the point: 'as constitutional law expands to more and more policy areas, and as it becomes "thicker" in each domain, so do the grounds for judicialized debate. The process tends to reinforce itself'. Sensing the growing confidence of judges in addressing broader political issues, interest groups, rights-conscious citizens and even political parties have also become more willing to continue their struggles in the judicial arena.

Of course, judicial activism has proceeded further in some democracies than in others. In comparative rankings of judicial activism, the United States invariably comes top (Holland, 1991). America is founded on a constitutional contract and an army of lawyers will forever quibble over the terms. The USA exhibits all the features contributing to judicial activism. These include a written constitution, federalism, judicial independence, no separate administrative courts, easy access to the courts, a legal system based on judge-made case law and high esteem for judges. The prominence of the Supreme Court has led one critic of 'government by judges' to dismiss it as 'a nine-man, black-robed junta' (Waldron, 2007, p. 309).

Fewer conditions of judicial autonomy are met in Britain, a country in which parliamentary sovereignty traditionally reigned supreme. Lacking the authority to annul legislation, judicial review in the British context normally refers to the capacity of judges to review executive decisions against the template provided by administrative law.

Even in Britain, however, judicial activism has increased, reflecting European influence. British judges were willing accomplices of the European Court as it established a legal order applying to all member states. The country's belated adoption of the European Convention on Human Rights in 1998, and the decay of the royal prerogative which once allowed the state to stand above the law, also encouraged judicial assertiveness. The establishment of a Supreme Court in 2009, albeit without the power of judicial review, reinforced the notion of judicial autonomy.

Formal statements of rights have also encouraged judicial expansion in other English-speaking countries. In Canada, a Charter of Rights and Freedoms was appended to the constitution in 1982, giving judges a more prominent role in defending individual rights. Similarly, New Zealand introduced a bill of rights in 1990, protecting 'the life and security of the person' and also establishing traditional but previously uncodified democratic and civil rights.

These charters pose a difficulty in countries with a tradition of parliamentary sovereignty, such as New Zealand and the UK. Ingenuity is needed to integrate a bill of rights with the supposed sovereignty of the legislature. Fortunately, New Zealand has delivered a clever solution. There, the Attorney General (a cabinet minister who bridges the political and judicial worlds) advises MPs on whether legislative proposals are consistent with basic rights. Technically, at least, parliament retains sole responsibility for adjusting its bills accordingly. Britain has adopted a similar halfway house. In theory, the legislature remains supreme but in practice MPs are unlikely to override a judicial opinion that a bill contradicts protected rights. In this way, sovereignty can be simultaneously defended and diluted.

Judicial independence and recruitment

Given the growing political authority of the judiciary, the question of maintaining its independence gains in importance. Liberal democracies accept judicial autonomy as fundamental to the rule of law but how is this independence to be achieved?

Security of tenure is of course important here. In Britain, as in the American federal judiciary, judges hold office for life during 'good behaviour'. America's constitution even stipulates that judges' pay 'shall not be diminished during their Continuance in Office'. Although the constitutional courts of Europe usually limit their judges to one term of seven to nine years, the position of the judge remains secure during this period.

But judicial autonomy depends on recruitment as well as security of tenure. If the selection of judges is controlled by politicians who appoint their own

placemen, the judiciary may just reinforce partisan authority, providing an integration rather than a separation of powers. This problem is particularly important when judicial tenure is short, limiting the period in which judges can develop their own perspective on the cases before them. Political systems have developed varying solutions to the issue of judicial selection; the main methods are shown in Figure 13.2.

At one extreme comes democratic election. This method is practised in some American states; it is certainly responsive, perhaps excessively so, to popular concerns (Bonneau and Hall, 2009). At the other extreme, co-option by judges already in post offers the surest guarantee of independence but can lead to a self-perpetuating elite. The danger is that the existing judges will seek out new recruits with an outlook resembling their own.

In between these extremes come the more conventional methods: appointment by the assembly, the executive and independent panels. The British government, for example, has recently ceded power of appointment to an independent commission, a decision justified by the relevant minister in the following way:

In a modern democratic society, it is no longer acceptable for judicial appointments to be entirely in the hands of a government minister. For example the judiciary is often involved in adjudicating on the lawfulness of actions of the executive. And so the appointments system must be, and must be seen to be, independent of government. (Falconer, 2006)

In practice, many countries now combine these orthodox methods, with the government choosing from a pool of candidates prepared by a professional body. In South Africa, for instance, the President of the Republic appoints senior judges after consulting

---

Figure 13.2 Methods of appointing judges

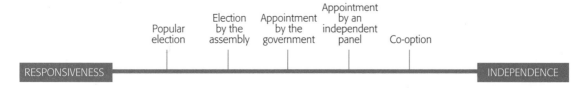

Popular election — Election by the assembly — Appointment by the government — Appointment by an independent panel — Co-option

RESPONSIVENESS — INDEPENDENCE

a Judicial Services Commission which includes representatives from the legal profession as well as the legislature.

Alternatively, and more traditionally, some judges on the senior court can be selected by one method while others are chosen by a different method. Thus, a third of the members of Italy's Constitutional Court are appointed by parliament in joint sitting, a third are nominated by the president and a third are selected by the judiciary itself.

For most courts charged with judicial review, selection still involves a clear political dimension. The stature of America's Supreme Court is such that appointments to it (nominated by the president but subject to Senate approval) are key decisions. Senate ratification can involve a set-piece battle between presidential friends and foes. In these contests, the judicial experience and legal ability of the nominee may matter less than ideology, partisanship and a clean personal history. Even so, Walter Dellinger, former acting US Solicitor General, argues that 'the political appointment of judges is an appropriate "democratic moment" before the independence of life tenure sets in' (Peretti, 2001).

A political dimension is also apparent in selection to constitutional courts. Typically, members are selected by the assembly in a procedure that can involve party horse-trading. For instance, eight out of the twelve members of Spain's Constitutional Court are appointed by the party-dominated parliament. In both America and Europe, then, political factors influence court appointments.

Below the level of the highest court, judicial autonomy raises the issue of **internal independence**. Guarnieri (2003, p. 225) emphasizes this theme. Noting that 'judicial organizations in continental Europe traditionally operate within a pyramid-like organizational structure', he argues that 'the role played by organizational hierarchies is crucial in order to highlight the actual dynamics of the judicial corps'. This issue arose in acute form in some Continental European countries after 1945,

when judges appointed under right-wing regimes continued in post, discouraging initiative by new recruits lower in the pyramid.

Guarnieri concludes that promotion and salary progression within the judiciary should depend solely on seniority, noting that such reforms were needed in Italy before younger 'assault judges' became willing to launch investigations into government corruption. Guarnieri's blanket solution may be extreme but, at any rate, it is important to recognize that the decisions of judges lower in the hierarchy will be influenced by any effects on their career prospects.

Administrative law

Where constitutional law sets out the fundamental principles governing the relationship between citizen and state, administrative law covers the rules governing this interaction in detailed settings. If a citizen (or other affected body) is in dispute with a public agency over a specific issue, such as obtaining a passport or eligibility for a welfare benefit, some standards must be developed enabling allegations of maladministration to be resolved. This task too has fallen to the judiciary; it is a role that grew massively in importance with the expansion of government in the twentieth century.

> **Administrative law** sets out the principles governing decision-making by public bodies and the remedies for breaching such rules. For example, America's Administrative Procedure Act (1946) requires courts to hold unlawful any agency action that is 'arbitrary, capricious, an abuse of discretion, or otherwise not in accordance with law'.

The issues involved here concern public law and have no clear analogy in the private sector. Typical questions asked in the area are:

▶ Competence: was an official authorized to make a particular decision?
▶ Procedure: was the decision made in the correct way (e.g. with adequate consultation)?
▶ Fairness: does the decision accord with natural justice?
▶ Liability: what should be done if a decision was incorrectly made or led to undesirable results?

> The **internal independence** of the judiciary refers to the autonomy of junior judges from their senior colleagues who often determine career advancement. Where this autonomy is limited, judicial initiative may be stifled.

How can administrative justice be realized? Liberal democracies handle the problem of legal regulation of the administration through a separatist or integrationist approach, with the chosen method reflecting and reinforcing differing conceptions of the state.

The first solution, common in codified legal systems, is to establish a separate system of administrative courts concerned exclusively with legal oversight of the bureaucracy. This **separatist approach** marks out a strong public sphere operating within a civil law framework. Where this approach is used, the work of civil servants is seen as legal in character, based on the uniform application of codes and leading naturally to judicial oversight.

> The **separatist approach** to administrative justice (as in France) is to establish special courts and laws to review the interaction between citizen and state. By contrast, the **integrationist approach** (as traditionally favoured in the United Kingdom) seeks to control the bureaucracy by reviewing disputes in ordinary courts, relying in large part on the ordinary law of the land.

France is the most influential example of the separatist model. It has developed an elaborate structure of administrative courts, headed by the Conseil d'État, founded in modern form in 1799 but with roots in the thirteenth century (Figure 13.3). The council is the final court of appeal within the hierarchy and also assesses administrative decisions

Figure 13.3 Administrative courts in France

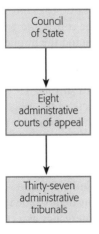

taken by government ministers and their officials as part of its original jurisdiction. This wide remit can lead to slow decisions, averaging about a year from inception to judgement.

Nonetheless, by developing its own case law, the Council has established general principles regulating administrative power. For example, it ruled in an asbestos case in 2004 that the state can be held responsible for failing to set appropriate standards protecting workers' health even if the employees affected work in the private sector. The Council's prestige, which exceeds that of the ordinary courts, expresses the autonomy of the public realm and also facilitates its capacity to check the executive.

The separatist solution speaks directly to the specific problems arising in public administration but runs the risk of boundary disputes over whether a case should be processed through administrative or ordinary courts. Such disputes can be especially awkward when, as is increasingly the case, a public task has been outsourced to a private contractor. Should a complaint about a private company allocating public housing under contract be processed by administrative or ordinary courts? In addition, special administrative courts reinforce a legalistic interpretation of public service which can lead to inflexible and unresponsive decision-making (as those with experience of the French bureaucracy will testify).

The second solution, favoured in Anglo-American countries with a common law tradition, reflects a less exalted view of public authority. The **integrationist approach** asserts that one set of courts should address both public and private law. The philosophy here is one law for all. That is, the same principles should span both sectors: for instance, employment in the public sector should be regulated by the same rules as apply to private firms. Ordinary courts should be able to arbitrate disputes between bureaucrats and citizens; no council of state is required.

One strength of this integrationist philosophy is that it prevents boundary disputes and simplifies the judicial system. Above all, the integrationist philosophy affirms a modest aspiration for the public realm; the state must abide by the same laws as its citizens. A. V. Dicey (1885) was the strongest exponent of this approach; his thinking was that special laws and courts for public business would in practice serve to advantage the government against the citizen.

In reality, special courts are rarely avoided entirely, even in the English-speaking world. The United States, for instance, has developed administrative courts dedicated to tax, military, bankruptcy and patent issues. Influenced by the strong public law tradition in the European Union, the United Kingdom introduced an Administrative Court in 2001 to provide judicial review of 'the decisions of inferior courts and tribunals, public bodies and persons exercising a public function' (Her Majesty's Court Service, 2005). Dicey seems to have lost this particular battle, defeated by the relentless expansion of regulation.

Note, however, that judicial review is only the final court of appeal for citizens protesting against an administrative decision. Normally, panels and tribunals closer to the decision offer an easier route of appeal. Thus, the first level of complaint is typically to an appeals panel operating within the department making the original decision. This can be followed by appeal to an external tribunal rather than a law court. These panels and tribunals review the substantive decision reached by the official, allowing the appellant to argue that the decision was wrong under the rules even if the correct rules were applied. By contrast, judicial review will normally focus solely on procedural issues – on whether the decision was reached by a competent official following the correct procedure.

Tribunals do have their strengths: they are inexpensive, cheap, flexible, substantive, informal and often speedy. They can also focus more on mediation and can redress the imbalance of legal knowledge between a government agency and a citizen, thus countering Dicey's concern about the inequality of expertise. So, in theory at least, the work of tribunals and courts should be complementary, with judicial intervention serving as a final court of appeal on matters of procedure.

However, tribunals themselves need to be seen to operate in a fair and consistent way, so just like the courts they tend to develop their own standards and rules. In effect, they too become a source of administrative law and a form of court, sometimes leading to complaints that they have become too formal and expensive to serve the practical purpose for which they were originally designed. Here, too, we see evidence of the inherent tendency for judicial authority to expand.

In some countries, citizens also have access to an ombudsman, a public official who can investigate a complaint about inadequate, if not illegal, behaviour by public authorities (see p. 357).

The twentieth-century expansion of government created not only new rights for citizens but also fresh opportunities for public servants to evade their obligations to those they serve. In a liberal state, administrative courts and tribunals make by their mere existence a worthwhile statement that public agents are expected to treat citizens fairly and reasonably. It is for such reasons that in 1982 Lord Diplock, a senior British judge, said that he regarded the development of administrative law 'as the greatest achievement of the English courts in my lifetime' (McEldowney, 2009, p. 3).

Law in authoritarian states

In authoritarian regimes, constitutions are feeble. The nature of such states is that any restraints on rule go unacknowledged; power, not law, is the political currency. As guardian of the law, the status of the judiciary is similarly diminished. In fact, it is often only in the transition to democracy that the old elite empowers the courts, seeking security for its own diminished future (Solomon, 2007).

Non-democratic rulers follow two broad strategies in limiting judicial authority. One tactic is to retain a framework of law but to influence the judges indirectly. Recruitment, training, evaluation, promotion and discipline procedures provide many opportunities for the regime to influence judges even while maintaining the facade of judicial independence.

In Indonesia, for example, the Ministry of Justice still administers the courts and pays judges' salaries; the justices understand the implications. More crudely, unsatisfactory judges can simply be dismissed. Egypt's President Nasser adopted this strategy with vigour in 1969. He got rid of 200 in one go: the 'massacre of the judges'. In Uganda, an extreme case, the killing was real rather than metaphorical; President Amin had his Chief Justice shot dead.

A second strategy, less subtle but to the point, is just to bypass the judicial process altogether. For instance, many non-democratic regimes use Declarations of Emergency as a cover to make

---

BOX 13.4

Article I of the Chinese constitution, 1982

1. The People's Republic of China is a socialist state under the people's democratic dictatorship led by the working class and based on the alliance of workers and peasants.
2. The socialist system is the basic system of the People's Republic of China. Sabotage of the socialist system by any organization or individual is prohibited.

Source: Tschentscher (2004).

---

decisions which are exempt from judicial scrutiny. In effect, a law is passed saying there is no law. Once introduced, such 'temporary' emergencies can drag on for decades.

Alternatively, rulers can make use of special courts that do the regime's bidding without much pretence of judicial independence; Egypt's State Security Courts are an example. Military rulers frequently extend the scope of secret military courts to include civilian troublemakers. Ordinary courts can then continue to deal with non-political cases, offering a thin image of legal integrity to the world.

Communist states offered a more sophisticated downgrade of constitutions and the judiciary. In Marxist theory, courts were viewed not as a constraint upon political authority but as an aid to the party in its mission of building socialism. Echoes of this perspective can still be found in official Chinese thinking. Like the Soviet Union, China has regularly introduced new constitutions, the fourth and most recent dating from 1982. Even though the current version begins by affirming the country's socialist status (Box 13.4), it is the least radical of the four. It seeks to establish a more predictable environment for economic development and to limit the ruling party's historic emphasis on class conflict, national self-reliance and revolutionary struggle. The leading role of the party is now mentioned only in the preamble, with the main text even declaring that 'all political parties must abide by the Constitution'. In the context of communist states, such a liberal statement is remarkable, even if it remains a poor

guide to reality. Amendments in 2004 gave further support to private property and human rights.

In addition to moderating the content of its constitution, contemporary China also gives greater emphasis to law in general. In the early decades of the People's Republic, legal perspectives were dismissed as 'bourgeois rightist' thinking. There were very few laws at all, reflecting a national tradition of unregulated power; the judiciary was essentially a branch of the police force. However, laws did become more numerous, precise and significant after the hiatus of the Cultural Revolution in the 1960s. In 1979, the country passed its first criminal laws; later revisions abolished the vague crime of counter-revolution and established the right of defendants to seek counsel. Law could prevail to the benefit of economic development.

Judges, too, have become more professional. By 2005, most judges were graduates, compared to only 7 per cent ten years earlier (Liebman, 2007). They now look to other legal decisions, and not always to the party elite, in forming their verdicts.

Reform notwithstanding, Chinese politics remains deeply authoritarian. Rule by law still means exerting political control through law rather than limiting the exercise of power. The courts are regarded as just one bureaucratic agency among others; legal judgements are not tested against the constitution and many decisions are simply ignored. Rulings are not published and difficult cases are often left undecided. Legal institutions remain less specialized, and legal personnel less professional, than in liberal democracies. Trial procedures, while improving, still offer only limited protection for the innocent. The death penalty remains in use, supposedly to strike hard against crime. The police remain largely unaccountable. Political opponents are still imprisoned without trial. Above all, party officials continue to occupy a protected position above the law. Politics continues to come first and power still trumps the constitution.

Law in illiberal democracies

By definition, constitutions and the law play second fiddle to elected authority in illiberal democracies.

The leader is elected within a constitutional framework but that environment has usually itself been shaped by the leader. More important, the exercise of power is rarely constrained by an independent judiciary. Rather it is the president who stands on high, defining the national interest under the broad authority granted to him by the voters:

How could it be otherwise for somebody who claims to embody the nation? In this view other institutions – such as congress and the judiciary – are nuisances that come attached to the domestic and international advantages or being a democratically elected president. Accountability to these institutions appears as an unnecessary impediment to the full authority that the president has been delegated to exercise (O'Donnell, 1994, p. 63).

Put differently, presidential accountability in an illiberal democracy is vertical (to the voters) rather than horizontal (to congress and the judiciary) (O'Donnell, 2003). In contrast to a liberal democracy, where the main parties have concluded that being ruled by law is preferable to being ruled by opponents, in an illiberal democracy the commanding figure still sees the constitution, the law and the courts as a source of political advantage. Legal processes operate more extensively than in authoritarian regimes but remain subject to political manipulation.

In Latin America, where illiberal democracy is common, several elected presidents have treated the constitution as a flexible document to be adapted to their own political needs. Many have sought to abolish term limits so that they can stand for re-election, providing a recurring source of tension between politics and the constitution.

Other South American constitutions have retained privileges for departing generals, thus perpetuating a sense of an additional institution remaining above the law. For instance, Chile's armed forces were initially granted immunity from prosecution in civilian courts, a tactic that effectively enabled former generals to escape justice for political murders committed during their tenure. In Argentina, similar legal exemptions dating from the 1980s formed a running political sore that festers to this day.

In addition to the difficulties of establishing the constitution as an effective political framework, the rule of law is held back throughout Latin America's illiberal democracies by deep-seated weaknesses in the judiciary. Prillaman (2000) chronicles the problems:

- Chronic inefficiency within the judicial system;
- The vulnerability of judges to political pressure;
- Inadequate and outdated laws;
- Insufficient resources and training;
- The public's lack of trust in legal remedies.

Judgements are slow to emerge and often ignored. The problem is circular: politicians are unwilling to grant real autonomy to an ineffective legal system, but until the judiciary acquires more responsibility its professionalism is unlikely to rise.

In many low-income countries with marked inequalities, the rule of law remains a distant idea. In some Latin America cities, the police probably commit almost as many crimes as they solve. Coordination between the police and judges is poor; sometimes both are in the pocket of drug barons. In Colombia, one in three judges received a death threat in the 1980s. Judges in Guatemala stand so directly in the firing line that they cannot obtain insurance (Dodson and Jackson, 2003, p. 248). In these conditions, informal arbitration, indigenous justice and lynchings may provide cheaper and faster remedies than appealing to a remote, ineffective and corrupt legal system.

However, the Russian experience shows that the law can gain ground, if only slowly and with difficulty, in at least some illiberal democracies. Russia's post-communist constitution of 1993 sets out an array of individual rights (including that of owning property); proclaims that 'the individual and his rights and freedoms are the supreme value'; and establishes a tripartite system of general, commercial and constitutional courts. The Constitutional Court, in particular, represented a major innovation in Russian legal thinking. Since 1993, the government has established detailed and lengthy codes appropriate for a civil law system. From 1998, criminal defendants who have exhausted all domestic remedies have even been able to appeal to the European Court of Human Rights (Sharlet, 2005, p. 147).

In contrast to many Latin America presidents, President Vladimir Putin supported the strengthening of law during his tenure. He was certainly not above selective use of the law for political ends but, as a law graduate once charged with promoting foreign investment in St Petersburg, he recognized the contribution that a coherent legal framework can make to economic revival. More to the point, he seemed to have calculated that uniform legal codes could help him to re-establish control over his country's corrupt bureaucrats and fragmenting republics while simultaneously strengthening Russia's international reputation.

Putin's youthful successor in the Kremlin, Dmitry Medvedev, was instinctively more sympathetic to the rule of law. Also a law graduate, he claimed that one purpose of a political system is precisely to ensure that judges can perform their functions independently (*Novaya Gazeta*, 2009).

Even in Russia, though, 'there has been and remains a considerable gap between individual rights on paper and their realization in practice' (Sharlet, 1997, p. 134). For instance:

- The conviction rate in criminal cases remains suspiciously high;
- Expertise and pay within the legal system are low, creating vulnerability to corruption;
- The police behave violently towards suspects;
- Conditions in prison are degrading;
- The state's responses to political violence, as in Chechnya, is brutal.

The further one treks beyond Moscow and St Petersburg, the larger the enforcement gap becomes. But we should be aware of judging the constitutional quality of post-communist Russia, and similar illiberal democracies, against contemporary Western standards. As Sharlet (1997, p. 134) reminds us:

While the Founding Fathers of the American republic quickly added the Bill of Rights to their newly ratified Constitution in the late eighteenth century, a number of these rights remained essentially 'parchment rights' and did not garner nationwide respect and judicial enforcement until well into the twentieth century. Is it surprising that Russia with its thousand-year authoritarian past and long tradition of legal nihilism should be

proceeding slowly in Rule of Law development? Surely it is more remarkable that Russia has made the progress it has, including in the uncharted territory of civil rights.

Legal pluralism

So far we have examined constitutions and law at the level of the territorial state. But law is found in other arenas, too: in the international system, in religious groups, in professional associations and in ethnic communities. The field of law supports a varied ecology and we need to introduce this diversity, with a particular eye on how different legal traditions interact within the same territory.

The key idea here is **legal pluralism**. The presence of multiple legal systems in a single territory complicates legal governance and creates potential conflicts between different codes. But it also offers individuals and groups the opportunity to live by laws expressing their own culture and identity. In this way, legal pluralism can support a multicultural society while also allowing actors to select a judicial forum appropriate to their situation (Melissaris, 2009).

Legal pluralism is the presence of more than one justice system within a single state. Examples include the coexistence of international and national law; of religious and secular law; and of indigenous and settler law (Griffiths, 1986).

As with other concepts in comparative politics, it is important to recognize their applicability to the past as well as the present. Religious and secular law inhabited their own spheres in pre-modern Europe, for instance, and the Catholic Church's Code of Canon Law runs to 250 pages. In a similar way, occupational guilds historically exercised considerable autonomy in recruiting, organizing and disciplining their members, often developing quasi-judicial committees and principles to help them in this task. Professional bodies, such as medical and indeed legal associations, continue in this fashion today. Legal pluralism is an established form of governance.

Nor should we suppose that the existence of non-state justice systems always raises acute or controversial problems. Individuals and organizations can agree to mediation and arbitration of disputes by chosen third parties, including private judges, if they so wish. For instance, two firms agreeing a contract, or two people entering a relationship, can agree in advance on a dispute-resolution procedure which they expect to be quicker, cheaper and perhaps more reliable than the standard judicial process. Indeed, the public courts can insist that these more informal mechanisms are employed first, thus producing an effective division of labour resembling that between tribunals and courts in administrative justice.

Three major sources of law which can impinge on national judicial systems are indigenous, Islamic and international law. We introduce each in turn.

Indigenous law

Indigenous communities in ex-colonies usually retain procedures and principles for resolving disputes which sit uneasily alongside the legal order imposed by the colonialists. In New Zealand, for instance, Maori norms of property ownership and inheritance differ from the conventional Western understanding of private property. Often, customary law is more concerned with the equilibrium of the community than with individual rights. In addition, it frequently supports retribution by the wronged as a valid way of restoring this balance.

Conflict between customary law, emphasizing community, and notions of human rights, emphasizing the individual, are not easily resolved. Throughout the Pacific region, these issues arise in relation to the rights of women, children and minorities and also in relation to the freedoms of speech, religion and movement.

The key to harmonizing indigenous law and human rights, suggests New Zealand's Law Commission (2006), is to focus on underlying values. For example, both traditions emphasize the inherent dignity of all people, although the ways in

> **Indigenous law** refers to the rules, norms and customs of groups native to an area, notably in former colonies. The United Nations Declaration on the Rights of Indigenous Peoples (2007) proclaims as a standard of achievement that 'indigenous peoples have the right to maintain and strengthen their distinct political, legal, economic, social and cultural institutions'.

which expression is given to this value differs. The Commission sees the creation of commentaries on customary law as an important method of educating judges and officials operating with the Western tradition. It regards such commentaries as preferable to recording custom in prescriptive codes – common-sense advice which nonetheless may reinforce the subordinate position of traditional customs.

Islamic law

The relationship between Islamic and national law is a particular issue in Muslim countries but also arises in the many non-Islamic societies with a Muslim minority (Shah, 2005). How far do governments in Muslim countries adopt Islamic law and how far are Muslims in non-Islamic countries subject to Islamic law?

> **Islamic law** is based on the Sharia, which is in turn derived from the Koran (Muhammad's revelations) and the Hadith (reports of what the prophet said and did). The Sharia and the Hadith are refined and adapted in Islamic jurisprudence, known as the *fiqh* (understanding of details). It is the *fiqh* that classifies all actions into one of five categories: obligatory, recommended, neutral, discouraged or forbidden.

The Sharia sets out the path for Muslims to follow. It is a code for life rather than a Western-style constitution: for example, 'liquor and gambling, idols and diving arrows are only a flighty work of Satan; give them up so that you may prosper'. Even so, severe punishments, pragmatically applied, are specified for those judged guilty against demanding standards of evidence.

As with all aspects of Islam, we should resist viewing Muslim legal thinking as a single, unchanging system. Some Muslim societies, such as Turkey and Uzbekistan, possess secular governments; others, such as Saudi Arabia, regard Islamic texts as their main source of law. Most Muslim countries fall in-between, with religious law coexisting alongside secular laws introduced by the state. Or Islamic law may apply only in certain territorial areas, such as some regions in Nigeria and parts of Pakistan.

Furthermore, like the justices of America's Supreme Court, Islamic legal scholars possess considerable flexibility to adapt and revise. In many ways, Islamic law is more 'an endless discussion on the duties of a Muslim' rather than a precise code implemented through the judicial system (Rahman, 1982, p. 32). Even when Sharia courts do exist, they are often confined to specific areas such as marriage and inheritance; secular courts cover a wider sphere of justice. In any case, the Sharia itself requires Muslims to obey secular laws, except when such rules require sinful acts. So legal pluralism is a possibility though, here more than elsewhere, pluralism implies pragmatism.

International law

International law is an additional component of legal pluralism in contemporary states. Traditionally, international law dealt only with the relations between states, but increasingly states have signed up to charters, conventions, declarations and covenants which create domestic obligations, for example in implementing human rights agreements.

Reflecting on this development, Held (2004, p. 125) judges that 'changes in the law of war, in human rights law, and in other legal domains have placed individuals, governments and non-governmental organizations under new systems of regulation – regulation which, in principle, recasts the legal significance of state boundaries'.

One way of integrating international agreements with national law is to pass a blanket provision stating that international law forms part of national law, even without any special mechanism of incorporation. Many constitutions are explicit on this point. Germany's constitution, for instance, states that 'the general rules of public international law are an integral part of federal law. They shall take precedence over the laws and shall create rights and duties for the inhabitants of the federal territory'.

International laws can apply directly to individuals, further complicating the legal environment within a state. The famous example here is the Nuremberg Charter used to try Nazi war leaders. Article 2 of the Charter declares:

The fact that internal law does not impose a penalty for an act which constitutes a crime under international law does not relieve the person who committed the act from responsibility under international law.

Article 4 goes on to state that:

The fact that a person acted pursuant to order of his Government or of a superior does not relieve him from responsibility under international law, provided a moral choice was in fact possible to him.

Since Nuremberg, the reach of international law into many less powerful states has extended. In the 1990s, the International Court of Justice set up new tribunals to try war crimes suspects from Rwanda and former Yugoslavia. In 1998, the Rwanda Tribunal became the first to convict a former head of state, Jean Kambanda, of crimes against humanity. The capacity of international legal norms to drive deeper into states may increase further with the development of the permanent International Criminal Court (ICC), established in The Hague in 2003 (Schabas, 2007).

Assessment

Legal pluralism creates both the possibility of conflicts and the means of reconciling them. For example, customary law may be based on the idea of male supremacy, a principle explicitly rejected in many national constitutions. But it is certainly impractical, and probably undesirable, to assimilate all legal orders to a single corpus of national law applying to every citizen within a territory. With legal systems, as with other dimensions of politics, coexistence is often possible with only limited conflict, particularly if each system of law is given priority in its own specialized domain (Berman, 2007). Just as governance builds on rather than replaces government, so legal pluralism can supplement the national constitution without threatening the latter's hallowed position.

> **International law** is traditionally defined as the system of rules which states (and other actors) regard as binding in their mutual relations. It derives from treaties, custom, accepted principles and the views of legal authorities. The term 'international law' was coined by the English philosopher Jeremy Bentham (1748–1832). Today, however, many international agreements create domestic obligations on states, for example, in limiting pollution.

Learning Resources for Chapter 13

Next step

Stone Sweet (2000) examines constitutional politics in five European political systems.

Further reading

Shapiro and Stone Sweet (2002) is a collection on political jurisprudence, including the United States, while Banks and O'Brien (2008) examine judicial policy-making. On the judiciary, Guarnieri and Perderzoli (2002) is a cross-national study. For the USA, D. O'Brien (2008a) examines the American Supreme Court; D. O'Brien (2008b) also usefully collates the views of American judges. Alter (2009) examines the European Court's political power. For the post-communist world, see Sadurski (2005) for constitutional courts in Eastern Europe. Peerenboom (2002) reviews China's long march towards the rule of law. Calleros-Alarcón (2008) assesses the judiciary in Latin America. Two books with a political perspective on administrative law are Hall (2005) for the USA and Loveland (2004) for the UK. Shah (2005) examines legal pluralism in the context of ethnic minorities.

Internet sources

Constitution Finder
Constitutions and charters
http://confinder.richmond.edu/

European Court of Justice
The official site and links to national sites
http://curia.europa.eu/

International Criminal Court
The official site
http://www2.icc-cpi.int/

Political Database of the Americas
Constitutions and much more in the Americas, North and South
http://pdba.georgetown.edu/Constitutions/constudies.html

Universal Declaration of Human Rights
The 1948 Declaration
http://www.un.org/en/documents/udhr/

www.palgrave.com
Companion Website
Visit the Companion Website to
'click and go'
www.palgrave.com/politics/hague

Chapter 14
Multilevel governance

Governance always incorporates a spatial dimension. Rulers need to extract resources from their territory while also retaining the willingness of the population to remain within the state's orbit. To achieve these ends, the modern state consists of an intricate network of organizations, typically consisting of the central government, its offices and representatives in the field, regional governments, and local authorities. The European Union provides an additional tier for its member countries. In examining the relationships between these layers, we seek to put flesh on the bones of the governance concept.

We begin by introducing the idea of multilevel governance, a term which seeks to capture the complexities of relationships across government levels. We then examine the federal solution to the territorial organization of power before turning to the special case of the European Union. This section is followed by a discussion of unitary states and the regional level within them. We then explore local government, the lowest tier in both federal and unitary states, and we conclude by examining the less intricate and more personal nature of central–local relations in authoritarian states and illiberal democracies.

Introducing multilevel governance

Multilevel governance is the term used to describe how policy-makers and interest groups in liberal democracies find themselves discussing, persuading and negotiating across multiple tiers, seeking to deliver coherent policy in specific functional areas such as transport and education. Where multilevel governance predominates, a policy-maker in a central department of education will spend more time on vertical relationships, talking to people from different tiers within the same field, than on horizontal coordination, engaged in discussion with people at the same level but working in a different policy area (Figure 14.1).

Communication is not confined to officials working at the same or adjacent level. Rather, international, national, regional and local officials in a given sector will form their own policy networks, with interaction across all

Multilevel governance applies the ideas of pluralism (see p. 231) and policy networks (see p. 233) to the relationships between tiers of government. It emerges when practitioners from several levels of government share the task of making regulations and forming policy, usually in conjunction with relevant interest groups (Hooghe and Marks, 2001). The term is commonly used in the European Union, whose presence adds a supranational tier to, and strengthens, existing governance networks within member states.

Figure 14.1 Coordination within and across tiers of government

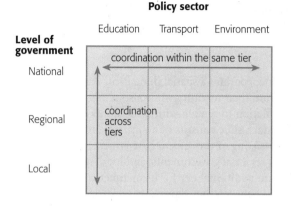

tiers. Thus, the leaders of major cities within EU countries will negotiate directly on matters of concern with the European Commission as well as with and through their national governments. The use of the term 'governance' rather than 'government' directs our attention to these relationships between institutions.

The idea of multilevel governance carries a further implication. It acknowledges that actors from a range of sectors – public, private and voluntary – help to regulate contemporary societies. Policy networks extend beyond officials working at different levels in the state. In education, for example, the central department will want to improve educational attainment in schools but to achieve its target it will need not only to consult lower tiers within the public sector (such as education boards) but also wider interests such as parents' associations, teachers' unions, private sector suppliers and educational researchers.

In fact, the multiple tiers of government involved in policy-making give more points of access and influence for these private groups. So the concept of multilevel governance denotes a pluralistic pattern of policy-making whose participants include relevant interest groups. The resulting networks resist hierarchical political control.

One strength of the concept of multilevel governance is its flexibility, particularly in embracing the international dimension. The European Union and intergovernmental entities such as the United Nations, the G20 and the International Monetary Fund provide an additional tier of governance, providing arenas where policies from climate change to bankers' bonuses are agreed, to be implemented (if not ignored or diluted) at national level. Older terms such as federal and unitary government, developed to describe institutions within states, do not extend as naturally in this way.

Rather like the concept of pluralism, multilevel governance can be portrayed in a positive or negative light. On the plus side, it implies a pragmatic concern with finding solutions through give-and-take among affected interests. On the negative side, it points to a complicated form of governance among insider groups, a form which resists both democratic control and penetration by less mainstream groups and thinking. Multilevel governance is a fashionable term but its popularity should not lead us to assume that the form of rule it describes is optimal.

Understanding multilevel governance requires an appreciation of the resources which each tier brings to the table. Typically, the representatives from the centre will possess larger budgets, strong political backing on high profile issues and the authority that flows from a national perspective. But, just like interest groups, officials from lower levels will possess their own power cards: detailed knowledge of the problem and the ability to judge the efficacy of the remedies proposed. If lower tiers are both resourced and enthused, they are in a position to make a difference; if not, they may lose interest, limiting the ability of the centre to achieve its policy goals.

It would be wrong to infer that power in multilevel governance is just the ability to persuade. Communication still operates in a constitutional framework that provides both limits and opportunities for representatives from each tier. If the constitution allocates responsibility for education to central government, local authorities are unlikely to build new schools until the Ministry of Education signs the cheque. Thus the formal allocation of responsibilities remains the rock on which multilevel governance is constructed. Multilevel governance develops from, without replacing, government.

BOX 14.1

The allocation of functions in the Canadian and German federations

	Canada	Germany
Exclusive jurisdiction (federal level)	The federal government exclusively controls 29 functions, including criminal law, the currency and defence.	The federal government's responsibilities include defence, citizenship and immigration.
Exclusive jurisdiction (provincial level)	The provinces control 'all matters of a merely local or private nature', including local government.	Few specific powers are explicitly granted to the *Länder* (states) which nonetheless implement federal laws 'in their own right'.
Concurrent jurisdiction (functions shared between levels)	Both the national and provincial governments can pass laws dealing with agriculture and immigration.	Concurrent powers include criminal law and employment. A constitutional amendment in 1969/70 created a new category of joint tasks, including agriculture.
Residual powers (the level responsible for functions not specifically allocated by the constitution)	The national parliament can make laws for the 'peace, order and good government of Canada'.	Any task not otherwise allocated remains with the *Länder*.

Note: Extensive reforms to the German constitution in 2006 sought to reduce the overlap in responsibilities between federal and *Länder* governments.

Federalism

Federalism is a form of multilevel governance which shares sovereignty, and not just power, between governments within a single state. It is a constitutional device, presupposing a formal political agreement establishing both the levels of government and their spheres of authority. So, like the constitutions within which they are embedded, **federations** are always a deliberate creation. In such a system, legal sovereignty is shared between the federal (or national) government and the con-

> **Federalism** (from the Latin *foedus*, meaning treaty) is the principle of sharing sovereignty between central and state (or provincial) governments; a **federation** is any political system that puts this idea into practice. A **confederation** is a looser link between participating countries which retain their separate statehood.

stituent subunits (often called states or provinces).

The key point about a federal partnership is that neither tier can abolish the other. It is this protected position of the states, not the extent of their powers, that distinguishes federations (such as the USA and Canada) from unitary governments (such as the UK and France). Multiple levels of government are integral to a federation, whereas in a unitary system sovereignty resides solely with the centre, with lower levels existing at its pleasure.

The constitution of a federal state allocates specific functions to each tier. The centre takes charge of external relations – defence, foreign affairs and immigration – and some common domestic functions such as the currency. The functions of the states are more variable but typically include education, law enforcement and local government. Residual powers often lie with the states, not the centre (Box 14.1). In nearly all federations, the states have a guaranteed voice in national policy-making through an upper chamber of the assembly. In that

Table 14.1 **Some major federations in liberal democracies**

	Year established as a federation	Area, thousand sq. km (rank in world)	Population, million (rank in world)	Number of states in federation
United States	1789	9,826 (9)	307 (4)	50
Switzerland	1848	41 (143)	8 (95)	26
Canada	1867	9,984 (8)	33 (39)	10
Brazil	1891	8,512 (11)	198 (6)	26
Australia	1901	7,687 (6)	21 (55)	6
Germany	1949	357 (69)	82 (17)	16
India	1950	3,288 (14)	1,166 (2)	28
Belgium	1993	30 (147)	10 (79)	3

Source: CIA (2009) for area and population.

chamber each state normally receives equal, or nearly equal, representation. The American Senate, with two senators per state, is the prototype.

The natural federal structure is for all the states within the union to possess identical powers under the constitution. However, some federations are less balanced. Asymmetric federalism arises when some states within a federation are given more autonomy than others, typically in response to cultural differences. Canada is a prime example. There, Quebec nationalists have long argued for special recognition for their French-speaking province; they view Canada as a compact between two equal communities (English- and French-speaking) rather than a contract between ten equal provinces.

Although asymmetric federalism is an understandable response to differences in power and culture between regions, the solution carries its own danger: a spiral of instability can develop as the less favoured states seek the status already granted to more privileged provinces.

Federations must be distinguished not just from unitary states but also from a less common format: **confederation**. In a confederation, the central authority remains the junior partner, acting merely as an agent of component states which retain their own sovereignty. So a confederation is more than an alliance but less than a federation. The classic case is the short-lived system adopted in 1781 in what is now the United States. The weak centre, embodied

in the Continental Congress, could neither tax nor regulate commerce and lacked direct authority over the people. It was the feeble nature of these Articles of Confederation that led to the creation of the federal United States in 1787.

Federalism is a recognized solution to the problem of organizing the territorial distribution of power. Elazar (1996, p. 426) counted 22 federations in the world, containing some two billion people or 40 per cent of the world's population (for some major examples see Table 14.1). Federalism is particularly common in large countries, whether size is measured by area or by population. Four of the world's largest states by area are federal: Australia, Brazil, Canada and the United States. In India, 10 out of 25 provinces each contain more than 40 million people; a federal arrangement is probably the only way to integrate such a large and varied country. Germany, Europe's largest country by population, exemplifies federalism on that continent.

There are two routes to a federation: first, by creating a new central authority ('coming together'); second, by transferring sovereignty from an existing national government to lower levels ('holding together'). Bryce (1919, p. 350) observed that 'federalism is an equally legitimate resource whether it is adopted for the sake of tightening or for loosening a pre-existing bond'. In practice, however, the tie is more often tightened than loosened; federalism almost always emerges as a compact between previously separate units combining to pursue a common interest. The United States, for instance, emerged from a meeting of representatives from 13 separate American states in 1787. Similar conventions, strongly influenced by the American experience, took place in Switzerland in 1848, Canada in 1867 and Australia in 1897/98.

So far, restructuring as a federation to hold a divided country together is a rare occurrence. Belgium is the main example. First established in 1830, Belgium has been beset by divisions between its French-speaking and larger and wealthier Dutch-speaking region. Constitutional revisions in 1970 and 1980 devolved more power to these separate groups. In 1993, the country finally proclaimed itself a federation comprising three main parts: first, pre-dominantly French-speaking Wallonia (which includes a small German-speaking community); second, Dutch-speaking Flanders; third, the Brussels region, centred on the bilingual but mainly French-speaking capital (Map 14.1). Thus far, the Belgian experience does suggest that federation can be an alternative to disintegration, a lesson of value to other states confronting internal divisions with a spatial dimension (Brans *et al.*, 2009).

What, then, provokes distinct peoples to set out on the journey to a federation? Motives are more often negative than positive; fear of the consequences of remaining separate must overcome the natural desire to preserve independence. Thus, Rubin and Feeley (2008, p. 188) suggest that federalism becomes a solution when, in an emerging state, 'the strong are not strong enough to vanquish the weak and the weak are not strong enough to go their separate ways'.

Historically, the most common incentive for coming together has been to secure the military and economic bonus of size, especially in response to strong competitors. Riker (1975, 1996) emphasized the military factor, arguing that federations emerge in response to an external threat. The American states, for instance, joined together partly because they felt themselves to be vulnerable in a predatory world.

However, economic factors have also encouraged federal formations. Both Australian and American federalists felt that a common market would promote economic activity. But just as the military case for forming new federations is currently rather

Map 14.1 Belgium

weak, given the paucity of orthodox wars, so federation is a convoluted way of securing gains from trade. Straightforward free trade areas (FTAs) between neighbouring countries are proving to be a more popular way forward. Unlike federations, FTAs such as the North American Free Trade Agreement entail no loss of sovereignty.

Military and economic arguments for forming new federations may have weakened but interest in ethnic federalism has grown. The Belgian experience shows that federations are useful for bridging ethnic diversity within a divided society; they are a device for incorporating such differences within a single political community. People who differ by descent, language and culture can nevertheless seek the advantages of membership in a shared enterprise. Thus, Switzerland integrates 23 cantons, two and a half languages (German and French, plus Italian) and two religions (Catholic and Protestant) into a stable federal framework.

Yet there is a danger in ethnic federations: namely, that they merely reinforce the divisions they were designed to accommodate. This risk is particularly acute when only two communities are involved. In these conditions, the gains of one group are the visible losses of another and the majority community may still be able to impose its will, defeating the original object of diffusing power. Citing Pakistan and Czechoslovakia, Watts (2005, p. 234) suggests that 'bipolar federations have invariably experienced serious tensions, instability and a high failure rate'. Even in Belgium, usually judged to be a federal success story, Deschouwer (2005, p. 105) reports that 'the granting of autonomy to the language groups ... has increased and deepened the differences between both communities and regional entities'. Federations may be more effective when they cut across, rather than entrench, ethnic divisions, thus marginalizing rather than reinforcing social divisions.

Dual and cooperative federalism

It is helpful to distinguish between dual and cooperative federalism. The former represents the federal spirit and remains a significant theme in American culture; the latter is an important ideal within European thinking and moves us closer to the realities of multilevel governance in contemporary federations.

Reflecting the original federal principle as conceived in the United States, **dual federalism** implies that the national and state governments operate independently, each tier acting autonomously in its own sphere, and linked only through the constitutional compact. Bryce (1919 p. 425) offered the image of two sets of machinery working well precisely because they avoid contact – the exact opposite of multilevel governance. In the circumstances of eighteenth-century America, such separation was a plausible objective; extensive coordination between federal and state administrations was judged to be neither necessary nor feasible.

Perhaps always a myth, dual federalism has long since disappeared, overwhelmed long before the arrival of terrorist threats by the demands of an integrated economy and world war. Even so, it expresses an implicit if unrealizable strand in federal thinking. Just as democracies are often judged against an unrealistic model of direct self-

> As originally envisaged in the USA, **dual federalism** meant that national and state governments retained separate spheres of action. Each level independently performed the tasks allocated to it by the constitution. **Cooperative federalism**, as practised in Germany, is based on collaboration between levels. National and state governments are expected to work together as partners in pursuing the interests of the whole.

government, so contemporary federations are often found wanting against the unattainable ideal of independent tiers.

The second approach is **cooperative federalism**. This interpretation is favoured in the main by European federations, especially Germany and German-influenced Austria. While federalism in the USA is based on a contract in which the states join together to form a central government with limited functions, the European form rests on the idea of cooperation between levels. Such solidarity expresses a shared commitment to a united society, binding the participants together. The moral norm is solidarity and the operating principle is **subsidiarity**: the idea that decisions should be taken at the lowest feasible level. The central government offers overall leadership but implementation is the duty of lower levels: a division rather than a separation of tasks.

> **Subsidiarity** is the principle that no task should be performed by a larger and more complex organization if it can be executed as well by a smaller, simpler body. The tenet emerged from Catholic social thought, where it was invoked to defend the role of the Church and voluntary associations against the encroachments of the welfare state.

Consider, for example, the German federation. Imposed by the Allies in 1949 as a constitutionally entrenched barrier against dictatorship, federalism represented a return to the country's strong regional roots (Gunlicks, 2003). It is reflected in the country's official title, the Federal Republic of Germany: under the Basic Law, Germany's federal character cannot be amended. Federalism quickly became an accepted part of the post-war republic.

From its inception, the German federation was based on interdependence, not independence. All the *Länder* (states) are expected to contribute to the success of the whole; in exchange, they are entitled to respect from the centre. The federal government makes policy but the *Länder* implement it, a division of administrative labour expressed in the constitutional requirement that 'the *Länder* shall execute federal laws as matters of their own concern'. Further, the constitution now explicitly defines some 'joint tasks', such as higher education, where responsibility is shared (Box 14.1).

Although German federalism remains far more organic than its American equivalent, its cooperative ethos has come under pressure from a growing perception that decision-making has become cumbersome and opaque. Accordingly, constitutional reforms finalized in 2006 sought to establish clearer lines of responsibility between Berlin and the *Länder*, for example by giving the states more autonomy in education and environmental protection. Although this package represents a move away from cooperative federalism towards greater subsidiarity, consultation remains embedded in German political practice. Multilevel governance cannot be legislated away, especially in a collaborative federation such as Germany.

An evolving balance

In most federations, the central government tended to gain influence for much of the twentieth century. Partly, this trend reflected the centre's financial muscle. The flow of money became more favourable to the centre as income tax revenues grew with the expansion of both the economy and the workforce. Income is mainly taxed at national level because otherwise people and corporations could move to low-tax states. By contrast, the states had to depend for their own independently raised revenue on sales and property taxes, a smaller and less dynamic revenue base.

The federal government now receives the lion's share of total public revenue, redistributing some of this money to the provinces through grants of various kinds (Box 14.2). In the USA, for instance, the centre's share of total government spending grew from 17 per cent in 1929, before the depression, to an estimated 54 per cent in 2009 (usgovernmentrevenue.com, 2009).

But the enhanced authority of the centre in federal systems was more than a financial matter. It also reflected the emergence of a national economy demanding overall coordination. Clearly, planning is needed to forestall the absurdity of highways ending at a state's borders or villains being expelled from a state rather than arrested there. When California experienced an electricity shortage in 2000, the federal government inevitably became involved as the state began to draw in power from surrounding areas. Over the twentieth century, the broader expansion of public functions also worked to the

BOX 14.2	
Financial transfers from the federal government to states	
Categorical grant	For specific projects (e.g. a new hospital).
Block grant	For particular programmes (e.g. medical care).
Revenue-sharing	General funding which places few limits on the recipient's use of funds.
Equalization grant	Used in some federations (e.g. Canada and Germany) in an effort to harmonize financial conditions between the states. Can create resentment in the wealthier states.

centre's advantage. Wars and depressions invariably empowered the national government. Such additional powers, once acquired, tended to be retained. In European federations, the post-1945 drive to complete a uniform welfare state based on national citizenship enhanced the national government still further.

From the 1980s, however, the trends became less clear cut. On the one hand, big projects run by the centre went out of fashion, partly because national governments found themselves financially stretched in eras of lower taxation and, latterly, financial crisis. Reflecting this trend, a number of courts also made some effort to encourage state autonomy. In the USA, a more conservative Supreme Court used the rights of states to strike down a number of congressional laws. For instance, in *United States* v. *Lopez* (1995) the justices declared unconstitutional a federal law banning possession of a gun within 1,000 feet of a school. Such matters were judged to be a state preserve.

On the other hand, the centre still sought to provide overall direction. Most obviously, in the twenty-first century national governments have led the response to the terrorist threat. In the USA, 'national control of domestic security eliminates a great deal of the discretion available to state and local government in areas that have previously been

CANADA

Form of government ■ a federal parliamentary democracy with ten provinces. Most Canadians live in Ontario or Quebec. A governor general (since 2005, the Haiti-born Michaëlle Jean) serves as ceremonial figurehead.

Legislature ■ the 308-seat House of Commons is the lower chamber. Unusually for a federation, the 105 members of the Senate, the upper chamber, are appointed by the prime minister rather than selected by the provinces.

Executive ■ the prime minister leads a cabinet whose members he selects with due regard for provincial representation.

Judiciary ■ Canada employs a dual (federal and provincial) court system, headed by a traditionally restrained Supreme Court. In 1982 the country introduced the Canadian Charter of Rights and Freedoms.

Electoral system ■ a plurality system with single-member districts. This produces large swings and distortions. Interest in electoral reform has developed in the provinces but not yet at national level.

Party system ■ the major parties are the Conservative Party of Canada and the Liberals. The Conservatives reunited in 2003 after a period of division and have formed a minority government since 2006. The other significant parties are the Bloc Québécois (BQ) and the left-wing New Democratic Party (NDP) (see Table 10.1 on p. 182).

Population (annual growth rate): 33.5m (+0.8%)
World Bank income group: high income
Political Rights score: ❶
Civil Liberties score: ❶
Human development index (rank/out of): 4/177
Freedom of the press index (rank/out of): 25/195
Perceived transparency index (rank/out of): 9/180

Note: For meaning and sources of scales and indexes, see p. xv. In all cases a score and rank of 1 is 'best'.

CANADA is a large country with a relatively small population. Its land mass is the second largest in the world but its population is little more than a tenth of its powerful American neighbour. Most Canadians live in urban settlements in a 100-mile strip bordering the United States. The country's economy depends heavily on the USA, a relationship reinforced by the formation of the North American Free Trade Agreement in 1994.

The United States therefore provides a natural contrast. Although both countries are settler societies, Canada never experienced America's radical break with the colonial power. The basis of its constitution remains the British North America Act (1867), now redesignated the Constitution Act. Not until the Constitution Act of 1982 was authority to amend the constitution returned to

Canada; indeed, the country's governor general is still formally appointed by the British monarch.

Where the American constitution is based on a philosophy of limiting government to protect the liberty of states and individuals, Canada's federation is more centralized and, unusually, operates within a parliamentary system in which members of the upper chamber are not selected by the provinces. The country has experienced neither slavery nor civil war; it has also followed a more orthodox path in policy development, with extensive public services premised on the principle of equality. In many senses, Canada is the more typical democracy.

In common with both the USA and Britain, Canada uses a plurality electoral system. However, the major parties (Liberal and Conservative) are more

American than British in organization and philosophy: they are election-fighting entities lacking a mass membership and strong central organization. They never acquired the sharp ideological differences which once characterized Britain's Conservative and Labour parties; as in the USA, the spoils of office were the prize for which the parties competed.

Yet, Canada's major parties receive less legal protection than their American equivalents and the Conservatives were reduced to a low ebb in the 1990s as the regional dimension intruded, with a populist party gaining support from dissatisfied voters in the resource-rich west. After reunification in 2003, the retitled Conservative Party of Canada was able to form a minority government in 2006. It was re-elected, again with a minority of seats, in 2008.

Further reading: Bickerton and Gagnon (2004), Brooks (2007).

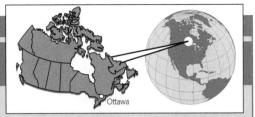
Ottawa

Federalism in Canada

The federal constitution of 1867 gave priority to Canada's national government, reserving to the provinces 'matters of a merely local or private nature'. As this phrase suggests, the document's authors thought of the provinces as little more than glorified municipalities. Since then, however, 'Canada has moved from a highly centralized political situation to one of the most decentralized federal systems in the world' (Landes, 1998, p. 102). What accounts for this transformation?

Canada's decentralizing trend, perhaps unique among federations, reflects the central issue of its politics: the place of French-speaking Quebec. From the sixteenth century, France and then Britain colonized the territories of Canada, inhabited at that time by around ten million indigenous people. Britain finally defeated the French in 1759. In contrast to the racial division in the USA, where blacks do not comprise a majority in any state, about 90 per cent of Canada's francophones live in Quebec and about 85 per cent of Quebec's population speaks French (Brooks, 2009, p. 196). Canada therefore provides a test case of federalism's ability to integrate a geographically concentrated minority.

For many Francophones, Canada consists of two founding peoples – the British and French – whose status should be equal. The assumption is that the country is a compact between two cultures rather than ten provinces. The conclusion is that Quebec, as a representative of one of the founding cultures, should receive

special recognition within the federation.

From the 1960s a revived nationalist party in Quebec sought to implement this vision. However, the federal response has been to decentralize power to all ten provinces, not just to Quebec. In Quebec itself, the Parti Québécois (PQ), elected to power in 1994, held a provincial referendum in 1995 on 'sovereignty association' for Quebec. This scheme would have

combined political sovereignty for Quebec with continued economic association with Canada. The proposal lost by the narrowest of margins. Subsequently, the issue of constitutional reform declined in intensity, with the PQ voted out of provincial office in 2003. However, in 2006, the House of Commons did declare that the Québécois 'form a nation within a united Canada'.

Multilevel governance, known in Canada as executive federalism, continues to operate even during these phases of intense debate over the

position of French-speaking Canada. As Brooks (2009, p. 204) puts it, 'divided jurisdiction has given rise to a sprawling and complicated network of relations linking the federal and provincial governments. This network is often compared to an iceberg, only a small part of which is visible to the eye'.

Although multilevel governance is often viewed favourably in the European Union, the secrecy and

unclear accountability of executive federalism in Canada have sparked significant criticism. In the context of a state with clear democratic traditions, executive federalism lacks any explicit base in law and the constitution. Even so, the practices of multilevel governance are surely an inherent feature of Canada's distinctive but long-lasting federation.

Further reading: Bakvis and Skogstad (2002), Stevenson (2009).

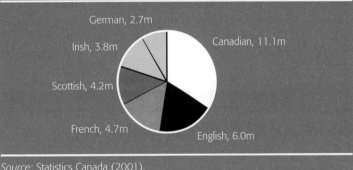

Self-reported ethnic origin of the population (six largest groups), 2001

German, 2.7m
Irish, 3.8m
Canadian, 11.1m
Scottish, 4.2m
French, 4.7m
English, 6.0m

Source: Statistics Canada (2001).

left free of federal interference' (Albritton, 2006, p. 14). Times of crisis overwhelm the niceties of federalism.

Any review of the changing balance between the tiers of a federation will show variation over time, reflecting both financial and political developments. Such changes indicate flexibility rather than instability; they are a means of adjustment which enhances the stability of the core federal bargain. Like constitutions, federations are reinterpreted for each generation. But where constitutions are adapted through the courts, federations also evolve through the murkier and more political means of multilevel governance. This manner of evolution may lack legitimacy but still enhances underlying stability.

Assessing federalism

What conclusions can we reach about the federal experiment (Box 14.3)? The case for federalism is that it offers a natural and practical arrangement for organizing large states. It provides checks and balances on a territorial basis, keeps some government functions closer to the people and allows for the representation of ethnic differences.

Federalism reduces overload in the national executive while the existence of multiple provinces produces healthy competition and opportunities for experiment. The states can move ahead even when the federal level languishes: early in the twenty-first century, for example, California and some other American states showed more concern with climate change than did the federal government.

Citizens and firms also have the luxury of choice: if they dislike governance in one state, they can always move to another. Above all, federalism reconciles two modern imperatives, securing the economic and military advantages of scale while retaining, indeed encouraging, cultural diversity.

But a case can also be mounted against federalism. Compared to unitary government, decision-making in a federation is complicated, slow-moving and indecisive. When a gunman ran amok in Tasmania in 1996, killing 35 people, federal Australia experienced some political problems before it succeeded in tightening gun control uniformly across the country. By contrast, unitary Britain acted speedily when a comparable incident occurred in the same year at a primary school in Dunblane, Scotland.

BOX 14.3

Federalism: strengths and weaknesses

Strength	Weakness
A practical arrangement for large countries	May be less effective in responding to security threats
Provides checks and balances	Decision-making is slow and complicated: 'trouble, expense and delay' (Bryce, 1919, p. 341)
Allows for the recognition of diversity	Can entrench divisions between provinces
Reduces overload at the centre	The centre experiences greater difficulty in launching national initiatives
Provides competition between provinces and allows citizens to move between them	How citizens are treated depends on where they live
Offers opportunities for policy experiments	Complicates accountability: who is responsible?
Allows small units to cooperate in achieving the economic and military advantages of size	May permit majorities within a province to exploit a minority
Brings government closer to the people	Basing representation in the upper chamber on states violates the principle of one person, one vote

Federalism can place the political interests of rival governments above the resolution of problems. Fiscal discipline becomes harder to enforce; several Latin American federations have struggled to control their free-spending (and free-riding) provinces. Extravagant spending by provinces, aware that they will be bailed out if necessary by the centre, can dent the fiscal strength of the state as a whole (Braun *et al.*, 2003).

Any final judgement on federalism must take a view on the proper balance between the concentration and diffusion of political power. Should power rest with one body to allow decisive action? If we accept this perspective, federalism is likely to be seen as an obstacle and impediment – and even as an anti-democratic device. Alternatively, should power be dispersed so as to reduce the danger of majority dictatorship? Through this lens, federalism will appear as an indispensable aid to liberty.

The European Union: a special case

Our understanding of federalism can be usefully tested against the challenging case of the European Union (EU). Leaving aside opinion on whether the EU ought to develop as a federation, to what extent can this singular entity already be regarded as possessing a federal rather than a merely intergovernmental character?

The case for admitting the EU to the federal family is certainly substantial. Shared sovereignty is the core feature of federalism and by this test the Union already possesses a broadly federal status. Like the United States, the European Union has a strong legal basis in the treaties on which it is founded. The influential European Court of Justice, just like America's Supreme Court, adjudicates disputes between levels of government. In both cases, court decisions apply directly to citizens, must be implemented by member governments and take priority over state laws.

In both regions, citizens of the component parts are also citizens of the whole. British passports, for instance, are adorned with 'European Union' as well as 'United Kingdom'. Externally, the EU is directly represented in international bodies such as the United Nations and it maintains over 130 diplomatic missions. A directly elected parliament exercises increasing influence in EU affairs. As with the American national government, the Union has specific policy responsibilities, notably for the single market. These are hardly signs of a mere intergovernmental organization.

In short, in Europe – as in America – sovereignty is already pooled. It is only British intransigence that insisted on the name 'European Union' rather than 'European Federation'. McKay's judgement from 1999 (p. 220) is certainly still relevant: 'we can conclude that although, after the implementation of Maastricht (1992), the EU remains an unusual and still evolving political entity, it also qualifies as a species of federal state'.

Yet the points against interpreting the EU as a federation are also substantial. In particular, to describe the EU as a federation would be to exaggerate its cohesion. Contrasts with the American exemplar are again striking:

- ◆ The USA possesses a single currency and freedom of movement but these goals have only been partly achieved within the EU;
- ◆ The EU is still governed by treaties between states whereas the United States was founded on a constitution;
- ◆ Where the USA was designed as a federation from the start, the EU was built on agreeing concrete policies, particularly for a single market, with federation as a faded aspiration;
- ◆ Where the USA fought a civil war to preserve its union, the EU has not faced this vital test nor, without its own military force, is it in any position to do so;
- ◆ The EU possesses a unicameral parliament whereas the USA, like the legislature of other federations, is bicameral.

In addition, we should note four additional points against a federal interpretation of the Union. First, the EU does not tax its citizens directly. Its main revenue source is a levy on the gross national income of member states. Second, member states have retained national control of the vital areas of foreign and defence policy, including the use of armed force. Third, member states retain individual membership of intergovernmental bodies such as the United Nations. Fourth, if the EU were a true federation with a coherent central government,

---

BOX 14.4

Methods for distributing power away from the centre

	Definition	Example
Deconcentration	Central government functions are executed by staff in the field	Most US federal civilian employees work away from Washington, DC
Decentralization	Central government functions are executed by subnational authorities	Local governments administer national welfare programmes in Scandinavia
Devolution	Central government grants some decision-making autonomy to lower levels	Regional governments in France, Italy and Spain

Note: Deconcentration and decentralization occur in federal as well as unitary states.

Henry Kissinger would not need to have asked his famous question, 'when I want to speak to Europe, who do I telephone?'.

Overall, we can conclude that the EU represents some pooling of its members' sovereignty and consists of institutions through which sovereignty is exercised. In these respects, the Union is certainly more than an alliance yet, as in the early decades of the United States, its members retain much of their traditional autonomy. Fundamentally, the members are still separate states and are recognized as such in the international system. If the EU is to be seen as a federation, it is certainly unique in its distribution of powers between the centre and its members.

One possible compromise is to interpret the Union as confederal in character (Warleigh, 1998). Nugent (2006, p. 553) provides a summary of this position:

Insofar as the EU is a union of previously sovereign states created by treaty in which supranational institutions exist but whose range of powers fall short of the powers exercised by their counterparts in federal systems, it may be thought of as a confederation.

Unitary states

Most states are unitary, meaning that sovereignty lies exclusively with the central government. In this hierarchical arrangement, the national government possesses the theoretical authority to abolish lower levels. Subnational administrations, whether regional or local, may make as well as implement policy, but they do so by leave of the centre. As a result of central supremacy, the national legislature in most unitary states has only one chamber since there is no need for a second house to represent entrenched provinces.

Unitary frameworks emerge naturally in societies with a history of rule by sovereign monarchs and emperors, such as Britain, France and Japan. Unitary structures are also the norm in smaller democracies, particularly those without strong ethnic divisions. In Latin America, nearly all the smaller countries (but none of the larger ones) are unitary. The countries of Eastern Europe have also chosen a unitary structure for their post-communist constitutions, viewing federalism as a device through which Russia sustained its dominance in the old Soviet Union.

After the complexities of federalism, a unitary structure may seem straightforward and efficient. However, the location of sovereignty is rarely an adequate guide to political realities; unitary government is often decentralized in its operation. Indeed in the 1990s many unitary states attempted to push responsibility for more functions on to lower levels. In practice, unitary states, just like federations, are best viewed through the lens of multilevel governance.

We can distinguish three broad ways in which unitary states disperse power from the centre: deconcentration, decentralization and devolution (Box 14.4). The first of these, **deconcentration**, is

Table 14.2 Subnational government in some unitary states, number of units by tier

	France	Italy	Netherlands	Norway	Poland	Sweden
Highest tier ('regions')	22	20	12	19	16	18
Middle tier ('provinces')	96	94	–	–	308	–
Lowest tier ('communes')	36,565	8,074	1,496	434	2,500	289

Note: Figures are from the late 1990s to the early 2000s. Labels used for a given tier vary by country.

purely an administrative matter, denoting the movement of central government employees away from the capital. The case for deconcentration is that it spreads the work around, reduces costs by allowing activities to move to cheaper areas and frees central departments to focus on policy-making rather than execution. Routine tasks such as issuing passports can be deconcentrated to an area with higher unemployment and lower costs.

The second, and politically more significant, way of dispersing power is through **decentralization**. This term means that policy execution is delegated to subnational bodies such as local authorities. Scandinavia is the classic example. There, local governments put into effect many welfare programmes agreed at national level. In a similar way, local government in the UK serves as the workhorse of central authority, implementing plans formed at the centre.

The third and most radical form of power dispersal is **devolution**. This occurs when the centre grants decision-making autonomy (including some legislative powers) to lower levels. In the United Kingdom, devolved assemblies were introduced in Scotland and Wales in 1999. The Scottish parliament, for instance, now controls policy in such areas as health, education, local government, social work and housing.

Spain is another example of a unitary state with extensive devolution. Its regions were strengthened in the transition to democracy following General Franco's death in 1975, and devolution has continued apace since, with Catalonia's status as a distinct nationality recognized in 2006. At least in theory, though, the framework is still unitary.

So even after devolution, the contrast with federations remains. Britain remains a unitary state because these new assemblies could be abolished by Westminster through normal legislation. As the English politician Enoch Powell (1912–98) observed, 'power devolved is power retained'.

Regional governance

The creation and expansion of the middle tier of government – the regional level standing between central and local authority – was an important trend in many unitary states since 1945 (and especially since the 1970s). As a result of this development, unitary states such as France, Italy and Poland now possess three levels of subnational government: regional, provincial and local (Table 14.2). The result is a multilevel system that is even more intricate than the two levels of subnational authority – state and local – within a federation.

The political significance of regions, while certainly increasing, remains highly variable. At its weakest, a region can be merely a spatial unit constructed by the centre to present figures on differences within a country and policies to reduce them. Regional planning of this kind became common in Western democracies in the 1950s and 1960s, initially as part of post-war reconstruction (Bickerton and Gagnon, 2008, p. 385). In this limited sense, regions are constructs of the national government: modified, amalgamated and sometimes, if rarely, deleted at the behest of planners. The inhabitants may know little, and care less, about their regional identity.

In most large unitary states, however, regions soon acquired a more substantial administrative base. They became a vehicle through which the centre could decentralize planning, with regional bodies taking responsibility for economic development and related public infrastructure, notably transport.

These structures were not necessarily directly elected; indeed, they were typically created by a push from the centre rather than a pull from the regions.

For example, in England, the Labour government elected in 1997 established regional Government Offices to implement central policies, and Regional Development Agencies (RDAs) to develop regional development plans. These bodies are unelected, with limited budgets and low visibility. They are a mechanism of decentralization – a device for reducing overload at the centre.

In the other large European unitary states, the coordinating function of administrative regions has advanced further. Regions are providing a valuable **mesolevel** perspective below that of the country as a whole but above that of local areas.

A key factor influencing the development of regional institutions is whether they are, or become, directly elected. Election creates a system of regional assemblies and executives which transforms regional governance into regional government. As a result, the regional level becomes more visible but, for better or worse, political and partisan factors come to intrude more directly into multilevel governance.

> The **mesolevel** is the intermediate, typically regional, layer of government located between national and local levels. 'Meso' comes from the Greek *mésos*, meaning middle.

France is an example of this transition. The 22 regions established in France in 1972 initially possessed extremely limited executive powers. However, their status was enhanced by a decentralization law passed in 1982 providing for direct election. The first round of these elections took place in 1986. Even though French regional bodies continue to operate with small budgets, Balme (1998, p. 182) comments that they are becoming arenas in which policies are formed.

Similar transitions have occurred elsewhere in continental Europe, reflecting a belief (at least among elites) that citizen participation in regional self-rule is intrinsically desirable. The case for direct election is perhaps strongest where regions are already important cultural entities, providing a focus for citizens' identities. In the United Kingdom, for example, attempts by the Labour government to create elected regional assemblies in England

foundered on public apathy. But assemblies were successfully introduced to Scotland and Wales, where national loyalties were already well-established.

The EU has encouraged the development of a regional level within its member states. The European Regional Development Fund, established in 1975, distributed aid directly to regions, rather than through central governments. The notion, somewhat exaggerated but significant at the time, was that the EU and the regions would gradually become the leading policy-makers, outflanking central governments which would be left with less to do in this new disposition.

The EU furthered such aspirations by introducing a Committee of the Regions and Local Communities in 1988. This body, composed of subnational authorities, proved to be merely consultative, however. National executives remain more central to the policy process than some of the more committed proponents of multilevel governance in the EU had originally envisaged (Bourne, 2003). New levels have been added without the subtraction of old ones.

Developments such as these demonstrate that the exclusive focus of sovereignty at the national level within unitary states is an increasingly poor guide to the realities of making and implementing coherent public policy.

Local government

Local government is universal, found in federal and unitary states alike. It is the lowest level of elected territorial organization within the state. Variously called communes, municipalities or parishes, local governments are 'where the day-to-day activity of politics and government gets done' (Teune, 1995b, p. 16). For example, 9/11 was certainly a global event but it was New York City officials who faced the immediate task of providing emergency services. Local government is where the citizen meets the state.

At their best, local administrations express the virtues of limited scale. They can represent natural communities, remain accessible to their citizens, reinforce local identities, offer a practical education in politics, provide a recruiting ground to higher posts, serve as a first port of call for citizens and dis-

BOX 14.5

Exploring the status of local government

Higher	Lower	Comment
In *European* democracies	In *New World* democracies (e.g. Australia, USA)	In Europe local governments often represent historic communities, but in the New World local government is more utilitarian in character
In *Northern Europe* (e.g. Scandinavia)	In *Southern Europe* (e.g. France, Italy)	Local governments administer the extensive welfare states found in Northern Europe but perform fewer functions in Southern Europe
When local governments possess *general competence* to represent their community	When local governments cannot act *ultra vires* ('beyond the powers')	General competence allows local authorities to take the initiative whereas *ultra vires* restricts them to designated functions
In *unitary states*	In *federations*	In federations, local government is the preserve of the states, creating diversity in its organization and reducing coherence

tribute resources in the light of specialist knowledge. Yet local governments also have characteristic weaknesses. They are often too small to deliver services efficiently, lack financial autonomy and are easily dominated by traditional elites.

The balance struck between intimacy and efficiency varies over time. In the second half of the twentieth century, local authorities were encouraged to become more efficient and customer-led, leading to larger units. For example, the number of Swedish municipalities fell from 2,500 in 1951 to 274 in 1974 (Rose, 2004, p. 168).

But around the turn of the century signs began to emerge of a rebirth of interest in citizen involvement, stimulated by the need to respond to declining turnout. In New Zealand, successful managerial reforms introduced in 1989 were followed by the Local Government Act (2002). This law outlined a more expansive, and possibly expensive, participatory vision for local authorities. Similarly, 'in the early 1990s, Dutch local government was preoccupied with a concern for effectiveness and efficiency. During the 1990s, however, the emphasis switched to the issue of public responsiveness' (Denters and Klok, 2005, p. 65). Norway resolved in 1995 that 'no further amalgamations

should be imposed against the wishes of a majority of residents in the municipalities concerned' (Rose, 2004, p. 168).

Status

The status of local government varies markedly across countries (Box 14.5). Consider, first, the contrast between European and New World democracies. In most of Europe, local authorities represent historic communities that predate the emergence of strong national governments. The origins of many Italian communes, for instance, can be dated to the twelfth century. Reflecting this position, European constitutions normally mandate some form of local self-government. Sweden's Instrument of Government roundly declares that Swedish democracy 'shall be realized through a representative and parliamentary polity and through local self-government'.

In the New World, by contrast, local government reveals a more pragmatic, utilitarian character. Local authorities were set up as needed to deal with 'roads, rates and rubbish'. Special boards (appointed or elected) were added to deal with specific problems such as mosquito control, harbours and land drainage. The policy style was apolitical: 'there is no

Figure 14.2 Average population of elected local authorities (lowest tier) in selected European democracies

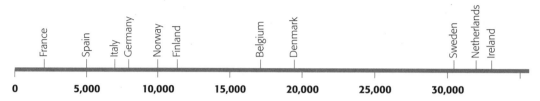

Note: Figures are from the late 1990s to 2003. Not shown: UK (137,000).

Sources: Adapted from John (2001), Denters and Rose (2005), Rose (2004).

Democratic or Republican way to collect garbage'. Indeed special boards were often set up precisely to be independent of party politics.

Second, the standing of local government varies within Europe on a broad north–south axis. In the northern countries, local authorities became important delivery vehicles for the extensive welfare states that matured after 1945. Services such as social assistance, unemployment benefit and education were funded by the state but provided locally, giving rise to such phrases as the welfare municipality and the local welfare state. In effect, local authorities became the government's front office, employing about one in four of the total workforce in Nordic countries (Rose, 2004, p. 169). In some countries, including Denmark, local authorities also act as tax collectors for the centre.

In southern Europe, by contrast, welfare states are less extensive, with the Catholic Church playing a greater role in providing care, while public services such as education remain under the direct control of the centre. In Italy, for instance, teachers are civil servants rather than employees of local councils. Also, communes in Southern Europe have remained small, especially in France (Figure 14.2). Limited scale precludes an extensive administrative role except when neighbouring areas form collaborative syndicates, as they often do, to supply utilities such as water and energy.

Third, **general competence** enhances both the authority and the standing of local authorities. Germany's Basic Law, for instance, gives local communities 'the right to regulate [all local matters] under their own responsibility and within the limits of the law'. The Dutch constitution states in a similar way that local communities have 'autonomous' powers to regulate their own affairs.

But in other countries, including the United Kingdom, councils could traditionally only perform those tasks expressly designated by the centre; any other act would be *ultra vires* (beyond the powers). In the United States, Dillon's Rule similarly restricts local governments to tasks delegated by their particular state. Some countries where *ultra vires* applies, including the United Kingdom and New Zealand, did establish a more liberal legal framework at the start of the twenty-first century but without granting the full power of general competence (Bush, 2005).

Fourth, local government tends to enjoy higher status in unitary states than in federations. The unitary nature of most European states allows direct links to form between powerful local administrations and the centre. By contrast, even in an era of multilevel governance, local authorities in federations tend to be creatures of the states, creating diversity but also reducing coherence. In these conditions local government is in constant danger of becoming the forgotten level.

Structure

The structure of local government has recently attracted attention, largely in an attempt to make

General competence is the authority of a local government to make regulations in any matter of concern to its area. Where general competence is lacking, local authorities are restricted to those tasks expressly mandated by higher authority.

BOX 14.6

Structures for local government

	Description	Examples
Council	Elected councillors form a council which operates through a smaller subgroup or through functional committees. The unelected mayor is appointed by the council or by central government.	Belgium, Netherlands, Sweden
Mayor–council	An elected mayor serves as chief executive. Councillors elected from local wards form a council with legislative and financial authority. This format is often subdivided into strong mayor and weak mayor systems.	About half the 7,000 cities in the USA, including Chicago and New York
Council–manager	The elected mayor and council appoint a professional manager to run executive departments.	About 3,000 American cities, including Dallas and Phoenix

Sources: Bowles (1998), Denters and Rose (2005), Mouritzen and Svara (2002).

---

decision-making clearer to local electorates in an era of falling turnout. In particular, efforts have been made to represent the mayor as the leading personification of the area. Just as political parties have sought to reverse a decline in membership by giving their supporters more say in the selection of candidates and leaders, so local governments in such countries as Italy, the Netherlands and the United Kingdom have encouraged turnout by experimenting with direct election of the mayor. A high profile mayor can enhance the area's visibility not just within the district itself but also, and equally importantly, among potential visitors and investors from outside. We see here a growing relationship between institutional design and the marketing of place.

There are, in fact, three broad ways of organizing local government: the council, mayor–council and council–manager formats (Box 14.6). The first and most traditional method concentrates authority in a college of elected councillors which is formally responsible for overseeing the organization's work. This full council often operates through powerful committees covering the main local services, as in Sweden and traditionally in England. In a slight variant, selected councillors and the mayor may combine to form a working body, as for example in Belgium and the Netherlands. In either case, the mayor is appointed by the council itself or by central

government. Whatever virtues this format may have, its collegiate character presents a rather opaque picture to the electorate; it is this council structure which has come under most scrutiny from reformers.

Accordingly, a second method of organization known as the mayor–council system has attracted attention. This model is more presidential than parliamentary. It is based on a separation of powers between an elected mayor, who is the chief executive, and an elected council with legislative and budget-approving powers. This highly political structure, used in many large American cities such as New York, permits a range of urban interests to be represented within its elaborate framework. The mayor and council often disagree, just as at national level the president is frequently in conflict with Congress. Again as at national level, the mayor is usually elected at large (from the entire area) while councillors represent specific neighbourhoods.

The powers awarded to the mayor and council vary considerably, defining strong mayor and weak mayor variants. In the strong mayor version, the mayor is the focus of authority and accountability, with the power to appoint and dismiss department heads without council approval. New York City is an example. In the weak mayor format, the council retains both legislative and executive authority, keeping the mayor on a closer leash. London's new mayor (directly elected since 2000) is a classic weak mayor, lacking the strong powers of his equivalent in New York (Sweating, 2003).

The third structure for local government, again originating in the United States, is the council–manager system. Unlike the mayor–council format, this arrangement seeks to depoliticize and simplify local government by separating politics from administration. This distinction is achieved by appointing a professional city manager, operating under the elected council and mayor, to administer the authority's work. Emerging in the USA early in the twentieth century in an attempt to curb corruption, the council–manager format has been widely adopted in the American west and south-west.

The model has corporate overtones, with the voters (shareholders) electing councillors (board of directors) to oversee a city manager (chief executive) who is responsible for cost-effective service delivery. However, the distinction between politics and administration is difficult to maintain in practice.

The enabling authority

What is it that local governments do? Broadly, their tasks are two-fold. The first is to provide an extensive and, for residents, significant range of local public services. These include libraries, local planning, primary education, provision for the elderly, refuse collection and water supply. The second task, more important in some countries than others, is the implementation of national welfare policies. However, a static description of functions fails to reveal how the role of local government has evolved since the 1980s, particularly in those countries where local authorities were traditionally large.

The major trend, especially prominent in the English-speaking world and Scandinavia, has been for municipal authorities to reduce their direct provision of services by delegating tasks to private organizations, both profit-making and voluntary. This transition from local government towards local governance reflects the emergence of new public management at national level (see p. 357). In Denmark, for example, many local governments set up user boards in primary schools. These boards were given block budgets and the authority to hire and fire staff (Bogason, 1996). In a similar way, private firms located in the commercial district of some American cities have taken over much of the responsibility for funding and organizing improvements to local services such as street-cleaning.

This transition is often presented as an evolution from providing to enabling. The **enabling authority** does not so much provide services as ensure that they are supplied. In theory, the authority becomes a smaller, coordinating body, more concerned with governance than government. More organizations become involved in local policy-making, many of them functional (e.g. school boards) rather than territorial (e.g. county councils). An increased concern with economic development, especially by attracting inward investment, often forms part of this more coordinating and strategic approach.

> The **enabling authority** is a term used to summarize one vision of local governance. Such an authority does not provide many services itself. Rather, its concerns are to coordinate the provision of services and to represent the community both within and beyond its territory. An enabling authority is strategic, contracting out service provision to private agencies, whether voluntary or profit-making.

Relationships with the centre

We must ask an additional question about local government: how is it integrated into the national structure of power? This question is key to appreciating the operation of multilevel governance within unitary states. The answer reveals cross-national contrasts in notions of public authority. In particular, the relationship between centre and locality usually takes one of two forms: dual or fused. Broadly, this distinction matches that between dual and cooperative traditions in federalism

In a **dual** approach, local government is seen as an organization separate from the centre: public authority is divided rather than integrated. It is as if there were two spheres of authority, connected for

> A **dual** system of local government (as in Britain) maintains a formal separation of central and local government. Although the centre is sovereign, local authorities are not seen as part of a single state apparatus. In a **fused** system (as in France), municipalities form part of a uniform system of administration applying across the country.

Figure 14.3 Multilevel governance in a unitary state: France

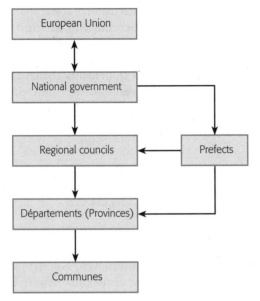

practical reasons only – an equivalent to dual federalism. Local governments retain free-standing status, setting their own internal organization and employing staff on their own conditions of service. Employees tend to move horizontally – from one local authority to another – rather than vertically, between central and local government. Ultimate authority rests with the centre, but local government employees do not regard themselves as working for the same employer as central civil servants. National politicians rarely emerge from local politics.

Traditionally, Britain was regarded as the best example of this dual system. Even though the country is unitary, with sovereignty focused on the centre, local government is regarded as more than a sub-branch of national authority. This separation reflects history. Even before the rise of the modern state, local magistrates administered their local communities. The spirit of self-government survives in a perception that central and local government are

A **prefect** is an official appointed by the central government to oversee the implementation of national policy in a particular area. The prefectoral system was originally designed to encourage policy uniformity and local allegiance.

distinct, if intensely interdependent, spheres. In the Nordic countries, too, local authorities are still viewed as self-governing units operating with discretionary authority within a unitary framework, even though much of their detailed work involves implementing national policy.

Under a **fused** system, by contrast, central and local government combine to form a single sphere of public authority. Both levels express the leading position of the state. In some European countries, such as Belgium and the Netherlands, the local mayor is even appointed by the national government and is responsible to the centre for maintaining local law and order. In addition, central and local authority are fused in the office of the **prefect**. In theory, a prefectoral system signals central dominance by establishing a clear hierarchy running from national government through the prefect to local authorities.

France is the classic example of this fused approach (Figure 14.3). The system was established by Napoleon early in the nineteenth century and consists of 96 *départements* in France, each with its own prefect and elected assembly. Napoleon called prefects 'emperors with small feet'. The framework is uniform and rational but in practice the prefect must now cooperate with local and regional councils rather than simply oversee them. The prefect has ceased to be the local emperor and is instead an agent of the *département*, representing interests upwards as much as transmitting commands downwards. The French model remains influential. Many other countries have adopted it, including all France's ex-colonies and several post-communist states. The office of prefect is also the oldest government institution at regional level within Scandinavian countries (Bjørna and Jennsen, 2006).

One expression of a fused system is the ease with which politicians move between, and frequently straddle, the national and the local. In Belgium, two out of three MPs also hold local political office (Winter and Brans, 2003, p. 51). In France, too, national politicians often become or remain mayor of their home town. This simultaneous occupancy of posts at different levels is known in France as the *cumul des mandats* (accumulation of offices). Even after the rules were tightened in 1985 and 2000, the most popular *cumul* – combining the office of local mayor with membership of the National Assembly –

is still permitted. It is an entrenched tradition reflecting the fused character of French public authority.

Cities

In both unitary and federal states, the governance of large urban areas has emerged as an issue complicating territorial governance within countries. The interdependence of cities and suburbs means that both need to be treated as a single metropolitan area, whatever the traditional boundaries. Within cities themselves, rich and poor – as well as native and immigrant – coexist uneasily, creating demands for public services. In addition, the international competitiveness of the capital calls for reinforcement through public policy.

Just as the need for planning stimulated the emergence of regional government in the second half of the twentieth century, so too is it now driving the development of techniques for governing large city regions. As Keating (2008, p. 73) suggests, the new century has seen a revival of the idea of metropolitan government for city regions.

As Bull and Newell report (2005, p. 158), Italy provides an example of one response to these problems:

Urbanization and industrialization over the post-war decades led to an increasing concentration of population and economic activity in a small number of urban areas, giving rise to strategic needs not always met by existing divisions of competence. Law no. 142 (1990) thus denoted specific large cities as 'metropolitan areas', and made it possible for the communes within such areas to come together to form metropolitan cities.

Similar responses are found elsewhere. The special status of London within the United Kingdom has been reflected in its acquisition of a measure of regional self-government. Since 2002, the new Greater London Authority, complete with an elected mayor and 25-member elected assembly, has promoted the city as an investment and cultural centre as well as controlling strategic planning and most public transport.

The international role of capital cities such as London means that their representatives merit regular communication with the centre. As an important component of the national brand, the performance of the capital is significant for the centre but the capital's international connections means it can in practice become semi-detached from its national moorings. As in other political relationships, the interests of the centre and the capital overlap but are far from identical. Inevitably, though, the capital is treated somewhat differently from other cities, producing an equivalent to asymmetric federalism.

Central–local relations in authoritarian states

Studying the relationship between centre and periphery in authoritarian states confirms the relative insignificance of institutions in non-democracies. In these regimes, the distinction between local government and local power is fundamental. The former is weak: authority flows from the top down and bottom-up institutions of representation are subordinate. When national power is exercised by the military or a ruling party, these bodies typically establish a parallel presence in the provinces, where their authority overrides that of formal state officials. For a humble mayor in such a situation, the main skill required is to lie low and avoid offending the real power-holders. Little of the pluralistic policy-making suggested by the notion of multi-level governance takes place and the more general description, central–local relations, is more accurate.

But it would be wrong to conclude that authoritarian regimes are highly centralized. Rather, central rulers – just like medieval monarchs – often depend on established provincial leaders to sustain their own, sometimes tenuous, grip on power. Central–local relations therefore tend to be more personal and less structured than in a liberal democracy. The hold of regional strongmen on power is not embedded in local institutions; such rulers command their fiefdoms in a personal fashion, replicating the authoritarian pattern found at national level. Central and local rulers are integrated by patronage: the national ruler effectively buys the support of local bigwigs who in turn maintain their position by selectively distributing resources to their own supporters. Patronage, not institutions, is the rope that binds.

It was perhaps only some communist regimes, notably the Soviet Union, which achieved real political centralization. In communist states, the leading role of the party always took precedence over local concerns. As long as the party itself remained highly centralized, national leaders could command outlying areas through the party hierarchy. Technically, the Union of Soviet Socialist Republics was a federation but in reality any attempt by a republic to apply its constitutional right to 'freely secede from the USSR' would have been crushed by force. As Chechnya has discovered, the same rule continues in contemporary Russia.

Central–local relations in China, the principal remaining communist state, take a rather different form. Despite its vast scale and multinational population, China has never adopted even the pretence of a federal solution. It remains a unitary and even imperial state governed, in theory, from Beijing.

Certainly, the structure is far from uniform. It includes two Special Administrative Regions (Hong Kong and Macao) which are ex-colonial regions returned to Beijing's control in the 1990s. These regions are ruled under the formula 'one country, two systems'. There are also five administrative regions (including Tibet and Inner Mongolia) which encompass national minorities. These areas are ruled from Beijing in an imperial fashion, with garrisons to protect against national uprisings. In addition, four large municipalities (including Shanghai and Beijing itself) are directly controlled.

With those exceptions, subnational government takes the form of 22 provinces (the largest containing over 80 million people), with further subdivisions into either counties and townships, or cities and districts. Provinces have gained substantial practical autonomy as the moral authority of, and funding from, the centre has declined. Provincial and city governments have spearheaded local economic development, stimulated by the desire of local political elites not just to achieve personal wealth but also to improve the resource base of their administrations.

As in the Soviet Union, the party itself provides a method of integrating centre and periphery. In particular, the circulation of party leaders between national and provincial posts helps to connect the two tiers, providing China's equivalent to the French *cumul des mandats*. Several provincial leaders serve on the party's central politburo; most members of this key group have worked in top provincial posts in their career. As Saich (2004, p. 160) comments, 'ultimately, Beijing has the power of control over 7,000 appointments and this makes it difficult for any provincial leader to defy the centre for too long'.

Central–local relations in China may not deliver the intricate policies generated by multilevel governance in liberal democracies but 'when the centre really wishes to implement a policy and moves coherently, local officials will comply even at significant cost to their own economic interests' (Saich, 2004, p. 161). Successes such as the one-child policy and economic reform demonstrate the capacity of party leaders in Beijing to implement central policy throughout this large and populous land.

Central–local relations in illiberal democracies

An illiberal democracy provides a difficult environment within which to foster central–local relations. The personal relationship between leader and people lends itself to an intermittent and unstructured engagement by the president in local affairs: indifference combined with the occasional intervention. The focus remains on the national level. In Venezuela, for instance, critics allege that 'the paternalist mentality created by easy oil money induces Venezuelans to look to the central government, which administers the revenue, for quick solutions to their problems' (Ellner, 2004, p. 15). This orientation is of course encouraged by the populist style of President Hugo Chávez himself. For such reasons, Romero (1997, p. 32) regards centralism – along with paternalism and populism – as a core feature of what he calls 'degraded democracy' in Venezuela.

At the same time, many illiberal democracies are located in poor countries where subnational administrations in remote districts simply lack the resources to provide effective governance. As in many authoritarian regimes, powerful landowners and businessmen may run the local show, often with tacit or explicit support from the central elite. Thus a nominally centralized system may coexist with a practical decentralization of power. As in authoritarian regimes, the connections between centre and periphery, and therefore between capital and the countryside, operate on a personal basis.

The astonishing trajectory of federalism in Russia's illiberal democracy illustrates these themes. The post-communist era experienced the most remarkable decentralization of power under Boris Yeltsin, followed by considerable recentralization under Vladimir Putin. As Hahn (2006, p. 148) writes, this was a game played for high stakes: 'the success or failure of Russia's transformation into a stable state with a viable market democracy will depend much on the creation of an effective and balanced federal system'. The challenge was to integrate a country of massive size containing numerous religions and national minorities.

Unlike China, post-communist Russia inherited a tradition of at least formal federalism from the old Soviet Union. Communist theory and practice had also encouraged the development of national groups within the USSR. These traditions were amplified by Boris Yeltsin. 'Take as much sovereignty as you can swallow,' he told the regions in 1990, as part of his tactical campaign to undermine Mikhail Gorbachev's authority in Moscow. A parade of sovereignties then marched across Russia, as republics declared their autonomy in what they hoped would become a Russian confederation. In the eyes of republican leaders, Russia was to be constructed *snizu vverkh*: from the bottom up.

Yeltsin continued on a confederal path after becoming president in 1991, even though the 1993 constitution gave priority to the centre. Ignoring the federal principle that all provinces should possess the same powers, Yeltsin signed bilateral treaties between 1994 and 1998 with about half of the 89 geographical units in the federation. These short-term agreements, probably inconsistent with the constitution, included specific and highly variable deals on how taxation and spending were to be shared with the centre. Many republics launched their own constitutions, again often contradicting federal law. Some districts within republics themselves became federal subjects, rather as if Seattle were able to elect its own senators in addition to those chosen to represent Washington state. All this amounted to asymmetric federalism on a grand scale.

Important political reasons underpinned this seemingly cavalier approach. Hahn (2006, p. 152) judges that Yeltsin's 'compromise with regional native elites prevented or at least forestalled separatism (except in Chechnya), civil war and even the dissolution of Russia'. Certainly, these agreements represented a unique moment in federalism's history. However, it was difficult to see how the patchwork resulting from this parade of treaties could provide a stable foundation for a federal state.

That, at any rate, was the view of Vladimir Putin. As president, he gave high priority to consolidating the **power vertical**. He achieved this goal in three ways:

▶ By ending nearly all the bilateral treaties struck by his predecessor and seeking to replace them with a more uniform system of revenue-sharing.

▶ By passing a law requiring any future treaties to be approved by both houses of the legislature.

▶ By creating, in 2000, seven extra-constitutional federal *okrugs* (districts) to oversee lower-level units. Each *okrug* is responsible for between 6 and 15 regions. These overlords ensure that branches of the federal government in the regions remain loyal to Moscow and that regional laws are rendered consistent with national ones.

As is often the case with illiberal democracies, these reforms can be read in various ways. First, President Putin created a more symmetrical federation and enhanced the authority of the centre throughout the land. In essence, he created a federation from what had become a confederation.

Second, the reforms also strengthened Putin's own political position. He staffed the *okrugs* with his own trusted appointees, often drawn from military or police backgrounds, and used them to mobilize support for his own re-election.

Third, he increased the capacity of the state to govern the Russian people. In that sense, the reforms

> The **power vertical** is a Russian phrase denoting central control over lower levels of government within the federation.

contributed to Putin's project of creating what he termed a 'sovereign democracy' in Russia. In Putin's eyes, a sovereign democracy is not built on the uncertain pluralistic foundations of multilevel governance. Rather, a sovereign democracy gives priority to the interests of Russia herself, interests which include an effective central state capable of controlling its population. On that foundation, Russia can strengthen its position in what it has long perceived to be a hostile world.

Learning Resources for Chapter 14

Next step

Bache and Flinders (2004) offer a comparative perspective on multilevel governance.

Further reading

Karmis and Norman (2005) bring together the classic texts on federalism. Comparative studies of federalism include Burgess (2006), Galligan (2006) and Hueglin and Fenna (2006). Menon and Schain (2006) compare the EU and the USA, Stevenson (2009) examines Canada, Bhattacharyya (2009) considers Asia, while Brans *et al.* (2009) survey Belgium. Gagnon and Tully (2001) is a comparative study of multinational democracies, focusing on federalism. Kavalski and Zolkos (2008) address the neglected topic of federations that failed. Denters and Rose (2005) and John (2001) survey local governance, while Dollery *et al.* (2008) discuss local government reform in Anglo-American countries. Ross and Campbell (2008) address federalism and local politics in Russia.

Internet sources

Centre for Studies on Federalism
Promotes scientific research, information and diffusion of knowledge, documentation and education in studies of federalism.
http://www.csfederalismo.it

Forum on Federations
Seeks to enhance federalism's contribution to maintaining and constructing democracy
http://www.forumfed.org/

Institute of Intergovernmental Relations, Queen's University
Research on federalism and intergovernmental relations in Canada and beyond
http://www.queensu.ca/iigr/

International Association of Centers for Federal Studies
An association of centres for federal studies
http://www.iacfs.org/

Committee of the Regions, European Union
Provides local and regional authorities with a voice in the European Union. Includes online studies
http://www.cor.europa.eu/

www.palgrave.com
Companion Website
Visit the Companion Website to
'click and go'
www.palgrave.com/politics/hague

Chapter 15
Legislatures

Legislatures are symbols of popular representation in politics. They are not governing bodies, they do not take major decisions and usually they do not even initiate proposals for laws. Yet they remain a foundation of both liberal and democratic politics. This significance arises from their representative role: 'legislatures join society to the legal structure of authority in the state. Legislatures are representative bodies: they reflect the sentiments and opinions of the citizens' (Olson, 1994, p. 1). As the liberal English political theorist John Locke (1632–1704) observed:

It is in their legislative, that the members of a commonwealth are united, and combined together into one coherent living body. This is the soul that gives form, life, and unity, to the commonwealth: from hence the several members have their mutual influence, sympathy, and connexion: and, therefore, when the legislative is broken, or dissolved, dissolution and death follows. (Locke, 1690, sec. 212)

In these ways, legislatures help to mobilize consent for the system of rule. As liberal democracy spreads throughout the world, so more legislatures are gaining the political weight which comes from performing this function of standing for the people.

How did legislatures acquire this significance? In brief, the origin of parliaments lies in the ancient royal courts of Europe. There, monarchs would judge important legal cases and meet with noblemen of the realm. Gradually these assemblies became more settled, coming to represent the various estates – the clergy, the nobility and the towns – into which society was then divided. In the thirteenth and fourteenth centuries, kings began to consult estate leaders more consistently on issues of war, administration, commerce and taxation.

Although the initiative for calling these colloquia lay with the king, a principle of Roman law was sometimes invoked in justification. This notion was *quod omnes similter tangit, ab omnibus comprobetur* (what concerns all, should be approved by all). So these early European assemblies were viewed as possessing a right to be consulted long before they became modern legislatures with the sovereign authority to pass laws.

A **legislature** is a multimember representative body which considers public issues and 'gives assent, on behalf of a political community that extends beyond the executive authority, to binding measures of public policy' (Norton, 1990, p. 1). The words used to denote these bodies reflect their origins: assemblies gather, congresses congregate, diets meet, dumas deliberate, legislatures pass laws and parliaments talk.

Figure 15.1 Population and assembly size, 2009

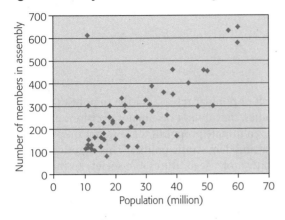

Notes: For bicameral assemblies, the size of the lower chamber is used. Analysis is confined to countries with populations in the range 10–60 million.

Source: CIA (2009).

Where European parliaments accumulated powers gradually and with difficulty, most modern constitutions celebrate the importance of the legislature. In the debates surrounding the American constitution, for instance, James Madison declared that 'in republican government, the legislative power necessarily predominates' (Hamilton, 1788d, p. 265). A leading role for the assembly was judged to be an essential defence against executive tyranny; in consequence, the list of powers awarded to Congress was longer and more detailed than that given to the president. Few other legislatures are as important as the American Congress but the principle of expressing the popular will through an assembly has become a fundamental tenet of liberal democracy.

Contemporary legislatures contribute to detailed governance as well as to broad expressions of the popular will. Indeed, one purpose of this chapter is to show how a modern assembly, with a well-resourced committee system and professional members with some autonomy from party, can improve the quality of legislation, scrutinize the actions of the executive and hold influential hearings on matters of public concern. It is in these detailed ways, as much as in partisan debates on the floor, that the contemporary assembly can show its mettle.

Structure

Only two things can be said with certainty about every assembly in the world: how many members and chambers it has (Blondel, 1973). In this section, we examine these important aspects of assembly structure.

Size

The size of an assembly, as indicated by the number of members in the more important lower chamber, reflects a country's population (Figure 15.1). In China, the world's most populous country, the cumbersome National People's Congress has almost 3,000 members. By contrast, the assembly in the South Pacific island of Tuvalu (population 12,373) contains just 15 representatives.

Size rarely indicates strength. Rather, giant assemblies are rendered impotent by their inability to act cohesively. They are in constant danger of being taken over by more coherent actors such as political parties or even by their own committees. Ruling communist parties, as in China, preferred a large legislature precisely because it was easier to control. There is also some evidence that large assemblies mean more hands in the till, leading to more and less efficient public spending (Chen and Malhotra, 2007).

By contrast, a very small chamber – say under 100 – offers opportunities for all deputies to have their say in a collegial environment. A tiny chamber may be entirely appropriate for small island communities such as Tuvalu. In practice, as Figure 15.1 shows, few lower houses possess more than 500–600 members, and this is probably a fair estimate of the maximum size for an effective body.

Number of chambers

Should a legislature have one chamber or two? If the latter, what role should the second chamber play and how should its members be selected? These old questions acquired practical significance in the 1990s as a fresh wave of democratization raised anew issues of institutional design.

Unicameral legislatures are the contemporary norm. By 2009, 114 of the world's 191 national parliaments (60 per cent) possessed only one chamber (IPU, 2009d). This proportion rose in the second half of the twentieth century as several smaller democracies abolished their second chamber, notably New Zealand in 1950, Denmark in 1954, Sweden in 1971 and Iceland in 1991. Movements from unicameral to bicameral status, such as Tunisia's creation of a second chamber in 2005, are rare.

Many smaller post-colonial and post-communist states have also embraced a single chamber. By contrast, **bicameral** legislatures are most often found in larger countries and in democracies; they are universal in federations where the second chamber typically expresses the voice of the component states (Uhr, 2006). Note, however, that many bicameral legislatures do occasionally meet in common session, not least for ceremonial purposes such as swearing in the head of state.

The choice between one and two chambers is not

> Although some European assemblies originally contained multiple chambers, one for each feudal estate, parliaments today are **unicameral** (one chamber) or **bicameral** (two chambers). The first or lower chamber is typically called the chamber of deputies, national assembly or house of representatives. The second or upper chamber is usually known as the senate ('camera' in this context comes from the Greek *kamara*, meaning a vaulted chamber).

just a technical matter of institutional design. Fundamentally, the decision reflects contrasting visions of democracy. Unicameral parliaments are justified by a majoritarian reading of popular control. The proposition is that an assembly based on direct popular election reflects the popular will and should not be obstructed. The radical French cleric Abbé Sieyès (1748–1836) put the point well: 'if a second chamber dissents from the first, it is mischievous; and if it agrees, it is superfluous' (Lively, 1991). Also, a single chamber is more accountable, economical and decisive, lacking the petty politicking and point-scoring which becomes possible as soon as two houses with distinct interests are created.

But the defenders of bicameral parliaments reject both the majoritarian logic of the Abbé and the penny-pinching of accountants. Bicameralists stress the liberal element of democracy, arguing that the upper chamber offers checks and balances. It can defend individual and group interests against a potentially oppressive majority in the lower house. The second chamber can also serve as a house of review, revising bills (proposed laws), scrutinizing constitutional amendments and eliminating intemperate legislation: in short, a second chamber for second thoughts. To adopt the terms used by the British statesman Edmund Burke (1729–97), the upper house can be a 'deliberative assembly of one nation' rather than a mere 'congress of ambassadors'.

So the power to delay can be presented as a positive virtue. For example, James Madison (1751–1836), one of America's founding fathers, suggested that an upper house afforded protection against 'an excess of law-making' (Hamilton, 1788e). It can offer a modern approximation to the traditional idea of a council of elders, often debating in a less partisan style than the lower house. Reflecting these points, Robert Cecil, thrice British prime minister in the nineteenth century, declared that the House of Lords 'represents the permanent, as opposed to the passing, feelings of the nation' (Russell, 2001).

A second house can also share the workload of the lower chamber, conduct detailed committee work and assist with appointments (e.g. to the judiciary). In performing these detailed tasks, an upper chamber can contribute to the effective functioning of a modern legislature.

Where legislatures do consist of two chambers, the question arises of the relationship between them. Usually, the lower chamber dominates. This format of **weak bicameralism** is typical of parliamentary government where the government's survival depends on maintaining the assembly's support and one chamber becomes the focus of such accountability. This task of sustaining or voting down the government falls naturally to the lower house, with its popular mandate. The dominance of the first chamber can also be seen in other ways, however. It often has special responsibility for money bills, is the

> **Weak bicameralism** arises when the lower chamber dominates the upper house, providing the primary focus for government accountability, as in most parliamentary systems. In **strong bicameralism**, found in a few federations with presidential government, the two chambers are more balanced in their powers (Lijphart, 1999).

Table 15.1 Selection to the upper chamber in some liberal democracies

	Chamber	Members	Term (years)	Method of selection
Australia	Senate	76	6	Direct election by single transferable vote in each state
Germany	Bundesrat	69	–	Appointed by state governments
Ireland	Senate	60	5	Appointed by the PM (11), elected from vocational panels (43) and from two universities (6)
Japan	House of Councillors	242	6	Direct election by a mixed-member majoritarian system
Netherlands	Senate	75	4	Elected by and from provincial councils, using party list PR
USA	Senate	100	6	Direct election by plurality voting in each state

Source: IPU (2009d).

forum where major proposals are introduced, and is entitled to override vetoes or amendments proffered by the second chamber.

In presidential systems, by contrast, the president is directly elected and his continuation in office does not depend on the legislature's confidence. This independent survival means that there is no need for the executive's accountability to focus on a single chamber. **Strong bicameralism** can emerge in these conditions, especially when combined with federalism. The American Congress is the best illustration of this more balanced arrangement. With its constitutional position as representative of the states, the Senate plays a full part in the country's legislative and budget-making processes.

Selection of the second chamber

A bicameral structure raises the question of how the members of the second chamber should be chosen. Some divergence with the lower house is needed to avoid mirroring the party balance in the first chamber. The three main methods are:

◆ Direct election (used by 35 per cent of all seats in upper houses);

◆ Indirect election through regional or local governments (also 35 per cent);

◆ Appointment, usually by the government (27 per cent) (IPU, 2009d).

Even when members of the upper chamber are elected, a contrast with the lower house is still normally achieved by providing its members with a longer tenure: typically five or six years compared to four or five in the lower chamber (Table 15.1). The election cycle can also be staggered: American Senators are granted a six-year term, with a third of the seats up for election every two years. By contrast, the entire membership of the House of Representatives, the lower chamber, must stand for re-election on an unusually short two-year cycle.

A federal structure also produces a natural divergence between chambers. In federations, Canada excepted, elections to the upper chamber are organized by state, with smaller states deliberately overrepresented. The American Senate contains two members for each of 50 states, meaning that California (population 36.8 million) has the same representation as Nevada (2.6 million). In more recent federations, membership is also weighted towards the smaller states but to a lesser extent.

Functions

Representation, we have suggested, is the key function of legislatures. But deliberation and legislation follow close behind. Other functions, crucial to some but not all assemblies, are authorizing expenditure, making governments and scrutinizing the executive (Box 15.1). In discussing these roles, we will see how the significance of parliaments in liberal democracies extends well beyond the narrow task of simply converting bills into laws.

Representation

If the essence of assemblies is that they represent society to government, how can we judge whether, and how well, that function is fulfilled? What features would a fully representative assembly exhibit?

Clearly, members of the assembly can and do defend the interests, and express the views, of the electors they represent. This detailed casework provides a major component of the members' workload and often provides satisfaction to members themselves. But our main concern here is with the broader representative function of the legislature as a whole.

One interpretation of representation, plausible at first sight, is that an assembly should be a **microcosm** of society. The idea here is that a legislature should be society in miniature, literally 'representing' society in all its diversity. Such a parliament would balance men and women, rich and poor, black and white, even educated and uneducated, in the same mix as in the population. How, after all, could a parliament composed entirely of middle-aged white men go about representing young black women (or vice versa)? To retain society's confidence, the argument continues, an assembly should reflect social diversity, standing in

A legislature would be a **microcosm** (literally, miniature world) if it formed a model of society, precisely reflecting its social diversity. An exact microcosm is impractical but there may still be value in ensuring that all major social groups achieve some parliamentary presence.

BOX 15.1

Functions of legislatures

Representation	Most members articulate the goals of the party under whose label they were elected
Deliberation	Debating matters of moment is the classic function of Britain's House of Commons
Legislation	Most bills come from the government but the legislature still approves them and may make amendments in committee
Authorizing expenditure	Parliament's role is normally reactive, approving or rejecting a budget prepared by the government
Making governments (see pp. 326–34)	In most parliamentary systems, the government emerges from the assembly and must retain its confidence
Scrutiny	Oversight of government activity and policy is growing in importance and is a task well-suited to the assembly's committees

---

for society and not just acting on its behalf (Phillips, 1995).

Several studies support this view. For instance, Alonso and Ruiz-Rufino (2007) found that in post-communist democracies, ethnic protest is less common in those countries where ethnic minorities have achieved significant and effective representation in parliament.

The notion that an assembly should mirror society was popular in some states in eighteenth-century America, where it was held to provide an approximation to the assemblies of ancient Athens. In 1778, for instance, the citizens of Essex County, Massachusetts, issued this comment on their state's proposed constitution:

Representatives should have the same views and interests with the people at large. They should think, feel, and act like them and in fine, should be an exact miniature of their constituents. They should be (if we may use the expression) the whole body politic, with all its property, rights and privileges reduced to a smaller scale, every part being diminished in just proportion. (Kramnick, 1987, p. 44)

But there is a considerable difficulty in implementing the views expressed in Essex County. An exact transcript of society could only be achieved by quota or random selection, dispensing with election altogether (as with juries). If such a practice were implemented, we would have to accept that parliaments, like juries, would contain their fair share of the addicted, the corrupt and the ignorant. Even the well-intentioned citizens of Essex County baulked at including women (due to their 'lack of promiscuous intercourse with the world') and slaves (who 'have no will').

Whether elected or not, representatives would need to be replaced regularly lest they become tainted by the very experience of office, a point that led the American politician John Adams (1735–1826) to proclaim that 'where annual election ends, there slavery begins'. In reality, the assembly as microcosm is an impractical and probably undesirable goal.

Today, a few countries reserve some seats for particular groups (such as New Zealand Maori) (Krook, 2007). **Reserved seats** do ensure at least some diversity within the assembly. Alternatively, and more frequently, an institution-wide or party-based quota for minorities or women can be imposed.

In the main, though, contemporary representation operates through parties. Victorious candidates owe their election to their party and they vote in parliament largely according to its commands. In New Zealand, Labour members must agree to abide by

Reserved seats are restricted to candidates from a particular group, typically minorities or women. Pakistan's first constitution (1956), for instance, stipulated that 3 per cent of seats in all assemblies were to be reserved for women. Appointment was by election from those elected to ordinary seats. Reserved seats are a separate mechanism from quotas applying to the assembly as a whole, or to the individual parties represented within it.

the decisions of the party caucus. In India, an extreme case, members lose their seat if they vote against their party, the theory being that they are deceiving the voters if they switch parties after their election. The party has become the vehicle of representation and the prism through which electors view candidates.

Elsewhere, party discipline is combined with at least some independence for members. In France and Germany, for instance, party obligations must be reconciled with the constitutional requirement that members of the legislature owe allegiance to the nation and not to any group within it. Even in these democracies, however, party voting remains the norm, though it is not enforced with the eagerness found in New Zealand and India.

Deliberation

Many legislatures serve as a deliberative body, considering public matters of national importance. This function contrasts sharply with the microcosm and party views of representation and offers an additional perspective on the contribution assemblies can make to a well-functioning political system.

In the eighteenth and nineteenth centuries, before the rise of disciplined parties, deliberation was regarded as the core activity. Members were expected to serve as trustees of the nation, applying exceptional knowledge and intelligence to the matters before them. What matters is the quality of debate, not whether it is representative.

The Irish-born politician Edmund Burke offered the classic account of deliberation. Elected Member of Parliament for the English constituency of Bristol in 1774, Burke admitted in his victory speech that he knew nothing about his constituency and had played little part in the campaign. But, he continued,

Parliament is not a congress of ambassadors from different and hostile interests; which interests each must maintain, as an agent and advocate against other agents and advocates; but Parliament is a deliberative assembly of one nation, with one interest, that of the whole; where, not local purposes, not local prejudices, ought to guide, but the general good, resulting from the general reason of the whole. You choose a member indeed; but when you have chosen him, he is not a member for

Bristol, but he is a member of Parliament. (Burke, 1774)

Deliberation of course continues today, with its status demonstrated by legislators' immunity from prosecution, in particular for statements made in performance of their duties. However, the deliberative style varies across countries in a manner captured in a contrast between **debating** and **committee-based legislatures**.

In a debating legislature such as Britain's, deliberation takes the form of general discussion in the chamber. Key issues eventually make their way to the floor of the House of Commons where they are discussed with passion and often with flair. Floor debate is the arena for national political discussion, forming part of a continuous election campaign. One of the achievements of the Commons is precisely its ability to combine effective deliberation, at least on vital issues, with strong partisanship.

> In a **debating legislature**, such as the British House of Commons, floor debate is the central activity; it is here that major issues are addressed and parties gain or lose ground. By contrast, in a **committee-based legislature**, such as the American Congress, most work takes place in committees. There, members engage in the specialized craft of transforming bills into laws, conducting hearings and scrutinizing the executive.

Appropriately, it was the English political philosopher John Stuart Mill (1806–73) who made the case for a debating assembly:

I know not how a representative assembly can more usefully employ itself than in talk, when the subject of talk is the great public interests of the country, and every sentence of it represents the opinion either of some important body of persons in the nation, or of an individual in whom such bodies have reposed their confidence. (Mill, 1861, p. 353)

By contrast, in committee-based assemblies such as the American Congress and the Scandinavian parliaments, deliberation is less theatrical, taking the form of policy discussion in committees. The task is to improve the government's proposals while also providing measured scrutiny of its actions. This deliberative style makes its own contribution to governance: less dramatic than a set-piece debate but often more constructive.

Legislation

Naturally enough, most constitutions explicitly assert the legislative function of parliaments. The end of absolute executive power is affirmed by giving to parliament, and to it alone, the right to make laws. Arbitrary government is replaced by a formal procedure for law-making. The painstaking process for passing bills into law signals the importance attached to government by rules rather than individuals. Where authoritarian rulers govern by decree, in a democracy bills are scrutinized and authorized by a national congress.

But we must be careful here. Legislation is rarely the function in which 'legislatures' exert most influence. Indeed, after 50 years the European Parliament – admittedly a special case – does not fully control the formal law-making process in the European Union (see Timeline and Box 15.2). In most liberal democracies, effective control over legislation rests with the government. Bills pass through the assembly without being designed or even transformed there.

In party-dominated Australia, for instance, the government treats the legislative function with virtual contempt. On a single night in 1991 it sought to put 26 bills through the Senate in three hours flat. In the era before New Zealand adopted proportional representation, one prime minister boasted that if an idea came to him while shaving, he could have it on the statute book by the evening, truly a case of slot-machine law.

In Britain, similarly, the governing party dominates law-making. Ninety-seven per cent of bills proposed by government between 1945 and 1987 became law. As Rose (1989, p. 173) said of Britain, 'laws are described as Acts of Parliament but it would be more accurate if they were stamped "Made in Whitehall"'. In the party-dominated parliaments of Britain and some of its ex-colonies, the legislative function is reduced to quality control: patching up errors in bills prepared in haste by ministers and civil servants. In legislation, at least, these assemblies are reactive rather than active.

By contrast, committee-based parliaments in Continental Europe do play a more positive role in

▶ **TIMELINE**

THE EUROPEAN PARLIAMENT

1952	Assembly of the European Coal and Steel Community established as an instrument of scrutiny, with the right to dismiss the Commission in some circumstances. Assembly members are drawn from national legislatures.
1962	The Assembly is renamed the European Parliament (EP).
1970	The EP gains more influence over the budget.
1975	The EP wins the right to propose modifications in areas where expenditure is not mandated by previous agreements.
1979	First direct elections. Average turnout 62 per cent.
1980	Isoglucose judgement by the European Court requires the EP to be consulted on proposed laws.
1986	The Single European Act initiates cooperation and assent procedures which give the EP more influence over legislation.
1992	The Maastricht Treaty requires members of the Commission to be approved by the EP. A new co-decision procedure gives the EP some veto authority over legislation.
1997	The Treaty of Amsterdam extends the co-decision procedure and formalizes the EP's right to veto the nominee for Commission president.
1999	All 20 commissioners (the Santer Commission) resign rather than face dismissal by the EP for mismanagement. Fifth direct elections. Average turnout 50 per cent.
2004	Sixth direct elections. Average turnout 46 per cent.
2009	Seventh direct elections. Average turnout 43 per cent
2009	The Treaty of Lisbon further extends the co-decision procedure.

Further reading: Corbett et al. (2005), Judge and Earnshaw (2003), Nugent (2006).

law-making. Coalition governments, influential committees and an elite commitment to compromise combine to deliver laws acceptable to all sides. In a few European countries, this more flexible approach is reflected not just in substantive discussion of bills but also in their initiation through agenda-setting initiatives (see p. 190). In Switzerland, for instance, a bill can originate not just from the executive but also from members of either house of the federal assembly or from any canton.

But it is in presidential systems, including the United States, that the assembly achieves most autonomy in making laws. The separation of powers and personnel inherent in a presidential regime limits executive influence over the legislature. This institutional separation is often reinforced by divided government. That is, the party in the White House may lack a majority in at least one chamber of Congress, further reducing the legislature's willingness to convert the administration's proposals into laws. In Latin America, where parties are weaker

BOX 15.2

The European Parliament

The European Parliament consists of a maximum of 751 members directly elected every five years from 375 million electors in the 27 member states, with smaller countries granted a measure of over-representation. No country may hold more than 96 or less than 6 members. Unusually and expensively, the Parliament is a multisite body, holding sessions in Brussels and Strasbourg. In addition, some staff are based in Luxembourg.

Election campaigns are second-order contests, with national issues to the fore. Turnout has declined steadily, reaching a low of 43 per cent in 2009. Limited public interest is regarded as contributing to the EU's lack of democratic authority, though in reality turnout is broadly comparable to that of American mid-term congressional elections.

The Parliament's scope has increased gradually and it now attracts the attentions of many lobbyists. Originally, it was not required to provide its assent for most proposals but, under the Treaty of Lisbon (2009), its right of co-decision now covers the vast majority of EU legislation.

Nonetheless, the parliament's role remains more limited and focused on technical regulation than that of national assemblies. In some areas, such as Economic and Monetary Union, its function is still largely consultative. It must still be questioned whether the Parliament fully performs the core legislative function of symbolically granting popular consent to executive policies.

and proportional representation is the norm for congressional elections, the president's party may be no more than a minor player in the legislature.

Yet even in presidential systems the initiative in framing bills usually lies with the executive. Certainly, in the American Congress only members of the House of Representatives can formally introduce bills. But the executive can easily find a friendly representative to initiate a bill on its behalf. The political reality is that bills are developed by the administration and then transformed in Congress if indeed they do not expire in its maze of committees. 'You supply the bills and we work them over,' one

member of Congress reportedly said to an administration official. The executive proposes, as in most political systems, but Congress disposes, usually by saying no.

Inevitably, this pluralistic process reduces the coherence of America's legislative programme. As President Kennedy said, 'it is very easy to defeat a bill in Congress. It is much more difficult to pass one' (Eigen and Siegel, 1993, p. 82). The difficulty American and other presidents experience in securing approval for their bills stands in marked contrast to the tighter control over the legislative programme exerted by the ruling party or coalition in parliamentary systems.

Although the process by which a legislature transforms a bill into law naturally varies from one democracy to another, Figure 15.2 offers a general outline. The overall procedure is explicitly deliberative, involving several readings (debates) as the bill moves from the floor to committee and back again.

Bicameral legislatures face an additional hurdle in realizing the legislative function. What happens if the second chamber amends a bill passed by the lower house? There must be some means of resolving such discrepancies. In almost all countries, the initial step is for the amended bill to return to the lower chamber for further discussion. But if the bill continues to shuttle between houses in this way until an agreed version emerges, as in Italy's strongly bicameral legislature, the danger is that it will be delayed or never become law at all. In Italy, for instance, a bill on rape introduced in 1977 did not become law until 1995.

To resolve this problem, most legislatures develop a procedure for short-circuiting the endless shuttle (Box 15.3). The most popular arrangement is to employ a special conference committee, containing an equal number of members from each chamber, to produce an agreed bill. This compromise version must then be approved or rejected by the main chambers without further modification. The American, French and German legislatures are among those employing this device. Conference committees are sometimes described as third chambers, for it is here that the final deals are struck and the decisive compromises made. They are frequently a vital arena for resolving, or at least reaching a compromise on, important national issues.

BOX 15.3

Resolving differences in the versions of a bill passed by each chamber

	Comment	Example
Conference or mediation committee	A joint committee of both chambers negotiates a compromise version which is then voted on by each house	Many countries, including France, Germany, Switzerland and the USA
Lower house is decisive	The lower house decides whether to accept or reject amendments from the upper house	Czech Republic, Spain, United Kingdom
Vote of a joint session of both chambers	The larger lower chamber exerts more weight in a joint vote	Australia, Brazil, India, Norway
Indefinite shuttle	Amended versions continue to shuttle between chambers until agreement is reached (if ever)	Italy is the main example of this rare procedure

Source: Adapted from Tsebelis and Money (1997), Table 2.2a.

Authorizing expenditure

This is one of the oldest functions of parliament and of the lower house in particular. The origin of European assemblies, after all, lay in the monarch's requirement for money. Since, as Spencer Walpole (1881, p. 4) wrote, the necessities of kings are the opportunities of peoples, assemblies were able to establish the right to raise grievances before granting supply (that is, revenue). In Britain, this tradition continued until 1982 in the form of 'supply days' during which the opposition could raise any issues it wished.

The power to authorize spending may be one of parliament's oldest functions but in many democracies it has become nominal. Even more than the law-making function, budgetary control forms part of the myth rather than the reality of parliamentary authority. Lack of real financial control is a major weakness of the modern assembly. Typically, the executive prepares the budget which is then reported to parliament but rarely modified there.

For the legislature to possess the power of the purse, suggests Wehner (2006), a large number of background conditions must be fulfilled:

- The assembly must be able to amend the budget (as opposed to, say, just being authorized to make cuts);
- The assembly must possess an effective committee system;
- The assembly must be granted sufficient time to consider the budget in detail;
- The assembly must have access to background information underlying the budget;
- The executive must be limited in its ability to alter budget allocations during implementation;
- The **reversionary budget** must differ from the government's own proposals.

Inevitably, few countries meet all these conditions. Among liberal democracies, the United States and Scandinavian countries come closest. At the other extreme, legislative control is particularly limited in Australia, France, South Africa and the United Kingdom. In general, parliamentary approval is after the fact, serving to confirm budget compromises worked out between government departments. In

A **reversionary budget** is the default (typically, last year's) budget which takes effect should the legislature fail to approve a new one in time.

many democracies, the budget is a done deal once it reaches the assembly. If the parliament began to unpick any part of the budget, the whole package would fall apart.

The United States is once more the great exception to the thesis of executive control of the purse. Congress remains central to the confused tangle that is American budget-making. The sums involved here are massive: the budget proposed for the fiscal year 2010 amounted to $3.6 trillion – about ten times Sweden's gross domestic product. Under America's constitution, all money spent by executive departments must be allocated under specific expenditure headings approved by Congress. No appropriations by Congress means no government programme. As Flammang *et al.* (1990, p. 422) wrote, 'without the agreement of members of Congress, no money can be doled out for foreign aid, salaries for army generals or paper clips for bureaucrats'.

The result is that the annual American budget has become an elaborate game of chicken. The executive and the legislature each hopes the other side will accede to its own proposals before the money runs out. Each year between 1978 and 1996, Congress failed to pass a complete budget by its own deadline, forcing agencies to operate under a reversionary budget. This rather alarming method of allocating enormous sums supports the proposition that financing the modern state is, like the law-making function, too important to be left to the assembly's many hands.

Scrutiny

The final function of legislatures is scrutiny (oversight) of the executive. John Stuart Mill emphasized this role as early as 1861:

The proper office of a representative assembly is to watch and control the government: to throw the light of publicity on its acts, to compel a full exposition and justification of all of them which any one considers questionable; [and] to censure them if found condemnable. (1861, p. 258)

However, in many countries such activity has only been growing in significance and value in recent decades.

To emphasize the scrutiny function is to accept that the executive, not the legislature, must govern. But given adequate resources and professional support

Figure 15.2 Typical steps in making a law

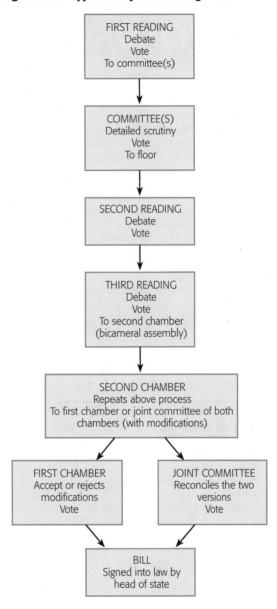

Source: Adapted from Mahler (2007), Table 4.9.

the assembly can restate its key role as representative of the people by acting as a watchdog over the administration. Effective monitoring can compensate for the downgrading of the assembly's legislative and expenditure functions, providing a new direction to parliament's work which appeals to younger generations of educated and committed members.

UNITED KINGDOM

Form of government ■ a parliamentary liberal democracy with a largely ceremonial monarchy.

Legislature ■ the House of Commons (646 members) is the dominant chamber. The House of Lords, the composition of which has been under review since 1997, acts in a revising and restraining capacity.

Executive ■ the Cabinet is the top decision-ratifying body; the prime minister selects and dismisses its members. Meetings of full cabinet are largely formal; its effective work is conducted in committee.

Judiciary ■ based on the common law tradition. In 2009, the introduction of a supreme court, albeit without the authority to veto legislation, strengthened the autonomy of the judiciary.

Electoral systems ■ the House of Commons is still elected by the single-member plurality method. A range of systems are used for elections to other bodies such as the Scottish Parliament, the Welsh Assembly and the European Parliament.

Party system ■ Traditionally a two-party system, the dominance of the Conservative and Labour parties has been challenged by the rise of the Liberal Democrats.

Population (annual growth rate): 61.1m (+0.3%)
World Bank income group: high income
Political Rights score:
Civil Liberties score: ①
Human development index (rank/out of): 16/177
Freedom of the press index (rank/out of): 28/195
Perceived transparency index (rank/out of): 16/180

Note: For meaning and sources of scales and indexes, see p. xv. In all cases a score and rank of 1 is 'best'.

The **UNITED KINGDOM** is a liberal democracy whose political system has nonetheless been in transition. Traditional models portrayed Britain as a centralized, unitary state; as a two-party system; as an exemplar of parliamentary sovereignty in which ministers were held to account by the assembly; and as a political system whose uncodified constitution offered little formal protection of individual rights. Yet the accuracy of all these images came under review, particularly after the election in 1997 of a reforming Labour administration.

The centralized and even the unitary character of the United Kingdom was put in question by the creation in 1999 of new assemblies for Scotland and Wales. The reform was asymmetric, with the Scottish parliament receiving more devolved powers than the Welsh assembly. Since 2007, Scotland has been governed by the Scottish National

Party, a left-leaning nationalist party advocating secession from the United Kingdom. Wales is governed by a coalition between Labour and Plaid Cymru, the Welsh nationalists. Devolution to Northern Ireland was reinstated in 2007, reflecting the ending of armed conflict between Catholic and Protestant groups and the UK government.

In the United Kingdom as a whole, the two-party system based on the Conservative and Labour parties has been challenged by the rise of the centre-left Liberal Democrats. In the 2005 election, the Liberal Democrats won six million votes and 62 seats; the share of the vote accruing to the two major parties fell to 68 per cent.

Parliamentary sovereignty has been dented by British membership of the European Union and a more assertive judiciary. Individual rights now receive clearer protection, exerted through the

judiciary, from the incorporation into British law of the European Convention on Human Rights.

Ministerial accountability has been complicated by the delegation of government tasks to semi-independent agencies. In a particularly significant reform, the 1997 Labour government immediately took steps to delegate monetary policy to the Monetary Policy Committee of the Bank of England.

The cumulative impact of these developments remains to be established and in any case needs to be set against the state's determination to ensure domestic security in a world of terrorism. What is clear is that many of the old assumptions about British politics have ceased to apply; in a more complicated and fragmented polity, replacement clichés may be harder to find.

Further reading: Bogdanor (2009), Dunleavy *et al.* (2006), King (2009).

The British parliament

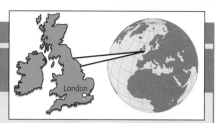

The new era of transition in British politics has impinged on its assembly. Traditionally, Britain's Parliament (one of the world's oldest) mixed omnipotence and impotence in a seemingly impossible combination. Omnipotence, because parliamentary sovereignty, allied to an uncodified constitution, meant there could be no higher authority in the land. Impotence, because the governing party exercised tight control over its own backbenchers, turning Parliament into an instrument rather than a wielder of power. How then has the mother of parliaments adapted to this time of change?

In the twenty-first century, Parliament's position has become less certain. The tired rituals of adversary politics in the House of Commons have become less convincing, not least for the many members – forming a majority of the House – who were elected for the first time in 1997 or later.

The notion that Parliament still possesses sovereignty still carries weight but, like many assemblies, Britain's legislature runs the risk of being left behind by international integration; by competition from the media as an arena of debate; and by the indifference of prime ministers who choose to spend less time in the House.

In addition, an expenses scandal which erupted in 2009 damaged the standing of the House. The fact that dubious expenses claims came to light showed that even MPs could not control the flow of information while the outcome was an end to self-policing of expenses by the House itself.

But not all developments are a reponse to crisis. MPs themselves have become more professional and committed; the era of the amateur is over. Members devote more time to an increasing volume of constituency casework and receive more back-office support. The number of late sittings has been cut. Select committees (and now subcommittees) have established themselves in the debate over policy and contribute to scrutinizing the executive. The prime minister now appears twice a year before a select committee for a more detailed discussion than is possible during weekly Question Time in the chamber.

The Vote Bundle

The daily papers of the House of Commons are known as the Vote Bundle. Its main sections are:

- Summary agenda;
- Order of business;
- Future business;
- Papers available today;
- Order of business in Westminster Hall;
- Public Bill Committee Proceedings;
- Votes and proceedings;
- Questions for oral or written answer;
- Private business;
- Notices of motions;
- Notices of amendments.

Source: Adapted from House of Commons Information Office (2008).

Overall, Cowley (2006, p. 49) judges that 'the Commons has become more efficient in what it does, but it has not necessarily become much stronger or more effective as a result'.

As an upper chamber in what remains a unitary state, the House of Lords occupies an uncertain position. Historically, its base consisted of hereditary peers, but the introduction of life peerages in 1958 led to some recovery in the chamber's standing. The abolition of all but 92 hereditary peers in 1999 served to further increase the chamber's confidence. Since no single party possesses a majority in the Lords, it is in a position to adopt an independent line.

When finally agreed, reform is likely to involve a substantial measure of election to the Lords, a development which may well make the Lords more assertive in challenging the executive.

Yet even as Britain's Parliament updates its skills, it will surely continue to do what it has always done best: acting as an arena for debating issues of central significance to the nation, its government and its leaders. Even in an era of reform, the House of Commons has retained its position as a classic debating assembly, reinforced by the less partisan style in the Lords.

Further reading: Cowley (2006), Norton (2005), Rush (2005).

A modern assembly possesses three main instruments with which to monitor the executive: first, questions and interpellations; second, emergency debates and confidence votes; and, third, committee investigations. As Box 15.4 indicates, the availability of these devices varies between parliamentary and presidential systems. The box may appear to suggest more opportunities for scrutiny in parliamentary systems but such a conclusion would be misleading. In a parliamentary format, backbench members of ruling parties will normally see their task as that of sustaining the government, thus limiting their room for manoeuvre. By contrast, legislators in a presidential system (and in the European Parliament) can be freer with criticism precisely because they know the survival of the executive is assured. We consider each of these monitoring instruments in turn.

Questions refer to direct queries of ministers. In many parliamentary systems, oral and written questions are mainstays of oversight. In Britain, for example, members of the House of Commons ask over 70,000 questions a year, keeping many civil servants busy as they prepare answers for their ministerial masters. Prime Minister's Question Time, a weekly event, remains a theatrical joust between the PM and the leader of the opposition. In other parliaments, however, questions are accorded lower status. French ministers often fail to answer them at all.

But in some assemblies in continental Europe, including Finland, France and Germany, the **interpellation** provides an alternative form of interrogation. An interpellation is a substantial form of question demanding a prompt response which is followed by a short debate and a vote on whether the government's answer is deemed acceptable. This technique, often linked to a vote of no confidence or censure motion, brought down several governments in the French Third (1870–1940) and Fourth (1946–58) Republics.

Emergency debates are a further, and higher-profile, way in which parliament can call the executive to account. Normally a minimum number of members, and the Presiding Officer (Speaker), must

An **interpellation** is an enquiry of the government, interrupting normal business, which is followed by a debate and usually a vote on the assembly's satisfaction with the answers given.

BOX 15.4		
Techniques for scrutinizing the executive		
	Parliamentary government	**Presidential government**
Questions and interpellations on the floor	✔	✗
Emergency debates and votes of confidence	✔	✗
Committee investigations	✔	✔

approve a proposal for such a debate. Although the event usually ends with a government win, the significance lies in the discussion itself and the fact of its being called. An emergency debate creates publicity and demands a considered response from the government's spokesperson.

Votes of confidence or censure motions are the ultimate test which a legislature can pose to the executive in a parliamentary system. Such motions are not so much a form of detailed scrutiny as a decision on whether the government can continue at all. Again, special rules may apply: in France and Sweden, a majority of all members (not just those voting) is required to demonstrate the legislature's loss of confidence. In other cases, a confidence motion is not specifically designated but is simply any vote on which the government would feel obliged to resign if defeated. Defeat on a motion to approve the budget would be an example. In some countries, again including Sweden, votes of confidence can be directed against individual ministers as well as the government as a whole.

The final and most detailed way in which legislatures in both parliamentary and presidential systems exercise oversight is through **committee investigations**. The American Congress is the classic case. Exceptionally, the constitution gives Congress, rather than the executive, responsibility for such important matters as commerce, the currency, defence and taxation. Of course, Congress does not carry out these functions itself; it delegates the tasks to the bureaucracy. But because of its constitutional position, and the budgetary authority flowing from it, Congress possesses inherent powers of oversight. A British civil servant can afford to treat a parliamentary question as a minor distraction but the head of a government agency in the United States knows that next year's budget – and salaries – may depend on maintaining good relations with Congress. Because the floor of the house is an inappropriate venue for detailed scrutiny, committees are the key to this form of oversight.

Committees

Committees have grown in number and significance. They have become the workhorses of effective legislatures, offering detailed scrutiny of both the executive and its bills. Yet committee operations lack the profile accorded to meetings of the whole chamber. So what purposes do committees serve? And what makes them effective?

Committees are small workgroups of members, created to cope with the volume and detail of parliamentary business, particularly in the larger and busier lower chamber. They take the form of standing, select or conference committees (Box 15.5). Standing committees offer line-by-line examination of bills while select committees monitor the main executive departments. The growing status of select committees reflects the increasing importance of the scrutiny function in contemporary legislatures. Whatever the committee type, members are usually allocated in proportion to overall party strength. In operation, however, partisanship is often held in check, yielding a more cooperative outlook than on the floor.

The American Congress is unique in the impact of its committees. Although unmentioned in the constitution, committees rapidly became vital to Congress's work. 'Congress in session is Congress on public exhibition, whilst Congress in its committee rooms is Congress at work', wrote Woodrow Wilson (1885, p. 79). Bryce (1921, p. 68), a nineteenth-century British observer of American politics, described the House of Representatives as 'a huge

---

BOX 15.5

Parliamentary committees

Standing ('permanent') committee	Considers bills in detail.
Select committee	Scrutinizes the executive, ideally with one committee for each main government department.
	Ad hoc temporary committees investigate particular matters of public interest.
Conference or mediation committee	In bicameral legislatures, a joint committee usually reconciles differences in the versions of a bill passed by each chamber.

---

panel from which committees are selected'. Despite a resurgence of partisanship since the mid-1990s, Bryce's comment still applies. Congressional committees are uniquely well-supported, employing over 3,000 policy specialists. Further, each committee creates its own subcommittees: in the 108th Congress (2003–05), there were 86 subcommittees in the Senate and 88 in the House. Committees decide the fate and shape of most legislation.

In addition to their legislative function, Congressional committees are particularly important in providing detailed scrutiny of the administration. Through its committees, Congress achieves a unique level of involvement with government. Much committee work is as a partner rather than an overseer of the executive, but a few investigative committees have achieved national status. The House Committee on Un-American Activities in the 1940s and 1950s, and the Senate Watergate Committee in the 1970s, are the best-known examples.

Even in the USA, however, committee oversight is limited. It can only cast light on a few corners of a vast bureaucracy; Congress sometimes seeks to micromanage departments rather than setting broad targets; and reports can quickly be forgotten as the political spotlight shifts. In the United States, and even more elsewhere, the government's big battalions outnumber the limited forces available to the legislature.

As far as legislation is concerned, committees have less influence in party-dominated legislatures. In Britain's House of Commons, government bills are examined by standing committees which largely replicate party combat on the floor of the chamber. These committees, unlike those of Congress, do not challenge executive dominance in framing legislation. They are unpopular, unspecialized and under-resourced. However, like many other legislatures, the Commons has expanded its system of select committees of scrutiny. Since 1979, select committees have shadowed all the main government departments, probing government policy and monitoring its implementation.

But it is Scandinavia that provides the best example of influential committees operating in the context of strong parties and parliamentary government. Scandinavia's main governing style, sometimes called committee parliamentarianism, is one in which influential standing committees negotiate the policies and bills on which the whole parliament later votes. In Sweden, for instance, committees modify about one in three government proposals and have the right, sometimes exercised, to put their own proposals (including bills) to the Riksdag as a whole. The Riksdag's committees are partners in a remarkably deliberative law-making process (see p. 379).

The key to the influence of committees lies in the three factors of expertise, intimacy and support:

◆ Expertise emerges over time from committees with specialized responsibilities and a clear field of operation. Expertise is most likely to develop in permanent committees with continuity of operation and membership. Detailed knowledge is further encouraged if members are restricted to serving on a small number of committees.

◆ Intimacy emerges from small size (perhaps no more than a dozen members) and is again reinforced by stable membership. Particularly when meetings take place in private, a small group can encourage cooperation and consensus, overcoming adversary relationships between parties.

◆ Support refers to the use of qualified staff to advise committees. Expert researchers can

assist politicians in producing credible recommendations, countering the wall of knowledge available to the executive.

Significantly, all three factors are present in the American Congress.

Membership

Who are the members who populate the legislature? And how do they go about their work? Answering these questions requires a shift from an institutional to a more behavioural approach.

At least in liberal democracies, the central theme is the rise of the **professional politician**: the degree-educated legislator with limited experience outside politics who expects politics to provide both a full-time and a fulfilling career. The amateurs of yesteryear – local landowners representing 'their' territory, ageing trade unionists rewarded with a seat in the assembly for their final years, lawyers seeking some short-term political experience – have given way to career politicians who know no other job. In politics, as elsewhere, specialization is now necessary for success. Even when politicians have experience of other careers such as law, the earlier job is often chosen because it is a feeder occupation for politics.

Particularly in Europe, the rise of the professional has led to speculation about the growth of a **political class** with a background and interests removed from the people it represents. Like any other occupational group, legislators from all parties share a concern with improving their conditions such as hours of work, research support, pay and pension.

But parliamentarians are in a unique position to act on their common interests by simply voting themselves an enhancement – as shown by a damaging expenses scandal which engulfed Britain's House of Commons in 2009. Members of all parties,

> In Weber's renowned distinction (1918), **professional politicians** live off, and not merely for, politics. They are full-timers requiring an appropriate income, support, career development and pension. Professional politicians are sometimes said to form a **political class**, implying the existence of a group that possesses, and can potentially act on, its shared interests (Mosca, 1896).

Figure 15.3 Incumbent return rates to the national legislature

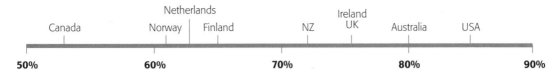

Note: Based on at least four elections between 1979 and 1994 to the lower or only chamber of the national parliament.

Source: Adapted from Matland and Studlar (2004).

it turned out, had been claiming on the public purse for personal expenses such as moat cleaning and piano tuning. The issue was not so much individual corruption as the flexible application of a system of allowances designed for a gentleman's club rather than a public institution. Britain's professional politicians had made short work of amateur regulation. Reports of corruption in other assemblies offer further support to the notion of a horizontal division between legislators and electors that at least supplements the traditional vertical distinction between parties.

In addition, incumbent members from all parties usually seek their own re-election. They can and do supply themselves with campaign resources (e.g. free mail) unavailable to their challengers, thus creating a powerful cartel against newcomers. Viewing politics purely as a clash between parties often leads to inadequate emphasis on this distinction within parties between incumbents and challengers. Like any other established class, politicians in post – of whatever party – are reluctant to upset the apple cart that has served them so well.

The transition to professional parliamentarians is seen clearly in many post-communist parliaments. There, the initial cohort of amateur politicians which dismantled the old regime is giving way to graduate members with political experience who can operate in a somewhat more structured environment. As Ilonski and Edinger (2007, p. 160) put it, the elite of transition is being supplanted by the elite of consolidation.

Politics as a profession implies a distinct view not just of representation but also of politics. It rejects the notion that governance is a task which ordinary citizens can and should undertake. It implies dissatisfaction with the idea that an assembly should draw together a representative sample of citizens 'different in nature, different in interests, different in looks, different in language' (Bagehot, 1867, p. 155). Rather, politics as a profession implies an emphasis on training, knowledge, experience and skill. Politics is a job, just like law, medicine and teaching.

Within the broad category of professional politician, the main contrast is between the American political entrepreneur and the more party-based careerist found in the parliaments of other liberal democracies. In the American Congress, candidates must compete against opponents from their own party in a primary; in office, they must build a personal profile and record of achievement which protects them from challenge and offers insurance should their party fall on hard times. And they must raise money for their campaign.

In most other liberal democracies, strong parties at both parliamentary and electoral level leave less room for independent action, resulting in loyal backbenchers rather than political entrepreneurs. Even when partisanship is important, however, younger and better-educated members are keen to make a difference. Although the French National Assembly remains a weak institution, Kerrouche (2006, p. 352) reports that even here 'deputies want to criticize, to attract media attention and to put forward alternative policies'. These aspirations are reflected in a substantial number of private members' bills and legislative amendments.

Of course, career politicians can only flourish in parliaments where re-election prospects are good. Generally, re-election is the norm in liberal democracies. Typically, most sitting legislators return for a new term following a general election (Figure 15.3; Best and Cotta, 2000). The question of the ideal level of turnover is difficult to answer with precision. On the one hand, the return rate should be high enough to sustain professional members, allowing the development of experience and expertise. On the other hand, it should not be so high as to create the 'three As' which Jackson (1994) associated with a surfeit of incumbency: arrogance, apathy and atrophy. Generally, turnover is greater in countries employing party-list proportional representation. This format allows party leaders to manage the order of candidates on the list so as to ensure a trickle of new members.

In countries employing plurality elections, the extent of turnover is less predictable and return rates can become indefensibly high. For instance, in the United States congressional elections of 2008, only 19 of 404 incumbent candidates in the House, and four of 27 Senators, were defeated (bear in mind, however, that incumbents under threat may opt for a tactical retirement). This **incumbency effect** is particularly striking in the USA. There, especially, existing members of Congress can exploit such resources as voters' recognition, public subsidies, financial backing, constituency service, their own experience and even (in the House of Representatives) the ability to manipulate the boundaries of their electoral districts. For these reasons, fresh candidates are most likely to win when an existing representative stands down, creating an **open seat**.

> The **incumbency effect** refers to the electoral bonus accruing to sitting members when they stand for re-election. In the United States, where this effect is large, an **open seat** is defined as one in which the existing representative has stood down, creating a more even contest.

Term limits provide a blunt solution to this incumbency effect. In Mexico, for example, members of the Chamber of Deputies are restricted to a single three-year tenure. Term limits are also now employed widely in states of the USA, although the Supreme Court declared in *U.S. Term Limits, Inc.* v. *Thornton* (1995) that states cannot impose term limits on their federal representatives.

Although popular with the public, term limits may create more problems than they solve. When members are automatically removed after each

> **Term limits** restrict elected politicians to a maximum number of periods in office, or ban re-election without a break. They enforce turnover at the price of reducing professionalism.

election, no parliamentary career is possible. The outcome is lame duck legislators lacking electoral accountability and concerned mainly to secure their next job. Carey *et al.* (2006) find that term-limited legislators in American states are, in fact, less responsive to their constituents. Ideally, turnover of legislators should be enforced by levelling the playing field, not by banning all experienced players.

Professional politicians are the leading category in most contemporary legislatures but they do not have it entirely their own way. One group, in particular, stands out in contrast to the now traditional political professional. **Celebrities-turned-politicians** exploit their fame in other fields to leapfrog into the legislature or (as with Governor Arnold Schwarzenegger of California) direct to executive office (Box 15.6).

It is tempting to regard celebrities-turned-politicians as an emerging group of post-professional politicians who exploit both their media-generated fame and their status as clean political outsiders to achieve quick political success (Beckman, 2007). Certainly, their presence in the assembly seems to convey a message that voters want to judge politicians by what they stand for, not just by their technical competence.

In an era in which electors have become less partisan and are less likely to watch television news, politicians as a class may find themselves driven to compete in the celebrity space (e.g. talk shows), rather than for the diminishing media coverage set aside for politics exclusively. The incumbency effect encourages even existing politicians with no other claim to fame to develop a high-profile image based on character and individuality – in other words, to adopt the mantle of the **politician-as-celebrity**.

But we should avoid easy generalization here. In particular, the celebrity-turned-politician is far from new. For example, American actress and singer Helen Gahagan Douglas was elected to the House of Representatives as early as 1944. India's Lok Sabha may contain more Bollywood stars than ever before but it is not self-evident that the liberal democratic

BOX 15.6

Actresses, athletes and astronauts: some celebrities in national legislatures

	Year of birth	Country	Source of celebrity
Helen Gahagan Douglas	1900	USA	Actress
John Glenn	1921	USA	Astronaut
Melina Mercouri	1925	Greece	Actress
Sonny Bono	1935	USA	Singer
Glenda Jackson	1936	UK	Actress
Bill Bradley	1943	USA	Basketball
Imran Khan	1952	Pakistan	Cricket
Sebastian Coe	1956	UK	Athletics
Govinda Arun Ahuja	1963	India	Actor
Tony Halme	1963	Finland	Pugilist
Tanja Saarela	1970	Finland	Beauty queen

Further reading: Corner and Pels (2003), Jones (2005), West and Orman (2003).

world (including India itself) is experiencing a mass migration from film studio to parliament. Rather, the appeal of celebrities-turned-politicians seems to lie partly in their outsider status and their very rarity, suggesting a natural limit to their ability to colonize the legislature. The status of outsider is inherently short-lived. The era of the professional legislator is far from over.

One final group of representatives is worthy of note: offspring who follow a parent into the

Celebrities-turned-politicians exploit the fame they have acquired in non-political arenas to ease their entry into political office, including the legislature. Such characters are distinct from **politicians-as-celebrities** whose style is to present themselves to the electors as if they are famous stars of stage and screen.

legislature. In Asia, political families often represent lineages with an established national reputation, or at least tight control over a particular electoral district. In India, for example, the Nehru-Gandhi dynasty is just one of several such dynasties. Before the 2009 election, more than a third of the members of the Japanese Diet were second-generation lawmakers, often inheriting the same seat as their family predecessor (Martin and Steel, 2008). In the Lebanon, too, clans such as the Gemayels and Mouawads are established on the political scene.

Beyond Asia, the phenomenon of second-generation legislators may simply reflect socialization: children growing up in a family where politics is viewed as an occupation are more likely to enter that profession themselves. This effect surely helps to explain why as many as a quarter of the candidates standing in the Australian election of 2001 had a close family member who had also stood for elective office (McAllister, 2003).

From one perspective, political families may be no more disturbing than family lines of physicians and accountants. Yet just as the notion of the professional politician gives rise to the concept of a political class, so too does the idea of political families encourage us to think in terms of a political caste. Both ideas imply a measure of closure in political recruitment and rest uneasily alongside the traditional interpretation of democracy as government by the people.

Legislatures in authoritarian states

Since assemblies are symbols of popular representation in politics, their significance in authoritarian regimes is inherently limited. Such assemblies generally function only as shadow institutions. Sessions are short and some members are appointed by the government. Members concentrate on raising grievances, pressing constituency interests and sometimes lining their own pockets. The rulers regard these activities as non-threatening because the real issues of national politics are left untouched. Yet legislatures are difficult to extinguish completely. A few traditional and dictatorial regimes excepted, most authoritarian regimes possess an assembly of some description. So why do non-democratic rulers bother with them at all? Their value is fourfold:

- A parliament provides a fig leaf of legitimacy, both domestic and international, for the regime. The ruler can say to visiting dignitaries and donors, 'Look! We too have an assembly, just like the British House of Commons and America's Congress!'
- The legislature can be used to incorporate moderate opponents into the regime, providing a forum for negotiating matters that do not threaten rulers' key interests.
- Raising constituents' grievances and lobbying for local interests provide a measure of integration between centre and periphery and between state and society. Such activity oils the political wheels without threatening those who control the machine.
- Assemblies provide a convenient pool of potential recruits to the elite. Behaviour in parliament provides a useful initial test of reliability.

Gandhi (2008, p. 181) offers a useful summary of the functions of parliaments in authoritarian regimes:

Legislatures under dictatorship serve as a controlled institutional channel through which outside groups can make their demands and incumbents can make concessions without appearing to cave in to popular protest.

To be sure, most communist regimes went to considerable lengths to produce statistically representative assemblies. Women and favoured groups such as industrial workers achieved greater representation than in Western legislatures. However, this feature reflected tight party control of the nomination process and the diluted political significance of the parliamentary body which typically met for only around ten days per year. In practice, a socially representative assembly more often indicated impotence than authority; for this reason, the fall in female representation after the end of communism should be interpreted sympathetically.

As communist regimes became somewhat more pluralistic as they matured, so their assemblies began to acquire modest significance. China

illustrates this trend. In the 12 years before Mao Zedong's death in 1976, the National People's Congress (NPC) did not meet at all. However, in the subsequent era of economic reform, the NPC began to emerge. A growing emphasis on the rule of law raised the status of the legislature which has now also begun to express popular hostility to corruption. Many votes are no longer unanimous, proceedings are less easily choreographed, some professional support is available to underpin Congress, and the party must anticipate the NPC's reaction to its proposals. Senior figures drafted into the assembly skilfully strengthened the NPC's position in Chinese governance, not by confrontation with the ruling party but by assisting the growth of the private sector and by making efforts to encourage national integration through links with subnational congresses (K. O'Brien, 2008).

However, the NPC, still the world's largest legislature, remains strongly hierarchical. Plenary sessions are still formal and infrequent. Even more than in committee-based assemblies in democracies, the NPC's influence operates through smaller subgroups. The most important of these is the Standing Committee, a group of about 150 members which meets regularly throughout the year. These subgroups remain sensitive to the party's interests; most members of the Standing Committee – as of the wider NPC – also belong to the party, giving the leadership an additional mechanism of control.

Of course, party domination of legislative proceedings is also found in parliamentary systems in liberal democracies, but there the party in command varies with election results. Although the NPC and its subgroups have become part of the Chinese power network, they still cannot be understood through Western notions of the separation of powers and parliamentary sovereignty.

Legislatures in illiberal democracies

The presence of an assembly is a defining feature of a democracy of any kind, liberal or illiberal. So legislatures certainly form part of the furniture of an illiberal democracy. Furthermore, their political position can be significant in areas that do not threaten the realities of presidential leadership: in representing local districts, for instance, and in passing routine legislation.

However, such assemblies operate in the shadow of executive authority. A nose for power will lead us away from the parliament and to the presidential office. There, we may discover an incumbent who governs by decree as well as by law and who may, *in extremis*, simply dissolve a recalcitrant legislature in search of more congenial arrangements.

The political environment of an illiberal democracy is particularly hostile to the notion that assemblies can hold the government to account through detailed scrutiny. On the contrary, the national leader considers himself responsible to the whole nation, not to what he sees as corrupt, partisan and parochial representatives in the assembly. In addition, many illiberal democracies are either new regimes or located in relatively poor countries; both factors militate against the development of a professional congress with a stable membership, extensive research support and a well-developed committee system. For example, Malawi's National Assembly employs a grand total of two researchers and two committee clerks; the equivalent figure for the United States Congress exceeds 3,000 (Nijzink *et al.*, 2000).

Diamond's observation about new democracies applies also to many illiberal democracies: 'these legislatures lack the organisation, financial resources, information service, experienced members and staff to serve as a mature and autonomous point of deliberation in the policy process' (1999, p. 98). Lacking capacity, parliaments also lack status relative to the dominant leader.

For instance, the position of legislatures in Latin America has undoubtedly strengthened in the post-military era of illiberal, and sometimes even liberal, democracy. As presidents have become more accountable, at least in the larger and more democratic countries, so assemblies have asserted the authority which flows from the separation of powers in a presidential executive. But it would be wrong to conclude that legislatures in these democracies have achieved, or will achieve, the exalted position of Congress in the United States. They still have considerable distance to travel before they can be said to 'restrain the prince and discipline the powerful' (Chalmers, 1990).

In the main, Latin American constitutions do not separate powers as completely as in the USA; rather, they still give presidents greater control over the budget and some latitude to govern through decrees. After Hugo Chávez assumed the Venezuelan presidency in 1998, he virtually dismantled Congress as part of his planning for a new constitution. In 2007, the National Assembly (stripped of opposition by an anti-Chávez boycott of an earlier election) meekly passed a law allowing the president to govern by decree for 18 months. While resources and professionalism have increased in many Latin American legislatures, they still live in the shadow of assertive presidents. For such reasons, electorates still prefer to take their chance with a strong-man president rather than an ill-disciplined and poorly regarded assembly.

In Russia's illiberal democracy, too, parliament (known as the Federal Assembly) occupies a secondary position. Certainly, the communist era of mute and meek assemblies has withered. Russia's post-communist constitution (1993) created a significant bicameral legislature which is now well-established. The State Duma (lower house) contains 450 members elected for a four-year term. The Federation Council (upper house) has 178 members – two selected by each of the 89 units of the federation. Laws take precedence over presidential decrees.

The weaknesses of the Federal Assembly lie more in its relationship with the executive. In the United States, the balance between congress and president is one of mutual checks; in Russia, authority is tilted to the government. Where America sought to limit presidential authority, the Russian tradition – characteristic of illiberal democracies – emphasizes strong government. Thus, the 1993 constitution states that Russia's president is not only 'guarantor of the constitution' but is also required to 'ensure the coordinated functioning and collaboration of bodies of state power'. So far, presidents have performed this role with no great regard for the legislature.

In addition, the limited autonomy of the Duma, at least compared to America's House of Representatives, is reflected in a generally inferior constitutional position. For instance, other actors (including the president) can introduce bills for its consideration and only the government can initiate money bills (Box 15.7).

Comparing Russia's State Duma and America's House of Representatives

	State Duma	House of Representatives
Members enjoy immunity from arrest	Yes	Yes
Consents to president's appointment of prime minister	Yes	No post of prime minister
Can bring down government	Yes	No
President can dissolve chamber	Yes	No
Initiates impeachment of president	Yes	Yes
External bodies can introduce bills	Yes	No
Members can introduce money bills	No	Yes
Can override presidential veto of legislation	Yes	Yes

Notes: 'Yes' may only apply in specific circumstances. Russia's system of government is formally semi-presidential, with the president sitting above the government.

As in other illiberal democracies, the exact political weight of Russia's parliament is difficult to judge and remains subject to change. Donaldson (2004, p. 230) suggested 'that the Russian parliament has become an important counter-weight to its presidency'. Writing just two years later, with Putin's party in the ascendancy within the Duma, Remington (2006, p. 58) judged that 'in the Putin era, parliament's independence has been reduced to virtually nil'. Perhaps so, but even President Putin himself claimed to find value in legislative institutions: 'today, we can justifiably call this period a time of strengthening the country's parliamentary and legal culture. One can speak about a modern State Duma as a working instrument of power' (quoted in Donaldson, 2004, p. 249). In Russia's illiberal democracy, more than in many authoritarian regimes, the legislature is expected to make itself useful – but no more.

Learning Resources for Chapter 15

Next step

Fish and Kroenig (2009) is an extensive reference work assessing the powers of national legislatures along the dimensions of autonomy, capacity, influence and powers.

Further reading

Olson (1994) and Loewenberg *et al.* (2002) offers useful comparative treatments of parliaments. Bicameralism and second chambers have attracted a flurry of interest: see Patterson and Mughan (1999), Uhr (2006) and Tsebelis and Money (1997). Committees are examined comparatively in Longley and Davidson (1998); see also Carey (2006). Cotta and Best (2007) provide a comparative treatment of long-term changes in parliamentary careers. Borchert and Zeiss (2003) is a comparative study of the political class as represented in the legislatures of liberal democracies. Corbett *et al.* (2005) survey the European Parliament. The most intensively studied legislature remains the American Congress: Davidson *et al.* (2009) and Dodd and Oppenheimer (2008) are standard texts.

Internet sources

Centre for Legislative Studies, University of Hull
Research, publication and education about legislatures
http://www.hull.ac.uk/cls/

Commonwealth Parliamentary Association
The parliaments of the Commonwealth
http://www.cpahq.org/

Inter-Parliamentary Union
The leading information source on, and links to, national parliaments
http://www.ipu.org/english/home.htm

Legislative Studies Quarterly
Includes titles and abstracts of articles in the journal
http://www.uiowa.edu/~lsq/

Chapter 16
The political executive

The **political executive** is the core of government, consisting of political leaders who form the top slice of the administration: presidents and ministers, prime ministers and cabinets. The executive is the regime's energizing force, setting priorities, resolving crises, making decisions and overseeing their implementation. Governing without an assembly or judiciary is perfectly feasible but ruling without an executive is impossible.

The political executive, which makes policy, must be distinguished from the bureaucracy, which puts policy into effect. Unlike appointed officials, the members of the executive are chosen by political means, most often by election, and can be removed by the same method. The executive is accountable for the activities of government; it is where the buck stops.

Democratic and authoritarian regimes are defined by the operation of their executive. Liberal democracies have succeeded in the delicate task of subjecting executive power to constitutional constraint. The government is not only elected but remains subject to rules which limit its power; it must also face regular re-election. In an authoritarian regime, by contrast, constitutional and electoral controls are absent or ineffective. The scope of the executive is limited not by the constitution but by political realities.

The executives of liberal democracies fall into three main groups: presidential, parliamentary and semi-presidential. In all three types, power is diffused. In presidential and semi-presidential regimes, the constitution sets up a system of checks and balances between separate executive, legislative and judicial institutions. In addition, the administration and the assembly can be under the control of different parties, providing a further limitation on the ability of the executive to monopolize power.

In parliamentary systems, the government is constrained in different ways. Its very survival depends on retaining the confidence of the assembly. In many cases, its freedom of action is limited further by the need to sustain a coalition between parties that have agreed to share the task of governing.

The central purpose of this chapter is to show how these restrictions on the exercise of power in liberal democracies operate in each of the three systems. The chapter concludes with a discussion of the less institutionalized executives found in authoritarian regimes and illiberal democracies.

The **political executive** forms the top tier of government. It directs the nation's affairs, supervises the execution of policy, mobilizes support for its goals and offers crisis leadership.

Presidential government

The world contains many presidents but fewer examples of **presidential government**. First, any dictator can style himself 'president' and many do so. Second, many presidents are elected in parliamentary systems to serve only as ceremonial head of state. For these two reasons, the existence of a president is an insufficient sign of a presidential system.

> **Presidential government**
> * Direct election of the president who steers the government and makes appointments to it;
> * Fixed terms of offices for the president and the assembly, neither of which can bring down the other;
> * No overlap in membership between the executive and the legislature;
> * The president serves as head of state.

Presidentialism proper is a form of constitutional rule in which a single chief executive governs using the authority derived from popular election, with an independent legislature (Figure 16.1). Almost always, this election takes the form of a direct vote of the people, with a limit on the number of times a president can be re-elected. The president directs the government and, unlike most prime ministers, also serves as ceremonial head of state. Because both president and legislature are elected for a fixed term, neither can bring down the other, giving each institution some autonomy. This separation of powers is the hallmark of the presidential system and is typically reinforced by a separation of personnel. Members of the executive cannot sit in the assembly, creating further distance between the two institutions. Similarly, legislators must resign their seats if they wish to serve in the government, meaning the president's ability to buy members' votes with the promise of a job is self-limiting.

Contrasting methods of election yield a further divergence in interests. Legislators depend only on the support of voters in their home district or state while the president (and the president only) is elected by a broader constituency, typically a national ballot.

So despite the focus on a single office, presidential government divides power. The system creates a requirement for the executive to negotiate with the legislature and, by this mechanism, seeks to ensure the triumph of deliberation over dictatorship. Defenders of the format argue that it captures the essence of democracy, setting constitutional limits on executive pretension. However, detractors suggest that presidentialism is a conspiracy against government. The dangers are threefold:

* That deliberation turns into stalemate;
* That the democratic will is thwarted by excessive fragmentation;
* That the system itself becomes unstable.

Presidential government predominates in the Americas. It is entrenched not just in the United States but also throughout Latin America. We must begin with the USA, where the format emerged, but we will then turn to Brazil as a more typical example.

United States

When the framers of the American constitution met in Philadelphia in 1787, the issue of the executive created a dilemma. On the one hand, the Founding Fathers wanted to avoid anything that might prove to be a 'foetus of monarchy'. After all, the American Revolution had just rid the new nation of England's George III. On the other hand, many delegates agreed with Alexander Hamilton that a single

Figure 16.1 Presidential government

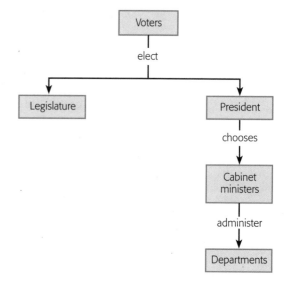

executive was needed for 'decision, activity, secrecy and dispatch'. Eventually, the founders settled on the presidency, an office capable of providing prompt action for a republic in which Congress was nonetheless expected to play the leading role.

But how should the occupant of this new, non-monarchical presidency be selected? Here the delegates were less clear. One possibility was to allow the national legislature to choose the chief executive. A subcommittee of the constitutional convention did canvass this possibility, which would have led to a form of parliamentary government. But the idea that the executive should be beholden to the assembly was not yet established, even in Britain. Instead, rather late in the proceedings, the delegates agreed to select the president through an electoral college whose members would be appointed by state legislatures. So the framers had stumbled across an essential feature of presidential government: separate election of executive and legislature (Dahl, 2001).

The case for separate selection was well made by James Madison (1781) in *Federalist Paper No. 51*:

In order to lay a due foundation for that separate and distinct exercise of the different powers of government, which to a certain extent is admitted on all hands to be essential to the preservation of all liberty, it is evident that each department should have a will of its own; and consequently should be so constituted that the members of each should have as little agency as possible in the appointment of the member of the others.

The founders were not, however, prepared to embrace direct election of the chief executive. On the contrary, the original purpose of the Electoral College had been to insulate the choice of president from influence by the 'excitable masses'. It is somewhat ironic, therefore, that today the president is effectively chosen by precisely the national vote that the delegates so feared. Each state is given a certain number of votes in the College, determined by its number of senators (two) plus its number of representatives in the House (based on the state's population). In all but two states, the leading presidential candidate then receives all its votes in the College, with the candidate winning a majority of College votes being declared president-elect. The College itself is now a mechanical counting device, not a site of decision.

The constitution also ensures that the president, once selected, remains secure in office, thus establishing the separate survival of executive and legislature which is another hallmark of presidential government. The president can only be dismissed by Congress through 'Impeachment for, and on Conviction of, Treason, Bribery, or other high Crimes and Misdemeanors'. So far, just two – including Bill Clinton in 1998 – have been impeached, though neither was convicted (Richard Nixon, however, resigned in 1974, anticipating conviction). Just as Congress cannot normally remove the president, neither can the president dissolve Congress and call new elections.

The constitution states that 'The executive Power shall be vested in a President of the United States of America'. In addition to a general obligation to 'take Care that the Laws be faithfully executed', the president is given explicit duties such as commander-in-chief. These express powers have been interpreted over time as giving the president additional implied powers – those without which he could not fulfil his constitutional duties.

These implied powers are independent of Congress and include the ability to issue executive orders and national security directives (Warber, 2006). Even in these areas, however, any administrative act which requires public expenditure must ultimately be authorized by Congress, and any executive act which offends the constitution may be struck down by the Supreme Court. In addition to express and implied powers, the president possesses further specific powers granted, and revocable, by Congressional statute (Box 16.1).

So although the American presidency is often seen as a symbol of power, the institution was designed as part of a concerted attempt to control executive pretension. As President Kennedy commented, 'the president is rightly described as a man of extraordinary powers. Yet it is also true that he must wield those powers under extraordinary limitations'. For instance, many of the president's powers are shared with Congress:

- The president is commander-in-chief but Congress retains the power to declare war;
- The president can make government appointments and sign treaties but only with 'the advice and consent' of the Senate;

BOX 16.1		

The American presidency: a classification of powers

	Definition	Example
Express powers	Powers explicitly listed in the constitution	'The President shall be Commander-in-Chief of the Army and Navy of the United States'
Implied powers	Powers held to derive from the president's explicit constitutional obligations	The president's obligation 'to preserve, protect and defend the Constitution' is taken to contain the notion of emergency powers
Statutory powers	Additional powers explicitly granted by Congress	Many highly specific grants by legislation, such as the authority to restrict imports from China

---

♦ The president 'recommends to Congress such measures as he shall judge necessary and expedient' but is offered no means to ensure his proposals are accepted;

♦ The president can veto legislation but Congress can override his objections;

♦ Congress, not the president, controls the purse strings.

Two crucial points flow from the president's constitutional position. First, to describe the relationship between the president and Congress as a separation of powers is misleading. In reality there is a separation of institutions rather than of legislative and executive powers. President and Congress share power: each seeking to influence the other but with neither in a position to dictate. This separated system, as Jones (1994) calls it, is subtle, intricate and balanced. It reflects a successful attempt by the founders to build checks and balances into American government.

The tension within the system, it is important to note, continues even when the same party controls both the White House and Congress. Whatever their party, members of Congress have different electoral interests from the president. Unlike the president's national constituency, legislators are elected without term limits from local areas for distinct terms of two years in the House and six years in the Senate (Box 16.2). The divergent interests resulting from these distinct constituencies mean that presidential

government is inherently less party-based than its parliamentary cousin.

This point, frequently misunderstood by foreign observers, is well stated by Mayhew in *Divided We Govern* (1991, p. 135): 'to suppose that an American party winning Congress and the presidency thereby wins the leeway of a British governing party is to be deluded by the election returns'. As he struggled to push his health care reforms through a reluctant Democratic Congress in 2009, President Obama would doubtless have agreed.

Second, in a system of shared control presidential power becomes the power to persuade (Neustadt, 1991). As President Truman said, 'the principal power that the president has is to bring people in and try to persuade them to do what they ought to do without persuasion'. In this task of persuasion, the contemporary president can follow two strategies: **going Washington** and **going public.**

Lyndon Johnson, a former leader of the Senate Democrats who succeeded to the presidency following President Kennedy's assassination in 1963, was a master of the Washington strategy. To secure

Going Washington means the American president engages in wheeling and dealing with members of Congress, assembling majorities for his legislative proposals. **Going public** occurs when the president exploits his unrivalled access to the mass media to influence public opinion and so persuade Washington indirectly (Kernell, 1997).

BOX 16.2

Separate election in the United States

	Electoral unit	Length of term	Limit on re-election
Presidency	A national vote, aggregated by state in an electoral college	4 years	Maximum of two terms
Senate	Direct popular vote in each of 50 states	6 years	No limit
House of Representatives	Direct popular vote in each of 435 districts	2 years	No limit

---

his bold domestic reforms, he leant heavily on members of Congress, using a potent combination of bullying, flattery and persuasion. He was, however, less successful with the wider public, lacking sparkle in front of a television camera. By contrast, 'the great communicator' Ronald Reagan (President, 1981–89) adopted the wider approach, seeking to communicate his agenda to the public and, indirectly, to influence Congress by his domination of the agenda. Wisely, Reagan also employed experienced aides to keep the pressure on key legislators.

The paradox of the American presidency – a weak governing position amid the trappings of omnipotence – is reflected in the president's support network. To meet presidential needs for information and advice, a conglomeration of supporting bodies has evolved, including the White House Office, the National Security Council and the Office of Management and Budget. Collectively known as the Executive Office of the President, these bodies provide far more direct support than is available to the prime minister in any parliamentary system, forming what is often called the institutional presidency (Burke, 2005). The days have long passed (they did once exist) when presidents asked family members to provide them with secretarial support, at no cost to the public purse.

Yet the massive apparatus of advice available to today's president has often proved to be a weakness. Some advisers are mere flatterers and many are political outsiders, appointed by the president at the start of his tenure before his eye for Washington's

politics is in. Far from helping the president, advisers sometimes end up undermining his position. The Watergate scandal in the 1970s destroyed the presidency of Richard Nixon; the Iran–Contra scandal in the 1980s laid siege to the reputation of Ronald Reagan.

One consideration here is that the presidential system lacks a strong cabinet to offer a counterbalance to personal advisers. In the USA, the cabinet goes unmentioned in the constitution; its meetings are little more than a presidential photo opportunity. Cabinet members often experience difficulty in gaining access to the president through his thicket of advisers.

Brazil

With democracy now established in parts of Latin America, students of presidential government must broaden their horizons beyond the USA. The United States remains the prototype but most working examples are now found to the south where the experience is rather less positive. This mixed performance reflects the difficulties of integrating a presidential system with two features, proportional representation and a multiparty system, which are absent in the USA. In short, comparative analysis shows that the USA is an unrepresentative case of presidential government.

A comparison between the USA and Brazil is particularly useful, demonstrating in particular the value of distinguishing between presidentialism in two-party and multiparty conditions. Where the American president is hemmed in with restrictions,

---

BOX 16.3

Comparing presidential powers in Brazil and the USA

	Brazil	USA
Can the president issue decrees?	Yes, in many areas. Valid for 60 days	No
Can the president initiate bills?	Yes, exclusively in some areas	No
Can the president declare bills urgent?	Yes	No
Can the president veto legislation?	Yes, in whole and part	Yes, but no **line-item veto**
How can Congress override a veto?	Absolute majority in joint meeting of both houses	Two-thirds majority in each house
President's control over the budget	Stronger	Weaker
Party system	Multiparty	Two-party
Does the president's party possess a majority in Congress?	No	Occasionally (12 years over the period 1969–2009)
Party discipline in Congress	Weak	Stronger

---

the Brazilian constitution appears to offer the country's president an arsenal of weapons (Box 16.3). First, Brazil's president can issue decrees – provisional regulations with the force of law – in specified areas. These decrees stay in effect for 60 days without parliamentary approval and can be renewed once. Second, he can declare bills to be urgent, forcing Congress to make a prompt decision on these proposals. Third, he (and in some areas he alone) can initiate bills in Congress. Fourth, he proposes a budget which goes into effect, month by month, if Congress does not itself pass a budget. The combined effect of these entitlements would appear to give Brazil's president ample means to govern.

A **line-item veto** is the ability to override a part – a line – of a bill without rejecting it in its entirety. Congress granted American presidents this power in 1996 but the Supreme Court declared the law unconstitutional two years later, stating that the constitution made no provision for the president to amend statutes.

Yet despite their panoply of formal powers, Brazilian presidents face the same problem as their North American colleagues: legislators who know their own interests. Indeed, Brazilian leaders experience even greater difficulty in bending Congress to their will. The explanation for this contrast lies in Brazil's fragmented multiparty system. In 2006, 20 parties were represented in the Chamber of Deputies and 12 in the Senate; as usual, the president's party was in a minority in each chamber.

Furthermore, party discipline within Brazil's Congress is exceptionally weak, reflecting the use of preference votes in the party-list electoral system. Deputies often switch party in midterm; unlike the country's soccer players, they do not even wait until the end of the season before transferring. Members are more concerned to obtain resources for their district than to show loyalty to their party. In Brazil, parties are not only more numerous but also less cohesive than in the USA, a contrast which complicates the president's task.

In responding to this partisan fragmentation, Brazil's presidents build informal coalitions. This requirement takes the form of appointing ministers from a range of parties in an attempt – often only partly effective – to extract loyalty from these parties' deputies. It is as though a Republican president in the United States, confronting a hostile Congress, were able to bolster his support by appointing a few Democratic legislators to his cabinet.

In forming coalitions, Brazilian presidents are assisted by a more flexible interpretation of the separation of institutions than is found in the USA. The United States is, in fact, exceptional within presidential systems in insisting on a strict separation of personnel between government and assembly. For instance, we certainly could not substitute 'the United States' for 'Brazil' in this quotation:

In Brazil, ministers will occasionally resign their government positions just before an important vote in the assembly, resume their legislative seats, vote and then resign their legislative seats and resume their ministerial posts again. (Cox and Morgenstern, 2002, p. 459)

Thus Brazil shows that the executive in presidential government does not need to be drawn from a single party. Like some other chief executives in the region, Brazilian presidents rely on a multiparty governing coalition as a technique for influencing the legislature. However, these coalitions are more informal, pragmatic, ineffective and unstable than the carefully crafted interparty coalitions which characterize parliamentary government in Western Europe. In presidential systems, after all, the collapse of a coalition does not mean the fall of a government, still less fresh elections, meaning the incentive to sustain a coalition is reduced.

So although Latin American constitutions appear to give the chief executive a more important political role, appearances are deceptive. The Latin American experience confirms that presidents operating in a democratic setting confront inherent difficulties in securing their programme. Mainwaring's assessment (1992, p. 112) remains valid:

My own view is that under democratic conditions, most Latin American presidents have had trouble accomplishing their agendas. They have held most of the power for initiating policy but have found it hard to get support for implementing policy. If my analysis is correct, it points to a significant weakness in democratic presidencies.

Assessing presidential government

In the final decades of the twentieth century, many countries emerged from military or communist rule to embrace democracy. Constitution-writers faced the question of whether to adopt a presidential or parliamentary form of government for their new democratic order. One way of forming an overall judgement of the presidential system is to ask what advice we would have provided.

We would need to begin by acknowledging the strengths of presidential rule:

◆ The president's fixed term provides continuity in the executive, avoiding the collapse of governing coalitions to which parliamentary governments are prone;
◆ Winning a presidential election requires candidates to develop broad support across the country;
◆ Elected by the country at large, the president rises above the squabbles between local interests represented in the assembly;
◆ A president provides a natural symbol of national unity, offering a familiar face for domestic and international audiences alike;
◆ Since a presidential system necessarily involves a separation of powers, it should also encourage limited government and thereby protect liberty.

But presidential government also carries inherent risks. Only one party can win the presidency; everyone else loses. All-or-nothing politics can lead to political instability, especially when political trust is still developing. In addition, fixed terms of office are too inelastic; 'everything is rigid, specified, dated', wrote Bagehot (1867). The deadlock arising when executive and legislature disagree means that the new political system may be unable to address pressing problems.

There is a danger, too, that presidents will grow too big for their boots. Latin American experience, for example, shows presidents frequently amending the constitution so as to continue in office beyond their one- or two-term limits.

Even worse, a frustrated or ambitious president may turn into a dictator; presidential democracies are more likely than parliamentary democracies to disintegrate (Cheibub, 2002). The USA remains the world's only case of stable presidential government over the long term – an exception to admire but not, it seems, a model that can be replicated elsewhere.

Presidential government involves betting the country on one person, thus inhibiting the development of the rule of law. Lijphart (2000, p. 267) regards the risks as altogether too great, judging presidentialism to be 'a strongly negative feature for the future of democracy'. He suggests that prudence mandates a parliamentary system governed by a broad coalition cabinet.

In practice, the choices made by new democracies seemed to reflect history and geography more than the wisdom of politics professors. Central European countries such as the Czech Republic and Hungary adopted the parliamentary form which dominates Western Europe, mindful no doubt of their decision to join the European Union. By contrast, post-military regimes in Latin American countries drew on their own political histories and the presence of the USA to the north in order to embrace a presidential system. Only time will tell if Latin America made the right choice.

Parliamentary government

Unlike presidential systems, in which the chief executive is separate from the legislature and independently elected, the executive in **parliamentary government** is organically linked to the assembly

> **Parliamentary government**
> - The governing parties emerge from the assembly and can be dismissed from office by a vote of no confidence.
> - The executive is collegial, taking the form of a cabinet (or council of ministers) in which the prime minister (premier, chancellor) was traditionally just first among equals. The cabinet typically contains around two dozen members and in larger governments not all ministers will be granted a seat.
> - A ceremonial head of state is normally separate from the post of prime minister.

(Figure 16.2). The government emerges from parliament and can be brought down by a vote of no confidence. By the same token the executive can, in nearly all cases, dissolve parliament and call fresh elections. If the paradox of presidentialism is executive weakness amid the appearance of strength, the puzzle of parliamentary government is to explain why effective government can still emerge from this mutual vulnerability of assembly and executive.

The puzzle is particularly acute in those countries where a historic separation of executive and legislative power means that serving cabinet members cannot be members of parliament. The British approach of selecting nearly all ministers from the assembly's ranks is far from universal. In some countries, such as Denmark, there is no such convention and in others, such as Sweden, ministers must resign their parliamentary seat (Box 16.4). Yet incompatibility rules still prove to be consistent with fairly stable governments.

The solution is clear: party provides the necessary unifying device, bridging government and legislature in a manner that presidential systems are designed to prevent. Where a single party wields a

Figure 16.2 Parliamentary government

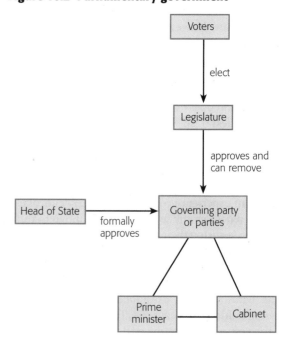

BOX 16.4

Compatibility rules

Can cabinet members also be members of parliament?	Examples
Yes, usually required	Ireland, United Kingdom
Yes	Denmark, Italy
No, incompatible	Belgium, Sweden

majority (as normally in Britain), government can be stable and decisive, perhaps even excessively so. But the British model of single-party majority government, facilitated as it is by a plurality electoral system, is exceptional. In many parliamentary systems, the assembly is elected by proportional representation, a system which rarely results in a majority of seats for one party. The outcomes here are a coalition or a minority administration.

So parliamentary government is as variable in operation as the presidential form. Just as the working of presidential government depends on whether the legislature is based on a two-party system (USA) or a multiparty system (e.g. Brazil), so too does the parliamentary system have two variants, one based on majority government (e.g. UK) and the other on either coalitions (e.g. Finland) or minority government (e.g. Denmark). We examine these forms separately.

Majority government

Britain is the classic example of parliamentary government based on a single ruling party with a secure majority. The plurality method of election customarily delivers a working majority in the House of Commons to a single party. The leader of this party becomes prime minister (PM), selecting 20 or so parliamentary colleagues from the same party to form the cabinet (ministerial council). Where the American cabinet is marginal to the president, the British cabinet is the formal lynchpin of the system; it is the focus of accountability to parliament, and even the strongest PM cannot govern without its support. The cabinet meets most weeks, chaired by

the PM. The monarch now sits above the entire political process, meeting regularly with the PM but rarely if ever intervening in political decisions.

Government accountability to the House is tight. Nearly all cabinet ministers are drawn from, and remain, members of the Commons. All ministers, including the PM, must regularly defend their policies in the chamber; further, the opposition will demand a vote of no confidence whenever it senses an advantage from launching a frontal attack. Should the government lose such a vote, it would be expected to resign, leading either to the opposition taking power or to fresh elections.

However, the key to the system's stability is that party discipline turns the cabinet into the master of the Commons rather than its servant. The governing party spans the cabinet and the assembly, securing its domination of the parliamentary agenda and timetable. The cabinet is officially the top committee of state but it is also an unofficial meeting of the party's leaders. As long as senior party figures remain sensitive to the views of their backbenchers (and often even if they do not), they can control the Commons. The government does indeed emerge from its parliamentary womb but it dominates its parent from the moment of its birth.

How does the ruling party achieve this level of control? Each party has a Whip's Office to ensure that backbenchers (ordinary MPs) vote as its leaders require. Even without the attention of the whips, MPs will generally toe the party line if they want to become ministers themselves. In a strong party system such as Britain's, a member who shows too much independence is unlikely to win promotion. In extreme cases, MPs who are thrown out of their party for dissent are unlikely to be re-elected by constituents for whom a party label is still key. Whatever their private views, it is in backbenchers' own interests to demonstrate public loyalty to their party.

Minority and coalition government

Many countries using parliamentary government elect their legislature by proportional representation, resulting in a situation where no single party gains a majority of seats. Here the tight link between the election result and government formation weakens. In this more fragmented situation, government takes one of three main forms (Müller and Strøm, 2000a):

- A majority coalition in which two or more parties with a majority of seats join together in government. This is the most common form of rule across Continental Europe; it characterizes Belgium, Finland, Germany and the Netherlands in particular.
- A minority coalition or alliance. These are formal coalitions or informal alliances between parties which, even together, still lack a parliamentary majority. Minority coalitions have predominated in Denmark since the 1980s. They were also found in Italy, especially before the transformation of the party system in the 1990s.
- A single-party minority government formed by the largest party. Single-party minority cabinets are common in Denmark, Norway and Sweden (Rasch, 2004, p. 130).

Figure 16.3 shows the party composition of West European governments in the second half of the twentieth century. Majority coalitions are most frequent, followed by single-party minority governments, minority coalitions and, least common, single-party majority governments.

Figure 16.3 Governments in Western Europe, 1945–99

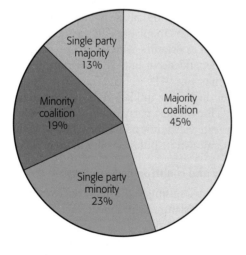

Notes: Based on 424 governments from 17 countries, including UK. Non-party administrations (3%) excluded.

Source: Adapted from Strøm and Nyblade (2007), Table 32.1.

Through both its statements and its silences, the constitution helps to account for these contrasts. The constitution lays out the hurdles a new government must clear before taking office. As Box 16.5 shows, some constitutions (and most recent ones) demand that the legislature demonstrates majority support for the new government through a formal vote of investiture. Spain and most post-communist countries of Eastern Europe are examples. Clearly, this requirement for a positive investiture vote by the assembly encourages the formation of a majority coalition with an agreed programme.

Significantly, some constitutions do not require a majority vote for a new administration. Since 1975, for instance, Sweden has adopted a less stringent test: a vote is held but the test is negative. The proposed prime minister can form a government as long as no more than half the members of the Riksdag object (Bergman, 2000).

In other countries, the constitution is entirely silent on the procedure for approving a new government. In these circumstances, the new administration takes office, and continues in power, until and unless it is voted down by the assembly. Denmark and Norway are examples.

These less demanding conventions – a negative investiture vote or none at all – facilitate the formation and survival of minority governments. Such administrations often receive the support of other parties in parliament which even outside office can continue to influence legislation through their presence on parliamentary committees. These parliamentary support parties, such as the Greens, may even make an agreement with the governing party to offer their support in specific policy areas (Bale and Bergman, 2006). Such circumstances constitute a parliamentary coalition without a governing coalition.

At what stage do parties declare their preferred partners? On occasion, their statement precedes the election, thus allowing voters to make a more informed judgement about the likely consequences of their own decisions. About a quarter of the governments formed in 20 parliamentary democracies between 1949 and 1995 were based on a pre-election coalition. Golder (2006) suggests these advance agreements secure a clear mandate for the government even in the context of a proportional electoral system.

More often, though, the party composition of government is decided after the election, through

Procedure for installing a government in parliamentary systems when no party possesses a majority of seats

	Description	Example
Positive investiture vote	To take office, a new government must obtain majority support in parliament	Spain, Finland
Negative investiture vote	A new government takes office unless voted down by a majority in parliament	Sweden
No investiture vote	No formal parliamentary vote is required before a new government takes office	Denmark

intricate negotiations between the leaders of the relevant parties. While this activity is underway, the outgoing government remains as a caretaker administration. On average, 30 days are needed before the new government takes office but much longer periods are possible: for instance, 208 days in the Netherlands in 1977 and 194 in Belgium in 2007. Let us examine how the search for a new government proceeds during these interregnums.

Some constitutions specify a procedure which the parties follow in forming a government. This often involves the head of state appointing an *informateur*, an experienced figure who explores the practical possibilities for the head of state. The *informateur* will most often recommend that the leader of the largest party be appointed *formateur*. The *formateur's* task is to form an administration through negotiation; this work helps not only to form but also to legitimize the new administration that emerges. Figure 16.4 shows how this process works in the typical case of Belgium.

The parties agreeing to go into coalition will next detail a joint programme in a lengthy public statement. Like constitutions, these package deals are often both opaque and lengthy; for instance, the agreement between the Christian Democrats and the Free Democrats in Germany following the 2009 election extended to 124 pages. These statements cover the policies to be pursued and the coalition's rules of conduct: for example, how it proposes to resolve disputes. Questions of office – which party

Figure 16.4 Government formation in Belgium

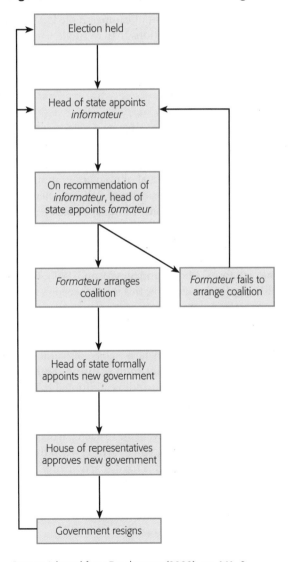

Source: Adapted from Deschouwer (2009), pp. 141–8.

obtains which ministry and whether that party alone determines the appointment – are also negotiated, with a party's bounty tightly reflecting its representation in parliament. Indeed, as Warwick and Druckman (2006, p. 635) observe:

One of the strongest empirical relationships in the social sciences is the linkage between the proportion of legislative seats a coalition party contributes to the total controlled by the government and the share of cabinet portfolios it receives in that government.

The compromises inherent in these deals mean that the rate of enactment of campaign pledges is somewhat lower in coalitions than in single party governments (Mansergh and Thomson, 2007). In a broader sense, though, coalitions tend to the centre, yielding a policy profile close to the typical voter.

Types of coalition

So much for the formalities of coalition formation. What though are the political realities? In particular, why do some parties end up in a governing coalition while others – with an equal or even larger number of seats – remain on the sidelines? Political scientists working within the rational choice approach have devoted considerable effort to answering this question, developing models which predict with about 40 per cent success which of many possible coalitions will form (Martin and Stevenson, 2001). By political science standards, this is a rather high level of predictive accuracy.

The most common type of coalition, it turns out, contains the smallest number of parties (typically two to four) needed to make a viable government. Party interest favours **minimum winning coalitions (MWCs)** because including additional parties in a coalition which already possesses a majority would simply dilute the number of posts and influence over policy that is available to each participant. As Riker (1962, p. 47) succinctly wrote, when the resource to be shared out is fixed, 'participants create coalitions just as large as they believe will ensure winning and no larger'. The rule of political meanness applies: only share when you must and then no more than necessary.

In addition, coalitions are usually based on parties with adjacent positions on the ideological spectrum.

BOX 16.6

Types of coalition government

Type	Definition
Minimum (or minimal) winning	Contains the smallest number of parties which together can secure a parliamentary majority
Oversized (or surplus majority)	Contains more parties than the minimum winning coalition
Grand	Formed by the two leading parties, usually from the left and the right, which together command a substantial majority of seats
Connected	Only contains parties that are located next to each other on an ideological spectrum

Note: Coalitions can be more than one type.

This test shapes which of many possible MWCs are chosen. In most Scandinavian countries, for example, coalitions usually draw exclusively on parties from within either the left-wing bloc or the right-wing bloc. Even where such clear blocs are lacking, the preference is still for **connected coalitions** – formed, that is, from parties adjacent to each other on an ideological and usually left–right scale. To combine two terms from Box 16.6, many cabinets are minimum connected winning coalitions. The rule of political meanness needs qualification: if you must share, do so with neighbours.

In addition, some parties, such as communist parties in Eastern Europe and extreme right-wing parties in Western Europe, are regarded as beyond the pale by the major players. In a sense, these pariah parties fall outside the established party system.

The tendency for neighbours to cooperate benefits centre parties which can jump either way. In Germany, for instance, the small liberal Free Democrat Party has participated in most coalitions, sometimes with the left-wing Social Democrats and since 2009 with the more conservative Christian Democrats. Either coalition could be presented as ideologically coherent. Such well-situated centre parties are known as swing or pivot parties. Germany, however, also has some experience of **grand coalitions** between the two leading parties; these rare episodes marginalize smaller parties like the Free Democrats.

Occasionally, **oversized coalitions** emerge, containing more parties than are needed for a majority. These arrangements typically emerge when the partners are uncertain about the stability of their pact. An influential example is the five-party rainbow coalition, ranging from the conservative National Coalition to the Left Alliance, which governed Finland between 1995 and 2003 (Jungar, 2002). The advantage of such enlarged administrations is that no single participating party may be able to form a majority in conjunction with a party not in the government, thus reducing the likelihood of defection. Oversized coalitions reflect the wise advice to keep your friends close but your enemies closer.

Durability of coalitions

We must address one final issue about coalitions. Such governments are frequently condemned as unstable, not least by English-speaking critics of proportional representation. How valid is this charge? In a few countries, certainly, government duration has been measured in months rather than years: an average of five months for the French Fourth Republic (1945–58) and eight months for Italian governments between 1948 and 1989. In these overcited examples, chronic political instability certainly contributed to poor governance.

But in most of Western Europe, coalition governments last a good deal longer, typically for several years (Strøm *et al.*, 2008). The whole purpose of coalitions is to ensure political, if not always governmental, stability by incorporating parties and the interests they represent into government. With stability as an explicit goal, the political style is deliberately consensual and cautious. Coalitions require negotiation over policy and posts but compromise is seen as a route to stability.

In some countries, additional conventions enhance durability. For example, coalition agreements in Austria, France and the Netherlands typically include a clause stating that the partners will call an election if they dissolve the coalition. This election rule, as it is called, raises the price of

dissolution and gives the partners an incentive to soldier on.

In Germany, two other procedures enhance durability. First, the constructive vote of no confidence requires an assembly to select a new prime minister before it can dispose of the incumbent. This rule prevents legislatures from acting destructively by bringing down a government without any thought to its successor. This mechanism has also been adopted in Hungary, Israel and Spain.

Second, Germany's chancellors can only request the president to dissolve the Bundestag and call fresh elections if they have first lost a vote of confidence. This regulation is meant to ensure the chancellor (unlike most prime ministers) cannot call an election for purely opportunistic reasons. As a result of these two rules, German coalitions typically survive the four years until the next scheduled election.

In post-communist Eastern Europe, however, coalitions have thus far proved to be less stable. Their average duration is barely half that found in the West (Baylis, 2007). Parties themselves are more pragmatic, with an uncertain social base and unclear ideology. The result is fragile coalitions vulnerable to short-term shifts in the political breeze. The west European model of stable coalitions, carefully crafted to avoid any threat to social stability, is difficult to replicate elsewhere.

Who governs?

Parliamentary government lacks the clear focus of the presidential system on a single chief executive. Rather, it involves a subtle and variable relationship between prime minister, cabinet and government ministers. Box 16.7 distinguishes between cabinet, prime ministerial and ministerial government. Examining the balance between these nodes in the governing network, and how they are changing over time, helps in appreciating the realities of parliamentary government.

For advocates of the parliamentary system, **cabinet government** is its key strength, encouraging more deliberation and so resulting in fewer mistakes than occur under a presidential format. When Olsen (1980, p. 203) wrote that 'a Norwegian prime minister is unlikely to achieve a position as superstar', many advocates of parliamentary government would have regarded his comment as praise. In theory, and sometimes in practice,

BOX 16.7

Location of decision-making in parliamentary government

	Description	Example
Cabinet government	Discussion in cabinet determines overall policy	Finland
Prime ministerial government	The PM is the dominant figure, dealing directly with individual ministers	Germany
Ministerial government	Individual ministers operate with little direction from the PM or the cabinet	Italy

parliamentary government involves collective leadership.

Finland provides a clear case of cabinet government. By law, the Finnish State Council is granted extensive decision-making authority. Both the prime minister and individual ministers are subject to constraints arising from Finland's complex multiparty coalitions. Prime ministers are primarily chairs of Council meetings, and it is at these meetings that decisions are reached and compromises made.

In many larger countries, the number and complexity of decisions means they cannot all be settled round the cabinet table. But scale of operation does not necessarily mean the end of cabinet government. Rather, we can sometimes speak of the emergence of a cabinet network, in which cabinet committees develop as important decision sites. Committees are small workgroups that focus on specific areas such as the budget, legislation or overall strategy. In addition to these standing committees, prime ministers also set up ad hoc committees to respond to specific issues such as labour disputes and terrorist acts. New Zealand has around 12 cabinet committees; Canada has eight.

So cabinet government, to the extent that it still exists, has often become government by the cabinet network, with the real decisions merely confirmed in the full meetings. Even committees largely ratify

decisions fixed up before the meeting through informal consultations usually led by the minister most directly concerned.

We move on now to the second row of Box 16.7: **prime ministerial government**. Germany is an example here, though the approach is called chancellor democracy in the country itself. The guiding principle is hierarchy rather than collegiality. The Bundestag (Germany's lower house) appoints a chancellor, not a party, and accountability to the Bundestag is mainly through the occupant of this office. The chancellor answers to parliament; ministers answer to the chancellor. The strong position of Germany's chief executive derives from the Basic Law (constitution) which states that the 'chancellor shall determine, and be responsible for, the general policy guidelines'.

Although there is a danger of inventing a golden age of cabinet government, several commentators suggest that parliamentary executives are, in general, moving in the direction of prime ministerial government. The proposition is that prime ministers have ceased to be first among equals and instead have become president-ministers. Fiers and Krouwel (2005, p. 128), for example, tell us that

within the last two decades, party leaders and prime ministers alike, both in Belgium and the Netherlands, acquired more prominent and powerful positions, transforming these consensus democracies into a kind of 'presidentialized' parliamentary system.

In similar vein, Poguntke and Webb (2005c, p. 340) conclude from a comparative study that 'leaders' power resources and autonomy within national political executives have increased and/or were already at a high level (compared to the type of collegial government that one associates with parliamentarism)'.

King (1994) identifies three factors at work here: increasing media focus on the premier, the growing international role of the chief executive and the emerging need for policy coordination as governance becomes more complex. Someone needs to bring government policy together and commit the country to international agreements with domestic consequences; that person is usually the prime minister. In addition, the prime minister is usually

BOX 16.8

Selecting the head of state in some parliamentary democracies

	Head of state	Method of selection	Tenure
Austria	President	Direct popular election by a two-round system	6 years
Germany	President	Election by a joint Bundestag and *Land* convention	5 years
India	President	Election by a college of federal and state assemblies	5 years
Spain	Monarch	Heredity (eldest male)	Life
United Kingdom	Monarch	Heredity (eldest male)	Life

leader of a party – and party leaders may also be growing in importance as their party's public face in the broadcast media.

Ministerial government, finally, arises when ministers operate without extensive direction from either prime minister or cabinet. This decentralized pattern can emerge either from respect for expertise or from the realities of coalition. Germany is an example of the importance attached to specialization. Although the chancellor sets the overall guidelines, the constitution goes on to say that 'each Federal Minister shall conduct the affairs of his department autonomously and on his own responsibility'. So Germany operates ministerial government within the framework of chancellor democracy. Ministers are appointed for their knowledge of the field and are expected to use their professional experience to shape their ministry's policy under the chancellor's guidance.

In many coalitions, parties appoint their own leading figures to head particular ministries, again giving rise to ministerial government. In the Netherlands, for instance, the prime minister neither appoints, dismisses nor reshuffles ministers. Cabinet members serve with but certainly not under the government's formal leader. In these conditions the premier's status is diminished, with ministers owing more loyalty to their party than to the prime minister or the cabinet. The chief executive is neither a chief nor an executive but rather a skilled conciliator.

Heads of state and parliamentary government

One hallmark of a parliamentary system is, in Bagehot's classic analysis (1867), the distinction between the **dignified** and **efficient** aspects of government. Unlike presidential systems, which combine the offices of head of state and head of government, parliamentary rule separates the two roles. Dignified or ceremonial leadership lies with the head of state; efficient leadership is based on the premier. This separation of roles creates more time for prime ministers to concentrate on running the country.

How then are heads of state selected? The position is either inherited (a monarchy) or elected (a presidency) (Box 16.8). At least in Europe and Asia, royal heads of state remain surprisingly numerous. Half the countries of Western Europe are constitutional monarchies, including Belgium, Denmark, the Netherlands, Spain and the United Kingdom. In some former British colonies such as Canada, a governor general stands in for the monarch.

Although monarchs are reluctant to enter the political arena in democratic times, royal influence can occasionally be significant, especially in times of crisis and transition. In the 1970s, for instance, King Juan Carlos helped to steer Spain's move to

'In such constitutions there are two parts: . . . first, those which excite and preserve the reverence of the population – the **dignified** parts, if I may so call them; and next the **efficient** parts – those by which it, in fact, works and rules . . . Every constitution must first gain authority and then use authority; it must first win the loyalty and confidence of mankind, and then employ that homage in the work of government.' (Bagehot, 1867, p. 6)

democracy. The King of Belgium also played a conciliatory role in his country's long march to federal
status, leading Senelle (1996, p. 281) to claim that
'were it not for the monarchy as symbol of the cohesion of the kingdom and therefore the visible incar-
nation of federal loyalty, the Belgian experiment
would be doomed to failure'.

Monarchies aside, most heads of state in parliamentary systems are elected, either by popular vote
(e.g. Ireland) or by parliament (e.g. Israel).
Alternatively, a special electoral college is used, often
comprising the national legislature plus representatives from regional or local government (e.g.
Germany). Elected presidents in a parliamentary
regime might be expected to have more latitude
than monarchs in addressing national issues but
Tavits (2008) suggests that direct election makes
little difference to their willingness to enter the
political arena.

Semi-presidential government

Presidential and parliamentary government provide
pure models of the political executive. By contrast,
the semi-presidential executive mixes both formats
to produce a new system with its own characteristics. Specifically, **semi-presidential government**
combines an elected president with a prime minister
and cabinet accountable to parliament (Figure 16.5).
Unlike the head of state in parliamentary systems,
the president in a semi-presidential executive is in
rather than above politics. As a two-headed system,
the semi-presidential executive creates a division of
authority within the executive itself and, for that
reason, an invitation to struggle between president
and prime minister.

Semi-presidential government, or the dual executive, combines an elected president performing political tasks with a prime minister who heads a cabinet
accountable to parliament. The prime minister,
usually appointed by the president, is responsible for
day-to-day domestic government but the president
retains an oversight role, responsibility for foreign
affairs and can usually take emergency powers.

The French political scientist Maurice Duverger
(1980) provided an influential definition of semi-
presidentialism. He described the system thus:

A political regime is considered semi-presidential if
the constitution which established it combines
three elements: (1) the president of the republic is
elected by universal suffrage; (2) he possesses quite
considerable powers; (3) he has opposite him,
however, a prime minister and ministers who
possess executive and governmental power and can
stay in office only if the parliament does not show
its opposition to them.

The 'quite considerable powers' of the president
are variable but often include special responsibility
for foreign affairs, appointing the prime minister,
initiating referendums, vetoing legislation and dis-
solving the assembly. In theory, the president can
offer leadership on foreign affairs while the prime

Figure 16.5 Semi-presidential government

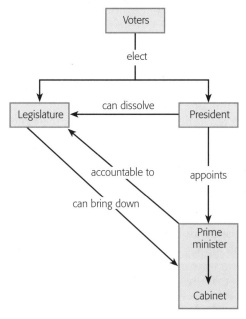

Note: Within semi-presidential government, Shugart and Carey
(1992) distinguish between premier-presidential and president-
parliamentary regimes. In the former, the cabinet is responsible
to parliament; the president cannot dismiss ministers unilaterally,
weakening the president. In the latter, the president as well as
the assembly exerts authority over the cabinet's composition,
strengthening the president.

minister addresses the intricacies of domestic politics through parliament.

If the United States exemplifies the presidential system, the French Fifth Republic provides the archetype of the semi-presidential executive. The 1958 constitution establishing the new regime was designed to provide stable governance in the context of a political crisis caused by a divisive colonial war in Algeria and a rebellious army. In addition, the unstable Fourth Republic, which had experienced 23 prime ministers in its short 12-year life, provided a model to avoid.

The new constitution created a presidency fit for the dominating presence of its first occupant, General Charles de Gaulle (President, 1959–69). Regarding himself as a national saviour, de Gaulle argued that 'power emanates directly from the people, which implies that the head of state, elected by the nation, is the source and holder of that power' (Knapp and Wright, 2006, p. 53). In office, de Gaulle's imperious style developed the office to, and perhaps even beyond, its constitutional limits.

Since a constitutional amendment of 1962, the president has been directly elected, thus fully establishing the semi-presidential form. The effect of this amendment, it is often argued, has been to create a powerful presidency where previously there had just been a powerful president. In a further amendment in 2000, the presidential term was reduced from seven to five years, with a two-term limit following in 2008.

The constitution certainly grants the French president extensive powers. The president:

- Is guarantor of national independence and the constitution;
- Takes emergency powers (not invoked since 1961);
- Heads the armed forces;
- Negotiates treaties;
- Calls referendums;
- Appoints some senior judges and civil servants;
- Presides over the Council of Ministers;
- Dissolves the National Assembly (but cannot veto legislation);
- Appoints (but cannot dismiss) the prime minister, in practice from the party winning assembly elections;
- Appoints other ministers on the recommendation of the PM, and dismisses them;
- Grants pardons;
- Can address parliament (since 2008).

In pursuing these roles, the president is supported by an influential personal staff in the Elysée Palace. So far, all six presidents in the Fifth Republic have sought to govern in expansive style, seeking to steer the ship of state rather than just to arbitrate conflicts emerging among the crew. The highly active approach of Nicolas Sarkozy, elected in 2007 with a supporting majority in parliament, exemplifies presidential activism.

What of prime ministers in France's semi-presidential executive? Although they must countersign most presidential decisions, their main concern is domestic affairs, casually dismissed by de Gaulle as 'the price of milk'. Appointed by the president but accountable to parliament, the prime minister's task is rarely straightforward. He or she (Edith Cresson was PM 1991–92) formally appoints ministers and coordinates their day-to-day work, operating within the president's style and tone. Since the government remains accountable to parliament, much of the prime minister's work focuses on managing the National Assembly. The ability of the assembly to force the prime minister and the Council of Ministers to resign after a vote of censure provides the parliamentary component of the semi-presidential executive.

Semi-presidential government held particular appeal to European countries facing international difficulties. Finland found a semi-presidential system helpful in managing its sensitive relationship with its large Russian neighbour. And a dual executive also proved attractive to east European states in the immediate aftermath of communism's collapse. As international pressures receded, however, so the president's star tended to wane. In 2000, Finland modified its constitution to strengthen the parliamentary element. Further, some post-communist countries, such as Hungary, have moved to a parliamentary form, through strong presidencies still characterize post-Soviet states. The semi-presidential executive was more than a transitional device but it did not threaten the pre-eminence of parliamentary government in Europe.

FRANCE

Form of government ■ a liberal democratic republic, headed by an elected president. The current republic, established in 1958, is the fifth republican regime since the revolution.

Legislature ■ weaker than in many liberal democracies, though marginally strengthened by constitutional reforms in 2008. The lower chamber, the National Assembly, contains 577 directly elected members. The 343 members of the Senate are indirectly elected through local government for a six-year term.

Executive ■ the semi-presidential executive combines a strong president, directly elected for a five-year term, with a prime minister who leads a Council of Ministers accountable to the assembly. Ministers cannot be members of the assembly.

Judiciary ■ French law is based on the Napoleonic Codes (1804–11). The Constitutional Court has grown in significance during the Fifth Republic and in 2008 acquired the power of judicial review.

Electoral system ■ a two-round system is used for both presidential and assembly elections, with a majority vote needed for victory on the first round.

Party system ■ left–right conflict remains a principle of French politics, though parties themselves have proved to be less stable. In the 2007 presidential election, Nicolas Sarkozy of the centre right was elected in a run-off against Ségolène Royal, leader of the Socialist Party.

Population (annual growth rate): 64.1m (+0.6%)	
World Bank income group: high income	
Political Rights score: ①	
Civil Liberties score: ①	
Human development index (rank/out of): 10/177	
Freedom of the press index (rank/out of): 43/195	
Perceived transparency index (rank/out of): 23/180	

Note: For meaning and sources of scales and indexes, see p. xv. In all cases a score and rank of 1 is 'best'.

Just how different is modern France? The case for French exceptionalism can be stated in three words: the French Revolution. The revolution of 1789 created a distinctive ethos within the country, centred on the idea of the nation. Expressed through a distinct language and culture, the nation is the fundamental source of political authority.

The state stands above mere partial interests, defining the long-term national will. Like other states built on revolution, notably the United States, France is an ideal as well as a country. But whereas American ideals led to pluralism, the French state is expected to be the leading player, uniformly implementing the revolution's ideals of liberty, equality and fraternity. All citizens possess the same rights and obligations and it is the state's task both to secure the rights and to extract the obligations.

As the country became more modern, urban and industrial after 1945, so French uniqueness declined. Retreat from empire left France, like Britain, as a middle-ranking power – albeit with a new base in the European Union. The creation of a new regional level of governance within France reduced the state's traditional centralization. Immigration from North Africa moderated the country's homogeneity, leading some to favour a more relaxed interpretation of citizenship. These changes led Hayward (1994, p. 32) to conclude that 'the revolutionary impulse is exhausted'.

Yet to portray France as just another democracy is to go too far. Inherited traditions still condition the way the country approaches its cosseted workforce, subsidized farmers and considerable but unequal affluence. Public discourse still assumes that the state must be capable of creating new jobs while simultaneously protecting the security of existing workers. Sovereignty is still presented as a cardinal virtue, with the result that globalization (and the USA specifically) is seen more as a threat than an opportunity. *Dirigisme* (state direction), suggests Wright (1997), has evolved rather than disappeared. Even if *l'exception française* is a myth, the legend itself still gives French politics its distinctive flavour.

Further reading: Cole *et al.* (2008), Knapp (2006), Stevens (2003).

The political executive in France

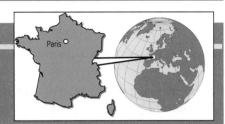

Paris

In France's semi-presidential executive the crucial relationship is between the president, on the one hand, and the prime minister and assembly, on the other. While the constitution may give control of foreign affairs to the president and reserve domestic policy to the prime minister, an interdependent world does not permit such pigeon-holing. France's relationship with the EU, for instance, encompasses both foreign and domestic affairs, complicating the decision-making process. Before one EU summit, Germany's chancellor insisted on meeting the French president and prime minister together, to speed negotiations. How then does France's complex political executive operate?

Presidents and prime ministers need to work in harmony, a task made easier when the party in the Elysée Palace also has a majority in the assembly. This has been the case for most of the Fifth Republic. Indeed, the reduction of the president's term to five years was partly an attempt to coordinate presidential and parliamentary election terms, limiting the likelihood of cohabitation.

When cohabitation does occur, as it has done three times since 1986, pres-

Cohabitation occurs in a semi-presidential executive when president and prime minister are drawn from different political camps. It intensifies competition between the two principals and places the president in the awkward position of leading both the nation and the opposition.

idential power tends to shrink. In these circumstances, prime ministers assert their constitutional duty to 'determine and direct the policy of the nation'. Crucially, though, cohabitation has not led to a crisis of the regime. The Fifth Republic has delivered the stability that its architects intended.

Just as the United States copes with power divided between the White House and Congress, so French experience confirms that the semi-presidential executive can provide stable government even when president and prime minister are drawn from different political blocs.

Cohabitation in the Fifth Republic, 1958–2006

	President	Party	Prime minister	Party
1986–1988	François Mitterrand	Socialist	Jacques Chirac	Gaullist
1993–1995	François Mitterrand	Socialist	Edouard Balladur	Gaullist
1997–2002	Jacques Chirac	Gaullist	Lionel Jospin	Socialist

Beneath the president and prime minister, the government's day-to-day political work is carried out by 19 senior ministers, supported by deputy ministers and ministers of state. There are four main reasons, however, why this group lacks even the public collegiality displayed by members of the British cabinet:

- Most (though not all) governments in the Fifth Republic have been coalitions, with ministers drawn from more than one party;
- The Council of Ministers (the cabinet), chaired by the president, is more ritual than discussion; its functioning resembles the

American rather than the British equivalent;
- Ministers are given a detailed specification of their responsibilities on appointment and often come to the job with a background in its area, thus generating an expectation that they can function autonomously;
- Interventions by the prime minister and the president are often to resolve disputes rather than to impose an overall agenda.

Ministerial autonomy is further enhanced by limited accountability to the assembly (ministers cannot be members of parliament though they do speak before it) and by a tradition of deferential treatment by the media, particularly on personal matters. These conditions encourage corruption, leading to Williams's description of France 'as the classic land of political scandal' (1970, p. 3).

Further reading: Elgie (2005), Godin and Chafer (2006), Hayward and Wright (2002).

The executive of the European Union

Characteristically, the executive of the European Union does not map neatly onto any of the executive types – presidential, parliamentary or semi-presidential – we have discussed. Nonetheless, its institutions are well-developed in comparison to mere intergovernmental organizations and its unique structures merit discussion.

As we might expect for a confederal entity, the EU's executive is based on a balance between transnational and intergovernmental forces. The key executive body, the European Commission, represents the common European interest. However, the Council of the European Union (also called the Council of Ministers) represents the member states and plays an increasingly important legislative and policy-making role. It is this blend of transnational (commission) and intergovernmental (council) ingredients which gives the executive its flavour.

Both the Commission and the Council perform legislative as well as executive functions. The Commission instigates legislative proposals while the Council must approve them. Indeed, the Council is sometimes seen as a second legislative chamber, representing the member states in the same way that Germany's state governments are directly represented in the Bundesrat. The sharp distinction drawn in many national constitutions between executive and legislative tasks is not matched in the EU.

The European Commission

The Commission is the EU's central executive body. Its structure, at least, resembles that of a national government in a parliamentary system. The Commission is headed by a president (the equivalent of a prime minister) who leads a college (cabinet) of commissioners (ministers). Like many national cabinets, the college meets weekly and reaches what are formally collective decisions. The 27 commissioners – a reduction is planned – operate with substantial autonomy. In practice, the working method comes closer to the ministerial rather than the collegial form of cabinet government.

The Commission is organized into departments known as Directorates General (DGs) and services (such as the Legal Service). These are equivalent to

---

The European Commission: Directorates General for Policies and External Relations, 2009

Policies	External Relations
Agriculture and Rural Development	Development
Competition	Enlargement
Economic and Financial Affairs	EuropeAid:
Education and Culture	Co-operation Office
Employment, Social Affairs and Equal Opportunities	External Relations
Energy and Transport	Humanitarian Aid
Enterprise and Industry	Trade
Environment	
Executive Agencies	
Maritime Affairs and Fisheries	
Health and Consumers	
Information Society and Media	
Internal Market and Services	
Justice, Freedom and Security	
Regional Policy	
Research	
Taxation and Customs Union	

Source: Europa (2009).

---

ministries in national governments. Each DG is responsible for a particular policy area and is headed by a Director General reporting to a commissioner (Box 16.9). Like national ministries, DGs are subdivided into divisions, known as directorates.

The 23,000 staff in the DGs are the Union's civil servants and, in that sense, the Commission forms an administrative bureaucracy as well as a political executive. Although the Commission employs the vast majority of EU staff, it remains tiny compared to national civil services. This fact reflects the EU's major role as a regulator rather than as an executor.

The EU's member states are primarily responsible for implementing policies developed by the Commission in Brussels, just as Germany's states give effect to policies agreed in Berlin. The Commission's job is to make regulations and oversee their execution without serving as the implementing agent itself.

Where the Commission does depart from the model of the parliamentary executive is in the manner of its appointment and the forms of its accountability. Rather than emerging from the European Parliament (EP), as we would expect from the parliamentary model, the president and commissioners are effectively nominated by the governments of the member states and only subject to approval by parliament. The nominees are interviewed by parliament which then votes on the proposed list as a whole. So we see here an example of the intergovernmental aspect of the European Union.

Again in contrast to parliamentary systems, the survival of the Commission is only loosely bound to its ability to maintain the parliament's confidence. Each college of commissioners is expected to see out its five-year term, with a new commission appointed following each parliamentary election. True, the EP is empowered to censure the Commission as a whole. In 1999, the college headed by Jacques Santer resigned six months before the end of its tenure, fearing censure for favouritism in appointments, financial mismanagement and lack of responsibility. The right of censure, like that of impeachment, provides a safety valve for difficult circumstances.

In pursuing the interests of the Union as a whole, the Commission possesses a substantial array of duties. It fulfils its function of promoting the common European interest by:

◆ Acting with the Court of Justice as guardian of the treaties;
◆ Exclusively proposing legislation;
◆ Managing the budget;
◆ Overseeing the implementation of policy by member states and European agencies;
◆ Representing the EU externally.

Historically, the Commission provided the motor of European integration, particularly in its development of the internal market during the 1980s. Now that the EU is more cautious about such grand initiatives, the Commission's glory days have passed. Nonetheless, like the bureaucracies of national governments, it remains a store-house of expertise and an institution capable of transforming political will into administrative direction. It is also the Union's main link with the interest groups on which policy-makers rely for information about developments in the member states. For these reasons, Nugent (2006, p. 190) concludes that 'the Commission is central and vital to the whole EU system'. Egeberg (2008, p. 235) goes on to draw a broader lesson:

For the first time in the history of international organizations, we can speak of a multi-purpose supranational executive with its own political leadership that is able to act relatively independently from national governments and councils of ministers.

Council of the European Union

But any assessment of the Commission must also bear in mind the intergovernmental Council of the European Union ('Council of Ministers'). The Council's responsibilities are to pass laws, in many areas jointly with the European Parliament; to coordinate the economic policies of the member states; to conclude international agreements; to approve the EU budget, jointly with the EP; to develop the EU's foreign and security policy; and to arrange for cooperation between member states in investigating cross-border crime (Europa, 2009).

The Council is a large forum in which varying groups of ministers from member states meet to formulate goals, agree policies, reach decisions and issue statements. It meets in nine different configurations, depending on topic (e.g. economic and financial affairs). The relevant minister from each member state attends particular meetings, supported by officials from the home government. In total, the Council meets around 90 times a year, typically for all day sessions which can contain over 100 participants, excluding interpreters. Decisions are reached by a qualified majority. The Council's president, supported by an extensive secretariat, seeks to build a consensus for particular initiatives and to inject coherence into proceedings.

Contrary to the hopes of the Union's founders, the significance of the Council of the European Union has not faded away as the EU has developed; on the contrary, its position has strengthened. Its legislative, strategic and policy-making character, and its focus on foreign policy and crime, give the Council a distinct position within the EU which both complements, and to an extent stands above, the Commission's more executive and administrative role. Certainly, as an intergovernmental body, the Council's position needs careful assessment in any overall judgement of the Commission's weight as a 'multipurpose supranational executive'.

In addition to the Council of the European Union, the European Council, consisting of the heads of government and the Commission president, meets at least twice a year. The European Council is a political and intergovernmental summit intended to steer the Union's development and especially its foreign policy. The emergence of the European Council has further strengthened the intergovernmental element of the EU. Under the Treaty of Lisbon, the European Council appoints a president for a tenure of two and a half years, renewable only once; the Council can also remove the incumbent. Significantly, this new post is popularly described as 'president of Europe'.

The executive in authoritarian states

In authoritarian states, formal executive structures – the executive, legislature and the judiciary – are less well-developed than in democracies. The top office may consist of a presidency (as in many civilian regimes) or a ruling council (as in many military governments) but the central feature of the authoritarian executive is its lack of institutionalization. The leader seeks to concentrate power on himself and his supporters, not to distribute it among institutions. Jackson and Rosberg's idea of **personal rule**

> Jackson and Rosberg (1982, p. 19) define **personal rule** as 'a system of relations linking rulers not with the "public" or even with the ruled but with patrons, associates, clients, supporters and rivals who constitute the "system". The system is "structured" not by institutions but by the politicians themselves. The fact that it is ultimately dependent upon persons rather than institutions is its essential vulnerability'.

(1982), although developed in the context of African politics, travels widely through the non-democratic world. Politics takes precedence over government and personalities matter more than institutions: a feast of presidents but a famine of presidencies.

This formula of strong politics amid weak institutions can itself become entrenched. More often, though, the result is a struggle over succession, insufficient emphasis on policy, and poor governance. In particular, the lack of a succession procedure (excepting hereditary monarchies) can create a conflict among potential inheritors not just after the leader's exit but also in the run-up. Authoritarian leaders keep their job for just as long as they can ward off their rivals. They must monitor threats and be prepared to neuter those who are becoming too strong. Politics comes before policy.

The price of defeat, furthermore, is high; politics can be a matter of life and death. When an American president leaves office, he can retire to his library to write his memoirs but ousted dictators risk a harsher fate. By necessity, therefore, the governing style of non-democratic rulers inclines to the ruthless.

We will use post-colonial Africa, the Middle East and post-communist countries in central Asia to illustrate these themes, before turning to the executive under communist rule.

Africa

Especially in the authoritarian era before the 1990s, post-colonial Africa illustrated the importance of personal leadership in non-democratic settings. Leaders were adept at using the coercive and financial resources of the regime to reward their friends and punish their enemies. As Sandbrook (1985) wrote of Mobutu Sese Seko during his dictatorial tenure as President of Zaire (1965–97):

> No potential challenger is permitted to gain a power base. Mobutu's officials know that their jobs depend solely on the president's discretion. Frequently, Mobutu fires cabinet ministers, often without explanation. Everyone is kept off balance. Everyone must vie for his patronage.

However, in post-colonial Africa, as in most authoritarian regimes, personal rule was far from absolute. Inadequately accountable in a constitutional sense, many personal rulers were highly constrained by other political actors. These included the military, leaders of ethnic groups, landowners, the business class, the bureaucracy, multinational companies and even factions in the leader's own court. To survive, leaders had to distribute the perks of office so as to maintain a viable coalition of support drawn from these groups. Enemies could be bought off by allowing them a share of the pie but their slice must not become so large as to threaten the big man himself. Mobutu himself set out the ground rules: 'if you want to steal, steal a little in a nice way. But if you steal too much to become rich overnight, you'll be caught' (Gould, 1980, p. 485).

The Middle East

In the Middle East, personal rule remains central to authoritarian rule. Shahs, sheikhs and sultans continue to rule oil-rich kingdoms in traditional patriarchal style. 'Ruling' rather than 'governing' is the appropriate term. In Saudi Arabia, for instance, advancement within the ruling family depends less on merit than on proximity to the family's network of advisers, friends and guards. Public and private are interwoven, each forming part of the ruler's sphere. Government posts are occupied on good behaviour, as demonstrated by unswerving loyalty to the ruler's personal interests.

Such systems of personal rule have survived for centuries, limiting the development of strong institutions. Leaving succession difficulties to one side, the paradox of Middle Eastern politics is that personal rule itself constitutes a stable regime, providing an exception to the general theme of instability in the authoritarian executive.

Central Asia

Personal rule also characterizes the post-communist states of central Asia such as Kyrgyzstan and Uzbekistan. While central Europe has moved in a democratic direction, many of the successor republics to the Soviet Union have seen the rise of authoritarian regimes with strong, personalized and non-accountable presidents. In these impoverished and mainly agricultural republics, where democracy has never flourished and experience of independent statehood is limited, rulers are concerned with power and voters with their daily struggle. Neither group cares greatly for structures of government.

In the central Asian republic of Uzbekistan, for example, the presidency is strongly personalized:

Power resides as much in the person of the president as in the office. The Uzbek presidency is not just a formal power position; it is also the center of an extensive informal network of regionally based, patron–client ties. The president is, in effect, the chief patron. (Easter, 1997)

Communist states

We might expect the institutions of government to have played a more central role in communist regimes. After all, these were political regimes par excellence, seeking to lead and transform society in a planned fashion.

Most communist states did have a clear structure of government, resembling the parliamentary form. A chairperson (prime minister) headed a presidium (cabinet). This presidium was, in turn, an inner steering body of a larger Council of Ministers which was itself formally 'elected' by the Supreme Soviet (parliament). An honorific post of state president also existed.

But in practice the ruling communist party dominated the formal institutions of state; the key post was general secretary of the party, not chairman of the presidium. The party secretary often confirmed his supremacy by taking a state post, whether prime minister or president. However, power remained rooted in the party; if the top leader lost his position as party secretary, he was politically doomed.

China offers a partial exception to this picture of a party-dominated executive in communist states. Chinese politics has always been more fluid and personal than in other communist states; some past leaders have not occupied any formal positions at all, whether in the party or the government. As is customary in communist countries, the state is led by the party. But the party itself is divided into factions based on personality and patronage. It is these factions within the party which provide political glue, binding the actors together in a predictable but non-institutionalized way.

Thus the Chinese case returns us to the theme of personal rule in authoritarian regimes. In China's factional environment, the top figures require cunning and patronage to prosper. Indeed, the evidence from China confirms that even this massive communist state can be ruled in a highly personal way. As Saich (2004, p. 83) observes:

Personal power and relations with powerful individuals are decisive throughout the Chinese political system. While this may decline as reforms become more institutionalized, most Chinese recognize that the best way to survive and flourish is to develop personal relationships (*guanxi*) with a powerful political patron.

The executive in illiberal democracies

The characteristic form of the executive in illiberal democracies is presidential rather than parliamentary. Where a prime minister in a parliamentary regime was traditionally first among equals, a presidential regime provides a natural platform for a leader who seeks to set himself apart from – and above – all others. In an illiberal democracy, the president operates without the full set of constitutional restraints which contain the chief executive of a liberal democracy. Instead, the president uses his direct mandate from the people and his claim to act in their long-term interests to cast a shadow over competing institutions such as the courts and the legislature without, however, reducing these bodies to token status. So we observe, once again, a form of personal rule.

This theme is illustrated in contemporary Russia. Formally, Russia is a semi-presidential regime arranged along French lines, with a directly elected president coexisting with a chairman of the government (that is, prime minister) who is nominated by the president and approved by the Duma (lower house).

In some minor respects, the Russian president's position is only slightly stronger than that of an American president. Both are limited to two four-year terms in office but the Russian leader can stand again after a term out. Both are subject to impeachment but the threshold is more demanding in Russia: a two-thirds majority in both parliamentary chambers plus confirmation by the courts. President Yeltsin narrowly avoided impeachment in 1999.

In reality, though, the Russian president can grasp the levers of power more easily than either an American or a French president. Under the 1993 constitution, the president acts as head of state, commander-in-chief and guarantor of the constitution. In the latter capacity, he can suspend the decisions of other state bodies. He can also issue decrees, though these can be overridden by legislation. In contrast to most semi-presidential systems, the president is empowered to remove ministers without parliamentary consent; and does so.

Russia's president is also charged with 'defining the basic directions of the domestic and foreign policy of the state' and with 'ensuring the coordinated functioning and collaboration of bodies of state power'. These broad duties affirm Russia's long tradition of executive power, a norm which both predates and was reinforced by the communist era. Strong government is regarded as a necessary source of effective leadership for a large and sometimes lawless country.

'The federal presidency is hegemonic', says Willerton (2005, p. 23), 'not only because its position is legally superior to that of other institutions, but because it possesses considerable independence and freedom of manoeuvre'. If there is any comparison at all with French semi-presidentialism, it is with the early days of the Fifth Republic, when de Gaulle was seen (and saw himself) as the guarantor of political order. But where the French president has since lost some ground as the country's politics has become more conventional, Vladimir Putin's tenure of Russia's presidency (1999–2008) saw a deliberate strengthening of executive power in the Kremlin.

Yet even after completing his tenure as president in 2008 to take up the office of prime minister, Vladimir Putin remained the pivotal figure in the country's government and politics. To a substantial extent, at least, power followed the man. The impact of the new president, Dmitri Medvedev, seemed to be marginal compared to that of his predecessor in the Kremlin. So in Russia's new and distinctly illiberal democracy, as in many others, it remains hazardous to seek to infer political realities from constitutional statements.

With its heavy artillery of supporting institutions, Russia's presidency is untypical of executive rule in illiberal democracies. Most often, illiberal democracy is found in smaller countries in Africa and Latin America, where presidential authority operates in a more personal way, often linked to effective use of patronage and a populist style. For instance, many African countries continue to find themselves locked into a situation where even elected presidents rule through personal relationships, preventing the growth of strong institutions that might encourage a transition from an illiberal to a liberal democracy. As Hyden (2006, p. 114) writes:

African rulers continue to see their interests as tied to local communities rather than to systems of abstract rule. They act at the level of the state as they do in their community. They rely on investments in personal reciprocity that are self-enforcing and hence not a matter for a court or any other third party to judge. They act in ways that go contrary to the principles of transparency and accountability.

These patronage networks, skilfully deployed, enabled 85 per cent of African presidents standing for re-election to secure victory between 1990 and 2005 (Posner and Young, 2007). Many African elections have become more competitive but the incumbent is still more likely to fall victim to term limits than to an opponent (Prempeh, 2008).

In some cases, including most French-speaking and some English-speaking African states, a semi-presidential form has been introduced as part of the transition from authoritarian rule. But 'form' is the operative word here. An executive president remains the dominant figure, as with President Musevini in Uganda. The prime minister and other ministers are

Vertical accountability exists when an actor at one level is overseen or is subject to sanction by an actor at another level. An example is a president subject to periodic re-election. **Horizontal accountability** exists when oversight or superintendence operates at the same level. An example is a president whose actions are subject to judicial review.

highly subordinate, such that the overall system is best characterized as presidential (Kirsche, 2007).

In the illiberal democracies of Latin America, similarly, accountability tends to be **vertical** (between the president and the voters) rather than **horizontal** (between the president and other political institutions such as the courts and congress). The concentration of authority in the presidency is both justified and reinforced by the weakness of other institutions. However, vertical accountability provides a broad and blunt device for holding the executive to account; horizontal accountability is needed if the president is to be pinned down in specific areas and the political system moved in a liberal direction (Mainwaring and Welna, 2003).

'US presidentialism', writes Philip (2003, p. 24), 'has been historically based on ideas of checks and balances, while Latin American presidentalism was often based on a search for leadership'. Philip cites the campaign slogan of a Brazilian politician from the 1940s: 'I steal but I get things done'. Even in recent times, many presidents have stolen from their own constitution, modifying its content to permit both their own re-election and government by decree. The leader still stands at the top of the tree, preventing both regression to dictatorship and progression to liberal democracy.

Learning Resources for Chapter 16

Next step

Lijphart (1992) remains an excellent collection on parliamentary and presidential government.

Further reading

Much work on the executive has focused on presidential government (including Latin America): for instance, Linz and Valenzuela (1994) and Mainwaring and Shugart (1997). On semi-presidential government, Elgie (1999, 2001) and Moestrup and Elgie (2005) offer comparative perspectives. On the American presidency, see helpful collections by Nelson (2009) and Ellis and Nelson (2006). Comparative but contrasting studies of parliamentary government include Strøm *et al.* (2008), Rhodes (2006b) and, on presidentialization, Poguntke and Webb (2005b). Helms (2005) compares the United States, Britain and Germany, thus contrasting presidential and parliamentary systems. For the selection of ministers, see Dowding and Dumont (2008). The executive in post-communist Europe is covered in White *et al.* (2003); see Willerton (2005) for Russia.

Internet sources

AmericanPresident.org
Covers the history and functions of the American presidency
http://www.americanpresident.org/

Cabinet Office, UK
An informative site, not least on cabinet committees
http://www.cabinetoffice.gov.uk/

Center on Institutions and Governance, University of Berkeley
Research and education on the origins, effects and evolution of institutions
http://igov.berkeley.edu/about.html

President of Russia
An informative site
http://www.kremlin.ru/eng/

Chapter 17
Public management

The study of public management focuses on the networks of central departments and public agencies that underpin the political executive. These networks provide advice to ruling politicians before policy is made and help to implement decisions once reached. The department secretary offering advice to the minister, the inspector checking tax returns, the health officer implementing a national anti-obesity strategy – all are part of the complex operation that is modern governance.

Traditionally, the study of public management focused on the central **bureaucracy**: the permanent salaried officials employed in central government departments to advise on, and administer, government policy. These elite officials, and the ministries they occupy, remain of obvious importance, but attention increasingly focuses on the wider governance beyond: in semi-independent agencies, local governments and even the non-governmental organizations to which the delivery of public programmes is increasingly subcontracted. For the time being, at least, the emphasis is as much on managing networks as on advising ministers.

A chapter on public management must therefore address agendas old and new. We begin by examining the evolution of the public sector, reviewing the forces shaping its development, before turning to the intricate organization of the contemporary public sector and the resulting issues of accountability raised by this complexity. We then discuss new public management, a philosophy which seeks to escape from traditional notions of bureaucracy, and we conclude by examining public management in authoritarian states and illiberal democracies.

Evolution

To appreciate modern bureaucracy, we must consider what preceded it. As with other aspects of government, the precursors varied between Europe and the New World. In Europe, clerical servants were originally agents of the royal household, serving under the personal instruction of the ruling monarch. Many features of modern bureaucracies – regular salaries, pensions, open recruitment – arose from a successful attempt to overcome this idea of public employment as personal service to the monarch.

Bureaucracy is, literally, rule by officials. The word 'bureau' comes from the Old French term *la bure*, meaning the brown woollen cloth on which the king's administrators laid out their accounts. The second half of 'bureaucracy' comes from the Greek *kratos*, meaning rule. Today, the term refers to the salaried officials who form the public administration or civil service.

The evolution of royal households into twentieth-century bureaucracies was a massive transformation, intimately linked to the rise of the modern state (Hyden, 1997). Today, we take the features of bureaucratic organization for granted, and even react against them, but in the early twentieth century the form was strikingly new: a phenomenon to be both admired and feared. The analysis presented by Max Weber exemplified this perspective, providing the traditional hierarchical view of public administration against which the newer ideas of networks and governance have formed (Box 17.1)

Weber's central claim was that bureaucracy made administration more efficient, providing the means by which the techniques of modern industry could be brought to bear on civil affairs:

The fully developed bureaucratic apparatus compares with other organizations exactly as does the machine with non-mechanical modes of production. Precision, speed, clarity, knowledge of files, continuity, discretion, unity, strict subordination, reduction of friction and of material and personal costs – these are raised to the optimum point in the strictly bureaucratic administration. (quoted in Kahlberg, 2005, p. 199)

While Weber's ideas proved to be highly influential in continental Europe, they carried less resonance in the New World. There, civil service development was more pragmatic. Lacking the European monarchical and state tradition, public management was initially considered to be a routine application of political directives. In the United States, the original philosophy was one of governance by the common man; almost every citizen, it was assumed, qualified for almost every public job. The notion of a professional civil service was considered somewhat elitist and undemocratic.

This populist theory of public management conveniently underpinned the **spoils system,** a term deriving from the phrase 'to the victor, the spoils'. The spoils system continued at least until 1883 when the Pendleton Act created a Civil Service Commission to recruit and regulate federal employees. So where a **merit system** had emerged in Europe in reaction to monarchy, in the USA it supplanted spoils.

BOX 17.1

Max Weber on bureaucracy

The German sociologist Max Weber (1864–1920) conceived of bureaucracy as a structured hierarchy in which salaried officials reach rational decisions by applying explicit rules to the facts before them. His model contains five features:

▶ Bureaucracy involves a carefully defined division of tasks;
▶ Authority is impersonal and decisions are reached by methodically applying rules to particular cases;
▶ People are recruited to serve in the bureaucracy based on proven or at least potential competence;
▶ Officials who perform their duties competently possess secure jobs and salaries and can expect promotion according to seniority and merit;
▶ The bureaucracy forms a disciplined hierarchy in which lower officials are subject to the authority of their superior.

Western bureaucracies reached their zenith in the twentieth century. The depression and two world wars vastly increased government intervention in society. The welfare state, completed in Western and especially Northern European countries in the decades following the Second World War, required a massive bureaucratic apparatus to distribute grants, allowances and pensions based on complex eligibility rules set by politicians. By 1980, public employment accounted for almost a third of the total workforce in Britain and Scandinavia, though much of this expansion took place at local level.

However, the final quarter of the twentieth century witnessed declining faith in government and bureaucracy. Where Weber had lauded the efficiency of the administrative machine, critics now judged

---

In a **spoils system**, elected politicians distribute government jobs to those with the foresight to support the winning candidate. In nineteenth-century America, the election of a new president led to a virtually complete turnover of employees in what was then a small federal government. In the contrasting **merit system**, public employees are recruited on merit by competitive examination.

that civil servants were engaged in unproductive games to increase the budgets and staffing of their particular sections (Niskanen, 1971). More to the point, public finances deteriorated in the 1970s. Seizing on this fiscal crisis, right-wing politicians such as Margaret Thatcher called for, and to an extent delivered, not just a reduced role for the state but also a change in the style of bureaucratic operation away from strict Weberian guidelines. Mrs Thatcher sought to refocus the bureaucracy on effective execution, emphasizing efficient management rather than bureaucratic application of formal rules.

More generally, the policy-forming community in many liberal democracies has widened, diminishing any monopoly which civil servants once exerted over policy advice and encouraging them to focus rather more on delivery – and specifically on the three Es of economy, efficiency and effectiveness (Box 17.2). In the twenty-first century, therefore, senior civil servants must be skilled in the arts of governance as well as government. Facing conflicting expectations derived from old and new philosophies, they must aim to:

- Show flexibility while abiding by rules;
- Deliver results while working within set procedures;
- Distil policy advice for ministers while managing complex networks;
- Act decisively while consulting widely;
- Help ministers realize political goals while also remaining neutral.

Recruitment

Recruitment to bureaucracies has evolved in tandem with the development of the civil service itself. The shift from a spoils to a merit system was a transition from recruitment by personal links with the ruler to open selection on merit. At least in theory, jobs became available to the whole population. Even though these reforms occurred in most democracies as long ago as the late nineteenth century, recruitment to the civil service remains an important theme today. Selection methods and employee profiles are scrutinized more carefully than in the private sector. Further, what counts as merit still

---

BOX 17.2

The three Es: economy, efficiency and effectiveness

	Definition	Objective
Economy	Minimize inputs	Spend less
Efficiency	Achieve maximum output of goods and services for a given input	Spend well
Effectiveness	Ensure that policy achieves its goals	Spend wisely

Source: National Audit Office (2006).

---

varies between countries, revealing contrasting ideas of a civil servant's role.

The main difference is between **unified** and **departmental** approaches. Britain exemplifies a unified (or generalist) tradition. Indeed, the United Kingdom pushes the cult of the amateur to extremes. Administration is seen as the art of judgement, born of intelligence and matured by experience. Specialist knowledge should be sought by bureaucrats but then treated with scepticism; experts should be on tap but not on top. A good administrator is expected to serve in a variety of departments and will be more rounded for having done so. Given this philosophy, it is natural for recruits to be sought for the civil service as a whole, not for a particular department.

An alternative method of pursuing the unified approach is to recruit to a *corps* (body) of civil servants rather than to a specific job in a ministry. France is an example here. It recruits civil servants

---

In a **unified** bureaucracy, recruitment is to the civil service as a whole, not to a specific job within it. Administrative work is conceived as requiring intelligence and education but not technical knowledge. By contrast, a **departmental** approach recruits people with technical backgrounds to a specific department or job.

through competitive examinations to such bodies as the Diplomatic Corps and the Finance Inspectorate. Although recruitment is to a specific *corps*, with a specialized title, it is in reality as much an enrolment into an elite encompassing both public and private realms. Even within the civil service, more than a third of *corps* members are working away from their home *corps* at any one time. At its highest levels, the French bureaucracy is clearly generalist albeit within a *corps* framework that provides a bow to specialized training.

Some unified civil services stress one particular form of technical expertise: law. In many European countries with a codified law tradition, legal training remains common among higher bureaucrats. Germany is a good illustration. There, over 60 per cent of top civil servants are lawyers, compared to just 20 per cent in the United States (where the civil service tradition is departmental). The German emphasis on law has influenced several other countries, including Denmark and Japan.

How does a departmental (or specialist) system differ from the unified approach? In a departmental system, recruiters look for specialist experts for individual departments. The Finance Ministry will recruit economists and the Department of Health will employ staff with medical training. Recruitment is to particular posts, not to an elite civil service or a *corps*. When staff leave, they often move to similar jobs in the private sector, rather than to different departments in government.

This emphasis on specific jobs and specialist expertise is common in countries with a weak state in which the administration lacks the status produced by centuries of service to pre-democratic rulers. The United States, New Zealand and the Netherlands are examples. In the Netherlands, each department sets its own recruitment standards, normally requiring prior training and expertise in its own area. Once appointed, mobility within the civil service itself is limited; staff who remain in public service usually stay in the same department for their entire career (Andeweg and Irwin, 2009, p. 176). The notion of recruiting talented young graduates to an elite, unified civil service, or even to a *corps*, is weak or non-existent.

One issue in recruitment to the public sector that led to some modification of strict selection on merit is **affirmative action**. The problem to which

affirmative action is presented as a solution is that in liberal democracies the typical senior civil servant is a male graduate from the dominant ethnic group and a middle- or upper-class family that was often itself active in public affairs (Aberbach *et al.*, 1981, p. 80). These findings disturbed those who considered that the members of a bureaucracy should be representative of the wider population (Kingsley, 1944).

A range of arguments has been invoked to support the thesis that a bureaucracy should reflect the social profile of the population. Broadly, these points match those advanced to promote the idea of the legislature as a microcosm (see p. 299):

▶ Civil servants whose work involves direct contact with specific groups will perform better at the job if they also belong to that category and literally speak the same language (e.g. Spanish-speakers in the USA);

▶ A public sector drawn from a range of religions and regions will encourage stability in divided societies;

▶ A diverse and representative bureaucracy, involving participation by all major social groups, will enhance the acceptability of decisions;

▶ Employment of minorities in the public sector will ripple through the labour market, including private companies;

▶ **Positive discrimination** will only be needed for a transitional period because, once a representative bureaucracy is established to overcome the legacy of the past, it will maintain itself naturally as minority civil servants become visible role models.

In the 1970s and 1980s, considerable efforts were made in the United States to ensure that staff profiles matched those of the wider population. Canadian governments, concerned since the 1960s to improve recruitment from French-speakers, also

---

Affirmative action consists of policies designed to overcome the legacy of past discrimination against particular groups. One such policy is **positive discrimination** – applying lower recruitment standards to the members of disadvantaged groups.

extended their recruitment efforts. However, such schemes never achieved the same popularity in Europe, perhaps because they would have involved accepting the inadequacy of the constitutional requirement of neutrality imposed on some civil services there. The Weberian philosophy of recruitment on merit was not to be moved.

Those who are more sceptical of affirmative action suggest that the correct solution to under-representation lies in improving the qualifications of the under-represented groups through education. Furthermore, affirmative action in the weaker sense of additional encouragement for minorities to apply for jobs can be adopted without embracing positive discrimination. The twin danger of positive discrimination is, first, that those denied jobs just because they belong to a majority group naturally become resentful, and, second, that those who are accepted just because they come from a minority background find themselves in an awkward position.

Organization

Here we examine the detailed organization of central government, looking at the cogs of the administrative machine. This section takes us into the heart of government, identifying the landmarks needed to map the elements of any particular state. Although structures – and labels – vary by country, we can distinguish between three main kinds of organization: departments, divisions and non-departmental public bodies (Box 17.3).

Departments

Government departments (or ministries) form the centrepiece of modern bureaucracies. Here we find the bodies pursuing the traditional tasks of government. In nearly all countries, a dozen or so established departments form the stable core of central government, covering such areas as finance, defence and foreign affairs. The total number varies but is typically between 12 and 24. The United States has 15 departments, each headed by a secretary of state appointed by the president.

Most countries followed a similar sequence in introducing departments (Figure 17.1). The first to be established are those performing core state

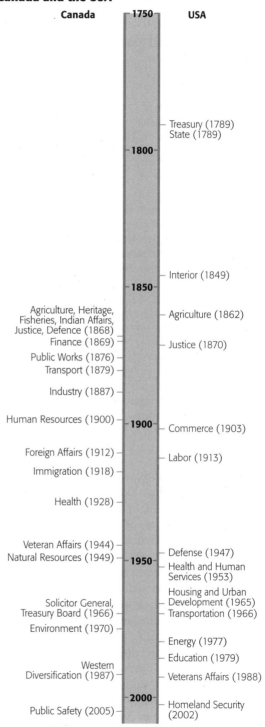

Figure 17.1 Founding of federal departments in Canada and the USA

Canada		USA
	1750	
		Treasury (1789)
		State (1789)
	1800	
		Interior (1849)
	1850	
Agriculture, Heritage, Fisheries, Indian Affairs, Justice, Defence (1868)		Agriculture (1862)
Finance (1869)		Justice (1870)
Public Works (1876)		
Transport (1879)		
Industry (1887)		
Human Resources (1900)	1900	Commerce (1903)
Foreign Affairs (1912)		Labor (1913)
Immigration (1918)		
Health (1928)		
Veteran Affairs (1944)		Defense (1947)
Natural Resources (1949)	1950	Health and Human Services (1953)
		Housing and Urban Development (1965)
Solicitor General, Treasury Board (1966)		Transportation (1966)
Environment (1970)		
		Energy (1977)
		Education (1979)
Western Diversification (1987)		Veterans Affairs (1988)
	2000	
Public Safety (2005)		Homeland Security (2002)

Sources: Rockman (2000), Tardi (2002, pp. 302–3).

The organization of government: departments, divisions and agencies

Department
>An administrative unit, sometimes known as a ministry, over which a minister exercises direct management control. Usually structured as a formal hierarchy and often established by statute.

Division
>An operating unit of a department, responsible to the minister but often with considerable independence in practice, especially in the USA. Also called sections and bureaus – and departments in countries where the larger unit is termed a 'ministry'.

Non-departmental public body
>Operates at one or more removes from the government, in an attempt to provide management flexibility and political independence. Sometimes called quangos – a term from America that originally meant a quasi non-governmental organization but which is often now taken to mean a quasi-governmental organization.

Figure 17.2 The structure of a typical government department

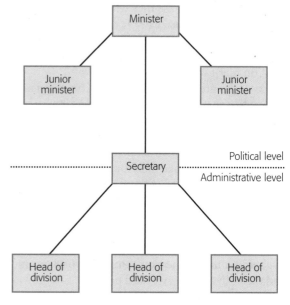

functions such as finance, law and order, defence and foreign affairs. These ministries are often as ancient as the state itself. In the United States, for instance, the Department of State and the Treasury each date from 1789. Later, countries added extra ministries to deal with new functions, including agriculture, commerce and labour. Later in the twentieth century came welfare departments dealing with social security, education, health and housing. More recent additions include the environment and, in a few countries, security.

Reflecting Weber's principles, the internal structure of departments is hierarchical (Figure 17.2). A single minister sits at the pinnacle, albeit often supported in large departments by junior ministers with divisional responsibilities. A senior civil servant, often known as the secretary or vice minister, is responsible for administration and for providing the

crucial bridge between political and bureaucratic levels.

Divisions

Departments are typically arranged into several divisions or sections, each responsible for an aspect of the organization's work. Thus an Education Department might include separate divisions for primary, secondary and higher education. Divisions are the operating units of departments, the sections within which the work gets done. They are the workhorses of government, the store of its experience and, in practice, the site where many important decisions are reached. Divisions are the state's engine room.

In some democracies, divisions acquire added importance because they are partially autonomous from their parent department. The extreme case is the USA, whose bureaucracy is the great exception to Weber's principle of hierarchy in departments. Even in their formal structure, American departments are more like multinational corporations, containing many divisions (often called 'agencies' in the USA) jostling within a single shell. The departments are merely the wrapping round a collection of disparate divisions and it is these bureaus which form the main operating units of the federal government. For example, the Department of Health and Human Services includes 11 divisions – called administrations, agencies, centers and services – within its skin (Box 17.4). The autonomy of bureaus within American departments, derived from their direct funding by Congress, is a major and often underestimated reason why American presidents experience such difficulty in imposing their will on Washington's complex administrative process.

Even in governments with more hierarchical departments, it would be naive to suppose that working practices correspond exactly to organization charts. Rarely does information move smoothly up and down the administrative pyramid. For instance, the 2,000 divisions in Germany's 14 federal ministries possess a concentration of expertise that enables them to block or at least circumvent reforms proposed from on high. A monopoly of knowledge creates the potential to neutralize change. In most liberal democracies, divisions within departments also possess their own ethos derived from long experience with their subject area. This entrenched in-house view breeds a natural cynicism towards the latest political initiative.

Non-departmental public bodies

So far, we have considered government ministries and the divisions typically nested within them. But there is another type of public organization that is growing in importance: the non-departmental public body. The essential feature of these entities is that they operate at one remove from government departments, with a formal relationship of at least semi-independence. Such bodies occupy an ambivalent position, created and funded by the government, but in contrast to divisions within a department they are free from day-to-day ministerial control. Once appointed by the government, the members of such boards are expected to operate with considerable autonomy.

Throughout the democratic world, these non-departmental bodies are expanding in number, complicating not just the academic task of mapping government but also the practical job of ensuring that the government as a whole acts coherently. Modern governance cannot be understood without delving deeper into the ecology of these non-departmental organizations.

BOX 17.4

Agencies within the Department of Health and Human Services, USA, 2009

Administration for Children and Families

Administration on Aging

Agency for Healthcare Research and Quality

Agency for Toxic Substances and Disease Registry

Centers for Disease Control and Prevention

Centers for Medicare & Medicaid Services

Food and Drug Administration

Health Resources and Services Administration

Indian Health Service

National Institutes of Health

Substance Abuse and Mental Health Services

Source: Department of Health and Human Services (2009).

Such bodies have long been prominent in the United States. There, 56 'independent establishments and government corporations' range from the Africa Development Foundation to the US Postal Service. These entities are distinct from bureaus in departments. Scandinavian countries, notably Sweden, also rely on non-departmental bodies to implement policy set by the ministry. A network of independent and relatively autonomous central boards – such as the Social Welfare Board, the National Labour Market Board and the National Pensions Board – executes official policy.

Non-departmental public bodies are established for a range of reasons:

- To provide protection from political interference in day-to-day operations;
- To operate with more flexibility (and at lower cost) than would be acceptable for a ministry;
- To acknowledge the professional status and autonomy of their staff;
- As a response to short-term pressure to do something about a problem.
- To allow ministries to focus on policy-making.

JAPAN

Form of government ■ a parliamentary liberal democracy with a ceremonial emperor.

Legislature ('Diet') ■ the 480 members of the House of Representatives are elected for a four-year term. The smaller upper house, the House of Councillors, is less significant.

Executive ■ an orthodox parliamentary executive, with a cabinet and prime minister accountable to the Diet.

Judiciary ■ the 15-member Supreme Court possesses the power of judicial review under the 1946 constitution but has proved unassertive in the face of LDP dominance.

Electoral system ■ under the mixed-member majoritarian system introduced in 1996, 300 members of the lower house are elected in single-member constituencies while the remainder are elected by proportional representation.

Party system ■ in 2009, the previously dominant LDP suffered a resounding defeat. It was replaced in office by the Democratic Party of Japan (308 seats), a party that embraced the spirit of reform without offering a clear reform programme.

Population (annual growth rate): 127.1m (−0.19%)
World Bank income group: high income
Political Rights score: ①
Civil Liberties score: ②
Human development index (rank/out of): 8/177
Freedom of the press index (rank/out of): 38/195
Perceived transparency index (rank/out of): 18/180

Note: For meaning and sources of scales and indexes, see p. xv. In all cases a score and rank of 1 is 'best'.

Until 2009, **JAPAN** offered one of the few surviving cases of a dominant party system in a liberal democracy. Either alone or in coalition, the LDP governed Japan for all but 11 months between 1955 and 2009. During this period, as Scheiner (2006, p. 1) points out, the opposition was unable to mount an effective challenge even though the LDP was unpopular with many voters.

How do we resolve the paradox of a party that was both successful and unpopular? The key lay in the LDP's willingness to use its control of an interventionist state to offer financial support and subsidies to those local areas which consistently elected the party's candidates. Because Japan's local governments depend heavily on central funding, their voters possess a strong incentive to support the party that serves their local interests. This network worked especially well in rural areas, which are over-represented in parliament.

The system was economically inefficient, generating unnecessary bridges, roads and dams throughout the land – and a large budget deficit for the state. The LDP's requirement for a steady flow of funds from the private sector also encouraged corruption. In elections to the Diet in 2009, however, this elaborate political construction collapsed. The LDP's share of the party vote declined from 38 to 27 per cent while its number of seats plummeted from 296 to 119. The LDP was replaced in office by the Democratic Party of Japan (which won 42 per cent of the party vote).

For students of comparative politics, the LDP's defeat came as no great surprise. Throughout the democratic world, dominant parties have lost ground, falling victim to more independent electorates, popular cynicism about pork barrel politics, factionalism and corruption, and the declining association of such parties with a national success story. In Japan, the LDP had provided the political front behind which senior bureaucrats and industrial corporations had marshalled post-war economic recovery, creating what is now the world's third largest economy. The goal of catching up with the West was widely shared and its achievement was a source of national pride.

However, a growth rate of 10 per cent in the 1960s declined to just 1.7 per cent in the 1990s as the effects of inefficient investment and an asset price bubble in the late 1980s required firms to reduce excess debt, capital and labour. Japan entered a recession in 2008 (CIA, 2009). Although the country coped relatively well with the global financial crisis, the LDP was by now dispirited, divided and poorly led. It experienced three changes of prime minister during 2006–09 but none of the successors to Junichiro Koizumi (prime minister, 2001–06) possessed his political appeal. Furthermore, a new electoral system introduced in 1996 meant that voters could no longer choose between different LDP candidates; a vote against the government now meant a vote for the opposition. Although the Democratic Party of Japan failed to offer a convincing policy alternative, it did not need to. After half a century, it was enough not to be the LDP.

Further reading: Johnson (2003), Martin and Steel (2008).

Public management in Japan

Tokyo

'The Japanese bureaucracy is probably more ballyhooed than any other bureaucracy in the world', write Rosenbluth and Thies (2004, p. 327). In particular, the civil service is usually accorded an important place in histories of the country's remarkably rapid economic growth in the 1950s and 1960s. How then did the bureaucracy lead rather than retard the development of the country's market economy?

Certainly, the bureaucracy as a whole remains relatively small, employing a lower proportion of the workforce than even the United States. In 2002, only 8 per cent of employees worked in the public sector, compared to 15 per cent in the USA and 30 per cent in Sweden (Handler *et al.*, 2005). One factor containing expansion was the scrap and build law (1964) which required an existing division within a ministry to be abolished if a new one was to be created.

However, the Japanese civil service possesses high status and motivates its recruits with the thought of good post-retirement jobs in the private sector and local government. The bureaucracy attracts able male recruits through open competition. Typically, only about 2,000 of the 30,000 applicants who take the higher civil service examination are recruited. Many come from just one department: Tokyo University's Law School.

The philosophy of the bureaucracy is unified rather than departmental but mobility is rare. Each group of recruits forms a distinct cohort within a ministry, progressing through the hierarchy but with a smaller proportion achieving promotion to the next level; the convention

is that staff should not expect to serve under anyone recruited later than them. The system is competitive and demanding but only highly rewarding at the top levels.

As Johnson (1995, p. 68) writes, senior bureaucrats form part of 'the economic general staff, which is itself legitimated by its meritocratic character'. The bureaucracy undoubtedly played a substantial role in post-war reconstruction. It was intertwined with the Liberal Democratic Party – conservative in all but name – and

Ministries of the Japanese government, 2009

Cabinet Office
Agriculture, Forestry and Fisheries
Board of Audit
Defence
Economy, Trade and Industry
Education, Culture, Sports, Science
   and Technology
Environment
Finance
Foreign Affairs
Health, Labour and Welfare
Internal Affairs and
   Communications
Justice
Land, Infrastructure and Transport

Source: Web Japan (2009).

big business. The professional economic bureaucracy, and in particular the Ministry of International Trade and Industry (MITI), was a significant factor in Japan's success. As post-war reconstruction began, MITI targeted specific growth industries such as cameras which were shielded from overseas competition until they became internationally successful. MITI operated mainly through dis-

cussion and persuasion, thus reducing the risk of major mistakes, but it could rely when necessary on the authority inherent in a highly regulated society.

In the post-war decades of high growth, Japan provided the pre-eminent example of how a small, merit-based bureaucracy, operating largely on the basis of persuasion, could guide rapid economic development within a predominantly market framework.

In the 1990s, state-led deflation painted the bureaucracy in a harsher light. A few civil servants were involved in bribery cases; these scandals made some large companies more wary of hiring retired bureaucrats. More fundamentally, in a global economy civil servants could no longer offer the same strategic direction to industry, given that the largest companies now operate on a world scale and that some overseas corporations are established within Japan.

Reflecting these developments, as well as a desire to improve coordination, the central bureaucracy was reorganized in 2001, with the number of departments reduced from 20 to 10; the once-mighty MITI becoming part of a new ministry. The Japan Fair Trade Commission acquired a more extensive role in enforcing competition, signalling greater emphasis on the interests of consumers rather than those of the large, export-oriented manufacturers that emerged during Japan's high growth phase.

Further reading: Kawabata (2007), Scheiner (2006).

BOX 17.5

A classification of regulatory bodies in the European Union

Type	Description	Example
European Regulatory Agency (ERA)	Established by European legislation. Can make proposals to the European Commission.	European Food Safety Authority
European Regulatory Network (ERN)	Coordinates national bodies that implement European legislation.	Committee of European Securities Regulators
Network of Independent Regulatory Agencies (NIRA)	Forums of national regulators in a specific sector.	Council of European Energy Regulators

Source: Thatcher and Coen (2008).

In many English-speaking democracies, the balance between the different kinds of non-departmental body changed considerably in and after the 1980s. Specifically, privatization eliminated many state-owned enterprises while demand for regulatory agencies increased. Today, the most important non-departmental bodies are not government corporations but agencies: public organizations operating separately from departments but charged (normally by statute) with delivering public services, or providing advice to government, or regulating an aspect of social life in which the public interest is at stake. We consider each in turn.

Service delivery agencies cover such activities as gathering intelligence, managing public buildings and providing driving licences. According to the school of new public management (see p. 357), specialist agencies, operating in a businesslike manner free from detailed political interference, should be more efficient at supplying services than a division of a government department.

Advisory bodies provide additional expertise to that available in a department. Unlike corporations and agencies, advisory boards are usually created by the sponsoring department without the backing of law. They are more informal and fluid – though often, in practice, long-lasting. Ministers seem to find them indispensable in providing information and advice on specialized topics. After all, a minister whose recommendations are based on those from an advisory committee possesses a useful insurance policy should the ideas come in for criticism.

From a governance perspective, *regulatory agencies* are the most important non-departmental bodies in contemporary liberal democracies. These agencies supervise natural monopolies (e.g. water supply) and such activities as adoption, broadcasting, elections, food standards and nuclear energy. Regulatory agencies are increasing in number in nearly all liberal democracies, partly to balance risks which cannot be well-judged by the private sector. For example, weighing the benefits of introducing a new drug against the danger of side effects is a task for public-minded experts rather than for self-interested drug companies. Britain has embraced regulatory agencies with particular gusto; the sector now employs over 20,000 people and costs around £1 billion per year.

The European Union, too, has achieved its policy objectives, in particular moving towards a single market, through issuing regulations. In a sense, the EU is best labelled as the ERS – the European Regulatory State (Box 17.5). The regulations it issues in such areas as chemical and food safety, competition and telecommunications exert global impact (Bach and Newman, 2007).

In general terms, then, charting the non-departmental public bodies in any liberal democracy confirms the complexity of contemporary governance. The rise of regulatory agencies, in particular, gives the lie to any simplistic claims of a diminished role for the state.

Accountability

The relationship between politicians and senior administrators has always been sensitive. Traditionally, the problem was posed as one of ensuring political control over non-elected officials: how could civil servants be prevented from obstructing the goals of freely elected governments? The problem of controlling bureaucratic power in a democracy was a particular concern of Max Weber. He identified the danger of public servants coming to dominate their elected masters, suggesting that

under normal conditions, the power position of a fully developed bureaucracy is always over-whelming. The 'political master' finds himself in the position of the 'dilettante' who stands opposite the 'expert', facing the trained official who stands within the management of administration. (quoted in Kahlberg, 2005, p. 211)

Today, Weber's observation is widely accepted. Commentators recognize that the bureaucracy's expertise, permanence, scale and control of implementation mean that it is bound to be more than a mechanical conduit for political directives. Senior public employees – department secretaries, heads of divisions, chairs of non-departmental public bodies – are invariably in a position to influence and elaborate policy.

The contemporary response to this political reality has been to reframe the issue as one of **accountability** rather than control (Mulgan, 2003). Increasingly, the philosophy is to encourage civil servants to defend their actions after the fact rather than to seek pre-emptive control over the actions themselves. In this way, accountability both acknowledges and potentially defuses Weber's fear of bureaucratic power – a neat move all round.

> **Accountability** can be used narrowly to refer to a reporting requirement ('to be called to account') or more broadly as a synonym for responsibility ('to be held to account'). In the latter sense, to be account-able is to be held responsible for one's actions by and often before another body. This body can express judgements about, and may be able to impose sanctions on, the actor.

BOX 17.6

Multiple accountabilities: deputy ministers (DMs, senior public officials) in Canada

Accountable to	Why?
Prime Minister	The PM appoints the DM
Minister	The DM is required to assist and serve the minister
Clerk of the Privy Council	The Clerk heads the Public Service and acts as the PM's DM
Treasury Board	DMs report to the Treasury Board on resource management
Public Services Commission	DMs report to the Public Services Commission on staffing issues
House of Commons committees	DMs give evidence to parliamentary committees
Committee of Senior Officials (COSO)	COSO oversees performance appraisal of DMs

Source: Bourgault (2002), p. 438.

For example, Polidano (1998, p. 35) argues that in a complex environment, where most policy-making involves coordination between several ministries, straight-line accountability to a minister no longer suffices. He suggests that 'bureaucrats can be prevented from complying with ministerial directions, however legitimate those directions may be. Multiple accountabilities are an inescapable part of the reality of government'.

Today, senior officials are accountable not just to ministers in their own department but also to the prime minister, the finance ministry and to the obligations inherent in agreements with other national and even international organizations. To take a specific example, 'the accountability system for deputy ministers [top civil servants] in Canada has been described as multiple, complex and at times contradictory' (Bourgault, 2002, p. 446). As elsewhere, the highest officials in Canada must march to many drums (Box 17.6).

What then are the main methods of overseeing public managers and calling their actions to account? Box 17.7 distinguishes between internal controls, operating within public organizations themselves, and external scrutiny, applied from outside. We examine each in turn.

Internal controls

The traditional form of internal control is, of course, ministerial direction. Ministers direct; public servants execute. Although no longer sufficient, hierarchical control by a minister remains an essential component of oversight. However, in practice, the capacity of ministers to exert such control is conditioned by two other factors: the reach of political appointments into the bureaucracy and the use ministers make of personal advisers.

In theory, the greater the number of appointments made by a minister within a department, the easier it should be to impose a specific direction. Recognizing that senior bureaucrats should possess political craft, many liberal democracies do now tend to staff important ministries with politically loyal and sympathetic civil servants. This practice, long familiar in Germany and Finland, is spreading to other Western democracies. Increasingly, politicians want civil servants who are, in Mrs Thatcher's famous phrase, 'one of us'.

Ministerial direction can also be aided by providing ministers with personal advisory staff. Because such advisers are not part of the department's permanent staff, they can act as their minister's eyes and ears, reporting back on issues which might otherwise be lost in the official hierarchy. In New Zealand, every minister's office featured a political adviser by 2006 (Eichbaum and Shaw, 2007). In France, ministers are aided by a cabinet: a group of about 15 to 20 people who form their personal advisory staff and work directly under their control (a cabinet in this sense of a ministerial advisory group is unconnected with the cabinet which forms the pinnacle of parliamentary government).

In addition to formal control by the minister, internal scrutiny is enforced by an army of regulators within government: the 'waste watchers, quality

---

BOX 17.7

Overseeing the bureaucracy

Internal controls
>   Ministerial direction
>   Regulators
>   Professional standards

External scrutiny
>   Legislature and judiciary
>   Ombudsman
>   Interest groups and the mass media

---

police and sleaze busters' as Hood *et al.* (1999) term them. Auditors inspect the books, standard-setters check performance, funding bodies assess outcomes and inspectors monitor everything from fire escapes to recycling rates. Contemporary ideology may preach a bonfire of regulations but modern practice is an overdose of inspection, resulting in cynicism among officials and occasionally requiring them to hit the target even if that means missing the point. To prevent the overdose from proving fatal, inspection is now beginning to operate with what is claimed to be a lighter touch, including a greater focus on key objectives – smart tape rather than red tape, allegedly (Hood *et al.*, 2004).

Even amid this regulatory avalanche, liberal democracies continued to rely on the professional standards of civil servants as a form of internal control. This mechanism is especially important in bureaucracies with a strong technical emphasis. In Norway and Sweden, for instance, many civil servants work in specialist directorates covering functions such as engineering, medicine and railways. These directorates give expression to professional expertise and are at least partially independent of ministries. Senior civil servants in these organizations respond to political signals without sacrificing their expert judgement – a good result but not one that is easily replicated elsewhere (Christensen and Peters, 1999).

External scrutiny

External scrutiny is an expanding if episodic form of accountability for public servants. Departments and agencies find themselves issuing extensive reports to outside bodies. However, external scrutiny tends to be intermittent and politically driven. When the heat is on, it is intense – but often there is none at all. The result is that accountability gaps and accountability overload can coexist within the same agency.

In the United States, bureaucrats have always been forthcoming in their appearances before the legislature; it is Congress, after all, that grants the appropriations. But even in Britain, where ministers alone were considered responsible to parliament for the actions of their officials, civil servants now appear before select committees. Slowly and shyly, and still with a concern to avoid embarrassing their minister, British public officials are becoming willing to report in public on their work.

As with other areas of politics, the judiciary is also growing in importance as an external arena in which the bureaucracy can be called to account. Administrative law gives the judiciary a tool for checking bureaucratic decision-making, allowing judges to overrule decisions that, for example, result from faulty procedures or which violate natural justice.

The **ombudsman** is a more recent addition to the mechanisms of external scrutiny. This watchdog was first introduced in Sweden in 1809, followed by Finland in 1919, other liberal democracies after 1945 and the European Union in 1995. Within countries, a single advocate may cover the entire public sector or, at the risk of reduced visibility and overlapping jurisdictions, separate commissioners may be appointed for specific areas. Ombudsmen must have strong powers of investigation if they are to succeed. In addition, the public must be aware of their existence and be prepared to complain to them. So far, these conditions have rarely been met beyond Scandinavia (Ansell and Gingrich, 2003).

Finally, interest groups and the mass media offer some check on bureaucratic bungling. Interest groups have an obvious vested interest in monitoring the detailed implementation of policy by

An **ombudsman** (grievance officer) is a public official appointed by the legislature to investigate allegations of maladministration in the public sector. These watchdogs originated in Scandinavia but have been emulated elsewhere though often with more restricted jurisdiction, resources and success.

public officials; indeed, this is one of their key activities. A vigorous mass media can also act as a selective check on the bureaucracy: regular television programmes, for example, now specialize in exposing public scandal and bureaucratic ineptitude. However, even more than with legislative oversight, scrutiny here tends to be selective and, in the case of the media, short-term. Exposés may encourage competence but rarely lead to structural reform; the specific case is resolved but bureaucratic complacency often remains.

New public management

'Government is not the solution to the problem; government is the problem.' This famous declaration by Ronald Reagan was one inspiration behind new public management (NPM), a creed which swept through the Anglo-American world of public management in the final decade of the twentieth century.

NPM remains of interest as a powerful critique of Weber's ideas about bureaucracy. It attracted many specialists who did not share the ideological perspective of Ronald Reagan; it was spoken of warmly by international bodies such as the Organisation for Economic Co-operation and Development; and it led to radical change in the public sectors of Australia, Canada, the United Kingdom and especially New Zealand.

The best way to approach NPM is to consider Osborne and Gaebler's *Reinventing Government* (1992), an exuberant statement of the new approach. Subtitled *How the Entrepreneurial Spirit is Transforming the Public Sector*, this American bestseller outlined ten principles which it advised government agencies to adopt to enhance their effectiveness (Box 17.8). Whereas Weber's model of bureaucracy was based on ideas of efficiency drawn from the Prussian army, Osborne and Gaebler were inspired by the freewheeling world of American business.

The authors cited with enthusiasm several examples of public sector organizations which followed their tips. One was the California parks department that allowed managers to spend their budget on whatever they needed, without seeking approval for individual items of expenditure. Another was the

Steer, don't row! Osborne and Gaebler's ten principles for improving the effectiveness of government agencies

- Promote competition between service providers;
- Empower citizens by pushing control out of the bureaucracy into the community;
- Measure performance, focusing not on inputs but on outcomes;
- Be driven by goals, not rules and regulations;
- Redefine clients as customers and offer them choices – between schools, training programmes and housing options;
- Prevent problems before they emerge, rather than offering services afterwards;
- Earn money rather than simply spend it;
- Decentralize authority and embrace participatory management;
- Prefer market mechanisms to bureaucratic ones;
- Catalyze all sectors – public, private and voluntary – into solving community problems.

Source: Adapted from Osborne and Gaebler (1992).

public convention centre which formed a joint venture with private firms to bring in well-known entertainment acts, with each side sharing both the risk and the profit.

The underlying theme was the gains achievable by giving pubic servants the flexibility to manage by results. And the significance of this empowerment, in turn, was the break it represented with Weber's view that the job of a bureaucrat was simply to apply fixed rules to cases. For its supporters, NPM was public management for a new century; Weber's model was dismissed as history. Public administration, it was alleged, had been displaced by public management.

While Osborne and Gaebler provided a convert's bible, Hood (1996) offered a more dispassionate and comparative perspective (Box 17.9). Hood showed that NPM penetrated furthest in Anglo-American countries and Scandinavia, where the public sector was most amenable to political control. By contrast, countries with a strong state and a high-prestige

bureaucracy, for example Germany, Japan and Spain, made less progress in implementing the new philosophy. In these states, where administration is conceived as a branch of law, civil servants still guard the public interest by applying legal codes to specific cases. Since the duties of civil servants are entrenched in extensive civil law codes, radical change is impossible without legislation. Such reforms as occurred have concentrated more on enhancing existing operations (e.g. improved budgeting) rather than radical restructuring or explicit performance measurement (Gualmini, 2008).

Within the more flexible Anglo-American framework, New Zealand stands out. It 'achieved what was probably the most comprehensive and radical set of public management reforms of any Western democracy' (Pollitt and Bouckaert, 2004, p. 280). In the 1980s and 1990s, successive governments – first Labour and then National – revolutionized the structure, management and role of the public sector. A remarkable coalition of business leaders, government economists and senior politicians from both major parties came together to force through unpopular but far from ineffective reforms.

One particular feature of the New Zealand model was its massive use of contracts (Boston *et al.*, 1995). This technique went far beyond the standard fare of using private firms to supply local services such as garbage collection. It extended to engaging private suppliers in sensitive areas such as debt collection. By such means, the Department of Transport, for

Components of new public management

- Managers given more discretion but held responsible for results;
- Performance assessed against explicit targets;
- Resources allocated according to results;
- Departments unbundled into more independent operating units;
- More work contracted out to the private sector;
- More flexibility in recruiting and retaining staff;
- Costs cut in an effort to achieve more with less.

Source: Adapted from Hood (1996).

example, reduced its direct employees from around 5,000 in 1986 to fewer than 50 in the mid-1990s, an astonishing transformation.

In addition, contracts were introduced within New Zealand's public sector to govern the relationships between purchasers (e.g. the Transport Department) and providers (e.g. Transit New Zealand, responsible for roads). Contractual arrangements within the public sector were an additional step, and a more direct challenge to Weber's model than simply contracting out services to the private sector.

What lessons can be learned from New Zealand's ambitious innovations in public administration? Mulgan (1997, p. 146) offered a balanced assessment:

The recent reorganization of the public service has led to greater clarity of government functions and to increased efficiencies in the provision of certain services to the public. At the same time, it has been expensive in the amount of resources consumed by the reform process itself and also in the added problems of coordination caused by the greatly increased number of individual public agencies.

In and beyond New Zealand, the rise of NPM was one reason why the accountability of public officials became more complex. When something goes wrong with a service provided by an agency operating under contract to a government department, who should take the blame: agency or department? In Britain, parliament has traditionally held ministers to account for all the actions carried out in their name. As *The Times* wrote on 15 February 1977, 'the constitutional position is both crystal clear and entirely sufficient. Officials propose. Ministers dispose. Officials execute'.

Yet as early as 1994 most British civil servants were working in one of about 100 semi-independent agencies. In theory, the minister sets the policy and the agency carries it out. But when a political storm blows up – when convicts escape from prison or a National Health Service hospital fails to clean its wards properly – it is still ministers who are hauled before parliament. Knowing this, ministers are inclined to interfere selectively with operational matters, contradicting the original purpose. Agency managers discover that they are not free to manage

after all, which reduces morale and increases turnover in the top posts (Pollitt and Bouckaert, 2004).

So traditional assumptions about responsibility can be found lurking under the gloss of new public management, further complicating the administrator's task. A Danish civil servant makes the point (Paulsen, 2007, p. 486):

The role of the civil servant is not one role but several. We want to be oriented towards new policy, and act with a willingness to take risks and try out new things. At the same time, we are not allowed to make any mistakes. If an unpleasant story ends up in the newspapers, and the mistake is yours, then you might have done some very good stuff, but it's very quickly forgotten.

The fragmentation produced by NPM led to a revived focus on **joined-up government** or a **whole-of-government** approach. Improved coordination between specialized public agencies offered the prospect of greater coherence across government policy as a whole, and also the capacity for ministers in central departments to re-establish control over what happens in the field. These newer reforms reflected awareness that policy problems are linked: for instance, poverty and a lack of educational attainment are one problem, not two.

Significantly, joined-up government made most progress in countries such as New Zealand where NPM had permeated furthest. While it is tempting to use the rise of the whole-of-government approach to pronounce the death of NPM, Christensen and Lægreid (2007, p. 12) are probably more accurate in concluding that 'what we are seeing is a rebalancing or adjustment of the basic NPM model in a more centralized direction without any fundamental change'. Joined-up government may prove to be a development rather than a repudiation of NPM. At a deeper level, it represents the

> **Joined-up government**, or a **whole-of-government** approach, seeks to improve the coordination of public policy across agencies. The aim is to prevent policies from undermining each other, to align the organization of government with its actual tasks, and to provide citizens with seamless access to services.

latest move in a perpetual battle within the public sector between those who seek decentralization in search of greater initiative and those who favour centralization in pursuit of enhanced coordination.

Public management in authoritarian states

Like the military, the bureaucracy is usually a more powerful force in non-democratic regimes than in democracies. By definition, institutions of representation – elections, competitive parties and freely organized interest groups – are weak under authoritarian rule, leaving more room for agencies of the state to prosper. A dictator can dispense with elections or even with legislatures but he cannot rule without officials to give effect to his will.

But the bureaucracy can be more than a dictator's service agency, not least in developing countries. Often in conjunction with the military, it can itself become a leading political force, claiming that its technical expertise and ability to resist popular pressure is the only route to long-term economic development. This assertion may have initial merit but eventually many bureaucracies in non-democratic regimes become bloated, over-politicized and inefficient, acting as a drag on rather than a stimulus to further progress. In the long run, bureaucratic regimes, like military governments, become part of the problem rather than the solution.

Certainly, the bureaucracy has played a positive role in most authoritarian regimes experiencing rapid economic growth. In the 1950s and 1960s, it helped to foster economic modernization in several regimes in the Middle East and North Africa. In conjunction with the military and a strong national leader such as Gamal Abdel Nasser (President of Egypt, 1956–70), modernizing bureaucracies were able to initiate state-sponsored development even against the opposition of conservative landowners.

O'Donnell (1973) introduced the term **bureaucratic authoritarianism** to describe Latin American countries which followed a similar course, under repressive military leadership, in the 1960s and 1970s. The high-performing economies of East Asia, such as Indonesia and Malaysia, provide more recent examples of the contribution that the bureaucracy can make to development in largely authoritarian settings.

But these instances of the bureaucracy instigating successful modernization are the exception. More often, the bureaucracy has inhibited rather than encouraged growth. The history of sub-Saharan Africa following independence provides a more sobering and representative assessment of the role of bureaucracy in non-democratic environments. After colonial rulers departed, authoritarian leaders used their control over public appointments as a political reward, denying the delicate distinction between politics and administration. This cavalier approach to public appointments extended to absorbing excess labour, especially among new graduates, into the administration. Public sector expansion was a method of buying support or at least preventing the public expression of opposition.

The outcome was uncontrolled growth of the civil service. By the early 1990s, public employment accounted for most non-agricultural employment in Africa (B. Smith, 1996, p. 221). Once appointed, public employees found that ties of kinship meant that they were duty-bound to use their privileged positions to reward their families and ethnic group, producing further growth of the civil service.

The fat bureaucracy that resulted proved to be incapable of acting as an effective instrument for development. Rather, the expanding administrative 'class' extracted resources from society for its own benefit, in that sense continuing rather than replacing the colonial model. With the main source of national wealth (e.g. commodity exports) under state control, public employment became the highway to riches, creating a bureaucratic bourgeoisie. Only towards the end of the twentieth century, under pressure from international agencies, were attempts made to rein in the public sector

> **Bureaucratic authoritarianism** was a term coined by O'Donnell (1973) to describe regimes in which technocrats in the bureaucracy imposed economic stability under the protection of a military government. Such regimes repressed popular movements. The concept was applied to Latin American countries such as Argentina and Brazil in the 1960s and 1970s.

through an emphasis on building **administrative capacity** (Turner and Hulme, 1997, p. 90).

Even where bureaucracy-led development has succeeded, the formula often outlasts its usefulness. Several East Asian states discovered at the end of the twentieth century that public administrators are more effective at building industrial capacity than at managing a mature, open economy with an expanding services sector. In Indonesia, for example, the Asian financial crisis of the late 1990s exposed the extent to which investment patterns had been distorted by crony capitalism, with access to capital depending more on official contacts than on rates of return.

> **Administrative capacity** refers to the bureaucracy's ability to address social problems through effective management and implementation of public policy.

The position of the bureaucracy in totalitarian systems in some ways echoed its role in authoritarian regimes. But one key difference marks out administration in the communist form of totalitarian rule: its sheer scale. The size of the bureaucracy under communism flowed from the totalitarian character of the guiding ideology. To achieve its theoretical mission of building a new society, the ruling party had to control all aspects of development, both economic and social, through the state. Most obviously, the private sector disappeared and the economy became an aspect of state administration.

Communist bureaucracies were intensely political, with the ruling party penetrating deeply into the administration. Indeed, the essence of communist rule lay in combining bureaucratic and political rule in one gigantic system. Reflecting Weber's concerns in the democratic world, the ruling party regarded the bureaucracy as both indispensable and potentially unreliable – as a force which through its control of implementation might one day come to dominate its political masters (Lewin, 1997).

Hence, the party sought to pacify the bureaucracy in the same way that it controlled the armed forces: by controlling all major appointments. This goal was achieved through the *nomenklatura*, a mechanism that provided a powerful incentive for ambitious careerists to gain and retain a sound reputation within the party. The *nomenklatura* continues to this day in China, where the list is now said to contain over eight million names (Manion, 2009, p. 435).

> The *nomenklatura* (list of names) was a large panel of trusted individuals from which ruling communist parties appointed people to posts in the bureaucracy.

The interpenetration of politics and bureaucracy in communist states caused significant problems for post-communist regimes in establishing a professional civil service based on political neutrality and merit-based recruitment (Gajduschek, 2007). In Hungary, for example, professionalism is increasing, helped by an expansion of higher education and an increase in public sector salaries, but political influences remain substantial. Elements of a spoils system remain as victorious parties, some with a base in the public sector itself, ensure their supporters occupy official posts. These bureaucrats then exploit the opportunities for bribery which compensate for what are often still low salaries.

Public management in illiberal democracies

The bureaucracy receives less attention than it deserves in discussion of illiberal democracies. The reason is understandable: illiberal democracies are typically founded on a personal relationship between president and people. This implicit contract works against the strengthening of rule-governed institutions, including a Weberian bureaucracy. Illiberal democracies are political, not bureaucratic, regimes.

Further, the rulers of illiberal democracies often present themselves in opposition to institutions such as the civil service. In Latin America, particularly, administrators frequently imitate the haughty remoteness of their long-gone colonial predecessors, producing a corrupt and unresponsive bureaucracy which provides a convenient target for populist politicians. Such rulers need enemies, and an inflexible civil service provides one. When the political leader of an illiberal democracy can secure the financial benefits from natural resources such as oil, he can spend these resources on maintaining a viable political coalition through patronage, thus further weakening formal institutions such as the civil service.

In Venezuela, for instance, Hugo Chávez introduced a new constitution in 1999 which defined the country's political system as 'democratic, participatory, elective, decentralized, responsible to the people, pluralist, based on term limits for elected officials and revocable mandates' (Alvarez, 2004, p. 152). The radical pretensions and inherent uncertainties of this new constitution contributed nothing to building an effective bureaucracy. Rather, the effect was to concentrate attention on the political realm – and on Chávez himself. His own local committees could distribute resources for greater short-term political gain than if the same resources were made available to a Weberian bureaucracy.

In many illiberal democracies, public management operates in a somewhat uncoordinated way, with separate bureaucratic islands serving the interests of their local managers rather than those of the public they ostensibly serve. Corruption inherited from the authoritarian order may continue unabated and jobs may be allocated on the basis of political rewards and ethnic ties.

Much routine work may continue to be conducted; illiberal democracies, after all, are far from failed states. Indeed, Nef (2003, p. 531) points out that the ending of authoritarian rule in Latin America led not just to privatization and fiscal prudence but also to some improvements 'in the quality and time of service rendered to customers in many of the countries'. But the real action lies in the political realm, and the bureaucracy as a whole often lacks the administrative capacity which international agencies – and sometimes even the political leadership itself – would like to see.

Russia's illiberal democracy illustrates but also qualifies these themes. More than in most such regimes, Russia's presidents have drawn on – rather than defined themselves in opposition to – the country's long tradition of state power. As Willerton (1997, p. 39) points out:

all past Russian political systems were characterised by a strong executive, with power concentrated on a small governing elite. An administrative bureaucracy supporting the political executive emerged under the Tatars [Turkic-speaking overlords of Russia, 1236–1452]. By the early eighteenth century Peter the Great had rationalised and professionalised that bureaucracy.

	Number	Examples
Federal ministries and agencies under the president ('the presidential bloc')	12	Internal Affairs, Foreign Affairs, Defence, Justice
Federal ministries under the government	11	Education and Science, Finance, Natural Resources, Transport
Other executive bodies under the government	12	Space Agency, Sport and Physical Culture, Tourist Agency

Source: President of Russia (2009).

In the post-communist era, securing control over these bureaucratic agencies required significant attention. In contrast to most liberal democracies, Russia never developed an integrated public bureaucracy with standard rules and merit-based appointments. Under communism, party and state became so intertwined that the collapse of the former came close to bringing down the latter. In the chaotic early years of post-communism, provision of public services inevitably devolved to the local level, fragmenting the administration of a large, diverse country.

The Civil Service Act (1995) did introduce more uniform provisions across the public sector, including for example a rigid grading structure, but the operation of Russia's bureaucracy still falls well short of Weber's standards. Even today, the legacy of inefficiency and corruption renders most of Russia's bureaucracy far less professional and responsive than, say, its American equivalent (Ágh, 2003, p. 545).

The result is problems of bureaucratic control in Russia which exceed those found in the United States, whose constitution at least vests sole executive power in the president. The Russian president also faces an additional issue: under the semi-presidential constitution of 1993, some key functions fall under direct presidential supervision but others are the responsibility of a government with its own prime minister (Box 17.10). Where the American president heads the executive branch, Russia's president stands above the government.

In an attempt to resolve these problems, Russia's post-communist presidents have developed a massive constellation of supervisory agencies, based in or reporting to the Kremlin. By 2009, the president's Executive Office contained 15 separate units, staffed in the main by loyal, competent and reliable supporters. These offices include the Presidential Control Directorate which 'oversees and checks that federal laws, decrees, orders and other presidential decisions are enforced by the federal executive bodies of power, the regional authorities, and organizations' (President of Russia, 2009). Frequent reorganization of the Executive Office suggests that its success remains incomplete.

Learning Resources for Chapter 17

Next step

Raadschelders *et al.* (2007) provide a comparative perspective on the civil services of the 21st century.

Further reading

Peters (2009) is a clear and comparative introduction to bureaucracy. Heady (2001) is an alternative. Osborne and Gaebler (1992) is an enthusiast's account of new public management, while Pollitt and Bouckaert (2004) offer a balanced comparative review. Page and Wright (2006) and Peters and Pierre (2004) provide collections on the changing role of senior civil servants in liberal democracies. Mulgan (2003) is a thoughtful review of the concept of accountability. Shafritz *et al.* (2003) provide a chronological selection of classics on American public administration. For Japan, Johnson (1995) remains an influential starting point; see also Kawabata (2007). With an emphasis on the relationship between administration and development, Turner and Hulme (1997) portray the role of bureaucracy in authoritarian regimes.

Internet sources

Administrative and Civil Service Reform, World Bank
Reviews the main debates on civil service management and reform
http://www.worldbank.org

AEI Center for Regulatory and Market Studies
A primary aim of the Reg-Markets Center is to gain a deeper understanding of how markets, laws and regulation contribute to economic well-being
http://www.reg-markets.org/

Sigma Programme
A joint initiative of the OECD and EU, this programme supports improvements in governance and public management
http://www.sigmaweb.org/

United Nations Online Network in Public Administration and Finance
Promotes effective public administration and efficient civil services
http://www.unpan.org/

www.palgrave.com
Companion Website
Visit the Companion Website to 'click and go'
www.palgrave.com/politics/hague

Part V
PUBLIC POLICY

Policy matters. In one country, government actions may be a major cause of human misery. In others, public policies can create conditions under which people can fulfil their potential. In this final part, therefore, our focus shifts from governments themselves to the policies they pursue – and to the success, or otherwise, with which they pursue them. We begin with a chapter on the policy process in which we review the core models of policy-making, the major stages of the policy process, policy instruments and regulation. We conclude with a chapter on a policy sector which influences all others: political economy. There, our coverage includes the comparative literature on varieties of capitalism and the financial crisis of 2007/09.

This part will enable you to:

▶ Analyse the main models, stages and instruments of public policy;
▶ Appreciate the significance of regulation as a policy instrument in liberal democracies;
▶ Understand variations in the organization of capitalist economies;

Chapter 18

The policy process

The task of policy analysis is to understand what governments do, how they do it and what difference it makes (Dye, 2007). Where political science examines the organization of the political factory, policy analysis examines the products emerging from it. So the focus is on the content, instruments, impact and evaluation of public policy. The emphasis is downstream, on implementation and results, as much as upstream, on the institutional sources of policy.

Because analysts are concerned with improving the quality and efficacy of public policy, the subject exudes a distinctly practical ethos. Policy analysts want to know whether and why a policy is working and how else its objectives might be pursued. Reflecting this interest, policy analysis is a subject that connects academic studies with political practice.

What, then, is a policy? As a plan of action, a policy covers both an aim (say, to discourage obesity) and a series of decisions, past or future, designed to achieve the objective (for example, reducing advertising of fast food). Policy can also take the form of explicit non-decisions: 'our policy is that nutritional choices should be left to the individual'. According to Colebatch (1998), policies exhibit coherence (policy as strategy), hierarchy (policy as instruction) and instrumentality (policy as means).

In understanding the policy process, it is important to avoid imposing rationality on a process that is often driven by political considerations, at least in high-profile sectors. Three points are noteworthy in this regard:

- Public policies are often contradictory. Governments can subsidize tobacco growers while also running anti-smoking campaigns.
- Policies can be nothing more than window-dressing – an attempt to be seen to be doing something but without any realistic expectation that the notional objective will be achieved.
- A policy statement may be a cover for acting in the opposite way. Leaders of low-income countries may dutifully inform international agencies of their support for a market economy while simultaneously bringing major corporations under their political control.

In short, public policy is a part as much as an output of politics. Policy and politics, we should remember, are words with the same root.

A **policy** is a broader notion than a decision. At a minimum, a policy covers a bundle of decisions. More generally, it reflects an intention to make future decisions in accordance with an overall objective.

BOX 18.1

Three models of policy-making

Rational model	Incremental model	Garbage-can model
Goals are set before means are considered	Goals and means are considered together	Goals are discovered through actions taken by the organization and are not specified separately
A good policy will achieve explicit goals	A good policy is one on which all the main actors agree	The garbage-can process does not resolve problems well but choices are sometimes made
Analysis is comprehensive; all effects of all options are addressed	Analysis is selective; the object is acceptable policy, not the best policy	Little analysis; the organization acts rather than decides
Theory is heavily used	Comparison with similar problems is heavily used	Trial and error, plus some memory of recent experiences, are used

Sources: Adapted from Lindblom (1959, p. 81) and Parsons (1995, p. 285).

Models of policy-making

In analysing policy-making, scholars have developed three models: the **rational** or synoptic model associated with Simon (1983), the **incremental** model developed by Lindblom (1979) and the **garbage-can** model, so named by Cohen *et al.* (1972). These accounts form an important part of the policy analysis tradition, with the first two models reflecting the views of politics discussed in Chapter 1.

In evaluating these perspectives, and in looking at policy analysis generally, it is important to distinguish between accounts of how policy should be made and descriptions of how it actually is made. Moving from left to right across Box 18.1 is, in part, a transition from the former to the latter. The rational model seeks to elaborate what would be involved in rational policy-making without assuming that its conclusions are reflected in what actually does happen. The incremental model, which views policy as a compromise between actors with ill-defined or even contradictory goals, can be seen either as an account of how politics ought to proceed (namely, peacefully reconciling different interests) or as a description of how policy is made. The garbage-can model, finally, is concerned just to describe the con-

siderable limitations of the policy-making process within many organizations; this perspective examines only what is, not what ought to be.

The lesson is that we should recognize the different functions these models perform rather than presenting them as wholly competitive. This point will become clearer as we discuss each perspective.

The rational model

Suppose we are in charge of secondary education and have decided to initiate a policy to improve students' performance. If we were to adopt a rational approach, we would first specify the outcomes sought, such as the proportion of students achieving a given level of qualifications. Then we would consider the most efficient means of maximizing that goal: would new schools, improved facilities, more teachers (or some combination thereof) deliver the objective and at what cost?

So the approach seeks to unpack the idea of rationality by examining how policy could emerge from a systematic search for the most efficient means of achieving defined goals. Specifically, it requires policy-makers to:

▶ Rank all their values;
▶ Formulate specific options;

- Check all the results of choosing each option against each value;
- Select the alternative that achieves most values.

This is an unrealistic counsel of perfection. It requires policy-makers to foresee the unforeseeable and measure the immeasurable. Even so, techniques such as cost–benefit analysis (CBA) have developed in an attempt to implement aspects of the rational model, and the results of such analyses can at least keep policy-makers on their toes (Boardman *et al.*, 2000).

> The **discount rate** is the factor by which the expected future benefits of a policy are reduced in order to estimate their present value. In general, a high discount rate will sharply reduce the current value of projects with long-term benefits, such as schemes to contain global warming (Stern, 2007).

Seeking to analyse the costs and benefits associated with each possible decision does have strengths, particularly when one from a small set of options needs to be chosen. Specifically, CBA brings submerged assumptions to the surface, benefiting those interests that would otherwise lack political clout. The benefit to the national economy from a new airport runway is factored in, not ignored in the welter of special interests.

In addition, CBA discourages symbolic policy-making which addresses a concern without attempting anything more specific. It requires explicit consideration of a **discount rate** so that the interests of future generations are not completely ignored. It contributes to transparent policy-making by forcing decision-makers to account for policies whose costs exceed benefits.

For such reasons, CBA has been formally applied to every regulatory proposal in the USA expected to have an impact on the economy exceeding $100m. It has also played its part in the development of risk-based regulation in the United Kingdom, under which many regulators seek to focus their efforts on the main dangers rather than mechanically applying the same rules to all. The principle is to incur expenditure where it can deliver the greatest reduction in risk (Hutter, 2005).

However, CBA, and with it the rational model of policy formulation, also possesses weaknesses. It underplays soft factors such as fairness and the quality of life. It ignores the distribution of costs and benefits. It is cumbersome, expensive and time-consuming. It does not automatically incorporate estimates of the likelihood that benefits will, in fact, be achieved. In the real political world, the conclusions from CBA are often sidestepped. A CBA of CBA would not always yield positive results.

The incremental model

Let us return to our example of improving students' educational performance. An incremental approach would start with interests rather than goals. As part of our regular meetings, we would consult with the various stakeholders: teachers' unions, parents' associations, educational researchers. We would hope that a consensus might emerge from these discussions on how extra resources should be spent. The long-term goals of this expenditure might not be measured or even specified but we would assume that a policy acceptable to all is unlikely to be disastrous. Such an approach is policy-making by evolution, not revolution; an increment is literally a small increase in an existing sequence.

The incremental model was developed by Lindblom (1959) as part of a reaction against the rational model. Rather than viewing policy-making as a systematic trawl through all the options, Lindblom judges that policy is continually remade in a series of minor adjustments, rather than as a result of a single, comprehensive plan. In reality, policy formulation rarely sails out on an open sea; mostly, it is a process of making small adjustments to modify the existing direction.

Incrementalism represents what Lindblom calls the science of muddling through: what matters is that those involved should agree on policies, not objectives. Agreement should be reached on the desirability of following a particular policy, even when objectives differ. Hence policy emerges from, rather than precedes, negotiation with interested groups.

This approach may not lead to achieving grand objectives but, by taking one step at a time, it does at least avoid making huge mistakes. Yet the model also reveals its limits when situations can only be remedied by strategic action. As Lindblom (1977, 1990) himself came to recognize, incremental policy formulation deals with existing problems rather than with avoiding future ones. It is politically safe but unadventurous; remedial rather than innovative. But the threat of ecological disaster, for instance, has arisen precisely from our failure to consider our long-term, cumulative impact on the environment. Incrementalism is policy-making for normal times.

The garbage-can model

How would the garbage-can model interpret policy-making to improve educational standards? The answer is that it would doubt the significance of such clear objectives. It would suggest that in the government's education department, separate divisions and individuals engage in their own routine work, interacting through assorted committees whose composition varies over time. Low educational attainment may be a concern of some staff and solutions may be available elsewhere in the organization, in the form of people committed to pet projects such as computer-based learning or a new way of teaching spelling. But whether the solution meets the problem, and is seen as a solution, and is acted on accordingly, is hit and miss – as random as the arrangement of the rubbish in the rubbish bin.

So the garbage-can model presents a rather alarming image of decision-making. Where both the rational and incremental models offer some prescription, the garbage-can expresses the perspective of a jaundiced realist. Policy-making is seen as partial, fluid, chaotic and incomplete. Organizations are conceived as loose collections of ideas rather than as holders of clear preferences; they take actions which reveal preferences more than they act on preferences. To the extent that problems are addressed at all, they have to wait their turn and join the queue. Actions, when taken, typically reflect the requirement for an immediate response in a specific area rather than the pursuit of a policy goal (Cohen *et al.*, 1972). At best, some problems are partly addressed some of the time (Bendor *et al.*, 2001). The organization as a whole displays limited overall rationality – and little good will come until we recognize this fact.

This model can be difficult to grasp, a fact that shows how deeply our minds seek to impose rationality on the policy process. Large, decentralized, public organizations such as universities are perhaps the best examples. On most college campuses, decisions emerge from committees which operate largely independently. The energy-saving group may not know what instruments can achieve its goals; the engineering faculty, full of imaginative tools, may not know the green committee exists. The committee on standards may want to raise admissions qualifications; the equal opportunity group to lower them for members of minorities.

Government is of course a classic example of an entity that is both large and decentralized. It is not a single entity but an array of ministries and agencies. Several government departments may deal with different aspects of a problem, with none having an overall perspective. Or one department may be charged with reducing pollution while another works to attract investments in new polluting factories. Clearly, the garbage-can model suggests that real policy-making is far removed from the rigours of rationality. Strong, sustained leadership is needed to impose a coherent response by government-as-a-whole even to a few key issues. In Britain, Tony Blair certainly advocated joined-up government but few would claim he succeeded in vanquishing the garbage-can.

Stages of the policy process

It is helpful to distinguish the five stages of the policy process shown in Figure 18.1: initiation, formulation, implementation, evaluation and review. Of course, these divisions are more analytical than chronological, meaning that in the real world they often overlap. So again we must keep a sharp eye on political realities and avoid imposing logical sequences on complex realities. Nonetheless, a review of these stages will provide a way to explore the particular focus of policy analysis.

Initiation and formulation

Why did governments expand public welfare for the first three decades after 1945 and then at least stabilize provision by the century's end? Why did many Western governments take companies into public ownership after the war and then start selling them back to the private sector in the 1980s and 1990s? These are questions about policy initiation and formulation – about the decision to make (or reverse) policy in a particular area and then to develop specific proposals within that area.

In all democracies, much of the agenda bubbles up from below, delivered by bureaucrats in the form of issues demanding immediate attention. These requirements include the need to fix the unforeseen impacts of earlier decisions, leading to the notion of policy as its own cause (Wildavsky, 1979, p. 62). For example, once a highway is opened, additional action will be needed to combat the spillover effects of congestion, accidents and pollution. Rather like legal decisions, public policy naturally tends to thicken over time; cases of withdrawal, such as the ending of prohibition in the United States, are unusual. In addition, much political business, including the annual budget, occurs on a regular cycle, dictating attention at certain times. So policymakers find that routine business always presses; they respond to, more than they shape, the agenda.

The broader process of policy initiation differs somewhat between the United States and European (and other party-led) liberal democracies. In the pluralistic world of American politics, success for a proposal depends on the opening of policy windows

Figure 18.1 Stages of the policy process

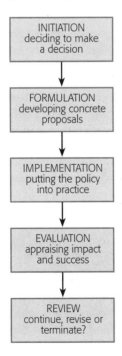

such as the opportunities created by the election of a new government. The policy window creates the potential for innovation – and even for a mild version of the critical junctures discussed in Chapter 3.

However, openings soon close: the cycle of attention to a particular issue is short, as both political debate and the public mood moves on. Thus, Kingdon (2003) suggests that **policy entrepreneurs** help to seize the moment. Like surfers, these initiators must ride the big wave by convincing the political elite not only of the scale of the problem but also of the timeliness of their policy aimed at its resolution.

> **Policy entrepreneurs** are 'advocates of proposals or for the prominence of an idea' (Kingdon, 2003, p. 122). They exert influence by raising the profile of their pet topic (automobile safety, world poverty); by framing how it is discussed ('yes we can'); and by showing how their ideas can be applied in fresh ways, to new areas and to current concerns.

From this perspective, interest group leaders succeed by linking their own preferred policies to a wider narrative: save the whale and you may be able to defuse criticism that you are failing to rescue the planet. Adopt our proposals for skills training and you will be seen to be addressing the bigger question of international competitiveness. So we should not portray current problems as bringing forth new solutions. Rather, existing schemes, serving the interests of their proponents, are frequently dusted down and offered as solutions to the crisis of the moment. The scheme of the moment typically emerges from a long, quiet gestation.

The concepts of policy entrepreneur and policy window offer insight into the free-wheeling, competitive public debate which governs policy initiation and formulation in the USA. However, these terms carry less resonance in the more structured, party-based democracies of Western Europe. Here the political agenda is under firmer, if still incomplete, control. Party manifestos and coalition agreements set out an agenda for government in more explicit and detailed form than in the USA. Detailed policies enter the public realm at a later point than in America.

In the extreme case of the European Union, the policy agenda is formally the preserve of the supranational, non-party European Commission. This body is granted the sole right of initiation, enabling it to fulfil its commitment to integration. Majone (2006, p. 231) makes the legal point:

The European Commission plays a very important role because of its monopoly of policy initiation. This monopoly has been granted by the founding Treaty and is carefully protected by the European Court of Justice. Hence, no national government can induce the Commission to make a specific proposal changing the status quo, unless that proposal also makes the Commission better off. Such tight control of the policy agenda has no analogue either in parliamentary or presidential democracies.

Normally, policy-formers operate within a narrow range of options. They will generally seek solutions which are consistent with broader currents of opinion and previous policies within the sector. Compare American and British attitudes to medical care. In the United States, both the Clinton and Obama administrations soon learned that health-care reform proposals which depart from the American preference for private provision generate considerable opposition from entrenched interests. In Britain, by contrast, over 60 years experience with the National Health Service have entrenched an expectation that medical care will be provided free at the point of care, and on a non-profit basis. Neither country could realistically adopt the other's approach, even it were demonstrably superior. Policy-makers rarely work with blank sheets; path dependence (see p. 75) applies to ideas as much as to institutions.

Implementation

After a policy has been agreed, it must be put into effect – an obvious point, of course, except that much traditional political science stopped at the point where government reached a decision, ignoring the myriad difficulties which arise in policy execution. Probably the main achievement of policy analysis has been to direct attention to these problems of implementation. No longer can execution be dismissed with Woodrow Wilson (1887) as 'mere administration'. Policy is as policy does.

Turning a blind eye to implementation issues can still be politically convenient. Often, the political imperative is just to have a policy; whether it works is neither here nor there. Coalition governments, in particular, are often based on elaborate agreements between parties on what is to be done. This bible must be obeyed even if its commandments are expensive and ineffective.

But there is a political risk in sleepwalking into implementation failure. For example, the British government's failure to prevent mad cow disease from crossing the species barrier to humans in the late 1980s was a classic instance of this error. Official committees instructed abattoirs to remove infective material from slaughtered cows but initially took no special steps to ensure these plans were carried out carefully. As a result of incompetence in slaughter-houses, the disease agent continued to enter the human food chain, killing over 150 people by 2009, and the government's standing suffered accordingly.

The **top-down** approach represents the traditional view of implementation. Within this perspective, the question posed was the classical problem of bureaucracy: how to ensure political direction of unruly public servants. Elected ministers had to be able to secure compliance from departments already committed to pet projects of their own. Without vigilance from on high, sound policies would be hijacked by lower-level officials committed to existing procedures, thus diluting the impact of new initiatives.

This top-down approach focuses excessively on control and compliance. Like the rational model of policy-making from which it springs, it may be unrealistic and even counter-productive. Hence the emergence of the contrasting **bottom-up** perspective, with its starting-point that policy-makers should seek to engage rather than control those who translate policy into practice. Writers in this tradition, such as Hill and Hupe (2002), ask: what if circumstances have changed since the policy was formulated? And what if the policy itself is poorly designed? Much legislation, after all, is based on

A **top-down** approach conceives the task of policy implementation as ensuring that policy execution delivers the outputs and outcomes specified by the policy-makers. By contrast, a **bottom-up** approach judges that those who execute policy should be encouraged to adapt to local and changing circumstances.

uncertain information and is highly general in content. Often, it cannot be followed to the letter because there is no letter to follow.

Many policy analysts now suggest that objectives are more likely to be met if those who execute policy are given not just encouragement and resources but also flexibility. Setting one specific target for an organization expected to deliver multiple goals simply leads to unbalanced delivery. Only what gets measured, gets done.

Furthermore, at street level – the point where policy is delivered – policy emerges from interaction between local bureaucrats and affected groups. Here at the sharp end, goals can often be best achieved by adapting them to local circumstances. For instance, education, health care and policing must surely differ between the rural countryside and multicultural areas in the inner city. If the policy is left unmodified, its fate will be that of the mighty dragon in the Chinese proverb: no match for the neighbourhood snake.

Further, local implementers will often be the only people with full knowledge of how policies interact. They will know that if two policies possess incompatible goals, something has to give. They will be aware that an excess of policy will lead to dilution, implying a need for local priorities if any single policy is to succeed. They will also know the significant actors in the locality, including the growing number of for-profit and voluntary sector agencies involved in policy execution. Implementation is often a matter of building relationships between organizations operating in the field, an art which is rarely covered in central manuals. The American politician Tip O'Neill (1912–94) said 'all politics is local', a phrase that applies with particular force to policy implementation.

So a bottom-up approach reflects an incremental view of policy-making in which implementation is seen as policy-making by other means. This approach reflects the contemporary emphasis on governance, with its stress on the many stakeholders involved in the policy process. The challenge is to ensure that local coalitions work for the policy rather than forming a conspiracy against it.

Evaluation

Just as policy analysis has increased awareness of the importance of policy implementation, so too has it sharpened our focus on evaluation. The task of policy evaluation is to work out whether a programme has achieved its goals and if so how cost-effectively.

Public policies, and the organizations created to put them into practice, lack the clear yardstick of profitability used in the private sector. How do we appraise a defence department if there are no wars and therefore no win–loss record? Is the office of crisis management doing its job if there were no crises last year? Which is the more successful police force: the one that solves most crimes or the one that has the fewest crimes to solve?

Evaluation is complicated further because goals are often modified during implementation, transforming a failing policy into a different but more successful one. This 'mushiness of goals', to use Fesler and Kettl's phrase (2008, p. 287), means that policy-makers' intent is often a poor benchmark for evaluation. Few programmes have such a specific objective as President Kennedy's commitment in 1961 to land a man on the moon and return him safely to earth 'before the decade is out' (mission accomplished, five months to spare).

The question of evaluation has often been ignored by governments. Sweden is a typical example. In the post-war decades, a succession of Social Democratic governments concentrated on building a universal welfare state without even conceiving of a need to evaluate the quality and cost-effectiveness with which services were delivered by an expanding bureaucracy. In France and Germany, and other continental countries where bureaucratic tasks are interpreted as the legalistic application of rules to cases, the issue of policy evaluation still barely surfaces – often to the detriment of long-suffering citizens.

Yet without some evaluation, governments are unable to learn the lessons of experience. In the United States, Jimmy Carter (President, 1977–81) did insist that at least 1 per cent of the funds allocated to any project should be devoted to evaluation; he wanted more focus on what policies achieved. In the 1990s, once more, evaluation began to return to the fore. For example, the Labour government elected in Britain in 1997 claimed a new pragmatic concern with evidence-based policy: what matters is what works. In some other democracies, too, public officials began to think, often for the first time, about how best to evaluate the programmes they administered.

Evaluation studies distinguish between **policy outputs** and **policy outcomes**. Outputs are easily measured by quantitative indicators of activities: visits, trips, treatments, beneficiaries. The danger here is that outputs turn into targets; the focus becomes what was done rather than what was achieved. So outcomes – the actual results– should be a more important component of evaluation than outputs. The stated purpose of America's Government Performance and Results Act (1993) illustrates the distinction:

The Act seeks to shift the focus of government decision-making and accountability away from a preoccupation with the activities that are undertaken – such as grants dispensed or inspections made – to a focus on the results of those activities, such as real gains in employability, safety, responsiveness, or program quality. (GAO, 2009)

However, outcomes are tricky. They are easier to define than to measure; they are highly resistant to change and, as a result, the cost per unit of impact can be extraordinarily high, with gains often only temporary. With social programmes, in particular, a creaming process often dilutes the impact: those who gain the most are those within the target group least in need of the support. For example, addiction treatment centres find it easiest to reach those users who would have been most likely to overcome their drug use anyway.

This stickiness of social reality means that attempts to 'remedy the deficiencies in the quality of human life' can never be a complete success. Yet they can be, and sometimes are, a total failure (Rossi *et al.*, 2003, p. 6). If our expectations of a policy's outcomes were more realistic, we might be less disap

Policy outputs are what government does; **policy outcomes** are what government achieves. Outputs are the activity; outcomes are the effects, both intended and unforeseen. Outputs are measured easily enough: so many new prisons are built, there is a specified increase in the state pension. Outcomes are harder to ascertain, such as a reduction in recidivism or in the number of elderly people living in poverty.

pointed with the limited results. So we can understand why agencies evaluating their own programmes often prefer to describe their outputs rather than their outcomes.

Just as policy implementation in accordance with the top-down model is an unrealistic goal, so judging policy effectiveness against specific objectives is often an implausibly scientific approach to evaluation. A more bottom-up, incremental approach to evaluation has therefore emerged. Here, the goals are more modest: the notion is that an evaluation should simply gather in the opinions of all the stakeholders affected by the policy, yielding a qualitative narrative rather than a barrage of output-based statistics. As Parsons (1995, p. 567) describes this approach, 'evaluation has to be predicated on wide and full collaboration of all programme stakeholders: agents (funders, implementers); beneficiaries (target groups, potential adopters); and those who are excluded ("victims")'.

In such a naturalistic evaluation, the varying objectives of different interests are welcomed. They are not dismissed as a barrier to objective scrutiny of policy. Unintended effects can be written back into the script, not excluded because they are irrelevant to the achievement of stated goals. This is a more pragmatic, indeed incremental, approach because the stakeholders might agree on the success of a policy even though they disagree on the standards against which it should be judged. The object of a bottom-up evaluation can simply be to learn from the project rather than to make uncertain judgements of success.

The danger of these naturalistic evaluations (and perhaps even of top-down evaluations) is that they become games of framing, blaming and claiming: politics all over again, with the most powerful stakeholder securing the most favourable write-up. To prevent the evaluation of a project from turning into nothing more than an application for continued funding, evaluation studies should always include some external assessors.

Review

Once a policy has been evaluated, or even if it has not, the three possibilities are: to continue, to revise or to terminate. Most policies, or at least the functions associated with them, continue with only minor revisions. Once a role for government is established, it tends to continue. But the agency charged with performing the function does change over time. In the United States, for instance, 426 separate agencies were established between 1946 and 1997 but a majority of these had been terminated by the end of the period, usually after a change of party in the White House (D. Lewis, 2002). So the observation that there is nothing so permanent as a temporary government organization appears to be wide of the mark. Functions continue but the agencies performing them can evolve, either because a task has been split between two or more agencies or because previously separate functions have been consolidated into a single organization.

Yet even if agency termination is surprisingly common, the intriguing question remains: why is policy termination so rare? Why does government as a whole seemingly prefer to adopt new functions than to drop old ones? Bardach (1976) suggests five reasons for the difficulties of policy termination:

▶ Policies are designed to last a long time, creating expectations of future benefits;
▶ Policy termination brings conflicts which leave too much blood on the floor;
▶ No one wants to admit the policy was a bad idea;
▶ Policy termination may affect other programmes and interests;
▶ Politics rewards innovation rather than tidy housekeeping.

Policy instruments

So far, we have treated policy in a general way: goals are (sometimes) set; outputs are (usually) achieved; outcomes are (occasionally) affected. But what are the instruments which give effect to policy? To put the question more broadly, how exactly do governments govern? The question is simple but useful, not least because a consideration of policy tools demonstrates the complexity of contemporary governance.

In thinking about the tools used to translate policy into practice, it is easy to overstate the importance of legislation and direct public provision. To be sure, parliament can establish a legal entitlement to a welfare benefit and then arrange

for local governments to pay out the relevant sum to those who satisfy eligibility rules. The welfare states of north European states developed in precisely this way and such state-administered mechanisms have generally proved to be popular with their electorates.

In reality, however, legislation and direct provision are just two of many policy instruments; what is more, these devices are becoming less prominent in an era of limited public resources and increased social complexity. Even when legislation provides a framework, it is increasingly fleshed out in lengthy and detailed delegated legislation issued by the sponsoring department.

A government's repertoire is remarkably wide-ranging. The lengthy list in Box 18.2 is by no means comprehensive; more detailed catalogues extend to over 30 tools (Osborne and Gaebler, 1992).

Leaving aside the provision of services, policy instruments can be classified as sticks (sanctions), carrots (rewards) and sermons (information and persuasion) (Vedung, 1998). Sticks include traditional command and control functions: banning this, requiring that. Carrots include positive financial incentives such as taxation and subsidies. Sermons include that stalwart of agencies seeking to demonstrate their concern to all and sundry: the public information campaign.

In addition to these traditional tools, market-based incentives have emerged as an interesting addition to the repertoire of policy instruments. Such mechanisms as tradable permits and auctions are increasingly used in environmental policy as a way of ensuring that any pollution rights available within a government-set ceiling reach those producers who generate most economic value from their pollution-creating activity. These producers will be the ones willing to pay the highest price for their licence.

In this way, the cap of a **cap and trade** system achieves the public good of limiting a particular pollutant; the trade allows the right to pollute to be

> In a **cap and trade** system, the government sets a limit on the total output of a particular pollutant and issues permits to that limit. These permits can then be bought and sold. The European Union Emission Trading System for carbon dioxide emissions is a major example.

BOX 18.2

A selection of policy instruments

Command and control	Example: reducing tobacco consumption
Legislation	Authorizing the health department to take measures to limit passive smoking
Regulation	Banning tobacco consumption in restaurants
Public services	Funding public health clinics to provide smoking cessation sessions
Private services	Paying private agencies to run smoking cessation clinics
Finance	
Taxation	Taxing tobacco products
Subsidies	Offering a rebate on purchases of nicotine replacement products
Advocacy	
Information	Launching a publicity campaign about the harmful effects of smoking
Persuasion	Launching a publicity campaign to encourage people to stop smoking
Civil society	Creating and funding anti-smoking groups in order to reshape the landscape of relevant interest groups

---

concentrated on producers who obtain greatest economic benefit from their allowance. The cost of the permit also provides an incentive to reduce pollution through, for example, technological innovation. However, it remains to be seen how effective such mechanisms prove to be over the long run (Cordes, 2002).

Given a range of tools, how should policy-makers choose between them? In practice, instrument selection is strongly influenced by past practice in the sector and by national policy styles. Nonetheless, more explicit criteria are available, including:

- Effectiveness: will the instrument achieve its goals?
- Efficiency: at what cost?
- Equity: is it fair?
- Appropriateness: does it fit the problem?
- Simplicity: is it manageable?

Since most policies use a combination of tools, the overall configuration should also be addressed. Instruments should not exert opposite effects and they should form a sequence such that, for example,

information campaigns come before direct regulation of behaviour (Salamon, 2002a).

Regulation

The final decades of the twentieth century witnessed an important shift in the delivery of public policy in many liberal democracies, especially in Europe. In social welfare, service delivery was increasingly contracted out to private agencies; in the economy, public industries were privatized. During the same period, public oversight became more intense in such sectors as banking, education, the environment, employment, scientific research and consumer protection. Together, these trends establish a changed rather than a diminished role for the state – and one which views the government as a regulator rather than provider.

So **regulation** has become a major policy instrument in contemporary liberal democracies. To understand the instruments of public policy, we must introduce the politics of regulation, comparing how different countries approach the task and

Public **regulation** consists of oversight of a particular social or economic sector particularly through making rules, enforcing them, and adjudicating disputes. Where general laws apply to society as a whole, much regulation focuses on specific areas, such as consumer protection.

Co-regulation entrusts the attainment of public objectives, in whole or in part, to groups which are recognized participants in the field (e.g. doctors' associations). **Self-regulation** is by the relevant groups themselves and may be independent of government. These terms are widely used by regulators in the European Union (Senden, 2005).

assessing the implications of the growing army of regulatory agencies.

A useful starting point is to contrast the British tradition of informal, cooperative regulation with the more rules-based American approach. This comparison gives us two styles of regulation, though neither country now fully exemplifies the mode traditionally associated with it.

We begin with Britain. Here, of course, regulation is far from new and a brief résumé of its origins is revealing (Moran, 2003). One of the first waves of public oversight of particular sectors occurred in the nineteenth century, aimed in part at mitigating the harshest effects of the Industrial Revolution. Regulatory bodies created in this Victorian burst of administrative innovation included the Factory Inspectorate (1833), the Poor Law Commission (1834) and the Prison Inspectorate (1835).

Although backed by statute, these early regulators quickly adopted an informal, cooperative style based on securing practical results rather than perfect compliance with procedures. This pragmatic approach, which recognized the power and wealth of the employers, initiated a gentlemanly British philosophy of regulation which remained dominant within the UK until the final third of the twentieth century. The underlying philosophy was reflected in advice given to some of the first factory inspectors:

Your best chance of success will be a courteous and conciliatory demeanour towards the mill-owners; and by impressing on their minds that the object of your visits is rather to assist them than to fish out grounds for complaint. (quoted in Moran, 2003, p. 43)

In contemporary terms, the British tradition is based on **co-regulation** (in conjunction with the regulated) or even the fostering of **self-regulation** (by those who are regulated). Safe working, for example, is not to be achieved through prescriptive rules imposed by inspectors but rather by encour-

aging the employer to adopt safety policies that identify and contain major risks. As one contemporary British regulator put it, 'visual inspection is a thing of the past in high hazard, large, complex facilities. You can't walk round a chemical plant and see much; all there is is shiny tanks and pipe-work' (quoted in Moran, 2003, p. 25). From this perspective, resort to law is a sign of regulatory failure rather than success.

There are undoubted strengths to the British approach. It recognizes that real expertise and effective control lies with the regulated and it seeks to obtain commitment to a substantive goal rather than conformity to a rulebook. But dangers have become apparent, too. The gentleman's club can easily turn into a secret society. Informal agreements can mutate into complacent conspiracies as each group – the regulator and regulated – seeks a comfortable life. The public interest, always amorphous and not directly at the table, is discretely side-lined. In addition, since regulated interests are more numerous, better resourced and more informed than the regulator, the format creates a particular danger of **regulatory capture**. The regulated can soon have the regulator in their pocket.

Regulatory capture arises when public agencies created to oversee particular industries come to serve the interests of those they supervise.

Eventually, the conspiracy unravels. Trains collide, chemical factories explode and financial advisers run off with their clients' money. These fiascos generate inescapable media coverage and a political requirement for more formal rules designed to prevent a recurrence. Given this weakness, it is perhaps unsurprising that the more formal, rules-based American style of regulation has proved to be more influential. Moran (2003, p. 17) again:

SWEDEN

Form of government ■ a unitary parliamentary democracy with a monarch serving as ceremonial head of state.

Legislature ■ the 349-member Riksdag ('meeting of the realm') plays a full part in the legislative process, supported by 15 influential committees. The parliament has been unicameral since 1971.

Executive ■ the government is headed by a prime minister who chairs weekly meetings of the cabinet.

Constitution and judiciary ■ the constitution consists of four entrenched laws: the Instrument of Government, the Act of Succession, the Freedom of the Press Act and the Fundamental Law on Freedom of Expression. The Supreme Court is traditionally restrained. The legal system is a blend of common and civil law.

Electoral system ■ the Riksdag is elected for a four-year term by party list proportional representation, with an additional tier of seats used to enhance proportionality. The national vote threshold to secure seats is 4 per cent.

Party system ■ the Social Democrats are the leading party, sharing their position on the left with the Left (formerly communist) Party and the Greens. However, a right-wing coalition, led by the conservative Moderates and including the Centre Party, the Christian Democrats and the Liberals, took office in 2006.

Population (annual growth rate): 9.1m (+0.2%)	
World Bank income group: high income	
Political Rights score: ❶	
Civil Liberties score: ❷	
Human development index (rank/out of): 7/177	
Freedom of the press index (rank/out of): 5/195	
Perceived transparency index (rank/out of): 1/180	

Note: For meaning and sources of scales and indexes, see p. xv. In all cases a score and rank of 1 is 'best'.

Sweden offers a high quality of life to its citizens. In particular, it combines a high standard of living with an exceptionally equal distribution of income, demonstrating with other Scandinavian countries that the twin objectives of mass affluence and limited inequality are compatible. Average life expectancy is about two years higher than in the UK and USA.

The country's economic strengths are considerable. As the CIA (2009) notes, 'aided by peace and neutrality for the whole of the 20th century, Sweden has achieved an enviable standard of living under a mixed system of high-tech capitalism and extensive welfare benefits. It has a modern distribution system, excellent internal and external communications, and a skilled labor force'.

Yet these strengths have been achieved with a relatively equal income distribu-

tion. The Gini coefficient, a measure of income inequality, is the lowest of all the 135 countries rated (CIA, 2009). The factors limiting income dispersion include:

■ A universal welfare system offering generous benefits;
■ Targeted support for groups vulnerable to poverty;
■ Relatively low differences in pre-tax incomes;
■ A progressive income tax (Palme, 2006).

Social and political stability has also contributed to Sweden's economic performance. This stability, in its turn, reflects limited internal diversity. Swedish is the foremost language, with Sami- and Finnish-speaking minorities; the dominant religion is Lutheran. A traditionally generous asylum policy has strength-

ened minorities from such countries as Syria and Iraq, but the national culture continues to emphasize equality and tolerance.

Lacking strong national, religious and ethnic divisions, the party system has been based around class and the left–right dimension. 'In no other country', writes Bergström (1991, p. 8), 'has the basic left–right scale accounted for so much of the party structure and electoral behaviour'. In particular, Sweden has exemplified the traditional five-party Scandinavian pattern of communist, social democratic, centre (formerly agrarian), liberal and conservative parties. Since the 1990s, the Greens and Christian Democrats have also achieved a place in the Riksdag. The Social Democrats have led in this party system, gaining support from the large public sector as well as the traditional working class.

Further reading: Heidar (2004), Lewin (2006).

The policy process in Sweden

Stockholm

In an influential analysis, Richardson et al. (1982) classified countries by their policy style – their preferred way of making policy. Of the two major dimensions of policy style, the first is whether a government seeks to anticipate problems or merely to react to them, fire brigade style. And the second is whether in forming policy a government attempts to reach a consensus through discussion with organized groups or, alternatively, is inclined to impose its decisions on society (Figure 18.2). Examining Sweden through this lens, Richardson et al. (1982) characterized the country's policy style as anticipatory and consensus-seeking. Is this interpretation still valid and how is it implemented in Swedish governance?

Anton's depiction (1969, p. 94) of Swedish policy-making as 'open, rationalistic, consensual and extraordinarily deliberative' remains fundamentally correct from a comparative perspective. In one sense, the accuracy of this characterization is surprising, since Sweden is a small unitary state with sovereignty firmly based on a unicameral parliament and a hegemonic social democratic party. On this potentially centralized foundation, however, Sweden has developed an elaborate negotiating democracy which is both culturally and institutionally secure.

One factor sustaining Sweden's distinctive policy process is the compact size and policy focus of the 12 departments of central government. Less than 5,000 staff are employed at these ministries; their core task is to 'assist the government in supplying background material for use as a

basis for decisions and in conducting inquiries into both national and international matters' (Regeringskansliet, 2009).

Most technical issues, and the services provided by the extensive welfare state, are contracted out to public agencies and local govern-

ment. This division of tasks requires extensive collaboration between public institutions and is sustained by high levels of transparency and trust.

Committees of enquiry (also called commissions) are the key device facilitating policy deliberation. Typically, the government appoints a committee to research a topic and present recommendations. Committees usually comprise a chair and advisers but can include opposition members of parliament; some enquiries are carried out by a single person. The commission consults with relevant interests and political parties. Next, its recommendations are published and discussed further. The relevant ministry then examines the report and, if appropriate, issues

a government bill (which is presented with a summary of comments received). The bill is then discussed in parliament, not least in one of the Riksdag's committees, where it may be modified before passing onto the statute book.

This rather slow policy-making

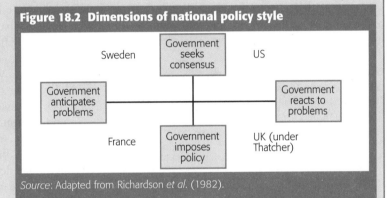

Figure 18.2 Dimensions of national policy style

Sweden — Government seeks consensus — US

Government anticipates problems — Government reacts to problems

France — Government imposes policy — UK (under Thatcher)

Source: Adapted from Richardson *et al.* (1982).

method is highly rational, in that information is collected and analysed, but also incremental, in that organized opponents of the proposal are given ample opportunity to voice their concerns.

However, public deliberation may contribute to blandness, and the strong emphasis on policy formulation may be at the expense of implementation. Still, the style is distinctively Swedish – and a useful comparison with the less measured policy-making style in other liberal democracies. In short, policy-making in Sweden provides us with an interesting deviant case.

Further reading: Lindvall and Rothstein (2006), OECD (2007).

America can claim copyright to the title 'regulatory state', for it is in the USA that the concept of regulation has been most closely studied, the regulatory agency most deeply institutionalized, and the idea of guiding the state's economic mission most historically entrenched.

Where many other democracies nationalized some key industries, America's aversion to direct public ownership led to a stronger focus on regulation. In particular, the United States developed the notion of **independent regulatory agencies** to make, implement and resolve disputes about the rules governing specialized sectors. These agencies are a distinct contribution to American governance, combining elements of legislative, executive and judicial power and lacking direct accountability to the political executive.

An **independent regulatory agency** is an American term for a public body established by Congress to make and apply rules for a particular sector. These agencies do not form part of a government department and their members can only be dismissed by the president for reasons set out in its founding law.

The earliest cohort of independent agencies emerged around the turn of the twentieth century as part of a deliberate attempt to counter the excessive partisanship of the spoils system. The hope was that these new bodies, operating outside the normal structure of government departments, would create impartial, professional and even scientific regulation without stifling the spirit of American enterprise. Further waves of agency creation followed in the New Deal and during the era of social reform in the 1960s. Examples include the Interstate Commerce Commission (1887), the Federal Reserve System (1913), the Securities and Exchange Commission (1934) and the Equal Employment Opportunity Commission (1965).

America's model of independent agencies has attracted interest as other countries (including Britain) have privatized large sections of industry, creating dominant corporations which need some form of oversight. Gilardi (2008, p. 4) observes that in Western Europe, 'at the beginning of the twenty first century, independent regulatory agencies are widely accepted as an appropriate institutional

model'. This growing interest in independent agencies reflects an attempt to depoliticize regulation – in other words, to reduce the scope of decision-making by elected politicians even as democratic values continue to be promoted in the abstract. The independent agency is tangible evidence of a shift not only from government to governance but also from democracy to expertise as a fount of authority.

Majone (1996) suggests two defences of this trend. First, autonomous agencies can adopt more consistent, credible and long-term policies than are feasible for politicians who remain subject to short-term electoral pressures. If an unelected central bank can control inflation more effectively than an elected government, the argument goes, then surely the bank should be given the job? Gilardi (2008) shows that in Western Europe, governments are most likely to delegate authority to regulatory agencies in areas where they need to increase the credibility of their own commitments and want to bind their successors.

Second, delegating political authority to specialized professional regulators is particularly appropriate for issues that are technical (e.g. telecommunications) rather than redistributive (e.g. taxation). There may well be a single best way of regulating mobile telephony even though the level of taxation is a political question for which there is no technical answer. As the regulatory state matures, so we may expect the shift from political to professional authority to become taken for granted.

It is doubtful, however, whether the particular model employed in the USA should be adopted elsewhere. As the successes of the more informal British approach remind us, regulation of a sector is not necessarily more effective than regulation with the sector. Formal rule-making in American agencies involves an official hearing with witnesses and counsel. As a policy instrument, issuing regulations becomes time-consuming and cumbersome, with a strong emphasis on procedures.

To be sure, American agencies have adopted informal and negotiated rule-making in some areas but, in comparison with Britain, the overall style remains highly legalistic, with frequent appeals to the courts (Peters, 2009a, p. 86). More direct and informal engagement by affected interests, as found in some European countries, would surely be beneficial, as would agreements with the sector that preclude the need to issue formal regulations in the first place. Co- and self-regulation have their place, not least because they are less expensive in time and money for the government.

In any event, the point is made: the philosophy and organization of regulation is an important aspect of the overall policy process. Regulation has become a characteristic policy instrument in contemporary liberal democracies, particularly as ideological preferences for purely public, or purely private, provision have lost their bite.

Public policy in authoritarian states

Compared with liberal democracies, policy analysis is less important to understanding the politics of authoritarian regimes and illiberal democracies. Nonetheless, it is important to understand the reasons for, and implications of, this contrast.

The central theme in the policy process of many non-democratic regimes is the subservience of policy to politics. Often, the key task for non-elected rulers is to play off domestic political forces against each other so as to ensure their own continuation in office, an art developed to its highest level by the cautious ruling families of the Middle East. Uncertain of their own long-term survival in office, authoritarian rulers may want to enrich themselves, their family and their ethnic group while they remain in control of the state's resources. These tasks of political survival and personal enrichment are hardly conducive to orderly policy development; rather, they demand a lack of transparency in policy presentation. As Hershberg (2006, p. 151) says,

To be successful, policies must reflect the capabilities – encompassing expertise, resources and authority – of the institutions and individuals charged with their implementation. Those capabilities are more likely to be translated into effective performance in environments characterized by predictable, transparent and efficient procedures for reaching decisions and for adjudicating differences of interest.

But it is precisely these 'predictable, transparent and efficient procedures' that non-democracies are often unable to supply. Frequently, opaque patronage is the main political currency; the age-old game of creating and benefiting from political debts works against clear procedures of any kind. The result is a conservative preference for the existing rules of the game, an indifference to policy and a lack of interest in national development. As Chazan *et al.* (1999, p. 171) note in discussing Africa, 'patriarchal rule has tended to be conservative: it propped up the existing order and did little to promote change. It required the exertion of a great deal of energy just to maintain control'.

In addition, rulers may simply lack the ability to make coherent policy. This weakness was especially common in military regimes whose leaders frequently lacked formal education and managerial competence. The generals sometimes seized power in an honest attempt to improve public policy-making but then discovered that governance was more complicated than they had imagined.

Policy inertia is therefore the standard pattern under authoritarian rule. Stagnation is reinforced when, as in many of the largest non-democracies, the rulers engage in **rent-seeking**, often using their control over natural commodities such as oil as their main source of revenue. In these circumstances, the government need not achieve the penetration of society required to collect taxes, nor need it concern itself with the development of human capital. Rather, a stand-off of mutual distrust develops between rulers and ruled, creating a context which is incompatible with the more sophisticated policy initiatives found in many liberal democracies. In the absence of effective social policy at national level, problems of poverty, welfare and medical care are addressed locally if at all.

> **Rent-seeking** occurs when people aim to obtain an income from selling a scarce resource without adding real value. Examples include government officials taking bribes to provide a licence to a company or a passport to a citizen. In such cases, civil servants sell their capacity to exercise discretion. Rent-seeking is mutually advantageous, benefiting both buyer and seller, but imposes a cost on the economy and society.

In addition, the absence of an extensive network of voluntary associations and interest groups in authoritarian states prevents the close coordination between state and society needed for effective policy-making and implementation. The blocking mechanism here is fear among rulers as much as the ruled. Saich (2009, p. 223) identifies these anxieties in the case of China's party elite:

While it is true that public discourse is breaking free of the codes and linguistic phrases established by the party-state, it is also clear that no coherent alternative vision has emerged that would fashion a civil society. From the party's point of view, what is lurking in the shadows waiting to pounce on any opening that would allow freedom of expression is revivalism, religion, linguistic division, regional and non-Han ethnic loyalties.

As always, however, it is important to distinguish between different types of authoritarian government. At one extreme, many military and personal rulers demonstrated immense concern about their own prosperity but none at all for their country's, leading to a policy shortage. At the other extreme, modernizing regimes whose ruling elite has a clear sense of the public good and a secure hold on power have followed long term policies, especially for economic development. Examples include Asia's developmental states (see p. 396) and communist regimes. Certainly, the Soviet Union attempted, and for a while achieved, a type of planning virtually without precedent in history. Every communist state formulated clearer national goals and targets than any democracy. The result was a decisive, ruthless and occasionally successful commitment to a single policy goal, notably industrialization.

Yet even in communist states, planning eventually yielded economic stagnation. The formula delivered production but low productivity and it emphasized quantity over quality. Communism may have been an ideology of transformation but, once the early revolutionary zeal was exhausted in countries such as the Soviet Union, policy development took second place to ensuring the rulers' political security. As in many non-communist authoritarian regimes, the dominance of politics over policy, and a relationship of suspicion between state and society, resulted in inertia, decay and collapse.

China is, of course, the major exception. It survives as an authoritarian regime partly because it has pursued policies leading to rapid economic development. The capacity of the party's top leadership in Beijing to form and implement coherent policy in the world's most populous country is a remarkable achievement. It owes much to political flexibility, to the country's authoritarian tradition and to the regime's continuing legitimacy – itself derived from sustained economic growth in urban areas.

The leadership's sensitivity to public concerns, unusual in authoritarian regimes, is seen not just in the achievement of economic development but also in attempts to limit its inegalitarian consequences. For example, the party's 2006 programme, Building a Harmonious Society, sought to reduce income inequality, improve access to medical care for rural-dwellers and urban migrants, extend social security and contain the environmental damage from industrialization (Saich, 2009). With less success, the party has also sought to address problems of corruption and the sense of a moral vacuum which contribute to popular dissatisfaction at local level with Chinese governance.

However, these attempts at long term and responsive policy-making are rarely found in authoritarian regimes. Indeed, these very successes may eventually prove to be the regime's undoing. From a sufficiently long-term perspective, the danger is that continued economic, educational and social advance will come to threaten the survival of authoritarian rule in China.

Public policy in illiberal democracies

The policy process in illiberal democracies falls between liberal democracies and authoritarian regimes. On the one hand, illiberal democracies inherently lack the strong institutions, legal framework and detailed connections with society that permit the sophisticated policy processes found in liberal democracies. On the other hand, these illiberal democracies cannot simply retreat from policy in the manner of many military regimes. There are elections to be won and popular dreams to be fed. Poverty and inequality generate the hope of a better life but simultaneously constrain the leader's ability to deliver.

The response of the rulers of illiberal democracies to these dilemmas is by no means uniform. However, one syndrome is for the leader to combine strong political control of key economic resources, particularly commodities, with a freer market in less sensitive sectors of the economy. In most cases, social and economic inequality is pronounced, with considerable wealth for a small group of well-connected business owners coexisting alongside unremitting poverty for a large sector of the population. Whether living in urban ghettos or remote rural areas, the poor must rely largely on self-help, with the government lacking the organization and resources needed to deliver an effective and uniform social policy. The populist leader both draws on, and claims he is the only means of overcoming, the glaring gap between the poverty of the many and the wealth of the few.

It is important to bear in mind that many illiberal democracies have emerged from an authoritarian past, creating major policy problems in the transition to a new order. Post-communist states provide the most dramatic examples of the policy transformation required of new democracies. When the communist order collapsed, an entire policy framework went with it; far from springing a leak, the communist boat sank. The task facing new leaders was to transform societies fuelled by power into societies based on rules, a project of enormous scale.

Under communism, large state-owned enterprises not only dominated the economy but also served as welfare providers, producing what Elster *et al.* (1998, p. 204) describe as a 'tight coupling' between the workplace and social policy. This elaborate, inefficient but functioning system could not be quickly replaced by market mechanisms in the economy or by social policy delivered through central or local governments.

In particular, a successful private economy, as in liberal democracies, is in fact an intricate public achievement. It requires entrepreneurs to show initiative, capital markets to provide resources for investment, consumers to spend money, courts to enforce property rights, bureaucrats to keep their fingers out of the pie, and a government to act as an umpire rather than a player. The policy challenges are multiple, simultaneous and, considered as a whole, enormous.

For example, after its chaotic transition from communism, Russia's post-communist illiberal democracy began to rebuild its capacity to govern an unequal and diverse society. A body of law was established which provided a more predictable environment for business investment. A recentralization of power encouraged the more uniform application of a newly codified legal system. The tax-take improved, offering an improvement in public revenues with the prospect of further gains if the economy itself continued to grow. The philosophy of social policy became more coherent, with a 'controversial 2005 reform that replaced the bulk of Soviet-era privileges (free or subsidised housing, transportation, medicine and the like for pensioners, students and others) with supposedly equivalent cash payments' (Twigg, 2005, p. 219).

Such reforms notwithstanding, policy-making in post-communist Russia remains subject to the political requirements of the ruling elite. The business environment has become more predictable but industrialists who pose a political threat to the president soon find that numerous rules and regulations are still invoked selectively against them. The state has disposed of many enterprises but rent-seeking continues; indeed, the government has tightened its control over the key resources of oil and gas. In 2006, for example, Russia's government provided its allies in charge of state-owned oil companies with a greater share of the Sakhalin-2 oil field in Siberia by simply rewriting the contract with Royal Dutch Shell. Political and economic power remain tightly interwoven, precluding – at least at the highest levels – uniform policy implementation.

As in other rent-seeking states, public control of export commodities enables the Russian state to sustain its own position even as it neglects the development of closer connections with the Russian population. Social problems such as poverty, alcoholism, violent crime and rural depopulation remain deep-rooted. Despite the attempt to modernize social policy, for many impoverished Russians the transition from communism must appear as a move from an authoritarian welfare state to an authoritarian state full stop.

As in many poor countries, even-handed policy implementation is impossible because many public officials are so poorly paid that corruption remains an essential tool for making ends meet. It may be true that sunlight is the best disinfectant but an escape from corruption and rent-seeking cannot be achieved just by calling for more transparency. The dilemma is that transparency requires broad-based economic development, but such development itself requires a reduction in corruption.

When we turn to illiberal democracies in the smaller states of Africa and Latin America, we find that the problems of building the capacity to execute policy are even greater. Perhaps the most appropriate policy agenda here is to strengthen the capacity of both the public sector and the private sector to deliver results of any kind. Without the ability to implement plans, policies themselves can yield only limited effects.

For instance, there is little point in adopting Western ideas of new public management within the bureaucracy; rather, the purpose should be to build up an orthodox civil service able to apply rules consistently and economically. As Adam Smith (1776) well understood, developing the market also requires enhancing the public infrastructure of transport, communication and education. In poor illiberal democracies, there need be no choice between improving the public or the private sector; both can and must develop together.

In Africa, however, attempts at **capacity building** have so far produced only limited results. Governments often lack the ability to implement their policies throughout the territory. They lack numbers on the ground and must often rely on traditional local leaders who are able to veto the implementation of a reform agenda. Whether its government is elected or not, a state that barely exists cannot be expected to engage in serious and effective policy-making and execution.

Encouraged by international organizations and an improvement in commodity prices, economic

> **Capacity building** consists in developing the long-term ability of organizations to achieve their objectives. Capacity building requires not just material and human resources but also the ability to use them effectively. The phrase is often encountered in discussion of plans to improve state capacity in developing countries.

growth has increased in many sub-Saharan states, particularly those that are more democratic. But even in the most successful cases, state capacity and the physical infrastructure remain limited, while poverty and corruption are still endemic. The transition from poverty, and from illiberal democracy, remains elusive.

Similarly, the smaller and more fragile illiberal democracies in Latin America find themselves immersed in a sea of difficulties which inhibit institutional development and the policy-implementing capacity flowing from it. Capacity building must be a major priority here too. For example, writing of the Andean states of Bolivia, Colombia, Ecuador, Peru and Venezuela where democracy has retained a toe-hold, Drake and Hershberg (2006, p. 20) note that:

reforms intended to increase the effectiveness or legitimacy of the state have sometimes sapped rather than strengthened state capacity ... Never very strong, the central government has been challenged by international and transnational actors; by domestic regional and local competitors; by purveyors of violence among criminals, guerrillas and paramilitaries; and by drug growers and traffickers.

In these circumstances, the task is to build the capacity of the state to implement policies of any kind.

Learning Resources for Chapter 18

Next step

Birkland (2005) is a clear and accessible introduction to theories and concepts in public policy.

Further reading

Stone (2001) and Fischer (2003) adopt critical but accessible approaches to public policy. Colebatch (1998) discusses the policy concept while Sabatier (2007) reviews theories of the policy process. On implementation, see Hill and Hupe (2002), and on evaluation, Fischer (2005). For policy instruments, see Salamon (2002b) and Eliadis *et al.* (2005). Peters (2009a) covers both the policy process and specific policy sectors in the USA. Rose (2004) is a comparative study of lesson-drawing in public policy. Majone (1996) and Moran (2003) are influential works on regulation. Moran *et al.* (2006) provide an extensive handbook on public policy.

Internet sources

Economics and Cost Analysis Support, Environment Protection Agency, USA
Analytical guidance on estimating the costs and benefits of environmental policy
http://www.epa.gov/ttn/ecas/

The Brookings Institution
An American private non-profit organization devoted to independent research and innovative policy solutions
http://www.brookings.org

Independent Evaluation Group, World Bank
An evaluation of the World Bank's support for capacity building in six African states
http://www.worldbank.org/ieg/africa_capacity_building/

www.palgrave.com
Companion Website
Visit the Companion Website to 'click and go'
www.palgrave.com/politics/hague

Political economy

Political economy is traditionally defined as the study of the causes of the wealth of nations. Specifically, the subject examines the policies governments follow in search of increased affluence for the countries they rule. In combining politics and economics, the topic is by nature interdisciplinary. As with other policy areas, the approach is also practical, responding to problems arising in the real world. The question is not just 'why?' but also 'what is to be done?' – about recessions, depressions, mass unemployment, inflation and financial crises.

As Weingast and Wittman write (2008, p. 3), 'over its long lifetime, the phrase "political economy" has had many different meanings'. Political economy can also refer to Marxist analysis of the impact of economic organization on politics; to studies of the impact of the economy on government popularity; and to all attempts to apply the methods of economic analysis to politics. Here, however, we treat political economy as an area of study rather than an approach, focusing on the subject's original concern with government policies for enhancing economic performance.

As background, we begin by introducing the core ideas of three key political economists: Adam Smith, John Maynard Keynes and Milton Friedman. We then inject a comparative dimension, examining the varied forms taken by capitalism in contemporary liberal democracies. After examining whether these differences between liberal democracies are declining, we conclude by discussing the distinctive political economies of authoritarian regimes and illiberal democracies.

Foundations

In this section, we review the work of three central figures in the development of political economy. Smith, Keynes and Friedman analysed economic problems but with a clear eye for both politics and policy. Their ideas have exerted considerable influence, but we will show also how they emerged in response to the conditions and challenges of their time. In this way, we will see both the relevance of ideas to politics and the importance of political circumstances as a forcing-house of ideas.

> The phrase **political economy** comes from seventeenth-century France when it referred to the financial management of the royal household. Today, the term refers to policy issues arising in the area where politics meets economics, with a particular focus on improving economic performance.

BOX 19.1		

Key thinkers in political economy

	Core prescription	Illustrative quotation
Adam Smith (1723–90)	Rely on the market's invisible hand to allocate resources to the areas where they will secure the highest return	'It is not from the benevolence of the butcher, the brewer, or the baker that we expect our dinner, but from their regard to their self-interest' (1776, p. 22)
John Maynard Keynes (1883–1946)	When demand is deficient, counter unemployment by boosting public spending	'If the Treasury were to fill old bottles with bank notes, bury them at suitable depths in disused coal mines which are then filled up to the surface with town rubbish, and leave it to private enterprise on well-tried principles of *laissez-faire* to dig the notes up again . . . there need be no more unemployment' (1936, p. 379)
Milton Friedman (1912–2006)	To bring inflation under control, restrict growth in the money supply	'Inflation is always and everywhere a monetary phenomenon' (1970, p. 16)

Adam Smith

The Scottish economist Adam Smith developed political economy as a field of study in the eighteenth century. He used the term to describe what is now called economics, proposing two objects for the subject: first, to enable the people to supply a plentiful revenue for themselves and, second, to endow the state with sufficient revenue to provide public services (Smith, 1776).

The emergence of political economy in Smith's time reflected the rise of the state, thus linking the subject to the broader discipline of politics. The central point here is that as the idea of a modern state began to develop, so too did the desire to understand how wealth was created for society at large, rather than just for a reigning monarch. This shift in approach reflected the growth of a commercial society in which a country's assets were coming to be measured by broader and more sophisticated tests than the mere accumulation of gold in the royal treasury.

The old mercantilist philosophy – that rulers should accumulate capital by ensuring a positive balance of trade with other countries – was giving way to a more dynamic philosophy in which trade between countries, and commerce within them,

were judged to be mutually rewarding. Developing and integrating a range of ideas already in circulation, Smith provided a powerful justification for this new commercial and liberal (but not yet democratic) society.

Specifically, he explained how the invisible hand of the market produces an efficient use of resources overall, even though individual producers and consumers act only in their own interests. Rather than regarding self-interested economic behaviour as ignoble, and selfishly neglectful of the public good, Smith judged that our interests as consumers are best served when the 'butcher, the brewer and the baker' also act in their own interests (Box 19.1).

High profits in a given sector encourage new entrants until profitability declines; conversely, low profits encourage the less efficient providers to depart. Provided the market is genuinely competitive, the outcome is a system that allocates funds to projects earning the highest return – an outcome that no planning agency in communist states was ever able to match.

As Gordon Brown (UK prime minister, 2007–) points out, Smith's position is more balanced and sophisticated than his contemporary image as a ruthless advocate of the free market suggests

(McLean, 2006). Smith was, for example, well aware of our capacity for empathy – our ability to place ourselves in the position of others – and regarded this natural human sympathy as the basis of social organization.

More specifically, Smith was fully aware of the danger of business cartels. He wrote that 'people of the same trade seldom meet together, even for merriment and diversion, but the conversation ends in a conspiracy against the public in some contrivance to raise prices' (1776, p. 232). He recognized the need to regulate against such sharp practices. In contemporary terms, 'Adam Smith's invisible hand of the free market utterly depends on the mailed fist of the sovereign state' (Jackson, 2007, p. 311).

Smith also saw a role for government in providing a public infrastructure, such as transport, which businesses needed to prosper. He also valued education as a means through which individuals can acquire a measure of enlightenment. For Adam Smith, as for Gordon Brown and Barack Obama, the market was a means for fulfilling deeper goals; it was not an end in itself.

John Maynard Keynes

While Smith's analysis still provides the theoretical basis for contemporary market economies, the circumstances of the twentieth century did require governments to attend to two major concerns: the rise of unemployment in the 1930s and of inflation in the 1970s. The first of these brought about an expanded role for government; the second, a reduction. The resolution of these issues extended the toolkit available to policy-makers and requires attention from students of politics as well as economics.

The English economist John Maynard Keynes offered a remedy for the problem of unemployment, at least in the drastic form it took in the depression of the 1930s. During this period, unemployment rates exceeded 25 per cent in some countries, far higher than during the recession of 2008/09.

The classical solution to the problem of recession had been to reduce wages so that employers would have more incentive to hire. At some low rate of pay, it was supposed, the labour market would clear. But Keynes recognized that lowering wages will, in the aggregate, reduce demand for the goods and services that employers provide. In this way, economies become trapped in a depression, locked into an unacceptable equilibrium of mass unemployment, deficient demand, excessive saving and inadequate investment.

In such conditions, Keynes advised, governments should prime the pump of recovery by increasing public spending. Through a multiplier effect, this injection of resources will circulate through the economy, gradually rebuilding confidence, demand, investment, employment and finally the revenues flowing into the government's own coffers. It is this multiplier effect, and the overall view of the economy it reflects, that distinguishes Keynes's thinking from mere make-work schemes.

The emphasis on governments' ability to manage aggregate demand promised a solution to what was still seen as capitalism's great weakness, at least compared to planned economies: the fluctuations of the business cycle. Indeed, Shonfield (1969, p. 64) suggested that 'control over the business cycle, which owes so much to Keynes's work, is probably the single most important factor in establishing the dynamic and prosperous capitalism of the post-war era'. Keynes seemed to have civilized the market, first demonstrating its superiority over totalitarian alternatives and then laying the foundations for post-war recovery. This was an achievement of the first order, and one that demonstrates the political significance of economic ideas (Hall, 1989).

Like Smith, Keynes never made a fetish of the market, fearing the 'empire of greed'. He even wrote that 'we are capable of shutting off the sun and the stars because they do not pay a dividend' (quoted in Skidelsky, 2009, p. 146). For Keynes, the fundamental objective was a diverse but harmonious society in which a balanced economy provides sufficient resources for individuals to live the good life. As Skidelsky (2009, p. 135) writes:

Keynes was not a socialist, but nor was he an uncritical admirer of capitalism. He saw it as a necessary stage to get societies from poverty to abundance, after which its usefulness would disappear . . . He wanted to preserve capitalism from its wreckers on both the extreme right and the extreme left. This aim underpinned his politics of the middle way . . . Capitalism was evolving new forms of public–private partnership which blurred the traditional separation of state and market and weakened the emphasis on maximising profit.

Milton Friedman

Eventually, however, the Keynesian revolution appeared to have run its course. By the dismal decade of the 1970s, a new tangle of political and economic problems had emerged: inflation (reaching double digits in the USA), government budget deficits, high rates of personal taxation, declining productivity growth and powerful trade unions.

Keynes's formula seemed to have limited relevance to this new era of economic stagnation combined with inflation. Indeed, Keynes's legacy had, in a way, become part of the problem. The very achievement of full employment had enhanced the bargaining power of trade unions, contributing to a cycle of price and wage increases. Viner's 1936 review of Keynes's work seemed to have been vindicated: 'in a world organized in accordance with Keynes' specifications, there would be a constant race between the printing press and the business agents of the trade unions, with the problem of unemployment largely solved if the printing press could maintain a constant lead' (quoted in deLong, 1995). Governments were now expected to deliver high employment, and leaders such as Richard Nixon gave it priority, even at the cost of inflation.

The logjam needed to be freed. Just as Keynes had suggested policies to resolve the unemployment problem, so a new guru – the American economist Milton Friedman – offered a remedy for the inflation of the 1970s. His solution lay in returning monetary policy to centre stage. In a contribution comparable in its impact to that of Keynes, Friedman (1970, p. 16) argued that 'inflation is always and everywhere a monetary phenomenon', in which 'substantial changes in prices are almost always the result of changes in the nominal supply of money'. As with other commodities, when money is plentiful, its value will go down (reflected in inflation, which means a given amount of money will buy less). But when money is tight, its value will stay high (reflected in stable prices).

So Freidman's solution to excessive inflation was clear and decisive. Restrict growth in the money supply and pay the short-term price of increased unemployment. In the long term, economic activity will recover in response to the stable and predictable environment which sound money provides.

Just as Keynes's deficit financing had advanced the cause of the left, so Friedman's monetarism gave an equivalent fillip to the right-wing administrations of Ronald Reagan and Margaret Thatcher. Like Keynes before him, Friedman's work modified the framework of economic policy-making, reinstating the importance of the money supply.

But where Keynes sought short-run solutions, Friedman's concern was with the long run. Friedman lacked Keynes's belief in the ability of policy-makers to fine-tune the economy; instead, he advocated a cautious, steady approach to the money supply. Where Keynes instinctively felt that policy-makers could improve market performance, Friedman was suspicious of political meddling; in that sense, his emphasis on sound money reflected a return to Adam Smith's belief in the wisdom of the market. Keynes was naturally sympathetic to government intervention; Friedman was not.

Many liberal democracies do now give their central banks responsibility for achieving a target level or range for inflation. For instance, the Reserve Bank in Australia is charged with securing an annual inflation rate of between 2 and 3 per cent, on average, over the economic cycle. These goals are achieved through manipulation of interest rates, rather than through what proved to be the excessively deflationary device of direct control over the supply of money.

Delegating the execution of monetary manipulation to appointed officials reduces the risk of monetary manipulation by governing parties more concerned with the political short run than the economic long run. The outcome is a reduction in direct government control but a further increment to predictability, giving additional confidence to investors. In other words, elected politicians have been put in their place, with sound results (Clark, 2005).

Varieties of capitalism

We can now use our discussion of the founding fathers to examine the political economies of contemporary liberal democracies, noting in particular the need to extend the discussion beyond the Anglo-American tradition established by these three

BOX 19.2

Varieties of capitalism: liberal and coordinated market economies

	Liberal market economy	Coordinated market economy
Basis of relationships between firms	Mainly formal market contracts	Discussion within collaborative networks, often industry-based, is more significant
Cross-shareholding between firms	Rare	Common
Source of capital for investment	Mainly shareholders and private equity	Banks and other companies more important
Priority of firms	Shorter-term profitability and responding to market changes	Long-term profitability, stability and market share are more important
Hiring and firing staff	More flexible	Less flexible
Strength of trade unions and employer organizations	Low	High
Leading sector	Market-led but service sector more important	Manufacturing is regarded as a core sector
Archetypal case	United States	Germany

Note: Coordinated economies are also described as organized market economies, social market economies or, with particular reference to Germany, Rhineland capitalism.

Source: Adapted from Hall and Soskice (2001).

leading figures. This task requires a comparison of liberal market economies as in the USA with coordinated market economies as in Germany (Box 19.2). In addition, we will introduce the idea of the developmental state associated with several Asian countries, notably Japan in its high growth phase after 1945.

As with other aspects of comparative politics, the study of political economy reveals important contrasts between countries. Just as democracy means different things in the USA and Germany, so too does the conception of what is entailed by a market economy. A market is not just an abstract idea; rather, it is itself an institution influenced by the culture and politics of the country in which it operates. The contrasts here show how economic policy

is shaped by national traditions and also provide potential opportunities for countries to learn from each other.

Hall and Soskice (2001) developed a broad but valuable contrast between liberal market economies and coordinated market economies (Box 19.2). It is worth relating this distinction to the thinkers we have just considered. Broadly, the liberal version corresponds to Adam Smith's construct of a free market as closely as can be expected from any system operating over 300 years later in an era of extensive regulation and active government. Milton Friedman, too, would align himself with the liberal form. Maynard Keynes, however, is a different case. Without seeking to put words in the master's mouth, his interest in a middle way, a balanced

FINANCIAL CRISIS IN THE USA, 2008–09

2008	**16 March**	JP Morgan Chase agrees to acquire Bear Stearns and accepts a $29 billion government loan.
	7 September	The government takes over Fannie Mae and Freddie Mac, government-sponsored enterprises which support the mortgage market.
	14 September	Bank of America acquires Merrill Lynch.
	15 September	Lehman Brothers files for bankruptcy – the largest in the country's history.
	17 September	The government effectively nationalizes AIG, the country's largest insurance company.
	18 September	Ben Bernanke, chairman of the Federal Reserve, tells members of Congress, 'if we don't do this [support the financial sector], we may not have an economy on Monday'.
	25 September	President Bush tells Congressional leaders, 'if money isn't loosened up, this sucker could go down'. The government places Washington Mutual (WaMu) into receivership – the largest bank failure in the country's history.
	29 September	Dow Jones Industrial Average declines 778 points, its largest ever daily fall in points.
	3 October	President Bush signs the Emergency Economic Stabilization Act, creating a government facility to purchase up to $700bn of troubled assets from financial institutions.
	16 December	Federal Funds interest rate reduced to 0.0–0.25 per cent.
2009	**17 February**	President Obama signs the American Recovery and Reinvestment Act, authorizing $787bn in tax cuts, increased welfare benefits and additional government spending.
	2 July	US unemployment reaches 9.5 per cent, the highest for 26 years.
	7 August	President Obama tells journalists, 'today we're pointed in the right direction . . . While we've rescued our economy from catastrophe, we've also begun to build a new foundation for growth'.

economy and a harmonious society would surely have encouraged him to examine with interest the idea of a coordinated market economy.

Liberal market economies

We begin with the liberal version. Here contractual market relationships are the business norm, whether for selling products and services, employing labour or raising finance. Competing firms operate in a flexible labour market, seeking to enhance profitability in order to satisfy the demands of their shareholders for a return. The government and the judiciary aim to ensure that contracts are enforced and disputes resolved, but their function is to umpire and to provide an impartial framework of regulation, rather than to play. Industry associations and trade unions seek to advise, but not to direct, their members. So economic actors, whether large corporations or individual employees, retain considerable autonomy, a feature which creates the potential for rapid, market-led restructuring when needed.

This liberal model is exemplified by the United States but it is also now found in other English-speaking countries, notably Australia, Britain, Canada and New Zealand. Note, however, that the movement of these latter countries in a liberal direction since the 1980s confirms that states do not

Financial crisis

Students of political economy must pay due attention to the financial crisis of 2008–09. During this period, the collapse of a financial bubble caused by ill-judged, opaque investments by banks in loans to American home-owners created enormous stresses in the world's financial system, stimulating a deep global recession and a massive response by governments. What does this crisis reveal about the relationship between governments and financial institutions?

Politically, the crisis strengthened the authority of national governments, including central banks. Domestically, the state's role as lender of last resort was strikingly demonstrated while the state's success in containing the financial crisis confirmed its continuing relevance. This achievement gave political rulers the authority to proceed with re-regulating the financial sector. In short, the balance between political and economic power seemed, at first glance, to have shifted back towards the former.

From an international perspective, too, it is significant that it was national governments rather than international organizations that led the response. Coordination between governments, and between central banks, was significant. But international financial institutions such as the International Monetary Fund, and indeed the European Union, were secondary players.

But in two respects the state's position was weakened rather than strengthened. First, governments damaged their own long-term financial position by supporting troubled banks and, in Keynesian fashion, funding spending to counter the recession. The sums involved here were gigantic. By July 2009, the American government had spent $4.7 trillion on bailouts of banks and insurance companies – more than one and a half times the value of Germany's gross domestic product (Kuhnhenn, 2009).

Second, government willingness to bail out the largest investment banks demonstrated the embedded position of these firms in the financial system. When a bank becomes too big or interconnected to fail, it sends a message to government and its own staff: we keep our profits in the good times but the government will pay for losses when times are bad. Banks are thereby encouraged to take greater risks and it remains to be seen how far this danger can be offset by tighter regulation. Adam Smith would surely have judged that too big to fail is simply too big.

Note, finally, that the origins of the crisis lay in the liberal market economy of the USA (see Timeline). Coordinated market economies, while far from unaffected, suffered less reputational damage.

Further reading: Gamble (2009), Tett (2009b).

necessarily occupy a permanent position in relation to these models.

Consider the American exemplar. In the USA, **shareholder capitalism** predominates: the shareholders own the firm and expect a continuing return on their investment (though, in practice, managers often gain sufficient control to secure a generous share of the profits). Expanding firms do not hesitate to take on additional labour, secure in the

knowledge that staff can be laid off should conditions worsen. Employees are mobile and willing to move for a better job. Hostile takeovers and corporate bankruptcies are interpreted as a signal from Adam Smith's invisible hand: they form 'the perennial gale of creative destruction' which Schumpeter (1943, p. 84) regarded as capitalism's essential strength. Failing companies may well declare themselves bankrupt but the managers can simply start another business.

Coordinated market economies

Unlike liberal market economies, the political economies of most Continental European countries display a less aggressive character. Here business

In **shareholder capitalism**, those who own the company seek to maximize the financial return on their investment and are willing to replace managers who fail to achieve this goal. This form is found in liberal market economies such as the USA.

relationships are less impersonal and contractual but more long-term and even familial. A business is more likely to raise funds from its bank than through the impersonal stock market; employees, once hired, are more likely to be retained through hard times.

In the model coordinated market economy, the private sector is seen less as an independent sphere of activity and more as an arena subject to control by social and political forces, including the government. In many such countries, these forces have included not just a strong socialist party but also an influential Catholic church; neither institution has favoured the free play of the market. In societies historically divided by class, religion and ideology, economic competition has been subject to political control in order to deliver social stability. Social cohesion and solidarity are core values. The market operates in a constrained way, reflecting a shared desire to prevent Smith's invisible hand from becoming a visible fist.

Who exactly provides the coordination? The actors vary by country, but include industrial associations in Germany, the dominant Social Democratic Party in Sweden and the state itself in France (Boyer, 1997). So coordination is not always a state-led activity; it can be led instead by powerful economic interests or by leading parties.

In a coordinated economy, leading firms belong to influential industry-wide associations that provide a forum for exchanging information. Companies hold shares in each other, forming a strong interlocking structure. Managers derive authority from their professional standing, not merely from the company they work for; in particular, engineers are accorded high status. The employment relationship is conceived as long term, giving employees a greater commitment to the business but also reducing the capacity for radical change. The state helps with coordination and the courts are prepared to intervene to ensure economic actors abide by broadly accepted standards, including civil law codes.

This coordinated or partnership model is exemplified by Germany but is also found in other European economies such as Austria, Belgium, Denmark, Finland, the Netherlands and Sweden. One indicator of a coordinated approach is that wage negotiations for specific types of job take place at national or sectoral level rather than within the firm (Box 19.3). At national level, a broad pact

---

BOX 19.3

Main level of wage negotiations in selected European countries

National level	Sectoral level	Company level
Belgium	Austria	Hungary
Finland	Germany	Poland
Ireland	Netherlands	United Kingdom

Source: Adapted from Avdagić and Crouch (2006, Table 11.2).

---

covering wages, prices and benefits may be agreed between the government and peak associations representing capital and labour. At sectoral level, the union covering an industry such as engineering may negotiate a package with an employers' federation whose members include all major engineering firms.

Let us look at the German exemplar. The coordination here is formally structured, creating engineered capitalism for an engineering economy. **Stakeholder capitalism** rather than shareholder capitalism predominates. Companies recognize obligations to a wide variety of stakeholders, including trade unions, banks, industrial associations, other companies, the local community and all levels of government. Many of these interests, furthermore, are represented on supervisory boards (Box 19.4). Wage inequalities are contained at a lower level than in the Anglo-American world.

Reflecting Germany's guild traditions, coordinating bodies such as trade associations are particularly important in specific industrial sectors. This feature has enabled post-war governments to remain in the background, avoiding comparisons with the interventionist Nazi era. Within manufacturing, the focus is on enhancing existing strengths rather than building new ones. Stakeholders such as trade unions and even creditors are naturally risk averse;

In **stakeholder capitalism**, companies acknowledge – and often incorporate into their deliberations – a wide range of interests, including employees, trade unions, the local community and the government. This form is found in coordinated market economies such as Germany.

BOX 19.4

Members of Volkswagen's Supervisory Board, 2009

▶ Ferdinand Piëch, Chair;
▶ Prime Minister and Economics Minister, State of Lower Saxony;
▶ Chair, Volkswagen Management Association;
▶ Three directors of Porsche AG;
▶ Five senior executives and directors from other German companies;
▶ Five chairs of Volkswagen Works Councils;
▶ Member of the executive committee, IG Metall (metalworkers' union);
▶ Chair, International Metalworkers' Foundation.

Note: Under the German format of codetermination, the supervisory board appoints and monitors the normal managing board as well as approving important decisions.

Source: Volkswagen AG (2009).

---

they do not gain as much as shareholders from successful new initiatives. Restructuring operates in a slower and more negotiated manner, with greater emphasis on fashioning a long-term solution acceptable to all partners. In Germany, bankruptcies and takeovers are regarded negatively, as a sign of past coordination failures. A firm in difficulty is more likely to be absorbed into a larger enterprise than to be closed down.

A coordinated economy is the industrial equivalent of the consensus politics which is found in most countries with this economic form. The representation of stakeholders within corporate governance parallels the power-sharing found in coalition governments. In both economic and political spheres, this support for balanced, negotiated, consensual governance reflects similar influences. These include: the fear of instability induced by Europe's violent past; the desire to reconcile what were once divisive cleavages of class and religion; and, in countries where Catholicism is strong, the Church's distrust of a market society of sovereign individuals. The similarities in economic and political organization resulting from this shared history shows the value of comparing the sectors and considering them as part of a single political economy.

One way of illustrating the difference between liberal and coordinated market economies is by contrasting their approach to private equity firms. These are companies that use financial resources to buy other firms with the intention of improving their performance and then selling them on, often in short order. Liberal market economies recognize the necessity for private equity. Like sharks in the sea and vultures over the ground, such companies cleanse the environment because of their ability to scent blood from a distance. Their role can be controversial but is broadly accepted as necessary.

In a coordinated market economy, attitudes to private equity are less welcoming. Private equity is judged to be a threat to national planning, industrial logic and long-term development. Coordinated economies prefer real engineering to financial engineering. In Germany, for example, Franz Müntefering, chairman of the SPD, compared private equity firms to locusts in a much-quoted speech in 2005: 'they remain anonymous, they have no face and descend like a swarm of locusts on a company, devour it and then fly on' (Koepk, 2005).

Müntefering's comments received substantial support from Germany's elite. Chancellor Schröder said, 'I would have put it differently but basically expressed the same thing'. Other leaders promised to 'fight against antisocial market capitalism', suggested that 'competition and social responsibility are not mutually exclusive' and bemoaned 'a neoliberal *zeitgeist* that measures every last aspect of our lives only by economic standards' (Koepk, 2005). Similar criticisms followed about the American origins of the global financial crisis (see Timeline).

Coordination within the economy does bring several potential economic advantages, offering a degree of stability and long-term planning for industrial economies needing to protect a legacy of past investment. In addition:

▶ Broadening the sphere of coordination from the individual firm to the industrial sector encourages investment both in training and in research and development. In liberal economies, by contrast, many firms free-ride by poaching staff and research produced by their competitors, leading to under-investment in these areas. So sectoral investment yields a collective benefit.

◆ Organizing such features as pensions and medical insurance at the level of the sector, rather than the company, allows for a pooling of risk. If companies form a single pensions scheme for all employees in their sector, individual workers will not lose their employer-funded pensions and medical insurance should their firm go bankrupt.

◆ Many coordinated economies operate under codified legal frameworks imposing detailed rules covering commercial practice. In Germany, Article 242 of the Civil Code establishes a norm of 'good faith' which the courts apply to business disputes. The existence of such commercial codes reduces legal costs. In liberal economies, notably the USA, contracting parties can insert any conditions they wish into an agreement. The result is more expensive deals – and more time in court.

The developmental state

We turn now away from the Western world and towards another variety of capitalism: the **developmental state**. This term is used to describe the institutional foundations of the rapid economic growth achieved by many countries in East Asia in the post-war era. Such a regime takes the form of a highly coordinated market economy, in which the state's legitimacy derives from economic success as much as popular election.

In a sense, the developmental state is a coordinated economy for an industrializing country, albeit with a more influential role for key politicians and bureaucrats and a more passive role for the population. The state's role in this configuration takes us away from Smith's pure free market and suggests that the government's role in a developing economy is more central, and certainly different from, its position in a developed economy.

We introduce the idea of the developmental state in the context of Japan. However, we should note that comparable strategies have been followed by

The **developmental state** leads a society to rapid industrialization by combining a powerful bureaucracy, which formulates national economic targets, with private ownership of the means of production. The main examples are East Asian states such as Japan and Korea in the post-war decades.

South Korea (which did not democratize until the 1990s) and, to a lesser extent, by illiberal democracies such as Malaysia.

Chalmers Johnson developed the notion of the developmental state as a variety of capitalism in *Japan: Who Governs? The Rise of the Developmental State* (1995). He suggested that after the Cold War the evident contrasts between Japanese and American capitalism no longer needed to be denied in the interests of anti-communist unity. Rather, the distinctive characteristics of Japan's political economy could be freely expressed.

According to Johnson, the state played an important coordinating role in Japan's post-war development. The bureaucracy targeted export-oriented manufacturing industries such as cameras and motorcycles. Close links between high-ranking government officials and senior managers in private firms sustained a powerful, cohesive elite capable of containing popular pressures on the government for greater consumption. The Liberal Democrats dominated the political landscape, effectively forestalling any radical opposition from gaining power through elections (see p. 352). Within industry, collaborative research at sectoral level provided a resource for the major firms. An undervalued currency encouraged exports while high tariffs and other trade barriers deterred imports.

Compared to the West, wages and benefits were low but distributed more equally; job security was high, with large firms providing secure employment in exchange for life-long loyalty. Profits were reinvested rather than paid out to shareholders. Efficient production rather than profitability, and investment rather than domestic consumption, were judged the keys for catching up. Johnson (1995, p. 68) summarized the central features of Japan's developmental state as 'a strong state, industrial policy, producer economics and managerial autonomy'.

At the very least, this governed market, as Wade (1990) called it, proved to be consistent with high economic growth for almost 30 years after the war, allowing Johnson (1995, p. 68) to declare that 'Asian capitalism seems destined to lie at the centre of what economists will teach their students in the next century'. Fifteen years on, we might think that Johnson got the region right, even if he should have emphasized China rather than Japan.

Convergence?

Our discussion so far has drawn attention to contrasts within the political economies of modern states. To what extent, though, are these differences receding as coordinated market economies face the challenge of international competition and developmental states adjust to the more market-led approach associated with developed status? Is the **convergence thesis** correct in maintaining that advanced economies are coalescing around the American model of a liberal market economy?

Certainly, the image of a global economy overwhelming historical differences in national capitalisms gained ground in the 1990s. Strange (1997, p. 183) offers a crisp account of this global perspective:

Given that the seeds of capitalism grew to maturity in very different gardens, would the forces of global structural change allow national differences to persist indefinitely? Or, alternatively, would the common logic of integrated world markets for more and more goods and services slowly but surely modify the old differences and bring national versions of capitalism ever closer to a common pattern? My bet was, and is, on the latter.

When we look at the recent standing of coordinated market economies, in particular, we can certainly find support for Strange's position. The coordinated model has come under significant stress. As in other liberal democracies, fewer employees now belong to trade unions, and fewer employers to trade associations, rendering more difficult the coordination required in a coordinated economy (Martin and Thelen, 2007). Germany is the world's largest exporter after China but overseas companies have become reluctant to invest in the country, citing over-regulation, high labour costs and an inflexible labour market. In 2003, Padgett (p. 142) judged that 'the capacity of the German model

The **convergence thesis** maintains that all developed economies are adopting a common format. The proposition is that a more global environment is forcing a liberal, pro-market response from each national economy.

for reconciling economic efficiency with traditional values may have reached its limits'. Three years later, Angela Merkel, the new Christian Democratic chancellor, agreed: 'we need change. We must keep what has proven its worth but change what burdens us'.

Equally, developmental states have been losing distinctiveness. Japan entered a decade of deflation in the 1990s and the Asian region as a whole experienced a massive financial convulsion in 1997. One reading of these difficulties is that policies aiding industrialization become counter-productive once development is achieved. Collaboration between firms and government departments, which once seemed highly constructive, begins to appear as secretive collusion. The Japanese notion of excessive competition was perhaps permissible in the building-up phase but seemed less appropriate once the economy had matured. Generally, developmental states can only place production before profit for so long. Banks must eventually go bankrupt if too many of their loans remain unpaid.

On this account, then, the crisis of the developmental state resembles the earlier crisis of the communist state: each hits the barrier of 'so far but no further'. In Weiss's incisive summary (1998, p. 65), 'by being developmentally effective, the state ends up digging its own grave'. The implication is that there is one formula for catch-up but another – more liberal than coordinated or developmental – for keep-up.

However, the advocates of varieties of capitalism are unpersuaded that convergence is taking place. Hall and Thelen (2008) rightly remind us that change does not equal convergence. Coordinated economies might be evolving, rather than converging, on the liberal model: 'in Germany, for example, the reforms made in a number of realms, including industrial relations, vocational training and social policy, do not signal a shift to the Anglo-Saxon model so much as they point to the development of new forms of coordination'. Other observers suggest that increasing foreign ownership of German firms encourages a more liberal approach without, however, dismantling the old mechanism of coordination (Milne, 2009). Furthermore, the origins of the financial crisis of 2008/09 in the United States undoubtedly dented the reputation of the liberal model. Suddenly, it became a model to avoid rather than one on which to converge.

Similarly, the distinctiveness of developmental states has declined but not dissolved. For Japan, Matsuura *et al.* (2004, p. 151) comment that 'much of the Japanese employment system remains intact for current workers' and that 'new institutional arrangements are emerging only slowly'. Change in South Korea has followed a comparable pattern: an evolution of the developmental state without convergence on the Anglo-American model of a liberal market economy. Despite democratization in the 1990s, Korea's political economy remains distinctive, leading Weiss (2004, p. 167) to postulate 'a more mature form of developmentalism: one that is now less propelled to catch up than by an emphasis on policies and institutions aimed at managing economic openness'.

So although Strange's convergence wager may yet come good, it does seem rather speculative. Prudence dictates that we avoid placing all our money on the superiority of one system of political economy. We need to reserve judgement over whether liberal market economies will out-perform over the long run and in all circumstances. As Perraton and Clift (2004a, p. 202) point out, 'economic performance typically depends on the period of comparison chosen: different economies have appeared to be top dog at different times which in itself should indicate that there is no one superior model'.

The political economies of authoritarian states

Liberal democracy and a market economy may form a natural pair but what type of government is best suited to a developing country? The question is clearly important. If authoritarian rule can be defended as an effective foundation for economic development, we will have a powerful critique of democracy's claims to be universally the best form of rule. After all, we would nearly all prefer to eat under a dictator than to starve in a democracy. In addition, we could reasonably anticipate that democracy is unlikely to consolidate in poor countries over the long term if the cost is slower economic development.

Reasons can certainly be found for supposing that authoritarian rule can facilitate development.

Industrialization requires massive investment in infrastructure such as transport, communications and education; initially, these can only be funded by the state. Even Adam Smith acknowledged the need for government to ensure provision of these collective goods.

In addition, authoritarian rulers can generate the surplus for investment by resisting short-term, electoral pressures for immediate consumption. Simply put, they can kick-start development because they can ignore the squeals of those whose consumption is initially limited.

Bearing such factors in mind, Huntington and Nelson (1976, p. 23) concluded that 'political participation must be held down, at least temporarily, in order to promote economic development'. Growth first, democracy later.

Overall, these theoretical claims are rarely reflected in empirical reality. A few non-democratic regimes initiate economic development but the majority do not. Many traditional rulers, such as the ruling families in the Middle East, continue to resist modernization. Other dictators, for example Nigeria's military 'lootocrats', set back economic development by decades through gross mismanagement.

Thus, a statistical study by Przeworski *et al.* (2000, p. 271) concluded that there is no 'cruel choice' to be made between democracy and development: 'we did not find a shred of evidence that democracy need be sacrificed on the altar of development'. These authors also found that, even in those cases where authoritarian regimes did achieve growth, this increase depended more on expanding the labour force to achieve growth. Democracies, by contrast, made more productive use of their inputs.

In the twenty-first century, furthermore, globalization has given developing countries access to private capital through multinational corporations and overseas banks. To access these resources, developing countries must convince lenders that their economy is market-friendly and that their politics are tolerably democratic. If leaders can succeed here, they need not extract as much capital from their own populations as authoritarian modernizers did in the last century.

In any event, studying the political economies of non-democratic regimes quickly confirms the importance of distinguishing between different types of authoritarian government. We will review the communist experience, and its legacy for contemporary states such as China and Vietnam, before turning to non-communist authoritarian regimes.

Communist states

Many communist states developed a **command economy** without precedent in history; each one formulated clearer national goals and targets than any democracy. The result was an often decisive and generally ruthless commitment to a single goal, notably industrialization.

Economically, this philosophy of the big push was not an unmitigated disaster. Notably in the USSR, it did prove successful at building the foundations of industrial development, albeit at a horrifying human price. Stalin's drive to industrialize Russia so as to protect it from attacks from the West transformed a society of peasants into a world industrial power within a generation. But the command economy was monstrously inefficient. The big push was a deliberately blinkered approach which ignored overall efficiency in order to achieve a specific target.

The underlying weakness was the absence of a price mechanism allowing a comparison of competing uses of capital. Physical allocation of resources by the planners of the command economy was no match for the signals provided by a market. This inherent weakness of any such grandiose planning was spotted long ago by Adam Smith. He noted the folly of the 'man of system who seems to think he can arrange the different members of a great society with as much ease as the hand arranges the different pieces upon a chessboard' (quoted in Deane, 1989, p. 69).

An anecdote illustrates the point. When Soviet leader Nikita Khrushchev first visited the United States, he was so impressed with the supermarkets that he asked his hosts: 'who is responsible for the supply of bread to New York City? I want to meet this brilliant man'. Khrushchev was a man of system who could not imagine that loaves could be supplied by Adam Smith's invisible hand rather than a single commissar.

In a communist **command economy**, also called a centrally planned economy, the national government set quotas for state-owned production units and allocated resources to them. The bureaucracy then implemented the plan.

Where, then, does the collapse of the command economy leave the remaining communist states, principally China and Vietnam? In both countries, rulers have certainly reduced the importance of central planning, yet they have only created some conditions of a market economy. Massive, and massively inefficient, state-owned enterprises still pervade the economy, soaking up labour and serving as an indirect welfare state. The expansion of the non-state sector has certainly stimulated continued growth, unleashing vibrant entrepreneurial activity. Yet party contacts still determine access to economic opportunities. To most eyes, internal as well as external, the system is inherently corrupt; it is certainly technically inefficient in that political criteria distort economic decisions, leading to huge misallocations of capital. The market decides – except when the party decides that it shouldn't. Business proceeds in accordance with rules – except when politics dictates that the rules are to be overridden (Clarke, 2007). These errors must eventually unwind, with damaging consequences for state-owned banks with enormous bad debts.

This idiosyncratic model is still delivering growth in what remain, for the most part, poor countries. As long as economic growth continues, nominally communist rulers may succeed in resolving the political tensions induced by corruption and increasing inequality. Even so, over the long term, economic growth will itself surely deliver a demand for more fundamental political reforms.

Other authoritarian states

Some non-communist authoritarian regimes have also initiated economic development. Examples include modernizing military regimes such as that of Gamal Abdel Nasser (president of Egypt, 1956–70) and Asian developmental states such as South Korea in its predemocratic phase. Echoing the communist experience, the explanation for these successes rests with the potential capacity of nondemocratic rulers to resist short-term pressures for immediate consumption, thereby generating resources for long-term industrialization.

Crucially, however, such cases are the exception. In this century as well as the last, non-communist authoritarian rule typically creates economic stagnation, leading to North's much-quoted comment

COUNTRY PROFILE

VENEZUELA

ILLIBERAL DEMOCRACY

Form of government ■ a federal and presidential republic with 23 states.

Legislature ■ the 167 members of the National Assembly are elected for a five-year term. An opposition boycott of the 2005 election meant that no opposition deputies were elected.

Executive ■ the president, directly elected for a six-year term, heads both the state and the government and chooses the members of the Council of Ministers. Term limits were removed by a constitutional amendment in 2009.

Constitution and judiciary ■ the constitution dates from 1999, with amendments approved in 2009. The judiciary is headed by the Supreme Tribunal of Justice whose members are elected by the National Assembly for a 12-year term. Considerable political intervention.

Electoral system ■ Mixed member proportional. Voting is legally required but abstention is common.

Party system ■ President Hugo Chávez's party is the United Socialist Party of Venezuela (PSUV), formed in 2006 by a merger of existing parties supporting the president. Two traditional and important parties are Democratic Action (AD), a left-of-centre but not a class-based organization, and the Social Christian Party (Committee for Free Elections, COPEI), a Christian Democratic party offering a right-of-centre approach.

Population (annual growth rate): 26.8m (+1.5%)

World Bank income group: upper middle

Political Rights score: ④

Civil Liberties score: ④

Human development index (rank/out of): 74/177

Freedom of the press index (rank/out of): 164/195

Perceived transparency index (rank/out of): 158/180

Note: For meaning and sources of scales and indexes, see p. xv. In all cases a score and rank of 1 is 'best'.

When Columbus arrived on the northern shores of Latin America in 1498, he was so impressed by the local buildings, constructed elegantly on stilts, that he was reminded of Venice – hence **Venezuela**. Today, a visitor to Caracas, the country's capital city, confronts a modern if dilapidated city surrounded by ever-expanding *barrios* (shanty towns) climbing almost vertically on the ravines around.

This contrast expresses the fundamental fact about Venezuela and many other countries on the continent: inequality. In a country rated as upper-middle income, over 40 per cent of the population live in poverty. The rich possess considerable wealth, displayed through European cars, manicured suburbs, gated communities and private planes.

Yet private affluence coexists with public squalor. Crime is endemic in most of this highly urban country, including Caracas. McCaughan (2004, p. 2) reports that 'the capital is literally falling apart as thieves filch metal from metro elevators, remove street lamps, dismantle apartment intercoms, steal electricity cables and even pickaxe cement barriers separating car lanes'. The point is not just the coexistence of poverty and crime but the simmering, and highly politicized, resentment connecting the two.

As part of Gran Colombia, full independence from Spain was achieved in 1819, with Venezuela becoming an autonomous country in 1830. 'The liberator' Simón Bolívar was the hero of this movement. Aspiring to create a

Latin American federation which would entrench individual rights, Bolívar's revolutionary spirit and unfinished project are still frequently invoked by Latin America's left.

For the first half of the twentieth century, Venezuela was governed by military, civilian or mixed dictatorships: some brutal, some modernizing, some both. In 1958, however, democracy of a sort was established and has continued ever since. The 1958 Pact of Punto Fijo was an agreement between the two major parties to marginalize other parties and to keep divisive issues off the agenda. This cartel was corrupt and inefficient, and became more so, eventually enabling Hugo Chávez to launch his own 'Bolivarian revolution'.

Further reading: Guevara (2005), McCaughan (2004).

Petro-populism in Venezuela

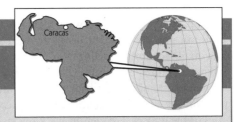

Caracas

Oil was discovered in Venezuela in 1914 and has proved to be the dominating feature of the country's economy. In 2008, the country's oil reserves remained the seventh largest in the world. Petroleum generates a third of Venezuela's gross domestic product and about 80 per cent of its exports. The country is one of the USA's leading suppliers. The oil industry was nationalized in 1976 and now directly provides most government revenue. How, then, has this vital resource impinged on the regime of Hugo Chávez?

Oil rents sustained the Punto Fijo cartel, enabling the colluding parties to share out the receipts through patronage. But the oil curse was also at work. The economy became increasingly unbalanced and inefficient, fluctuating with the oil price. It was against this background that Hugo Chávez, a former paratrooper, won the presidential election of 1998. He promised a Bolivarian revolution to bring social justice and clean government to the *barrios*: 'this is a different Venezuela, where the wretched of the earth know they can free themselves from their past. And this is a different Latin America'. The Chavistas cheered him on, especially but not only from the *barrios*.

Despite middle-class opposition, and many political twists and turns, Chávez has continued in power, winning a new term in 2006. A charismatic and intensely political figure, the president has retained considerable popular support while also marginalizing opposition through decisive and sometimes authoritarian influence over the economy, the military, the media and the justice system. He has sustained, but cannot institutionalize, his personalist illiberal democracy.

Chávez has proved to be as dependent on oil as the preceding regime. He has used the government's generous revenues to establish expensive *misiones* (social programmes) that have helped to reduce poverty. But easy money has

led to an indifference to more fundamental economic reforms: corruption, inflation and inefficiency are endemic. Chávez has created grass-roots organizations that bypass rather than consolidate state institutions.

Rather like a boxer who cannot fight without an opponent, Chávez depends on his wealthy enemies on the right to sustain his own political momentum. His regime is corrupt but this very fact enables him to rail against corruption. Eventually, his remarkable revolu-

tionary energy will surely exhaust a society more concerned with economic growth than firebrand politics. In the long run, Chávez's instinctive left-wing populism will be revealed as a symptom of, not a solution to, the deep-seated inequalities of his country and continent. And oil will be shown once more to be a hindrance, not a help, to balanced economic and political development.

Further reading: Gott (2005), McCoy and Myers (2006)

▶ TIMELINE

HUGO CHÁVEZ

1954	Born in Sabaneta, Venezuela.
1971	Enrols in the Academy of Military Sciences.
1975	Graduates from the Academy.
1982	Establishes a left-wing cell in the army.
1992	Leads a failed coup.
1994	Released from prison (where he studied Simón Bolívar).
1998	Elected president.
1999	Referendum ratifies new constitution.
2000	Re-elected president. Authorized by the assembly to legislate by decree for one year.
2001	National strike against decree laws.
2002	Removed from power by coup but returns two days later after street protests.
2004	Wins recall vote. Announces alliance with Cuba.
2006	Wins all seats in the National Assembly after opposition boycott. Re-elected president. Announces 'socialism for the twenty-first century'.
2007	Defeated in a referendum to amend constitution (including abolition of term limits).
2009	Term limits abolished after another referendum.

(1981, p. 20): 'the existence of the state is essential to economic growth; the state, however, is the source of man-made economic decline'.

Why does the typical authoritarian regime not engender sustained and substantial economic growth? The answer often lies in the political insecurities of the leaders. Frequently, their key task is to play off domestic political forces against each other to ensure their continuation in office, an art developed to its highest level by the cautious but shrewd ruling families of the Middle East. When expensive patronage becomes the main political game, coherent economic development is bypassed. The public sector often becomes bloated, with poorly paid employees engaging in rent-seeking to enrich themselves at the expense of business. A firm's success, and its tax burden, depends on its political contacts more than its business strengths. Economics and politics comprise a single arena, as in European monarchies before the era of commerce, resulting in inefficient use of capital. Alternatively, the ruler may just want to enrich himself, his family and his ethnic group by taking resources out of the economy and often out of the country.

Leaving aside the characteristic economic distortions of authoritarian regimes, the **resource curse** provides an additional aspect of under-performance in those dictatorships endowed with plentiful natural resources. Remarkably, far from out-performing other developing countries, countries rich in resources such as oil fall behind in economic growth (Sachs and Warner, 1995b). Certainly, most Middle Eastern countries such as Saudi Arabia have

escaped from low-income status. Even so, their generous endowment has acted as a brake on, rather than a stimulus to, sustained growth.

Why is it, then, that an abundance of natural resources seems to reduce economic growth? The factors involved are again political. One answer, of particular relevance to sub-Saharan Africa, is that such resources comprise a honeypot which encourages internal conflict as local warlords compete for control of mineral-rich enclaves in areas remote from the capital. The geographical concentration of these commodities intensifies conflict between resource-rich and resource-poor regions and groups, especially in the context of economies offering few other opportunities to acquire wealth.

However, the idea of the **rentier state** is an explanation with more widespread applicability, particularly in the Middle East. Rentier states obtain most of their revenue from exporting a natural resource, usually through licensing private, and often Western, contractors to secure the extraction. In economic terms, the rent-seeking government obtains an income from owning an asset to which it adds little value. For example, agricultural commodities may be exported raw, with processing elsewhere. In the contemporary world, the purest rentier states are Middle Eastern monarchies with oil and gas reserves (Figure 19.1).

The authoritarian rulers of these rentier states receive a direct income from overseas, reducing their

> The **resource curse** refers to low economic growth in countries with an abundance of natural commodities such as oil, gas and scarce minerals.

> A **rentier state** is a regime whose main funding is based on rent-seeking. These states obtain the bulk of their revenues from exporting such resources as oil and gas without adding value to these commodities (for rent-seeking, see p. 381).

Figure 19.1 Rentier states: governments with the highest share of natural resource revenues in their income

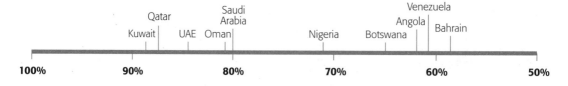

Source: Adapted from Herb (2005, p. 299).

need to raise taxes. And without taxation, pressures for representation are reduced. A portion of the resource rent can be distributed to the population as handouts or through providing jobs in a swollen public sector, thus buying popular acquiescence to a non-democratic regime.

For the future, we can certainly imagine a world in which intensifying conflict over a diminishing supply of natural resources takes place between resource-poor democracies and resource-rich authoritarian regimes. The Iraq invasion of 2003, for example, is sometimes interpreted in these terms. In this way, the resource curse may come to affect those living in liberal democracies as well as the inhabitants of those countries directly subject to it.

The political economies of illiberal democracies

In illiberal democracies, the operation of the economy is usually market-based but remains subject to political override. This intervention may take the form of a developmental regime, as in Asian countries such as Malaysia and Singapore. More often, the rulers of an illiberal democracy adopt an inconsistent approach, intervening in commercial decisions when political interests are at stake and using the economy as a means of buying or rewarding loyalty. Thus the operation of the market becomes more arbitrary and less efficient than in liberal democracies where a network of institutions, developed over generations, provides a more stable and credible framework for the conduct of business.

At the same time, economic intervention by the rulers of illiberal democracies is more limited than in authoritarian (especially communist) states. It is often restricted to politically sensitive areas. After all, in an illiberal democracy in which re-election is permitted, a president must face the voters at election time. This task is more palatable when living standards are growing. The ruler's claim to extensive authority is based on the proposition, 'only I can deliver'. In other words, an illiberal democracy creates a stronger alignment than does an authoritarian state between the interests of ruler and ruled.

In addition to these domestic considerations, astute leaders realize the value of a functioning market economy in attracting foreign investment and in ensuring their credibility with international organizations such as the International Monetary Fund. An illiberal democracy can create a political interest in a strong economic performance. As a discussion of Russia under Putin will show, in low- or middle-income countries an illiberal democracy with effective leadership can deliver economic growth.

After Vladimir Putin became president in 2000, economic policy became more orthodox than during the initial post-communist period under Boris Yeltsin. Putin modernized business law, improved tax collection, reduced inflation, increased foreign investment, ran a government budget surplus and generally provided a more stable environment within which the economy grew at an annual average of 6.7 per cent between 2000 and 2006 (Wagstyl, 2006, p. 2). At the very least, Putin provided a framework within which the economy could prosper from buoyant commodity prices. Even though many Russians still have little sympathy for the subtleties of a market economy, Putin's record was such that he was judged to be a good tsar.

But the president was also an intensely political figure. Given the population's desire for strong leadership and the potential threat from wealthy businessmen, it was just as well that Putin's political skills were so finely honed. Just as he improved the environment for routine business transactions, so too did he extend the Kremlin's control over the crucial oil sector. It is this combination of policies – encouraging the market where possible but overriding it when politically necessary – which characterizes economic management in illiberal democracies.

In 2003, for example, Putin launched a bruising attack on Mikhail Khodorkovsky, head of the country's largest oil company, Yukos. Khodorkovsky's business ambitions for his company threatened the government's command of the energy sector, while his political ambitions were also a concern to Putin. The businessman was jailed for fraud and later transferred to a Siberian penal colony located in a radioactive zone. Yukos was dismembered and taken over by the state. As Rutland (2005, p. 199) writes, 'the arrest of Russia's richest man and the near destruction of its largest and most successful private company grabbed the attention of Western observers, who feared that Russia was turning its back on the market economy'. In an illiberal democracy, just as in a fully authoritarian state, power and wealth are closely linked and industrialists must therefore learn to avoid overstepping the mark.

Learning Resources for Chapter 19

Next step

Hall and Soskice (2001) is an informed and influential collection on the varieties of capitalist organization in established democracies.

Further reading

Perraton and Clift (2004b) and Hancké *et al.* (2008) are also useful on varieties of capitalism. On the history of political economy, Heilbroner (1953) remains an outstanding account; see also Deane (1989) and Polanyi (1957). Hall (1989) is a comparative study of Keynes's impact. Friedman's monetarist outlook can be found in Friedman (1991); see Friedman (1962) for his underlying political perspective. Gamble (2009) examines the financial crisis of 2008/09. Johnson (1995) is the classic work on the developmental state; see Sachs and Warner (1995b) for the resource curse. Rutland (2005) reviews the Russian economy under Putin. Weingast and Wittman (2006) is an extensive handbook on political economy.

Internet sources

Glossary of Political Economy Terms by Paul M. Johnson, Auburn University
A helpful glossary
http://www.auburn.edu/~johnspm/gloss/

International Forum on Globalization
Examines the 'restructuring of global politics and economics'
http://www.ifg.org/index.htm

Martin Wolf, Financial Times
Influential and accessible columns by a leading commentator
http://www.ft.com/comment/columnists/martinwolf

World Bank
An informative site on developmental policy
http://www.worldbank.org

www.palgrave.com
Companion Website
Visit the Companion Website to 'click and go'
www.palgrave.com/politics/hague

References

These references, and those from the previous edition, are listed by chapter on the companion website.

A

Aberbach, J., Putnam, R. and Rockman, B. (1981) *Bureaucrats and Politicians* (Cambridge, MA: Harvard University Press).

Adams, F. (2003) *Deepening Democracy: Global Governance and Political Reform in Latin America* (New York: Praeger).

Ágh, A. (2003) 'Public Administration in Central and Eastern Europe', in *Handbook of Public Administration*, ed. B. Guy Peters and J. Pierre (London and Thousand Oaks, CA: Sage) pp. 536–48.

Agüero, F. (2004) 'Authoritarian Legacies: The Military's Role', in *Authoritarian Legacies and Democracies in Latin America and Southern Europe*, ed. K. Hite and P. Cesarini (Notre Dame, IN: University of Notre Dame Press) pp. 233–62.

Alavi, N. (2005) *We Are Iran: The Persian Blogs* (New York: Soft Skull Press).

Albritton, R. (2006) 'American Federalism and Intergovernmental Relations', in *Developments in American Politics 5*, ed. G. Peele *et al.* (New York and Basingstoke: Palgrave Macmillan) pp. 124–45.

Alexander, H. (2005) 'Comparative Analysis of Political Party and Campaign Financing in the United States and Canada', in *The Delicate Balance between Political Equity and Freedom of Expression: Political Party and Campaign Financing in Canada and the United States*, ed. S. Griner and D. Zovatto (Washington, DC: International IDEA), http://www.idea.int/publications/pp_can_usa/upload/Freedom_Full1.pdf, accessed 28 July 2006.

Allison, G. (1971) *Essence of Decision: Explaining the Cuban Missile Crisis* (Boston, MA: Little Brown).

Allison, G. and Zelikow, P. (1999) *Essence of Decision: Explaining the Cuban Missile Crisis* (New York: Longman)

Almond, G. (1983) 'Communism and Political Culture Theory', *Comparative Politics* (15) 127–38.

Almond, G. (1993) 'The Study of Political Culture', in *Political Culture in Germany*, ed. D. Berg-Schlosser and R. Rytlewski (New York: St. Martin's Press) pp. 13–26.

Almond, G. and Verba, S. (1963) *The Civic Culture* (Princeton, NJ: Princeton University Press).

Almond, G. and Verba, S. (eds) (1980) *The Civic Culture Revisited* (Princeton, NJ: Princeton University Press).

Alonso, S. and Ruiz-Rufino, R. (2007) 'Political Representation and Ethnic Conflict in New Democracies', *European Journal of Political Research* (46) 237–67.

Alter, K. (2009) *The European Court's Political Power: Selected Essays* (Oxford and New York: Oxford University Press).

Althaus, S. (2003) *Collective Preferences in Democratic Politics: Opinion Surveys and the Will of the People* (Cambridge and New York: Cambridge University Press).

Alvarez, A. (2004) 'State Reform Before and After Chávez's Election', in *Venezuelan Politics in the Chávez Era: Class, Polarization and Conflict*, ed. S. Ellner and D. Hellinger (Boulder, CO and London: Lynne Rienner) pp. 147–60.

Álvarez-Rivera, M. (2009) 'Elections to the German Bundestag', *Election Resources on the Internet*, http://electionresources.org/de/, accessed 22 November 2009.

American National Election Studies (2009) *Data Center*, http://www.electionstudies.org, accessed 18 November 2009.

Anderson, B. (1983) *Imagined Communities: Reflections on the Origins and Spread of Nationalism* (London: Verso).

Anderson, B. (1998) *The Spectre of Comparisons: Nationalism, South-East Asia and the World* (London and New York: Verso).

Anderson, C. (2009) 'Nested Citizens: Macropolitics and Microbehaviour' in *Comparative Politics: Rationality, Culture and Structure*, 2nd edn, ed. M. Lichbach and A. Zuckerman, (Cambridge and New York: Cambridge University Press) pp. 314–32.

Andeweg, R. and Irwin, G. (2009) *Governance and Politics of the Netherlands*, 3rd edn (Basingstoke and New York: Palgrave Macmillan).

Ansell, C. and Gingrich, J. (2003) 'Reforming the Administrative State', in *Democracy Transformed? Expanding Political Opportunities in Advanced Industrial Democracies*, ed. B. Cain, R. Dalton and S. Scarrow (Oxford and New York: Oxford University Press) pp. 164–91.

Anton, T. (1969) 'Policy-Making and Political Culture in Sweden', *Scandinavian Political Studies* (4) 82–102.

Arblaster, A. (2002) *Democracy*, 3rd edn (Buckingham and Philadelphia, PA: Open University Press).

Arendt, H. (1970) *On Violence* (London: Allen Lane).

Aristotle (1962 edn) *The Politics*, trans. T. Sinclair (Harmondsworth and Baltimore, MD: Penguin).

Armitage, D. (2005) 'The Contagion of Sovereignty: Declarations of Independence since 1776', *South African Historical Journal* (52) 1–18.

Arter, D. (1999) *Scandinavian Politics Today* (Manchester: Manchester University Press and New York: St Martin's Press).

Arter, D. (2003) 'Committee Cohesion and the "Corporate Dimension" of Parliamentary Committees: A Comparative Analysis', *Journal of Legislative Studies* (9) 73–87.

Arter, D. (2006) *Democracy in Scandinavia: Consensual, Majoritarian or Mixed?* (Manchester and New York: Manchester University Press).

Atton, C. (2004) *An Alternative Internet: Radical Media, Politics and Creativity* (Edinburgh: Edinburgh University Press).

Avdagić, S. and Crouch, C. (2006) 'Organized Economic Interests: Diversity and Change in an Enlarged Europe', in *Developments in European Politics*, ed. P. Heywood *et al.* (Basingstoke and New York: Palgrave Macmillan) pp. 196–216.

B

Bach, D. and Newman, A. (2007) 'The European Regulatory State and Global Public Policy', *Journal of European Public Policy* (14) 827–46.

Bache, I. and Flinders, M. (eds) (2004) *Multi-level Governance* (Oxford and New York: Oxford University Press).

Baer, M. (1993) 'Mexico's Second Revolution: Pathways to Liberalization', in *Political and Economic Liberalization in Mexico: At a Critical Juncture?*, ed. R. Roett (Boulder, CO and London: Lynne Rienner) pp. 51–68.

Bagehot, W. (1867) [1963 edn] *The English Constitution* (London: Fontana).

Bale, T. and Bergman, T. (2006) 'Captives No Longer, But Servants Still? Contract Parliamentarianism and the New Minority Governance in Sweden and New Zealand', *Government and Opposition* (41) 422–49.

Balfour, S. (2005) *The Politics of Contemporary Spain* (London and New York: Routledge).

Balme, R. (1998) 'The French Region as a Space for Public Policy', in *Regions in Europe*, ed. P. Le Galès and C. Lequesne (London and New York: Routledge) pp. 181–98.

Banks, C. and O'Brien, D. (2008) *Courts and Judicial Policymaking* (Upper Saddle River, NJ: Prentice Hall).

Barber, B. (1995) *Jihad vs McWorld* (New York: Ballantine Books).

Barber, J. (1972) *The Presidential Character: Predicting Performance in the White House* (Englewood Cliffs, NJ: Prentice Hall).

Barber, J. (1992) *The Pulse of Politics: Electing Presidents in. the Media Age* (New Brunswick, NY and London: Transaction Books).

Bardach, E. (1976) 'Policy Termination as a Political Process', *Policy Sciences* (7) 123–31.

Bardes, B., Shelley, M. and Schmidt, S. (2008) *American Government and Politics: The Essentials*, 2009/10 edn (Belmont, CA: Thomson Wadsworth).

Bardi, L. and Mair, P. (2008) 'The Parameters of Party Systems', *Party Politics* (14) 147–66.

Barry, B. (1988) *Sociologists, Economists, and Democracy* (Chicago, IL: University of Chicago Press).

Bartle, J. and Bellucci, P. (eds) (2008) *Political Parties and Partisanship: Social Identity and Individual Attitudes* (London and New York: Routledge).

Bates, R. (1998) 'The International Coffee Organization: An International Institution' in *Analytic Narratives*, ed. R. Bates, A. Greif, M. Levi, J.-L. Rosenthal and B. Weingast (Princeton, NJ: Princeton University Press) pp. 194–230.

Bates, R., Greif, A., Levi, M., Rosenthal, J.-L. and Weingast, B. (eds) (1998) *Analytic Narratives* (Princeton, NJ: Princeton University Press).

Baylis, T. (2007) 'Embattled Executives: Prime Ministerial Weakness in East Central Europe', *Communist and Post-Communist Studies* (40) 81–106.

BBC News (2009) *Obama Speaks of Hopes for Africa*, http://www.news.bbc.co.uk, accessed 8 August 2009.

BEA (Bureau of European Analysis) *State Economic Growth Slowed in 2007*, http://bea.gov.newsreleases/regional/grp_state/gsp_newsrelease.htm, accessed 20 December 2008.

Beckman, L. (2007) 'The Professionalization of Politicians Reconsidered: A Study of the Swedish Cabinet, 1917–2004', *Parliamentary Affairs* (60) 66–83.

Beetham, D. (2004) 'Freedom as the Foundation', *Journal of Democracy* (15) 61–75.

Bell, D. (1960) *The End of Ideology? On the Exhaustion of Political Ideas in the 1950s* (New York: Free Press).

Bellamy, R. (2008) *Citizenship: A Very Short Introduction* (Oxford and New York: Oxford University Press).

Bellin, E. (2005) 'Coercive Institutions and Coercive Leaders', in *Authoritarianism in the Middle East*, ed. M. Posusney and M. Angrist (Boulder, CO and London: Lynne Rienner) pp. 21–42.

Bendor, J., Moe, T. and Shorts, K. (2001) 'Recycling the Garbage Can: An Assessment of the Research Program', *American Political Science Review* (95) 169–90.

Bennett, W. Lance (2005) 'Social Movements Beyond Borders: Understanding Two Eras of Transnational Activism', in *Transnational Protest and Global Activism*, ed. D. della Porta and S. Tarrow (Lanham, MD: Rowman & Littlefield) pp. 203–26.

Bennett, W. Lance and Entman, R. (eds) (2001) *Mediated Politics: Communication in the Future of Democracy* (Cambridge and New York: Cambridge University Press).

Bentley, A. (1908) *The Process of Government* (Chicago, IL: University of Chicago Press).

Bentley, T., Jupp, B. and Stedman Jones, D. (2000) *Getting to Grips with Depoliticization* (London: Demos), http://www.demos.co.uk, accessed 6 June 2006.

Berger, S. and Compston, H. (eds) (2002) *Policy Concertation and Social Partnership in Western Europe: Lessons for the 21st Century* (New York and Oxford: Berghahn).

Berglund, F., Holmberg, S., Schmitt, H. and Thomassen, J. (2005) 'Party Identification and Party Choice' in *The European Voter: A Comparative Study of Modern Democracies*, ed. J. Thomassen (Oxford and New York: Oxford University Press) pp. 106–24.

Bergman, T. (2000) 'Sweden: When Minority Cabinets Are the Rule and Majority Coalitions the Exception', in *Coalition Governments in Western Europe*, ed. W. Müller and K. Strøm (Oxford and New York: Oxford University Press) pp. 192–230.

Berg-Schlosser, D. and Rytlewski, R. (1993) *Political Culture in Germany* (New York: St. Martin's Press).

Bergström, H (1991) 'Sweden's Politics and Party System at the Crossroads', *West European Politics* (14) 8–30.

Berman, P. (2007) 'Global Legal Pluralism', *Southern California Law Review* (80) 1155–1238.

Best, H. and Cotta, M. (2000) *Parliamentary Representatives in Europe, 1848–2000* (Oxford and New York: Oxford University Press).

Beyers, J., Eising, R. and Maloney, W. (eds) (2009) *Interest Group Politics in Europe: Lessons from EU Studies and Comparative Politics* (London and New York: Routledge).

Bhattacharyya, H. (2009) *Federalism in Asia: India, Pakistan and Malaysia* (London and New York: Routledge).

Bickerton, J. and Gagnon, A.-G. (eds) (2004) *Canadian Politics*, 4th edn (Peterborough, ON: Broadview Press).

Bickerton, J. and Gagnon, A.-G. (2008) 'Regions', in *Comparative Politics*, ed. D. Caramani (Oxford and New York: Oxford University Press) pp. 367–91.

Bielasiak, J. (2006) 'Regime Diversity and Electoral Systems in Postcommunism', *Journal of Communist and Transition Politics* (22) 407–30.

Biezen, I. van (2003) *Political Parties in New Democracies: Party Organization in Southern and East-Central Europe* (Basingstoke and New York: Palgrave Macmillan).

Binderkrantz, A. (2005) 'Interest Group Strategies: Navigating Between Privileged Access and Strategies of Pressure', *Political Studies* (53) 694–715.

Birch, S. (2007) 'Electoral Systems and the Manipulation of Elections', *Comparative Political Studies* (40) 1533–56.

Birkland, T. (2005) *An Introduction to the Policy Process: Theories, Concepts and Models of Public Policy Making,* 2nd edn (Armonk, NY and London: M. E. Sharpe).

Bishop, G. (2004) *The Illusion of Public Opinion: Fact and Artifact in American Public Opinion Polls* (Lanham, MD and Oxford: Rowman & Littlefield).

Bjørna, A. and Jennsen, S. (2006) 'Prefectural Systems and Central-Local Government Relationships in Scandinavia', *Scandinavian Political Studies* (29) 308–32.

Blais, A., Dobrzynska, A. and Massicotte, L. (2003) *Why is Turnout Higher in Some Countries than in Others?* (Ottawa, Ontario: Elections Canada), http://www.elections.ca/content.asp?section=loi&document=summary&dir=tur/tuh&lang=e&textonly=false, accessed 14 June 2006.

Blais, A., Massicotte, L. and Dobrzynska, A. (1997) 'Direct Presidential Elections: A World Summary', *Electoral Studies* (16) 441–55.

Blondel, J. (1973) *Comparative Legislatures* (Englewood Cliffs, NJ: Prentice Hall).

Blondel, J. (1993) 'Consensus Politics and Multiparty Systems', paper presented at the *Conference on Consensual Policymaking and Multiparty Politics*, Australian National University, 1993.

Blondel, J. (1995) *Comparative Government: An Introduction,* 2nd edn (Harlow and New York: Longman).

Boardman, A., Greenberg, D., Vining, A. and Weimer, D. (2000) *Cost-Benefit Analysis: Concepts and Practice,* 2nd edn (Englewood Cliffs, NJ: Prentice Hall).

Bogason, P. (1996) 'The Fragmentation of Local Government in Scandinavia', *European Journal of Political Research* (30) 65–86.

Bogdanor, V. (2009) *The New British Constitution* (London: Hart).

Bonneau, C. and Hall, M. (2009) *In Defense of Judicial Elections* (New York and London: Routledge).

Borchert, J. and Zeiss, J. (eds) (2003) *The Political Class in Advanced Democracies* (Oxford and New York: Oxford University Press).

Borón, A. (1998) 'Faulty Democracies? A Reflection on the Capitalist "Fault Lines"', in *Fault Lines of Democracy in Post-Transition Latin America,* ed. F. Agüero and J. Stark (Coral Gables, FL: University of Miami) pp. 41–66.

Börzel, T. and Sedelmeieir, U. (2006) 'The EU Dimension in European Politics', in *Developments in European Politics,* ed. P. Heywood, E. Jones, M. Rhodes and U. Sedelmeier (Basingstoke and New York: Palgrave Macmillan), pp. 54–70.

Boston, J., Martin, J., Pallot, J. and Walsh, P. (eds) (1995) *Reshaping the State: New Zealand's Bureaucratic Revolution* (Oxford and New York: Oxford University Press).

Bourchier, D. (2006) *Illiberal Democracy in Indonesia* (London and New York: Routledge).

Bourgault, J. (2002) 'The Role of Deputy Ministers in Canadian Government', in *The Handbook of Canadian Public Administration,* ed. C. Dunn (Don Mills, Ontario: Oxford University Press) pp. 430–49.

Bourgault, L. (1995) *Mass Media in Sub-Saharan Africa* (Bloomington, IN: Indiana University Press).

Bourne, A. (2003) 'Regional Europe', in *European Union Politics,* ed. M. Cini (Oxford and New York: Oxford University Press) pp. 278–93.

Bowler, S. and Donovan, T. (2002) 'Democracy, Institutions and Attitudes about Citizen Influence on Government', *British Journal of Political Science* (32) 371–90.

Bowles, N. (1998) *Government and Politics of the United States,* 2nd edn (Basingstoke: Macmillan).

Boyer, R. (1997) 'French Statism at the Crossroads', in *Political Economy of Modern Capitalism: Mapping Convergence and Diversity,* ed. C. Crouch and W. Streeck (London and Thousand Oaks, CA: Sage) pp. 71–101.

Brans, M., De Winter, L. and Swenden, W. (eds) (2009) *The Politics of Belgium: Institutions and Policy Under Bipolar and Centrifugal Federalism* (London and New York: Routledge).

Bratton, M. (1998) 'Second Elections in Africa', *Journal of Democracy* (9) 51–66.

Braun, D. with Walti, A., Bullinger, A.-B. and Ayrton, R. (2003) *Fiscal Policies in Federal States* (Aldershot and Burlington, VT: Ashgate).

Breslin, S. (2004) 'Capitalism with Chinese Characteristics: The Public, the Private and the International', *Working Paper No. 104,* Asia Research Centre (Perth: Murdoch University), http://www.arc.murdoch.edu.au/wp/wp104.pdf, accessed 20 March 2006.

Brewer, M. (2008) *Party Images in the American Electorate* (London and New York: Routledge)

Brewer, P., Aday, S. and Gross, K. (2003) 'Rallies All Round: The Dynamics of System Support', in *Framing Terrorism: The News Media, the Government and the Public,* ed. P. Norris, M. Kern and M. Just (London and New York: Routledge) pp. 229–54.

Brodsgaard, K. and Yongnian, Z. (eds) (2006) *The Chinese Communist Party in Reform* (London and New York: Routledge).

Brooker, P. (2009) *Non-Democratic Regimes: Theory, Government and Politics,* 2nd edn (Basingstoke and New York: Palgrave Macmillan).

Brooks, S. (2007) *Canadian Democracy: An Introduction,* 5th edn (Don Mills, Ontario and Oxford: Oxford University Press).

Brooks, S. (2009) *Canadian Democracy: An Introduction,* 6th edn (Don Mills, Ontario and Oxford: Oxford University Press).

Brown, A. (ed.) (2004) *The Demise of Marxism-Leninism in Russia* (London and New York: Palgrave).

Bryce, J. (1919) *The American Commonwealth,* Vol. 1 (London: Macmillan).

Bryce, J. (1921) *Modern Democracies,* Vol. 2 (New York: Macmillan).

Brzezinski, Z. (2002) 'Confronting Anti-American Grievances', *New York Times,* 1 September.

BSA (British Social Attitudes) (2009) *Contents List,* http://www.

britsocat.com/Body.aspx?control=BritsocatHome, accessed 16 September 2009.

Budge, I. (2006) 'Identifying Dimensions and Locating Parties: Methodological and Conceptual Problems' in *Handbook of Party Politics,* ed. R. Katz and W. Crotty (London and Thousand Oaks, CA: Sage) pp. 422–34.

Buhlungu, S., Daniel, J., Southall, R. and Lutchman, J. (eds) (2007) *State of the Nation: South Africa 2007* (Cape Town: HSRC Press).

Bull, M. and Newell, J. (2005) *Italian Politics: Adjustment under Duress* (Cambridge and Malden, MA: Polity).

Bull, M. and Rhodes, M. (eds) (2008) *Italy: A Contested Polity* (London and New York: Routledge).

Burea, G. de and Weiler, J. (eds) (2002) *The European Court of Justice* (Oxford and New York: Oxford University Press).

Burgess, M. (2006) *Comparative Federalism: Theory and Practice* (London and New York: Routledge).

Burkan, J. (2008) 'Legislatures on the Rise', *Journal of Democracy* (19) 124–37.

Burke, E. (1774) [1975 edn] 'Speech to the Electors of Bristol', in *Edmund Burke on Government, Politics and Society,* ed. B. Hill (London: Fontana) pp. 156–8.

Burke, J. (2005) 'The Institutional Presidency', in *The Presidency and the Political System,* 8th edn, ed. M. Nelson (Washington DC: CQ Press) pp. 399–424.

Bush, K. (2005) 'New Zealand: A Quantum Leap Forward?', in *Comparing Local Governance: Trends and Developments,* ed. B. Denters and L. Rose (Basingstoke and New York: Palgrave Macmillan) pp. 174–92.

Butler, A. (2004) *Contemporary South Africa* (Basingstoke and New York: Palgrave).

C

Cabinet Office (2008) *The National Security Strategy of the United Kingdom: Security in an Interdependent World,* http://interactive.cabinetoffice.gov.uk/documents/security/national_security_strategy.pdf, accessed 20 December 2008.

Cain, B. and Goux, D. (2006) 'Parties in an Era of Renewed Partisanship', in *Developments in American Politics 5,* ed. G. Peele, C. Bailey, B. Cain and B. Guy Peters (Basingstoke and New York: Palgrave Macmillan) pp. 37–52.

Calhoun, C. (1997) *Nationalism* (Buckingham: Open University Press).

Calhoun, J. (1851) [2007 edn] *Disquisition on Government,* ed. H. Cheek (South Bend, IN: St Augustine's Press).

Calleros-Alarcón (2008) *The Unfinished Transition to Democracy in Latin America* (London and New York: Routledge).

Camp, R. (2006) *Politics in Mexico: The Democratic Consolidation,* 5th edn. (Oxford and New York: Oxford University Press).

Campbell, A., Converse, P., Miller, A. and Stokes, D. (1960) *The American Voter* (New York: Wiley).

Canel, E. (1992) 'Democratization and the Decline of Urban Social Movements in Uruguay: A Political Institutional Account', in *The Making of Social Movements in Latin America: Identity, Strategy and Democracy,* ed. A. Escobar and S. Alvarez (Boulder, CO and Oxford: Westview) pp. 276–90.

Carey, J. (2006) 'Legislative Organization', in *The Oxford Handbook of Political Institutions,* ed. R. Rhodes, S. Binder and B. Rockman (Oxford and New York: Oxford University Press) pp. 431–54.

Carey, J., Niemi, R., Powell, L. and Moncrief, G. (2006) 'The Effects of Term Limits on State Legislatures: A New Survey of the 50 States', *Legislative Studies Quarterly* (31) 105–34.

Carothers, T. (2002) 'The End of the Transition Paradigm', *Journal of Democracy* (13) 5–21.

Carriûn, J. (ed.) (2006) *The Fujimori Legacy: The Rise of Electoral Authoritarianism in Peru* (University Park, PA: Penn State University Press).

Carty, K. (2002) 'Canada's Nineteenth-Century Cadre Parties at the Millennium', in *Political Parties in Advanced Industrial Democracies,* ed. P. Webb, D. Farrell and I. Holliday (Oxford New York: Oxford University Press) pp. 131–52.

Case, W. (1996) 'Can the "Halfway House" Stand? Semi-democracy and Elite Theory in Three Southeast Asian Countries', *Comparative Politics* (28) 437–64.

Chabal, P. and Daloz, J.-P. (2006) *Culture Troubles: Politics and the Interpretation of Meaning* (London: Hurst).

Chalmers, D. (1990) 'Dilemmas of Latin American Democratization: Dealing with International Forces', *Papers on Latin America, No. 18* (New York: Columbia University Institute of Latin American and Iberian Studies).

Chari, R., Murphy, G. and Hogan, J. (2007) 'Regulating Lobbyists: A Comparative Analysis of the United States, Canada, Germany and the European Union', *Political Quarterly* (78) 422–38.

Chazan, N., Lewis, P., Mortimer, R., Rothchild, D. and Stedman, S. (1999) *Politics and Society in Contemporary Africa,* 3rd edn (Boulder, CO: Lynne Rienner).

Chehabi, H. (2001) 'The Political Regime of the Islamic Republic of Iran', *Government and Opposition* (39) 48–70.

Chehabi, H. and Linz, J. (eds) (1998) *Sultanistic Regimes* (Baltimore, MD and London: Johns Hopkins University Press).

Cheibub, J. (2002) 'Minority Governments, Deadlock Situations and the Survival of Presidential Democracies', *Comparative Political Studies* (35) 284–312.

Chen, J. and Malhotra, N. (2007) 'The Law of 1/n: The Effect of Chamber Size on Government Spending in Bicameral Legislatures', *American Political Science Review* (101) 657–76.

Chesterman, S., Ignatieff, M. and Thakur, R. (eds) (2005) *Making States Work: State Failure and the Crisis of Governance* (Tokyo and New York: United Nations University Press)

ChinaToday.com (2009) *Communist Party of China,* http://www.chinatoday.com/org/cpc/, accessed 18 April 2009.

Christensen, T and Lægreid, P. (2007) 'Theoretical Approach and Research Questions' in *Transcending New Public Management: The Transformation of Public Sector Reforms,* ed. T. Christensen and P. Lægreid (Farnham: Ashgate) pp. 1–16.

Christensen, T. and Peters, B. Guy (1999) *Structure, Culture and Governance: A Comparison of Norway and the United States* (Lanham, MD and Oxford: Rowman & Littlefield).

CIA (Central Intelligence Agency) (2009) *The World Factbook,* https://www.cia.gov/cia/publications/factbook/index.html.

Cigler, C. and Loomis, B. (eds) (2006) *Interest Group Politics,* 7th edn (Washington: Congressional Quarterly Press).

Cini, M. (ed.) (2006) *European Union Politics,* 2nd edn (Oxford and New York: Oxford University Press).

Clapham, C. (2003) 'The Challenge to the State in a Globalized World', in *State Failure, Collapse and Reconstruction*, ed. J. Milliken (Malden, MA and Oxford: Blackwell) pp. 25–44.

Clark, S. (1995) *State and Status: The Rise of the State and Aristocratic Power in Western Europe* (Montreal and Kingston: McGill-Queen's University Press).

Clark, W. (2005) *Capitalism, Not Globalism: Capital Mobility, Central Bank Independence, and the Political Control of the Economy* (Ann Arbor, MI: University of Michigan Press).

Clarke, D. (2007) 'Legislating for a Market Economy in China', *The China Quarterly* (191) 567–85.

Clément, K. (2008) 'New Social Movements in Russia: A Challenge to the Dominant Model of Power Relationships', *Journal of Communist Studies and Transition Politics* (24) 68–89.

Coase, R. (1960) 'The Problem of Social Cost', *Journal of Law and Economics* (3) 1–44.

Cohen, J. (1997) 'Deliberation and Democratic Legitimacy', in *Deliberative Democracy: Essays on Reason and Politics*, ed. J. Bohman and W. Rehg (Cambridge, MA: MIT Press) pp. 67–92.

Cohen, M., March, J. and Olsen, J. (1972) 'A Garbage Can Model of Organizational Choice', *Administrative Science Quarterly* (17) 1–25.

Cole, A., Le Galès, P. and Levy, J. (eds) (2005) *Developments in French Politics 4* (Basingstoke and New York: Palgrave Macmillan).

Colebatch, H. (1998) *Policy* (Buckingham: Open University Press).

Colomer, J. (ed.) (2004a) *Handbook of Electoral System Choice* (Basingstoke and New York: Palgrave Macmillan).

Colomer, J. (2004b) 'The Strategy and History of Electoral System Choice', in *Handbook of Electoral System Choice*, ed. J. Colomer (Basingstoke and New York: Palgrave Macmillan) pp. 3–80.

Common Cause (2006) *About Us* (Washington, DC: Common Cause), http://www.commoncause.org/sitepp.asp?c= dkLNK1MQIwG&b=189955, accessed 28 June 2006

Commonwealth Secretariat (1997) *A Future for Small States: Overcoming Vulnerability* (London: Commonwealth Secretariat).

Conradt, D. (2008) *The German Polity*, 9th edn (New York: Longman).

Corbett, R., Jacobs, F. and Shackleton, M. (2005) *The European Parliament*, 6th edn (London: John Harper).

Cordes, J. (2002) 'Corrective Taxes, Charges and Tradable Permits', in *The Tools of Government: A Guide to the New Governance*, ed. L. Salamon (New York: Oxford University Press) pp. 255–81.

Corner, J. and Pels, D. (eds) (2003) *Media and the Restyling of Politics: Consumerism, Celebrity, Cynicism* (London and Thousand Oaks, CA: Sage).

Cotta, M. (2000) 'Defining Party and Government', in *The Nature of Party Government: A Comparative European Perspective*, ed. J. Blondel and M. Cotta (Basingstoke: Macmillan) pp. 56–95.

Cotta, M. and Best, H. (eds) (2007) *Democratic Representation in Europe: Diversity, Change and Convergence* (Oxford and New York: Oxford University Press).

Cottey, A., Edmunds, T. and Forster, A. (eds) (2003) *Democratic Control of the Military in Post-Communist Europe* (Basingstoke: Palgrave).

Cowley, P. (2006) 'Making Parliament Matter?', in *Developments in British Politics 8*, ed. P. Dunleavy, R. Heffernan, P. Cowley and C. Hay (Basingstoke: Palgrave Macmillan) pp. 36–55.

Cox, G. and Morgenstern, S. (2002) 'Latin America's Reactive Assemblies and Proactive Presidents', in *Legislative Politics in Latin America*, ed. S. Morgenstern and B. Nacif (Cambridge and New York: Cambridge University Press) pp. 446–68.

Creveld, M. van (1999) *The Rise and Decline of the State* (Cambridge and New York: Cambridge University Press).

Crick, B. (2000) *In Defence of Politics*, 5th edn (Harmondsworth: Penguin).

Crisp, B. (2000) *Democratic Institutional Design: The Powers and Incentives of Venezuelan Politicians and Interest Groups* (Stanford, CA: Stanford University Press).

Cross, W. and Young, L. (2004) 'The Contours of Political Party Membership in Canada', *Party Politics* (10) 427–44.

Crothers, L. and Lockhart, C. (eds) (2002) *Culture and Politics: A Reader* (Basingstoke: Palgrave Macmillan).

Crotty, W. (2006) 'Party Transformations: The United States and Western Europe', in *Handbook of Party Politics*, ed. R. Katz and W. Crotty (London and Thousand Oaks, CA: Sage) pp. 499–514.

Crouch, H. (1996) *Government and Society in Malaysia* (Ithaca, NY: Cornell University Press).

Cummings, S. (2005) *Kazakhstan: Power and the Elite* (London and New York: I. B. Taurus).

Curran, J. and Seaton, J. (2003) *Power Without Responsibility: The Press and Broadcasting in Britain*, 6th edn (London and New York: Methuen).

D

Dahl, R. (1957) 'The Concept of Power', *Behavioral Science* (2) 201–15.

Dahl, R. (1989) *Democracy and its Critics* (New Haven, CT and London: Yale University Press).

Dahl, R. (1993) 'Pluralism', in *The Oxford Companion to Politics of the World*, ed. J. Krieger (New York and Oxford: Oxford University Press) pp. 704–7.

Dahl, R. (1998) *On Democracy* (New Haven, CT and London: Yale University Press).

Dahl, R. (2001) *How Democratic is the American Constitution?* (New Haven, CT and London: Yale University Press).

Dahl, R., Shapiro, I. and Cheibub, J. (eds) (2003) *The Democracy Sourcebook* (Cambridge, MA: MIT Press).

Dalton, R. (1994) *The Green Rainbow: Environmental Groups in Western Europe* (New Haven, CT and London: Yale University Press).

Dalton, R. (2008a) *Citizen Politics: Public Opinion and Political Parties in Advanced Industrial Democracies*, 5th edn (Washington, DC: CQ Press).

Dalton, R. (2008b) 'Citizenship Norms and the Expansion of Political Participation', *Political Studies* (59) 76–98.

Dalton, R. and Gray, M. (2003) 'Expanding the Electoral Marketplace', in *Democracy Transformed? Expanding Political Opportunities in Advanced Industrial Democracies*, ed. B. Cain, R. Dalton and S. Scarrow (Oxford and New York: Oxford University Press) pp. 23–44.

Dalton, R. and Klingemann, H.-D. (eds) (2007) *The Oxford Handbook of Political Behaviour* (Oxford and New York: Oxford University Press).

Dalton, R. and Wattenberg, M. (2000) *Politics without Partisans: Political Change in Advanced Industrial Democracies* (Oxford and New York: Oxford University Press).

Dalton, R., McAllister, I. and Wattenberg, M. (2000) 'The Consequences of Partisan Dealignment', in *Parties without Partisans: Political Change in Advanced Industrial Democracies*, ed. R. Dalton and M. Wattenberg (Oxford and New York: Oxford University Press) pp. 37–63.

Davidson, B. (1992) *The Black Man's Burden: Africa and the Curse of the Nation-State* (Oxford and Harare: James Currey).

Davidson, R., Oleszek, W. and Lee, F. (2009) *Congress and Its Members*, 12th edn (Washington, DC: CQ Press).

Deane, R (1989) *The State and the Economic System: An Introduction to the History of Political Economy* (Oxford and New York: Oxford University Press).

DeLong, B. (1995) *The Inflation of the 1970s*, http://econ161. berkeley.edu/Econ_Articles/theinflationofthes.html, accessed 9 November 2009.

Dempsey, J. (2002) 'Civil Liberties in a Time of Crisis', *Human Rights* (29) 8–10.

Denters, B. and Klok, P.-J. (2005) 'The Netherlands: In Search of Responsiveness', in *Comparing Local Governance: Trends and Developments,* ed. B. Denters and L. Rose (Basingstoke and New York: Palgrave Macmillan) pp. 65–82.

Denters, B. and Rose, L. (eds) (2005) *Comparing Local Governance: Trends and Developments* (Basingstoke and New York: Palgrave Macmillan).

Department of Health and Human Services (2009) *About HHL,* http://www.hhs.gov/about/index.html#agencies, accessed 2 November 2009.

Derbyshire, J. and Derbyshire, L. (1999) *Political Systems of the World* (Oxford: Helicon).

Deschouwer, K. (2005) 'The Unintended Consequences of Consociational Federalism: The Case of Belgium', in *Power Sharing: New Challenges for Divided Societies,* ed. I. O'Flynn and D. Russell (London and Ann Arbor, MI: Pluto Press) pp. 92–106.

Deschouwer, K. (2006) 'Political Parties as Multi-level Organizations', in *Handbook of Party Politics,* ed. R. Katz and W. Crotty (London and Thousand Oaks, CA: Sage) pp. 291–300.

Deschouwer, K. (2009) *The Politics of Belgium: Governing a Divided Society* (Basingstoke and New York: Palgrave Macmillan).

DGB (Confederation of German Trade Unions) (2009) *Structure and Tasks,* http://www.dgb.de, accessed 1 October 2009.

Diamond, L. (1999) *Developing Democracy: Toward Consolidation* (Baltimore, MD and London: Johns Hopkins University Press).

Dicey, A. (1885) [1959 edn] *Introduction to the Study of the Law of the Constitution,* 10th edn (London: Macmillan).

Dickie, M. (2007) 'China Learns to Click Carefully', *Financial Times,* 13 November, p. 19.

Dickson, B. (2007) 'Integrating Wealth and Power in China: The Communist Party's Embrace of the Market Sector', *China Quarterly* (192) 827–54.

Dittmer, L. and Liu, G. (eds) (2006) *China's Deep Reform: Domestic Politics in Transition* (Lanham, MD and Oxford: Rowman & Littlefield).

Dodd, L. and Oppenheimer, B. (eds) (2008) *Congress Reconsidered,* 9th edn (Washington, DC: Congressional Quarterly Press).

Dodson, M. and Jackson, D. (2003) 'Horizontal Accountability and the Rule of Law in Central America', in *Democratic Accountability in Latin America,* ed. S. Mainwaring and C. Welna (Oxford and New York) pp. 228–65.

Dogan, M. and Pelassy, G. (1990) *How to Compare Nations* (Chatham, NJ: Chatham House).

Dollery, B., Garcea, J. and LeSage Jr, E. (eds) (2008) *Local Government Reform: A Comparative Analysis of Advanced Anglo-American Countries* (London and New York: Routledge).

Donaldson, R. (2004) 'Russia', *Journal of Legislative Studies* (10) 230–49.

Dooley, B. and Baron, S. (eds) (2001) *The Politics of Information in Early Modern Europe* (London and New York: Longman).

Dowding, K. and Dumont, P. (eds) (2008) *The Selection of Ministers in Europe: Hiring and Firing* (London and New York: Routledge).

Downs, A. (1957) *An Economic Theory of Democracy* (New York: Harper).

Drake, P. and Hershberg, E. (2006) 'The Crisis of State-Society Relations in the Post-1980s Andes', in *State and Society in Conflict: Comparative Perspectives on Andean Crises,* ed. R Drake and E. Hershberg (Pittsburgh, PA: University of Pittsburgh Press) pp. 1–40.

Duch, R. and Stevenson, R. (2008) *The Economic Vote: How Political and Economic Institutions Condition Electoral Results* (Cambridge and New York: Cambridge University Press).

Dunleavy, P., Heffernan, R., Cowley, P. and Hay, C. (eds) (2006) *Developments in British Politics 8* (Basingstoke and New York: Palgrave Macmillan).

Duverger, M. (1954) [1970 edn] *Political Parties* (London: Methuen).

Duverger, M. (1980) 'A New Political System Model: Semi-Presidential Government', *European Journal of Political Research* (8) 165–87.

Dworkin, R. (1977) *Taking Rights Seriously* (Cambridge, MA and London: Harvard University Press).

Dye, T. (2007) *Understanding Public Policy,* 12th edn (Englewood Cliffs, NJ: Prentice Hall).

Dyson, K. (1980) *The State Tradition in Western Europe: A Study of an Idea and Institution* (Oxford: Martin Robertson).

E

Eagleton, T. (1991) *Ideology: An Introduction* (London: Verso).

Easter, G. (1997) 'Preference for Presidentialism: Postcommunist Regime Change in Russia and the NIS', *World Politics* (49) 184–211.

Eberle, J. (1990) 'Understanding the Revolutions in Eastern Europe', in *Spring in Winter: The 1989 Revolutions,* ed. G. Prins (Manchester: Manchester University Press) pp. 193–209.

Eckstein, H. (1998) 'Russia and the Conditions of Democracy', in *Can Democracy Take Root in Post-Soviet Russia? Explorations in State-Society Relations,* ed. H. Eckstein, W. Reisinger and F. Fleron, Jr (Lanham, MD and Oxford: Rowman & Littlefield) pp. 349–81.

Edmonds-Poli, E. and Shirk, D. (2008) *Contemporary Mexican Politics* (Lanham, MD: Rowman & Littlefield).

Egeberg, M. (2008) 'European Government(s): Executive Politics in Transition', *West European Politics* (31) 235–57.

Eichbaum, C. and Shaw, R. (2007) 'Ministerial Advisers, Politicization and the Retreat from Westminster: The Case of New Zealand', *Public Administration* (85) 569–87.

Eigen, L. and Siegel, J. (1993) *The Macmillan Dictionary of Political Quotations* (New York: Macmillan).

Elazar, D. (1996) 'From Statism to Federalism: A Paradigm Shift', *International Political Science Review* (17) 417–30.

Eley, G. and Suny, R. (1996) 'From the Moment of Social History to the Work of Cultural Representation', in *Becoming National: A Reader*, ed. G. Eley and R. Suny (Oxford and New York: Oxford University Press) pp. 3–37.

Elgie, R. (2003) *Political Institutions in Contemporary France* (Oxford and New York: Oxford University Press).

Elgie, R. (2005) 'The Political Executive', in *Developments in French Politics 3*, ed. A. Cole, P. le Galès and J. Levy (Basingstoke and New York: Palgrave Macmillan) pp. 70–87.

Elgie, R. (ed.) (1999) *Semi-Presidentialism in Europe* (Oxford and New York: Oxford University Press).

Elgie, R. (ed.) (2001) *Divided Government in Comparative Perspective* (Oxford and New York: Oxford University Press).

Eliadis, P., Hill, M. and Howlett, M. (eds) (2005) *Designing Government: From Instruments to Governance* (Montreal and London: McGill-Queen's University Press).

Elkit, J., Svensson, P. and Togeby, L. (2005) 'Why is Voter Turnout Not Declining in Denmark?', paper prepared for delivery at the *Annual Meeting of the American Political Science Association*, Washington, DC.

Ellis, R. and Nelson, M. (eds) (2006) *Debating the Presidency: Conflicting Perspectives on the American Executive* (Washington, DC: CQ Press).

Ellner, S. (2004) 'The Search for Explanations', in *Venezuelan Politics in the Chávez Era: Class, Polarization and Conflict*, ed. S. Ellner and D. Hellinger (Boulder, CO and London: Lynne Rienner) pp. 7–26.

Elster, J. (1989) *Nuts and Bolts for the Social Sciences* (Cambridge and New York: Cambridge University Press).

Elster, J., Offe, C. and Preuss, U. (1998) *Institutional Design in Post-Communist Societies: Rebuilding the Ship at Sea* (Cambridge and New York: Cambridge University Press).

Endersby, J., Petrocik, J. and Shaw, D. (2006) 'Electoral Mobilization in the United States', in *Handbook of Party Politics*, ed. R. Katz and W. Crotty (London and Thousand Oaks, CA: Sage) pp. 316–36.

Engels, F. (1844) [1999 edn] *The Condition of the Working Class in England in 1844*, ed. D. McLellan (Oxford and New York: Oxford University Press).

Esarey, A. (2006) *Speak No Evil: Mass Media Control in Contemporary China* (New York: Freedom House), http://www.freedomhouse.org/uploads/special_report/33.pdf, accessed 6 March 2006.

Esman, M. (1996) 'Diasporas and International Relations', in *Ethnicity*, ed. J. Hutchinson and A. Smith (Oxford and New York: Oxford University Press) pp. 316–20.

Esser, F. and Pfetsch, B. (eds) (2004) *Comparing Political Communication: Theories, Cases and Challenges* (Cambridge and New York: Cambridge University Press).

ETUC (European Trade Union Federation) (2006) *What is the 'European Social Model' or 'Social Europe'?*, http://www.etuc.org/a/111, accessed 10 December 2006.

Eulau, H. (1963) *The Behavioral Persuasion in Politics* (New York: Random House).

Europa (2009) *The European Commission*, http://www.europa.eu, accessed 28 October 2009.

Eurostat (2008) *Key Figures on Europe*, 2007/08 edn, http://epp.eurostat.ec.europa.eu, accessed 20 December 2008.

Evans Jr, A. (2005) 'A Russian Civil Society?', in *Developments in Russian Politics 6*, ed. S. White, Z. Gitelman and R. Sakwa (Basingstoke and New York: Palgrave Macmillan) pp. 96–113.

F

Falconer, C. (2006) 'History', *Judicial Appointments Commission*, http://www.judicialappointments.gov.uk/about/history.htm, accessed 4 August 2006.

Farcau, B. (1994) *The Coup: Tactics in the Seizure of Power* (Westport, CT: Praeger).

Farnen, R. and Meloen, J. (eds) (2000) *Democracy, Authoritarianism and Education* (Basingstoke: Palgrave).

Farr, J. (1995) 'Remembering the Revolution: Behavioralism in American Politics Science' in *Political Science in History: Research Programs and Political Traditions*, ed. J. Farr, J. Dryzek and S. Leonard (Cambridge and New York: Cambridge University Press) pp. 198–224.

Farrell, D. (2001) *Electoral Systems: A Comparative Introduction* (London and New York: Palgrave).

FDC (Forum for Democratic Change) (2007) *One Uganda, One People*, http://www.fdcganda.org/, accessed 9 January 2007.

Feldman, O. (1993) *Politics and the News Media in Japan* (Ann Arbor, MI: University of Michigan Press).

Fernando J. and Heston A. (1997) 'NGOs between States, Markets and Civil Society', *Annals of the American Academy of Political and Social Sciences* (554) 8–19.

Fesler, J. and Kettl, D. (2008) *The Politics of the Administrative Process*, 4th edn (Washington, DC: CQ Press).

Fiers, S. and Krouwel, A. (2005) 'The Low Countries: From "Prime Minister" to President-Minister', in *The Presidentialization of Politics: A Comparative Study of Modern Democracies*, ed. T. Poguntke and P. Webb (Oxford and New York: Oxford University Press) pp. 128–58.

Finer, S. (1970) *Comparative Government* (Harmondsworth and New York: Penguin).

Finer, S. (1997) *The History of Government from the Earliest Times*, 3 vols (Oxford and New York: Oxford University Press).

Fink, A. (2008) *How To Conduct Surveys: A Step-by-Step Guide*, 4th edn (Thousand Oaks, CA and London: Sage).

Finley, M. (1985) *Democracy Ancient and Modern* (London: Hogarth Press).

Finnemore, M. (1996) *National Interests in International Society* (Ithaca, NY: Cornell University Press).

Fiorina, M. (1981) *Retrospective Voting in American National Elections* (New Haven, CT: Yale University Press).

Fischer, F. (2003) *Reframing Public Policy: Discursive Practice and Deliberative Practices* (Oxford and New York: Oxford University Press).

Fischer, F. (2005) *Evaluating Public Policy* (Chicago: Nelson-Wood).

Fish, M. (2005) *Democracy Derailed in Russia: The Failure of Open Politics* (Cambridge and New York: Cambridge University Press).

Fish, S. and Kroenig, M. (2009) *The Handbook of National Legislatures: A Global Survey* (Cambridge and New York: Cambridge University Press).

Fisher, J. and Eisenstadt, T. (2004) 'Comparative Party Finance: What Is To Be Done?' *Party Politics* (10) 619–26.

Fishkin, J. (1991) *Democracy and Deliberation: New Directions for Democratic Reform* (New Haven, CT and London: Yale University Press).

Fishkin, J. and Laslett, P. (eds) (2003) *Debating Deliberative Democracy* (Oxford and New York: Blackwell).

Flammang, J., Gordon, D., Lukes, T. and Smorsten, K. (1990) *American Politics in a Changing World* (Pacific Grove, CA: Brooks/Cole).

Foley, M. (1999) 'In Kiev They Fine a Journalist $1m and Cut Off All the Phones', *The Times*, 2 April, p. 45.

Foweraker, T., Landman, T. and Harvey, N. (2003) *Governing Latin America* (Cambridge and Malden, MA: Polity).

Franklin, M. (1992) 'The Decline of Cleavage Politics', in *Electoral Change: Responses to Evolving Social and Attitudinal Structures in Western Countries*, ed. M. Franklin, T. Mackie and H. Valen (Cambridge and New York: Cambridge University Press) pp. 383–405.

Franklin, M. (2004) *Voter Turnout and the Dynamics of Electoral Competition in Established Democracies* (Cambridge and New York: Cambridge University Press).

Freedom House (2009) *Freedom in the World,* http://www.freedomhouse.org, accessed 11 September 2009.

Friedman, M. (1962) *Capitalism and Freedom* (Chicago and London: University of Chicago Press).

Friedman, M. (1970) 'A Theoretical Framework for Monetary Analysis', in *Milton Friedman's Monetary Framework: A Debate with His Critics*, ed. R. Gordon (Chicago and London: University of Chicago Press) pp. 1–62.

Friedman, M. (1991) *Monetarist Economics* (Oxford and Cambridge, MA: Basil Blackwell).

Friedrich, C. (1937) *Constitutional Government and Politics* (New York: Harper).

Fukuyama, F. (1992) *The End of History and the Last Man* (New York: Free Press).

Fukuyama, F. (2004) *State Building: Governance and World Order in the Twenty-First Century* (Ithaca, NY: Cornell University Press).

Fuller, G. (2002) 'The Future for Political Islam', *Foreign Affairs* (81) 48–60.

Fuller, L. (1969) *The Morality of Law* (New Haven and London: Yale University Press).

Fund for Peace (2009) *Failed States Index,* http://www.fundforpeace.org, accessed 9 September 2009.

G

Gagnon, A.-G. and Tully, J. (eds) (2001) *Multinational Democracies* (Cambridge and New York: Cambridge University Press).

Gajduschek, G. (2007) 'Politicization, Professionalization, or Both? Hungary's Civil Service System', *Communist and Post-Communist Studies* (40) 343–62.

Gallagher, M. and Mitchell, P. (eds) (2005) *The Politics of Electoral Systems* (Oxford and New York: Oxford University Press).

Gallagher, M., Laver, M. and Mair, P. (2006) *Representative Government in Modern Europe: Institutions, Parties, and Governments*, 4th edn (New York and London: McGraw-Hill).

Gallie, W. (1956) 'Essentially Contested Concepts', *Proceedings of the Aristotelian Society* (56) 157–97.

Galligan, B. (2006) 'Comparative Federalism', in *The Oxford Handbook of Political Institutions*, ed. R. Rhodes, S. Binder and B. Rockman (Oxford and New York: Oxford University Press) pp. 261–80.

Gambetta, D. (2005) 'Can We Make Sense of Suicide Missions?', in *Making Sense of Suicide Missions,* ed. D. Gambetta (Oxford and New York: Oxford University Press) pp. 259–300.

Gamble, A. (2009) *The Spectre at the Feast: Capitalist Crisis and the Politics of Recession* (London and New York: Palgrave Macmillan).

Gandhi, J. (2008) *Political Institutions Under Dictatorship* (Cambridge and New York: Cambridge University Press).

GAO (General Accountability Office) (2009) *Reports on the Government Performance and Results Act*, http://www.gao.gov/new.items/gpra/gpra.htm, accessed 11 August 2009.

Gavin, N. and Sanders, D. (2003) 'The Press and its Influence on British Political Attitudes under New Labour', *Political Studies* (51) 573–91.

Geddes, B. (2003) *Paradigms and Sand Castles: Theory Building and Research Design in Comparative Politics* (Ann Arbor, MI: University of Michigan Press).

Geertz, C. (1963) 'The Integrative Revolution: Primordial Sentiments and Civil Politics in the New States' in *Old Societies and New States: The Quest for Modernity in Asia and Africa*, ed. C. Geertz (NY: Free Press) pp. 105–57.

Geertz, C. (1973) [1993 edn] 'Thick Description: Toward an Interpretative Theory of Culture', in *Interpretation of Cultures*, ed. C. Geertz (London: Fontana) pp. 1–33.

Geffen, S. van (2001) *The Court Rules: Modelling and Testing Supreme Court Influence on Policy* (Assen: Van Gorcum).

Gellner, E. (1983) *Nations and Nationalism* (Oxford and Cambridge, MA: Blackwell).

George, A. (1969) 'The Operational Code: A Neglected Approach to the Study of Political Leaders and Decision-making', *International Studies Quarterly* (13) 190–222.

George, A. and Bennett, A. (2004) *Case Studies and Theory Development in the Social Sciences* (Cambridge, MA: MIT Press).

Gerth, H. and Mills, C. Wright (1948) *From Max Weber* (London: Routledge & Kegan Paul).

Geys, B. (2006) 'Explaining Voter Turnout: A Review of Aggregate-Level Research', *Electoral Studies* (25) 637–63.

Gilardi, F. (2008) *Delegation in the Regulatory State: Independent Regulatory Agencies in Western Europe* (Cheltenham: Edward Elgar).

Ginsberg, B. (1982) *The Consequences of Consent* (Reading, MA: Addison Wesley).

Ginsborg, P. (2003) *A History of Contemporary Italy: Society and Politics, 1943–1988* (Basingstoke: Palgrave Macmillan).

Ginsburg, R. (1992) [2004 edn] 'Speaking in a Judicial Voice: Reflections on *Roe* v. *Wade*', in *Judges on Judging: Views from the Bench*, ed. D. O'Brien (Washington, DC: CQ Press) pp. 194–200.

Girard, P. (2006) *Paradise Lost: Haiti's Tumultuous Journey from Pearl of the Caribbean to Third World Hotspot* (Basingstoke and New York: Palgrave).

Gitelman, Z. (2005) 'The Democratization of Russia in Comparative Perspective', in *Developments in Russian Politics 6*, ed. S. White, Z. Gitelman and R. Sakwa (Basingstoke and New York: Palgrave Macmillan) pp. 241–56.

Glynn, C., Herbst, S., O'Keefe, G. and Shapiro, R. (1998) *Public Opinion* (Boulder, CO and Oxford: Westview Press).

Goban-Klas, T. and Sasinka-Klas, T. (1992) 'From Closed to Open Communication Systems', in *Democracy and Civil Society in Eastern Europe*, ed. P. Lewis (London: Macmillan and New York: St Martin's Press) pp. 76–90.

Godin, E. and Chafer, T. (eds) (2006) *The French Exception* (Oxford: Berghahn Books).

Goede, M. de (2005) *Virtue, Fortune and Faith: A Genealogy of Finance* (Minneapolis, MA: University of Minnesota Press).

Golder, S. (2006) 'Pre-Election Coalition Formation in Parliamentary Democracies', *British Journal of Political Science* (36) 193–212.

Goldsmith, J. and Wu, T. (2006) *Who Controls the Internet? Illusions of a Borderless World* (New York and Oxford: Oxford University Press).

Goldstone, J. (1991) 'An Analytical Framework', in *Revolutions of the Late Twentieth Century*, ed. J. Goldstone, T. Gurr and F. Moshiri (Boulder, CO and Oxford: Westview) pp. 37–51.

Gong, T. (2002) 'Dangerous Collusion: Corruption as a Collective Venture in Contemporary China', *Communist and Postsocialist Studies* (35) 85–103.

Goodin, R. and Klingemann, H.-D. (1996) 'Politics Science: The Discipline' in *A New Handbook of Political Science*, ed. R. Goodin and H.-D. Klingemann (Oxford and New York: Oxford University Press) pp. 3–49.

Goodwin, J. and Jasper, J. (2003) 'Editors' Introduction', in *The Social Movements Reader: Cases and Concepts*, ed. J. Goodwin and J. Jasper (Malden, MA and Oxford: Blackwell) pp. 3–7.

Gordon, S. (2005) *Campaign Contributions and Legislative Voting: A New Approach* (London and New York: Routledge).

Gott, R. (2005) *Hugo Chávez and the Bolivarian Revolution* (London and New York: Verso).

Gould, D. (1980) 'Patrons and Clients: The Role of the Military in Zaire Politics', in *The Performance of Soldiers as Governors*, ed. I. Mowoe (Washington, DC: University Press of America) pp. 473–92.

Graber, D. (2005) *Mass Media and American Politics*, 7th edn (Washington, DC: CQ Press).

Green, D. (2002a) 'Constructivist Comparative Politics: Foundations and Framework', in *Constructivism and Comparative Politics*, ed. D. Green (Armonk, NY and London: M.E. Sharpe) pp. 3–59.

Green, D. (ed.) (2002b) *Constructivism and Comparative Politics* (Armonk, NY and London: M.E. Sharpe).

Green, D. and Shapiro, I. (1994) *Pathologies of Rational Choice Theory: A Critique of Applications in Political Science* (New Haven, CT: Yale University Press).

Greenwood, J. (2007) *Interest Representation in the European Union*, 2nd edn (Basingstoke and New York: Palgrave Macmillan).

Gregorian, V. (2004) *Islam: A Mosaic, Not a Monolith* (Washington, DC: Brookings Institution Press).

Griffiths, J. (1986), 'What is Legal Pluralism?', *Journal of Legal Pluralism* (24) 1–55.

Grugel, J. (2002) *Democratization: A Critical Introduction* (Basingstoke: Palgrave Macmillan).

Gualmini, E. (2008) 'Restructuring Weberian Bureaucracy: Comparing Managerial Reforms in Europe and the United States', *Public Administration* (86) 75–94.

Guarnieri, C. (2003) 'Courts as an Instrument of Horizontal Accountability: The Case of Latin Europe', in *Democracy and the Rule of Law*, ed. J. Maravall and A. Przeworski (Cambridge and New York: Cambridge University Press) pp. 223–41.

Guarnieri, C. and Pederzoli, P. (2002) *The Power of Judges: A Comparative Study of Courts and Democracy*, trans. C. Thomas (Oxford and New York: Oxford University Press).

Guehenno, J.-M. (1995) *The End of the Nation-State* (Minneapolis, MN and London: University of Minnesota Press).

Guevara, A. (2005) *Chávez, Venezuela and the New Latin America: An Interview with Hugo Chávez* (Melbourne and New York: Ocean Press).

Guo, G. (2007) 'Organizational Involvement and Political Participation in China', *Comparative Political Studies* (40) 457–82.

Gunlicks, A. (2003) *The Länder and German Federalism* (Manchester and New York: Manchester University Press).

Gunther, R. and Montero, J. (2009) *The Politics of Spain* (Cambridge and New York: Cambridge University Press).

Gunther, P. and Mughan, A. (eds) (2000) *Democracy and the Media: A Comparative Perspective* (Cambridge and New York: Cambridge University Press).

Gunther, R., Montero, J. and Botella, J. (2004) *Democracy in Modern Spain* (New Haven, CT and London: Yale University Press).

Gunther, R., Montero, J. and Linz, J. (eds) (2002) *Political Parties: Old Concepts and New Challenges* (Oxford and New York: Oxford University Press).

Gurr, T. (1980) *Why Men Rebel* (Princeton, NJ: Princeton University Press).

Guthrie, J. (2008) 'Trader Who Won a Green Gamble', *Financial Times*, 19 November, p. 18.

H

Habermas, J. (1975) *Legitimation Crisis* (Boston, MA: Beacon Press).

Habermas, J. (1978) *Knowledge and Human Interests*, 2nd edn, trans. J. Shapiro (London: Heinemann Education).

Hadenius, A. and Teorell, J. (2007) 'Pathways from Authoritarianism', *Journal of Democracy* (18) 143–56.

Hagopian, F. and Mainwaring, S. (eds) (2005) *The Third Wave of Democratization in Latin America: Advances and Setbacks* (New York and Cambridge: Cambridge University Press).

Hahn, G. (2006) 'Reforming the Federation', in *Developments in Russian Politics 6*, ed. S White, Z. Gitelman and R. Sakwa (Basingstoke and New York: Palgrave Macmillan) pp. 148–67.

Hall, D. (2005) *Administrative Law: Bureaucracy in a Democracy,* 3rd edn (Upper Saddle River, NJ: Prentice Hall).

Hall, P. (ed.) (1989) *The Political Power of Economic Ideas: Keynesianism across Nations* (Princeton, NJ: Princeton University Press).

Hall, P. and Soskice, D. (2001) 'An Introduction to Varieties of Capitalism', in *Varieties of Capitalism: The Institutional Foundations of Comparative Advantage,* ed. P. Hall and D. Soskice (Oxford and New York: Oxford University Press) pp. 11–70.

Hall, P. and Thelen, K. (2008) 'Institutional Change in Varieties of Capitalism', *Socio-Economic Review,* Advance Access, http://ser.oxfordjournals.org, accessed 31 July 2009.

Hallin, D. and Mancini, P. (2004) *Comparing Media Systems: Three Models of Media and Politics* (Cambridge and New York: Cambridge University Press).

Hamilton, A. (1788a) [1970 edn] *The Federalist,* No. 70, intro W. Brock (London: Dent and New York: Dutton) pp. 357–63.

Hamilton, A. (1788b) [1970 edn] *The Federalist,* No. 84, intro W. Brock (London: Dent and New York: Dutton) pp. 436–45.

Hamilton, A. (1788c) [1970 edn] *The Federalist,* No. 45, intro W. Brock (London: Dent and New York: Dutton) pp. 233–8.

Hamilton, A. (1788d) [1970 edn] *The Federalist,* No. 51, intro W. Brock (London: Dent and New York: Dutton) pp. 263–7.

Hamilton, A. (1788e) [1970 edn] *The Federalist,* No. 62, intro W. Brock (London: Dent and New York: Dutton) pp. 314–20.

Hamilton, A. (1788f) [1970 edn] *The Federalist,* No. 69, intro W. Brock (London: Dent and New York: Dutton) pp. 350–6.

Hamilton, R. (1987) 'The Elements of the Concept of Ideology', *Political Studies* (35) 18–38.

Hancké, B., Rhodes, M. and Thatcher, M. (eds) (2008) *Beyond Varieties of Capitalism: Conflict, Contradictions and Complementarities in the European Economy* (Oxford and New York: Oxford University Press).

Handler, H., Koebel, B., Reiss, P. and Schratzenstaller, M. (2005) *The Size and Performance of Public Sector Activities in Europe,* Internet Documents in Economics Access Service, http://ideas. repec.org, accessed 23 June 2009.

Hansen, M. (1991) *The Athenian Democracy in the Age of Demosthenes* (Oxford and Cambridge, MA: Blackwell).

Hare, T. (1873) *The Election of Representatives, Parliamentary and Municipal,* 4th edn (London: Longmans, Green, Reader & Dyer).

Hartlyn, J. (1998) 'The Trujillo Regime in the Dominican Republic', in *Sultanistic Regimes,* ed. H. Chehabi and J. Linz (Baltimore, MD and London: Johns Hopkins University Press) pp. 85–112.

Hartz, L. (1955) *The Liberal Tradition in America* (New York: Harcourt, Brace).

Hatzfeld, J. (2005) *A Time for Machetes: The Rwandan Genocide – The Killers Speak* (London: Serpent's Tail).

Hay, C. (2002) *Political Analysis: A Critical Introduction* (Basingstoke and New York: Palgrave).

Hay, C. (2007) *Why We Hate Politics* (Cambridge and Malden, MA: Polity).

Hay, C., Lister, M. and Marsh, D. (2005) *The State: Theories and Issues* (Basingstoke and New York: Palgrave Macmillan).

Hayward, J. (1994) 'Ideological Change: The Exhaustion of the Revolutionary Impulse', in *Developments in French Politics,* ed. R. Hall, J. Hayward and H. Machin (Basingstoke: Macmillan) pp. 15–32.

Hayward, J. (2004) 'Parliament and the French Government's Domination of the Legislative Process', *Journal of Legislative Studies* (10) 79–97.

Hayward, J. and Wright, V. (2002) *Governing from the Centre: Core Executive Coordination in France* (Oxford and New York: Oxford University Press).

Hazan, R. (2002) 'Candidate Selection', in *Comparing Democracies 2: New Challenges in the Study of Elections and Voting,* ed. L. LeDuc, R. Niemi and P. Norris (London and Thousand Oaks, CA: Sage) pp. 108–26.

Heady, F. (2001) *Public Administration: A Comparative Perspective,* 6th edn (New York: Marcel Dekker).

Heclo, H. (1974) *Modern Social Policies in Britain and Sweden* (New Haven, CT and London: Yale University Press).

Heclo, H. (1978) 'Issue Networks and the Executive Establishment', in *The New American Political System,* ed. A. King (Washington, DC: American Enterprise Institute) pp. 87–124.

Heidar, K. (ed.) (2004) *Nordic Politics: Comparative Perspectives* (Oslo: Universitetsforlaget)

Heilbroner, R. (1953) [2000 edn] *The Worldly Philosophers: The Lives, Times and Ideas of the Great Economic Thinkers,* 7th edn (London and New York: Penguin).

Held, D. (2004) *Global Covenant: The Social Democratic Alternative to the Washington Consensus* (Cambridge and Malden, MA: Polity).

Held, D. (2006) *Models of Democracy,* 3rd edn (Cambridge: Polity).

Hellinger, D. (2003) 'Political Overview: The Breakdown of *Puntofijismo* and the Rise of *Chavismo*', in *Venezuelan Politics in the Chávez Era: Class, Polarization and Conflict,* ed. S. Ellner and D. Hellinger (Boulder, CO and London: Lynne Rienner), pp. 27–54.

Helms, D. (ed.) (2000) *Institutions and Institutional Change in the Federal Republic of Germany* (Basingstoke: Palgrave).

Helms, L. (2005) *Presidents, Prime Ministers and Chancellors: Executive Leadership in Western Democracies* (Basingstoke and New York: Palgrave Macmillan).

Her Majesty's Court Service (2005) *The Administrative Court,* http://www.hmcourtsservice.gov.uk/cms/admin.htm, accessed 5 August 2006.

Herb, M. (1999) *All in the Family: Absolutism, Revolution and Democracy in the Middle Eastern Monarchies* (Albany, NY: State University of New York Press).

Herb, M. (2005) 'Princes, Parliaments, and the Prospects for Democracy in the Gulf', in *Authoritarianism in the Middle East,* ed. M. Posusney and M. Angrist (Lynne Rienner: Boulder, CO and Oxford) pp. 169–92.

Herbst, J. (2001) 'Political Liberalization in Africa after 10 Years', *Comparative Politics* (33) 357–75.

Herbst, J. (2004) 'Let Them Fail: State Failure in Theory and Practice', in *When States Fail: Causes and Consequences,* ed. R. Rotberg (Princeton, NJ: Princeton University Press) pp. 302–18.

Herbst, S. (1998) *Reading Public Opinion: How Political Actors View The Political Process* (Chicago and London: University of Chicago Press).

Hershberg, E. (2006) 'Technocrats, Citizens and Second-Generation Reforms: Colombia's Andean Malaise', in *State and Society in Conflict: Comparative Perspectives on the Andean Crisis,* ed. P. Drake and E. Hershberg (Pittsburgh, PA: University of Pittsburgh Press) pp. 134–56.

Hetherington, M. (2004) *Why Trust Matters: Declining Political Trust and the Demise of Political Liberalism* (Princeton, NJ: Princeton University Press).

Heywood, A. (2007) *Political Ideologies: An Introduction,* 4th edn (Basingstoke and New York: Palgrave Macmillan).

Heywood, P. (1995) *The Government and Politics of Spain* (Basingstoke: Macmillan).

Hill, L. (2002) 'On the Rightness of Compelling Citizens to "Vote": The Australian Case', *Political Studies* (50) 80–101.

Hill, M. and Hupe, P. (2002) *Implementing Public Policy: Governance in Theory and Practice* (London and Thousand Oaks, CA: Sage).

Hindmoor, A. (forthcoming) 'Rational Choice' in *Theory and Methods in Political Science,* 3rd edn, ed. D. Marsh and G. Stoker (Basingstoke and New York: Palgrave Macmillan).

Hirschl, R. (2002) 'The Political Origins of Judicial Empowerment through Constitutionalization: Lessons from Israel's Constitutional Review', *Comparative Politics* (33) 315–35.

Hite, K. and Cesarini, P. (eds) (2004) *Authoritarian Legacies and Democracies in Latin America and Southern Europe* (Notre Dame, IN: University of Notre Dame Press).

Hix, S. (2005) *The Political System of the European Union,* 2nd edn (Basingstoke: Palgrave Macmillan).

Hobbes, T. (1651) [1968 edn] *Leviathan,* ed. M. Oakeshott (Toronto: Crowell-Collier).

Holland, K. (1991) 'Introduction', in *Judicial Activism in Comparative Perspective,* ed. K. Holland (Basingstoke: Macmillan) pp. 1–11.

Holmes, L. (1997) *Postcommunism: An Introduction* (Cambridge and Malden, MA: Polity).

Hood, C. (1996) 'Exploring Variations in Public Management Reform in the 1990s', in *Civil Service Systems in Comparative Perspective,* ed. H. Bekke, J. Perry and T. Toonen (Bloomington, IN: Indiana University Press) pp. 268–87.

Hood, C., James, O., Scott, C., Jones, G. and Travers, T. (1999) *Regulation inside Government: Waste-Watchers, Quality Police and Sleaze-Busters* (Oxford and New York: Oxford University Press).

Hood, C., Rothstein, H. and Baldwin, R. (2004) *The Government of Risk: Understanding Risk Regulation Regimes* (New York and Oxford: Oxford University Press).

Hooghe, L. and Marks, G. (2001) *Multilevel Governance and European Integration* (Lanham, MD: Rowman & Littlefield).

Horiuchi, Y. (2004) *Institutions, Incentives and Electoral Participation in Japan: Cross-Level and Cross-National Perspectives* (London and New York: Routledge).

Horowitz, D. (2002) 'Constitutional Design: Proposals versus Processes', in *The Architecture of Democracy: Constitutional Design, Conflict Management and Democracy* (Oxford and New York: Oxford University Press) pp. 15–36.

Horowitz, D. (2006) 'Constitutional Courts: Primer for Decision-Makers', *Journal of Democracy* (17) 125–37.

House of Commons Information Office (2008) *The Vote Bundle,* http://www.parliament.uk/parliamentary_publications_and_archives/factsheets/p16.cfm, accessed 1 December 2009.

Howe, H. (2001) *Ambiguous Order: Military Forces in African States* (Boulder, CO and London: Lynne Rienner).

Hrebenar, R. (1997) *Interest Group Politics in America,* 3rd edn (Englewood Cliffs, NJ: Prentice Hall).

Hueglin, T. and Fenna, A. (2006) *Comparative Federalism: A Systematic Inquiry* (Peterborough, Ontario: Broadview Press).

Hughes, C. (1916) *Addresses of Charles Evans Hughes* (New York: Putnam's).

Hull, A. (1999) 'Comparative Political Science: An Inventory and Assessment since the 1980s', *Political Science and Politics* (32) 117–24.

Huntington, S. (1968) *Political Order in Changing Societies* (New Haven, CT and London: Yale University Press).

Huntington, S. (1970) 'Social and Institutional Dynamics of One-Party Systems', in *Authoritarian Politics in Modern Society: The Dynamics of Established One-Party Systems,* ed. S. Huntington and C. Moore (New York and London: Basic Books) pp. 3–47.

Huntington, S. (1991) *The Third Wave: Democratization in the Late Twentieth Century* (Norman, OK and London: University of Oklahoma Press).

Huntington, S. (1993) 'Clash of Civilizations', *Foreign Affairs* (72) 22–49.

Huntington, S. (1996) *The Clash of Civilizations and the Making of World Order* (New York: Simon & Schuster).

Huntington, S. (2004) *Who Are We? America's Great Debate* (New York: Free Press).

Huntington, S. and Nelson, J. (1976) *No Easy Choice: Political Participation in Developing Countries* (Cambridge, MA: Harvard University Press).

Hutter, B. (2005) 'Risk Management and Governance', in *Designing Government: From Instruments to Governance,* ed. P. Eliadis, M. Hill and M. Howlett (Montreal and London: McGill-Queen's University Press) pp. 303–21.

Hutton, W. (2006) *The Writing on the Wall: China and the West in the 21st Century* (Boston, MA: Little, Brown).

Hyden, G. (1997) 'Democratization and Administration', in *Democracy's Victory and Crisis,* ed. A. Hadenius (Cambridge and New York: Cambridge University Press) pp. 242–62.

Hyden, G. (2006) *African Politics in Comparative Perspective* (Cambridge and New York: Cambridge University Press).

I

Ibarra, R (2003) *Social Movements and Democracy* (London: Palgrave Macmillan).

IDEA (International Institute for Democracy and Electoral Assistance) (2006) *Engaging the Electorate: Initiatives to Promote Voter Turnout From Around the World,* http://www.idea.int/publications/vt_ee/index.cfm, accessed 13 June 2006.

IDEA (International Institute for Democracy and Electoral Assistance) (2008) *Direct Democracy,* http://www.idea.int, accessed 17 April 2009.

Ignatieff, M. (2002) 'Intervention and State Failure', *Dissent* (49) 114–23.

Ignazi, P. (2006) *Extreme Right Parties in Western Europe* (Oxford and New York: Oxford University Press).

Ilonski, G. and Edinger, M. (2007) 'MPs in Post-Communist and Post-Soviet Nations: A Parliamentary Elite in the Making', *Journal of Legislative Studies* (13) 142–63.

Immigrant Voting Project (2009) *Current Immigrant Voting Rights*, http://www.immigrantvoting.org, accessed 27 September 2009.

Inglehart, R. (1971) 'The Silent Revolution in Europe: Intergenerational Change in Post-Industrial Societies', *American Political Science Review* (65) 991–1017.

Inglehart, R. (1990) *Culture Shift in Advanced Industrial Society* (Princeton, NJ: Princeton University Press).

Inglehart, R. (1997) *Modernization and Postmodernization: Cultural, Economic and Social Change in 43 Societies* (Princeton, NJ and London: Princeton University Press).

Inglehart, R. (1999) 'Postmodernization Erodes Respect for Authority, but Increases Support for Democracy', in *Critical Citizens: Global Support for Democratic Governance*, ed. P. Norris (Oxford and New York: Oxford University Press) pp. 236–56.

Inglehart, R. (2000) 'Political Culture and Democratic Institutions', paper prepared for the *Annual Conference of the American Political Science Association*, Washington, DC.

Inoguchi, T. (2002) 'Broadening the Basis of Political Capital in Japan', in *Democracies in Flux: The Evolution of Social Capital in Contemporary Society*, ed. R. Putnam (Oxford and New York: Oxford University Press) pp. 359–92.

Institute for Comparative Social Research (2003) *Future of Democracy in Russia in the Hands of Silent Majority*, http://www.ru/print.php?id=541, accessed 13 December 2006.

Internet Society of China (2002) *Public Pledge of Self-Regulation and Professional Ethics for the Chinese Internet Industry*, http://www.isc.org.cn/20020417/ca102762.htm, accessed 30 April 2006.

Internet World Stats (2009) *Internet Usage Stats: The Big Picture*, http://www.internetworldstats.com/stats.htm, accessed 24 April 2009.

Ipsos-Mori (2008) *Hansard Society: Audit of Political Engagement 6*, http://www.ipsos-mori.com/_assets/politicaltrends/pdf/ape-6-topline.pdf, accessed 7 April 2009.

IPU (Inter-Parliamentary Union) (2009a) *Women in National Parliaments*, http://www.ipu.org/wmn-e/classif.htm, accessed 7 September 2009.

IPU (Inter-Parliamentary Union) (2009b) *Parline Database on National Parliaments*, http://www.ipu.org/parline-e/parline-search.asp, accessed 22 November 2009.

IPU (Inter-Parliamentary Union) (2009c) *Denmark: Last Elections*, http://www.ipu.org/parline-e/reports/2087_E.htm, accessed 28 November 2009.

IPU (Inter-Parliamentary Union) (2009d) *Parliaments at a Glance*, http://www.ipu.org/parline-e, accessed 30 November 2009.

Ivaldi, G. (2006) 'Beyond France's 2005 Referendum on the European Constitutional Treaty', *West European Politics* (29) 47–69.

Iyengar, S., Peters, M. and Kinder, D. (1982) 'Experimental Demonstrations of the "Not-So-Minimal" Consequences of Television News Programs', *American Political Science Review* (76) 848–58.

J

Jackson, K. (1994) 'Stability and Renewal: Incumbency and Parliamentary Composition', in *The Victorious Incumbent:*

A Threat to Democracy? ed. A. Somit, R. Wildenmann and B. Boll (Aldershot and Brookfield, VT: Dartmouth) pp. 251–77.

Jackson, R. (1990) *Quasi-states: Sovereignty, International Relations and the Third World* (Cambridge and New York: Cambridge University Press).

Jackson, R. (2007) 'Sovereignty and its Presuppositions: Before 9/11 and After', *Political Studies* (55) 297–317.

Jackson, R. and Rosberg, C. (1982) *Personal Rule in Black Africa: Prince, Autocrat, Prophet, Tyrant* (Berkeley, CA: University of California Press).

Jamieson, K. and Waldman, P. (2003) *The Press Effect: Politicians, Journalists and the Stories that Shape the Political World* (Oxford and New York: Oxford University Press).

Janis, I. (1982) *Groupthink: Psychological Studies of Policy Decisions and Fiascoes*, 2nd edn (Boston, MA: Houghton Mifflin).

Jasiewicz, K. (2003) 'Elections and Voting Behaviour', in *Developments in Central and East European Politics 3*, ed. S. White, J. Batt and P. Lewis (Basingstoke and New York: Palgrave Macmillan) pp. 173–89.

Jayanntha, D. (1991) *Electoral Allegiance in Sri Lanka* (Cambridge and New York: Cambridge University Press).

John, P. (2001) *Local Governance in Western Europe* (London and Thousand Oaks, CA: Sage).

Johnson, C. (1995) *Japan: Who Governs? The Rise of the Developmental State* (New York and London: Norton).

Johnson, D. (2003) 'A Tale of Two Systems: Prosecuting Corruption in Japan and Italy', in *The State of Civil Society in Japan*, ed. F. Schwartz and S. Pharr (Cambridge and New York: Cambridge University Press) pp. 257–80.

Johnson, D. (ed.) (2009) *Campaigning for President: Strategy and Tactics, New Voices and New Techniques* (London and New York: Routledge).

Johnson, J. (2001) 'Path Contingency in Postcommunist Transformations', *Comparative Politics* (33) 253–74.

Jones, C. (1994) *The Presidency in a Separated System* (Washington, DC: Brookings Institution).

Jones, J. (2005) *Entertaining Politics: New Political Television and Civic Culture* (Lanham, MD: Rowman & Littlefield).

Jones, M. (1995a) 'A Guide to the Electoral Systems of the Americas', *Electoral Studies* (14) 5–21.

Jones, M. (1995b) *Electoral Laws and the Survival of Presidential Democracies* (Notre Dame, IN: University of Notre Dame Press).

Jordan, A., Wurzel, R. and Zito, A. (2005) 'The Rise of "New" Policy Instruments in Comparative Perspective: Has Governance Eclipsed Government?' *Political Studies* (53) 477–96.

Joyce, P. (2002) *The Politics of Protest: Extra-Parliamentary Politics in Britain since 1970* (London: Palgrave Macmillan).

Judge, D. and Earnshaw, D. (2003) *The European Parliament* (Basingstoke and New York: Palgrave Macmillan).

Jungar, A. C. (2002) 'A Case of a Surplus Majority Government: The Finnish Rainbow Coalition', *Scandinavian Political Studies* (25) 57–83.

K

Kahlberg, S. (ed.) (2005) *Max Weber: Readings and Commentary on Modernity* (Malden, MA and Oxford: Blackwell).

Karmis, D. and Norman, W. (eds) (2005) *Theories of Federalism: A Reader* (New York and Basingstoke: Palgrave Macmillan).

Karp, J. and Banducci, S. (2008) 'Political Efficacy and Participation in 27 Democracies: How Electoral Systems Shape Political Behaviour', *British Journal of Political Science* (38) 311–44.

Karp, J., Banducci, S. and Bowler, S. (2007) 'Getting Out the Vote: Party Mobilization in a Comparative Perspective', *British Journal of Political Science* (2007) 91–112.

Katz, R. (1997) *Democracy and Elections* (Oxford and New York: Oxford University Press).

Katz, R. and Crotty, W. (eds) (2006) *Handbook of Party Politics* (London and Thousand Oaks, CA: Sage).

Katz, R. and Mair, P. (1995) 'Changing Models of Party Organization and Party Democracy: The Emergence of the Cartel Party', *Party Politics* (1) 5–28.

Kavalski, E. and Zolkos, M. (eds) (2008) *Defunct Federalisms: Critical Perspectives on Federal Failure* (London and New York: Routledge).

Kavanagh, D. and Butler, D. (2005) *The British General Election of 2005* (Basingstoke and New York: Palgrave Macmillan).

Kawabata, E. (2007) *Contemporary Government Reform in Japan* (London and New York: Palgrave Macmillan).

Keating, M. (2008) '30 Years of Territorial Politics', *West European Politics* (31) 60–81.

Kegley, C. and Blanton, S. (2009) *World Politics: Trends and Transformations*, 12th edn (Belmont, CA: Wadsworth).

Keitetsi, C. (2004) *Child Soldier* (London: Souvenir Press).

Kelly, R. (2003) 'Not as Daft as You Thought', *New Statesman*, 2 June, http://www.newstatesman.com/200306020008, accessed 1 September 2009.

Kernell, S. (1997) *Going Public: New Strategies of Presidential Leadership*, 3rd edn (Washington, DC: CQ Press).

Kerrouche, F. (2006) 'The French *Assemblée Nationale*: The Case of a Weak Legislature', *Journal of Legislative Studies* (12) 336–65.

Keshavarzian, A. (2005) 'Contestation without Democracy: Elite Fragmentation in Iran', in *Authoritarianism in the Middle East: Regimes and Resistance,* ed. M. Posusney and M. Angrist (Boulder, CO and London: Lynne Rienner) pp. 63–90.

Keynes, J. (1936) *The General Theory of Employment, Interest and Money* (London: Macmillan).

Khadiagala, G. (1995) 'State Collapse and Reconstruction in Uganda', in *Collapsed States: The Disintegration and Restoration of Legitimate Authority,* ed. W. Zartman (Boulder, CO and London: Lynne Rienner) pp. 33–47.

Khatchadourian, A. (2004) 'The Terror at Jaslyk', *The Nation* (web only), http://www.thenation.com/doc/20040426/khatchadourian, accessed 1 April 2006.

King, A. (1994) 'Ministerial Autonomy in Britain', in *Cabinet Ministers and Parliamentary Government,* ed. M. Laver and K. Shepsle (Cambridge and New York: Cambridge University Press) pp. 203–25.

King, A. (ed.) (2002) *Leaders' Personalities and the Outcomes of Democratic Elections* (Oxford and New York: Oxford University Press).

King, A. (2009) *The British Constitution* (Oxford and New York: Oxford University Press).

King, G., Keohane, R. and Verba S. (1994) *Designing Social Inquiry: Scientific Inference in Qualitative Research* (Princeton, NJ: Princeton University Press).

King, S. (2007) 'Sustaining Authoritarianism in the Middle East and North Africa', *Political Science Quarterly* (122) 433–60.

Kingdon, J. (2003) *Agendas, Alternatives and Public Policy*, 2nd edn (New York: Longman).

Kingsley, J. (1944) *Representative Bureaucracy* (Yellow Springs, OH: Antioch).

Kirchheimer, O. (1966) 'The Transformation of the Western European Party Systems', in *Political Parties and Political Development,* ed. J. LaPalombara and M. Weiner (Princeton, NJ: Princeton University Press) pp. 177–200.

Kirsche, L. (2007) 'Semi-Presidentialism and the Perils of Power-Sharing in Neopatrimonial Regimes', *Comparative Political Studies* (40) 372–94.

Kitschelt, H. (2007) 'Growth and Persistence of the Radical Right in Post-Industrial Democracies: Advances and Challenges in Comparative Research', *West European Politics* (30) 1176–1206.

Kitschelt, H., Manfeldova, Z., Markowski, R. and Toka, G. (1999) *Postcommunist Party Systems: Competition, Representation and Inter-Party Competition* (Cambridge and New York: Cambridge University Press).

Kjær, A. (2004) *Governance* (Cambridge: Polity).

Klapper, J. (1960) *The Effects of Mass Communication* (New York and London: Free Press).

Kleinfeld, R. (2006) 'Competing Definitions of the Rule of Law', in *Promoting the Rule of Law Abroad: In Search of Knowledge,* ed. T. Carothers (Washington, DC: Carnegie Endowment for International Peace) pp. 31–74.

Klijn, E.-H. and Skelcher, C. (2007) 'Democracy and Governance Networks: Compatible or Not?', *Public Administration* (85) 587–608.

Knapp, A. and Wright, V. (2006) *The Government and Politics of France,* 5th edn (London and New York: Routledge).

Knutsen, O. (1996) 'Value Orientations and Party Choice: A Comparative Study of the Relationship between Five Value Orientations and Voting Intention in Thirteen West European Democracies', in *Wahlen und Politische Einstellungen in Westlichen Demokratien,* ed. O. Gabriel and W. Falter (Frankfurt: Peter Lang) pp. 247–319.

Kobach, K. (1997) 'Direct Democracy and Swiss Isolationism', *West European Politics* (20) 185–211.

Koepk, P. (2005) 'Social Market and Sad', *Atlantic Monthly*, http://www.atlantic-times.com/archive_detail.php?record ID=098, accessed 15 July 2009.

Kolinsky, E. (2002) 'Party Governance, Political Culture and the Transformation of East Germany since 1990', in *Continuity and Change in German Politics: Beyond the Politics of Centrality? A Festschrift for Gordon Smith,* ed. S. Padgett and T. Poguntke (London and Portland, OR: Cass) pp. 169–83.

Kommers, D. (2006) 'The Federal Constitutional Court: Guardian of German Democracy', *Annals of the American Academy of Political and Social Science* (603) 111–28.

Kopecky, P. (2006) 'Political Parties and the State in Post-Communist Europe: The Nature of Symbiosis', *Journal of Communist Studies and Transition Politics* (22) 251–73.

Kornhauser, W. (1959) *The Politics of Mass Society* (Glencoe, IL: Free Press).

Korosteleva, E. (2004) 'The Quality of Democracy in Belarus and Ukraine', *Journal of Communist and Transition Politics* (20) 122–42.

Kostadinova, T. (2002) 'Do Mixed Electoral Systems Matter? A Cross-National Comparison of Their Effects in Eastern Europe', *Electoral Studies* (21) 23–34.

Kramnick, I. (1987) 'Editor's Introduction', in J. Madison, A. Hamilton and J. Jay, *The Federalist Papers* (London: Penguin) pp. 11–81.

Krook, M. (2007) 'Candidate Gender Quotas: A Framework for Analysis', *European Journal of Political Research* (46) 367–94.

Krouwel, A. (2003) 'Otto Kirchheimer and the Catch-All Party', *West European Politics* (26) 23–40.

Krueger, R. and Casey, M. (2000) *Focus Groups: A Practical Guide for Applied Research,* 3rd edn (Thousand Oaks, CA and London: Sage).

Kudrle, R. and Marmor, T. (1981) 'The Development of Welfare States in North America', in *The Development of Welfare States in Europe and America,* ed. P. Flora and A. Heidenheimer (New Brunswick, NJ and London: Transaction) pp. 187–236.

Kühn, Z. (2006) 'The Judicialization of European Politics', in *Developments in European Politics,* ed. P. Heywood, E. Jones, M. Rhodes and U. Sedelmeier (Basingstoke and New York: Palgrave Macmillan) pp. 216–36.

Kuhnhenn, J. (2009) 'US Financial Market Bailout Tab Hits $4.7 Trillion', *Associated Press,* http://www.google.com/hosted news/ap/article, accessed 22 July 2009.

Kulik, A. (2007) 'Russia's Political Parties: Deep in the Shadow of the President' in *When Parties Prosper: The Uses of Electoral Success,* ed. K. Lawson and P. Merkl (Boulder, CO: Lynne Rienner) pp. 27–42.

L

Lakatos, I. (1978) *The Methodology of Scientific Research Programmes: Philosophical Papers* Vol. 1, ed. J. Worrall and G. Curie (Cambridge and New York: Cambridge University Press).

Landes, R. (1998) *The Canadian Polity: A Comparative Introduction,* 5th edn (Scarborough, Ontario: Prentice Hall Canada).

Landes, R. (2002) *The Canadian Polity: A Comparative Introduction,* 6th edn (Scarborough, Ontario: Prentice Hall Canada).

Langer, A. (2006) 'A Historical Exploration of the Personalisation of Politics in the Media: The British Prime Ministers, 1945–1999', paper delivered to the *56th Annual Conference of the Political Studies Association,* Reading, England.

Langman, L. (2006) 'The Social Psychology of Nationalism', in *The Sage Handbook of Nations and Nationalism,* ed. G. Delanty and K. Kumar (London: Sage) pp. 71–83.

LaPalombara, J. (1974) *Politics within Nations* (Englewood Cliffs, NJ: Prentice Hall).

Lasswell, H. (1936) *Politics: Who Gets What, When, How?* (New York: McGraw Hill).

Latouche, S. (1996) *The Westernization of the World* (Cambridge and Cambridge, MA: Polity).

Laver, M. (1983) *Invitation to Politics* (Oxford: Martin Robertson).

Laver, M. and Schofield, N. (1998) *Multiparty Government: The Politics of Coalition in Europe* (Ann Arbor, MI: University of Michigan Press).

Law Commission (2006) *Custom and Human Rights in the Pacific,* http://www.lawcom.govt.nz/, accessed 12 October 2009.

Lawson, C. (2004) 'Fox's Mexico at Mid-term', *Journal of Democracy* (15) 139–53.

Lawson, K. (2001) 'Political Parties and Party Competition', in *The Oxford Companion to Politics of the World,* 2nd edn, ed. J. Krieger (Oxford and New York: Oxford University Press) pp. 670–3.

Lazarsfeld, P. and Merton, R. (1948) [1996 edn] 'Mass Communication, Popular Taste and Organized Social Action', in *Media Studies: A Reader,* ed. P. Marris and S. Thornham (Edinburgh: Edinburgh University Press) pp. 14–24.

LeDuc, L., Niemi, R. and Norris, P. (eds) (2009) *Comparing Democracies 3: New Challenges in the Study of Elections and Voting* (Thousand Oaks, CA and London: Sage).

Le Galès, P. (2008) 'Territorial Politics in France' in *Developments in French Politics 4,* ed. A. Cole, P. Le Galès and J. Levy (Basingstoke and New York: Palgrave Macmillan) pp. 156–71.

Leib, E. (2004) *Deliberative Democracy in America: A Proposal for a Popular Branch of Government* (University Park, PA: Pennsylvania University Press).

Leites, N. (1960) *American Foreign Policy* (London: George Allen).

Lesch, A. (2004) 'Politics in Egypt', in *Comparative Politics Today: A World View,* 8th edn, ed. G. Almond, G. Bingham Powell, K. Strøm and R. Dalton (New York: Longman) pp. 581–632.

Lewin, L. (2004) 'Sweden: Introducing Proportional Representation from Above', in *Handbook of Electoral System Choice,* ed. J. Colomer (Basingstoke and New York: Palgrave Macmillan) pp. 265–78.

Lewin, L. (2006) *Ideology and Strategy: A Century of Swedish Politics* (Cambridge and New York: Cambridge University Press).

Lewin, M. (1997) 'Bureaucracy and the Stalinist State', in *Stalinism and Nazism: Dictatorships in Comparison,* ed. I. Kershaw and M. Lewin (Cambridge and New York: Cambridge University Press) pp. 53–74.

Lewis, D. (2002) 'The Politics of Agency Termination: Confronting the Myth of Agency Termination', *Journal of Politics* (64) 89–120.

Lewis, P. (2007) 'Political Parties', in *Developments in Central and East European Politics 4,* ed. S. White, J. Batt and P. Lewis (Basingstoke and New York: Palgrave Macmillan) pp. 174–92.

Lewis-Beck, M., Norpoth, H. and Jacoby, W. (2008) *The American Voter Revisited* (Ann Arbor, MI: University of Michigan Press).

Lichbach, M. (2009) 'Thinking and Working in the Midst of Things: Discovery, Explanation and Evidence in Comparative Politics' in *Comparative Politics: Rationality, Culture and Structure,* 2nd edn, ed. M. Lichbach and A. Zuckerman (Cambridge and New York: Cambridge University Press) pp. 18–71.

Lichbach, M. and Zuckerman, A. (eds) (2009) *Comparative Politics: Rationality, Culture and Structure,* 2nd edn (Cambridge and New York: Cambridge University Press).

Lieberman, E. (2005) 'Nested Analysis as Mixed-Method Strategy for Comparative Research', *American Political Science Review* (99) 435–52.

Liebman, B. (2007) 'China's Courts: Restricted Reform', *China Quarterly* (191) 620–38.

Lijphart, A. (1968) *The Politics of Accommodation: Pluralism and Democracy in the Netherlands* (Berkeley, CA: University of California Press).

Lijphart, A. (1977) *Democracy in Plural Societies: A Comparative Exploration* (Berkeley, CA: University of California Press).

Lijphart, A. (ed.) (1992) *Parliamentary versus Presidential Government* (Oxford and New York: Oxford University Press).

Lijphart, A. (1999) *Patterns of Democracy: Government Forms and Performance in Thirty Six Countries* (New Haven, CT and London: Yale University Press).

Lijphart, A. (2000) 'The Future of Democracy: Reasons for Pessimism but also Some Optimism', *Scandinavian Political Studies* (23) 265–72.

Lijphart, A. (2002) 'The Evolution of Consociational Theory and Consociational Practices, 1965–2000', *Acta Politica* (37) 11–20.

Lindblom, C. (1959) 'The Science of Muddling Through', *Public Administration* (19) 78–88.

Lindblom, C. (1977) *Politics and Markets* (New York: Basic Books).

Lindblom, C. (1979) 'Still Muddling, Not Yet Through', *Public Administration Review* (39) 517–26.

Lindblom, C. (1990) *Inquiry and Change: The Troubled Attempt to Understand and Shape Society* (New Haven, CT and London: Yale University Press).

Lindvall, J. and Rothstein, B. (2006) 'Sweden: The Fall of the Strong State', *Scandinavian Political Studies* (29) 47–63.

Linz, J. (1975) [2000 edn] *Totalitarian and Authoritarian Regimes* (Boulder, CO and London: Lynne Rienner).

Linz, J. and Valenzuela, A. (eds) (1994) *The Failure of Presidential Democracy* (Baltimore, MD: Johns Hopkins University Press).

Lippman, W. (1922) *Public Opinion* (London: Allen & Unwin).

Lipset, S. (1960) [1983 edn] *Political Man* (New York: Basic Books).

Lipset, S. (1990) *Continental Divide: The Values and Institutions of the United States and Canada* (London and New York: Routledge).

Lipset, S. and Rokkan, S. (1967) 'Cleavage Structures, Party Systems and Voter Alignments', in *Party Systems and Voter Alignments*, ed. S. Lipset and S. Rokkan (New York and London: Free Press) pp. 1–65.

Listhaug, O. and Grønflaten, L. (2007) 'Civic Decline? Trends in Political Involvement in Norway, 1965–2001', *Scandinavian Political Studies* (30) 272–99.

Lively, J. (1991) 'Sièyes, Emmanuel Joseph', in *The Blackwell Encyclopaedia of Political Thought*, ed. D. Miller (Oxford and Cambridge, MA: Blackwell) pp. 475–6.

Locke, J. (1690) [1970 edn] *Two Treatises of Government*, ed. P. Laslett (Cambridge and New York: Cambridge University Press).

Loewenberg, G., Squire, P. and Kiewit, D. (eds) (2002) *Legislatures: Comparative Perspectives on Representative Assemblies* (Ann Arbor, MI: University of Michigan Press).

Longley, L. and Davidson, R. (eds) (1998) *The New Roles of Parliamentary Committees* (London: Frank Cass).

Loveland, I. (2004) *Constitutional Law, Administrative Law and Human Rights: A Critical Introduction*, 3rd edn (Oxford and New York: Oxford University Press).

Lowenstein, D. (2006) 'Legal Regulation and Protection of American Parties', in *Handbook of Party Politics*, ed. R. Katz and W. Crotty (London and Thousand Oaks, CA: Sage) pp. 456–70.

Lowi, T. (1969) *The End of Liberalism* (New York: Norton).

Lukes, S. (1974) [2005 edn] *Power: A Radical View*, 2nd edn (Basingstoke and New York: Palgrave Macmillan).

Lundell, K. (2009) *Electoral Systems in the Postwar Era* (London and New York: Routledge).

Lust-Okar, E. and Zerhouni, S. (eds) (2008) *Political Participation in the Middle East* (Boulder, CO: Lynne Rienner).

Lutz, D. (2007) *Principles of Constitutional Design* (Cambridge and New York: Cambridge University Press).

Lutz, J. and Lutz, B. (2004) *Global Terrorism* (London and New York: Routledge).

Lyon, D. (2003) *Surveillance after September 11* (Cambridge and Malden, MA: Polity).

M

Macedo, S., Berry, J., Alex-Assensoh, Y., Brintnall, M. and Campbell, D. (2005) *Democracy at Risk: How Political Choices Undermine Citizen Participation, and What We Can D About It* (Washington, DC: Brookings).

Mackenzie, G. and Labiner, J. (2002) *Opportunity Lost: The Rise and Fall of Trust and Confidence in Government After September 11* (Washington, DC: Center For Public Service, Brookings Institution), http://www.brookings.edu/gs/cps/oppotunityfinal.pdf, accessed 15 April 2006.

Mackenzie, W. (1958) *Free Elections: An Elementary Textbook* (London: Allen & Unwin).

Macpherson, C. (1977) *The Life and Times of Liberal Democracy* (Oxford and New York: Oxford University Press).

Maddex, R. (2007) *Constitutions of the World*, 3rd edn (Washington, DC and London: CQ Press).

Madison J. (1781) [1970 edn] 'The Federalist, No. 51', in *The Federalist or, The New Constitution*, intro. W. Brock (London: Dent and New York: Dutton) pp. 263–7.

Magone, J. (2008) *Contemporary Spanish Politics*, 2nd edn (London and New York: Routledge).

Magyar, K. (1992) 'Military Intervention and Withdrawal in Africa: Problems and Perspectives', in *From Military to Civilian Rule*, ed. C. Danopoulos (London and New York: Routledge) pp. 230–48.

Mahler, G. (2007) *Comparative Politics: An Institutional and Cross-National Approach*, 5th edn (Upper Saddle River, NJ: Pearson).

Mahoney, J. (2003) 'Knowledge Accumulation in Comparative Historical Research: The Case of Democracy and Authoritarianism' in *Comparative Historical Analysis in the Social Sciences*, ed. J. Mahoney and D. Rueschmeyer (Cambridge and New York: Cambridge University Press) pp. 337–72.

Mahoney, J. and Rueschmeyer D. (eds) (2003) *Comparative Historical Analysis in the Social Sciences* (Cambridge and New York: Cambridge University Press).

Mainwaring, S. (1992) 'Presidentialism in Latin America', in *Parliamentary versus Presidential Government*, ed. A. Lijphart (Oxford and New York: Oxford University Press) pp. 111–17.

Mainwaring, S. and Shugart, M. (eds) (1997) *Presidentialism and Democracy in Latin America* (Cambridge and New York: Cambridge University Press).

Mainwaring, S. and Welna, C. (eds) (2003) *Democratic Accountability in Latin America* (Oxford and New York: Oxford University Press).

Mair, P. (1994) 'Party Organizations: From Civil Society to the State', in *How Parties Organize: Change and Adaptation in Party Organizations in Western Democracies,* ed. R. Katz and P. Mair (Thousand Oaks, CA and London: Sage).

Mair, P. (1996) 'Comparative Politics: An Overview', in *A New Handbook of Political Science,* ed. R. Goodin and H. Klingemann (Oxford and New York: Oxford University Press) pp. 309–35.

Mair, P. (2006) 'Cleavages', in *Handbook of Party Politics,* ed. R. Katz and W. Crotty (London and Thousand Oaks, CA: Sage) pp. 371–5.

Mair, P. (2007) 'Left-Right Orientations' in *The Oxford Handbook of Political Behaviour,* ed. R. Dalton and H-.D. Klingemann (Oxford and New York: Oxford University Press), pp. 206–22.

Mair, P. (2008) 'The Challenge to Party Government', *West European Politics* (31) 211–34.

Mair, P. (2009) 'Left-Right Orientations' in *The Oxford Handbook of Political Behavior,* ed. R. Dalton and H.-D. Klingemann (Oxford and New York: Oxford University Press) pp. 206–22.

Mair, P. and van Biezen, I. (2001) 'Party Membership in Europe, 1980–2000', *Party Politics* (7) 5–22.

Majone, G. (1996) *Regulating Europe* (London and New York: Routledge).

Majone, G. (2006) 'Agenda Setting', in *The Oxford Handbook of Public Policy,* ed. M. Moran, M. Rein and R. Goodin (Oxford and New York: Oxford University Press) pp. 228–50.

Maloney, W. (2009) 'Interest Groups and the Revitalization of Democracy', *Representation* (45) 277–88.

Mandelbaum, M. (2007) *Democracy's Good Name: The Rise and Risks of the World's Most Popular Form of Government* (New York: PublicAffairs).

Manion, M. (2009) 'Politics in China', in *Comparative Politics Today: A World View,* 9th edn, ed. G. Almond, G. Bingham Powell, R. Dalton and K. Strøm (New York and London: Pearson Longman) pp. 418–65.

Mann, M. (1986) *The Sources of Social Power, Volume 1: A History of Power from the Beginning to AD 1780* (Cambridge and New York: Cambridge University Press).

Mann, M. (1997) 'Has Globalization Ended the Rise and Fall of the Nation-State?', *Review of International Political Economy* (4) 472–96.

Mann, T. and Cain, B. (eds) (2005) *Party Lines: Competition, Partisanship and Congressional Redistricting* (Washington, DC: Brookings).

Manor, J. (2006) *World Bank Aid That Works: Successful Development in Fragile States* (Washington, DC: World Bank).

Mansergh, L. and Thomson, R. (2007) 'Election Pledges, Party Competition and Policy Making', *Comparative Politics* (39) 311–30.

Manza, J. and Uggen, C. (2008) *Locked Out: Felon Disenfranchisement and American Democracy* (Oxford and New York: Oxford University Press).

March, D. and Olsen, J. (1984) 'The New Institutionalism: Organizational Factors in Political Life', *American Political Science Review* (78) 734–49.

Marsh, D. and Rhodes, R. (eds) (1992) *Policy Networks in British Government* (Oxford and New York: Oxford University Press).

Marsh, D. and Stoker, G. (eds) (2010) *Theory and Methods in Political Science,* 3rd edn (Basingstoke and New York: Palgrave Macmillan).

Marshall, T. (1987) [2004 edn] 'The Constitution: A Living Document', in *Judges on Judging: Views from the Bench,* ed. D. O'Brien (Washington, DC: CQ Press) pp. 178–82.

Martin, C. and Thelen, K. (2007) 'The State and Coordinated Capitalism: Contributions of the Public Sector to Social Solidarity in Post-Industrial Societies', *World Politics* (60) 1–36.

Martin, L. and Stevenson, R. (2001) 'Government Formation in Parliamentary Democracies', *American Journal of Political Science* (45) 33–50.

Martin, S. and Steel, G. (eds) (2008) *Democratic Reform in Japan: Assessing the Impact* (Boulder, CO: Lynne Rienner).

Martin, V. (2003) *Creating an Islamic State: Khomeini and the Making of a New Iran* (London: I. B. Taurus).

Marx, K. (1875) *Critique of the Gotha Programme,* Part IV, http://www.marxists.org, accessed 25 March 2006.

Marx, K. and Engels, F. (1845/6) *The German Ideology,* http://www.marxists.org, accessed 9 August 2009.

Marx, K. and Engels, F. (1848) [1967] *The Communist Manifesto,* intro. G. Stedman Jones (Harmondsworth: Penguin).

Mason, A. (1993) 'The Role of the Courts at the Turn of the Century', *Journal of Judicial Administration* (3) 12–18.

Mason, R. (2006) 'The Media' in *Developments in American Politics 5,* ed. G. Peele, C. Bailey, B. Cain and B. Guy Peters (Basingstoke and New York: Palgrave Macmillan) pp. 165–81.

Matland, R. and Studlar, D. (2004) 'Determinants of Legislative Turnover: A Cross-National Analysis', *British Journal of Political Science* (34) 87–108.

Matsuura, K., Pollitt, M., Takada, R. and Tanaka, S. (2004) 'Institutional Restructuring in the Japanese Economy since 1985', in *Where Are National Capitalisms Now?* ed. J. Perraton and B. Clift (Basingstoke and New York: Palgrave Macmillan) pp. 133–53.

Matthews, T. (1989) 'Interest Groups', in *Politics in Australia,* ed. R. Smith and L. Watson (Sydney: Allen & Unwin) pp. 211–27.

Mayhew, D. (1991) *Divided We Govern: Party Control, Lawmaking and Investigations, 1946–1990* (New Haven, CT and London: Yale University Press).

McAllister, I. (2003) 'Australia: Party Politicians as a Political Class', in *The Political Class in Advanced Democracies,* ed. J. Borchert and J. Zeiss (Oxford and New York: Oxford University Press) pp. 26–44.

McAllister, I. and Studlar, D. (2002) 'Electoral Systems and Women's Representation: A Long-Term Perspective', *Representation* (39) 3–14.

McCaughan, M. (2004) *The Battle of Venezuela* (London: Latin America Bureau).

McChesney, R. (1999) *Rich Media, Poor Democracies* (Urbana, IL: University of Illinois Press).

McCormick, J. (2008) *Understanding the European Union: A Concise Introduction,* 4th edn (Basingstoke: Palgrave Macmillan).

McCoy, J. and Myers, D. (eds) (2006) *The Unravelling of Representative Democracy in Venezuela* (Baltimore, MD: Johns Hopkins University Press).

McCreery, D. (2002) 'State and Society in Nineteenth Century Goiás', in *Studies in the Formation of the Nation State in Latin America,* ed. J. Dunkerley (London: Institute of Latin American Studies) pp. 133–60.

McEldowney, J. (2009) 'Administrative Law', in *The Concise Oxford Dictionary of Politics*, 3rd edn, ed. I. McLean and A. Macmillan (Oxford and New York: Oxford University Press).

McFaul, M. (2005) 'The Electoral System', in *Developments in Russian Politics 6*, ed. S. White, Z. Gitelman and R. Sakwa (Basingstoke and New York: Palgrave Macmillan) pp. 61–79.

McGarry, J. and O'Leary, B. (2006) 'Consociational Theory, Northern Ireland's Conflict and its Agreement – Part 1', *Government and Opposition* (41) 43–63.

McKay, D. (1999) *Federalism and European Union: A Political Economy Perspective* (Oxford and New York: Oxford University Press).

McKay, D. (2009) *American Politics and Society*, 7th edn (Chichester: Wiley).

McLean, I. (2006) *Adam Smith, Radical and Egalitarian: An Interpretation for the 21st Century* (Edinburgh: Edinburgh University Press).

Meehan, J. (ed.) (1995) *Feminists Read Habermas: Gendering the Subject of Discourse* (London and New York: Routledge).

Meguid, B. (2008) *Party Competition between Unequals: Strategies and Electoral Fortunes in Western Europe* (New York and Cambridge: Cambridge University Press).

Melissaris, E. (2009) *Ubiquitous Justice: Legal Theory and the Space for Legal Pluralism* (Farnham: Ashgate).

Melleuish, G. (2002) 'The State in World History: Perspectives and Problems', *Australian Journal of Politics and History* (48) 322–35.

Melvin, N. (2000) *Uzbekistan: Transition to Authoritarianism on the Silk Road* (Reading: Harwood).

Menon, A. and Schain, M. (eds) (2006) *Comparative Federalism: The European Union and the United States in Comparative Perspective* (Oxford and New York: Oxford University Press).

Meredith, M. (2006) *The Fate of Africa: From the Hopes of Freedom to the Heart of Despair* (New York: Public Affairs).

Michels, R. (1911) [1962 edn] *Political Parties* (New York: Free Press).

Mickiewicz, E. (2008) *Television, Power and the Public in Russia* (New York and Cambridge: Cambridge University Press).

Migdal, J. (2001) *State in Society: Studying How States and Societies Transform and Constitute One Another* (Cambridge and New York: Cambridge University Press).

Milbrath, L. and Goel, M. (1977) *Political Participation: How and Why Do People Get Involved in Politics*, 2nd edn (Chicago, IL: Rand McNally).

Milgram, S. (1974) *Obedience to Authority: An Experimental View* (New York: Harper & Row).

Mill, J. (1861) [1991 edn] 'Considerations on Representative Government', in *Collected Works of John Stuart Mill*, Vol. 19, ed. J. O'Grady and B. Robson (Toronto: University of Toronto Press and London: Routledge) pp. 371–577.

Miller, R. (2005) *Party Politics in New Zealand* (South Melbourne, Victoria: Oxford University Press).

Miller, W. (1995) 'Quantitative Methods', in *Theory and Methods in Political Science*, ed. D. Marsh and G. Stoker (Basingstoke and New York: Macmillan) pp. 154–72.

Mills, C. Wright (1956) *The Power Elite* (New York and Oxford: Oxford University Press).

Milne, R. (2009) 'Bitter Feuds at Deutschland AG Herald Change', *Financial Times*, 14 August, p. 19.

Mitchell, A. (1982) 'The Local Campaign, 1977–79', in *Political Communications: The General Election Campaign of 1979*, ed. R. Worcester and M. Harrop (London: Allen & Unwin) pp. 36–42.

Moestrup, S. and Elgie, R. (eds) (2005) *Semi-presidentialism outside Europe* (London and New York: Routledge).

Möller, T. (2007) 'Sweden: Still a Stable Party System?' in *When Parties Prosper: The Uses of Electoral Success*, ed. K. Lawson and P. Merkl (Boulder, CO: Lynne Rienner) pp. 27–42.

Moore, Barrington, Jr (1966) *Social Origins of Dictatorship and Democracy: Lord and Peasant in the Making of the Modern World* (Boston, MA: Beacon Press).

Moran, M. (2003) *The British Regulatory State: High Modernism and Hyper-Innovation* (Oxford and New York: Oxford University Press).

Moran, M., Rein, M. and Goodin, R. (eds) (2006) *The Oxford Handbook of Public Policy* (Oxford and New York: Oxford University Press).

Morel, L. (2007) 'The Rise of "Politically Obligatory" Referendums: The 2005 French Referendum in Comparative Perspective', *West European Politics* (30) 1041–67.

Morlino, L. (1995) 'Italy's Civic Divide', *Journal of Democracy* (6) 173–7.

Mosca, G. (1896) [1939 edn] *The Ruling Class* (New York: McGraw-Hill).

Mouritzen, P. and Svara, J. (2002) *Leadership at the Apex: Politicians and Administrators in Western Local Governments* (Pittsburgh, PA: University of Pittsburgh Press).

Mughan, A. (2000) *Media and the Presidentialization of Parliamentary Elections* (Basingstoke: Palgrave).

Mulgan, R. (1997) *Politics in New Zealand*, 2nd edn (Auckland: Auckland University Press).

Mulgan, R. (2003) *Holding Power to Account: Accountability in Modern Democracies* (Basingstoke: Palgrave Macmillan).

Müller, W. and Strøm, K. (eds) (2000a) *Coalition Governments in Western Europe* (Oxford and New York: Oxford University Press).

Müller, W. and Strøm, K. (2000b) 'Coalition Governance in Western Europe', in *Coalition Governments in Western Europe*, ed. W. Müller and K. Strøm (Oxford and New York: Oxford University Press) pp. 559–92.

Muñoz, H. (2006) 'The Growing Community of Democracies', in *Democracy Rising: Assessing the Global Challenge*, ed. H. Muñoz (Boulder, CO and London: Lynne Rienner) pp. 1–8.

Munro, W. (1925) *The Governments of Europe* (New York: Macmillan).

Murrie, M. (2006) 'Broadcasters Getting Online, Staying On Air', *eJournal USA* (11), http://usinfo.state.gov/journals/itgic/0306/ijge/ijge0306.htm, accessed 28 April 2006.

Mutz, D. (2006) *Hearing the Other Side: Deliberative Versus Participatory Democracy* (Cambridge and New York: Cambridge University Press).

N

Nassmacher, K. (ed.) (2001) *Foundations of Democracy: Approaches to Comparative Political Finance* (Baden Baden: Nomos Verlag).

Nassmacher, K. (ed.) (2006) 'Regulation of Party Finance', in *Handbook of Party Politics*, ed. R. Katz and W. Crotty (London and Thousand Oaks, CA: Sage) pp. 446–55.

National Audit Office (2006) *The Role of the National Audit Office,* http://www.nao.org.uk/about/role.htm#meeting, accessed 12 November 2006.

Nef, J. (2003) 'Public Administration and Public Sector Reform in Latin America', in *Handbook of Public Administration,* ed. B. Guy Peters and J. Pierre (London and Thousand Oaks, CA: Sage) pp. 523–35.

Nelson, M. (ed.) (2009) *The Presidency and the Political System,* 9th edn (Washington, DC: CQ Press).

Neustadt, R. (1991) *Presidential Power and the Modern Presidents* (New York: Free Press).

Newton, K. (2006) 'May The Weak Force Be With You: The Power of the Mass Media in Modern Politics', *European Journal of Political Research* (45) 209–34.

Nicholson, P. (1990) 'Politics as the Exercise of Force' in *What is Politics?* ed. A. Leftwich (Cambridge and Malden, MA: Polity) pp. 41–52.

Nijzink, L., Mozaffar, S. and Azevedo, E. (2000) 'Parliament and the Enhancement of Democracy on the African Continent: An Analysis of Institutional Capacity and Public Perceptions', *Journal of Legislative Studies* (12) 311–35.

Niskanen, W. (1971) *Bureaucracy and Representative Government* (Chicago: Aldine, Atherton).

Norris, P. (1999a) 'The Growth of Critical Citizens and Its Consequences', in *Critical Citizens: Global Support for Democratic Governance,* ed. P. Norris (Oxford and New York: Oxford University Press) pp. 257–72.

Norris, P. (ed.) (1999b) *Critical Citizens: Global Support for Democratic Governance* (Oxford and New York: Oxford University Press).

Norris, P. (2000) *A Virtuous Circle: Political Communication in Postindustrial Societies* (Cambridge and New York: Cambridge University Press).

Norris, P. (2002) *Democratic Phoenix: Reinventing Political Activism* (Cambridge and New York: Cambridge University Press).

Norris, P. (2004a) *Electoral Engineering: Voting Rules and Political Behaviour* (Cambridge and New York: Cambridge University Press).

Norris, P. (2004b) 'Will New Technology Boost Turnout?', in *Voter Turnout in Western Europe since 1945: A Regional Report* (Stockholm: IDEA) pp. 42–50.

Norris, P. and Inglehart, R. (2004) *Sacred and Secular: Religion and Politics Worldwide* (Cambridge and New York: Cambridge University Press).

Norris, P., Kern, M. and Just, M. (eds) (2003) *Framing Terrorism: The News Media, the Government and the Public* (London and New York: Routledge).

North, D. (1981) *Structure and Change in Economic History* (New York: Norton).

Norton, P. (ed.) (1990) *Legislatures* (Oxford and New York: Oxford University Press).

Norton, P. (2005) *Parliament in Britain* (Basingstoke: Palgrave Macmillan).

Novaya Gazeta (2009) *Medvedev's Declaration,* http://www.novayagazeta.ru, accessed 3 October 2009.

NRA (National Rifle Association) (2006) *A Brief History of the NRA,* http://www.nra.org/aboutus.apx, accessed 9 December 2006.

Nugent, N. (2006) *The Government and Politics of the European Union,* 6th edn (Basingstoke and New York: Palgrave Macmillan).

Nurmi, H. and Nurmi, L. (2002) 'The 2000 Presidential Election in Finland', *Electoral Studies* (21) 473–9.

O

Oakes, L. (1997) *Prophetic Charisma: The Psychology of Revolutionary Religious Personalities* (Syracuse, NY: Syracuse University Press).

Oates, S. (2005) 'Media and Political Communication', in *Developments in Russian Politics 6,* ed. S. White, Z. Gitelman and R. Sakwa (Basingstoke and New York: Palgrave Macmillan) pp. 114–29.

Oates, S. (2006) *Television, Democracy and Elections in Russia* (London and New York: Routledge).

O'Brien, D. (2008a) *Storm Center: The Supreme Court in American Politics,* 7th edn (New York: Norton).

O'Brien, D. (ed.) (2008b) *Judges on Judging: Views from the Bench,* 3rd edn (Washington, DC: CQ Press).

O'Brien, K. (2008) *Reform without Liberalization: China's National People's Congress and the Politics of Institutional Change* (Cambridge and New York: Cambridge University Press).

Ocitti, T. (2006) *Press, Politics and Public Policy in Uganda: The Role of Journalism in Democratization* (Lewiston, NY: Edwin Mellen).

O'Donnell, G. (1973) *Modernization and Bureaucratic Authoritarianism: Studies in South American Politics* (Berkeley, CA: California University Press), http://ark.cdlib.org/ark:/13030/ft4v19n9n2/, accessed 3 November 2006.

O'Donnell, G. (1994) 'Delegative Democracy', *Journal of Democracy* (5) 55–69.

O'Donnell, G. (2003) 'Horizontal Accountability: The Legal Institutionalization of Mistrust', in *Democratic Accountability in Latin America,* ed. S. Mainwaring and C. Welna (Oxford and New York: Oxford University Press) pp. 34–54.

O'Donnell, G., Schmitter, P. and Whitehead, L. (eds) (1986) *Transitions from Authoritarian Rule* (Baltimore, MD and London: Johns Hopkins University Press).

OECD (Organisation for Economic Co-operation and Development) (2007) *Policy Brief: Sweden,* http://www.oecd.org, accessed 23 December, 2009.

OECD (Organisation for Economic Co-operation and Development) (2009) *National Accounts of OECD Countries* (Paris: OECD).

O'Flynn, I. (2006) *Deliberative Democracy and Divided Societies* (Edinburgh: Edinburgh University Press).

O'Harrow, R. (2005) *No Place to Hide* (New York: Free Press).

Ohmae, K. (1995) *The End of the Nation State: The Rise of Regional Economies* (New York: Free Press and London: HarperCollins).

Olsen, J. (1980) 'Governing Norway: Segmentation, Anticipation and Consensus Formation', in *Presidents and Prime Ministers,* ed. R. Rose and E. Suleiman (Washington, DC: American Enterprise Institute) pp. 203–55.

Olson, D. (1994) *Legislative Institutions: A Comparative View* (New York: M.E. Sharpe).

O'Neill, S. (2009) 'The Real War in Mexico: How Democracy Can Defeat the Drug Cartels', *Foreign Affairs* (88) 63–77.

Opello, W. and Rosow, S. (2004) *The Nation-State and Global Order: A Historical Introduction to Contemporary Politics,* 2nd edn (Boulder, CO and London: Lynne Rienner).

Onuf, N. (1989) *World of Our Making: Rules and Rule in Social Theory and International Relations* (Columbia, SC: University of South Carolina Press).

Orren, K. and Skowronek, S. (1995) 'Order and Time in Institutional Study: A Brief for the Historical Approach' in *Political Science in History: Research Programs and Political Traditions,* ed. J. Farr, J. Dryzek and S. Leonard (Cambridge and New York: Cambridge University Press) pp. 296–317.

Osborne, D. and Gaebler, T. (1992) *Reinventing Government: How the Entrepreneurial Spirit Is Transforming the Public Sector* (New York and London: Penguin).

Osiander, A. (2001) 'Sovereignty, International Relations and the Westphalian Myth', *International Organization* (55) 251–89.

Ostrogorski, M. (1902) *Democracy and the Organisation of Political Parties* (London: Macmillan).

Ottaway, M. (2003) *Democracy Challenged: The Rise of Semi-Authoritarianism* (Washington, DC: Carnegie Endowment for International Peace).

Owen, R. (1993) 'The Practice of Electoral Democracy in the Arab East and North Africa: Some Lessons from Nearly a Century's Experience', in *Rules and Rights in the Middle East,* ed. E. Goldberg, R. Kasaba and J. Migdal (Seattle, WA: University of Washington Press) pp. 17–40.

Owen, R. (2004) *State, Power and Politics in the Middle East,* 3rd edn (London and New York: Routledge).

P

Padgett, S. (2003) 'Political Economy: The German Model under Stress', in *Developments in German Politics 3,* ed. S. Padgett, W. Paterson and G. Smith (Basingstoke and New York: Palgrave Macmillan) pp. 121–42.

Page, E. and Wright, V. (eds) (2006) *From the Active to the Enabling State: The Changing Role of Top Officials in European Nations* (Basingstoke: Palgrave Macmillan).

Paine, T. (1791/2) [1984 edn] *Rights of Man* (Harmondsworth: Penguin).

Palme, J. (2006) 'Income Distribution in Sweden', *Japanese Journal of Social Security Policy* (5) 16–26.

Palmer, M. (2003) *Breaking the Real Axis of Evil: How to Oust the World's Last Dictators by 2025* (Lanham, MD: Rowman & Littlefield).

Panebianco, A. (1988) *Political Parties: Organization and Power* (Cambridge and New York: Cambridge University Press).

Park, H. (1976) 'Changes in Chinese Communist Ideology', in *Comparative Communism: The Soviet, Chinese and Yugoslav Models,* ed. G. Bertsch and T. Ganschow (San Francisco: W. H. Freeman) pp. 144–50.

Parkin, F. (2002) *Max Weber,* revised edn (London and New York: Routledge).

Parkinson, J. (2006) *Deliberating in the Real World: Problems of Legitimacy in Deliberative Democracy* (Oxford and New York: Oxford University Press).

Parsons, C. (forthcoming) 'Constructivism' in *Theory and Methods in Political Science,* 3rd edn, ed. D. Marsh and G. Stoker (Basingstoke and New York: Palgrave Macmillan).

Parsons, T. (1967) 'On the Concept of Political Power', in *Sociological Theory and Modern Society,* ed. T. Parsons (New York and London: Free Press) pp. 286–99.

Parsons, W. (1995) *Public Policy: An Introduction to the Theory and Practice of Policy Analysis* (Brookfield, VT and Aldershot: Edward Elgar).

Patterson, S. and Mughan, A. (eds) (1999) *Senates: Bicameralism in the Contemporary World* (Columbus, OH: Ohio State University Press).

Pattie, C., Seyd, P. and Whiteley, P. (2004) *Citizenship in Britain: Values, Participation and Democracy* (New York and Cambridge: Cambridge University Press).

Paul, T. (ed.) (2004) *The Nation-State in Question* (Princeton, NJ: Princeton University Press).

Paulsen, B. (2007) 'The Question of Roles and Identities in Public Administration', *Public Administration* (30) 469–90.

Pearl, S. (2003) 'No Subject' (*Gmane Culture Studies Mailing List Archive*), http://article.gmane.org/gmane.culture.studies. literature. slavic/2220, accessed 5 April 2006.

Pedahzur, A. (2005) *Suicide Terrorism* (Cambridge and Malden, MA: Polity Press).

Peerenboom, R. (2002) *China's Long March Toward Rule of Law* (Cambridge and New York: Cambridge University Press).

Pelly, M., Stephens, T. and Wilkinson, M. (2005) 'Former Leaders Call for Debate', *Sydney Morning Herald,* 25 October.

Pennings, P., Keman, H. and Kleinnijenhuis, J. (2006) *Doing Research in Political Science: An Introduction to Comparative Methods and Statistics,* 2nd edn (Thousand Oaks, CA and London: Sage).

Peregudov, S. (2001) 'The Oligarchical Model of Russian Capitalism', in *Contemporary Russian Politics: A Reader,* ed. A. Brown (Oxford and New York: Oxford University Press) pp. 259–68.

Peréz-Liñán, A. (2006) 'Evaluating Presidential Runoff Elections', *Electoral Studies* (25) 129–46.

Peretti T. (2001) *In Defence of a Political Court* (Princeton, NJ: Princeton University Press).

Perlmutter, A. (1981) *Modern Authoritarianism* (New Haven, CT: Yale University Press).

Perlmutter, A. (1997) *Making the World Safe for Democracy: A Century of Wilsonianism and its Totalitarian Challenges* (Chapel Hill, NC: University of North Carolina Press).

Perraton, J. and Clift, B. (2004a) 'So Where Are National Capitalisms Now?', in *Where Are National Capitalisms Now?,* ed. J. Perraton and B. Clift (Basingstoke and New York: Palgrave Macmillan) pp. 195–261.

Perraton, J. and Clift, B. (eds) (2004b) *Where Are National Capitalisms Now?* (Basingstoke and New York: Palgrave Macmillan).

Peters, B. Guy (1998) *Comparative Politics: Theory and Methods* (London: Macmillan and New York: New York University Press).

Peters, B. Guy (1999) *Institutional Theory in Political Science: The 'New Institutionalism'* (London and New York: Pinter).

Peters, B. Guy (2009a) *American Public Policy: Promise and Performance,* 8th edn (Washington, DC: CQ Press).

Peters, B. Guy (2009b) *The Politics of Bureaucracy: An Introduction to Comparative Public Administration,* 6th edn (London and New York: Routledge).

Peters, B. Guy and Pierre, J. (eds) (2003) *Handbook of Public Administration* (London and Thousand Oaks, CA: Sage).

Peters. B. Guy and Pierre, J. (eds) (2004) *The Politicization of the Civil Service in Comparative Perspective* (London and New York: Routledge).

Petracca, M. (1992) 'The Rediscovery of Interest Group Politics', in *The Politics of Interests: Interest Groups Transformed*, ed. M. Petracca (Boulder, CO and Oxford: Westview) pp. 3–31.

Pharr, S. and Putnam, R. (eds) (2000) *Disaffected Democracies: What's Troubling The Trilateral Countries?* (Princeton, NJ: Princeton University Press).

Philip, G. (2003) *Democracy in Latin America* (Cambridge: Polity and Malden, MA: Blackwell).

Phillips, A. (1995) *The Politics of Presence* (Oxford and New York: Oxford University Press).

Pierson, P. (2004) *Politics in Time: History, Institutions and Social Analysis* (Princeton, NJ and Woodstock: Princeton University Press).

Poguntke, T. and Webb, P. (2005a) 'The Presidentialization of Politics in Democratic Societies: A Framework for Analysis', in *The Presidentialization of Politics: A Comparative Study of Modern Democracies*, ed. T. Poguntke and P. Webb (Oxford and New York: Oxford University Press) pp. 1–25.

Poguntke, T. and Webb, P. (eds) (2005b) *The Presidentialization of Politics: A Comparative Study of Modern Democracies* (Oxford and New York: Oxford University Press).

Poguntke, T. and Webb, P. (2005c) 'The Presidentialization of Contemporary Democratic Politics: Evidence, Causes, and Consequences', in *The Presidentialization of Politics: A Comparative Study of Modern Democracies*, ed. T. Poguntke and P. Webb (Oxford and New York: Oxford University Press) pp. 336–56.

Polanyi, K. (1957) *The Great Transformation: The Political and Economic Origins of Our Time* (Boston, MA: Beacon Press).

Polidano, C. (1998) 'Why Bureaucrats Can't Always Do What Ministers Want: Multiple Accountabilities in Westminster Democracies', *Public Policy and Administration* (13) 35–50.

Political Studies Review (2006) 'Review Symposium of Steven Lukes, *Power: A Radical View*' (Basingstoke and New York: Palgrave Macmillan, 1974 [2005 edn]). (4) 115–75.

Polity IV Project (2009) *Political Regime Characteristics and Transitions, 1800–2008*, http://www.systemicpeace.org, accessed 10 September 2009.

Pollitt, C. and Bouckaert, G. (2004) *Public Management Reform: A Comparative Analysis,* 2nd edn (Oxford and New York: Oxford University Press).

Porta, D. della and Diani, M. (1999) *Social Movements: An Introduction* (Malden, MA and Oxford: Blackwell).

Porta, D. della, Kriesi, H. and Rucht, D. (eds) (1999) *Social Movements in a Globalizing World* (London: Macmillan and New York: St Martin's Press).

Posner, D. and Young, D. (2007) 'The Institutionalization of Political Power in Africa', *Journal of Democracy* (19) 109–23.

Posusney, M. (2005) 'The Middle East's Democracy Deficit in Comparative Perspective', in *Authoritarianism in the Middle East: Regimes and Resistance*, ed. M. Posusney and M. Angrist (Boulder, CO and London: Lynne Rienner) pp. 1–20.

Posusney, M. and Angrist, M. (eds) (2005) *Authoritarianism in the Middle East: Regimes and Resistance* (Boulder, CO and London: Lynne Rienner).

Prempeh, H. (2008) 'Presidents Untamed', *Journal of Democracy* (19) 109–23.

President of the United States (2002) *National Security Strategy of the United States of America* (Washington, DC), http://www.whitehouse.gov/nsc/nss.html, accessed 5 January 2006.

President of Russia (2009) *President of Russia*, http://www.kremlin.ru/eng/, accessed 11 November 2009.

Prillaman, W. (2000) *The Judiciary and Democratic Decay in Latin America: Declining Confidence in the Rule of Law* (Westport, CT: Praeger).

Pryor, K. (2003) *A National State of Confusion* (New York: Salon.com), http://dir.salon.com/story/opinion/feature/2003/02/06/iraq_poll/index.html, accessed 2 May 2006.

Przeworski, A. (1991) *Democracy and the Market: Political and Economic Reforms in Eastern Europe and Latin America* (Cambridge and New York: Cambridge University Press).

Przeworski, A. and Teune, H. (1970) *The Logic of Comparative Social Inquiry* (New York: Wiley).

Przeworski, A., Alvarez, M., Cheibub, J. and Limongi, F. (2000) *Democracy and Development: Political Institutions and Well-Being in the World, 1950–1990* (Cambridge and New York: Cambridge University Press).

Psephos (2006) *Election to the Chamber of Deputies, 2006*, http://psephos.adam-carr.net, accessed 12 December 2006.

Psephos (2009) *Adam Carr's Election Archive*, http://psephos.adam-carr.net, accessed 12 November 2009.

Putnam, R. (1976) *The Comparative Study of Political Elites* (Englewood Cliffs, NJ: Prentice Hall).

Putnam, R. (1993) *Making Democracy Work: Civic Traditions in Modern Italy* (Princeton, NJ: Princeton University Press).

Putnam, R. (2000) *Bowling Alone: The Collapse and Revival of American Community* (New York: Simon & Schuster).

Putnam, R. (ed.) (2002) *Democracies in Flux: The Evolution of Social Capital in Contemporary Society* (Oxford and New York: Oxford University Press).

Putnam, R., Pharr, S. and Dalton, R. (2000) 'What's Troubling the Trilateral Countries?', in *Disaffected Democracies: What's Troubling the Trilateral Countries?*, ed. S. Pharr and R. Putnam (Princeton, NJ: Princeton University Press) pp. 3–30.

Pye, L. (1985) *Asian Power and Politics: The Cultural Dimensions of Authority* (Cambridge, MA: Harvard University Press).

Pye, L. (1995) 'Political Culture', in *The Encyclopaedia of Democracy*, ed. S. Lipset (London and New York: Routledge) pp. 965–9.

Q

Qualter, T. (1991) 'Public Opinion', in *The Blackwell Encyclopaedia of Political Science*, ed. V. Bogdanor (Oxford and Cambridge, MA: Blackwell) p. 511.

Qvortrup, M. (2005) *A Comparative Study of Referendums: Government by the People,* 2nd edn (Manchester: Manchester University Press).

Qvortrup, M. (2008) 'Citizen Initiated Referendums (CIRs) in New Zealand: A Comparative Appraisal', *Representation* (44) 69–78.

R

Raadschelders, J., Toonen, T. and Van der Meer, F. (eds) (2007) *The Civil Service in the 21st Century: Comparative Perspectives* (London and New York: Palgrave Macmillan).

Ragin, C. (1987) *The Comparative Method: Moving Beyond Qualitative and Quantitative Strategies* (Berkeley, CA and London: University of California Press).

Ragin, C. (1994) 'Introduction to Qualitative Comparative Analysis', in *The Comparative Political Economy of the Welfare State*, ed. T. Janoski and A. Hicks (New York and Cambridge: Cambridge University Press) pp. 299–319.

Ragin, C., Berg-Schlosser, D. and de Meur, G. (1996) 'Political Methodology: Qualitative Methods', in *A New Handbook of Political Science*, ed. R. Goodin and H. Klingemann (Oxford and New York: Oxford University Press) pp. 749–68.

Rahat, G. (2007) 'Candidate Selection: The Choice before the Choice', *Journal of Democracy* (18) 157–71.

Rahman, F. (1982) *Islam and Modernity: Transformation of an Intellectual Tradition* (Chicago, IL: University of Chicago Press).

Rainer, H. and Siedler, T. (2006) 'Does Democracy Foster Trust?' ISER Working Paper 2006–31 (Colchester: University of Essex).

von Ranke, L. (1824) [1887 edn] *Histories of the Latin and Teutonic Peoples from 1494 to 1514* (London: Chiswick Press).

Rasch, B. (2004) 'Parliamentary Government', in *Nordic Politics: Comparative Perspectives*, ed. K. Heidar (Oslo: Universitetsforlaget) pp. 127–41.

Regeringskansliet (Government Offices of Sweden) (2009) *How the Government and Government Offices Function*, http://www.regeringen.se/sb/d/2856, accessed 6 August 2009.

Reilly, B. (2007) 'Democratization and Electoral Reform in the Asia-Pacific Region: Is There an "Asian Model" of Democracy?', *Comparative Political Studies* (40) 1350–71.

Remington, T. (2004) 'Politics in Russia', in *Comparative Politics Today: A World View*, 8th edn, ed. G. Almond, G. Bingham Powell, K. Strøm and R. Dalton (New York and London: Pearson Longman) pp. 366–417.

Remington, T. (2006) 'Parliamentary Politics in Russia', in *Developments in Russian Politics 6*, ed. S. White, Z. Gitelman and R. Sakwa (Basingstoke and New York: Palgrave Macmillan) pp. 40–60.

Reno, W. (2003) 'The Politics of Insurgency in Collapsing States', in *State Failure, Collapse and Reconstruction*, ed. J. Milliken (Malden, MA and Oxford: Blackwell) pp. 83–104.

Reynolds, A., Reilly, B. and Ellis, A. (2005) *Electoral System Design: The International IDEA Handbook* (Stockholm: International Institute for Democracy and Electoral Assistance), http://www.idea.int/publications/, accessed 11 June 2006.

Rhodes, R. (1996) 'The New Governance: Governing without Government', *Political Studies* (44) 652–67.

Rhodes, R. (2006a) 'Policy Network Analysis', in *The Oxford Handbook of Public Policy*, ed. M. Moran, M. Rein and R. Goodin (Oxford and New York: Oxford University Press) pp. 424–47.

Rhodes, R. (2006b) 'Executives in Parliamentary Government', in *The Oxford Handbook of Political Institutions*, ed. R. Rhodes, S. Binder and B. Rockman (Oxford and New York: Oxford University Press) pp. 323–43.

Rhodes, R., Binder, S. and Rockman, B. (eds) (2006) *The Oxford Handbook of Political Institutions* (Oxford and New York: Oxford University Press).

Richardson, J., Gustafsson, G. and Jordan, G. (1982) 'The Concept of Policy Style' in *Policy Styles in Western Europe*, ed. J. Richardson (London: Allen & Unwin) pp. 1–16.

Riches, W. (2004) *The Civil Rights Movement: Struggle and Resistance*, 2nd edn (Basingstoke: Palgrave Macmillan).

Riker, W. (1962) *The Theory of Political Coalitions* (New Haven, CT and London: Yale University Press).

Riker, W. (1975) 'Federalism', in *The Handbook of Political Science*, Vol. 5, ed. F. Greenstein and N. Polsby (Reading, MA: Addison-Wesley) pp. 93–172.

Riker, W. (1990) 'Political Science and Rational Choice' in *Perspectives on Positive Political Economy*, ed. J. Alt and K. Shepsle (Cambridge and New York: Cambridge University Press) pp. 182–97.

Riker, W. (1996) 'European Federalism: The Lessons of Past Experience', in *Federalizing Europe? The Costs, Benefits and Pre-conditions of Federal Political Systems*, ed. J. Hesse and V. Wright (Oxford and New York: Oxford University Press) pp. 9–24.

Riker, W. and Ordeshook, P. (1973) *Introduction to Positive Political Theory* (Englewood Cliffs, NJ: Prentice Hall).

Rockman, B. (2000) 'Administering the Summit in the United States', in *Administering the Summit*, ed. B. Guy Peters, R. Rhodes and V. Wright (London: Macmillan) pp. 245–62.

Rokkan, S. (1970) *Citizens, Elections, Parties* (New York: McKay).

Romero, A. (1997) 'Rearranging the Deck Chairs on the Titanic: The Agony of Democracy in Venezuela', *Latin America Research Review* (32) 7–36.

Rose, L. (2004) 'Local Government and Politics', in *Nordic Politics: Comparative Perspectives*, ed. K. Heidar (Oslo: Universitetforlaget) pp. 164–82.

Rose, R. (1989) *Politics in England: Change and Persistence*, 5th edn (Basingstoke: Macmillan).

Rose, R. (1991a) 'Comparing Forms of Comparative Analysis', *Political Studies* (39) 446–62.

Rose, R. (1991b) *The Postmodern President*, 2nd edn (Chatham, NJ: Chatham House).

Rose, R. (1999) 'Living in an Antimodern Society', *East European Constitutional Review* (8) 68–75.

Rose, R. (2000) 'A Supply-Side View of Russia's Elections', *East European Constitutional Review* (9) 53–59.

Rosenbluth, E. and Thies, M. (2004) 'Politics in Japan', in *Comparative Politics Today: A World View*, 8th edn, ed. G. Almond, G. Bingham Powell, K. Strøm and R. Dalton (New York: Pearson Longman) pp. 318–65.

Rosenfeld, G. (2005) *The World Hitler Never Made: Alternate History and the Memory of Nazism* (Cambridge and New York: Cambridge University Press).

Ross, C. and Campbell, A. (eds) (2008) *Federalism and Local Politics in Russia* (London and New York: Routledge).

Ross, M. (2009) 'Culture in Comparative Political Analysis' in *Comparative Politics: Rationality, Culture and Structure*, ed. M. Lichbach and A. Zuckerman (Cambridge and New York: Cambridge University Press) pp. 134–61.

Rossi, P., Freeman, H. and Lipsey, M. (2003) *Evaluation: A Systematic Approach*, 7th edn (Thousand Oaks, CA and London: Sage Publications).

Rotberg, R. (ed.) (2004) *When States Fail: Causes and Consequences* (Princeton, NJ: Princeton University Press).

Rothchild, D. (1997) *Managing Ethnic Conflict in Africa: Pressures and Incentives for Cooperation* (Washington, DC: Brookings Institution Press).

Rothstein, B. (1996) 'Political Institutions: An Overview' in *A New Handbook of Political Science*, ed. R Goodin and H.-D. Klingemann (Oxford and New York: Oxford University Press) pp. 205–22.

Rothstein, B. (2002) 'Sweden: Social Capital in the Social Democratic State', in *Democracies in Flux: The Evolution of Social Capital in Contemporary Society*, ed. R. Putnam (Oxford and New York: Oxford University Press) pp. 289–332.

Rothwell, D. (1986) 'Risk-Taking and Polarization in Small Group Communication', *Communication Education* (35) 182–7.

Rousseau, J.-J. (1755) [1988 edn] *Rousseau's Political Writings*, ed. A. Ritter and J. Bondanella (New York and London: Norton).

Rousseau, J.-J. (1762) [1913 edn] *The Social Contract* (London: Dent and New York: Dutton).

Roy, O. (1994) *The Failure of Political Islam* (London: I. B. Taurus).

Rubin, E. and Feeley, M. (2008) 'Federalism and Internationalism', *Publius* (38) 167–91.

Rueschmeyer, D., Rueschmeyer, M. and Wittrock, B. (1998a) 'Contrasting Patterns of Participation and Democracy', in *Participation and Democracy: Comparisons and Interpretations*, ed. D. Rueschmeyer, M. Rueschmeyer and B. Wittrock (Armonk, NY and London: M. E. Sharpe) pp. 266–84.

Rueschmeyer, D., Rueschmeyer, M. and Wittrock, B. (eds) (1998b) *Participation and Democracy: Comparisons and Interpretations* (Armonk, New York and London: M. E. Sharpe).

Rush, M. (2005) *Parliament Today* (Manchester: Manchester University Press).

Russell, B. (1938) *Power: A New Social Analysis* (London: Allen & Unwin).

Russell, M. (2001) 'What Are Second Chambers For?', *Parliamentary Affairs* (54) 442–58.

Rutland, P. (2005) 'Putin's Economic Record', in *Developments in Russian Politics 6*, ed. S. White, Z. Gitelman and R. Sakwa (Basingstoke and New York: Palgrave Macmillan) pp. 186–203.

S

Sabatier, P. (ed.) (2007) *Theories of the Policy Process*, 2nd edn (Boulder, CO: Westview).

Sachs, J. and Warner, A. (1995b) 'Natural Resource Abundance and Economic Growth', Working Paper 5398 (Cambridge, MA: National Bureau of Economic Research).

Sadurski, W. (2005) *Rights before Courts: A Study of Constitutional Courts in Postcommunist States of Central and Eastern Europe* (Dordrecht: Springer).

Safire, W. (1993) *Safire's New Political Dictionary* (New York: Random House).

Saich, A. (2004) *Governance and Politics of China,* 2nd edn (Basingstoke and New York: Palgrave).

Saich, A. (2009) *Web Update for Governance and Politics of China*, http://www.palgrave.com/politics/saich/docs/update1.pdf, accessed 10 July 2009.

Saikal, A. (2003) *Islam and the West: Conflict or Cooperation?* (Basingstoke and New York: Palgrave Macmillan).

Sait, E. (1938) *Political Institutions: A Preface* (New York: Appleton-Century).

Sakwa, R. (2002) *Russian Politics and Society,* 3rd edn (London and New York: Routledge).

Salamon, L. (2002a) 'The New Governance and the Tools of Public Action: An Introduction', in *The Tools of Government: A Guide to the New Governance,* ed. L. Salamon (New York: Oxford University Press) pp. 1–47.

Salamon, L. (ed.) (2002b) *The Tools of Government: A Guide to the New Governance* (New York: Oxford University Press).

Sandbrook R. (1985) *The Politics of Africa's Economic Stagnation* (Cambridge and New York: Cambridge University Press).

Santa-Cruz, A. (2005) *International Election Monitoring, Sovereignty and the Western Hemisphere: The Emergence of an International Norm* (London and New York: Routledge).

Sartori, G. (1976) *Parties and Party Systems: A Framework for Analysis* (Cambridge and New York: Cambridge University Press).

Sartori, G. (1994) *Comparative Constitutional Engineering: An Inquiry into Structures, Incentives and Outcomes* (Basingstoke: Macmillan).

Saward, M. (2006) 'The State and Civil Liberties in the Post-9/11 World' in *Developments in British Politics 8*, ed. P. Dunleavy, R. Heffernan, P. Cowley and C. Hay (Basingstoke and New York: Palgrave Macmillan) pp. 212–30.

Scarrow. S. (2002a) 'Germany: The Mixed-Member System as a Political Compromise', in *Mixed-Member Electoral Systems: The Best of Both Worlds,* ed. M. Shugart and M. Wattenberg (Oxford and New York: Oxford University Press) pp. 5–69.

Scarrow, S. (ed.) (2002b) *Perspectives on Political Parties: Classic Readings* (Basingstoke and New York: Palgrave Macmillan).

Scarrow, S. (2006) 'Party Subsidies and the Freezing of Party Competition: Do Cartel Mechanisms Work?', *West European Politics* (29) 619–39.

Schabas, W. (2007) *An Introduction to the International Criminal Court*, 2nd edn (Cambridge and New York: Cambridge University Press).

Schattschneider, E. (1942) *Party Government* (New York: Farrar & Reinhart).

Schedler, A. (2005) 'From Electoral Authoritarianism to Democratic Consolidation', in *Mexico's Democracy at Work: Political and Electoral Dynamics,* ed. R. Crandall, G. Paz and R. Roett (Boulder, CO and London: Lynne Rienner) pp. 9–38.

Schedler, A. (ed.) (2006) *Electoral Authoritarianism: The Dynamics of Unfree Competition* (Boulder, CO and London: Lynne Rienner).

Scheiner, E. (2006) *Democracy without Competition in Japan: Opposition Failure in a One-Party Dominant State* (Cambridge and New York: Cambridge University Press).

Schmidt, V. (2002) *The Futures of European Capitalism* (New York and Oxford: Oxford University Press).

Schöpflin, G. (1990) 'Why Communism Collapsed', *International Affairs* (66) 3–17.

Schudson, M. (1998) *The Good Citizen: A History of American Civic Life* (Cambridge, MA and London: Harvard University Press).

Schuman, R. (1950) *Declaration of 9 May, 1950*, http://www.robert-schuman.org, accessed 20 December 2008.

Schumpeter, J. (1943) *Capitalism, Socialism and Democracy* (London: Allen & Unwin).

Scott, W. (2007) *Institutions and Organizations: Ideas and Interests*, 3rd edn (London and Thousand Oaks, CA: Sage).

Segal, J. and Spaeth, H. (2002) *The Supreme Court and the Attitudinal Model Revisited* (New York and Cambridge: Cambridge University Press).

Seligson, M. (2005) 'Democracy on Ice: The Multiple Challenges of Guatemala's Peace Process', in *The Third Wave of Democratization in Latin America: Advances and Setbacks*, ed. F. Hagopian and S. Mainwaring (New York and Cambridge: Cambridge University Press) pp. 202–34.

Senden, L. (2005) 'Soft Law, Self-regulation and Co-regulation in European Law: Where Do They Meet?', *Electronic Journal of Comparative Law* (9), http://www.ejcl.org, accessed 28 October 2009.

Senelle, R. (1996) 'The Reform of the Belgian State', in *Federalizing Europe? The Costs, Benefits and Preconditions of Federal Political Systems*, ed. J. Hesse and V. Wright (Oxford and New York: Oxford University Press) pp. 266–324.

Seyd, P. and Whiteley, P. (2002) *New Labour's Grassroots: The Transformation of the Labour Party Membership* (Basingstoke and New York: Palgrave Macmillan).

Seznec, J. F. (2003) 'Stirrings in Saudi Arabia', in *Islam and Democracy in the Middle East*, ed. L. Diamond, M. Plattner and D. Brumberg (Baltimore, MD and London: Johns Hopkins University Press) pp. 76–83.

Shafritz, J., Hyde, A. and Parkes, S. (eds) (2003) *Classics in Public Administration*, 5th edn (Belmont, CA: Thomson Wadsworth).

Shah, P. (2005) *Legal Pluralism in Law: Coping with Cultural Diversity in Law* (London and New York: Routledge Cavendish).

Shapiro, M. (1987) 'Review of Rasmussen's "On Law and Policy in the European Court of Justice: A Comparative Study in Judicial Policy-making"', *American Journal of International Law* (81) 1007–11.

Shapiro, M., and Stone Sweet, A. (2002) *On Law, Politics and Judicialization* (Oxford and New York: Oxford University Press).

Sharlet, R. (1997) 'The Progress of Human Rights', in *Developments in Russian Politics 4, ed.* S. White, A. Pravda and Z. Gitelman (Basingstoke: Macmillan) pp. 129–48.

Sharlet, R. (2005) 'In Search of the Rule of Law', in *Developments in Russian Politics 6*, ed. S. White, Z. Gitelman and R. Sakwa (Basingstoke and New York: Palgrave Macmillan) pp. 130–47.

Shepherd, R. (2006) 'The Denim Revolt that can Rid Europe of Tyranny', *Financial Times*, 17 March, p. 19.

Shepsle, K. (2006) 'Rational Choice Institutionalism' in *The Oxford Handbook of Political Institutions*, ed. R. Rhodes, S. Binder and B. Rockman (Oxford and New York: Oxford University Press) pp. 23–38.

Shin, M. and Agnew, J. (2008) *Berlusconi's Italy: Mapping Contemporary Italian Politics* (Philadelphia, PA: Temple University Press).

Shirk, D. (2005) *Mexico's New Politics: The PAN and Democratic Change* (Boulder, CO and London: Lynne Rienner).

Shively, W. (forthcoming) *Power and Choice: An Introduction to Political Science*, 12th edn (New York and London: McGraw-Hill).

Shonfield, A. (1969) *Modern Capitalism* (Oxford and New York: Oxford University Press).

Shugart, M. and Carey, J. (1992) *Presidents and Assemblies: Constitutional Design and Electoral Dynamics* (Cambridge and New York: Cambridge University Press).

Shugart, M. and Wattenberg, M. (eds) (2000) *Mixed-Member Electoral Systems: The Best of Both Worlds* (Oxford and New York: Oxford University Press).

Silva, P. (ed.) (2001) *The Soldier and the State in South America* (London: Palgrave).

Silvia, S. and Schroeder, W. (2007) 'Why Are German Employers' Associations Declining? Arguments and Evidence', *Comparative Political Studies* (40) 1433–59.

Simon, H. (1983) *Reason in Human Affairs* (Oxford and Cambridge, MA: Blackwell).

Skidelsky, R. (2009) *Keynes: The Return of the Master* (London and New York: Penguin).

Skocpol, T. (1979) *States and Social Revolutions: A Comparative Analysis of France, Russia and China* (Cambridge and New York: Cambridge University Press).

Skocpol, T. (2003) 'Doubly Engaged Social Science: The Promise of Comparative Historical Analysis' in *Comparative Historical Analysis in the Social Sciences*, ed. J. Mahoney and D. Rueschmeyer (Cambridge and New York: Cambridge University Press) pp. 407–28.

Slaughter, A.-M. (2003) 'Governing the Global Economy through Government Networks', in *The Global Transformations Reader*, 2nd edn, ed. D. Held and A. McGrew (Cambridge and Malden, MA: Polity) pp. 189–203.

Slaughter, A.-M. (2004) *A New World Order* (Princeton, NJ: Princeton University Press).

Smith, A. (1776) [1993 edn] *An Inquiry into the Nature and Causes of the Wealth of Nations*, ed. K. Sutherland (Oxford and New York: Oxford University Press).

Smith, A. (2009) *Ethno-symbolism and Nationalism: A Cultural Approach* (London and New York: Routledge).

Smith, B. (1996) *Understanding Third World Politics* (London: Macmillan).

Smith, M. (1995) *Pressure Politics* (Manchester: Baseline Books).

Smooha, S. (2002) 'The Model of Ethnic Democracy', *Nations and Nationalism* (8) 475–503.

Solomon, P. (2007) 'Courts and Judges in Authoritarian Regimes', *World Politics* (60) 122–45.

Sørensen, G. (2004) *The Transformation of the State: Beyond the Myth of Retreat* (Basingstoke and New York: Palgrave Macmillan).

SouthAfrica.info (2009) *The Constitution of South Africa*, http://www.southafrica.info/about/democracy/constitution.htm, accessed 29 November 2009.

Sparks, A. (2009) *Beyond the Miracle: Inside the New South Africa* (Chicago: University of Chicago Press).

Spruyt, H. (2005) *Ending Empire: Contested Sovereignty and Territorial Partition* (Cornell, NY: Cornell University Press).

Statistics Canada (2001) *2001 Census of Canada*, http://www12.statcan.ca/english/census01/home/index.cfm, accessed 15 December 2006.

Steen, A. (1995) *Change of Regime and Political Recruitment: The*

Parliamentary Elites in the Baltic States (Bordeaux: ECPR Workshop on Political Recruitment).

Steinmo, S. (2003) 'The Evolution of Policy Ideas: Tax Policy in the Twentieth Century', *British Journal of Politics and International Relations* (5) 206–36.

Stepan, A. (2001) *Arguing Comparative Politics* (Oxford and New York: Oxford University Press).

Stern, N. (2007) *The Economics of Climate Change: The Stern Review* (Cambridge and New York: Cambridge University Press).

Stevens, A. (2003) *Government and Politics of France*, 3rd edn (Basingstoke and New York: Palgrave Macmillan).

Stevens, A. (2007) *Women, Power and Politics* (Basingstoke and New York: Palgrave Macmillan).

Stevenson, G. (2009) *Unfulfilled Union: Canadian Federalism and National Unity*, 5th edn (Montreal and Kingston: McGill-Queen's University Press).

Stimson, J. (1991) *Public Opinion in America: Moods, Cycles and Swings* (Boulder, CO and Oxford: Westview Press).

Stimson, J. (2004) *Tides of Consent: How Public Opinion Shapes American Politics* (Oxford and New York: Oxford University Press).

Stoker, G. (2006) *Why Politics Matters: Making Democracy Work* (Basingstoke and New York: Palgrave Macmillan)

Stoker, G. and Marsh, D. (forthcoming) 'Introduction' in *Theory and Methods in Political Science*, 3rd edn, ed. D. Marsh and G. Stoker (Basingstoke and New York: Palgrave Macmillan) pp. 14–29.

Stone, D. (2001) *Policy Paradox: The Art of Political Decision Making*, rev. edn (New York: Norton).

Stonecash, J. (2005) *Political Parties Matter: Realignment and the Return of Partisan Voting* (Boulder, CO: Lynne Rienner).

Stone Sweet, A. (2000) *Governing with Judges: Constitutional Politics in Europe* (Oxford and New York: Oxford University Press).

Stouffer, S. (1966) *Communism, Conformity and Civil Liberties* (New York: Wiley).

Strange, S. (1997) 'The Future of Global Capitalism; Or, Will Divergence Persist Forever?', in *Political Economy of Modern Capitalism: Mapping Convergence and Diversity*, ed. C. Crouch and W. Streeck (London and Thousand Oaks, CA: Sage) pp. 182–91.

Street, J. (forthcoming) *Mass Media, Politics and Democracy*, 2nd edn (Basingstoke and New York: Palgrave).

Strøm, K. and Nyblade, B. (2007) 'Coalition Theory and Government Formation' in *The Oxford Handbook of Comparative Politics*, ed. C. Boix and S. Stokes (Oxford and New York: Oxford University Press) pp. 782–804.

Strøm, K., Müller, W. and Bergman, T. (eds) (2008) *Cabinets and Coalition Bargaining: The Democratic Life Cycle in Western Europe* (Oxford and New York: Oxford University Press).

Sundberg, J. (2002) 'The Scandinavian Party Model at the Crossroads', in *Political Parties in Advanced Industrial Democracies*, ed. P. Webb, D. Farrell and I. Holliday (Oxford and New York: Oxford University Press) pp. 181–216.

Sweating, D. (2003) 'How Strong Is the Mayor of London?', *Policy and Politics* (31) 465–78.

T

Tálos, E. and Kittel B. (2002) 'Austria in the 1990s: The Routine of Social Partnership in Question?', in *Policy Concertation and Social Partnership: Lessons for the 21st Century*, ed. S. Berger and H. Compston (New York and Oxford: Berghahn) pp. 35–50.

Tardi, G. (2002) 'Departments and Other Institutions of Government', in *Canadian Public Administration*, ed. C. Dunn (Don Mills, Ontario: Oxford University Press) pp. 281–304.

Tarrow, S. (1998) *Power in Movement: Social Movements and Contentious Politics*, 2nd edn (Cambridge and New York: Cambridge University Press).

Tavits, M. (2008) *Presidents with Prime Ministers: Do Direct Elections Matter?* (Oxford and New York: Oxford University Press).

Tetlock, P. and Belkin, A. (1996) *Counterfactual Thought Experiments in World Politics* (Princeton, NJ and London: Princeton University Press).

Tett, G. (2009a) 'Why the Idea of Living Wills is Likely to Die a Quiet Death', *Financial Times*, 14 August, p. 28.

Tett, G. (2009b) *Fool's Gold: How Unrestrained Greed Corrupted a Dream, Shattered Global Markets and Unleashed a Catastrophe* (London: Little, Brown).

Teune, H. (1995a) 'Preface', *Annals of the American Academy of Political and Social Sciences* (540) 8–10.

Teune, H. (1995b) 'Local Government and Democratic Political Development', *Annals of the American Academy of Political and Social Sciences* (540) 11–23.

Thatcher, M. and Coen, D. (2008) 'Reshaping European Regulatory Space: An Evolutionary Analysis', *West European Politics* (31) 806–36.

Thomas, C. (ed.) (2001) *Political Parties and Interest Groups: Shaping Democratic Governance* (Boulder, CO and London: Lynne Rienner).

Tilly, C. (1975) 'Reflections on the History of European State-Making', in *The Formation of National States in Western Europe*, ed. C. Tilly (Princeton, NJ: Princeton University Press) pp. 3–83.

Tilly, C. (1978) *From Mobilization to Revolution* (Reading, MA: Addison-Wesley).

Tilly, C. (1997) 'Means and Ends of Comparison in Macrosociology', *Comparative Social Research* (16) 43–53.

Tilly, C. (2004) *Social Movements, 1768–2004* (Boulder, CO: Paradigm Publishers).

Tocqueville, A. de (1835) [1966 edn] *Democracy in America* (New York: Vintage Books).

Tocqueville, A. de (1856) [1954 edn] *The Ancien Regime and the Revolution in France* (London: Fontana).

Tracey, M. (1998) *The Decline and Fall of Public Service Broadcasting* (New York and Oxford: Oxford University Press).

Transparency International (2009) *Global Corruption Report*, http://www.transparency.org/policy_and_research/surveys_indices/cpi/2009, accessed 9 September 2009.

Tremewan, C. (1994) *The Political Economy of Social Control in Singapore* (Basingstoke: Macmillan).

Tripp, A. (2000) *Women and Politics in Uganda* (London: James Currey).

Tripp, A. and Kang, A. (2008) 'The Global Impact of Quotas', *Comparative Political Studies* (41) 338–61.

Trotsky, L. (1932/3) [1965 edn] *The History of the Russian Revolution*, Vol. 1, trans. M. Eastman (London: Gollancz).

Tschentscher, A. (2004) *China Constitution* (International Constitutional Law Project), http://www.oefre.unibe.ch/law/icl/ch00000_.html, accessed 16 August 2006.

Tsebelis, G. (2002) *Veto Players: How Political Institutions Work* (Princeton, NJ: Princeton University Press).

Tsebelis, G. and Money, J. (1997) *Bicameralism* (Cambridge and New York: Cambridge University Press).

Turner, M. and Hulme, D. (1997) *Governance, Administration and Development* (London: Macmillan).

Twigg, J. (2005) 'Social Policy in Post-Soviet Russia', in *Developments in Russian Politics* 6, ed. S. White, Z. Gitelman and R. Sakwa (Basingstoke and New York: Palgrave Macmillan) pp. 204–20.

U

Uhr, J. (2006) 'Bicameralism', in *The Oxford Handbook of Political Institutions*, ed. R. Rhodes, S. Binder and B. Rockman (Oxford and New York: Oxford University Press) pp. 474–94.

UNESCO (United Nations Educational, Scientific and Cultural Organization) (2002) *Universal Declaration on Cultural Diversity*, http://www.unesco.org/education/imld_2002/unversal_decla.shtml#2, accessed 14 April 2006.

UNHCR (United Nations High Commission for Human Rights) (1966) *United Nations Covenant on Civil and Political Rights*, http://www.unhcr.ch, accessed 9 February 2006.

United Nations (2009) *Growth in United Nations Membership, 1945–2009*, http://www.un.org/Overview/growth.htm, accessed 1 August 2009.

United Nations Development Programme (UNDP) (2009) *Human Development Report*, http://hdr.undp.org/reports/global/2009/pdf/HDR05_HDI.pdf, accessed 3 April 2009.

United States Election Project (2008) *Voter Turnout*, http://elections.gmu.edu, accessed 28 December 2008.

usgovernmentrevenue.com (2009) *Total Budgeted Government Revenue*, http://www.usgovernmentrevenue.com, accessed 13 October 2009.

V

Valentino, B. (2004) *Final Solutions: Mass Killing and Genocide in the 20th Century* (Ithaca, NY: Cornell University Press).

Van den Berghe, P. (1981) *The Ethnic Phenomenon* (New York: Elsevier).

Vanhanen, T. (1997) *Prospects of Democracy: A Study of 172 Countries* (London and New York: Routledge).

Vartiainen, J. (2004) 'Scandinavian Capitalism at the Turn of the Century', in *Where are National Capitalisms Now?*, ed. J. Perraton and B. Clift (Basingstoke and New York: Palgrave Macmillan) pp. 111–32.

Vedung, E. (1998) 'Policy Instruments: Typologies and Theories', in *Carrots, Sticks, and Sermons: Policy Instruments and Their Evaluation*, ed. M.-L. Bemelmans-Videc, R. Rist and E. Vedung (New Brunswick, NJ: Transaction) pp. 21–52.

Verba, S. (1987) *Elites and the Idea of Equality: A Comparison of Japan, Sweden and the United States* (Cambridge, MA and London: Harvard University Press).

Verba, S., Nie, N. and Kim, J. (1978) *Participation and Political Equality: A Seven-Nation Comparison* (New York and Cambridge: Cambridge University Press).

Verba, S., Scholzman, K. and Brady, H. (1995) *Voice and Equality: Civic Voluntarism in American Politics* (Cambridge, MA and London: Harvard University Press).

Visser, J. (2006) 'Union Membership Statistics in 24 Countries', *Monthly Labor Review Online* (129), http://www.bls.gov, accessed 3 October 2009.

Volkswagen AG (2009) *Bodies: Working at Volkswagen*, http://www.vw-personal.de/content/www/enflarbeiten/organe/aufsichtsrat.html, accessed 26 February 2009.

W

Wade, R. (1990) *Governing the Market* (Princeton, NJ: Princeton University Press).

Wagstyl, S. (2006) 'Growth Figures Mask Nerves', *Financial Times*, 21 April, p. 2.

Waldron, J. (2007) *Law and Disagreement* (Oxford and New York: Oxford University Press).

Walker, J. (1991) *Mobilizing Interest Groups in America: Patrons, Professionals and Social Movements* (Ann Arbor, MI: University of Michigan Press).

Walpole, S. (1881) *The Electorate and the Legislature* (London: Macmillan).

WAN (World Association of Newspapers) (2008) *World Press Trends*, http://www.wan-press.org, accessed 19 September 2009.

Wang, X. (2002) 'The Postcommunist Personality: The Spectre of China's Market Reforms', *The China Journal* (47) 1–17.

Warber, A. (2006) *Executive Orders and the Modern Presidency: Legislating from the Oval Office* (Boulder, CO and London: Lynne Rienner).

Warleigh, A. (1998) 'Better The Devil You Know? Synthetic and Confederal Understandings of European Integration', *West European Politics* (21) 1–18.

Warwick, P. and Druckman, J. (2006) 'The Portfolio Allocation Paradox: An Investigation into the Nature of a Very Strong but Puzzling Relationship', *European Journal of Political Research* (45) 635–65.

Waters, M. (2000) *Globalization*, 2nd edn (London and New York: Routledge).

Watt, E. (1982) *Authority* (London: Croom Helm).

Wattenberg, M. (2000) 'The Decline of Party Mobilization', in *Parties without Partisans*, ed. R. Dalton and M. Wattenberg (Oxford and New York: Oxford University Press) pp. 64–76.

Watts, R. (2005) 'Comparing Forms of Federal Partnerships', in *Theories of Federalism: A Reader*, ed. D. Karmis and W. Norman (New York and Basingstoke: Palgrave Macmillan) pp. 233–54.

Weale, A. (2007) *Democracy*, 2nd edn (Basingstoke and New York: Palgrave Macmillan).

Weaver, R. and Rockman, B. (eds) (1993) *Do Institutions Matter? Government Capabilities in the United States and Abroad* (Washington: The Brookings Institution).

Webb, P. and White, S. (2007a) 'Political Parties in New Democracies: Trajectories of Development and Implications for Democracy' in *Party Politics in New Democracies*, ed. P. Webb and S. White (Oxford and New York: Oxford University Press) pp. 347–50.

Webb, P. and White, S. (eds) (2007b) *Party Politics in New Democracies*, ed. P. Webb and S. White (Oxford and New York: Oxford University Press).

Webb, P., Farrell, D. and Holliday, I. (eds) (2002) *Political Parties in Advanced Industrial Democracies* (Oxford and New York: Oxford University Press).

Weber, M. (1905) [1930 edn] *The Protestant Ethic and the Spirit of Capitalism* (London: Allen & Unwin).

Weber, M. (1918) [1990 edn] 'The Advent of Plebiscitarian Democracy', in *The West European Party System*, ed. P. Mair (Oxford and New York: Oxford University Press) pp. 31–7.

Weber, M. (1921–22) [1978 edn] *Economy and Society: An Outline of Interpretive Sociology*, ed. G. Roth and C. Wittich (Berkeley, CA: University of California Press).

Weber, M. (1922) [1957 edn] *The Theory of Economic and Social Organization* (Berkeley, CA: University of California Press).

Weber, M. (1923) [1946 edn] 'The Social Psychology of the World Religions', in *From Max Weber: Essays in Sociology*, ed. and trans. H. Gerth and C. Wright Mills (Oxford and New York: Oxford University Press) pp. 267–301.

Web Japan (2009) *Governmental Structure*, http://www.web-japan.org/factsheet/index.html, accessed 2 December 2009.

Wehner, J. (2006) 'Assessing the Power of the Purse: An Index of Legislative Budget Institutions', *Political Studies* (54) 767–85.

Weiler, J. (1994) 'A Quiet Revolution: The European Court of Justice and its Interlocutors', *Comparative Political Studies* (26) 519–34.

Weingast, B. (1998) 'Political Stability and Civil War: Institutions, Commitment and American Democracy' in R. Bates, *Analytic Narratives* (Princeton, NJ: Princeton University Press).

Weingast, B. and Wittman, D. (eds) (2006) *The Oxford Handbook of Political Economy* (Oxford and New York: Oxford University Press).

Weingast, B. and Wittman, D. (2008) 'The Reach of Political Economy' in *The Oxford Handbook of Political Economy*, ed. B. Weingast and D. Wittman (Oxford and New York: Oxford University Press) pp. 3–28.

Weiss, L. (1998) *The Myth of the Powerless State: Governing the Economy in a Global Era* (Cambridge: Polity).

Weiss, L. (2004) 'Developmental States Before and After the Asian Crisis', in *Where Are National Capitalisms Now?*, ed. J. Perraton and B. Clift (Basingstoke and New York: Palgrave Macmillan) pp. 154–68.

Weiss, T. and Gordenker, C. (1996) 'Pluralizing Global Governance' in *Nongovernmental Organizations, The United Nations and Global Governance*, ed. T. Weiss and C. Gordenker (Boulder, CO and London: Lynne Rienner) pp. 17–50.

Weissberg, R. (2002) *Polling, Policy and Public Opinion: The Case Against Heeding 'The Voice of the People'* (London and New York: Palgrave Macmillan).

Wendt, A. (1999) *Social Theory of International Politics* (Cambridge and New York: Cambridge University Press).

West, D. and Orman, J. (2003) *Celebrity Politics* (Upper Saddle River, NJ: Prentice Hall).

White, S. (2005a) 'The Political Parties', in *Developments in Russian Politics 6*, ed. S. White, Z. Gitelman and R. Sakwa (Basingstoke and New York: Palgrave Macmillan) pp. 80–95.

White, S. (2005b) 'Russia: The Authoritarian Adaptation of an Electoral System', in *The Politics of Electoral Systems*, ed. M. Gallagher and P. Mitchell (Oxford and New York: Oxford University Press) pp. 313–32.

White, S. (2007) 'Russia's Client Party System' in *Party Politics in New Democracies*, ed. P. Webb and S. White (Oxford and New York: Oxford University Press) pp. 21–52.

White, S., Batt, J. and Lewis, P. (eds) (2003) *Developments in Central and East European Politics 3* (Basingstoke: Palgrave Macmillan).

White, S., Gitelman, Z. and Sakwa, R. (eds) (2005) *Developments in Russian Politics 6* (Basingstoke and New York: Palgrave Macmillan).

White House (2006) *National Security Strategy, March 2006*, http://www.whitehouse.gov/nsc/nss/2006/, accessed 24 August 2006.

Wiarda, H. (ed.) (2004) *Comparative Politics: Critical Concepts in Political Science*, 6 vols (London and New York: Routledge).

Wigbold, H. (1979) 'Holland: The Shaky Pillars of Hilversum', in *Television and Political Life*, ed. A. Smith (London: Macmillan) pp. 191–231.

Wildavsky, A. (1979) *The Art and Craft of Policy Analysis* (Boston, MA: Little, Brown).

Wilde, R. (2007) *Territorial Administration by International Organizations* (Oxford and New York: Oxford University Press).

Willerton, J. (1997) 'Presidential Power', in *Developments in Russian Politics*, ed. S. White, A. Pravda and Z. Gitelman (Basingstoke: Macmillan) pp. 35–60.

Willerton, J. (2005) 'Putin and the Hegemonic Presidency', in *Developments in Russian Politics 6*, ed. S. White, Z. Gitelman and R. Sakwa (Basingstoke and New York: Palgrave Macmillan) pp. 18–39.

Williams, P. (1970) *Wars, Plots and Scandal in Post-War France* (Oxford: Oxford University Press).

Williams, R. (1962) *Communications* (Harmondsworth and New York: Penguin).

Willnat, L. and Aw, A. (eds) (2009) *Political Communication in Asia* (London and New York: Routledge).

Wilson, A. (2006) *Ukraine's Orange Revolution* (New Haven, CT: Yale University Press).

Wilson, G. (1990) *Interest Groups* (Oxford and Cambridge, MA: Blackwell).

Wilson, G. (2003) *Business and Politics: A Comparative Introduction*, 3rd edn (Basingstoke: Macmillan).

Wilson, W. (1885) *Congressional Government* (Boston, MA: Houghton Mifflin).

Wilson, W. (1887) 'The Study of Administration', *Political Science Quarterly* (2) 197–222.

Winham, G. (2005) 'The Evolution of the Global Trade Regime', in *Global Political Economy*, ed. J. Ravenhill (Oxford and New York: Oxford University Press) pp. 87–115.

Winter, L. and Brans, M. (2003) 'Belgium: Political Professionals and the Crisis of the Party State', in *The Political Class in Advanced Democracies*, ed. J. Borchert and J. Zeiss (Oxford and New York: Oxford University Press) pp. 45–66.

Woerkens, M. van (2002) *The Strangled Traveler: Colonial Imaginings and the Thugs of India*, trans. C. Tihanyi (Chicago, IL: University of Chicago Press).

World Bank (1997) *World Development Report: The State in a Changing World* (Oxford and New York: Oxford University Press).

World Bank (2009) *Country Groups,* http://web.worldbank.org/WBSITE/EXTERNAL/DATASTATISTICS/0,,contentMDK:20421402~pagePK:64133150~piPK:64133175~theSitePK:239419,00.html, accessed 9 November, 2009.

Wright, V. (1997) 'La Fin du Dirigisme?', *Modern and Contemporary France* (5) 151–5.

Y, Z

Yin, R. (2003) *Case Study Research: Design and Methods,* 3rd edn (Thousand Oaks, CA and London: Sage).

Yin, R. (ed.) (2004) *The Case Study Anthology* (Thousand Oaks, CA and London: Sage).

Zakaria, E (2003) *The Future of Freedom: Illiberal Democracy at Home and Abroad* (New York and London: Norton).

Zartman, W. (ed.) (1995a) *Collapsed States: The Disintegration and Restoration of Legitimate Authority* (Boulder, CO and London: Lynne Rienner).

Zartman, W. (1995b) 'Posing the Problem of State Collapse', in *Collapsed States: The Disintegration and Restoration of Legitimate Authority,* ed. W. Zartman (Boulder, CO and London: Lynne Rienner) pp. 1–14.

Zartman, W. (1995c) 'Putting Things Back Together', in *Collapsed States: The Disintegration and Restoration of Legitimate Authority,* ed. W. Zartman (Boulder, CO and London: Lynne Rienner) pp. 267–74.

Zhao, S. (ed.) (2006) *Debating Political Reform in China: Rule of Law vs. Democratization* (Armonk, NY and London: M.E. Sharpe).

Zirakzadeh, C. (1997) *Social Movements in Politics: A Comparative Study* (London and New York: Longman).

Index

Note: entries in orange type indicate a definition.